MORAL EDUCATION:
THEORY AND APPLICATION

MORAL EDUCATION:

THEORY AND APPLICATION

Edited by
Marvin W. Berkowitz
Marquette University

Fritz Oser
University of Fribourg

LEA LAWRENCE ERLBAUM ASSOCIATES, PUBLISHERS
1985 Hillsdale, New Jersey   London

Lawrence Erlbaum Associates, Inc., Publishers
365 Broadway
Hillsdale, New Jersey 07642

Library of Congress Cataloging in Publication Data
Main entry under title:

Moral education.

Includes bibliographies and indexes.
1. Moral education — Addresses, essays, lectures.
I. Berkowitz, Marvin W., 1950- . II. Oser, Fritz.
LC268.M687 1985   370.11′4   85-6855
ISBN 0-89859-557-6

Printed in the United States of America
10 9 8 7 6 5 4 3 2 1

Contents

List of Contributors

Marvin W. Berkowitz, *Marquette University*
Augusto Blasi, *University of Massachusetts-Boston*
Steven Brion-Meisels, *Judge Baker Guidance Center, Boston*
Daniel Candee, *Harvard University*
Rainer Döbert, *Free University, Berlin, West Germany*
Lutz Eckensberger, *University of Saarland, West Germany*
Wolfgang Edelstein, *Max-Planck-Institute for Human Development and Education, Berlin, West Germany*
Frederick Gordon, *Harvard University*
Alexandra Hewer, *Harvard University*
Ann Higgins, *Harvard University*
Otfried Höffe, *University of Fribourg, Switzerland*
Monika Keller, *Max-Planck-Institute for Human Development and Education, Berlin, West Germany*
Lawrence Kohlberg, *Harvard University*
Guido Küng, *University of Fribourg, Switzerland*
Thomas Lickona, *State University of NY College at Cortland*
Mordecai Nisan, *The Hebrew University of Jerusalem, Israel*
Gil G. Noam, *McClean Hospital, Boston*
Gertrud Nunner-Winkler, *Max-Planck-Institute, Munich, West Germany*
Fritz Oser, *University of Fribourg, Switzerland*
Clark Power, *University of Notre Dame*
James R. Rest, *University of Minnesota*
Siegfried Reuss, *Max-Planck-Institute for Human Development and Education, Berlin, West Germany*
Andre Schläfli, *University of Fribourg, Switzerland*
Robert L. Selman, *Harvard University*
Susanne Villenave-Cremer, *University of Saarland, West Germany*

Preface

If one were to take a poll asking people whether they would vote for or against morality, one would expect a rather overwhelming endorsement. There is little disagreement that people should behave morally, should respect moral rules and should be concerned about justice and responsibility. There is, however, a great deal of disagreement about what constitutes morality and how it can be stimulated in an individual and/or social group. This is specially noticeable in theoretical, practical and empirical approaches to moral education.

Perhaps the historically most volatile issue in moral education has centered about what the content of such training should be. Should it be based upon prevailing political trends? Should it be based upon loyalty to some other social frame of reference, e. g., a religion or an economic organization? Should it be based on forms of retribution? This controversy was rendered obsolete with the advent of moral education based upon Lawrence Kohlberg's theory of moral reasoning development. Moshe Blatt's (Blatt & Kohlberg, 1975) pioneering attempts at bringing developmental theory to the classroom formed the basis for Kohlberg's argument that moral education should be free of the content controversy by orienting instead to the natural progression of stages of reasoning development that themselves are not tied to any particular moral content but rather to progressively more adequate forms of moral problem solving. Such a conception attracted claims of relativism and irresponsibility, but Kohlberg and his colleagues have amply demonstrated that (1) his model is diametrically incompatible with a relativist stance while (2) also avoiding the problems that plague indoctrinative moral education (Kohlberg & Mayer, 1972). The sequence of development is fixed and universal, and although content is correlated to particular stages, that relationship is indirect and imperfect. It is the individual who constructs the content implications of his or her stage of moral reasoning, and therefore indoctrination is inappropriate.

Initially, Kohlberg and his colleagues claimed that all one need do in moral education is change the stage or structure of an individual's moral reasoning, and changes in moral behavior, ego and personality style would occur. Unfortunately, while relationships between these facets of human development have been both theoretically and empirically laid out, the relationships are more complex than originally assumed. In 1978 Kohlberg acknowledged that moral education curricula based upon his theory needed revision if they were to optimally impact on general human moral growth.

Three general trends in Kohlberg's work can be noted. First, there is the development of a stage model of morality that dates back to Kohlberg's earliest work. Second, there is the construction of a general model of moral education. And third, there is the elaboration of the conception of the Just Community form of moral education. It is this third trend which represents an attempt to resolve the problems that Kohlberg acknowledged in the preceding generation of moral education efforts. It addresses the total person, including personality, cognition, ego and behavior. It acknowledges the role of peer conformity and the power of the collective in affecting moral growth. And it includes consideration of particular content.

Nonetheless, as moral education entered the 1980s, many important problems remained. The question of the legitimacy of the highest stage is still being considered. The problem of the relationship between judgment and action is receiving much attention and reformulation as well. The role of affect in moral functioning has been sorely overlooked until very recently. A further issue is the implication of the particular realm of one's life (family, school, peer group, workplace, church) for the form and effectiveness of moral education. Finally, how can self-acknowledged moral transgressions in typical individuals be incorporated into the theory?

This volume reflects these problems. It also reflects Kohlberg's work in seven predominant ways. First, and most directly, it presents current work stemming from the Kohlberg camp, including Kohlberg's latest thinking on the Just Community approach to moral education (chapter 2) as well as the work of his students and colleagues.

A second way that this volume reflects Kohlberg's work is a bit more indirect than the first. The history of Kohlberg's theorizing, research and practice has been marked by the non-linearity of its path. Revisions, revisitations, and reformulations abound. Criticisms, reflections and adjustment are the norm. And, ultimately, thoughtful assessment and integration result (cf. Kohlberg, Levine, & Hewer, 1983). This volume attempts to honor the spirit of openness, reflection and dialectical scientific growth that is so pronounced in Kohlberg's work. We have attempted to do so by including chapters that are not simply representations of, as Jack Fraenkel (1976) has dubbed it, the *Kohlberg bandwagon*. Rather we have included the views of "friendly" critics, i.e., revisionists who acknowledge the value of Kohlberg's thinking but are not blind to possibilities for improvement and refinement. Hence the closing set of chapters is entitled "Critiques and Revisions." We have not limited our inclusion of critical perspectives to this one section, however. Throughout the volume new thinking, revision and critique proliferate. In the opening section on "Theoretical Perspectives and Philosophical Foundations," we include James Rest's (chapter 1) expansion of Kohlberg's model, Otfried Höffe's (chapter 3) philosophical analysis of Kohlberg's grounding assumptions, Monika Keller and Siegfried Reuss' (chapter 4) synthesis of Kohlberg's cognitive-structural approach with discourse ethics, and Kohlberg's own revision of his theory of the Just Community as well.

A third way in which the volume attempts to represent the spirit of Kohlberg's work is by recognizing, as he has from the beginning of his career (Kohlberg, 1958) to his current three volume magnum opus (Kohlberg, 1981, 1984, in preparation), that theory, research and practice cannot and should not be separated. Hence the subtitle of this book, *Theory and Application*, and the organization of the chapters into three sections: theory, application and critique. The research focus is a theme that runs throughout the three sections. For example, Rest (chapter 1) reports an ongoing investigation of professional moral education in a dental school setting as an example of his theoretical model in the theory section. The application section actually represents a mixture of pure application, as exemplified by Power's (chapter 9) description of the democratization of a large urban high school, applied research (see Oser and Schläfli, chapter 11, on moral education in a bank apprenticeship program), to pure research with educational implications, for example Berkowitz's chapter (8) on moral discussion. Nisan's chapter (17) on the notion of limited morality in the Critique section also represents a fine synthesis of theory, research and application. All of the authors in this collection represent approaches to moral education and moral development that encompass theory, research and practice.

Kohlberg's approach to moral education can be described as quite broad. Even in his dissertation (Kohlberg, 1958) he acknowledged the descriptive, accelerative and remediating sides of moral education. His subsequent work traversed such discrepant yet related terrain as prison reform, cross-cultural description, school intervention, and parent effects on child development. In honoring this fourth spirit of Kohlberg's work, i.e., of education broadly defined, we have attempted to include in this collection educational interventions and applications in four areas: the school, the family, the workplace and in clinical-developmental intervention. We do not consider this list to be exhaustive either. Indeed, in yielding to space limitations we eventually abandoned our plans for sections on political issues and on sociological influences. We should also note that some of the chapters in this collection were not easily categorized.

The reader will probably be able to suggest alternative placements for a few of the chapters. We readily acknowledge this and merely claim to have made the most appropriate assignments possible.

When one first visits Kohlberg' Center for Moral Education and Development at the Harvard Graduate School of Education, one is invariably struck with the eclectic nature of the moral education enterprise. One finds the scholars there struggling to synthesize Piaget and Durkheim, Dewey and Habermas, the Israeli kibbutz and urban American high schools. Furthermore, the traditional Friday afternoon roundtables are equally likely to be presented by a psychologist, an educator, a philospher, a theologian, a sociologist, an administrator or a psychotherapist. And astonishingly all are welcome and all are relevant. We have attempted to represent this fifth aspect of Kohlberg's work by including chapters by philosophers (e.g., Otfried Höffe and Guido Küng), psychologists (e.g., Steven Brion-Meisels & Robert Selman, and Augusto Blasi), educators (e.g., Clark Power, and Fritz Oser & Andre Schläfli), psychotherapists (e.g., Gil Noam and Alexandra Hewer) and others.

Yet a sixth aspect of Kohlberg's work has been its international orientation. Both the theoretical origins of Kohlberg's thinking (Piaget, Dewey, Durkheim, Socrates, Rawls, Kant, Mead) and the geographic locations of his research (United States, Israel, Mexico, Turkey, Taiwan, etc.) represent an international focus. This volume is also clearly and intentionally international as well. The contributors are from the United States, Switzerland, Germany and Israel, four of the countries where most of the current work in Kohlbergian moral education is being done. Included in the representation of European authors are two perspectives that may be new to many American readers, that of discourse ethics (cf. Habermas, 1984) and action theory (cf. Eckensberger & Reinshagen, 1980). These perspectives have become quite popular in European circles and are only now being introduced to American audiences. It is our hope that this volume will expedite the process of introduction.

Kohlberg has historically focused much of his research and application on the adolescent, even though his theoretical work spans early childhood to old age (cf. Kohlberg, 1973; Kohlberg & Gilligan, 1971; Kohlberg & Kramer, 1969). We have emphasized the adolescent in this collection as a seventh aspect of the spirit of Kohlberg's work. While there are chapters that are not specific to any particular developmental group (e.g., Nisan, chapter 17; Blasi, chapter 19; Rest, chapter 1) and others that refer to both younger (e.g., Keller & Reuss, chapter 4) and older individuals (e.g., Candee, chapter 12; Higgins & Gordon, chapter 10), the modal emphasis is clearly on adolescence.

We would also like to point out that his volume, while heavily focused on Kohlberg's work from both supportive and critical perspectives, is not limited to Kohlbergian emphases. Both Nisan (chapter 17) and Blasi (chapter 19) introduce ideas that need no connection to traditional cognitive-developmental education to be meaningful and valid. Furthermore, Villenave-Cremer and Eckensberger (chapter 7) offer a highly radical reinterpretation of Kohlberg's thinking. Finally, Brion-Meisels and Selman (chapter 15) present a model of interpersonal negotiation that is based upon the development of social thinking, and not specifically upon moral thinking.

Moral education continues to be a growing field. We hope that his collection of essays and research reports will familiarize our readers with new ideas they may not have bèen aware of previously. We have avoided rehashing the traditional work that is well documented elsewhere (e.g., Hersh, Paolitto & Reimer, 1979; Kohlberg, 1981; Mosher, 1980; Scharf, 1978) and focused our efforts on new directions in the field. Many of the authors in this collection will be new to our readers and many other such scholars had to be excluded simply on the basis of space limitations. This collection therefore may best be depicted as a representation of the best of a large body of ongoing research and practice in moral education.

Marvin W. Berkowitz
Fritz Oser

REFERENCES

Blatt, M. & Kohlberg, L. (1975). The effects of classroom moral discussion upon children's level of moral judgment. *Journal of Moral Education, 4*, 129–161.

Eckensberger, L. H. & Reinshagen, H. (1980). Kohlberg's Stufentheorie der Entwicklung des Moralischen Urteils. Ein Versuch ihrer Reinterpretation im Bezugsrahmen handlungstheoretischer Konzepte. In L. H. Eckensberger & R. K. Silbereisen (Eds.), *Entwicklung sozialer Kognitionen* (pp. 65–131). Stuttgart: Klett-Cotta.

Fraenkel, J. R. (1976). The Kohlberg bandwagon: Some reservations. *Social Education, 40*, 216–222.

Habermas, J. (1984). *Theory of communicative action. Vol. 1: Reason and rationality in society.* (T. McCarthy, Trans.). Boston: Beacon Press.

Hersh, R., Paolitto, D., & Reimer, J. (1979). *Promoting moral growth: From Piaget to Kohlberg.* New York: Longman.

Kohlberg, L. (1958). *The development of modes of moral thinking and choice in years ten to sixteen.* Unpublished doctoral dissertation, University of Chicago.

Kohlberg, L. (1973). Continuities in childhood and adult moral development revisited. In P. B. Baltes & K. W. Schaie (Eds.), *Life-span developmental psychology: Personality & socialization* (pp. 180–204). New York: Academic.

Kohlberg, L. (1978). Revisions in the theory and practice of moral development. In W. Damon (Ed.), *New directions for child development: Moral development* (pp. 83–88), No. 2. San Francisco: Jossey-Bass.

Kohlberg, L. (1981). *Essays on moral development. Vol. 1: The philosophy of moral development.* San Francisco: Harper & Row.

Kohlberg, L. (1984). *Essays on moral development. Vol. 2: The psychology of moral development.* San Francisco: Harper & Row.

Kohlberg, L. (in preparation). *Essays on moral development. Vol. 3: The education of moral development.* San Francisco: Harper & Row.

Kohlberg, L. & Gilligan, C. F. (1971). The adolescent as philosopher: The discovery of the self in a postconventional world. *Daedalus, 100,* 1051–1086.

Kohlberg, L. & Kramer, R. (1969). Continuities and discontinuities in childhood and adult moral development. *Human Development, 12,* 93–120.

Kohlberg, L., Levine, C., & Hewer, A. (1983). *Moral stages: A current formulation and a response to critics. Contributions to human development* (Vol. 10). New York: S. Karger.

Kohlberg, L. & Mayer, R. (1972). Development as the aim of education. *Havard Educational Review, 42,* 449–496.

Mosher, R. L. (Ed.). (1980). *Moral education: A first generation of research and development.* New York: Praeger.

Scharf, P. (Ed.) (1978). *Readings in moral education.* Minneapolis: Winston Press.

THEORETICAL PERSPECTIVES AND PHILOSOPHICAL FOUNDATIONS

An Interdisciplinary Approach to Moral Education

James R. Rest
University of Minnesota

Hardly anyone opposes in principle an interdisciplinary approach to anything. Like an *international* conference, an *interdisciplinary* approach carries the presumption that people with different perspectives will enrich each other and synergistically create something more valuable and comprehensive than any one group working alone. However, my own experience with interdisciplinary meetings has often been disappointing. Participants in interdisciplinary gatherings seem to spend an inordinate amount of time disentangling each other's specialized lingo, and struggling with different fundamental starting points; and even when some product does emerge, it is often a patchwork of compromises and a clutter of inconsistent ideas.

A number of us at the University of Minnesota from different disciplines have been working together for several years now, and we hope to do better than the typical interdisciplinary team. I would like to be able to tell you that we have a proven formula for success. However, what we actually have are some ideas and proposals that seem to have been working reasonably well so far in guiding research and program development. I will describe some features of this general approach, some of the inevitable issues that need to be confronted, and some of the options we are trying.

Right at the start, the prospects for constructive interdisciplinary collaboration may be improved by two conditions: (1) If the team can agree on some practical goal towards which all are contributing; and (2) If the team can agree on some plan for dividing the work and drawing upon the special expertise of the various participants. At the University of Minnesota, our practical goal has been to prepare graduate students studying for careers in the helping professions (dentists, nurses, counseling psychologists, etc.) to deal with the inevitable moral and value dilemmas that they will face in their future jobs. We all accept this as the overriding goal towards which we are working. Each group has subgoals and special agendas that it brings to this enterprise, making this worthwhile for each member as an individual. For example, I, as a research psychologist, also see it as an opportunity for carrying out research on a particular psychological model of morality. On the other hand, professionals teaching in the particular area—such as the faculty in the dental school—see this interdisciplinary activity as contributing to the overall strength of their professional program and as maintaining professional standards. Philosophers and lawyers can see it as providing real-life case studies in applied ethics, worthy of large investments of time in analyzing the issues and proposed solutions.

As the overriding goal, I would stress the importance of preparing students to deal with the moral dilemmas encountered in their professional life. Focusing on some external condition in the real world that we all think is important has allowed us to avoid a stalemate on unsettled theoretical issues. All of us probably do not have the same set of fundamental axioms about reality or goodness or rightness, and yet we can move ahead insofar as some activity or analysis seems to contribute towards our practical goal. Of course it is important to be constantly working towards clarifying the theoretical issues (such as the relation of applied ethics to the traditional grand theories of moral philosophy, the relation of cognition and emotion in the psychology of morality, the bounds of responsibility of professionals). Nevertheless, without final or complete answers to these questions, we are not paralyzed. It is hoped that our practical work helps our theoretical work too.

As the second condition for productive interdisciplinary collaboration, it is also important to have some agreement about a division of labor and a plan for orchestrating the contributions from the various participants. As an illustration, a plan of coordination has been evolving at the University of Minnesota, started by a colleague in the School of Dentistry, Dr. Muriel Bebeau. Dr. Bebeau involved wider circles of participants, enlisted expertise from various disciplines, and cultivated support in the School of Dentistry for a moral education program.

Dr. Bebeau asked professional dentists to describe the kinds of moral dilemmas that dentists encounter on the job. After interviewing a number of dentists, she made a list of such dilemmas. This list was sent out to hundreds of dentists as a survey, so as to identify which moral dilemmas are perceived by the professional community as the most recurrent and important ones. The responses to this survey identified the "top 10" moral dilemmas in dentistry. Dr. Bebeau then dramatized these dilemmas—like a radio drama—in the form of a scripted dialogue between a dentist and a client conversing in the dentist's office (Bebeau, Rest, Speidel, Yamoor, & Eberhardy, 1982). Over the course of the dialogue, some moral dilemmas for the dentist would be presented. School of Dentistry faculty were involved in checking these dramatized dilemmas for realism as well as on technical points. Professionals in the field agreed that the finished product was representative of the kinds of dilemmas that new students were likely to face on the job. For example, one of the dramatized dilemmas concerns a woman, Margaret Herrington, who comes into the dentist's office on her first visit, having moved from another town. In the course of the examination, we see that, although Ms. Herrington has had extensive and costly dental work by her previous dentist, the work is seriously deficient and must be redone. The drama builds to a point where the dentist in the dramatization is suggesting to Ms. Herrington that she needs to have a lot of new dental work done. Ms. Herrington is surprised at this news and begins to challenge the new dentist to tell her why this is necessary. At this point, the listener is asked to role-play the dentist in that situation to show how the situation should be handled. Students in the dental program listened to these dramatizations and were asked to respond. Some of the students were so absorbed in handling the technical aspects of the situation (e.g., Do the symptoms indicate periodontal disease? How many crowns will have to be redone? Might oral surgery be necessary?) that they missed the moral issues: Who is going to pay for redoing all this work—Ms. Herrington who has already paid once to have the job done? Who is this previous dentist and how did such inferior work occur? Does the new dentist have a responsibility to the profession to check up on this colleague? And so on.

Thus the students were confronted with these dilemmas and gave their responses. Some of these responses were tape-recorded and replayed for the School of Dentistry faculty. Faculty were amazed and flabbergasted by the ways that some of their students said they would deal with these dilemmas. Faculty heard some students say that fellow dentists should never criticize each other's work, and that, in effect, dentists had a professional responsibility to hide each other's malpractice from the public. Faculty heard some students say that the only accommodation they would make to Ms. Herrington's problem was to offer her long-term monthly payments but would still charge her the full amount. (I should hasten to add that the School of Dentistry at the University of Minnesota has an outstanding reputation for preparing good clinicians, and that entrance into the dentistry program is highly competitive). When faculty heard how unprepared some of their students were to meet the moral dilemmas that inevitably face them on the job, the School of Dentistry made a commitment to build components of moral education into its curriculum.

So far, this story about the School of Dentistry has illustrated how an educational psychologist, Dr. Bebeau, collaborated with faculty in a professional program. Simply presenting some student responses (even without extensive test development, data analysis, or research) was a very effective demonstration to faculty that something needed to be done. Currently we are trying to implement a systematic program of curriculum development and research. To do this involves the contributions of other areas of expertise as well. For instance, the hypothetical dilemmas evoke many different proposals for solution. To claim that one solution is better than another is essentially a philosophical enterprise. So when we have a variety of proposed solutions to a dilemma, we call in colleagues with training in the "normative" disciplines (philosophy, theology, and law) to examine the adequacy of certain solutions and arguments, and to identify the critical features of the "better" in contrast to the less adequate, solutions. The philosophers are not asked to give us a short historical essay on how Aristotle or Kant might respond to the problem, but are asked to help build a taxonomy for scoring responses to these dilemmas and to present arguments for the greater adequacy to some responses.

The description so far includes the professionals in the field (e.g., faculty in the School of Dentistry), colleagues from the normative disciplines (philosophy, theology, law), and psychology. However, I have much more to say about the role psychology has to play, since I am a psychologist. And so for the remainder of this paper I will emphasize the psychological contribution to an interdisciplinary project.

In very general terms, I see four basic contributions of the psychologist to an interdisciplinary team: first, to use existing psychological theory and research to characterize the variables and processes that are most likely involved in the production of moral behavior; second, to draw upon psychology's many techniques and research strategies for collecting information in order to characterize what the students initially are like, and to monitor the process and outcomes of intervention; third, to devise models of the psychological processes which "experts" intuitively use in moral decision making and which distinguish them from the less expert; and fourth, to clarify the mechanisms and conditions of change so that we can help "novices" function more like the "experts."

While I cannot claim to have complete or final answers to any of these issues, I do have some proposals and some research that I'd like to discuss now (for more extensive discussions, see Rest, 1983a and, in press). First, I have a particular view about what existing psychological theory and research has to tell us about the variables and processes that are involved in the production of moral behavior. I propose that existing psychological research supports the view that the production of moral behavior involves four major component processes. This four-component model arises from a review of the morality literature for the Mussen *Handbook* (Rest, 1983b). The four major processes as indicated in Table 1.1 are: (1) interpreting the situation in terms of recognizing what actions are possible for the actor and how each course of action affects all the parties involved; (2) figuring out what one ought to do—applying moral ideals to the situation to determine the moral course of action; (3) choosing among moral and non-moral values to decide what one actually intends to do; and (4) implementing what one intends to do.

Note that I am denying that moral behavior is produced by a single, unitary process such as stages of moral reasoning, or empathy, or reinforcement contingencies. I think one-variable theories of morality are untenable. Two people who are similar on one process (e.g., moral reasoning) need not be similar on

TABLE 1.1
Major Component Processes in the Production of Moral Behavior

Component I

Major functions of the process: To interpret the situation in terms of how one's actions affect the welfare of others.

Exemplary research: (Response to emergencies) Staub (1978, 1979); Schwartz (1977); (Social cognition development) Shantz (1983); Selman (1980); (Empathy) Hoffman (1977, in press).

Cognitive-affective interaction: Drawing inferences about how the other will be affected, and feeling empathy, disgust, etc. for the other.

Component II

Major functions: To formulate what a moral course of action would be; to identify the moral ideal in a specific situation.

Exemplary research: (Cognitive developmental) Piaget (1932/1965); Kohlberg (1969, 1976); DIT research (Rest, 1979); Damon (1977); (Social psychology "norms") Berkowitz & Daniels (1963); Schwartz (1977); (Post-Piagetian) Keasey (1978).

Cognitive-affective interaction: Both abstract and attitudinal-valuing aspects are involved in the construction of systems of moral meaning; moral ideals are comprised of both cognitive and affective elements.

Component III

Major functions: To select among competing value outcomes of ideals, the one to act upon; deciding whether or not to try to fulfill one's moral ideal.

Exemplary research: (Decision-making models, and factors which affect decision-making) Pomazal & Jaccord (1976); Lerner (1971); Schwartz (1977); Isen et al., (1978); (Theories of moral motivation) Wilson (1975); Aronfreed (1968); Bandura (1977b); Kohlberg (1969); Hoffman (in press); Durkheim (1961); Rawls (1971).

Cognitive-affective interactions: Calculation of relative utilities of various goals; mood influencing outlook; defensive distortion of perception; empathy impelling decisions; social understanding motivating the choice of goals.

Component IV

Major functions: To execute and implement what one intends to do.

Exemplary research: (Ego strength and self regulation) Mischel and Mischel (1976); Krebs (1967); Staub (1979).

Cognitive-affective interaction: Task persistence as affected by cognitive transformation of the goal.

other processes (e.g., moral sensitivity or moral motivation). A person who performs one process with great facility need not have great facility in other processes. Although one process might interact and influence another process, the processes ought to be distinguished from each other as performing different functions, all of which are necessary for the production of moral behavior. Deficiency in any process can result in moral failure. Therefore, it follows that moral education should be aimed at improving proficiency in all of the processes.

Note that the components represent the *processes* involved in the production of a moral act, not general *traits* of people. Assessing how a subject interprets a particular situation (Component I) does not commit us to the view that the subject generally interprets situations in certain ways. The four components are not presented as four virtues that make up an ideal person; rather they are the major units of analysis in tracing how a particular course of action was produced in the context of a particular situation.

Note also that there are different affect and cognition interactions in every component. I assume that there are no pure cognitions without affects, nor pure affects without cognitions. Just as each component involves different cognitive processes, so also each component involves different cognition-affect interactions. There is not just one kind of relation between cognition and affect. In fact, as a matter of personal history, I was pushed into the four-component model as I tried to make sense out of the variety of studies on cognition-affect relations. Although each of these studies does indeed present a view of cognition-affect relationships, the studies are not addressing the same relationship (nor the same cognitions and the same affects). For instance, Hoffman (1977, in press) describes the interaction of cognition and affect in terms of how different "conceptions of the other" influence the emotion of empathy. A different kind of cognition-affect interaction is described by Kohlberg (1969) in talking about the feelings and motives that parallel cognitive structures, since both cognitions and affects are involved in a person's system of meaning. Isen, Clark, Karp, and Shalker (1978) refer to yet another interaction in describing how mood can influence memory processes. Mischel and Mischel (1976) describe how cognitive reconstructions of reward objects can influence a person's willingness to persevere at tedious tasks. As Table 1.1 suggests, these different interfaces of cognitions and affects point to the necessity of positing different processes, each with distinctive cognitive and affective interfaces.

THE FOUR COMPONENTS

Now let us consider each of the components in more detail.

Component I.   Component I, interpreting the situation, involves imagining the possible courses of action in a situation and tracing the consequences of action in terms of how they affect the welfare of all the parties involved.

Four findings from psychological research stand out in regard to Component I. The first finding is that many people have great difficulty in interpreting even relatively simple situations. Research on bystander reactions to emergencies shows this. For example, research by Staub (1978, 1979) shows that helping behavior is related to the ambiguity of the situation—if subjects are not clear about what's happening, they don't volunteer to help as much. A second finding is that striking individual differences exist among people in their sensitivity to the needs and welfare of others. This is shown in social psychological research by

Schwartz (1977) on a variable he describes as "Awareness of Consequences." A third finding is that the ability to make inferences about the needs and wants of others—and about how one's actions would affect others—is a developmental phenomenon. People get better with age in being able to make inferences about others. The vast emerging field of "Social Cognition" is relevant here and documents this point (Selman, 1980; Shantz, 1983). A fourth finding is that a social situation can arouse strong feelings even before extensive cognitive encoding. Feelings can be activated before one fully understands a situation (Zajonc, 1980). Hoffman (1977) has emphasized the role of empathy in morality, and views the arousal of empathy as a primary response which need not be mediated by complex cognitive operations. Hoffman's account is particularly interesting in suggesting how this primary affective response comes to interact with and be modified by cognitive development to produce more complex forms of empathy. The general point here, however, is that aroused affects are part of what needs to be interpreted in a situation, and therefore part of Component I processing.

Recently Dr. Bebeau and I have been collaborating in the School of Dentistry project to develop instruments for measuring Component I specifically in regard to social situations encountered in the dentistry profession (Bebeau et al., 1982). The "radio dramas" I mentioned earlier are used to provide subject responses. A scoring guide is being developed to assess what we call "moral sensitivity." A low score on moral sensitivity occurs if the subject is unaware of the *moral* problem and focuses exclusively on the technical problems, or is not aware of possible courses of action which might help others, or doesn't take account of special characteristics or needs of the patient. We are about to begin some systematic validating studies, but currently the research is far enough along to indicate that our measure does produce a range of scores, that interrater reliability is good, that internal consistency is adequate, and that moral sensitivity (Component I) is definitely different from moral reasoning (the "DIT," a measure of Component II). I might mention that in the development of our scoring taxonomy, the professional community (faculty from the School of Dentistry) were very much involved, and also that we sought out philosophical and legal input. I believe that moral sensitivity is a component that can be dramatically improved (if it is initially low) by moral education programs in professional schools. These programs can acquaint students with the most recurrent and important moral dilemmas that they will face in their jobs, can furnish students practice in imagining possible lines of action in response to a dilemma and tracing the consequences, and can make them aware of differing points of view. One of our next activities in the dental school project is to conduct pre-post test evaluations of "sensitizing" sessions.

Component II. The function of Component I processes is to identify possible courses of action and their consequences. The function of Component II is to identify which course of action is the *moral* action (or the one best satisfying moral ideals). Cognitive developmental research—notably that influenced by Piaget and Kohlberg—primarily deals with Component II processes. For me, the most important theoretical points about the cognitive developmental approach are fourfold. (1) Development is characterized in terms of a person's progressive understanding of the purpose, function, and nature of social cooperation, instead of in terms of learning more social rules, or being more willing to sacrifice oneself. (2) The lasting effects of social experience are portrayed in terms of increased understanding of the rationale for establishing cooperative arrangements, particularly as to how each of the participants in the cooperative system are reciprocating the burdens and benefits of that system. Therefore, the residue of social experience in long-term memory is characterized in terms of general concepts of justice (or "schemes of cooperation"). At first, children become aware of fairly simple schemes of cooperation, involving only a few people who know each other through face-to-face encounters, and who reciprocate in concrete, short-term exchanges. Gradually they become aware of more complicated schemes of cooperation, involving long-term, society-wide networks, institutionalized role systems, divisions of labor, and law-making and law-enforcement systems (see Rest, 1979, for further discussion). The various schemes of cooperation (or "justice structures") are called "stages" of moral reasoning, each characterized in terms of its distinctive notion of justice—that is, progressive awareness of the possibilities and requirements for arranging cooperation among successively wider circles of participants. Each stage is viewed as an underlying *general* framework of assumptions about how people ought to act towards each other. (3) There are a finite number of basic "schemes of cooperation," these can be identified, and are essentially like Kohlberg's descriptions of the six stages. Furthermore, the stages comprise an ordered sequence such that the latter stages are elaborated from the earlier. (4) When a person is faced with a particular new social situation and is trying to figure out what would be the moral course of action, the person calls from long-term memory those general knowledge structures in order to aid in identifying the most important considerations, to prioritize the conflicting claims of various people, and to judge which course of action best fulfills one's ideal of justice. And so a moral judgment for a particular situation involves assimilating the situation to general social knowledge represented by the "stages" of moral judgment.

Now I don't believe that these general justice structures (or stages) are the *only* determinants of which course of action is morally right. For example, some research by Mordecai Nisan (1984) indicates that the prevailing social norms of a community can affect one's judgment about what is morally right. Work by Lawrence (1978) indicates that religious or political ideology can overrule one's concepts of justice; also some of my recent work (Rest, 1981) indicates that there are many complicating linkages between "stages" and action advocacy. Nevertheless, research on the six-stage model of moral judgment originally proposed by Kohlberg has been one of the most productive and significant research enterprises in all of social-personality development. Of course, it is not possible to present the documentation here. However, I would like to draw on just a few findings from the vast research on moral judgment that are especially relevant to the potential targets of our moral education efforts.

The most widely used assessment technique for studying moral judgment in late adolescence and adulthood is the Defining Issues Test (DIT). The DIT is a multiple choice test derived from Kohlberg's general approach, but with some different properties from Kohlberg's test. Details about the test characteristics of the DIT are reviewed in several other places (e.g., Rest, 1979). Table 1.2 presents the average scores on the DIT of several groups.

Notice that there is a definite age-education trend: The students in junior high have low scores, the college students have medium scores, and the graduate students have high scores. In some studies, age and education account for almost 50% of the variance in scores (Rest, 1979). Notice also that the moral philosophy/political science graduate students have the highest scores—this makes some intuitive sense if we regard moral philosophers as experts in moral reasoning. Notice that the average college student is about 22 points below the moral

TABLE 1.2*
Selected Groups in Moral Judgment
Development*

Average P-Index	Group
18.9	Institutionalized delinquent boys, average age = 16.1
21.9	Average junior high student
23.5	Prison inmates
28.2	Adults with senior high education
31.8	Average senior high school student
40.0	Average of adults in general
41.6	Navy enlisted men
42.3	Average college student
42.8	Students in graduate business school
46.4	Staff nurses
46.8	College volunteers for community service project
49.5	Practicing medical physicians
50.2	Medical students
52.2	Advanced law students
59.8	Seminarians in liberal Protestant seminary
65.2	Moral philosophy and political science doctoral students.

*DIT scores are expressed here in terms of the P-Index which represents the relative importance that a subject gives to "principled" considerations in making a moral decision—in other words, the degree to which a subject takes a philosophical perspective in deciding what ought to be done in a moral dilemma. The score is determined by the percentage of Stage 5 and 6 items that a subject ranks as more important than items at lower stages.

philosophy students and that the average junior high student is about 21 points below the college student. This indicates that the average college student is as far from thinking like a moral philosopher as the junior high student is from the college student. One of the important implications of these data for moral educators is that the natural assimilative frameworks of meaning used by most adolescents and young adults to make "moral sense" of social situations is dramatically different from the operative frameworks of moral philosophers. Ethics instruction that disregards the natural assimilative framework of the students and assumes either too much or too little cognitive elaboration is likely to seem artificial and irrelevant to the students and unlikely to connect with their natural ways of thinking.

In the data that we have on various groups of subjects, we find that DIT scores are more highly correlated with years of formal education than with chronological age. For example, a group of adults who are 50–60 years old and have only a high school education have DIT scores similar to current high school students; adults who have college educations and who are 50–60 years old have scores similar to current college students. In other words, the cross-sectional data suggest that, generally, a person's moral judgment score increases while he or she is in formal schooling; and, after a person ends his/her formal education, the moral judgment score levels off. In some longitudinal data, presented in Fig. 1.1, we see the growth curves for two groups: Both groups were schoolmates in high school (in 1972), but after graduation one group went on to college and the other group did not. Each group was tested at two-year intervals (1974, 1976, 1978, 1980) and you can see that the non-college group leveled off and reached a plateau in young adulthood, whereas the college group continued to increase in DIT scores and become increasingly divergent from the non-college group. Five other longitudinal studies of DIT scores during the college years also show significant increases (see Rest, 1983a, for citations). (I might also mention that in Kohlberg's longitudinal sample, formal education is also powerfully correlated with his test of moral judgment—Colby, Kohlberg, Gibbs, & Lieberman, 1983.) This suggests that formal education is a powerful determinant of moral judgment development. The main problem right now is that we don't know what specifically it is about formal education or the college environment that is primarily responsible for this effect. Is it the formal curriculum? Is it the social interaction and extracurricular activities? Is it the general intellectual stimulation? Is it a personality self-selection factor that college students have? The gains in college cannot be attributed solely to moral education courses in college because most college students who show gains do not take these courses. Moreover, when subjects do take moral education courses, even when the experimental groups gain significantly more than the control groups, the gains are not large (typically one-tenth to one-twentieth of the effective range of the moral judgment tests); and the final scores of the "treated" groups are still far below the scores of moral philosophy/political science doctoral students. There is good news and

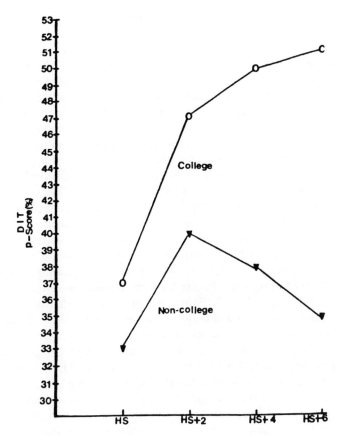

FIG. 1.1   Longitudinal change in DIT score in the college-bound group and in the non-college group.

bad news in these findings. The good news is that the intervention studies suggest that our ways of assessing moral judgment must be reflecting something fundamental and basic to natural development rather than reflecting merely the surface learning of a special terminology, or mastering certain tricks of argument, or being able to drop the names of moral philosophers and their theories. The bad news is that to date our moral education courses are not spectacularly powerful. Currently we have some studies focused on the conditions and mechanisms of change (Rest, 1979, 1983a; Spickelmier, 1983; Volker, 1980).

I'd like to mention one last set of findings. This is that moral judgment as measured by the DIT is significantly related to behavior. Blasi (1980) recently completed a review of studies linking behavior to moral judgment, studies that primarily used Kohlberg's test. A number of behavioral studies using the DIT are reviewed in Rest, 1979. Of these studies, the most pertinent one to our moral education project is that linking the DIT to clinical ratings of medical interns, as discussed by Candee, this volume (cf. Sheehan, Husted, Candee, Cook, & Bargen, 1980). The most intriguing point is that the general quality of work of medical interns was significantly related to moral judgment. This finding is all the more impressive when we recognize that very few psychological variables have been found to predict the quality of a doctor's performance. The work of Candee and Sheehan has been at least a minor sensation among researchers in the health sciences and I know of several new projects that are eager to follow up this finding. This research supports the view that development in moral judgment should be an important component in the education of health professionals. Health professionals who score high on moral judgment are rated as doing a better overall job than those who score low.

Along with many other psychologists following Kohlberg's lead, the University of Minnesota project in the School of Dentistry has initiated an intervention program to foster development in moral judgment that emphasizes peer discussion of controversial moral dilemmas. Dr. Bebeau conducts this work and she has drawn heavily from the educational program at Alverno College, particularly from Dr. Marcia Mentkowski. I must leave the elaboration of this program to them (Bebeau & Speidel, 1983; Earley, Mentkowski, & Shafer, 1980; Mentkowski & Strait, 1983) and will only mention that the faculty in the School of Dentistry are heavily involved in this activity.

Further work on the moral judgment variable will attempt to go beyond the DIT and Kohlberg's test. Both Kohlberg's test and the DIT were designed to rough out the major markers of development over the life span; they are extremely coarse-grained. We would like to have finer-grained characterizations of people's thinking that is especially relevant to the most pertinent issues of a particular profession, and the concepts and problem-solving strategies that specifically deal with those issues. We don't just want to know whether subjects are employing a "principled" perspective (i.e., using Stages 5 and 6), but want a more detailed model of the psychological processes used by "experts." Here is where people from the normative disciplines (philosophy, law, theology) can be helpful by providing criteria and rationales for identifying "expert" problem-solving. Practitioners in the field provide instances of problem-solving which the psychologist can then model and describe.

Component III.   Component III involves deciding what one actually intends to do by selecting among competing values. Typically, a person is aware of a number of possible outcomes of different courses of action, each representing different values and activating different motives. And, it is not unusual for nonmoral values to be so strong and attractive that a person chooses a course of action that preempts or compromises the moral ideal. For instance, Damon (1977) asked young children how 10 candy bars *ought* to be distributed as rewards for making bracelets. In interviews, the children described various schemes for a fair distribution of rewards, explaining why they thought a particular distribution *ought* to be followed. However, when these same children *actually* were given the 10 candy bars to distribute, they deviated from their espoused schemes of fair distribution, and instead gave *themselves* a disproportionate number of candy bars. Thus the children's espoused moral ideals were compromised by other motives, in this case, by desire for those tasty candy bars.

Given that a person is aware of various possible courses of action in a situation, each leading to a different kind of outcome or goal, why then would a person ever choose the moral alternative, especially if it involves sacrificing some personal interest or enduring some hardship? What motivates moral behavior? A large number of answers to this question have been proposed. I'll briefly list some of the theories of moral motivation (see Rest, 1983b, for a more complete discussion):

1. People behave morally because evolution has bred altruism into our genetic inheritance (e.g., Wilson, 1975).

2. "Conscience makes cowards of us all"—that is, shame, guilt, conditioned negative affect, fear of God motivates morality (e.g., Aronfreed, 1968; Eysenck, 1976).

3. There is no special motivation to be moral; people just respond to reinforcement and/or modeling opportunities and "learn" social behavior (Bandura, 1977b; Goldiamond, 1968).

4. Social understanding of how cooperation functions and one's own stake in making it work leads to moral motivation (e.g., Dewey, 1959; Piaget, 1932/1965; "liberal enlightenment").

5. Moral motivation is derived from a sense of awe and self-subjugation to something greater than the self—identification with a crusade, dedication to one's country or collective, reverence for the sacred (e.g., Durkheim, 1961; Erikson, 1958).

6. Empathy is the basis for altruistic motivation (e.g., Hoffman, 1977).

7. The experience of living in just and caring communities can lead to understanding how cooperative communities are possible and to moral commitment (e.g., Rawls, 1971; Kohlberg, this volume).

8. Concern for self integrity and one's identity as a moral agent is what motivates moral action (Blasi, this volume).

These eight theories about moral motivation indicate the diversity of views on the issue. None of these views is supported by very complete or compelling research evidence at this point, and an enormous amount of work needs to be done on this component of morality.

At present, the interdisciplinary project at the University of Minnesota has no elaborate educational intervention designed to foster moral motivation. Of course, to the degree that moral motivation is affected by social understanding, our educational program does try to make clear to the students their stake in maintaining cooperative systems and professional standards. Moreover, in a tentative way, we are trying to expose students to respected professionals who obviously are technically competent and "successful" in their careers (in the usual sense of "success"), but in addition, are sensitive and concerned about the moral issues of their profession. In the future we hope to invite respected practitioners from the community to speak to students about moral dilemmas they have faced in their practice. The basic idea is that the students will respect these professionals, aspire to be like them, and will develop an ideal image of their professional selves not only as technically competent but also as active moral agents in a wider social world. Hopefully by fostering these aspirations, we will have some impact on their moral motivation.

Component IV. This component involves executing and implementing a plan of action. As popular wisdom advises, good intentions are often a long way from good deeds. Component IV involves figuring out the sequence of concrete actions, working around impediments and unexpected difficulties, overcoming fatigue and frustration, resisting distractions and other allurements, and keeping sight of the eventual goal. Perseverance, resoluteness, competence, and "character" are virtues of Component IV. Psychologists sometimes refer to these processes as involving "ego strength" or "self-regulation skills." A biblical term for failure in Component IV processes is "weakness of the flesh." However, firm resolve, perseverance, iron will, strong character, ego strength, and so on can be used for ill or good. Ego strength comes in handy to rob a bank, prepare for a marathon, rehearse for a piano concert, or carry out genocide.

In one study of Stage Four "Law and Order" subjects on Kohlberg's measure, those with high "ego strength" cheated less than Stage Four subjects with low ego strength. Presumably the former had "the strength of their convictions," whereas the latter had convictions but didn't act on them (Krebs, 1967). Various other lines of research also suggest that a certain inner strength, an ability to mobilize oneself to action, is a factor in moral behavior. D. E. Barrett and M. R. Yarrow (1977) found that social assertiveness was an important component in children's "prosocial" behavior. Perry London (1970) interviewed people who were involved in saving persecuted Jews in Nazi Germany, and was struck by their adventurousness as well as their caring.

Research with young children has described techniques for enhancing persistence in tasks that require effort, for supplying the "oomph" to improve one's follow-through (Masters & Santrock, 1976; Mischel, 1974). Self regulation is enhanced by training children to verbalize messages to themselves, such as, "This is fun, really fun!" Individuals who act as cheerleaders to themselves are able to increase their persistence and follow-through. Bandura states that expectations of efficacy determine "whether coping behavior will be initiated, how much effort will be expended, and how long it will be sustained in the face of obstacles and adverse experiences" (1977a). With older subjects, Rational Emotive Therapy (Ellis, 1977) employs basically the same technique as that of Masters and Santrock, attempting to increase persistence by engendering expectations of efficacy and goal-mindedness. While these techniques may be effective with children and patients in therapy, there is, however, some question about their appropriateness for wide-scale use in professional schools.

In the University of Minnesota's interdisciplinary project, we have not yet addressed the issues of assessing Component IV or of designing special interventions focusing on Component IV. However, it does seem likely that we may be helpful in increasing students' ability to carry through on their moral commitments. For one, we can alert students to the most recurrent moral problems they will encounter, and thus reduce the surprise and confusion when the problems do arise. Also we can provide practice in problem-solving and equip them with problem-solving tools. Furthermore, we can present occasions for clarifying their moral aspirations which may strengthen their resolve.

In conclusion, the four-component model has provided a programmatic structure for the psychologist's contribution to our interdisciplinary project. In short, we want to develop assessment instruments for each component, to study its nature and the conditions for change, and to develop interventions to facilitate development in each component. My presentation of the four-component model has been lopsided in attending more to Component II, moral judgment. However, that is where most research and educational activity has been. This account has also heavily emphasized the contribution of the research psychologist in the interdisciplinary team—likewise, this imbalance is due to my having more to say about that role. Nevertheless I hope you have some sense of how other disciplines and specialties fit in. The experienced professional in the field is necessary to define the problem and its setting, to participate in defining more adequate solutions, to model the professional as both technically competent and morally responsible, to deliver parts of the curriculum. The philosopher/lawyer/theologian is necessary for the analysis of solutions, and for identifying features which mark solutions as more or less adequate. The educational psychologist contributes to the development of curriculum materials and classroom activities, and to the training of effective teaching skills. The project that we have begun in the School of Dentistry is intended to have application in other settings as well. Currently at the University of Minnesota, some of these ideas are being used in Nursing (Crisham, 1979) and Counseling Psychology (Volker, in preparation). More generally, our work illustrates how research can feed into an educational project, and how an educational project makes research possible.

REFERENCES

Aronfreed, J. (1968). *Conduct and conscience*. New York: Acadmic.

Bandura, A. (1977a). Self efficacy: Toward a unifying theory of behavioral change. *Psychological Review, 84*(2), 191ff.

Bandura, A. (1977b). *Social learning theory*. Englewood Cliffs, NJ: Prentice-Hall.

Barrett, D. E. & Yarrow, M. R. (1977). Prosocial behavior, social inferential ability, and assertiveness in children. *Child Development, 48*, 475–481.

Bebeau, M., Rest, J., Speidel, M., Yamoor, C., & Eberhardy, J. (1982, March). *Assessing student sensitivity to ethical issues in professional problems.* Paper presented at the annual meeting of the I.A.D.R., New Orleans, LA.

Bebeau, M. & Speidel, M. (1983). *Faculty and course development for a problem-oriented course in professional responsibility.* Final Report to American Fund for Dental Health. (Available from M. Bebeau, Department of Health Ecology, University of Minnesota. Health Science Building A, 15–136, Minneapolis, MN 55455.)

Berkowitz, L. & Daniels, L. R. (1963). Responsibility and dependency. *Journal of Abnormal and Social Psychology, 66,* 429–436.

Blasi, A. (1980). Bridging moral cognition and moral action: A critical review of the literature. *Psychological Bulletin, 88,* 1–45.

Colby, A., Kohlberg, L., Gibbs, J., & Lieberman, M. (1983). A longitudinal study of moral judgment. *SRCD Monograph, 48*(1 & 2).

Crisham, P. (1979). *Moral judgment of nurses in hypothetical and nursing dilemmas.* Unpublished doctoral dissertation, University of Minnesota.

Damon, W. (1977). *The social world of the child.* San Francisco: Jossey-Bass.

Dewey, J. (1959). *Moral principle in education.* New York: Philosophical Library.

Durkheim, E. (1961). *Moral education.* New York: The Free Press.

Earley, M., Mentkowski, M., & Shafer, J. (1980). *Valuing at Alverno: The valuing process in liberal education.* Milwaukee, WI: Alverno Productions.

Ellis, A. (1977). Rational emotive thearpy: Research data that supports the clinical and personality hypothesis of RET and other modes of cognitive-behavioral therapy. *The Counseling Psychologist, 7,* 2–42.

Erikson, E. (1958). *Young man Luther.* New York: Norton.

Eysenck, H. J. (1976). The biology of morality. In T. Lickona (Ed.), *Moral development and behavior.* (pp. 108–123). New York: Holt, Rinehart & Winston.

Goldiamond, I. (1968). Moral development: A functional analysis. *Psychology Today, 2*(4), 31ff.

Hoffman, M. L. (1977). Empathy, its development and prosocial implications. In C. Keasey (Ed.), *Nebraska symposium on motivation* (Vol. 25) (pp. 169–218). Lincoln: University of Nebraska Press.

Hoffman, M. L. (in press). Affective and cognitive processes in moral internalization. In E. T. Higgins, D. Ruble, & W. Hartup (Eds.), *Social cognition and social behavior.* New York: Cambridge University.

Isen, A. M., Clark, M., Karp, L., & Shalker, T. E. (1978). Affect, accessibility of material in memory, and behavior: A cognitive loop? *Journal of Personality and Social Psychology, 36,* 1–13.

Keasey, C. B. (1978). Children's developing awareness and usage of intentionality and motives. In C. B. Keasey (Ed.), *Nebraska symposium on motivation* (Vol. 25) (pp. 219–260). Lincoln: University of Nebraska.

Kohlberg, L. (1969). Stage and sequence: The cognitive-developmental approach to socialization. In D. Goslin (Ed.), *Handbook of socialization theory and research* (pp. 347–480). Chicago: Rand McNally.

Kohlberg, L. (1976). Moral stages and moralization: The cognitive-developmental approach. In T. Lickona (Ed.), *Moral development and behavior: Theory, research and social issues* (pp. 31–53). New York: Holt, Rinehart & Winston.

Krebs, R. L. (1967). *Some relations between moral judgment, attention, and resistance to temptation.* Unpublised doctoral dissertation, University of Chicago.

Lawrence, J. A. (1978). *The component procedures of moral judgment-making.* Unpublished doctoral dissertation, University of Minnesota.

Lerner, M. J. (1971). Observer's evaluation of a victim: Justice, guilt and veridical perception. *Journal of Personality and Social Psychology, 20,* 127–135.

London, P. (1970). The rescuers: Motivational hypotheses about Christians who saved Jews from the Nazis. In J. Macaulay & L. Berkowitz (Eds.), *Altruism and helping behavior*. New York: Academic.

Masters, J. C. & Santrock, J. (1976). Studies in the self-regulation of behavior: Effects of contingent cognitive and affective events. *Developmental Psychology, 12*, 334–348.

Mentkowski, M. & Strait, M. J. (1983). *A longitudinal study of student change in cognitive development and generic abilities in an outcome-centered liberal arts curriculum*. Final Report to the National Institute of Education. (Available from M. Mentkowski, Alverno College, 3401 South 39th Street, Milwaukee, WI 53215.)

Mischel, W. (1974). Processes in delay of gratification. In L. Berkowitz (Ed.), *Advances in social psychology* Vol. 7, New York: Academic.

Mischel, W. & Mischel, H. (1976). A cognitive social-learning approach to morality and self-regulation. In T. Lickona (Ed.), *Moral development and behavior* (pp. 84–107). New York: Holt, Rinehart & Winston.

Nisan, M. (1984). Social norms and moral judgment. In W. Kurtines & J. Gewirtz (Eds.), *Morality and moral development* (pp. 208–224). New York: Wiley.

Piaget, J. (1965). *The moral judgment of the child*. (M. Gabain, Trans.). New York: The Free Press (originally published, 1932).

Pomazal, R. J. & Jaccord, J. J. (1976). An informational approach to altruistic behavior. *Journal of Personality and Social Psychology, 33*, 317–327.

Rawls, J. (1971). *A theory of justice*. Cambridge, MA: Harvard University.

Rest, J. R. (1979). *Development in judging moral issues*. University of Minnesota.

Rest, J. R. (1981, April). *Action advocacy in hypothetical moral dilemmas*. Paper presented at the biannual meeting of S.R.C.D., Boston, MA.

Rest, J. R. (1983a). *The relation of moral judgment development to formal education*. Technical Report, Minnesota Moral Research Project. (Available from J. Rest, 206A Burton Hall, University of Minnesota, Minneapolis, MN 55455.)

Rest, J. R. (1983b). Morality. In J. H. Flavell & E. M. Markman (Eds.), *Cognitive development*, volume in P. H. Mussen (Ed.), *Handbook of child psychology*, 4th edition (pp. 556–629). New York: Wiley.

Rest, J. R. (1984). The major components of morality. In W. Kurtines & J. Gewirtz (Eds.), *Morality and moral development*. (pp. 24–38). New York: Wiley.

Schwartz, S. H. (1977). Normative influences on altruism. In L. Berkowitz (Ed.), *Advances in experimental social psychology* (Vol. 10) (pp. 221–279). New York: Academic.

Selman, R. L. (1980). *The growth of interpersonal understanding*. New York: Academic.

Shantz, C. U. (1983). Social cognition. In J. H. Flavell & E. M. Markman (Eds.), *Cognitive development*, volume in P. H. Mussen (Ed.), *Handbook of child psychology*, 4th edition (pp. 495–555). New York: Wiley.

Sheehan, T. J., Husted, S. D., Candee, D., Cook, C. D., & Bargen, M. (1980). Moral judgment as a predictor of clinical performance. *Evaluation and the Health Professions, 3*, 393–404.

Spickelmier, J. (1983). *College experiences and moral judgment development*. Unpublished doctoral dissertation, University of Minnesota.

Staub, E. (1978, 1979). *Positive social behavior and morality* (Vol. I and II). New York: Academic.

Volker, J. (1980). *Moral reasoning and college experience*. Unpublished master's thesis, University of Minnesota.

Volker, J. (in preparation). *Moral sensitivity in counseling-psychology students*. Unpublished doctoral dissertation, University of Minnesota.

Wilson, E. O. (1975). *Sociobiology: The new synthesis*. Cambridge, MA: Belkap Press of Harvard University.

Zajonc, R. B. (1980). Feeling and thinking: Perferences need no inferences. *American Psychologist, 35*, 151–175.

2 The Just Community Approach to Moral Education in Theory and Practice

Lawrence Kohlberg
Harvard University

For the last 12 years, I, along with other academicians, have been involved in developing and researching an approach to moral education that we have called "the Just Community approach." The first thing I want to stress is that the approach assumes a much different relationship between theory and practice than did our first efforts in moral education, i.e., classroom hypothetical dilemma discussion. These early efforts generated disputes and questions as to whether academicians should involve themselves in programs in the schools or prisons. Nevertheless there was a sense that moral education was a wave of the future in America. Foundations were eager to fund moral education projects and a number of school systems were eager to be the sites of such projects. None of us felt we had an established theory and research base for moral education but I at least felt such a base could only be developed through engaging in the process. I agreed with Dewey when he said of education, "One can never have a science of bridge-building before building bridges."

Moral education in terms of moral stages was launched in 1968 when Blatt finished his thesis (Blatt & Kohlberg, 1975). The Blatt approach involved having children discuss hypothetical moral dilemmas and showing with that kind of Socratic discussion that on the average one-third of the children moved up one stage or there was a one-third stage change in most of the children (what I henceforth have called "the Blatt effect"), which has now been replicated in about 100 classrooms. The moral stages are described in Table 2.1. A hypothetical dilemma, the Heinz dilemma, and examples of stage responses are presented in Table 2.2. The manual for scoring stages is currently in press (Colby, Candee, Gibbs, Hewer, Kaufman, Kohlberg, Power, & Speicher-Dubin, in press). The Blatt approach was the classical way of going from research to

TABLE 2.1
Definition of Moral Stages

I. Preconventional level

At this level the child is responsive to cultural rules and labels of good and bad, right or wrong, but interprets these labels either in terms of the physical or the hedonistic consequences of action (punishment, reward, exchange of favors) or in terms of the physical power of those who enunciate the rules and labels. The level is divided into the following two stages:

Stage 1: *The punishment-and-obedience orientation*. The physical consequences of action determine its goodness or badness regardless of the human meaning or value of these consequences. Avoidance of punishment and unquestioning deference to power are valued in their own right, not in terms of respect for an underlying moral order supported by punishment and authority (the latter being stage 4).

Stage 2: *The instrumental-relativist orientation*. Right action consists of that which instrumentally satisfies one's own needs and occasionally the needs of others. Human relations are viewed in terms like those of the market place. Elements of fairness, of reciprocity, and of equal sharing are present, but they are always interpreted in a physical pragmatic way. Reciprocity is a matter of "you scratch my back and I'll scratch yours," not of loyalty, gratitude, or justice.

II. Conventional level

At this level, maintaining the expectations of the individual's family, group, or nation is perceived as valuable in its own right, regardless of immediate and obvious consequences. The attitude is not only one of *conformity* to personal expectations and social order, but of loyalty to it, of actively *maintaining*, supporting, and justifying the order, and of identifying with the persons or group involved in it. At this level, there are the following two stages:

Stage 3: *The interpersonal concordance or "good boy—nice girl" orientation*. Good behavior is that which pleases or helps others and is approved by them. There is much conformity to stereotypical images of what is majority or "natural" behavior. Behavior is frequently judged by intention—"he means well" becomes important for the first time. One earns approval by being "nice."

Stage 4: *The "law and order" orientation*. There is orientation toward authority, fixed rules, and the maintenance of the social order. Right behavior consists of doing one's duty, showing respect for authority, and maintaining the given social order for its own sake.

III. Postconventional, autonomous, or principled level

At this level, there is a clear effort to define moral values and principles that have validity and application apart from the authority of the groups or persons holding these principles and apart from the individual's own identification with these groups. This level again has two stages:

Stage 5: *The social-contract legalistic orientation*, generally with utilitarian overtones. Right action tends to be defined in terms of general individual rights, and standards which have been critically examined and agreed upon by the whole society. There is a clear awareness of the relativism of personal values and opinions and a corresponding emphasis upon procedural rules for reaching consensus. Aside from what is constitutionally and democratically agreed upon, the right is a matter of personal "values" and "opinion." The result is an emphasis upon the "legal point of view," but with an emphasis upon the possibility of changing law in terms of rational considerations of social utility (rather than freezing it in terms of stage 4 "law and order"). Outside the legal realm, free agreement and contract is the binding element of obligation. This is the "official" morality of the American government and constitution.

Stage 6: *The universal-ethical-principle orientation*. Right is defined by the decision of conscience in accord with self-chosen *ethical principles* appealing to logical comprehensiveness, universality, and consistency. These principles are abstract and ethical (the Golden Rule, the categorical imperative); they are not concrete moral rules like the Ten Commandments. At heart, these are universal principles of *justice*, of the *reciprocity* and *equality* of human *rights*, and of respect for the dignity of human beings as *individual persons* ("From Is to Ought," pp. 164/5).

TABLE 2.2
Examples of Responses at Each Stage to the Heinz Dilemma

In Europe, a woman was near death from a very bad disease, a special kind of cancer. There was one drug that the doctors thought might save her. It was a form of radium that a druggist in the same town had recently discovered. The drug was expensive to make, but the druggist was charging 10 times what the drug cost him to make. He paid $200 for the radium and charged $2000 for a small dose of the drug. The sick woman's husband, Heinz, went to everyone he knew to borrow the money, but he could get together only about $1000 which was half of what it cost. He told the druggist that his wife was dying, and asked him to sell it cheaper or let him pay later. But the druggist said, ''No, I discovered the drug and I'm going to make money from it.'' Heinz got desperate and broke into the man's store to steal the drug for his wife.

STAGE 1
TOMMY AT AGE 10:
Heinz shouldn't steal; he should buy the drug. If he steals the drug, he might get put in jail and have to put the drug back anyway.

But maybe Heinz should steal the drug because his wife might be an important lady, like Betsy Ross, she made the flag.

STAGE 2
TOMMY AT AGE 13:
Heinz should steal the drug to save his wife's life. He might get sent to jail, but he'd still have his wife.

(''Tommy, you said he should steal the drug for his wife. Should he steal it if it were a friend who was dying?'')

That's going too far. He could be in jail while his friend is alive and free. I don't think a friend would do that for him.

STAGE 3
TOMMY AT AGE 16:
If I was Heinz, I would have stolen the drug for my wife. You can't put a price on love, no amount of gifts make love. You can't put a price on life either.

STAGE 4
TOMMY AT AGE 21:
When you get married, you take a vow to love and cherish your wife. Marriage is not only love, it's an obligation. Like a legal contract.

STAGE 5
KENNY AT AGE 25:
I think he was justified in breaking in because there was a human life at stake. I think that transcends any right that the druggist had to the drug.

DID THE DRUGGIST HAVE RIGHT TO CHARGE THAT MUCH WHEN NO LAW SETTING LIMIT?

He has a legal right, but I don't think he had a moral right to do it. The profit was excessive, it was 10 times what he bought it for.

(Continued)

TABLE 2.2 (*Continued*)

IS IT THE HUSBAND'S DUTY OR OBLIGATION TO STEAL THE DRUG FOR HIS WIFE IF HE CAN GET IT NO OTHER WAY?

Again, I think the fact that her life was in danger transcends any other standards you might use to judge his actions.

(WHY?)

Well supposedly man is the supreme being and we are the most valuable resource on the planet, it is important to preserve a human life.

SUPPOSE IT WAS SOMEONE DYING WHO WASN'T EVEN CLOSE. BUT THERE WAS NO ONE ELSE TO HELP HIM. WOULD IT BE RIGHT TO STEAL DRUG FOR SUCH A STRANGER?

It's something he should do. In order to be consistent, yes, I would have to say. Something he should do again from a moral standpoint.

WHAT IS THIS MORAL STANDPOINT?

Well, I think every individual has a right to live and if there is a way of saving an individual I think an individual should be saved if he wants to be.

WHAT DOES THE WORD MORALITY MEAN TO YOU?

I think it is acting so as to, I have to get my thinking straight on that. Nobody in the world knows the answer. I think it is presuming or recognizing the right of the individual to do, well, basically it is recognizing the rights of other individuals, not interfering with those rights, act as fairly, it is going to sound corny, but as you would have them treat you, as you would expect them to treat you, fairly and honestly. I think it is basically to preserve the human being's right to existence, I think that is the most important. Secondly, the human being's rights to do as he pleases, again without interfering with somebody else's rights.

STAGE 6
JOAN AGE 32:

NOW THE FIRST QUESTION IS, WHAT DO YOU SEE AS THE PROBLEM IN THIS SITUATION?

The problem for Heinz seems to be that his wife is dying and that he's caught in between obeying societal law of not stealing and committing a crime that would result in saving his wife's life. I would like to think that here's a conflict for the druggist as well. Anytime there are conflicts in a situation. . . . As soon as more than one person knows about a situation, O.K., that there's shared conflicts and the conflicts of each person sort of play off one another. And I think that the conflicts can be resolved to some extent by kind of pooling—so that as soon as more than one person becomes aware of the conflict that there are automatically problems to be resolved by each, things to be considered by each; and each person then has the power to affect what happens in the conflict. If I were Heinz I, you know, would keep trying to talk with the druggist . . . I have a hard time thinking of any decision as being static and it seems to me that dialogue is very important and a continuing dialogue in this kind of situation. But if it came to a point where nothing else could be done, I think that in consultation with his wife, if he and his wife decided that that would be an acceptable alternative for Heinz, then yes he should. Because I think that ultimately it comes down to a conflict of duties. On the other hand, Heinz, I think as, just by virtue of being a member of the human race, has an obligation, a duty to protect other people I guess that's a way to put it.

(*Continued*)

TABLE 2.2 (*Continued*)

And when it gets down to a conflict between those two, I think that the protection of human life is more important.

IS IT IMPORTANT FOR PEOPLE TO DO EVERYTHING THEY CAN TO SAVE ANOTHER'S LIFE?

No. I have this natural responsibility I'm talking about—to preserve your dignity, integrity, as an autonomous human being. And now when I think 'Do I have a responsibility to save your life?' I think that depends a lot. If I'm walking down the street, yes. I would do anything I could to save somebody else's life. I mean if I saw somebody walking in front of a car, I would jerk that person out of the way of the car. That would be the way I would react automatically. But, in other situations it depends. If you are terminally ill and you have decided that you would prefer rational suicide, or would prefer to not go through any more chemotherapy, any number of those things, I don't feel that I have the right to intrude on that position of yours, to say that you must take this chemotherapy, it's going to extend your life for a week longer, or a month longer or something. I don't see myself doing that, no.

LET ME ASK YOU THIS QUESTION: IN LOOKING AT THE ORIGINAL SITUATION OF HEINZ AND THE DRUG AND DECIDING WHETHER TO STEAL OR NOT, IS THERE ANY ONE CONSIDERATION THAT STANDS OUT IN YOUR MIND ABOVE ALL OTHERS, IN MAKING A DECISION OF THIS SORT?

I would say that there are two things. The first thing is that no person has the right to make a decision that affects the dignity and integrity of another person without there being cooperative discussion among the people involved. Number one. The second thing is that, you know, in this very strange situation where it would come down to being, you know, the single person's decision, and I have trouble conceiving that as ever happening, then it comes down to preserving the dignity and integrity. . . and for the reason of life usually is involved in that, of another person. So I guess I'm saying that, well. . . I'm not saying that preserving life is *the* essential or ultimate thing. I think that preserving a person's dignity and integrity are the important things.

IF HEINZ DOESN'T LOVE HIS WIFE, SHOULD HE STEAL THE DRUG FOR HER?

I don't think that he should steal it out of a sense of love. I think that Heinz should steal the drug, if it comes down to that far-reaching point, out of a sense of responsibility to preserve life, not out of love. I think responsibility, as I'm using it here, means a recognition of dignity, on the part of every living being, but I could narrow it down, if you like, to persons. And responsibility is really something that's entailed in that recognition. If I respect you as a creature with dignity and your own unique, special being, in recognizing that I won't intrude on you, I won't purposefully harm you—there's this whole series of negatives that go along with being responsible and there's also some positives. And that's to recognize you as being unique, important and integral, in some sense, and to do what I can to preserve all that.

SUPPOSE THE PERSON DYING IS NOT HIS WIFE BUT A STRANGER. SHOULD HEINZ STEAL THE DRUG FOR A STRANGER?

Yes.

IS IT A DUTY OR OBLIGATION FOR HEINZ?

When I think of my being obliged to do something, I think of another person as having a special claim, a claim that goes beyond the sort of minimal claims we all have on one another. To me that's obligation. And responsibility is what I naturally feel for every person. It's not imposed on me from the outside, it's part of my nature as a human being.

practice; it simply applied classical Piagetian developmental psychology theory and the results of training studies using cognitive conflict and exposure to the next stage up to the classroom. The Blatt approach had a pure research basis; for example the studies of Rest (1973) on comprehension, preference and assimilation and the Turiel (1966) experimental studies in which children were exposed to advice at different stages with pro and con arguments on an issue and then pre and posttested for change, with change being mainly to the next stage up. Blatt took this research-based approach to the classroom and found, somewhat to my surprise, that a little moral discussion would move children up a third of a stage. I asked him to replicate it a number of times, which he did in many different ways. We were finally convinced that the stages were influenceable by this kind of Socratic moral discussion. Some of the moral education interventions that followed the Blatt studies are reported in Mosher (1980) or summarized by Lockwood (1978).

The philosophic rationale for the practice of Socratic dilemma discussion also seemed straightforward from a theoretical standpoint (Kohlberg, 1981). It rested on two arguments about moral development as the aim of moral education. The first argument, more Deweyite, considers development as defining the process of education. It claims that the development approach is a further alternative to relativistic individualism on the one side and indoctrination on the other side. Paradigmatic of relativism was Rath's and Simon's values clarification or values realization. Like Protagoras and the Sophist in the days of Socrates, the values clarifiers helped the individual student to express and organize his values while being relativistic about recognizing that other students had other values. Given its premises and procedures the values clarifier was powerless if the student's values included genocide, as an extreme example, or cheating on exams at the more likely level.

At the other extreme was indoctrination, usually rationalized through a ''bag of virtues,'' as I irreverently termed this approach. In the American studies of Hartshorne and May (1928 30) the three cardinal virtues were named honesty, service, and self-control. In today's Peoples Republic of China, the virtues include courtesy, cleanliness with regard to the environment, loyalty, and cleanliness of thought. Such an approach is arbitrary in its content. It is indoctrinative in its approach. In contrast, the developmental approach appeals to rational autonomy in both its intent or theory and in its method, which is Socratic.

The second argument, more debatable, rests on the premise that a higher stage is a better stage culminating in a Stage 5 of universal human rights, and democratic agreement and contract, a liberal philosophy basic to any Constitutional democracy, and a Stage 6 which, in Jürgen Habermas' (1979) version represents discursive will formation in a paradigm of universal dialogue and which, in my version, represents ideal role-taking or ''moral musical chairs.'' In Kohlberg (1981) I call this endpoint ''Justice as Reversibility'' and liken the sociomoral operations of justice like reciprocity and equality to the reversibility Piaget finds in operational logico-mathematical thought. Higher stages are not only formally better, but they lead in some situations and under some conditions to a universal consensus on choice, the aim of reasoning and argumentation about justice. This lends support to the Socratic faith in the universality of rational justice.

What I have described really is a straight movement from developmental psychology and philosophy to practice, what I call a one-way street model. A psychologist takes a theory, developed and tested by pure developmental psychology research, and then starts to apply the theory and make prescriptions from the theory to classroom practice, and then evaluates the effect by summative rather than formative research. I had never really felt that that was a viable way of relating research to practice in moral education. I rather believed that you had to be in reciprocal collaboration with teachers. The theorist, as consultant, searches for concepts and methods which aid the teacher in making the decisions he or she faces rather than making prescriptions to teachers based on deductions from developmental psychology theory and research. The one-way street model of relating theory to practice rests on what I have called the "psychologist's fallacy," i.e., to believe that what is important for developmental psychology research is what is important for practitioners in the classroom. I think Skinnerian behavior modification was, at least until recently, a good example of the psychologist's fallacy of application of preformed theory based on pure research findings to prescriptions for educational practice. Practically I came to realize the lack of utility of the one-way street approach from a Stone Foundation study by Colby, Kohlberg, Fenton, Speicher-Dubin, and Lieberman (1977). In the study, Fenton and I trained a number of teachers to do hypothetical moral discussion in connection with their social studies courses, using Fenton's text books. We found a Blatt effect in about half the classrooms. In those classrooms there were two specific elements: first, a Socratic approach by the teacher that really did ask probing questions for reasons, and second, a stage mixture in classes, i.e., children had to be reasoning at more than one stage, or sizeable numbers at at least two stages, to get change. Our research results indicated the operation was a success in the sense that it showed that ordinary classroom teachers, or at least half of them, reproduced the Blatt effect without being elaborately trained and motivated psychology graduate students. However, while the intervention operation was a success, the patient died; that is, we went back a year later and found that not a single teacher continued to do moral discussion after the commitment to the research had ended. In other words, it didn't speak enough to the teachers' and students' needs, even though it did lead to a one-third stage change.

One answer to this problem was to integrate moral discussion with teachers' curriculum goals in English and social studies. Some teachers were really innovative about curriculum, and would include and develop English literature and social studies curricula, not as in the Stone Study (just to have discussions and move people up a stage) but rather to relate moral discussion about literature and history to the way in which children experienced and thought about literature or history. Such integration of moral discussion with curriculum was carried out in the 1970s and is summarized in Mosher's (1980) book on moral education. So that is one way of getting moral development theory into education and into practice when it really can be seen by teachers to relate to curricular goals that they already have, such as sensitivity to literature.

Besides integration with the curriculum there were more fundamental limits to the dilemma discussion approach to be surmounted before we would really have a viable kind of practice. In the first place was the question of the relation of judgment to action, or what you might call the relationship of reasoning in hypothetical dilemmas to reasoning in real life dilemmas. Research studies empirically demonstrated a relationship between judgment and action (Kohlberg, 1984), but we really don't know from those studies whether change in moral judgment from educational programs would actually lead to change in moral action. So the first issue was our and the teachers' concerns for action. The second issue was the concern for content as well as for structure. The teachers I consulted with in the Cambridge Cluster school, a Just Community alternative high school, said that moral education has to deal with content as well as structure, that the old teaching of virtues approach is in a sense justified, as has been argued by Richard Peters (1981). To oversimplify, Peters set up a two-stage process, early socialization into virtues and then later, moral education as rational reflection that goes on around hypothetical moral dilemmas and other discussions. Thus the rational, structural, formal approach really only comes to play when the child has already been socialized.

The philosophic issue involved in education for content as well as structure is the issue of indoctrination. Common sense would say that teachers should help children to see that stealing is wrong or a violation of certain fundamental rights of other students and teachers and would probably be willing to accept an indoctrinative approach to this content. Unwilling to accept indoctrination, we do accept what we now call an advocacy approach to the teaching of moral content. But, what are its limits? I have accepted the idea that the teacher is and should be an advocate for certain moral content. The teacher in real life has to go beyond being a process facilitator, a Socratic questioner or a Carl Rogers reflector and supporter of development. This latter stance is quite workable for hypothetical moral dilemmas, but if there is an actual episode of stealing, the teacher is going to advocate for what we hope is the right answer in this moral decision.

Following, for instance, Downey and Kelley's (1978) review of the indoctrination issue in moral education, we may consider indoctrination in terms of (a) the content of what is taught, (b) the method of teaching and (c) the intent of the teacher. In terms of *content* teaching, Darwinian evolution is not indoctrination because its content is within limits verifiable; teaching Creationism is a content which is not verifiable. Within broad limits I believe principles of justice represent content on which it is possible to reach some rational consensus, a consensus in America expressed by the Declaration of Independence's enumeration of equal rights to life, liberty and opportunity in the pursuit of happiness. In terms of manner or *method*, moral advocacy of justice can be by the method of appeal to reasons which the teacher himself accepts, rather than by the use of the teacher's authority. In terms of *intention*, advocacy of justice by the teacher can and should be based on an attitude of respect for the student, as an autonomous moral agent, i.e., advocacy should be just in its method and intent, not only in its content. Philosophically what prevents advocacy from being indoctrination is the establishment of participatory democracy in the classroom or in the school. The teacher can only advocate as one, the first among equals, from a rational point of view, and not through reliance on authority or power. The teacher should be one member of a democratic political community, in which each person has one vote. The best assurance that teacher advocacy stays within these bounds is participatory democracy in the classroom or the school. As I shall illustrate later, effective teacher advocacy in a Just Community school rests on use of reasons of fairness or community, usually at a relatively advanced stage in a context of controversy about the rightness of a particular rule or policy. We shall illustrate cases where teachers have strong moral opinions about use of drugs, school attendance or cheating which cannot directly be imposed on students in a Just Community school through authority, but only become influential insofar as they are couched in terms of considerations of justice or community. Furthermore, I shall illustrate that there is an ongoing dialogue about the rights of the minority or the individual and the rights of the community manifested in majority vote. In these schools, this dialogue includes discussions of what the students in the Scarsdale Alternative School, another Just Community high school, call teacher intimidation, i.e., the fact that, when a teacher advocates, he or she is also perceived by students as having power through academic authority in grading, college recommendations, etc.

A NOTION OF JUSTICE

The linkage of democracy to the justice side of the Just Community approach, and to that aspect of justice we call non-indoctrination is quite clear: it is the linkage of justice to a small political community based on equal political rights. It is also clear why school democracy might succeed in developing just action as well as judgment where hypothetical dilemma discussions seem to have failed. First, in a democratic school students would make decisions about real-life dilemmas and actions, ones they have to make for the school's survival as a community. They have to take responsibility for rules and a discipline process which they come to through discussion, reasoning and argumentation about fairness. Second, they would be confronted by teachers and peers about discrepancies between their public judgments and reasoning and their actual action. If they voted or agreed to a rule, a violation of that rule could be confronted by teachers and peers as a gap in self-consistency, as a "hypocrisy", rather than as ignoring an authority-made rule.

While non-indoctrinative, our approach may be called socializing or "socialization". This is so because, unlike hypothetical moral dilemma discussion, it does involve the use of group criticism, reward, and discipline.

The ideal of justice which guides our definition of a Just Community is theoretically articulated at what we have tentatively identified as a sixth stage of justice reasoning and judgment. What we take to be a Stage 6 response to the Heinz dilemma is presented in Table 2.2.

We may summarize this interview around several points. First, this woman, Joan believes in actual dialogue or full communication and a correlated reversible role-taking, or "moral musical chairs", in coming to a solution. Second, she follows Kant in thinking that a decision must be universalizable (cf. Höffe, this volume). Third, she has a single general principle for resolving moral dilemmas, responsibility to other human beings as autonomous moral beings possessing dignity and integrity. This single general principle is clearly distinguished from a general rule to preserve life since she spontaneously says that it need not dictate keeping a person alive under conditions such as our euthanasia dilemma. Fourth, this prinicple defines both rights and caring responsibilities, or integrates the two. Fifth, she is non-relativist but not an absolutist; for instance, she does not define the preservation of human life as an absolute in all situations. Instead she takes a moral point of view which she thinks everybody should take to resolve moral dilemmas.

While a number of normative moral theories of justice, including some forms of utilitarianism, meet our formal criteria of Stage 6 universalized reversible general principles (Kohlberg, 1984) the theories of justice which have guided our theoretical efforts are modern developments of the Kantian deontological or formalistic tradition, as formulated by Rawls (1971), Habermas (1979) and Kohlberg (1981). At the heart of these theories is the attitude or principle of universalized and generalized respect for individual human personality and autonomy enunciated by our example of a Stage 6 response to the Heinz dilemma (Table 2.2). Central to these "Stage 6" theories is an idealized method of arriving at consensus between rational moral actors as distinct from a Stage 5 democratic majority rule method.

For Rawls, the idealized method is one of a social contract by rational actors in an "original position" under a "veil of ignorance" such that they choose principles of justice and rightness which they would accept if they did not know what position in society they were to have, well born or poor, black or white, male or female. In Kohlberg's (1981) formulation the method is one of "ideal role taking" or "moral musical chairs", i.e., a second order Golden Rule, whereby the claim of each person involved is considered while interpreting this claim based upon his or her requirement to consider or role take the claims of others involved. For Habermas, the method is one of "discursive will formation'' or mutual modification of claims and needs in light of the claims and needs of others through a dialogue process which is manifested in an ideal communication situation free of domination or manipulation. The principles of social justice which would be agreed to in such a process of reaching ideal consensus would be, following Rawls, first the maximum liberty compatible with the like liberty of others and, second, equity or equal opportunity and the distribution of status, power, and goods that does not accept inequality except insofar as the distribution is acceptable from the point of view of the least advantaged.

These modern formulations of Kant explicitly add a second equity or ideal equality principle to Kant's first liberty principle of justice. According to Kant, ''Freedom (independence from constraints of another's will) insofar as it is compatible with the freedom of everyone else in accordance with a universal law, is the one sole and original right that belongs to every human being by virtue of his humanity''. Modern libertarians like Nozick accept this principle, but they don't accept Rawls' equality principle. Our ''Stage 6'' theoretical conception of justice uses the basic principles of liberty and equality embodied in the U.S. Constitution or in the structure of a participatory democracy school deciding on issues of justice or rightness; and our ideal notion of the process of dialogue among students and teachers that goes on in such a democracy is one of ''ideal role-taking'' in our terms, and ideal communication in Habermas' terms. I should add that our conception of Stage 6 as an ideal terminus of moral development has been associated with the hypothesis that there is a monotonic increase from stage to stage in the correspondence between justice judgments and actual action. The empirical support for this assumption is documented in Kohlberg (1984) and, with regard to the particular case cited as Stage 6 in Table 2.2, in chapter 6 of that volume. Obviously we do not assume that students or teachers will always or even often engage in Stage 6 reasoning, dialogue, decision-making or action. We do, however, feel that this ideal of justice offers the psychologically optimal experience of role-taking and dialogue between persons at various stages, one which stimulates the development of justice reasoning from stage to stage, a conception that modifies the ''plus one'' strategy associated with the Blatt approach. The ''plus one'' assumption is further modified by the Walker (in press) finding that conflicting ''plus two'' pro and con role-playing leads to as much change to the next stage up as does ''plus one'' role playing, and by the finding of Berkowitz and Gibbs (1983) that ''transactive dialogue'' leads to movement to the next stage up independent of the ''plus one'' effect.

A NOTION OF COMMUNITY

We have so far discussed the philosophy and psychology of the ''right'' or the just which generates our thinking about the Just Community. We now turn to the philosophy and psychology of ''the good'', i.e., a philosophy of community, which guides our efforts. Inspired by Rousseau, the French Revolution added to liberty and equality the phrase "fraternity." Going beyond respect for rights, "the good" includes the ideals of altruism or responsibility of persons to and for one another and for participation in the affairs of the community. Community as a central moral ideal has been defined in various ways by more "organic" moral philosophers from Plato to Rousseau to Hegel, including Durkheim (1973), Royce (1982), Dewey (1966), Mac Murray (1961), and Habermas (1979).

There is a strong reason for concern in the 1980s about youth's motivation and ability to actively participate in the larger democratic community. The diagnosis given in 1978 by Lasch is that we live in "The Culture of Narcissism," more popularly known as the "Me Generation." Not necessarily unjust or immoral, the youthful student and citizen is privatistic or apathetic about the civic community, and about the public good, focusing instead on his or her own concerns and ideals of happiness. Dewey spoke forcefully for the need for school democracy to educate a sense of responsibility to participate in the civic community for the public good.

Dewey's general philosophy of moral development stresses a conception of moral character centering on what we may call "responsible altruism" or "social responsibility." Dewey (1960) rejects "a list or catalogue of virtues" as characterizing "conventional or customary, as opposed to reflective, morality" in favor of a notion of virtue as "wholehearted, persistent and impartial interest." He claims that "virtuous traits interpenetrate one another, this unity is the very idea of the integrity of character." With regard to good action he says,

A union of benevolent impulse and intelligent reflection is the interest most likely to result in conduct that is good. But in this union the role of thoughtful inquiry is quite as important as that of sympathetic affection.

Our discussion points to the conclusion that neither egoism nor altruism nor any combination of the two is a satisfactory principle. Selfhood is not something which exists apart from association and intercourse. The interests that are formed in the social environment are far more important than are the adjustments of isolated selves.

We must realize the fact that regard for self and regard for others are both secondary phases of a more normal and complete interest, regard for the welfare and integrity of the social groups of which we form a part.

The family, for example, is something other than one person, plus another, plus another. It is an enduring form of association in which each member gets direction for his conduct by thinking of the whole group and his place in it, rather than an adjustment of egoism and alturism.

In a justly organized social order, the very relation which persons bear to one another demand the kind of conduct which meets the needs of others while they also enable him to express and fulfill the capacities of his own being. Services, in other words would be reciprocal and cooperative in their effect." (Dewey, 1960, pp. 163–164)

In the developmental or progressive view of Dewey, democracy in the school is a necessary bridge between the family and the outside society in providing experiences of democratic participation and community leading to the development of social responsibility. Dewey says:

> The term community (has) both a eulogistic or normative sense, and a descriptive sense. . . . In social philosophy, ... society is conceived as one by its very nature. The qualities which accompany this praiseworthy community of purpose and welfare (and) loyalty to public ends are emphasized. On a more descriptive level, community is (1) the number and variety of commonly shared interests in a group and (2) a cerain amount of interaction and cooperative intercourse with other groups. These two elements both point to democracy. The first signifies not only more numerous and varied points of common interest, but greater reliance upon the recognition of mutual interests as a factor in social function. A democracy is more than a form of government, it is a mode of living such that persons who participate in an interest have to refer their own action to that of others. (Dewey, 1966, pp. 82–83)

I have relied on Dewey in articulating a general view of "development as the *aim* of (moral) education." (Kohlberg, 1981) So too, I have relied on Dewey's idea of democratic community as the *means* of moral education.

Going beyond moral formalism, then, Dewey stressed more than the cooperative role-taking of the rights and viewpoints of other individuals or groups, which he, G. H. Mead (1934) and I (Kohlberg, 1984), view as psychologically central to development through moral justice stages. He spoke also of a sense of participation in, and responsibility for, a larger shared whole, i.e., "the Community" or "the public good."

Dewey's theory of democratic community, while helpful, has not, to my satisfaction, sufficiently defined a theory of moral community appealing to and developing adolescent moral idealism while also meeting the teachers' sense of their own and the student's moral responsibility. It has, however, been central to the work of Mosher (1980) in consulting with the Brookline School-Within-a-School, a democratic alternative high school discussed in this paper only in terms of research results (cf. Power, this volume).

A philosophy and psychology of community more directly appealing to adolescents' aspirations for moral solidarity than Dewey's philosophy of democratic cooperation is that of Royce (1982). Like Dewey, Baldwin and Mead, Royce had a theory of the early origin of the self in a social community through processes of communication and imitation which led to development in both definition of a self and a reciprocal definition of the social other (Hart & Kohlberg, in press).

In Erikson's (1964) insightful map of human development, the adolescent capable of abstract or formal thought and of constructing or committing himself to an ideology confronts the problem of the self's identity, and finds a solution in the virtue of *fidelity* to another person, to a group and to a cause. Royce (1982) calls this virtue "loyalty." In the *Philosophy of Loyalty*, he says:

The first truth is this, we have first learned what we ought to, what our ideal should be, and in general about the moral law through some authority external to our wills. But if we ask 'What reason can I now give myself why my duty is my duty?' then no external authority can give one any reasons, only a calm and reasonable view of what it is that I myself really will can decide such a question. Your duty is what you yourself will to do insofar as you clearly discover who you are, and what your place is in the world. Kant called this first principle the Principle of the Autonomy or self-direction of the rational will of each moral being. But now there stands beside the principle of autonomy a second principle equally inevitable and important. Left to myself I can never find out what my will is . . . . .

Following Baldwin (Hart & Kohlberg, in press) Royce says:

We first learn what our will is by imitating the will of others, but we never really imitate. Even by imitation, we often learn how to possess and then carry out our own self will. Social conformity gives us social power. Such power brings us to a consciousness of who and what we are. Now for the first time we begin to have a will of our own and hereupon we may discover this will to be in sharp conflict with the will of society. This is normally what happens to most of us in youth. At any moment we may meet new problems of right and wrong relating to our plans of life. We hereupon look within; at what we call our conscience, to find out what our duty is. But as we do so, we discover too often what wayward and blind guides our own hearts are. So we look without to the social world. Neither within nor without, then do I find what seems to me a settled authority or harmonious plan of life unless indeed one happy sort of union takes place between the inner and the outer, between my social world and myself, between my natural waywardness and the ways of my fellows. This happy union is the one that takes place whenever my social conformity, my docility as an imitative creature, turns into exactly what I shall call *loyalty* . . . .

Suppose a being whose social conformity has been sufficient to enable him to learn the social arts and have influence over others. This being must aquire a good deal of self will. By merely consulting convention, on the one hand, and his disposition to be somebody on the other, he can never find any one final and consistent plan of life. But now suppose there appears in this man's life someone of the greater social passions, such as patriotism exemplifies. Let his country be in danger, whether the patriotic mood is justified does not matter for the moment. But one reason why men may love this spirit involving war is that when it comes it seems at once to define a plan of life, a plan which solves the conflicts of self will and conformity. This plan has two features (1) it is through and through a social plan obedient to the general will of the country (2) it is through and through an exaltation of the self, of the inner man who now feels glorified through his sacrifice, dignified in his self-surrender. As a mere fact of human nature, then, there are social passions which actually tend to do two things at once (1) to intensify our will, our self consciousness and sense of dignity and value and (2) to make obvious to us that this our will has no purpose but just to do the will of some social power. This social power is the cause to which we are loyal. Thus loyalty, viewed merely as a personal attitude, solves the paradox of our ordinary existence by showing outside of ourselves the cause which is to be served and inside of ourselves the will which delights to do this service and is not thwarted by but enriched and expressed in such service . . . . A man is loyal when he has some *cause* to which he is loyal, when he *willingly devotes* himself to this cause and when he exercises this devotion by acting steadily in the service of his cause. (Royce, 1982, pp. 279–288)

Working with a similar theory of the social self, Mead (1934) notes the same social psychological phemonenon first found in youth and calls it "the fusion of the Me", i.e., the (social defined) self or object of social expectations, and the "I", i.e., the personally willing response to the "Me" in a social situation.

Royce deals with two issues. The first is that loyalty requires a social community.

Loyalty is social, it concerns other men. If one is loyal to a cause one has at least possible fellow servants. Since a cause tends to unite the many fellow servants in one service, it consequently seems to the loyal man to have a sort of superpersonal quality about it. You can love an individual. But you can be loyal only to a tie that binds you and others into some sort of unity and one is loyal to individuals only through the tie. The cause to which loyalty devotes itself always has this union of the personal and seeming superindividual about it. It binds many individuals into one service. Loyal lovers, for instance, are loyal not merely to one another as separate individuals but to their love, to their union which is something more than either of them viewed as "distinct individuals." By loyalty I mean the practically devoted love of an individual for a community. (Royce, 1982, p. 280)

Royce obviously also has to deal with the fact that loyalties to causes or groups are often at strife with one another. He said, "If loyalty is a supreme good, the mutually destructive conflict of loyalties is in general a supreme evil" (Royce, 1982, p. 291).

Royce's proposed solution to this problem is to invoke a second-order principle, "loyalty to loyalty." "A cause is good not only for me but for mankind, insofar as it is essentially a *loyalty to loyalty*, that is an aid furtherance of loyalty in my fellows."

Rather than invoking "loyalty to loyalty," our philosophy of a Just Community would stress loyalty to universal principles of justice and responsibility as the solution to this problem, the same problem addressed by Dewey's second criterion of communication and cooperation between groups in his definition of community.

A third more vivid concept of community, although not necessarily democratic, comes from Durkheim (1973). Durkheim's central conceptions are (1) that the group, society or community is a whole or collectivity greater than the sum of its individual parts, and (2) that the experience of membership in the whole induces moral sentiments and actions by the individual. On the one side these moral sentiments are sentiments of respect for group norms and rules, "the spirit of discipline", a respect in turn derived from respect for the group which makes them. On the other side they are "the spirit of altruism," the willingness to freely give up the ego's interests, privileges and possessions to the group or other members of it. We have found Durkheim's theory useful for both practice and theory though it makes what I consider two central philosophic mistakes. While the group or the collective may not truly be a metaphysical whole different from the individuals and relations which compose it, individuals particularly at my conventional moral reasoning Stages 3 and 4 often think that the collective is such a whole, as do postconventional thinkers like Durkheim and Royce. In that sense, a classroom or small school community is often able to engage in adolescents a sense of altruism and responsibility which friends and family may not. In a similar sense norms experienced as collective may be able to inspire feelings of obligation which the individual adolescent's own judgment or that of other individuals may not.

Following Durkheim, then, we have stressed that "the good" as altruism is cultivated by a "sense of community" by a feeling of group cohesion or solidarity, by a shared valuing or attachment to the school community and each of its members.

Our "Just Community" efforts at moral education, have from the start oriented to "the good" of altruism, i.e., of attachment and caring for others and the group, largely relying on an adaptation of Durkheim's concepts, as well as to concepts of "the right," i.e., of justice and the impartial or "cognitive" role-taking involved in the development of stages of justice reasoning. As Wallwork (1983) notes, Durkheim stresses an emotionally involved altruism as the core of morality and its internal acceptance. Like modern authors such as Hoffman (1976), Durkheim noted the presence of empathy in very young children, as well as attachment and efforts at helping behavior. Durkheim says "A bond of constant communication is established between the consciousness of the child and the other's consciousness. What happens to the latter reverberates in the former. He is thus naturally induced to act so as to prevent or soften others' sorrows". (1973, p. 220).

Empathy and sympathy are transformed to altruism, according to Durkheim, when the individual transcends himself and feels and acts as a member of a group or as part of a social whole that is not simply an association of individuals but rather a union implying devotion to a group as a whole as well as to its individual members. As Wallwork (1983) states,

> Durkheim sometimes implies that other-regard is not a sufficient condition of morality because one needs in addition to be devoted to a group that is reality sui generis qualitatively distinct from each of its members. His considered view, however, seems to be that devotion to society involves devotion to its members, who are not merely means to a larger end but constitute elements or parts of a whole that does not exist without them. To act for the group is to act on behalf of its

individual members and conversely to act for another individual is to act for the group to which you and the other person belong, even if it is only a dyad. On the side of obligation, while Durkheim holds a Kantian view of obligation, he believes we cannot experience the raison d'etre of obligatory principles like promise-keeping, truthfulness and justice unless we feel a sense of solidarity with others in the social group that are held together by such principles.

INTEGRATING JUSTICE AND COMMUNITY

Wallwork (1983) critiques my theory of the development of stages of judgments of justice as ignoring this affective altruistic concern for "the good." This same critique is central to Gilligan's (1982) critique of my moral theory as ignoring altruism, care of "response." Like Durkheim, and unlike Gilligan, our theory of the Just Community does not make a typological dichotomy between justice and care, or assume that both are not present in both sexes. For Durkheim, the collectivity was both the authority behind "the right" of rules and obligations as well as the object of altruistic aspiration toward "the good." Durkheim's double-aspect theory of morality is even clearer in our Just Community theory. Through participatory justice and democracy, a sense of the group as valuable and united, the source of altruism and solidarity, is enhanced. Through collective acts of care and responsibility for the welfare of the group and each of its members, the sense of justice is enhanced. Both are advocated by teachers in a community designed to include teachers and the student peer group, morally two rather different groups in most American schools. More than merely advocacy of justice and community by teachers and students, moral development also occurs in the Just Community through discovery of a small world which is in fact fair and communitarian. Following Durkheim, the teacher's role is largely to point out to students or help them discover the existence of this "moral reality."

While inspired by Durkheim's (1961) theory of moral education, we questioned the non-democratic and indoctrinative aspects of it. For Durkheim the teacher is the supreme authority in the classroom, the dispenser of punishment and reward, and the representative or "priest" of the national society which is the major collective source and object of morality.

While Durkheim's theory of moral education centered on the bourgeois national state, it actually represents the clearest statement of the practice of moral education in the Marxist-Leninist states. I recently had the opportunity to interview two Chinese teachers about the practice of moral education in the People's Republic of China. They described the Chinese classroom as one which maintains its collective character as a homeroom even though various subject matter teachers circulate through it to teach their specialities. A single home room teacher is the homeroom group's leader who plans classroom activities with an elected student committee. The classroom of 35 to 40 students is in turn divided into six small groups, each with an elected leader. Each small group is responsible for the moral behavior of its members, as this may pose problems from the point of view of the leader. Each subgroup is collectively in competition with each other, vying for designation by the teacher as the best behaved group of the class. These practices embody Durkheim's theory of moral development through building the spirit of discipline or group norms and the spirit of attachment through the sense of community or group cohesion. Like Durkheim, it relies on the use of collective responsibility as well as upon the authority of the teachers as both representing the spirit of the group and as the priest or respresentative of the wiser society which awards the teacher authority in its name. Like Royce it stresses loyalty, but a single loyalty, to the state and the party.

As I pointed out in an article on the moral atmosphere of the school (Kohlberg, 1970), the Soviet, Cuban and Chinese systems represent the most effective form of indoctrinative moral education found in the modern world. It is an interesting fact that the "scientific" version of Marxist theory has not spelled out the practice of collective moral education as clearly as did Durkheim's; presumably because it bypasses the direct study of the culture of the group to deal with its economic and technological infra-structure.

As I wrote in Kohlberg (1971), collective moral education is compatible with participatory democracy, as appeared in my observation of the kibbutz. The kibbutz we have studied over 10 years was founded in 1948 by a group of left wing or Hashamir Hatzair Americans. For a variety of reasons it took as one mission the task of socializing and educating not only its own children but also city-born adolescents, mostly Oriental Jews who were having difficulties with schools and the law. Our ten-year study shows that these adolescents, mostly Stage 2 on entrance to the kibbutz high school, caught up in moral judgment to their kibbutz-born counterparts and were just as likely as adults to be members of the kibbutz, some reaching Stage 5 like some of their kibbutz-born counterparts (Kohlberg, 1984). To me it was challenging to see the success of collective moral education in an adult community governed by participatory democracy existing in a still larger society which was capitalistic and parliamentarian.

EXAMPLE OF A JUST COMMUNITY: CAMBRIDGE CLUSTER SCHOOL

Our first two efforts at using Dewey-Piaget democracy and Durkheimian collective moral education, like the kibbutz experiment, focused heavily on remedial moral education for preconventional adolescents and young adults. The first effort was a prison experiment, reported in a book by Hickey and Scharf (1980) entitled *Toward a Just Correctional System*. Our second effort, the Cambridge Cluster school also focused heavily on disadvantaged or "street" kids, 50% of whom were black, who were at risk in terms of making it in school or in conventional society. On entrance, most were scored at Stage 2 or 2/3. The school did succeed by certain criteria. All the students moved to the conventional stages. At graduation, on the average, they were reasoning at Stage 3/4. More than three-fourths of them went on to college, a striking finding given the minimal likelihood of higher education for them at the time they entered the school.

The considerable success of the school is highlighted by some of its failures. The success of a Just Community school rests on the importance of membership in it to the individual students who compose it, i.e., to its sense of community. Its primary negative sanction is group criticism. Such criticism was not very effective in the Cluster school, partly because it only ran half of the school day and students had friends outside the Cluster school. In residential settings, and in smaller group units than the Cluster unit of 60, group criticism is much more powerful. As a result of the weakness of group criticism as a sanction at Cluster, continued violation of the community-made rules has led to the final sanction, expulsion from the voluntary Cluster school back to the larger regular high school in which it was housed. The first student expelled, at the end of the first year was Greg. Greg had violated every rule of the school, including fighting, causing disturbances, stealing and cutting classes. In spite of all these violations Greg desperately wanted to belong to the school and about half of the students were willing to tolerate his misbehavior because they liked him and knew he really cared for the school. His caring for the school was manifested particularly in enforcement of rules which he did not violate. He did not smoke marijuana, against which there was a democratic rule, and he enforced the rule by making a citizen's arrest of a fellow student, grabbing the tell-tale sack of marijuana and hauling the offending student, Rich, to the discipline committee (D.C.) made up of five students and one teacher. The D.C. voted to tell Rich's parents and warn him and them that one more offense would lead to expulsion. Rich appealed the D.C. ruling to a meeting of the entire community, which Greg happened to chair. Despite the fact that Greg was out to get Rich, he chaired an extremely fair meeting, allowing all of Rich's friends to speak and ending with a vote to revoke the D.C. decision to tell Rich's parents. Sweat rolled down Greg's brow the entire time as he tried to hold his biases and emotions in check.

Greg finally came up for expulsion for having cut more than 10 classes after having been warned by the D.C. The D.C., following the rules, voted to expel him. Greg then appealed the expulsion to the community. In the staff meeting preceding the community meeting, I proposed that the manner in which Greg was handled was a test of the strength of the schools' sense of community. To retain Greg, it could and should accept collective responsibility for him, i.e., that the other students could and should support and pressure him to come to class. The majority of the staff saw it as a different test of the schools' strength of community. If the school was a community it should uphold its rules and expell Greg, or the rules would lose all meaning. In the staff meeting and in the following community meeting, the forces of law and order carried the day by a slight majority. Greg's defense was that this was the only school he ever cared about. When the vote went against him this tough young man wept. He had an option to reapply in the fall, which he did, but his sense of belonging was gone. He repeatedly and senselessly broke rules and was again expelled. He never returned to the regular school but moved his life to the streets. Three years later he was sent to Walpole Prison for armed robbery and later was accused of murder. Besides our own sense of failure, Greg's story informs us of the overwhelming importance for many adolescents of belonging to a community, particularly for those adolescents with little family community at home.

THE DEVELOPMENT OF THE JUST COMMUNITY

I will tell one other episode from the story of the Cambridge Cluster School which more directly explains our intervention theory and our method of research that is tied to the theory. Following my own translation of Durkheim, my role in community meetings, and the role which I strove to teach the staff, was to speak not for myself but as representing the spirit, traditions and future of the community. In this spirit I would (1) advocate making a rule or developing a collective norm important to the school and (2) attempt to tie this norm to the welfare and spirit of community of the group.

In the first year of Cluster school there were repeated episodes of theft. The issue was raised in a community meeting by the staff. Students agreed it should be made a disciplinary offense although they voiced the Stage 2 opinion that if someone was stupid enough to leave something around it was that person's fault if it was stolen. Not happy with leaving the matter there, I said, "Maybe somebody can explain why the stealing is going on? Don't people think it's wrong and a violation of the community?" Students were not very responsive to this appeal. One student said "I don't think you should worry about that. The fact is that it happened. To worry about why it happened isn't worth it." Yet I persisted: "I think ripping off is not an individual business; it is a community business. It is not a discipline issue as much as some feeling by the community that people have to have some level of trust, which is inconsistent with anybody ripping off from anybody else in the community." Only one student saw my point. The others believed making a rule against stealing was the best that could be done. They voted for the rule and with that the meeting ended. But the problem of stealing persisted. Discussions about the necessity for building trust and mutual care continued throughout the first year.

Cluster members began the second year optimistically. However, in October there was another stealing incident. Nine dollars was taken during a class from someone's purse, and no one would admit who took the money. A community meeting was convened to discuss the theft. One group of students came to the meeting with a proposal that each member of the school should chip in 15¢ to make up for the $9 stolen from the girl's purse. Phyllis, a girl from this group, offered a rationale for reimbursing the stolen money. "It's everyone's fault that she don't have no money. It was stolen because people just don't care about the community." They think "they are all individuals and don't have to be included in the community." "Everybody should care that she got her money stolen," and therefore, "we decided to give her money back to her."

Not everyone agreed with the proposal. Bob was worried that if they adopted the proposal, "then anyone can say I lost $10." Jill asked, "How do you know whether to believe someone who says her money has been stolen?" Bob and Jill both thought the fault lay not with the community but with the girl for having left her pocketbook unattended. "She gives you a chance to steal it; if you had it in your arms, wouldn't you be thinking about stealing it?" In response, Phyllis reiterated her point. She began with the assumption that Cluster ought to be a community and its members ought to trust one another. If people could not be trusted, it was the group's failure, and they would have to pay for the fault. Staff members and students both pointed out that the community should put pressure on the guilty party to return the money. Thus they adopted a compromise: "If the money is not returned anonymously by a certain date, everyone will be assessed 15¢." The combined proposal was voted in and in fact proved effective. The person who stole the money eventually admitted it. There were no thefts in the school in the three years after the meeting.

In comparing these two meetings we do not think that development in individual moral judgment between the first and second year can alone account for the change in stealing behavior. A review of the transcripts will show some individuals reasoning at Stage 2 and Stage 3 in each meeting. What has changed dramatically is the social or collective norms in the context of which judgments are being made. We maintain that in its second year Cluster School progressed toward becoming a Just Community. Phyllis' statements marked the change. They revealed a Stage 3 structure not only of Phyllis' individual moral judgment but of the moral atmosphere of the Cluster community. Phyllis did not simply speak for herself as an individual with personal opinions; she spoke for the whole school, exhorting the other members to live up to the normative values of caring and trust. In her view students were obligated *qua* members of the community to live up to these expectations. Thus caring and trust were no longer perceived as simply being the staff's bag of virtues but were seen as values that the community as a whole was beginning to share. We refer to these shared values as "collective normative values," distinguishing them from values expressed in individual moral judgments.

Phyllis' linking of stealing to the values of caring and trust was a departure from the students' tendency in the first year to deal with the issue by making a rule against stealing. A rule simply states that a given action is proscribed and that its perpetrators will be punished. Phyllis' statement presumed the existence of a norm—a generalized expectation that no one would steal. That norm was linked to the community values of caring and trust, so that there was a generalized expectation that not only would individual members not steal the property of others, but they would also actively care for the property of others and see that no one else stole it.

What gave force to these normative values was their being perceived as necessary for creating a community in the school. During the first year, some of the staff and I suggested that the issue of stealing be viewed as "a violation of the community," but only one student responded to that. By the second year, students were concerned with whether the school was "really a community." This concern presupposed the recognition that "this school is supposed to be a community." We believe this recognition was crucial for the resolution of the stealing problem. In the students' past experience, stealing had been a common occurrence. Given their stages of development, they could not be expected to take responsibility for the property of others unless they valued Cluster as a social context different from the city streets or the hall of the larger school. Participating in a community which drew them into close association with one another allowed them to realize that their actions had consequences for a solidarity group they really cared about.

The issue of stealing led to the creation of a collective norm preventing stealing behavior because it was linked to two communitarian norms, those of trust and of collective responsibility, and hence the value of community itself. This did not happen spontaneously; it was partly a response to advocacy by myself and other members of the staff. This advocacy, however, was ineffective in the first year of the school, yet meaningful in the second year. Power's (1979) dissertation documents in detail the longitudinal formation of the collective norms of property, trust and collective responsibility at Cluster for four years. It documents the growth of these collective norms both in stage, from Stage 2/3 to Stage 3/4, and in phase or degree of institutionalization. The *phases* of institutionalization of a norm are described in Table 2.3. At a high phase, a norm is not only expected of the self and others, but active enforcement of the norm through persuasion or taking a stand when others are deviating is additionally considered to be required. Analyses of both community meeting transcripts and longitudinal interviews of individuals showed similar patterns of development. The *stages* of collective norms are described in Table 2.4.

The fact that one norm would develop in stage and phase was no guarantee that another norm would. The Cluster school never developed a norm against smoking marijuana or coming to class high that was anything more than a "be cool, be discrete" norm about drug use.

A norm which was intermediate between the norm of respect for property and the drug use norm in terms of development of phase was the norm of racial and ethnic integration. The issue of integration was central to me and some of the staff since our experiment hoped to deal with a central problem of urban schools;

TABLE 2.3
Phases of the Collective Norm

Phase 0:   No collective norm exists or is proposed.

COLLECTIVE NORM PROPOSAL
Phase 1:   Individuals propose collective norrms for group acceptance.

COLLECTIVE NORM ACCEPTANCE
Phase 2:   Collective norm is accepted as a group ideal but not agreed to. It is not an expectation for behavior.

    a) some group members accept ideal
    b) most group members accept ideal

Phase 3:   Collective norm is accepted and agreed to but it is not (yet) an expectation for behavior.

    a) some group members agree to collective norm
    b) most group members agree to collective norm

COLLECTIVE NORM EXPECTATION
Phase 4:   Collective norm is accepted and expected. (Naive expectation)

    a) some group members expect the collective norm to be followed
    b) most group members expect the collective norm to be followed

Phase 5:   Collective norm is expected but not followed (Disappointed expectation)

    a) some group members are disappointed
    b) most group members are disappointed

COLLECTIVE NORM ENFORCEMENT
Phase 6:   Collective norm is expected and upheld through expected persuading of deviant to follow norm.

    a) some group members persuade
    b) most group members persuade

Phase 7:   Collective norm is expected and upheld through expected reporting of defiant to the group.

    a) some group members report
    b) most group members report

---

i.e., racial integration and genuine equality of opportunity for black and minority students.

Our philosophy of community suggested that the school be a single community integrating not only teachers and students but peer cliques which usually compete with or reject one another in regular high schools (as later quotations in this paper will clearly illustrate). From Dewey's defintion of democratic community, our emphasis on integration represented an effort to attain his second criterion of democratic community, open and cooperative relations between different groups, which implies a need for diversity in the context of community. From the point of view of justice, some of the staff and I felt that Stage 6 justice

TABLE 2.4
Stages of Collective Normative Values and the Sense of Community
Valuing

Collective Normative Values	*Sense of Community Valuing*
STAGE 2	
There is not yet an explicit awarenesss of collective normative values. However, there are *generalized expectations* that individuals should recognize concrete individual rights and resolve conflicts through exchange.	There is no clear sense of community apart from exchanges among group members. Community denotes a collection of individuals who do favors for each other and rely on each other for protection. Community is valued insofar as it meets the concrete needs of its members.
EXAMPLES:	*EXAMPLES:*
1. Do not "rat" on another group member. Ratting or reporting another group member to authorities is disapproved of because it exposes the rule breaker to likely punishment. 2. Do not bother others. Live and let live. 3. Help others out when you want to.	The community is like a "bank." Members meet to exchange favors but you cannot take more than you give.
STAGE 3	
Collective normative values refer to relationships among group members. Membership in a group implies living up to *shared expectations*. Conflicts should be resolved by appeal to mutual collective normative values.	The sense of community refers to a set of relationships and sharings among group members. The group is valued for the friendliness of its members. The value of the group is equated with the value of its collective normative expectations.
EXAMPLES:	*EXAMPLES:*
1. Members of a group should be able to trust each other with their possessions. 2. Members of a group should care about other members of the group.	1. The community is a family in which members care for each other. 2. The community is honorable because it helps others.
STAGE 4	
Collective normative values stress the community as an entity distinct from its individual members. Members are *obligated* to act out of concern for the welfare and harmony of the group.	The school is explicitly valued as an entity distinct from the relationships among its members. Group commitments and ideals are valued. The community is perceived as an organic whole composed of interrelated systems that carry on the functioning of the group.
EXAMPLES:	*EXAMPLES:*
1. Individuals not only are responsible for themselves but share responsibility for the whole group. 2. Individuals should participate in the political organization of the group by making their opinions known and by being informed voters.	Stealing affects "the community more than the individual because that is what we are. We are not just a group of individuals."

justified a certain degree of reverse discrimination. Various interpretations (Blocker & Smith, 1980) of Rawls (1971) have interpreted the Rawls notion of equality of opportunity, especially in education, as justifying reverse discrimination, since in the original position under the veil of ignorance, Rawls' difference principle would justify inequalities from the point of view of representative persons who were the least advantaged. The distribution of educational abilities among minorities of educational and other talents is a matter of chance rather than merit, and "impartial" standards of educational selection may be modified to produce educational equity rather than strict equality of educational opportunity. Other members of the staff did not agree with this but it was left to the community to decide. Initially the Cluster school membership had been determined by a notion of proportional representation allowing about 25% of the students to be black, the same proportion of black students as was found in the Cambridge school population. In the second year, a democracy class led by Elsa Wasserman (1975) became involved in the issue of reverse discrimination. There were 47 white students in the school and 18 black students. The black students wanted more equal representation in the community. But there were already six students on the waiting list, only one of whom was black. The democracy class proposed that all six openings be filled by blacks. The following is adapted from an edited full transcript of the resulting community meeting as reported in Wasserman (1975), as well as in Power, Higgins, Reimer and Kohlberg (in press).

Two students chaired the meeting, one black and one white. One of the students stated the issue in the following words:

> All right, this is about admisson of six new students to Cluster School. There's six openings and there's only one black person on the waiting list. And there's room for six more people. In Democracy class a lot of people wanted all the rest of the people that would come to Cluster School to be black.

A white student immediately asked the implications for the white students on the waiting list:

> Does that mean that there's only one black on it now, but you want to get five more blacks to jump in front of the rest of the waiting line?

The students responded loudly, both supporting and opposing this reply. One chairperson stopped the commotion saying:

> Wait, I just want to stop this. I don't want no one jumping out of hand, because disturbances are going to be going like crazy, because I ain't in no mood for no one jumping out of hand in this meeting. I'm going to go around (and call on each in turn).

A black student presented a Stage 3 point of view:

> I'm going to try to tell you how I feel about the situation. Because, you see, I'm one of the people that wants some black people to come in . . . From what I see I feel I would be more comfortable with them here. I want them here. I want to let some new black people come in and experience the school.

A white student responded by a Stage 2/3 elaboration of the issue of fairness to the white students already on the waiting list in terms of "first come first served":

> Yesterday, right, you were talking in democracy, you were saying there's six openings, right. If they were all black people, it would be fair to let them in. I don't care if there were six black people on the waiting list, they could come in, but these five white people, they were first, right?

Other white students argued at Stage 3 and 4 that fairness meant considering the discomfort of black students, now in the minority, who felt uncomfortable:

> It doesn't matter to me whether they're black or white, they're people. But why can't everybody just accept the fact that blacks would feel more comfortable and get a better education with more blacks in school? And why can't we just let the people that have signed up be black and come to the school, because that will improve (the situation of) all the blacks in the school.

In response to questions by some of the white students as to why more blacks had not volunteered to enter the school, a black student replied:

> What would we say about how no black kids are signed up? One reason why they don't is they look at this school and see all these white people and they say this school is for whities. I don't want to go here 'cause there ain't going to be nobody here that I know. And no black people are ever going to sign up as long as they see there's only 18 black kids and 47 whites. Now how they going to feel signing up to go to this school?

A white student asked why the black students felt uncomfortable in the school. A black student responded at Stage 3.

> Well, I'm going to tell you why I feel uncomfortable. Before I knew who was here, I phoned Cambridge Latin and I didn' want to sign up with Latin, so I heard about Cluster and I came down. This is my first year in this school and I don't know who's here. Never in my life have I seen as many of you who have outnumbered me and mine, anyway. OK, then I get to know them. I say, these whites are all right, you know. And my opinions changed, they changed just a little bit, all right? And then I go home and I look, I listen to the news and I see what the whities are

doing to the blacks. For what? Because they want to learn. And then I come back here and I try to get some of my brothers and sisters into this school so they can be helped like I'm being helped. And what do I hear? No. Because they don't want to hear it. Why can't they just give us 18 blacks a little personal satisfaction within ourselves to have some more of us so we can be together? All right! (*Applause*)

After some angry exchanges, a white student tried to pull together the feelings of the community in a Stage 3/4 statement:

All the people in this community right now are all saying in some way or another—usually they don't want to say it—but they're expressing feelings that they care about the other people and how their education goes and how their working in this community goes. And I feel that the blacks in this community can't work as well and feel as comfortable without more blacks in this community. It's not fair. Everybody knows that everybody in this school, no matter how it sounds no, cares about the other people. Then why can't you allow six more blacks in, 20-whatever blacks will be able to get a good education in this school and a good sense of democracy and just everything. And you know, why can't we just let six more blacks in, it would help the whole thing. The whole community, the whole school would be helped by that.

After further intense discussion, an almost unanimous vote was made to give priority to the six black students who had applied later to the meeting.

In terms of individual justice reasoning, arguments for and against reverse discrimination were at about the same level, Stage 3 or Stage 3/4. Recognition of the needs of blacks was at this level as was the opposing concern for the impartiality of the standard "first come, first served." The essential determining factor in the vote was that expressed by the white student at the end, the concern for a better community and a caring for the black students now in the community and realizing their discomfort as members of the community. Both the white student and some of the black students proposed a norm of integration in the "we prescriptive mode" of degree of collectiveness and tieing the norm to a sense of valuing solidarity and the welfare of the school, i.e., to the sense of community (Phase 1 in Table 2.3; Degree 15 in Table 2.7). While I myself felt that the decision was fair on Stage 5 or Stage 6 grounds, it was clearly debatable and the faculty was divided on it. In any case, the decision was arrived at democratically without strong advocacy by the faculty for the integrative or reverse discrimination solution.

A more controversial set of meetings on integration occurred in a later year of school, as reported in Kohlberg (1980). While the meeting just described initiated a norm of integration (Phase 3 in Table 2.3), the phase of the norm remained low the next year. Blacks and whites sat separately in community meetings and most black students enrolled in the class of the only black teacher, overcrowding it. Evidently the norm of integration was not at a high phase of institutionalization, in part because of the strong and rather exclusive sense of solidarity of the black students. The staff in general were concerned about this and thought it necessary to confront this visible but silent self-segregation and to advocate for a higher phase of sense of obligation to the norm of integration.

The meeting transpired, in part, as follows:

BILL (black staff member):
There are at least two groups that I know of, I mean it looks that way, maybe it is just that they are intellectually different, but there is a group which includes Colin; there is another group which includes Leslie, and maybe Phyllis and maybe Bill and they don't want to have anything to do with each other. They have different interests and I don't see how you can have a community if you have people separate, and I think maybe in that group. I wonder why no one wants to talk about why they feel they want to be in one group and not in a whole group. Do you feel like that is sort of private, and you don't want to talk about it?

BETSY (white student):
There are two groups and there are at least some in one group who refuse to even consider anything that the other group says. There is no ground that we can meet these people on. If there was a way for all groups to get together and to interact, that would be much better. Some people said that we should have had a retreat by now, we should have. You can't meet these people, they go to different classes, they are different groups. There is no common ground yet.

JOE (black student):
That's true the only time that people get together in a group is on a retreat, when we are high.

LARRY (the author):
That is the problem that this community meeting is supposed to be working on, but I don't think that we can say we can't work on it at a community meeting and go off on a retreat and get high or something. We've got to work it through to some extent here. I would like Tema to say why not.

TEMA (white student):
It isn't that people don't understand each other, but they never talk to each other. They just assume that people are prejudiced in their ideas or viewpoints and that is ridiculous because they never even talk to these people.

ARTHUR (white staff):
I can see why maybe getting high on a retreat makes it a lot easier to relate to some other people in the community. But I also am being pulled the other way in saying we have to learn to confront one another's innermost thoughts and being and communicate without the extra help of a drink to be sociable or a reefer or whatever it is that makes the barriers start to fall down. There ought to be other ways, too, of doing that, during the school day. When my core class split up into two groups, some people stayed with Betsy and some people came with me. Originally some of the black kids in the group were staying with Betsy, but when they saw that they were going to be the only two or one or three black kids in that group, they got up and they all went on with me.

CHARLIE (black student):
I am like that too. I am not prejudiced, but I went in the class over there, I was the only black one in there, and I wasn't scared to be there, but I'm not going to be the only chocolate chip in a vanilla cone. I have to be in a class that is mixed, I can't be in a class with all whites and one me.

EDDIE (black student):
I'm not prejudiced. Let them go their way and we go ours.

ANN (white consultant):
I wanted to ask Eddie about his idea of community—that you'll go your way and I'll go mine.

EDDIE (black student):
What do you mean, I don' understand?

ANN:
What does community mean to you if everyone goes their own way?

EDDIE:
They are humans, that's what it is supposed to be like. You want me to come in here, right, say 'Hi Karl, how are you doing, how are you feeling?'. Well, I don't care. It is just ridiculous, and you will never get it like that.

ANN:
Why not?

EDDIE:
You want to know why? If I knew why then I could solve all the problems in the world.

As Charlie (a black student) replied to Arthur (a teacher), "I'm not going to be the only chocolate chip in a vanilla cone. I have to be in a class that's mixed, I can't be in a class with all whites and one me." Charlie understandably fears loss of his identity in an all-white class. We might say he resists the expectation of positive integration not because it isn't part of Stage 3 ideas of "being a good community member," which he accepts, but because the sacrifice may be too great. In contrast, Eddie takes a more Stage 2 position in level of social responsibility (Table 2.4). He says, "You go your way, I'll go my way, I won't interfere with you if you don't interfere with me." He refers to Karl, a white student he doesn't like, not just because Karl is white but because of his barefoot hippy style, which is anathema in the black subculture. Eddie says to Ann, a white consultant: "You want me to come in there and say, 'Hi Karl, how are you doing, how are you feeling?' Well, I don't care. It is just ridiculous and you'll never get it like that." Asked why not, he answers, "If I knew why, I could solve all the problems in the world." Eddie may not be able to answer the question that would solve all the problems in the world, but soon he is able to answer the question that can solve the problem of Karl.

A few months later, Karl came before the community meeting because he had registered for only two courses during the day, the two Cluster core courses. The Cambridge High school requires a minimum of four courses. Karl needed the four courses and three more to graduate that year. Karl said he did not care if he graduated and didn't see why Cluster School was bothering him when the principal and the high school didn't care. Karl said, "I don't care about graduating and I'm not interested in high school. I'm only here for Cluster."

EDDIE:
If you don't like high school, why don't you take the seven courses so you can graduate?

KARL:
I can't graduate this year—it would be too many courses.

EDDIE:
Why didn't you take more courses last year so you could graduate this year?

KARL:
I didn't think about it, I *didn't* care.

EDDIE:
If you don't care about yourself, we have to care about you for you. What are you here in school for now? What are you going to do after high school?

KARL:
I don't need to graduate to do what I want to do, to play rock.

EDDIE:
Do you think you're being a good example in Cluster?

KARL:
No. Do you think you are a good example?

EDDIE:
I guess we're even. I guess if you're not going to worry about yourself I'm not going to worry about you. But you should think about it.

From my theoretical point of view, the staff and I were not advocating a liberal political ideology of integration but rather the fundamental principles or values of a Just Community school. In other words, we were advocating the ideas of justice and community immanent in the school itself. We were advocating justice and community at the fourth and fifth stage in which these ideals should be manifest in the entire community and not simply in cliques of friends and racial compatriots. Between the two meetings, Eddie's thinking about community had moved up a stage in response to community expectations at the third and fourth stages.

To us this meeting is more controversial than the first. It, along with related meetings, tying the norm of integration to the value of community, was successful in its outcome. However, it involved strong staff confrontation and advocacy and caused considerable discomfort to some students in its process. The staff supported a norm of integration against a norm of privacy or freedom of association. This process helped to achieve the second of two major outcomes at Cluster school. The first was the development of a sense of social responsibility, e.g., toward property or of "honesty" discussed in connection with the stealing meetings. The second was the high proportion of students to go on to college, including the economically disadvantaged blacks. The norm of integration brought both races and social classes closer together so that the disadvantaged developed "middle class" educational aspirations. This educational focus at Cluster school, emerging from the community process, is discussed at more length in Power and Higgins (1981).

Some of the difficulties and unresolved dilemmas in the Cluster school experiences are discussed by Reimer and Power (1980). Others involved (1) tension among the staff, with which I became involved and which had no director, (2) lack of time for staff training and (3) the arrival of a new headmaster in the Cambridge High School. The program continues, but in a smaller and somewhat modified form.

JUSTICE AND CONVENTION IN THE JUST COMMUNITY: SCARSDALE ALTERNATIVE SCHOOL

Much less turbulent development of a Just Community model has gone on since 1978 at the Scarsdale (New York) Alternative High School, which is part of the Scarsdale High School. There has been a staff director in the school with good political relations with the larger school administration, and there has been great staff cohesiveness and much staff training. In addition, the student population tends to be a much easier group to work with.

The students at this school are almost all upper middle class and aimed toward the best colleges. The staff of the school, extraordinarily able, adopted the Just Community model in 1978 after two years of attendance at the Harvard Summer School Institute on Moral Education. In addition to staff attendance at the Harvard Institute, at least one of the students has attended each year as well, due to the belief that a non-indoctrinative approach requires that students critically understand the theory governing the staff's participation and teaching.

The initial issue facing democracy at Scarsdale in September, 1978, was the use of drugs and alcohol on a forthcoming orientation outing or retreat. The students agreed not to use "dope" on the retreat. The staff urged that students, as well as staff, have responsibility for enforcing the rule, not merely for obeying it. After much discussion, the students decided that, in the abstract, they had the responsibility to enforce the rule, that they should enforce it, but that, in practice, they couldn't be expected to police their friends. Thus, they wouldn't vote that they *would* enforce the rule (Phase 4 in Table 2.3).

After the retreat I raised the question as to whether students had actually obeyed the rule they voted on. A mild discipline was agreed upon in case anyone wished to admit violations. Soon, 20 students spoke up admitting they had violated the rule. Their attitudes ranged from the feeling that they were civilly disobedient champions of individual rights to a sense of penitence at having let the community down. Some of the "upright" students castigated the "sinners"; other upright students castigated these "moralists" for hurting the feelings of the sinners. In the end, the dominant feeling was that everyone, saint and sinner, cared about one another and the community and that it could survive confrontation with a sense of solidarity and community.

During the next week, the students and staff proceeded to consider making a rule about coming "high" to class. In previous years, this issue had been dealt with by teachers, who would suspend the student for the day if they thought he was obviously high. Some students argued that a person had a right to get high, that is, that such a rule was an unwarranted restriction of freedom. This led to a lengthy metaphysical excursion to generate a definition of the word "rights." The staff and many students agreed that being high was a violation of the obligation to participate in the school community and in the class: therefore it was not just the individual student's own business. Some individualistically-oriented students did not see the point. For example, one such student said, "I don't see how it's different than making a rule against picking my nose in class. Picking my nose is offensive to others, but I should still have a right to do it." Another student tried to explain that picking one's nose didn't hurt the community or the common good, whereas coming high to class did. In the end, the rule was approved.

Through this process a high phase of a collective norm against the use of drug and alcohol during school hours was developed, and few violations have occurred since. However, students equally clearly see the restriction of drugs and alcohol use as limited to school participation during the day, and they say so openly at meetings and in writing.

The issue of drugs that we have chronicled at Scarsdale has involved much discussion of justice, but the collective norm established has been more in the line of Durkheim's "spirit of discipline" i.e., a norm of convention or of organizational functioning, than being directly a justice norm. As stated by Turiel (1983, p. 34):

> Social conventions are behavioral uniformities which coordinate the activities of individuals within social systems—they act by providing people with knowing what to expect of each other. Social-centered acts are symbolic of elements of social organization, conventions are validated by consensus and therefore are relative to the societal content. In addition to the variation of conventions from one social system to another, they may be altered by consensus or general social useage within a social system.

In contrast with convention, moral prescriptives are not perceived to be alterable by consensus: The individual's moral prescriptives (e.g. regarding killing and the value of life) are determined by factors inherent to social relationships, as opposed to a particular form of social organization. An individual's perception of an act such as the taking of a life as a trangression is not contingent on the presence of a rule but rather stems from factors intrinsic to the event, e.g., the consenquence to the victim. This means that moral issues are not perceived as relative to the societal context. The moral theories formed by individuals are based on concepts regarding the welfare of persons, the rights of persons and justice in the sense of comparative treatment of individuals and means of distribution.

Turiel argues that even young children sharply distinguish between norms of convention and norms of justice and that the levels of development of judgments of convention are different from the stages of justice reasoning. Turiel is clearly making an important distinction. The norm against drug use discussed so far is more or less a norm of convention. Norms of convention take on their force in the Scarsdale Alternative School because of their association with democratic agreement and the sense or value of community, not because of their intrinsic or universal nature. It is rather for reasons of rights and justice, even if somewhat undeveloped or misguided ones, that there is opposition to the drug rule as violating individual rights.

The distinction between conventional norms and justice norms is obviously important in evaluating the long range impact of Just Community education. Philosophically we can endorse life-long judgments and actions of *justice*, whereas we need not endorse lifelong actions of adherence to *conventions* like regular class attendance or being drug free in the school. These conventional norms stressed by school administrators and teachers are not only organizationally useful to the high school but are useful to the student in obtaining an education. In the traditional high schools we have studied, these conventional norms do not have strong moral meaning or value for most students. In the Just Community schools, they do take on moral meaning as enhancing the school community and as representing what Royce would call the virtue of loyalty to the school community. As conventional norms of drug use and attendance are relative to time and place, they do not directly define long range aims of moral development as an aim of education. In contrast, norms of justice, democracy and responsible caring (collective responsibility) do represent norms which not only signify school loyalty but also life-long norms for the morally developing human being, norms continuing beyond their high school lives. We did not make the distinction between norms of convention and norms of justice and responsible care in discussing the Cambridge Cluster School, because it was only norms of justice and care that developed to a high degree of collectiveness and a high phase in Cluster. This, for instance was the case for stealing, clearly a norm of justice which students could understand, without advocacy by teachers, as hurting one another. In contrast, the norms of convention advocated by teachers at

Cambridge Cluster School did not "take" or become high in degree of collectiveness or phase of enforcement. In Scarsdale, teacher advocacy was effective in developing a phase of adherence to conventional drug and attendance norms, including student confrontation of those who violated the norms. Whether the success of the Scarsdale School in creating a sense of school loyalty leading to confrontation of and possible disloyalty to a deviant friend is a controversial issue is best discussed around a norm of justice rather than a norm of convention.

At Cluster school, teacher advocacy of a phase of enforcing a norm against stealing by confronting a suspected transgressing friend seems to us non-controversial because respect for property rights is a basic norm of justice.

In Scarsdale, where students come from well-off homes and where family and community socialization provided firm norms against stealing, there were no incidents of stealing. Since 1978, when the Just Community approach was inaugurated, the only episode of "stealing" involved the disappearance of a few students' sandwiches from the communal refrigerator. Although stealing was not an issue in Scarsdale, another form of injustice was: cheating.

JUDGMENT AND ACTION IN THE JUST COMMUNITY

Cheating.   High school cheating is a particularly interesting form of injustice to study for a number of theoretical reasons. In the first place it has been a paradigmatic focus of study of student moral behavior since Hartshorne and May (1928–1930). We have repeatedly noted in other writings (Kohlberg, 1984) that Hartshorne and May found that cheating behavior could not be explained by a general trait or virtue of honesty but rather seemed to be situation specific. Their conclusion that cheating was situation specific included the finding that risk of detection was one important factor in the likelihood that cheating would continue. Another finding was a classroom effect, i.e., some classroom groups cheated markedly less than others, a finding which we identify as a "moral atmosphere" effect. Still another finding was that individual students would cheat in one situation but not another, e.g., there was little correlation between one experimental test of cheating and another.

These findings have led our analysis to the level of individual personality. They have led us to question the fruitfulness of the Aristotelian tradition of postulating discrete fixed character-traits or virtues like Hartshorne and May's virtues of honesty, service and self-control. Instead, at the individual personality level, we have postulated stages (and types or substages) of general justice reasoning or of a sense of justice as an important influence on cheating behavior. We have done so, in part, as a result of reviewing a range of studies indicating a monotonic decline of cheating with moral stage (Kohlberg, 1984, ch.7).

We have not, however, felt that stimulating the development of justice reasoning stages through moral dilemma discussion is in itself a sufficient approach to affecting moral actions such as cheating. In fact, while Blatt (Blatt and

Kohlberg, 1975) was successful in stimulating upward movement in stage of moral reasoning through hypothetical dilemma discussion, he did not find a decrease in Hartshorne and May experimental cheating tasks as a result.

Theoretically, our Just Community approach aims to change individual action by changing the moral atmosphere of the school. As this situational atmosphere interacts with individual moral judgment and action, it influences not only judgments of rightness or justice but also individual judgments of the self's moral responsibility which mediate between deontological judgments of the rightness or justice of an action and the felt necessity or responsibility of acting in accordance with the judgment of rightness in a specific situation. In our theory of judgment and action (Kohlberg, 1984), inconsistencies between deontological choice and a judgment of responsibility of ''I have to'' or ''I'll feel self blame if I don't'' are reported. These include not only inconsistencies due to ''quasi-obligations'' to *others*, but also ''quasi-obligations'' or responsibilities *to the self and to self-interest*. These judgments of responsibility are heavily related to group and situational factors such as peer group collective norms which may be counter-norms, that is norms counter to acting in line with the deontically right, as was true for the Watergate and My Lai situations. On the other hand, judgments of responsibility deriving from these peer group collective norms may also support judgments of responsibility that lead to fair and beneficial action.

In the case of cheating at schools like Scarsdale High School, most students and teachers are aware of a ''hidden'' or unspoken curriculum about cheating which presents a double message. On the one hand, teachers, parents and even peers strongly expect and positively evaluate academic success and competition, a pressure which influences students to use illicit means (cheating) to achieve. Peers in particular not only condone the use of illicit means to get good grades but may actually expect help and cooperation through cheating. Thus there are peer ''counter norms'' of helping and ignoring cheating, conflicting with official or teacher-based norms against cheating. A student in the regular Scarsdale High School expressed his or her view of this in an anonymous letter to the local newspaper, which said in part:

> . . . Scarsdale's biggest problem is that nobody is happy. Priding itself on being a great prep school, they have created a hellish atmosphere. . . . The past year three to five students tried to kill themselves and at least four students (that I know of) were institutionalized for mental problems. . . . Most of these problems were due to the unbearable pressure. This pressure is evident in many facets of the school. What people do for good grades is unbelievable. Obviously, there is much cheating in Scarsdale. As an aware student, I approximate that 95% of the students will cheat without guilt whenever they need something. This habit is something that is taught to them by the school, not dissuaded at all. . . .

As noted, in Kohlberg (1984) we have reviewed studies indicating that there is a monotonic decline in cheating by moral stage. Stage 4 students cheat less than Stage 3 students, Stage 3 less than Stage 2. We interpret this judgment-action relationship situationally. It is not so much a matter that Stage 4 subjects judge cheating wrong and unfair (deontic judgment) and Stage 3 or Stage 2 subjects do not, but that Stage 4 subjects judge that they have a responsibility not to cheat in the particular situation whereas lower stage subjects do not. Lower stage students are more likely to have excuses or "quasi-obligations" which make cheating permissible on Stage 3 or Stage 2 grounds. For instance, Stage 3 subjects have "quasi-obligations" to uphold the expectations of parents that they receive good grades and they have a quasi-obligation to the expectations of friends for help in cheating or the expectation that students as a group support one another in cheating and don't in any way bring the teacher's attention to cheating. Stage 4 students are more likely to be sensitive to the unfairness to noncheaters of cheating and to the trust and implicit contract with the teacher for not cheating. Like Stage 3 students, however, refraining from cheating at Stage 4 will depend upon making a judgment of responsibility to not cheat in the particular situation. If many others are cheating, responsibility to noncheating students and to the teacher is weakened. In summary, judgments of responsibility are largely dependent upon situational moral atmosphere or group norm factors.

It should be noted that developing a peer-supported norm against cheating is more difficult than developing one against stealing. Peer group norms about stealing from one another do develop readily because peers are clear victims of unfairness in stealing. In the case of cheating, those most concerned or victimized are the teachers, and peer group norms supportive of cheating can be generated in an atmosphere in which the students are a "we group" distinct from the teachers as a "they group." Strong collective norms against cheating can usually only develop if the peer group and the teacher groups are seen as members of a common community, making community norms fair to teachers as well as to students. This is, in fact what happened in Scarsdale.

In 1982, the director held a core or advisory group meeting in which students discussed cheating occurring when they had been in the regular Scarsdale High School and the moral atmosphere that made it acceptable. In answer to the director's question "Is cheating widespread at the Alternative School or at the High School?" Tamson answered: "It's very common at the high school; there's the opportunity to cheat and get away with it. Teachers can't really keep their eyes on every student. There's a feeling 'Your friend is going to help you if you don't know the answer.'"

Thus Tamson identifies not only the situational risk factor identified by Hartshorne and May, but the existence of a Stage 3 or possible Stage 4 counter-norm to honesty. The norms of friendship and affiliation, especially strong at Stage 3, create a peer "counter-norm" to honesty. In the cheating situation, not only peer norms but parental expectations act as "quasi-obligations" which prevent judgments of responsibility to do "the right thing." In this core group, Richy experienced the Stage 3 "quasi-obligation" of fulfilling parental expectations and "making them feel happy." He said, "I got a lot of pressures from my parents and in the ninth grade I was saying 'OK, It's your first year of high school, you have to do well' and I was just cheating because I wanted to do well and I wanted to make my parents happy.'' Going on to describe how other students acted, he said, ''I just know there has to be in other people's minds that parental pressure 'I have to do good on this test or my dad is going to kill me.' That's how it was for me so I cheated.''

Going on to describe the moral atmosphere of the high school, a male student in the advisory group said, ''At the end of the test, people would be walking up to hand it in and say, 'Hey what's the answer to number 8?' You sit there and tell the answer right in front of the teacher and nobody really cared and it helped you out a lot.'' We pointed out earlier that, in experimental cheating studies, not only peers but adults seem not to care about cheating. If adults do not express strong expectations and trust in student honesty, conventional stage children are not sensitized to having a responsibility not to cheat.

A female student corroborated the idea that, in the high school, teachers didn't seem to care about cheating and that made it ''all right.'' She said, ''I was in the French class at the high school and the teacher walked out and we had an open discussion about the test until she came back.''

Another student interpreted the teachers' attitude not as not caring about cheating but as daring students to cheat, and having an attitude of self-confirming mistrust toward students. She said, ''At the high school they assume you're going to cheat. The teacher says 'Don't cheat' and it's almost like inviting it. They'd say 'Keep your eyes on the test, I don't want any eyes wandering around' and so it's always a challenge, 'let's see if we can beat this teacher'.''

The net combination of these factors was to create a moral atmosphere in the regular high school where no one had a responsibility not to cheat. A female student said, ''I'd think the atmosphere at the high school was that everyone around you is cheating; it pressures you into it because they're going to get a 90 and you're going to get an 80. It's a lot of pressure to be like them and to get a good grade too.''

For some students, the atmosphere of the high school was such that it desensitized them from making a deontic moral judgment of rightness at all.

A female student stated that ''When I was in the high school I didn't make generalizations about people cheating at all. I cheated for myself and I never gave it too much thought.''

Other students make justice judgments that it's not unfair to cheat. ''It never seemed to hurt anyone else. It wasn't a matter of making someone else pass or fail, you are just doing better.'' A student, Karen, made a final judgment. ''I think it is a social norm at the high school, no one would confront anyone else because most likely they cheat also, and the teachers, it doesn't even seem to bother them.''

Students also agreed that cheating was less frequent in the alternative school even without a formal democratic norm about cheating, because of smaller classes and greater trust between teachers and students. Nevertheless cheating still occasionally occurred, they agreed, especially with regard to copying homework.

The advisory group meeting just discussed occurred in late 1982. It came as a result of two cases of cheating discussed in the school. One student had been discovered by a math teacher to have cheated on a math exam and a group of four students were reported by an English teacher to have cheated on an English essay test. Both cases were brought before the fairness or student-teacher discipline committee. It was strongly recommended by the fairness committee that the alternative school would have a lengthy discussion on cheating to develop rules and consequences about cheating.

The issue of making a rule against cheating was relatively noncontroversial when it came before the community meetings. Most of the students thought cheating was unjust and that having a rule against cheating was just and would lead students to make a judgment of responsibility or obligation not to cheat. As stated by one student:

> It really bothers me to have cheating going on because it's intruding on my rights. If there's cheating, for the people who do work hard it makes them seem like they're not working hard because others are copying papers and get the same grades and do nothing. If there was a rule which said we realize cheating is wrong, and it's your obligation not to cheat, it would make everyone feel the obligation.

This student sees cheating as unfair and violating the rights of other students who work for their grades, a common form of conventional (Stages 3 and 4) justice reasoning. To translate this reasoning into a judgment of responsibility or obligation, however, requires community agreement.

Another student continued, "I disagree that under pressure circumstances people have to cheat. I was under a lot of pressure too and I was hysterical I was going to fail this test. It was just memorization and I had these crib sheets and this teacher said 'No cheating goes' and I couldn't cheat so I got a 67. What I'm saying is that cheating isn't necessary. The reason for cheating is that people are lazy and don't want to study so they make up crib sheets. It's not responsible". This student then denies the necessity or "quasi-obligation" to cheat and makes a judgment of responsibility not to cheat.

Other students gave reasons against cheating not in terms of fairness or justice but in terms of community valuing. A male student argued, "It goes with being in a community. Ending cheating is a good direction for our community, it's for the benefit of our community". Speaking for "we the community," this student proposed a collective norm against cheating. The director advocated a shared norm against cheating by invoking the value of such a norm of the mutual trust and solidarity of a community, including teachers and peers:

> Cheating is an issue that can really divide our community, students against teachers in terms of cheating. There are students who join teachers' ranks but it sounds like

on the issue that it's me and you. Because obviously teachers don't participate in cheating. Peter, you were asking for reasons in this school. It's because it's fundamental to our school that there's trust within the community. You know my attitude when I give a test, it's based on trust. I would hate to mistrust people in the community and when people say it's not so bad cheating on a little test because you won't even take it again and it's not relevant to your later life it ignores a division about trust which can divide the community.

Just as a collective norm against stealing arose at Cambridge Cluster school through teacher and student advocacy of the norm as necessary for community trust and solidarity, so this staff member advocated a norm against cheating in the Scarsdale Alternative School.

Another teacher advocated a norm against cheating, less in terms of community and more in terms of the injustice of cheating cited by some students, as we quoted earlier, but questioned by other students. He said, "You have to see that cheating is hurting other people as a way to get ahead. I can't imagine you can think that's a principle you can live by despite all the temptation we talked about." While making a rule against cheating was soon agreed upon, the question of how to enforce this rule was extremely controversial. The teachers proposed that not only the faculty but the other students had the responsibility to enforce the rule by confronting any student seen cheating. As we noted in connection with the drug issue, the Scarsdale faculty were from the start concerned that the students share in responsibility for enforcement of agreed upon norms. In our theoretical language, they were determined that the norm should reach Phase 6 or 7, i.e., persuasion to desist from rule violation or to confront someone who had violated the rule. This was obviously controversial, not only for the students, but for an outside observer and consultant like Kohlberg. The rationale for the faculty's expectation that students confront one another over cheating was that teachers and students belonged to a common community and that it was not fair to the faculty to leave it to them to be the policemen or enforcers of a rule arrived at democratically. As stated by one of the teachers:

> Is it fair in a democratic school to make these rules and then shuffle down to the teacher's corner for their enforcement? There are certain rules that we make and the problem of who finds out about violation of them and who enforces them doesn't arise. But others that are hard to enforce like this one, I would say if we can't enforce it together we can't make it together. We don't own it. It's all our responsibility to deal with the cheating problem. If John sees someone cheating why is it any different from my seeing someone cheating?

Using this logic the faculty made the following proposals:

1. If a student knows that another student cheated, it is the student's responsibility to confront the student whom they know cheated.
2. The student who cheated should discuss the situation with the teacher of the class.

3. If the student who cheated refuses to discuss the matter with the teacher, the student who did the confronting has the responsibility to discuss the issue with the teacher.

4. The teacher has the responsibility to fail the student for the given assignment.

5. The teacher has the responsibility to bring the student before the Fairness Committee.

This effort of the staff to make students responsible for enforcing the cheating rule and being loyal to the school as a whole obviously contradicts the very powerful norms of loyalty and trust between friends. While it is possible to conceptualize these norms of loyalty to friends at a third stage of caring for individual mutual relations, and loyalty to the community as Stage 4, interpersonal norms of loyalty and trust are also basic to fourth and fifth stage concerns about friendship as well as to concerns about solidarity in the school community. The first image which the notion of confrontation and reporting friends may conjure up is that of Soviet or Chinese ideologies and practices of reporting deviance to state authorities and an invasion by the community in the whole private realm of friendship and intimacy. While this was not the perception of any of the Scarsdale students and faculty, there were many students who nonetheless had hesitation about confronting other students who were cheating.

One of the students said, "For someone to turn somebody in who they saw cheating, I would just go through a lot of pain, it would be personal hell." Another student responded, "At first, I felt like I didn't want all that responsibility but I think we do have a lot of responsibility to each other, a responsibility to the community and in a way to each other."

The director articulated more clearly this student's justification for confrontations, the justification that in a Just Community students have more responsibility for the character of their friends or for serving as moral mentors to one another. She said, "I think that sometimes we confuse what it means to be a good friend and that sometimes the best way you can show your caring and friendship is to show this responsibility and help your friend to act more honestly and not to violate the trust of the school".

A number of students saw the rightness of confrontation in this light, that cheating was unfair or wrong and that it was right to confront a friend who was cheating, but while right, it was a very difficult thing to do emotionally. A student noted, "I don't think anybody really thinks that cheating is not wrong. I'd think most people think it's right to turn someone in but it's really hard to do. We've friends and you don't want to hurt their feelings. It would be easier if this proposal is passed. Then I won't let myself look away if I see someone cheating." Another student added, "I would really feel intimidated about confronting some people in the community if I saw them cheating."

Other students felt that making an agreement to confront a student was asking too much. One student said, "It would be hard to confront. I think it should be left up to the person, not up to the rule.'' The director responded, ''We all value friendships but I think we need to hear how people could value their friendship and still be able to confront someone cheating.''

A student responded with reasoning that is transitional from Stage 3 to Stage 4, both individually and in her valuing of the community and its norms. She said, ''I would be able to do it because I would expect a friend to do it to me. It's not fair to the community because the community would fall apart if people thought they could cheat and others would feel I can't make that commitment. You just have to harden yourself and say, 'You have to do it.' The community has to be based on honesty.'' Another student was more skeptical saying, ''We're talking about establishing a rule that is going to work and I'm not sure it's going to work for me.'' One of the teachers responded, ''It's been my concern that we'd make a phony rule. Why don't we just do this? Let's trust everyone to vote honestly. Let's be aware of the reasons not to be able to confront somebody else. If you really believe you should have the responsibility to confront and you believe you can do that vote 'Yes.' If you don't believe it for yourself or for the community than vote it down. I think we have to trust that people will vote honestly.''

After further student discussion for and against the rule requiring that students confront one another, a vote was taken in which a large majority voted for the rule.

The reader, like Kohlberg, will probably experience considerable conflict about the meeting. Strong teacher advocacy led to a vote for students to confront one another about cheating. Cheating was perceived as unfair and a norm against it was carried to Phase 7 in its strength of institutionalization. By democratic agreement, an honor code against cheating was set up much like that at West Point, the army academy, though the West Point honor code was decreed by the adult officers and then signed by students as the price of admission to West Point. The price of the code, however, could easily be the weakening of ties of loyalty and trust between intimate friends, and considerable internal conflict and pain for members of a friendship pair. The question is whether enhancing the ''virtue'' of honesty and strengthening trust between teacher and students is worth such a price.

To address this question, we shall report an incident which occurred in the director's core group. Some weeks after passing the rule against cheating and requiring student confrontation, the director asked how the new policy was going. At the time, Wendy, a sophomore in her core group, said she felt she had to admit she had cheated on homework since the rule had been made. She felt that she had to say it to remain a part of the community. She said if she didn't admit to breaking the rule she couldn't feel close to the community but by admitting it she was prepared to take the consequences and knew that she would be accepted by the community for admitting it. At that point several students asked her if she had thought about the rule when she was breaking it and her response was ''yes, I knew I was breaking the rule but I also knew I was not doing well in this class; I was behind. I obviously made the wrong decision to cheat but I did it and I'm sorry.'' After a few members focused on that issue, Wendy said that during the cheating discussions in her core group she had become very bothered. She said, ''I feel like I'm a hypocrite because although I knew I cheated I'm extremely bothered by someone else who also has cheated and who has not said anything.'' Several students asked her what she felt her obligation was. Going back to her knowledge of what the community meeting on cheating had decided. Wendy said ''I know I'm supposed to confront the person.'' Then the director asked if she would like a friend or someone else to help her confront the person who cheated. Wendy said to the core group, ''You know Amy has a very strong will and personality, much stronger than mine. So although I knew it was wrong I couldn't say no to Amy.'' Wendy added that because her friendship with Amy was extremely important to her and that a refusal to permit Amy to copy might jeopardize their friendship, she didn't want to make an issue out of what Amy was doing. At that point the students discussed why Wendy felt that her friendship depended on letting Amy copy her work. Wendy's response was, ''Everyone here knows Amy and knows how determined she is and she is just someone you (at least I) can't tell what to do.'' At that point the core group focused on discussing with Wendy and Lissy, another student, how they were going to confront Amy about what happened.

After the core group meeting, Lissy and Wendy immediately went to talk to Amy about the discussion during core group. As a result of their discussion, in the community meeting that immediately followed core group Amy spoke up and apologized to the community for cheating.

In an ordinary group of society, this conflict would be a ''no-win'' dilemma. In a Just Community school, however, Wendy and Lissy's concern that a friend who cheated confess need not entail a destruction of loyalty and trust between the two friends. Impelled to loyalty by the community, Wendy and Lissy did appeal to Amy's own sense of loyalty to the community and in making that appeal may have been able to strengthen the friendship between Wendy and Amy. Wendy, while feeling close to Amy, also had felt intimidated by her strong personality, an intimidation which left Lissy conflicted about what her friendship might be with Amy. Because of strong support that the core group and the community gave one another, they were able to resolve the issue of confronting a friend about rule violations in a way which supported, rather than destroyed the friendship between Wendy and Amy. This is only possible because Amy, the friend who initiated the act of cheating, also felt loyal to the community. It also rested on the fact that admission of a rule violation or receiving a confrontation for rule violation in a Just Community school does not lead to harsh sanctions by an arbitrary authority but leads to consequences determined by the peer fairness committee which Wendy, Lissy, and Amy see as moderate and fair. It also depends on the sense that admission of a rule violation before the group or community does not make the person who confesses the object of harsh criticism and reduction of status or membership in the group. The act of admitting a rule violation is seen by most of the community as a positive sign of caring for the community. It is responded to by group emotional support and reassurance of the confessor's solid standing of membership in the group. The group feels this way because the rule violator's concern about the community is sufficiently strong to lead to admission of rule violation. In spite of the fact that the confrontation of one student by another is often a painful emotional process, its resolution can be one of a stronger sense of solidarity both between the friends involved and between the members of the core group and community.

Although the reader may agree with the fact that a conflict between personal loyalty to a friend and upholding a group rule could be resolved in a Just Community school in a way which strengthens rather than weakens ties of friendship, the whole process of open admission of rule violation with its possible consequence and group criticism may still seem a negative process similar to that in authoritarian communities such as in the People's Republic of China. Such a feeling derives from genuine validity of the strong American tradition of respect for privacy in personal matters which would exclude such personal issues from open public discussion even in a community tied together with such a feeling of mutual goodwill. We believe that, on reflection, however, the preference of the Just Community approach for open public discussion over concealment and gossip in indirect discussion can be justified as not in violation of personal privacy. The rules involved are public rules democratically agreed upon by the community and the infringement of these rules is also a public matter. The issue is quite different from opening up personal issues concerning a student's home and out of school life to public scrutiny and criticism. It did not imply "big brother" monitoring of the students' personal lives and of the morality of the totality of the students' lives by teachers and the group. Public discussion is restricted to issues of fairness in the school life of the community rather than a monitoring of the student's total personal and moral life. Furthermore, unlike models of moral education in authoritarian and totalitarian countries, public group discussion is not used as a form of humiliation and emotional ostracism; it culminates in reaffirmation of the individual's worth to the community and his or her continued membership in it.

As an example, personal sexual behavior is not made the subject for public discussion, rules or criticism since it is felt that that would be an intrusion into the student's personal privacy. If students bring their sexual problems or relationships to teachers in seeking advice, the information is held in strict confidence. The only time in which sexual relations have been discussed as a public issue has been in connection with rooming assignments on the annual school retreat. It is understood and agreed upon that males and females will be assigned separate rooms during the retreat.

In summary, at the Scarsdale Alternative School, honesty or just action with regard to cheating is developed or maintained by a high phase norm against it tied to valuing the community. This involves controversial confrontation. Usually this is a confrontation concerning the gap in an individual between judging what is right by an endorsement, through a vote, of a rule or norm and taking responsibility in line with this judgment. Such controversy is relieved if confrontation occurs in the community of one's peers in an atmosphere of fairness and care and of some sense of Royce's "loyalty to loyalty," or of an ideal of open dialogue and ideal role-taking. This leaves open, however, another controversial issue: minority rights.

Civil Disobedience.   In the discussion above, a student said, "I voted against the procedure of confrontation. I believe in the rule but I don't believe in how we've agreed to enforce it. You should never report on a fellow student, we need to be loyal to each other." In the case of the drug rule, most of us would feel that the minority should abide by the decision of the majority. But in this case, a minority voter does not feel compelled to abide by the majority rule for reasons of conscience, so he is willing to be civilly disobedient. Here, more strongly than in the rule about drugs, we enter the realm of postconventional reasoning pro and con. At the center of many discussions by staff and students at Scarsdale is the relation between majority rule and minority rights, loosely the issue at the transition from Stage 4 to Stage 5. One episode involving this issue was the civil disobedience of a teacher against a majority vote to continue a tense community meeting about expulsion of a student at the cost of cancelling regular afternoon classes. His statement announcing that he would hold regular classes is presented as Table 2.5. A student response to it is listed as Table 2.6. I would call both Stage 4/5, in transition from conventional to principled morality.

The upshot of this conflict was that the teacher was asked to appear before the student/staff discipline or fairness committee which "disciplined" him by asking for acknowledgment to the community that he had been in error or that his action was not legitimate civil disobedience. He did this with grace, his passions of the moment being cooled.

As the student's letter indicates, "civilly disobedient" nonparticipation in a voluntary participating community is a different matter than civil disobedience in a pluralistic democratic state, which is nonvoluntary in the sense that the citizen has no option as to whether or not to belong to the state. Upholding community can be done in a civilly disobedient way by a member but this was not this teacher's mode of response. What is more important than the "right" resolution of this issue by the community is the fact that it involved students in an "abstract" or principled moral issue and in argumentation about civil disobedience in the context of real life school decisions.

Expulsion and Membership.   Let me cite a fourth episode from the Alternative School which demonstrated that the Just Community approach could indeed work where as it had failed in the expulsion of Greg from the Cambridge Cluster School. I shall cite a community meeting I attended in Scarsdale in 1983.

TABLE 2.5
Staff Letter to SAS Community

Dear SAS Majority,

I speak for myself alone in this letter. If some of you in the Minority in today's final vote on schedule changes agree with me, I'd of course be delighted.

To the best of my memory, the American Revolutionists were upset at King George because he wouldn't take them seriously. So they dumped some tea into Boston Harbor, I believe it was, and raised hell generally. I am upset likewise; you didn't seem to take me seriously, so I plan to follow my ancestors' example (one graduated from Harvard in the late 1600's) and raise a little hell myself.

Why am I upset?

1. You voted today to meet from 1:00 to 1:45. Though I was opposed, I was one of maybe a half dozen people waiting at 1:00. We began about 1:20.

2. Despite my pleas for much needed time, both last week and again today, you agree to meet right through Math 11 Regents class time.

3. Despite my saying it was cruel both to me and to my Math 11 students, you condemned us to two hours together tomorrow.

4. Because of this, you are telling me I must cancel Physics tomorrow, though I believe that class is at least as important as Math 11.

5. Call me cynic if you will, but I am convinced that a substantial number of you voted to continue the meeting in large part because you wanted to get out of class and that you voted for Friday's schedule change for the same reason.

6. Though many of you are aware of my dislike of working under pressure and extend your sincerest sympathies, especially around Regents time, your actions say you don't care.

I promised you I'd raise hell. How?

1. I will *not* meet Math 11 for two hours Friday. I will be in room 39, F block as usual, but not E.

2. I will be in the yellow room for Physics tomorrow during E block as usual. If you are in either Social Action or in Political Philosophy and also in Physics, you'll have to make a choice.

3. If you continue to tamper with scheduled math time, I will not assume responsibility for Regents preparation.

Sorry. I can't seem to get your attention.

The issue at hand was whether to expel Lisa, a first-year tenth grade student, which would mean she would be returning to the regular high school where she had been unhappy and had done poorly. The staff, in a staff meeting had unanimously decided that such a return would be best for the school community and possibly for Lisa herself. Until she became aware of the threat of expulsion, she had regularly cut classes in spite of many reminders. She had frequently been verbally abusive to the staff, something almost unheard of in that school. The teachers felt she had not made the necessary commitment to the alternative school to work effectively with her, and that she was taking away time and energy that other students should receive.

Because it was the first expulsion issue in three years, discussion of Lisa's expulsion precluded other personal discussion in the small core group meetings

TABLE 2.6
Student Response to Staff Civil Disobedience

"OF THE NATURE OF DISOBEDIENCE"

—Anonymous

The principle upon which the 'participatory democracy' system of government that our school had adopted is self explanatory: Any policy decision necessitates the participation of all. The purpose being, that "all"—the total group affected by such decision—have input into these same decisions which "all" will have to abide by. In order for such a system to function effectively then, "all" must act within the means of the system or else act to change the system—these are the only two rational alternatives. Furthermore, any action taken outside the system's apparatus must be accordingly dealt with as an act of protest and rebellion deserving a reaction by the system, or the community which upholds the system.

Last week in community meeting (the appropriate forum for legislative action) there was a hotly contested issue debated by the community. The subject matter is not significant to this discussion but the repercussions of the decision are.

Majority-rule decision-making depends on each member's voting for what he genuinely believes to be in the community's best interest. Implied explicitly in this system is the obligation for each member of the community to live with community-made decisions, regardless of his personal opinions. Involvement in any voluntary system entails allegiance to that system at all times, not merely convenient times. Further, such a system requires that all participants faithfully trust the community's ability to legislate, or else they are obligated to change the system or leave the system. As long as "all" agree the system is legitimate "all" must unconditionally exercise and not act outside the provisions of the system. Whether participatory democracy is good or bad is unimportant until that issue is examined under a formal proposal. What is important is obedience to a system for the sake of law and order.

Disobedience toward the system, in the form of direct violation of community-made policy is a direct attack on the system, not merely that particular policy, and must be dealt with in order to preserve the system. Mr. D. Potter, an active and vocal participant in the system, has committed such a violation of the system in his disavowal of a community decision. As said above, the nature of his gripe is irrelevant here; moreso, the significance of his action lies in the theoretical nature of such behavior that violates directly a basic premise of the democratic system. Mr. Potter participated in the system up to the crucial point, the test of the system's effectiveness and at this junction he made the fatal decision to use his own discretion and abandon the system. He stayed in the system until the system no longer suited his personal preferences and then he made his own rules. His refusal to honor the majority-rule concept of justice strips the system of all justice and authority because all other members are infringed on and chaos results. The will of the community is ignored by such a usurpation of the community's power. Such action is an attack on the community and set a lethal precedent for anarchy. In rebelling against the system he must either be acknowledged as correct in his action, in which case the system must be changed, or he must be reprimanded.

The system has means for voicing minority discontent but cannot tolerate deviance that operates independent of the system for this is true tyranny. Mr. Potter, in his action, presumes to be in position of greater insight than the community and thus had appointed himself acting decision and policy maker. A real gripe, which we must assume precipitated such action, can be voiced in no more destructive way than by belligerent, self-centered despotism. It closes all channels for discussion and compromise. It makes a mockery of every member's opinion and power with the community. When individuals take justice into their own hands the result is rule by the most powerful and silencing of all minority or other opinions. In a sense, Mr. Potter has provided a healthy atmosphere for just the sort of injustice he himself feels victimized by. If the system is in need of repair then this kind of action is singularly appropriate but if indeed the system is valid and worth preserving, such vigilance stands in direct opposition to justice and cannot be tolerated.

which preceded the school-wide community meeting. I attended a core group meeting where students took varying attitudes. Some felt Lisa had passed all bounds and that upholding the standards of the school required her expulsion. Others knew of her family difficulties and of her almost complete lack of close friends, and worried about her return to the regular high school. One student said that the school was a very strong community and should give her the support and the prodding which could keep her attending class and being a member of the school.

The larger community meeting began with the director's statement that it was the community's decision. She asked students to think about the issue from Lisa's point of view, from the staff's point of view and from the point of view of the whole community. Then a spokesperson for the staff read a report recommending and giving the reasons for expulsion. Lisa was then asked to express her view. Her initial response was quite instrumental and self-protective, a statement suggesting Stage 2. She didn't like the regular high school, and for the past week, she pointed out, she had attended classes regularly. When asked why she had developed the improved attitude, she said "Out of fear."

The two students chairing the meeting asked for student discussion. Many hands went up. One of the first to speak was Sharon. She elaborated her view that because the school was a strong community it should form a support group for Lisa. Even if Lisa wasn't self-disciplined enough to come to class regularly, others could help her and put some daily pressure on her to come to class. Others made comments supportive of Sharon's position. One student said he took pride in the community and would value it less if no attempt was made to keep and support Lisa. Other students were more "hard-nosed". One student commented, "No one else had an attendance problem like Lisa's. Why should the community tolerate it?" Another student said, "I didn't know this was supposed to be a therapeutic community." A student responded to this saying, "It's not a therapeutic community. It's a community. That means we all care about each member of the school, with or without problems."

After more discussion, Lisa, who was crying, was asked to comment. She talked about her desire to have another chance to stay in the school. It was as if a dawning Stage 3 awareness was growing as to what the school could be for her, a place where people cared. There was discussion among the other students that being a caring community sounded good but who would really take the responsibility. A number of students individually volunteered to take this responsibility. Alternatives were outlined on the blackboard: Stay in the school; stay in the school on probation with an individual contract to be worked out with the staff; expulsion with the chance to return the following year if she did well in the regular school. Lisa, when asked what she would vote for, answered "Stay in the school on probation." Extensive discussion followed with an indication that some staff members were changing their minds. When a vote was called for 1 1/2 hours later Lisa asked to leave the room so she would not know who voted against her. Eventually she agreed to stay. Of the 76 voting members present all but 4 voted for Lisa to stay.

In the days after the meeting a contract between Lisa, her advisor, and a support group of students was worked out. Lisa met once a week with this support group. For the rest of the year she not only attended all classes but her work improved and her use of abusive or disrespectful language disappeared.

At a meeting after school, a number of the observers, the staff and I held a debriefing meeting. One visiting private school department chairman asked me, "Dr. Kohlberg, don't you worry that adults who are a little older should put so much power in the hands of students?." Staff members answered for me. They had been convinced in this particular case that the students had made a more fair or just decision than they had come to. The justice of the decision, however, rested not only on democratic discussion but on the strong and high-stage sense of community of the students. In most schools, a teacher or an administrator faces a "no-win" choice. If they opt for the needs of a troubled kid, they weaken the rules and welfare of the larger group. In Lisa's situation, the option that was best for the troubled student actually strengthened the group's sense of community and its sense of responsibility for its rules such as for attendance and participation. Perhaps quite wisely, the teachers did not accept this solution until they saw it genuinely coming from the students.

In comparison to the Cambridge Cluster School students at the time of Greg's expulsion, the students at the Scarsdale Alternative School had a stronger sense of community and a stronger norm of collective responsibility for individual members, leading to a different outcome in the Scarsdale decision than at Cambridge.

ASSESSING THE JUST COMMUNITY

Our discussion of the Just Community approach to moral education in this paper has been largely anecdotal and historical. We have, however, developed more extensively elsewhere a systematic research approach to the study of the moral atmosphere of the schools discussed (Higgins, Power, & Kohlberg, 1984). We have continued to use our standard or "classical" moral dilemma method longitudinally with three democratic alternative schools and with comparison groups in the corresponding regular high schools. In both Cambridge and Scarsdale, the "Just Community" alternative school students advanced more than an average of one-fourth stage per year. This result is equivalent to the "Blatt effect" emerging from hypothetical dilemma discussion, and does not correspond to our central goals in the Just Community interventions. Our focus was rather primarily upon the development of the group and its moral atmosphere rather than upon individual moral judgment. Reports by students and teachers of student behavior tended to confirm the ethnographic analysis we made of the school moral atmosphere. We reported this in our discussion of stealing at the Cambridge Cluster School and of drugs in the Cambridge and Scarsdale Alternative schools. Our formulation of school moral atmosphere was partly based on Durkheim's theorizing insofar as this was compatible with our observations of group development in the Cluster and Scarsdale schools. As we have noted, Durkheim saw the first element of morality as "the spirit of discipline" including both group norms of justice (norms against violating the rights of individuals, such as norms against stealing or cheating) and norms of convention, following Turiel's (1983) distinction. These would include the drug rule, rules of attendance, etc. Related to "the spirit of discipline," but more important to Durkheim, was the underlying sense of community or valuing of the group united by solidarity that Durkheim called "the spirit of altruism." They are particularly expressed and developed in decisions based on collective responsibility such as collective restitution for theft in the Cambridge Cluster school and collective support toward Lisa in the Scarsdale Alternative School. Student and teacher advocacy for a degree of collective responsibility both comes from, and in turn stimulates, a sense of group solidarity or a sense of community. Recommended by Durkheim, I had observed it in practice in our Israeli kibbutz (Kohlberg, 1971).

The first hypothesis of our Durkheim-inspired research approach was that there were collective norms in the Just Community schools and that these would be more clearly collective and shared both over time and in comparison to the regular high schools. Durkheim had simply postulated that norms were collective; we set out to observe the degree to which group members expressed collective, as distinct from individual or personal, moral norms. Table 2.7 indicates the the degree of collectiveness of a norm used in our research. There are three dimensions to the table. The first goes from "I" to "we," i.e., the speaker's perspective develops from individual advocacy or judgment to being a spokesperson for the group. The second dimension is the constituency of the norm, e.g., its centering on other members of the group. The third dimension is the prescriptivity or oughtness of the norm, a prescriptivity which, according to Durkheim, increases with the collectiveness of a norm and its centrality to group solidarity.

To illustrate this "degree of collectiveness" dimension, as evident in the speech of the student spokespersons for collective restitution at the Cambridge Cluster School, we shall cite some typical interview material from the moral atmosphere study. The moral atmosphere study centered on student responses to "practical" or everyday school dilemmas including issues of justice (theft), of "conventional" aspects of discipline (drug use), and of "altruism" or of acts of helping, usually thought to go beyond rights and duties. The altruistic dilemma is presented in Table 2.8.

Before considering student responses to the dilemma, I would like to ask the reader to think of his own response to Billy's dilemma. Most high school stu-

TABLE 2.7
Degree of Collectiveness of Norms

1.	I—Rejection:	No one can make a rule or agreement in this school which would be followed or taken seriously. *Descriptive.* I as an individual. No group constituency.
2.	I—Conscience:	An action in accordance with the norm should not be expected or demanded by the group because it should be left to each individual's free choice. *Prescriptive.* Could be descriptive. I as an individual.
3.	I—No Awareness:	Does not perceive the existence of a shared norm concerning this issue and does not take a position pro or con about the groups' developing such a norm. Also does not have an individual norm concerning this issue. *Descriptive.* I as an individual. Group constituency.
4.	I—Individual:	An action should be performed which is in accordance with the norm where this action is not defined or implied by membership in the group. There is no suggestion that the task of the group is or should be to develop or promote the norm. *Prescriptive.* I as an individual. *Constituency*—universal, applied to people in the group as much as to people outside the group.
5.	I—Individual Ambiguous:	An action should be performed which is in accordance with the norm where this action is implied by membership in the group. *Prescriptive.* I as an individual. *Constituency*—ambiguous but seems to apply to people in the group more than to those outside.
6.	Authority:	An action should be performed because it is expected or demanded by the teacher, administrator whose authority derives from his/her status or the law which makes the teacher a superior member of the group. *Prescriptive or Descriptive.* Teacher as authority. Group constituency.
7.	Authority-Acceptance:	An action should be performed because it is expected by authority or law with the clear implication that the group accepts this authority and thinks promoting and upholding the norm is in the interest of the group's welfare. *Prescriptive.* Teacher as authority. Group constituency. The speaker perspective is the individual speaking as if he or she and others have internalized the norm.
8.	They-Aggregate (I disagree):	They the group or a substantial subgroup, have a tendency to act in accordance with a norm in a way that the individual speaker does not share or disagrees with. *Prescriptive or Descriptive.* I, as a member of the group. Group constituency.

(*Continued*)

TABLE 2.7 (*Continued*)

9.	I and They— Aggregate:	They and I have a tendency to act in the same way in accordance with a norm. *Prescriptive or Descriptive.* I and they, as members of the group. Group constituency.
10.	Limiting or Proposing I:	The speaker thinks the group or all members of the group should follow or uphold this norm better or should have this new norm. (This category overlaps with Phase I—Proposing). *Prescriptive.* I, as a member of the group. Group constituency.
11.	Spontaneous— Collective:	They or they and I think that group members should act in accordance with the norm *because* they feel naturally motivated to do so due to the sense of belonging to the group. *Descriptive.* They and I as members of the group. Group constituency.
12.	They—Limited Collective:	They think that group members should act in accordance with the norm without the speaker identifying himself with that normative expectation. The speaker can differentiate his own normative perspective. *Prescriptive.* They, as members of the group. Group constituency.
13.	I and They— Limited Collective:	Both I and they, as members of the group, think that group members should act in accordance with the norm. *Prescriptive.* I and they, as members of the group. Group constituency.
14.	Implicit—We Collective:	The members of this group think that all of us should act in accordance with the norm. *Prescriptive.* Speaker perspective is group member *qua* group member.
15.	We Explicit— Collective:	We, the members of this group, think that we should act in accordance with the norm. *Prescriptive.* We (explicitly stated), members *qua* members. Group constituency.

dents and adults do not think that Billy has any responsibility or duty to drive Harry to his interview. That would be an act of altruism which goes beyond justice, rights and duties. At Stage 6 the obligatory or just and the good come closer together. If Billy and Harry enter into ideal dialogue or role-taking or if Billy imagines himself under Rawls' "veil of ignorance" in deciding what is fair, imagining he could equally be in either position, it would be fair to take responsibility for driving Harry.

TABLE 2.8
Caring Dilemma

The college Harry applied to had scheduled an interview with him for the coming Saturday morning at 9:00 a.m. Since the college was 40 miles away from Harry's town and Harry had no way of getting there, his guidance counselor agreed to drive him. The Friday before the interview the guidance counselor told Harry that his car had broken down and was in the repair shop until Monday. He said he felt badly but there was no way he could drive him to his interview. He still wanted to help him out so he went to Harry's homeroom and he asked the students if there was anyone who could drive Harry to the college. No one volunteered to drive him. A lot of students in the class think Harry shows off and talks too much and don't like him. The homeroom teacher says he has to take his children to the dentist at that time. Some students say they can't use the family car, others work, some don't have their licenses. One student, Billy, knows he can use his family car but he wonders whether he should do something for Harry when the few students in class who know him best say they are busy or just can't do it. Besides, he would have to get up really early on a Saturday morning which is the only morning during the week he can sleep late.

1.   SHOULD BILLY VOLUNTEER TO DRIVE HARRY TO THE COLLEGE?
      WHY OR WHY NOT?

Let us return from the philosophy of this decision to high school students' responses to this dilemma as they illustrate the moral atmosphere, collective norms and the valuing of community in various schools.

In response to this dilemma, Betsy, a Cambridge Cluster School student said: "Anyone who is in Cluster knows they should help out . . . there is the general feeling and everyone knows that." SHOULD SOMEONE HELP OUT? "Yes, they should because Cluster School is a community. Because you have a responsibility to the students in this school. You are supposed to think of them as part of the school and part of the community, so you should do it."

Betsy's response depicts a group with a high degree collective norm, degree 14. Her statement exemplifies the three aspects of the highest two levels of the collectiveness of the helping norm. When Betsy says "you are supposed to," she is speaking as one member of a collective to other members of the collective and she is representing the point of view of the group as a whole. This aspect of her response we called *speaker's perspective*. Betsy is Level IV because her statement "you have a responsibility to the kids in this school" doesn't come from her as an individual, but is a statement from the perspective of the group, representative of the collective norm. The speaker's perspective defines the group *for* whom the subject is speaking or representing. The *group constituency* defines the group membership of the persons *to* whom the subject is speaking or prescribing a rule or action. In this example it is clear to whom Betsy is speaking; she is prescribing *to* the members of the Cluster School. The third aspect is that the *norm is stated prescriptively* in terms of an obligation. We distinguish norms which are prescriptive from norms which are aggregate or stated as descriptive of the behavior of individuals or groups. Aggregate norms reflect a "statistical tendency'' rather than a clearly shared idea of obligation. Betsy's response to the dilemma thus illustrates Durkheim's conception of a collective norm of altruism. It also illustrates Durkheim's view that altruism toward others often derives from a valuing of the collectivity and its solidarity rather than from an individually generated sentiment of sympathy.

Table 2.9 sketches out the degree to which respondents value the community or the solidarity of the group. Betsy illustrates Level IV, the highest degree of community valuing. In answer to why people in her school help out on the caring dilemma, Betsy said: "Yes, they should because Cluster is a community. Because you have a responsibility to the kids in this school, even if you don't like them all that much, you are in school and you're with them every day, you know, you are supposed to think of them as part of the school and part of the community, so you should do it."

We categorized her response as being at Level IV, in terms of her idea that the school is a community which expects members to help each other because they are all members of the same group. This implies an awareness and valuing of community which creates moral obligations and norms. The interviewer asked: WHAT DOES IT MEAN WHEN YOU SAY, WE ARE A COMMUNITY, SO WE ARE SUPPOSED TO HELP EACH OTHER? "Because everyone is supposed to be one, it is our school, it is not a school that all these separate people go to that don't care about each other."

Betsy's response indicates three aspects of this level of community valuing. First is the idea that a community implies a strong degree of unity, a oneness, or

TABLE 2.9
Degree of Community Valuing

I.	*Instrumental Extrinsic:*	The school is valued as an institution that helps the individual to meet his own academic needs.
II.	*"Espirit' de Corp" Extrinsic:*	The school is valued as an institution that helps the individual and that the individual feels some loyalty toward *as manifest* in team spirit and support of teams or groups in school.
III.	*Spontaneous Community Intrinsic:*	The school is valued as the kind of place in which members feel an inner motivation to help others in the group community and the community generates special feelings of closeness among members.
IV.	*Communal Intrinsic:*	The school as a community is valued for its own sake. Community can obligate its members in special ways and members can expect special privileges or responsibilities from the group and other members.

solidarity. Second is it expresses the idea of personal identification with the group and its objectives, "it's our school." Third is the feature that membership in the group means mutual caring about one another as group members.

As a contrast to Betsy's sense of a collective moral norm of altruism linked to a valuing of a solidarity community, we may cite the response of Rob, a member of the regular high school at the same Stage (3/4) as Betsy on our classical hypothetical moral dilemmas. Rob said: "He should help out. I would wait till after class, I would keep it quiet so nobody might know about it and then I could help the kid. Then nobody would say anything to me because they would not know about it. I just believe in helping people."

Here Rob was clearly making an individual moral judgment to help. He observed a peer group norm which would operate in the opposite direction of helping, a "counter norm" to norms of morality and altruism. Rob would expect disapproval from the peer group for helping a deviant or unpopular student. This peer group norm is classified as an aggregate norm (refer to Table 7 on the degree of collectiveness of a norm). An aggregate norm arises from statistical observation that students don't help unpopular students or don't want to associate with them. It is neither strictly prescriptive, or obligatory, nor is it the result of shared decisions and discussion leading to a "we perspective."

As noted, Rob was clearly aware that his norm of helping is individual. When asked if his school should have a shared agreement to help he said: "Yah, right. Like it is not a law, but everybody knows that it is good to help someone out. But people just don't care about anybody else." Focusing on the theme of a lack of a sense of community and caring at the high school he commented that "Seventy-five percent of them wouldn't care. They are worried about their own problems probably." Rob, as an individual, held a norm of helping but was conspicuously aware of the discrepancy between his individual norm of helping and the absence of any collective norm of helping. He said:

> It's really - it should be an agreement with yourself, you know. It is like, I have strong feelings toward other people. I don't like to think bad things and I never say anything bad about anybody, and it is more of an agreement with yourself than with anybody, you couldn't make an agreement with somebody about something like this.

Not only was Rob aware of the discrepancy between his individual norm of helping and the lack of any collective norm but also his response indicates that he thought it was impossible to develop shared moral norms on issues such as helping. This is scored as Degree I on our scale, explicit rejection of the possibility of developing a shared norm (see Table 2.7).

In contrast to Betsy, Rob did not see a shared valuing of community. He individually valued the school but others did not.

I don't consider this school a community. Too many people hold grudges against each other, because maybe they look different or act different. Or some kids come to school to be with their friends or to be stoned, and some kids come to do work. Like the kids who get stoned might stand around and see someone with a lot of books walk by and laugh. But they won't laugh when graduation comes. No, most people think of themselves, really.

HOW DO YOU THINK THINKING ABOUT THE COMMUNITY WOULD AFFECT THAT?

If they did think about it, I don't really know, because I don't know if they ever did, like I said only people in committees and stuff would think about it and talk about it, and those would be a small minority.

IN HANDLING ISSUES ABOUT RESPECTING OTHER PEOPLE'S PROPERTY AND TRUSTING OTHER PEOPLE, DO YOU THINK THE SCHOOL IS REALLY A COMMUNITY?

Well not really, because in a way like we own this school and a lot of kids mess it up. Like write on the walls, there is no need for that, there is paper to write on. I don't know, some people do and some people don't. I don't really know the percentage.

These comments suggest that Rob was between Degree I and Degree II in his thinking about the value of the school (see Table 2.9). He, as an individual, attached some value to the school as an organization and said "in a way like we own this school and a lot of kids mess it up." He felt some ownership of the school and found vandalism or injury to it offensive. He also valued its major function, academic learning, even though he saw many other students as not doing likewise. Thus, there is a contrast between his individual valuing of the school as an organization and his perception of the attitudes of most of the students in this regard.

The moral atmosphere research model we have described uses Durkheim's concepts of collective norms and group solidarity or community spirit. Durkheim has admitted limitations from the point of view of moral and social philosophy. Rather than totally integrating our theory of individual ontogenetic stages of justice and rights with a more compatible theory of democratic community like that of Dewey and Mead, however, we have found Durkheim's collectivistic theory a more powerful addition to justice stage theory in guiding intervention and research with democratic school communities. Our moral atmosphere research assumes that collective norms and the sense of community can be assigned a moral stage as can classical moral dilemma individual responses, as was done in Table 2.4.

The stages commonly found in high school students, Stage 2, 3, and 4, are defined in Table 2.4. Stage 5 is as yet undefined but would obviously integrate more clearly the values of individual rights with the collective welfare stressed in Stage 4 definitions of collective norms and community.

Some signs of this integration are reflected in the moral atmosphere interview responses of a Scarsdale Alternative School student:

> Like in community meeting there is a big difference in me now. Before I thought about what was good for me in the meeting. I don't think consciously selfish. I just thought we should each vote for what we each wanted and then you combine them and the best comes out somehow. Not I try to distinguish what is best for me from what is best for all of the students or the community and to decide on that basis.

The shift she describes is from a theory of pluralistic interest group democracy governed by an "invisible hand" to a search for a consensus or Rousseau's "general will," a search never successfully showed by political states although it may be in voluntary communities.

With regard to the experimental or alternative school as a voluntary community, our Scarsdale student said: "I think if you're being into the school, you're being into something that give up certain rights or functions for the chance of belonging here. But there are different limits, there is no way the community should decide everything, many things should be left to individual decision."

Leaving philosophic issues aside for the moment, the reader will see that the moral atmosphere on all our "Durkheimian" dimensions of the three democratic alternative schools is quite similar and quite different from the regular high schools in their communities. This is indicated by the results reported in Table 2.10.

RESPONSE TO HABERMAS

Habermas (1979) has approached the issue of moral education from a somewhat different, but not entirely incompatible, perspective from that presented here. I would like to conclude by taking up some of his comments, presented to me informally. First, Habermas points out that the approach is an effort to guide the "unstudied curriculum" and is in a certain sense a model of socialization which is something broader than education in the formal and pedagogical sense, in particular because it involves the use of democratic discipline, approval and disapproval. I would note, however, that the model endeavors to stay within the limits of education and to address the danger of indoctrination usually taken for granted as part of the socialization process in the family.

Second, Habermas has pointed out that there is a degree of illusoriness in a democratic process in the classroom or alternative school which is often in contradiction to the actual authoritarian character of the broader school structure, the home or the street. I have only anecdotal data on the way in which students cope with these contradictions. If the model is picked up and researched more extensively, we would hope this question would be addressed more directly.

TABLE 2.10
Moral Atmosphere Results for Six Schools

District	Brookline		Cambridge		Scarsdale	
Type of School	Brookline High School Traditional	School Within a School (Democratic)	Cambridge High School Traditional	Cluster School (Democratic)	Scarsdale School Traditional	Scarsdale Alternative (Democratic)
1. Frequency of perceived prosocial choice for others	54%	73%	46%	83%	65%	81%
2. Frequency of predicted prosocial behavior of others	29%	51%	34%	56%	29%	72%
3. Modal degree of collectiveness or norms (1–15)	3;5	11	3;5	13	3;5	11
4. Mean stage of collective norms	2/3(272)*	3/4(342)	2/3(239)	3(309)	3(290)	3/4(337)
5. Mean phase of collective norms	0	5	0	4	0	6
N =	23	16	16	20	19	12

*(MMS)-Moral Maturity Score

Finally, I will take up Habermas' most important comments, those concerning the different moral functions of the Just Community approach. The first major function Habermas lists is the creation of a setting for problem-solving or conflict-resolving moral discourse. Habermas calls the social structure of the discourse egalitarian or symmetrical. This terminology comes from Habermas' theory of an "ideal speech situation," a concept used to define a "universal speech ethic." An ideal speech situation involves the possibility of unlimited discussion in which moral claims can be "redeemed" or *justified* by open argumentation of a sort similar to that elaborated by moral philopophers. Such an ideal speech situation must involve not only unlimited discussion but discussion that is free from distorting influences, especially open domination and strategic or manipulative behavior. Symmetry implies that speakers have the same chance to employ regulative speech acts to recommend and forbid, to criticize, etc. The just or democratic norm of our Just Community is necessary if not sufficient to define a Habermas "ideal speech" situation, one which in the end is defined by my moral theory as a Stage 6 process of ideal role-taking in dialogue or "moral musical chairs." In Habermas' ideal speech situation, discussion must be able to move to a level of "theoretical" redemption or justification of moral validity claims. Habermas uses as an example of such discourse the interchange between Dawes and the anonymous student presented in tables 2.5 and 2.6 about the rightness of "civil disobedience" in a voluntary school community. Habermas claims that these exchanges occur "in the context of moral justification." Habermas sees a second more common moral function of the Just Community in "the context of moral discovery." He assigns Phyllis' speech about collective responsibility and restitution to this category of discovering what is the right thing to do. As Habermas elaborates this distinction, Phyllis' act of discovery is a discovery of the facts of living in a solidarity community. In this context, stealing is a violation of trust where it is not seen as such in the nonsolidarity community of the larger high school. In the "context of discovery" all the members of the community make group decisions together and feel responsible for what happens in the group, e.g., the act of stealing. In a certain sense Phyllis' act of discovery is a perception or intuition of a moral "fact," the fact of collective solidarity and responsibility, its violation by the theft and the "fact" of responsibility of each group member to do something about it. This "moral discovery," Habermas says, rests not so much on the egalitarian, democratic element of the Just Community which allows opportunity for symmetrical moral argumentation, but rather on the effort "to promote a network of interaction which functions as a *context of solidarity.*"

We have stressed a Durkheimian interpretation of our focus upon "a sense of community" or a sense of collective solidarity and the formation of collective norms. Habermas provides us with a slightly different interpretation, based upon his theory of discourse ethics, but one which mirrors our emphasis on developing the Just Community approach as a contributor to moral action. He stresses the "context of solidarity" as (a) creating moral discoveries or insights like that of

Phyllis, but more importantly (b) the motivation to act in accordance with these moral insights. He concludes his comments as follows: "Summarizing my rather loose considerations, I would propose to distinguish carefully between the following four functional aspects of a "Just Community". This design

(1) provides a setting for problem solving discourses which is supposed to serve as a context for both
   a) justifying and
   b) discovering moral insights; (and)
(2) promotes a context of solidarity which is supposed to serve as a motivational backing for both
   a) the cognitive purpose of gaining moral insights and
   b) the ego-developmental purpose of becoming autonomous, that is, of knowing how to act with good moral reasons.

In elaborating this list, he says:

> The context of solidarity is supposed to serve *ego-developmental* rather than pure cognitive purposes. To put it differently: the community turns out to function as a socialization device which can supplement and reinforce procedures of parental autonomy training. I use "autonomy" here in the Kantian sense where the term implies the insight that a valid norm is not "given" to us, but has to be *created* by reasonable moral subjects.

We would not make the dichotomy between "cognitive moral development" and "ego development" which Habermas makes, nor, as we noted earlier, do we call our form of moral education supplementary socialization to that of parental autonomy training. These differences in terminology from that of Habermas are discussed in Kohlberg (1984). I do want to stress, however, that Habermas agrees with me that what he calls 'collective socialization' is in the service of moral autonomy, not conformity or heteronomy. Students are learning, we believe, not that "I must conform to the group" but that "we are legislating norms and if we all legislate these norms we must all act upon them", i.e., the Kantian notion of autonomy. We have developed a typological assessment of autonomy, distinct from moral stage (Colby, et al., in press; Kohlberg, 1984) and are planning to assess development in the democratic schools on this measure. Thus we hope to deal with the most common criticism of our communitarian education for justice, i.e., that it encourages simply conformity to the group. In any case, our theory of intervention and our theory of formative evaluation research is a circular and somewhat eclectic one, as we stressed in our initial remarks about theory and practice being a two-way street. As we continue, I hope the theory will be what Lakatos (1978) describes as the progressive "content adding" spiral of valuable scientific theories as research programs, rather than being of the degenerative or static type which he also describes.

ACKNOWLEDGMENT

This paper is a summary of a forthcoming lengthier work: *Democracy and Schooling: The Moral Atmosphere of Three Experimental Schools* by Clark Power, Ann Higgins, Joseph Reimer and Lawrence Kohlberg. New York, Columbia University Press 1985 (in press). In addition to acknowledging the contribution of my fellow researchers, I would like to acknowledge the support of the Danforth and Ford Foundations for the development of this work.

REFERENCES

Berkowitz, M. W. & Gibbs, J. C. (1983). Measuring the developmental features of moral discussion. *Merrill-Palmer Quarterly, 29,* 399–410.

Blatt, M. & Kohlberg, L. (1975). The effects of classroom discussion upon children's level of moral judgment. *Journal of Moral Education, 4,* 129–161.

Blocker, H. Q. & Smith, E. (1980). *John Rawls' theory of justice: An introduction.* Columbus, OH: Ohio State University.

Colby, A., Kohlberg, L., Candee, D., Gibbs, J. C., Hewer, A., Kaufman, K., Power, C., & Speicher-Dubin, B. (in press). *The measurement of moral judgment.* New York: Cambridge University.

Colby, A., Kohlberg, L., Fenton, E., Speicher-Dubin, B., & Lieberman, M. (1977). Secondary school moral discussion programmes led by social studies teachers. *Journal of Moral Education, 6,* 90–117.

Dewey, J. (1960). *Theory of moral life.* New York: Holt Rinehart & Winston.

Dewey, J. (1966). *Democracy and education.* New York: MacMillan Free.

Downey, M. & Kelly, A. V. (1978). *Moral education: Theory and practice.* London: Harper and Row.

Durkheim, E. (1973). *Moral education.* New York: Free Press.

Erikson, E. (1964). *Insight and responsibility.* New York: Norton.

Gilligan, C. (1982). *In a different voice: Psychological theory and women's development.* Cambridge, MA: Harvard University.

Habermas, J. (1979). *Communication and the evolution of society.* Boston: Beacon Press.

Hart, D. & Kohlberg, L. (In press). The theories of the development of the social self of Mead and Baldwin. In L. Kohlberg (Ed.), *Child psychology and childhood education: A cognitive-developmental view.* New York: Longman.

Hartshorne, H. & May, M. A. (1928–1930). *Studies in the nature of character* (Vols. 1–3). New York: MacMillan.

Hickey, J. & Scharf, P. (1980). *Toward a just correctional system.* San Francisco: Jossey-Bass.

Higgins, A., Power, C., & Kohlberg, L. (1984). The relationship of moral atmosphere to judgments of responsibility. In W. Kurtines & J. Gewirtz (Eds.), *Morality, moral behavior and development.* (pp. 74–106). New York: Wiley Interscience.

Hoffman, M. L. (1976). Empathy, role-taking, guilt and development of altruistic motives. In T. Lickona (Ed.), *Moral development and behavior: Theory of research and social issues* (pp. 124–143). New York: Holt Rinehart and Winston.

Kohlberg, L. (1970). The moral atmosphere of the school. In N. Overley (Ed.). *The unstudied curriculum: Its impact on children* (pp. 104–127). Association for Supervision and Curriculum Development, Washington, DC.

Kohlberg, L. (1971). Cognitive-developmental theory and practice of collective moral education. In

M. Wolins & M. Gottesman (Eds.), *Group care: An Israeli approach - The education path of Youth Aliyah* (pp. 342–379). New York: Gordon and Breach.

Kohlberg, L. (1980). High school democracy and education for a just society. In R. L. Mosher (Ed.), *Moral education: A first generation of research and development* (pp. 20–57). New York: Praeger.

Kohlberg, L. (1981). *Essays on moral development, Volume One: The philosophy of moral development.* San Francisco: Harper and Row.

Kohlberg, L. (1984). *Essays on moral development, Volume Two: The psychology of moral development.* San Francisco: Harper and Row.

Lakatos, J. (1978). *The methodology of scientific research programs.* Cambridge, England: Cambridge University.

Lockwood, A. (1978). The effects of values clarification and moral development curricula on school age subjects: A critical review of recent research. *Review of Educational Research, 48,* 325–364.

MacMurray, J. (1961). *Persons in relation.* London: Faber and Faber.

Mead, G. H. (1934). *Mind, self and society.* Chicago: University of Chicago Press.

Mosher, R. L. (Ed.) (1980). *Moral education: A first generation of research and development.* New York: Praeger.

Peters, R. S. (1981). *Moral development and moral education.* London: Allen and Unwin.

Power, C. (1979). *The moral atmosphere of a just community high school: A four year longitudinal study.* Unpublished doctoral dissertation, Harvard University.

Power, C. & Higgins, A. (1981). *The moral atmosphere and learning.* Cambridge, MA: Harvard University Moral Education Research Foundation.

Power, C., Higgins, A., Reimer, J., & Kohlberg, L. (In press). *Democracy and schooling: The moral atmosphere of three experimental schools.* New York: Columbia University.

Rawls, J. (1971). *A theory of justice.* Cambridge, MA: Harvard University.

Reimer, J. & Power, C. (1980). Educating for democratic community: Some unresolved problems. In R. L. Mosher (Ed.), *Moral education: A first generation of research and development* (pp. 303–320). New York: Praeger.

Rest, J. R., (1973). The hierarchical nature of moral judgment. *Journal of Personality, 41,* 86–109.

Royce, J. (1982). *The philosophy of Josiah Royce* (edited by J. Roth). Indianapolis: Hackett.

Turiel, E. (1966). An experimental test of the sequentiality of developmental stages in the child's moral judgment. *Journal of Personality and Social Psychology, 3,* 611–618.

Turiel, E. (1983). *The development of social knowledge, morality and convention.* New York: Cambridge University.

Walker, L. (in press). The validity of stages of moral reasoning. In L. Kohlberg and D. Candee (Eds.) *Research in moral development.* Cambridge, MA: Harvard University.

Wallwork, E. (1983). *Moralization in Durkheim and Kohlberg.* Unpublished manuscript, Syracuse University.

Wasserman, E. (1975). Implementing Kohlberg's "Just Community" in an alternative high school. *Social Education, 40,* 203–207.

3 Autonomy and Universalization as Moral Principles: A Dispute with Kohlberg, Utilitarianism and Discourse Ethics

Otfried Höffe
University of Fribourg (Switzerland)

Authoritarian education is no longer possible. One does not necessarily have to be a representative of radical antiauthoritarian education to agree with this point. Parents and teachers cannot simply make requirements without justifying them to their children or without convincing them and often leaving them enough freedom to choose. In this respect, the domain of education and its theory, i.e., pedagogy, reflect the general social and cultural situation of modern times, a situation whose key word is "freedom." In the name of freedom, many wars have been and are still being fought, political revolutions have been plotted, and economic and social changes have been and are being demanded. These revolutions and changes are not only concerned with liberation from slavery or bondage, nor solely with religious liberty and freedom of conscience, nor the equal rights of hitherto discriminated groups. The struggle for freedom has penetrated even into education and its theory.

Yet upon closer examination, one discovers that the validity of the principle of freedom has lost some of its obviousness and hence the key function of freedom is not taken for granted anymore. I will present only three examples. *First,* many critics have considered education that claims to take freedom most seriously, namely antiauthoritarian education (cf. Engelmayer, 1973; Neill, 1960), to be in fact a threat to freedom (cf. Classen, 1973). It is considered to be a threat to the freedom of others because the rejection of any kind of authority implies the rejection of obligations which protect the freedom of others. Their argument is that even the freedom of people raised by the antiauthoritarian method is endangered, because, without the acceptance of obligations, no self-reliable personality can be formed. *Second,* a refusal of the principle of freedom is latently present in the victim mentality. This means that one always has the impression of being a victim of childhood traumas, a victim of negative experiences at school or in the family, a victim of the economic situation as well as of social expectations. Even individuals ruining the lives of their partner or children, of their parents or colleagues, consider themselves more as guiltless victims than as responsible actors (cf. the psychotherapeutical states of Jaeggi, 1981). The *third* threat to freedom comes from a sociological attitude which, according to Skinner (1971), no longer considers man as an autonomously acting subject, but rather talks of behavior which can always be traced back to the environment. If a strict behaviorism successfully encroaches on pedagogy, the notion of freedom will be discarded from its vocabulary. The highest goal of education is socialization, that is, assimilation to a social context. Wherever this assimilation does not succeed, such an approach leads us to talk about deviant behavior which cannot be blamed on the agent but is due to the circumstances under which this person grew up and suffered.

The restriction of the principle of freedom is obvious but is not undisputed. It is through the theory of moral education that the principle could regain its key role. The predominant contemporary theory of moral education is based on the studies of Piaget (1932/1948) which have been incorporated by Rawls (1963, 1971) in the context of his Theory of Justice. Kohlberg's (1969, 1971, 1973, 1981) further development of these studies has been decisive for pedagogy. The background of all three representatives is Kant's ethics with its principle of freedom and autonomy.

In reference to Piaget and Rawls, Kohlberg distinguishes three levels in the development of moral judgment, each composed of two stages. The levels and stages have a hierarchical order. Consequently, their sequence cannot be inverted. According to Kohlberg (1981), the first (Preconventional) level contains the stage of punishment and obedience (Stage 1) and that of individual instrumental purpose and exchange (Stage 2); the second (Conventional) level contains the stage of mutual interpersonal expectations, relationships, and conformity (Stage 3) and that of social system and conscience maintenance (Stage 4); in the third (Postconventional) and principled level we find the stage of prior rights and social contract or utility (Stage 5) and finally, that of universal ethical principles (Stage 6) as they are formulated, for instance, in the ethics of Kant and Rawls, who define morality in terms of autonomy and universality (universalizability). It should be noted, however, that, in recent formulations, Kohlberg (1984) presents only five stages.

Kohlberg's assertion of the third (Postconventional) level is not controversial; however, his claim that the sixth stage is the highest one of moral development is often criticized. The criticism reflects the current general discussion of ethics between (a) utilitarians, (b) Kantians and (c) representatives of discourse ethics (Apel, 1973, 1980a, 1980b; Habermas, 1976, 1983a, 1983b). Unlike Kohlberg (and Kant) the utilitarians consider the sixth stage, autonomy according to universalizable principles, as unnecessary, whereas representatives of discourse ethics such as Apel and Habermas think that the sixth stage is insufficient and postulate a higher, seventh stage (Apel, 1980a, 1980b; Habermas, 1976). In a recent publication, Habermas (1983b) renounces a seventh stage, but insists on the deficiency of the principle of universalizability and claims a principle of discourse ethics beyond that of universalizability (Habermas, 1983a).

At first sight, the dispute concerning the moral principle seems to be irrelevant for pedagogy and merely a task for philosophers. But indeed the controversy determines the main goal of education. Shall it ultimately be based on social welfare (utilitarianism), on autonomy (Kant, Rawls, Kohlberg) or on discourse (Habermas)?

Since the philosophical dispute between utilitarians, representatives of discourse ethics and Kohlberg is pedagogically relevant, one has to ask how it could be settled. Kohlberg, like Piaget, considers himself to be an empirical psychologist and sociologist and therefore one is tempted to settle the argument empirically and to let Kohlberg's concept of development, including Stage 6, stand the test. Many students and professors of psychology and sociology seem to have discovered, through Kohlberg, theoretical guidelines for new empirical research.

However, Kohlberg makes at least two empirical claims. *First,* he claims that the sequence of the stages is irreversible, each following stage presupposes the preceding one. This point is affected neither by the utilitarian rejection of a sixth stage nor by the postulate of a seventh stage by Apel and Habermas. Hence it is not controversial in the debate on the principle of freedom. As far as the two first levels are concerned, the thesis of irreversibility is trivial anyway. It confirms simply the well known fundamental task of education, namely, that the child does not know and recognize the patterns of behavior of the group and culture at birth, but rather must learn them. This process of learning is nothing else but the assimilation to existing social morals, thus the transition from the preconventional to the conventional level. *Second,* and less trivially, Kohlberg claims that moral development ultimately comes to an end only with the development of the sixth stage. This claim can be interpreted in two ways, one of which is empirical and the other teleological. The empirical interpretation has three variations: individual, social and historical.

According to the empirical-individual interpretation, each adult would have to reach the sixth stage. This is obviously not the case for Stage 6, not even for Stage 5; and in that respect, utilitarianism has no superiority over Kohlberg and discourse ethics. Besides, Kohlberg does not claim that everybody actually reaches Stage 6.

According the the empirical-social interpretation, a society (culture) would consider only individuals who have reached Stage 6 to be fully morally developed. Such a claim is not confirmed by experience. Not every culture sees autonomy as the highest principle of moral judgment nor as the criterion for a full moral development. According to Magnis-Suseno (1981), it is amazing how well the morality of Java, for example, corresponds to Kohlberg's third stage and part of the fourth stage but not to his fifth and sixth stages. From the viewpoint of an empirical-social interpreter, Kohlberg's theory of moral development is not independently valid but is relative to a given culture.

According to the Javanese counterevidence, for some cultures it is not only the sixth but even the fifth stage that is contested as a criterion for moral maturity. Hence in this respect as well, the controversy between Kohlberg's principle of freedom, Apel's and Habermas' principle of discourse, and utilitarianism cannot be settled by empirical testing.

Finally, the empirical interpretation of Kohlberg's theory could be considered from a sociohistorical point of view. One could propose that humanity develops in a direction that will find its perfection in Stage 6. An argument against this position is that the moral development in different cultures (be it the Western World or the Middle and the Far East) is not homogeneous and therefore we cannot claim a uniform development. In addition, it may be mentioned that one cannot predict the future by conclusions of the past.

Since the different empirical interpretations lead to a negative result, we have to consider the teleological interpretation, according to which the development of moral judgment reaches its highest point only at Stage 6. The morality defined by autonomy and universalization is the stage where moral development has reached its pefection. This implies that (1) the moral judgment of Stage 5 is incomplete and not fully developed and (2) that, unlike discourse ethics, more advanced moral development is not possible and therefore an illusion.

Such a claim must mainly be confirmed by arguments of philosophical ethics, not by arguments of empirical psychology or empirical pedagogy. Obviously this does not mean that the claim is of an ideological nature or that it is empirically irrelevant. Unlike an ideology, the claim, on the one hand, is confirmed or questioned by rational arguments and not by subjective opinions. On the other hand, the justification of the sixth stage as the stage of perfection (completion) of moral development has important implications for pedagogical theory and practice as well as for psychology and criticism of society, i.e., the moral development of an individual or a society, especially its basic legal order, can be considered complete only when the principle of freedom has been recognized as the criterion of moral judgment of personal and public actions as well as of social institutions.

In the following paragraphs, I would like to develop an argument of philosophical ethics. In spite of the provisionality of the argument, I hold the following four theses: (1) that the justification of the sixth stage as the highest stage of moral development begins with a conceptual analysis which proves morality to be a valid obligation in a categorical and unrestricted way; (2) that two complementary moral principles ensue from the concept of categorical obligation, i.e., the universalization of the principles of action and the autonomy of the will. Therefore I argue counter to utilitarianism (3) that Stage 6, defined in terms of universalization and autonomy, is necessary for a full development of moral judgment, and I argue counter to discourse ethics (4) that this stage is sufficient for such a definition of moral maturity.

MORALITY AS CATEGORICAL IMPERATIVE

The question of when moral development can fundamentally be considered completed is to be answered by the concept of morality itself. Therefore the argumentative solution of the dispute between (a) utilitarianism, (b) Kant-Rawls-Kohlberg and (c) discourse ethics starts with a conceptual analysis—which can only be dealt with very briefly here. The analysis of the notion of morality has a presupposition, namely that individuals are responsible for their actions. It further has three basic elements: Morality is (1) an evaluation of responsible actions, and its character is (2) imperative and (3) categorical.

Morality as Evaluation of Responsible Action

Whoever evaluates human action morally presupposes that, unlike reflexes and physiological processes, human action might be voluntary. This implies that the agent is responsible for his actions; he himself is the author.

The moral judgment itself—according to the first element of the concept, is an evaluation of responsible practice which can either be good and right and in this respect a success, or it can be bad, wrong or evil and therefore a failure. In fact, we do make the agent responsible for his or her actions and we do evaluate them. We accept, reward, honor, admire, applaud and appreciate good actions and we reject, reproach, criticize, correct, accuse, condemn and despise bad actions. And this (positive or negative) evaluation does not only concern actions of others but also our own—in the form of self-criticism or a bad conscience.

The Imperative Character of Morality

Since human action does not always correspond to what is considered morally good and right, morality has the character of a claim which can be ignored or of an imperative which can be denied. Therefore the second element of the concept of morality is the "ought" (imperative) character. This does not only count for a morality with direct commandments and prohibitions, such as the Decalogue. The imperative character of morality can also have the form of an ideal like the biblical parables, an ideal which ought to be imitated but often enough is not achieved. Thus, ideals as well have the character of a claim or an imperative.

The Categorical Character of Morality

The evaluation of an action as successful (good and right) or as a failure (bad or evil) can have different aspects. In general, we can construct three different aspects or dimensions of evaluation, where two are pre-moral and one is moral. The three aspects are in an objective sequence which cannot be reversed, and which reveals moral evaluation to be the highest kind of evaluation.

First, the success or failure of an action can concern its objective adequacy with respect to its intentions, goals and purposes. We then talk of technical, tactical or strategic rightness or of a technical, tactical or strategic good which means a limited range of rightness—the action is not completely right in itself, but only with respect to its intentions. We also speak of a conditional, hypothetical good, i.e., the action as a whole is good only if the intentions are good, if not, it is bad. Therefore the good is conditioned by something else, namely the intentions. One could also say that the technical good follows and is subordinated to the intentions.

Because the technical good is secondary, the question of the rightness goes further back to the intentions. This implies that *secondly* we examine the adequacy of concrete intentions to intentions of the second order, be it the natural interest of every individual in his well being (pragmatic rightness, Preconventional level of Kohlberg) or the adequacy of the prevailing customs (positive moral, a given ethos, social rightness, Conventional level of Kohlberg). In this case, the good and the right still have a limited range and hypothetical validity. For the action as a whole and as such is not right in itself, but only under the presupposition and condition of something else, namely personal well being or prevailing customs. Therefore, Kohlberg is right when he claims that moral development is not completed with this level and that there has to be a third level after the Preconventional and the Conventional ones.

From the first two dimensions of evaluation, the technical and the pragmatic-hypothetical dimension, the third and properly moral dimension is at first only negatively distinguished, namely through the suppression of the limitations and the conditions of evaluation. Not only are the means being evaluated as good or right, so are the intentions, both concrete intentions, and even more the intentions of the second order expressed by the concrete ones. Because in this case, by definition, all restrictions and conditions of evaluation are suppressed, the third element of the concept of morality is an unconditioned, categorical good and right.

Although the moral dimension of evaluation is at this juncture only negatively and formally determined, it can already be considered as necessary and sufficient and therefore the principally highest dimension of evaluation. The dimension is necessary; if the conditions, especially the intentions, are good, then the conditioned is good. If not, it is bad. Thus the unconditioned good is the presupposition for the goodness of the conditioned good. On the other hand, the third dimension is sufficient to complete the evaluation of responsible action, for the unconditioned good can fundamentally not be surpassed by its definition. Therefore the third dimension is not only accidentally but fundamentally the highest dimension of evaluation. A furthergoing and higher dimension is inconceivable.

In the same way, the concept of a fundamentally highest moral stage is defined by the unconditioned good. Only that moral evaluation is not relativized to an individual, to a culture or to a history, but is the fundamentally highest stage of development which is not connected to any conditions or presuppositions of evaluation, but is the unconditioned good and right.

If we summarize the three fundamental elements of the preceding conceptual analyses, we can say that the "essence" of morality consists in the evaluation of responsible practice which has on the one hand an imperative character ("you *shall* do or not do what corresponds to the moral evaluation") and on the other hand is unconditionally and categorically valid (the moral good is not only good *under the condition of* something else but is good in itself). Taking away the first element as being a self-evident presupposition and emphasizing the second and third, we come to the conclusion that morality is an unconditional and therefore categorical imperative. This is an insight that we owe to Kant (1785/1968; esp. sec. 1 and 2; cf. Höffe, 1983, chap. 9).

TWO COMPLEMENTARY MORAL PRINCIPLES: UNIVERSALIZATION AND AUTONOMY

After having outlined the concept of morality, we shall now derive the highest moral criterion. Methodically speaking, the conceptual ("metaethical") criterion has a normative-ethical consequence. Two complementary principles result from the concept of morality as categorical imperative: the universalization of principles of action and the autonomy of will.

The Universalization of the Principles of Action as the Highest Criterion of Morality

Because the moral good in the strict sense (Kohlberg's highest level of moral development) is not conditioned in its goodness by momentary moods and intentions of the agent, it is valid in an ultra-momentary and an ultra-subjective way. What is ultra-momentarily and ultra-subjectively valid in the strict sense is by definition generally valid. Hence, the moral criterion that we search for is universal validity or universalizability.

The Object of Universalization. Of which object can the universalizability be demanded? According to a first but rather naive assumption, it is the concrete action that should be universalizable. However, a concrete action always takes place in an individual situation which is influenced by personal and social circumstances. The composition of these circumstances is different in every situation which makes a universalization impossible. Additionally, one can object that the composition of the circumstances in relation to the momentary action is given and is therefore not the responsibility of the agent. According to our preceding brief conceptual analyses, we can argue that morality is the evaluation of responsible practice. Therefore the evaluation cannot concern the concrete action as a whole because the concrete action has circumstantial aspects which are beyond the agent's responsibility. The evaluation can only regard that "part" of the action which is due to the agent.

According to a second assumption (e.g., Habermas, 1983a, p. 75 ff.), the needs and interests of the agents should be universalizable. But we find similar counter-arguments against this assumption. First, the concrete composition of needs and interests are quite different with every individual, even with every phase of life of the same person. They therefore cannot be universalized. Second, the needs and interests have physiological, social, cultural and many other reasons which can only partially but not completely be imputed to the agent. Since morality concerns responsbility, it cannot demand the universalization of all needs and interests.

According to a third assumption which is accepted by most of the contemporary representatives of the principle of universalization (e.g., Singer, 1971, chap. 13), the factually observed rules of action should be universalizable. First, this opinion is contested by some of its absurd consequences, consequences that have also been used to argue against Kant's categorical imperative but which are really due to a misunderstanding of Kant. According to W. K. Frankena (1963), rules like the left shoe-lace should be tied first or whistle in the dark if you are alone are universalizable and thus morally demanded by the categorical imperative. Obviously, such rules do not have to be observed from a moral point of view and, therefore, the critics of Kant say the categorical imperative cannot be the right moral principle. This criticism is right in what it asserts (those rules are certainly not morally demanded) but it is wrong in what it imputes (since according to Kant's categorical imperative only certain kinds of rules of action are obligatory).

Still another argument against the opinion that the moral question of universalization might be put to any kind of rules of action can be found. It is part of the concept of morality (as the unconditioned good) that its obligations, for example not to cheat, are ultimately recognized neither by chance nor for self-interest nor by threats of punishment. For, in relation to actions that are performed by accident, for selfinterest or under fear of punishment, there are always actions that are even better. Only that action which wills the morally commanded or morally permitted as such cannot be surpassed by a better one. Therefore, we shall not put the question of the universalizability to the observable rules of action but to the fundamental principle set by the agent itself. Kant calls these principles of action maxims.

In the controversies concerning the categorical imperative, the object of universalization is often misunderstood. Moreover, the criterion of morals derived from the conceptual analysis cannot be sufficiently defined until after having explained the object of universalization. Finally, this task must be fulfilled in order to be able to settle the controversy between (a) utilitarianism (b) Kant-Rawls-Kohlberg and (c) discourse ethics. Therefore, we shall sive some further explanation of the concept of maxim and its significance for ethics and a theory of moral development.

Maxims.   Kant (1788) means by maxims subjective principles of action which contain a general determination of will and include several practical rules: (1) As subjective principles, they differ with every individual. (2) As determinations of will, they do not designate schemes of order which an objective observer may impute to the agent; they are principles which are recognized by the agent himself. (3) As principles which include several rules, maxims contain the mode according to which one leads his life as a whole, in relation to certain fundamental aspects of personal and social life such as indigence, weariness of life or offense.

Because of their relation to certain domains of life and types of situation, maxims distinguish themselves from an even higher stage of generalization such as the forms of life (bioi) of Aristotle or the modes of existence of Kirkegaard. Maxims are fundamental attitudes which provide a common direction towards a number of different concrete intentions and actions. A maxim, for example, is the intention to live considerately or inconsiderately, to answer offenses with revenge or with generosity, to act helpfully or indifferently in situations of need.

Morality in its highest stage demands first the examination of whether those principles of action can be universalized and second living only according to such principles which are strictly universalizable and therefore objective laws. Consequently the categorical imperative as the highest criterion of morality reads as follows: "Act only according to that maxim by which you can at the same time will that it should become a universal law" (Kant, 1785, p. 421).

Maxims establish the directing principle of judgment for a whole sphere of life for all situations of need, e.g., helpfulness or indifference. The principle of judgment is mediated with the regularly recurring kinds of situations within the general sphere of life. Practical rules such as jumping into the water when somebody is drowning deal with the changing conditions of life. Depending on the situation and the abilities of the agent, the practical rules are different even though they follow the same maxim; whereas a well-trained swimmer will jump into the water, a non-swimmer will not. In spite of the same principle of judgment, there have to be different rules (norms) of helpfulness or indifference, of considerateness or inconsiderateness, of revenge or generosity. On the other hand, a single principle of action can be based on two different maxims. Therefore it is not the widespread ethics of rules and norms, but the ethics of maxims which is the adequate form of moral philosophy and of a theory of the highest stage of moral development.

The Significance of Ethics of Maxims.   Ethics of maxims are superior to any ethics of norms in different respects. The reason for that superiority is prior to the controversies concerning the principle of freedom. Whoever disagrees with

Kohlberg and is contented with the fifth stage or demands a seventh stage cannot close his mind to the following arguments (cf. Höffe, 1984, chap. 4,I):

(1) Since maxims as general principles of will abstract from the changing circumstances of the action, they extract the normative pattern from the concrete action. Thus the normatively determining factor without the modification of changing factors of the situation becomes clear. Since ethics of maxims distinguish, in a concrete action, between the two fundamentally different elements: on the one hand the normative element (such as helpfulness) and on the other hand the descriptive element (I see that somebody is drowning and I can/cannot swim), they render possible the insight that human actions may be different (the swimmer jumps into the water and the non-swimmer gets help) but still have a common moral (help) or immoral (indifferent) quality. At the same time, an ethical relativism or a rigid dogmatism of rules and norms is being avoided. The maxim (helpfulness or indifference) means exactly the moment of unity which contradicts relativism. At the same time the necessity to adjust the maxim to the particular of the respective situations is in contradiction to a dogmatism of norms (always try to save drowning persons even though you might not be able to swim or the current might be too strong). Maxims only indicate the general outline; for a concrete action we need contextualization, a productive process of interpretation and evaluation (What happened? By which means can I organize in order to help?). It is the practical judgment (in the tradition of Plato and Aristotle: prudence) which realizes this evaluation according to direction to the maxims.

(2) Maxims are general principles of life and therefore they do not reduce the individual to an immense variety of rules or an infinite number of singular actions. Through maxims the parts of a life are jointed to uniform contexts of sense whose moral or non-moral quality is tested by the categorical imperative. Whereas the "injection" of practical rules in education comes close to an act of training, the orientation towards normative principles, that is maxims, makes a reasonable self-determination of man possible with the necessary freedom to take differences in temperament, abilities, socio-cultural circumstances, and momentary situational factors into consideration.

(3) Because Maxims abstract from the changing circumstances of a person and the society, they reveal the character of the person. It is not norms in the sense of concrete rules of action but rather the maxims that are principles of living which render a more evaluation of a person (which is different from a physical, intellectual or psychological evaluation) possible and which qualify him or her as considerate, as egoistical, as righteous, etc. Therefore the maxims are a far more adequate object for questions of moral identity than norms and hence, for questions of moral education and the evaluation of man.

The Autonomy of the Will

The explanations of the categorical imperative as the highest standard of morality cannot be completed without mentioning a common misunderstanding. The universalizability of maxims is not only identified as a criterion but as a principle of morality. This identification, however, is irritating or at least inexact because, for ethics, the question of principles has a double meaning. On the one hand we search for the highest criterion of all moral action which, according to our preceding considerations, is the categorical imperative. On the other hand we search for the ultimate reason why a responsible being is at all able to act according to the categorical imperative or the highest stage of morality. We are looking for the principle of the moral personality which is to be found in the self-determination (autonomy) of will. The condition of the possibility that someone's actions can be moral consists of the ability of the will to determine itself according to self-set rules, called maxims.

Both aspects of the question concerning principles are linked to each other. The categorical imperative is the law which determines the autonomy of will; the autonomy of will makes it possible to live according to the demands of the categorical imperative.

The notion of autonomy (freedom) which is decisive for the sixth stage of moral development is subjected to many midunderstandings; therefore we shall offer further explanation of it.

Freedom, in general, means self-determination: the self-determination of the individual, of the group or of the political community. The concept of self-determination has two aspects. Negatively speaking, self-determination means to be free from alien laws; to be independent of determination through natural, social and political factors. Positively it means self-legislation; the individual, the group or the political community determines the content of their activities themselves.

At first, freedom was a particular legal determination which meant a privilege for a limited number of people in the Germanic as well as in the Greco-Roman worlds. In contrast to the slaves, the free people lived for themselves as full members of a community. They were independent of foreign power and they were, in contrast to foreigners, protected against violation or oppression by a foreign power.

Through the influence of Stoic and Judeo-Christian thought as well as through the influence of philosophers and political movements of modern times, freedom has become a universal claim to which any individual or any social or political community is entitled. The double meaning of freedom, however, has kept its validity until today. Political freedom is composed of freedom from alien power, along with the guarantee of the freedom through an authorized public power such as the institutions of law and state.

In discussing the highest stage of moral development, it is not always clearly seen that the universalized freedom occurs on two levels: (1) as self-determination of action (freedom of action) and (2) as self-determination of will (freedom of will). The freedom of action itself has two aspects. From a socio-political point of view, it means the right and the possibility to act according to one's own will and convictions without coercion; from a psychological point of view, freedom of action means the ability to act or not act in a conscious and voluntary and hence in an independent and responsible way. Success or failure of the action can be blamed on the agent and he can be held responsible.

With respect to moral freedom, freedom of action is the first and elementary stage. There can be no moral freedom without a conscious and voluntary and thus responsible action, i.e., without the freedom of action. Education aimed towards freedom of action is therefore the first and indispensable goal of any moral education. On the other hand, freedom of action is merely an elementary stage and moral freedom contains a higher stage of freedom, namely the ability to take responsibility, not according to any kind of rules but according to autonomous principles, i.e., maxims, and to follow not any but only universalizable maxims.

Moral freedom or autonomy of will consists in the fact that the will is *ultimately* not determined by something else, such as the power of the drives and passions, feelings of sympathy or antipathy, or social constraints. Such a determination by something else (heteronomy) would be the exact opposite of autonomy. Positively speaking, autonomy means that the will gives itself its own laws.

Self-legislation does not mean, as the existentialists tend to think (Sartre, 1946, pp. 22–24) that man, in order to be free, has to strip off his various psychological and social conditions and has to live a life "out of nothing," independent of any factors of determination. Indeed, there is always a multitude of conditions but they are not unchangeable facts. Individuals can put themselves in relation to the conditions by naming, judging and accepting or rejecting them. Attempts can be made to change them through educational, self-educational, therapeutic, social and political procedures. But most importantly, and this is what is meant by the principle of autonomy, the sensual drives and the historical-social factors may not be the *ultimate* factors of determination of action. Whoever by principle always follows his or her momentary inclinations, and this only because they are momentary inclinations, acts just as immorally as someone who acts fundamentally according to historical and social conventions.

With the principle of autonomy of will, which goes back to Kant, morality has been based on a new foundation. The ground of morality is neither to be discovered in a benevolent self-love nor in a moral sense and even less in a physical sense, since in all these cases we only relate to factual and accidental moods of the subject and not to something which is strictly universally valid. The ultimate basis of morality is also not the sense of justice either (Rawls, 1963), because the sense of justice itself is something that is derived and conditioned. If it is derived from autonomy, it is moral (in the sense of the highest stage), otherwise it is not. An action is only unconditional if the will is autonomous and hence is free.

CRITICISM OF UTILITARIANISM

From the concept of morality as categorical imperative, a double moral principle results: on the one hand, the demand to act according to universalizable maxims;

on the other hand, the origin of such action lies in the autonomy of will. On this basis, the controversy concerning the highest moral principle can be settled: Is Kohlberg's sixth stage, as utilitarianism claims, not necessary for a full development of moral conscientiousness or, as discourse ethics claims, is it insufficient?

First, I discuss utilitarianism whose point of departure is the natural interest of each man in his own well-being (cf. Bentham, 1789, Chap. I, 1, p. 11). This point is followed by the morally decisive step from the individual well-being to the common well-being (Bentham, 1789, p. 11). The strong feature of utilitarianism consists in the fact that it binds an altruistic attitude, namely, an orientation towards the common well-being with empirical knowledge (of the consequences of an action) and its meaning for the happiness of the individuals involved. Because of this empirical-pragmatic side, many moral philosophers think that utilitarianism is superior to Kant's ethics. Yet at a closer look, this impression of superiority turns out to be an illusion, and the converse, that it is inferior, is true.

A first objection against utilitarianism belonging to the philosophy of law and stages rather than ethics is the following: utilitarianism cannot resolve the problems of political justice adequately. (cf. Höffe, 1984, p. 151). For according to utilitarianism it is not impossible that under certain, though not very probable, circumstances, slavery, a feudal society, or even a police or military state is not only morally tolerated but even required, i.e., if it produces an increase of the common well-being. Utilitarianism represents a sort of a collective egoism which allows for an oppression of minorities, including a violation of inalienable human rights insofar as it would cause an improvement of the well-being of the majority and therefore a positive balance of the collective happiness. In addition, utilitarianism considers two public decisions leading to the same public profit as morally equivalent, even though one of the decisions might divide the profit among a few people and the other among many or all of the interested parties.

If one takes Kant's principle of universalizability and applies it according to the requirements of philosophy of law and state, not to personal but to public action, the categorical imperative becomes a request for legislators to organize public life in agreement with strictly universally valid principles. And human rights are universally valid because they are by definition independent of sex and color, of origin, race and language, of religious and political background, i.e., they are valid independent of any particular determination. Whatever excludes any particular determination is eo ipso universally valid. Therefore it is possible to justify with Kant (cf. Höffe, 1983 chap. 10), but not with utilitarianism, the core of political justice which is human rights.

Moreover, utilitarianism does not care for what reasons and motives one promotes the common well-being, regardless of whether it is to achieve a good reputation or out of fear of punishment in cases such as the omission of help. Such reasons would be nothing other than hidden variations of self-interest ("fear of punishment") and conventional morality ("good reputation") and it would contradict the principle of autonomy. Because whoever does something (or omits something) out of fear of punishment or because of his good reputation, does not give to himself (auto . . .) the law (. . . nomos) of his action, but rather receives it from outside from the existing order of law or from the social conventions, he acts not autonomously, but heteronomously. Briefly, the relativization of self-interest and conventional morality in utilitarianism is not radical enough. The fundamentally highest stage in the development of moral judgment has yet to be achieved.

Furthermore, classical utilitarianism claims the common well-being as a moral criterion but it does not sufficiently justify it. According to Bentham (1789, Chap. 1, pp. 11, 13–14), a direct proof is impossible and an indirect proof is only indicated. Mill's (1863, Chap. 4) proof has two logical errors: On the one hand, he equates the desired with the desirable, and on the other hand he equates personal happiness with common happiness. Whoever looks for an adequate philosophical justification could rely exactly upon the criterion of universalization belonging to the sixth stage of moral development which utilitarianism claims not to be necessary.

The fulfillment of the needs and interests of a person, and consequently his well-being, can contradict the fulfillment of the needs and interests of another person. Both persons, for example, may want to possess the same object. But if the well-being of one individual can contradict the well-being of another, the maxim opposed to utilitarianism namely, to pursue only personal well-being, cannot be considered as a universal law. And therefore, according to the moral criterion "act only according to universalizable maxims," an antiutilitarian lifestyle which is bound only to self-interest is immoral and, e contrario, an attitude that is not merely bound to self-interest is moral. Utilitarianism is correct in considering not the personal but the common well-being as the moral issue. But in accepting this issue, the reason and standard is not to be found in happiness, as the utilitarians such as Bentham (1789, Chap. I, p. 1) would claim; it lies rather in universalizability.

CRITICISM OF DISCOURSE ETHICS

The criticism, as opposed to the one of utilitarianism, claiming that the capability of moral judgment is not yet fully developed in the sixth stage, comes from discourse ethics. They criticize Rawls (Habermas, 1983a, p. 76), Kohlberg (Apel, 1980a, p. 59; Habermas, 1976, p. 74) and Kant (Apel, 1980b, p. 78; Habermas, 1983a, p. 76) for their monological application of the principle of universalization, and they demand instead a "cooperative effort" and a "consensual settlement of conflicts" (Habermas, 1983a, p. 77). Thus, they demand a "standpoint" that goes beyond Kant's categorical imperative and beyond Kohlberg's sixth stage, a standpoint "in which the individual considers his basic moral obligation to be principally bound to the reciprocity of demands and to the responsibility in a community of communication among responsible beings'' (Apel, 1980b, p. 70).

I hold two arguments against the demand to go beyond the stage of a universalistic morality. *First*, it is *impossible* for Apel and Habermas to go beyond the sixth stage, be it from a logical or from a moral point of view, since their discourse ethics presupposes the concept of morality as a categorical imperative as well as the universalizability (of maxims) as the highest criterion of morality. *Second*, even in the interest of discourse ethics, it is *not necessary* to go beyond the categorical imperative and the criterion of universalization; because they are not at all, as Apel and Habermas assume, connected to a monological interpretation, they admit as well a communicative interpretation. Furthermore, such an interpretation is admitted to be necessary.

The Categorical Imperative and Generalizability as Presuppositions of Discourse Ethics

Real and Ideal Discourse.   According to discourse ethics, it does not matter whether, in an observable discourse (real historical discourse), a factual consensus succeeds or fails. On the one hand, lack of time and fundamental disagreement can prevent a consensus. On the other hand, each real consensus depends on intellectual and emotional circumstances as well as on structures which may prevent a reasonable agreement and which may discriminate between the participants of the current discourse and even more so, those who do not participate. Therefore, Apel and Habermas are right not to overemphasize the process of historical discourse and not to claim it to be the highest moral principle. Since historical discourses are at best an attempt to apply the principle of universalization approximately and to apply it in a situation which, we have to assume at any time, threatens us as individuals, as groups and as cultures through intellectual and emotional deception.

An Argumentative Circle?   Because of the insufficiencies of any real-historical discourse, Apel and Habermas do not propose *any* discourse but rather, specifically, an ideal discourse as the basic norm. But the ideal discourse distinguishes itself from the real one by certain preconditions of structural features which as a whole, constitute the ideal. The conditions of this ideal ensure that the participants of the discourse acknowledge each other's equal rights and try not to deceive each other, but, instead, intend to communicate on an honest and unconstrained level. But such conditions (honesty instead of fraud, freedom from constraint instead of constraint) are exactly those obligations which ought first to be justified as moral by means of the criterion of morality. Therefore, discourse ethics seems to get into a logical, rather than hermeneutical, argumentative circle: That which ought to be proved by the ideal discourse (certain self-set principles of action like honesty or freedom from constraints to be morally valid) is hidden in the premises of the discourse, namely, in the conditions and structural features which constitute the discourse as an ideal one. Thus, the moral principles for which a criterion has yet to be found are already present in the definition of this criterion; a discourse, which according to the representatives of discourse ethics is the only one of use as a moral criterion, namely the ideal discourse, presupposes moral principles as valid even though they have yet to be proven morally valid in the ideal discourse.

Apel (1981) has defended himself against the logical circle objection with the remark that the different steps of justification of the application were not clearly distinguished. Indeed, one has to distinguish different steps of the justification of morality with Apel. But in doing so, the suspicion of a circle is not invalidated but rather is specified.

Three steps of argumentation must be distinguished. (1) Systematically speaking, the most fundamental step consists in the so-called "transcendental-pragmatic ultimate justification." It is carried out as a self-reflection of the argumentative discourse and shows that the language-bound argumentation cannot be avoided and that the "consensual" or "ideal" communication is the condition for the possibility of any language-bound argumentation. This argumentation, which Apel outlines more than he stringently proves, is supposed to lead to the ideal communication as the fundamental norm. Since the fundamental norm is supposed to consist in the ideal communication and since the ideal communication is supposed to be a stage above the categorical imperative and the criterion of universalization, we need, according to the representatives of discourse ethics (in this case according to Apel), a seventh stage of moral development which goes beyond Kohlberg's sixth stage.

(2) In the next step of the argument, these obligations which are part of the fundamental norm of the ideal communication are explained and therefore have "all along" been recognized in an ideal communication. Principles such as freedom from constraint and honesty are here proved as moral obligations.

(3) In the last step, i.e., the step of application, further obligations are proven to be moral in the context of an ideal communication, i.e., of an ideal discourse, namely those obligations which are more specific than the principles of freedom from coercion and honesty.

The Categorical Imperative and the Principle of Generalization as Unnoticed Presuppositions. By means of the distinction of the three stages of justification, one can more precisely formulate the logical problem of argumentation of discourse ethics, in this case Apel's variant. If the first step of justification, the self-reflection of the inevitable language-bound argumentation, is supposed to lead to an ideal communication as the fundamental norm of all morality, Apel makes an unjustified presupposition. The self-reflection of the language-bound argumentation shows that it becomes possible only under the conditions of an ideal communication. This implies that the goal of argumentation, the fundamental norm of all morality, is not yet attained. The proof whether language-bound argumentation even has a moral relevance is still lacking, so the ultimate presupposition of the language-bound argumentation cannot be considered as a principle or criterion of morality.

Only under the presupposition that the language-bound argumentation indeed is a case, even a paradigmatic case, of morality in its highest level, discourse ethics achieves its goal, namely to justify a criterion or a fundamental norm of morality. It may be true that language-bound argumentation is a (paradigmatic) case of morality. But this has to be expressly proven. In any case, the transition from the pragmatics of language as self-reflection of language-bound argumentation to ethics as the justification of a criterion or morality, or in other words, the identification of the language-bound argumentation with the moral dimension, is the fundamental ethical problem of (Apel's) discourse ethics. This fundamental problem, however, is not solved by a self-reflection of argumentation but by a genuine (meta-)ethical discussion, namely, with an analysis of the concept of morality. Without this analysis, the identification of the ideal communication or the ideal discourse as the model and example of morality in its highest stage cannot be justified. Therefore, the objection that discourse ethics cannot fulfill its ethical pretensions remains valid despite the distinction of three principal steps of argumentation. Even in the first principal step, something is presupposed to be evident (justified) which in fact first has to be proven; i.e., the concept of morality.

The step of argumentation presupposed by discourse ethics implies the proper ethical argument. According to the analysis of the concept sketched above, it leads to an understanding of morality as a categorical imperative. Moreover, discourse ethics also presupposes the same understanding of morality with its two aspects, imperative character and categorical validity, even though it is obviously not explicitly justified.

First, ideal communications or the ideal discourses are not always and necessarily recognized because we can, and often do, argue technically, strategically or pragmatically. But anyway, we ought not only act technically, strategically or pragmatically but also according to a fundamental norm which is the ideal communication; which means that the fundamental norm of discourse ethics cannot deny its demanding, that is its imperative, character.

Secondly, we are not asked in an ideal communication if we have a spontaneous desire or expect an advantage from it; for otherwise we would be placing desire and advantage, pragmatic and strategical evaluation above the consensual communication. The call for a consensual communication is rather unrestricted and unconditional; it is categorically valid and the ideal communication as a whole has the meaning of a categorical imperative.

Discourse ethics not only presupposes the concept of morality as a categorical imperative, it also recognizes the criterion of universalization, since according to the claim that the fundamental norm of morality consists of the ideal communication, the consensual communication is not simply valid for this or that subject according to its accidental moods or social culture in which the individual has been brought up. Considered as a basic norm, the ideal communication claims to be principally valid for all persons and hence claims to be a strictly universal law. Consequently, the highest moral criterion for discourse ethics consists not in the communication or the discourse but in the categorical imperative and the criterion of universalization.

If I am correct, the ethical reflections of Habermas have undergone a development which, at its most recent level, begins to recognize in a subtle and unobtrusive way the methodical significance of the universalization which it claimed to have. According to Habermas (1983a), the principle of universalization has the role of a "basic principle which renders possible a consensus" ("konsensermöglichendes Brückenprinzip"). In this claim the expression "to render a consensus possible" is decisive. If the principle of universalization renders the consensus possible, this implies that from the point of view of logical argumentation, the consensus is the argued, and the principle of universalization is the argument (reason). In doing so, Habermas recognizes the principle of universalization as having priority over the discourse.

The principle of universalization is not the "bridge" leading to a consensus but the pillar upon which the bridge, the consensus, is built. The principle does not have the role as Habermas thinks, of a bridge but the role of a pillar or a foundation. Moreover, discourse ethics does not furnish justification for this principle out of the concept of morality as a categorical imperative.

Is the Categorical Imperative a Solipsistic Principle?

The reason why the philosophers of discourse ethics propose a seventh stage of moral development which goes beyond Kant, Rawls and Kohlberg is their opinion that the categorical imperative and the criterion of universalization are monological (solipsistic) moral principles. The objection of the so-called solipsism, which is mainly aimed against Kant is wrong, because, according to Kant, the criterion of morality consists in the strict notion of universalization of maxims. Strictly speaking, universalizable maxims however are valid for a community of individuals, and indeed for the largest possible community excluding no current or future living members, wherever they may live. Whoever declares the categorical imperative with the universalization of maxims to be the criterion of his or her actions, recognizes eo ipso all persons with their needs and interests as having basically the same rights. Such a person asks which needs and interests, or more precisely which principles of satisfaction of needs and interests, can be universalized and are therefore morally legitimate.

The further question, i.e., how to find out which maxims have the quality of universality, is important, but it is a problem of application and not of justification. Whether I in the concrete situation resolve the problem alone or together with others, whether I convince the other person or the other person convinces me or a third person convinces both of us, all of those questions are secondary for the theory of argumentation. Even if I think about the universalizability of maxims alone, my deliberations are not in a fundamental sense solipsistic or monological, as Apel and Habermas suggest. There may be many reasons not to trust one's own judgment. Imagine, for example, the intellectual, emotional and social limits which nobody can escape. Therefore it may be better to find out together with others which maxim can be universalized and therefore deserve the consent of all in a real discourse and which maxim will actually lead to the agreement of all in an ideal discourse. In this case, it is also not the common debate, not the discourse, that decides the morality of a maxim but the kind of arguments calling for a consensus, namely the universalizability of the morality of a maxim.

Granted it is not only in science and philosophy that language and communication are currently experiencing a boom stronger than ever before. Among the manifold reasons for this development we certainly have to name the obviousness with which we, at least "in principle," recognize democracy (participation) as a feature of political structure. On the other hand, many things are not vehemently defended unless their existence is threatened. This is without doubt the case for language and communication. We shall not underestimate the dangers of impoverishment of language or even speechlessness. The preponderance of nonverbal and very often oversimplified forms of communication, the increase of television, propaganda and comics, the advance of technical language and pseudotechnical language, the superabundance of attractions, obligations and functional imperatives of industry-"culture" threaten our language ability and the willingness to have intensive personal relations and nonfunctional discourses.

In this situation, it makes sense to emphasize along with Apel and Habermas the fundamental and extensive importance of language and communication. It is also right to argue against an individualistic, and in favor of a communicational, understanding of freedom. True freedom always implies the acceptance of other people as free persons having equal rights. In view of the different needs and interests of people, communicational freedom naturally implies the willingness to respect that diversity. Concrete norms of action are therefore not the result of a monological and ahistorical process of subsumption. They are even less the result of pure power and arbitrariness. They are much more the result of an historical process of communication. It is therefore a task of the basic legal order to bind legislation institutionally to a formation of will in the context of a communicational process. But such a plea for language, communication and argumentation neither makes it possible nor necessary to go beyond the categorical imperative and the principle of freedom as the highest stage of morality.

REFERENCES

Apel, K. O. (1973). Das apriori der Kommunikationsgemeinschaft und die Grundlagen der Ethik. In K. O. Apel (Ed.), *Transformation der Philosophie*, Vol. 2 (pp. 358–435).

Apel, K. O. (1980a). Geschichtliche Phasen der Herausforderung der praktischen Vernunft und Entwicklungsstufen des moralischen Bewusstseins. In *Funkkolleg praktische Philosophie/Ethik, Studienbegleitbrief,* Vol. 1 (pp. 38–60). Weinheim-Basel: Beltz.

Apel, K. O. (1980b). Kants Vernunftethik und ihre inneren Grenzen. In *Funkkolleg praktische Philosophie/Ethik, Studienbegleitbrief* Vol. 2 (pp. 62–81). Weinheim-Basel: Beltz.

Apel, K. O. (1981). Ist die philosophische Letztbegründung moralischer Normen auf die reale Praxis anwendbar? In K.-O. Apel (Ed.), *Praktische Philosophie/Ethik,* Studienbegleitbrief 8 (pp. 72–100). Weinheim: Beltzverlag.

Bentham, J. (1789). *An introduction to the principles of morals and legislation* (Ed. by J. H. Burns & H. L. A. Hart, London, 1970). London: The Althone.

Classen, J. (1973). *Antiauthoritäre Erziehung in der wissenschaftlichen Diskussion.* Heidelberg: Quelle and Meyes.

Engelmayer, O. (Ed.) (1973). *Die Antiauthoritätsdiskussion in der Pädagogik.* Neuburgweiher: Karlsruhe.

Frankena, W. K. (1963). *Ethics.* Englewood Cliffs, NJ: Prentice-Hall.

Habermas, J. (1976). Moralentwicklung und ich-identität. In J. Habermas (Ed.), *Zur Rekonstruktion des historischen Materialismus,* (pp. 63–91). Frankfurt/M.: Suhrkamp.

Habermas, J. (1983a). Diskursethik-notizen zu einem begründungsprogram. In J. Habermas (Ed.), *Moralbewusstein und kommunikatives handeln* (pp. 53–125). Frankfurt/M.: Suhrkamp.

Habermas, J. (1983b). *Moralbewusstsein und kommunikatives handeln.* Frankfurt/M.: Suhrkamp.

Höffe, O. (1983). *Immanuel Kant. Leben, Werk, Wirkung.* München: Beck.

Höffe, O. (1984). *Ethik und Politik. Grundmodelle und-probleme der praktischen Philosophie* (2nd Edition). Frankfurt/M: Suhrkamp.

Jaeggi, E. (1981). Lauter Opfer-keine Täter? *Merkur, 35,* 335–337.

Kant, I. (1785). Grundlegung zur Metaphysik der Sitten. In *Akademieausgabe,* Vol. 4, Berlin: Walter de Gruyter and Co., 1968.

Kant, I. (1788). Kritik der praktischen Vernunft. In *Akademieausgabe,* Vol. 5. Berlin: Walter de Gruyter and Co., 1968.

Kohlberg, L. (1969). Stage and sequence: The cognitive developmental approach to socialization. In D. A. Goslin (Ed.), *Handbook of socialization theory and research* (pp. 347–480). Chicago: Rand McNally.

Kohlberg, L. (1971). From is to ought: How to commit naturalistic fallacy and get away with it in the study of moral development. In T. Mischel (Ed.), *Cognitive development and epistemology* (pp. 151–235) New York: Academic.

Kohlberg, L. (1973). The claim to moral adequacy of a highest stage of moral judgment. *Journal of Philosophy, 70,* 630 646.

Kohlberg, L. (1981). *Essays on moral development, Vol. 1: The philosophy of moral development.* San Francisco: Harper and Row.

Kohlberg, L. (1984). *Essays on moral development, Vol. 2: The psychology of moral development.* San Francisco: Harper and Row.

Magnis-Suseno, F. (1981). *Javanische Weisheit und Ethik, Studien zu einer östlichen Moral.* München-Wien: Oldenbourg.

Mill, J. S. (1863). *Utilitarianism.* (Edited by M. Warnock, 1962) London: Collins, Fontana.

Neill, A. S. (1960). *Summerhill. A radical approach to child rearing.* New York: Hart.

Piaget, J. (1932). *Le jugement moral chez l'enfant* (The moral judgment of the child). Paris: Alcan.

Rawls, J. (1963). The sense of justice. *The Philosophical Review, 72,* 281–305.

Rawls, T. (1971). *A theory of justice.* Cambridge: Harvard University.

Sartre, J.-P. (1946). *L'existentialisme est un humanisme.* Paris: Nagel.

Singer, M. G. (1971). *Generalization in ethics. An essay in the logic of ethics, with the rudiments of a system of moral philosophy* (2nd Ed.). New York: Atheneum.

Skinner, B. F. (1971). *Beyond freedom and dignity.* New York: Knopf.

The Process of Moral Decision-Making: Normative and Empirical Conditions of Participation in Moral Discourse

Monika Keller
Siegfried Reuss
Max-Planck-Institute for Human Development and Education
Berlin, West Germany

This paper represents an attempt to interrelate moral philosophy, moral development and moral education. Before we discuss our topic, a remark concerning the
way in which we approach the problem is in order. Any attempt to establish a
direct deductive connection between moral philosophy, moral psychology and
education would disregard the fact that each domain has its own specific way of
conceptualizing its problems. Rather, it appears appropriate to analyze the natural emergence of moral reasoning and decision-making in the light of a normative
theory of moral reasoning while at the same time highlighting the necessary
empirical conditions for participation in moral discourse. In the following we
shall outline the principles of a theory of discursive ethics. In the light of this
framework we shall analyze the development of reasoning about an everyday
moral conflict. Finally, some ideas for a concept of analytical moral education
are put forward.

ASPECTS OF A NORMATIVE THEORY
OF MORAL REASONING

The moral educational position presented here in terms of both moral philosophy
and psychology is based on the argument that moral education is communication-
oriented action. The discourse principle hereby sets the standard for communica-
tion-oriented action. This principle means that action is morally justifiable only if
it is judged as right from the perspective of all those concerned. Thus, communicative action is dependent on the consent of those concerned. It must be
distinguished from instrumental or strategic action (Habermas, 1981). These

forms of actions are regulated by goal-adequacy (functionality) or rules of prudence only. Goal-rational action leaves open the question of how specific goals, means, or strategies and consequences can be justified in the light of an actor's responsibility towards others. As moral beings, we are not objects of a decision, even though that decision might prove to be to our advantage. The *principle of justification* implies that we, as moral subjects, may request justification and investigate any course of action which concerns us. This makes the task of justification the focus within a theory of moral decision-making. Justification means generalization (Hare, 1963; Singer, 1961). Whoever treats person A differently from person B will be obliged to justify this; i.e., he or she must be able to point out a relevant difference between A and B which would be acceptable to those involved. This principle of justification implies the *principle of fairness*: given equal conditions, we can request equal treatment.

The consent of all persons concerned may not be given until a fair balance between one's own and others' interests and a fair distribution of efforts and sacrifices which are tied to the pursuit of certain goals is achieved.

Moral discourse is based on certain procedural rules: a) Each potential participant in a discourse must be free to include his or her own needs, interests, feelings, and convictions and to express these freely and unrestrictedly, and b), on principle, each participant has to be free to make any declaration or criticism he or she desires.

Since all practical communication would break down if existing norms could be criticized at liberty, or if all norms had to be justified at the same time, the burden of justification must fall upon the person who doubts the existing norm or practice. Therefore, any discourse is bound to a reasonable use of these procedural rules. It is in everybody's best interest that the particular needs and normative beliefs brought to the discourse remain subject to rational criticism and the consent of those concerned.

It would make a case for a heteronomous morality if one were to make an appropriate interpretation of "justified interests" directly dependent on existing norms. The validity of particular norms must continually be measured in view of (1) the consequences which result from their general observance to the satisfaction of each individual's interest, and (2) whether those consequences can be accepted willingly by all those concerned (Habermas, 1983). The consideration of these consequences in relation to each concrete individual's specific needs and conditions is a central component of the principle of universalization, which constitutes an autonomous morality.

Therefore, to be morally justifiable, any decision must be well-grounded. One may differentiate between *prima facie reasons* which relate to *typical* situations and *carefully weighed reasons* which do justice to the *special* circumstances of a situation. The change from prima facie to carefully weighed reasons creates a need for a two-step process of justification. This process is based on a complex definition of the situation (Oser, 1981) which makes allowance in both a differentiated and comprehensive way for the relative power of any relevant view. The individual faced with a decision must try to convince everyone concerned "which reasons within *a certain type* and *which types* of reasons are superior to others" (Baier, 1958, p. 96).

The validity of specific norms is restricted by the particular conditions of the situation. The definition of those conditions obviously cannot be left to the individual who may just be looking for a way to avoid the normative pressure of expectations. Any argument brought forward in order to neutralize existing prima facie obligations and to allow the pursuit of particular interests against the justified claims of others is nonvalid and can always be rejected. If someone wants to question the validity of an accepted norm, this can only be done legitimately by suggesting certain external or internal (psychological) conditions of a situation which, in the eyes of the decision-making subject and of those concerned, are more important (Singer, 1961).

The principle of universalization as a guiding principle of action implies that the claim for autonomy cannot be indicated unless the actor is willing to hypothetically take the role of all persons concerned by the action. One can fully agree with a rule of action only if one is willing to apply it to oneself (Baier, 1958; Hare, 1963). The rational core of the golden rule is based on this principle.

PSYCHOLOGICAL PREREQUISITES
OF DISCURSIVE ETHICS

Moral decision-making has to rely on a differentiated definition of the situation, including all relevant points of view. In order to achieve a situation-adequate definition of a conflict, the participants of the discourse must be open to the view that others have about a situation and to the specific viewpoints which they may assert regarding certain conditions as reasons for or against a specific course of action.

An appropriate definition of the situation with regard to the moral aspects involved requires access to the psychological-normative dimension of the "inner world" of self and other. The process of defining a situation appropriately implies the development of complex social-cognitive abilities in the form of differentiation and coordination of perspectives. The definition of the situation involves cognitive processes and feelings (Denzin, 1980), in the light of which certain aspects of the situation gain specific valencies. Discursive moral decision-making involves empathy and prosocial feelings. Feelings, either nonmoral or even moral, are not in themselves valid arguments. Rather, the only argument which is truly valid is the articulation of these feelings in normative convictions, which may elicit a rationally motivated consent of all those concerned.

The individual perspectives of those concerned are constituted of certain viewpoints. A central normative viewpoint is that of the constitution and maintenance of a "good relationship." An adequate understanding of a concept of a "good relationship" has to be interpreted in the framework of discursive ethics. In the case of conflicting interests and norms, it is necessary to transcend the context of particular relationships and to seek the consent of all those concerned by a course of action. This implies overcoming any discriminant exclusivity by which outsiders are excluded from the community of moral subjects.

The totality of viewpoints relevant for the definition of the situation and the process of moral decision-making depends on the social-cognitive repertoire conceptually available to a person at a given point in his or her development, that is, on his or her repertoire of categorical differentiations. In order to systematically elaborate this repertoire, it would be necessary to explicate the *framework of a theory of action.* In this contribution it will suffice to differentiate the following relevant aspects: the understanding of (a) persons, relationships, situations, and special circumstances; (b) the interpretation of needs, interests, expectations, feelings, motives, intentions, goals, means, and consequences of action, and (c) specific contextual rules, procedural rules, evaluative standards, principles, and metaprinciples.

From a cognitive-developmental and educational point of view, we have to explore which concept of relationship and which categorical differentiations are available at a given point in development, which structural properties characterize them, and how they are used in the process of moral decision-making.

INTERPERSONAL MORAL REASONING: AN EMPIRICAL DEVELOPMENTAL APPROACH

In the following we shall present empirical data on children's moral reasoning in order to illustrate the developmental aspects of a discourse theory of morality as outlined in the preceding section. Interpersonal moral reasoning is assessed in an interview about an everyday moral conflict. The subjects range in age from 7 to 14.[1] The story is a slightly modified version of Selman's (1980) friendship-dilemma.

> The heroine (or hero for male subjects) of the story has promised to visit her best friend on a certain day. Some time later she receives an invitation by a third child, a "newcomer," to go to the cinema (circus), which coincides in time exactly with the visit promised to the friend. The story includes a number of psychological details to which the subject can refer spontaneously: Both friends have known each other for quite some time; they meet regularly on a certain day of the week; the

---

[1]Data were selected from a longitudinal sample of 120 subjects, interviewed at the ages 7, 9 and 12 years. Some 13 and 14 year old subjects were also included in order to assess higher level reasoning more adequately.

promise is for this point in time. The friend wants to show her toys (or, alternatively, play new records), but also hints at problems with her parents which she wants to discuss. The "newcomer," who adds to the invitation an offer of Coca Cola and hot dogs, has moved into the neighborhood only recently and has no friends. The heroine and the newcomer seem to get along well; the friend dislikes the newcomer.

The story thus contains conflicting interpersonal and moral obligations:

1. The moral obligation of the promise.
2. Interpersonal obligations related to the friendship.
3. Altruistic obligations, related to the situation of the third child.

Apart from these obligations, attractive offers engage hedonistic self-interest: toys/records vs. cinema/circus, hot dogs and Coca Cola.

A 45-minute interview allows various aspects of interpersonal and moral reasoning to be assessed. Compared to Selman's (1980) procedure, we are interested in the specifically moral aspects of the conflict resolution. With respect to Kohlberg (1976, 1981) the focus is on moral reasoning about an everyday conflict which is affectively close to the subject's experience. Furthermore, we are interested in the relevance of moral judgment structures for the negotiation of conflicting claims in practical-moral decision-making. The repertoire of categorical differentiations according to which the subject interprets the different perspectives involved in the conflict is assessed with regard to the following topics: the spontaneous definition of the situation, the hypothetical action decision and the reasons and justifications given for it, the moral evaluation of a decision, the anticipation of short- and long-term consequences for the persons concerned (specifically actor and friend) of a decision violating interpersonal expectations and moral rules, the discourse or negotiation strategies used to avoid such consequences or to compensate for them by strategies of justification and (material) restitution.

Thus, during the interview the perspectives of the participants in the conflict have to be differentiated and coordinated with regard to the specific conditions of the situation and possible solutions of the conflict. Furthermore the interview itself is a discourse, in which the interviewer makes the subject reconstruct the different viewpoints within the situation, and, by doing so, becomes in a sense the advocate of the persons affected by a decision.

DEVELOPMENTAL LEVELS OF
INTERPERSONAL-MORAL REASONING

In the following, three developmental levels of interpreting the interpersonal conflict are outlined. They represent three types of conceptualization of relationships in which the aforementioned principle of discourse is actualized in different ways. Two forms of relationships, neither of which is successful in establishing a moral balance between oneself's and others' interests, or between competing obligations, shall be compared with a kind of relationship in which this balance is achieved. The types of relationships are assumed to form a developmental hierarchy. However, a strict developmental logical reconstruction is not within the scope of this paper (see Keller, 1984; Keller & Maute, 1983; Keller & Reuss, 1984).

Level A.   A relationship is totally unbalanced when the *discourse principle* (the consent of all those concerned) is absolutely disregarded. Individuals are not seen as moral subjects who have to justify their actions from the perspectives of others. In this case the necessity of a moral balance between one's own and others' interests cannot yet be understood. The major viewpoint, on which the definition of the situation and action plans are based at this premoral level, rests on the simple fact that self and others are seen as having certain wishes, interests, feelings, and expectations, which are related to the gratification of empirical needs. This implies a certain understanding of the conflict which is seen in the fact that different offers are being made to the heroine, one of which she has to choose: The friend wants to play with her, the newcomer wants to go to the cinema with her. These interests are compared on an equal basis, and confront the heroine either with two equally tempting or two equally negative alternatives (either both are fun, she wants to do both, i.e., play with the toys and go to the movie and have Coke and hot dogs; or she does not want to leave anyone out).

The violation of interests has negative consequences for those concerned. The perspective of the friend may have more power than that of the newcomer which is not yet fully differentiated. Only the friend is conceptualized as a partner in the sense that one likes to play with her. In addition, within the framework of this particular play relationship, the interests of the friend assume empirical but not normative importance. The date between the friends becomes part of the definition of the situation, because it generates an expectation on the side of the friend. However, the meaning of the expectation is reduced to the simple fact that the friend is waiting. If the heroine does not come to the friend, "the friend will go to her house and look for her."

For this reason, the date is not yet defined as an obligation resulting from the fact that the heroine has committed herself by the promise given. Rather, the situation is interpreted such that a demand has been made from the outside: "Her friend told her to come." The violation of friend's interests and expectations results in certain nonmoral emotional reactions: The friend feels bad, sad, unhappy, may be very angry, or may even want to end the relationship ("she will never play with her again"). Certain quasi-moral emotions or evaluations can already come up: "The friend thinks it's very bad, not very nice." Consequences of the violation of the friend's interests by going to the movie can be anticipated. Thus, the heroine may experience empathic or guilt feelings towards the friend: "She feels bad because she's thinking about her friend"; "she is thinking about what the friend will do, or that she's alone at home, and she's thinking she should have gone to the friend." The quality of certain needs, interests, emotions and evaluations is not yet defined by the normative criteria of a "good relationship." The meaning of "good relationship" is interpreted with regard to particular needs, interests, and feelings empirically attributable to self and other.

At this level of development, a moral balance between self's and others' interests, expectations, and feelings is not being sought in a discursive manner, because the question of *justification*—as an acceptance of empirical needs based on good reasons—has not yet appeared or has not yet assumed moral quality. Even though children may have already developed a sensitivity to the fact that the friend should be told of an unforeseen change in plans ("just to let her know, so she won't wait"), the conversation with the friend is restricted to the mere fact of informing her about the action: "I'd tell her that I'm going to the movie." If the interviewer hypothetically takes the perspective of the friend and asks the subjects: "What if the friend says: 'but you promised'," there will either be no answer, or the subject will refer merely to the empirical needs: "But I want to go to the movie, it's so nice."

In many cases, damage will be done to communicative standards. The actor will not look for communicative interaction, or will even avoid it deliberately from fear that the friend's anticipated resistance will ruin a good opportunity. One has the impression that inability to attend to one's own interests leads to avoidance of such situations of discourse. Indeed, in the case of communication after the completed action, the heroine may attempt to hide the action or some part of it (e.g., whom she went to the movie with). The dominant motive may be the heroine's fear of consequences for herself ("that the friend will be very angry towards her") and/or breaking up the relationship ("that she will never play with her again"). It may already be understood that lying is bad, but such an observation will not be linked to specific norms of relationship and/or truthfulness. It will be related instead to the disturbing consequences which such an action may have for oneself.

Level B. A relationship-structure is also unbalanced when a complex coordination of perspectives has already taken place and the perspectives of the generalized other can be adopted, but the establishment of a moral balance between self's, others', and mutual interests is not achieved because the individuals define themselves too exclusively as mutually related to each other (compare Selman's [1980] friendship level III of "intimate friendship" or Kohlberg's [1976] conventional "good boy—nice girl" morality).

In the process of moral decision-making the "good" friendship becomes a primary determinant of the moral definition of the situation as well as of possible solutions to the conflict. Friendship is now understood as a system of mutual expectations. It implies trust and reliability, as well as special concern for each other within the framework of an intensive, lasting emotional relationship. This understanding of friendship creates a sensitivity to special viewpoints (circumstances) of the conflict situation, which are not attended to in the premoral coping with the conflict. The wish of the friend to talk to the *heroine* is now being interpreted in the sense that she might have problems which could be solved in a talk. Since the mutual support in solving problems is an important sign of intimate friendships, friends' needs for a talk represent specific circumstances which imply a special obligation, and therefore prove important in the process of decision-making. Decisions about actions are constructed explicitly by reference to rules of fairness and ideals about how a good, loyal and trustworthy friend behaves: "If she promised, it would be very unfair not to go. If she's a good friend, she should go to see her. She doesn't want to be a promisebreaker or a traitor"; "When you promise your best friend something, you really have to keep that promise or at least talk to your friend before you change or break the promise . . . if you just break the promise—just like that—without talking to your friend—I don't think she'll trust you in the future . . . if nobody trusted each other this wouldn't be a good world" (Tr, G, 13).[2]

The consequences of violating the obligation one has to a friend are interpreted in terms of failing trust and reliability ("friend won't trust her any more, will think she can't depend on her, or that she's not a reliable friend"). The feelings of the friend are sometimes revealed by a *hypothetical role switch*: "If I were he, I would be very hurt and disappointed"; "There goes my best friend who promised to come see me, with a boy I don't like" (Tr, G, 13, 32). The friend interprets the action of going to the movie in a way that implies the heroine wants to give up the old relationship in favor of a new one; that is, she is afraid of loosing her closest friend. As a result of this triangle, the perspective of "jealousy" appears. On the one hand, the new child is being looked at as an intruder in the intimate relationship; on the other hand, the claim of the newcomer for integration in a relationship may be understood and the child may be seen as someone who has to be integrated into a relationship. From the perspective of the heroine, not only empathic, but also normative moral feelings are actualized by failing to keep up obligations towards the friend. Feelings of guilt and shame are anticipated, such as "having a guilty conscience" or even psychosomatic reactions, like a "tummy ache." The heroine may adopt a moral perspective regarding her action (thinking about what she did right or wrong, that she hasn't been a good friend). Thus, self-evaluative standards are developed, which are based on the concept of the "good relationship."

The *discourse principle* assumes a special importance in the case of conflicting interests and/or norms because of the validity of the evaluative standards of a

---

[2]The first number in all subject codes refers to the age of the subject.

good relationship. The heroine is aware of the fact that a decision connected with her obligations towards her friend can only be made with the friend's consent. Action decisions should not be justified after the fact. On the contrary, a chance to discuss the problem with the friend should be looked for spontaneously. This discourse differs from the type described previously in that it is straightforward: One asks the friend if she would mind changing the date. This is presented as a wish or request, and is explained (to the friend) by indicating the specific circumstances of the situation: either the "unique opportunity," or the situation of a newcomer who is alone and has no friends, or both: "Then he would tell him, well, poor Petur has no friends, it was the last time the movie was playing, it was a popular movie, and well, it was really a tempting offer" (Tr, G, 12, 55). The friend also may be asked to imagine a switch of roles: "What would you do (have done) in my situation?"

One should emphasize here that the flexibility for situation-specific handling of one's own interests, as well as handling competing obligations is still limited in this type of relationship. The hypothetical reasons for practical decisions favor the obligations and responsibilities towards the friend, even if an obligation towards the new child, or a conflicting self-interest is recognized. Those circumstances of the situation which focus on the position of the friend are dominant. Only if the friend's consent is secured will an alternative decision be made. Concrete competing obligations as well as one's own interests cannot be presented to the friend as legitimate facts, but are brought to her attention with a request for understanding. They are not yet, as in the next stage, tied to general norms; therefore, a normatively justified balance will not yet occur. Since at this level no balance can be reached between self's and others' interests, a decision in favor of the interests of the self works out to violate the moral balance, which can only be restored by subsequent justification, such as apologizing by giving reasons and asking forgiveness. In the case of violation of discursive standards, feelings of guilt caused by offending the relationship and/or the norm of truthfulness result. There are also attempts to restore the moral balance by reconfirming the loyalty to the friendship.

Level C.   For our third—balanced—form of relationship we will not differentiate among the complete network of categorical differentiations that can be created. Instead, we will show how the concept of a "good relationship" emphasizes legitimate individual freedom in moral decision-making, while at the same time preserving the shared standards of a "good relationship." A new form of moral balance is established in the tension between mutually accepted friendship norms such as solidarity and reliability, and the need for autonomous moral decision-making. This takes into account the claims of the self as well, being one among all concerned. This new flexibility is tied to general moral and interpersonal norms which have now become explicit. At the same time, such norms are limited in their validity; their specific meaning has to be established in the context of a given specific situation: "Friendship doesn't mean always being together and doing everything together. You have to have some freedom, I think it's quite normal to do things by yourself" (J, 14, 63). The friend's claim—even in the case of having given a promise—is valid only if her needs deserve real priority, as, for example, in the case of urgent problems. This validity has to be examined in a previous conversation. There is a full understanding of *discursive standards*: "If you didn't say anything at the moment and only said, well, I can't come, then it would make it much easier right then, if you said, for example, my parents say I can't come, or something. But, if she found out another way or somehow by chance, that would be bad, because then she'll feel she's been lied to, so it's better to say something before, and also because it's important for the friendship" (J, 13, 26); ". . . well, my friend, she always tells me when she can't come over, and she also explains, and I do the same with her. The same holds for a birthday. If I'm invited and I have a date with my friend (at the same time), I explain it to her, and she understands. If she didn't understand, I'd be rather surprised" (B, 14, 15).

Particular conditions of the situation are clarified in a conversation with the friend. In comparison with the previous level, one's own claims can be supported normatively and therefore can be seen as justified under specific circumstances. The reasoning gives preference to the friend if the case is justified by its urgency. Only if the problems are urgent and cannot be solved at another point in time, do the obligations take preference: "If she (the friend) says no, well, then I want to hear her arguments" (B, 14, 24). The friend is now expected to have an understanding of the specific situation: on the one hand, of the new child's situation ("well, a person who's alone feels lonesome and shouldn't be left to be an outsider" [J, 14, 38]); on the other hand, the friend is expected to understand justified self-interest ("a good friend shouldn't be jealous because I talk to someone else, you have to have freedom, I think . . . You shouldn't be envious of your friends" [B, 14, 34/66]). This norm is also valid for the self: "If my friend told me, you know, that we could meet another day, we could talk over the problems, then I would fully accept it" (B, 14, 27). Behind this is the (implicit) norm that friends have to be understanding of each other's needs.

The legitimacy of the friend's needs can be weighed against the legitimacy of the needs of others as well as the legitimacy of one's own justified interests. Not only does the heroine have the moral duty to include the perspective of her friend, but the friend likewise has the moral duty to consider the situation of the heroine as well as that of the newcomer.

Our data show that the first type of relationship (Level A) is predominant in 7- to 9-year-olds. The second type of relationship (Level B) is characteristic of 12-year-olds, while the third type (Level C) begins to appear in 14-year-olds. It should be noted that the moral balance between conflicting claims achieved in our third type of relationship refers to a conflict at the immediate interpersonal level of a friendship relationship. Complex institutional conditions in the context of social systems would pose different conditions for the establishment of a moral balance.

In the following section we will attempt to interpret the forms of reasoning just presented in the context of the principles and components of a theory of discursive ethics as outlined in the first part of this chapter.

DEVELOPMENTAL LEVELS IN RELATION TO PRINCIPLES AND STRATEGIES OF JUSTIFICATION

Level A. This type of relationship contains two sublevels which were not explicitly differentiated within this paper. At the first sublevel, the child uses empirical needs and interests as a reason for her satisfaction. Consequences of action relate to satisfaction or nonsatisfaction of these claims. If the self has his or her own needs satisfied, the consequences of the action are felt to be positive, even if negative consequences for others are evident. To obtain the consent of those affected by an action is not seen as necessary; no need for justification exists as yet. Information about one's intention or action—if verbalized at all— refers to simple statements of fact or to needs ("I went to a movie"; "I went to a movie because it's fun"; "I want to go to a movie"). No differentiation can be made between explanation and justification. Moral standards of interpersonal relationships are not yet developed.

At the second sublevel, the subject experiences him or herself as an object of justified claim of the other. The conditions are that the perspectives of others are not only differentiated, but are also related to the perspective of the self. There is an understanding that actions concerning others have to be explained to them. But justification of action is related to concrete expectations and claims of others. Unlike the earlier level, however, the perspectives of others are taken into account in an action plan. Again, prudent considerations resulting from antici- pated negative consequences can lead to explanation (justification) only after the norm-violating action has been performed (e.g., not saying anything, lying, excuses, apologies, making up by compensatory actions).

Level B. In the second type of relationship, coordination of perspectives appears in a more developed form, stemming from the self's ability to view him or herself as the object of expectations of generalized others. In other words, the self is now subject to normative claims shared by self and others (Mead, 1934). Only at this point does the moral subject orient to the internalized norms and standards of the self-evaluative system. Negative consequences of a course of action follow from the incongruence between actions and the standards of the self-evaluative system. These standards are based on norms of reciprocity, such as the golden rule. The restriction of this developmental level consists in the still rigid definition of norms according to the communality of generalized claims and expectations. Subjects at this level do not yet incorporate the demands of specific circumstances or situations that might justify a decision in one's own interest or of a third person even in the case of an obligation, such as a promise given. While the legitimate course of action is now defined by reference to norms of reciprocity, the communality of these norms, however, is not yet based upon procedural rules, a step necessary for any negotiation of the validity of certain obligations in specific situations. Such an omission limits the application of the golden rule at this level. On the other hand, if the child or the adolescent hypothetically takes the perspective of those concerned, this is primarily based on reciprocal normative expectations and not—as before—on the mere assumption of factual needs and interests.

Level C.   In the third form of relationship, the validity of norms can be limited by regarding specific conditions of the situation. Legitimate and justified exceptions to prima facie duties become possible. The self is faced with the task of establishing the appropriate conditions for applying a norm. This presupposes a certain flexibility in moral decision-making to take into consideration, in a balanced form, one's own interests and obligations as well as the interests and claims of the other persons concerned. In the case of conflicting claims, this requires one to enter into a discourse with the goal of coming to a justified agreement, that is, an agreement shared by those concerned. Consequences of action still result from the violation of the reciprocal norms as internalized in the self-evaluative system, but also, although not represented in our data, from the violation of self-set standards.

ASPECTS OF A CONCEPT OF ANALYTICAL
MORAL PEDAGOGY

The first section of this presentation dealt with the normative, the second section with the empirical prerequisites for participation in moral discourse. Taking into account this dual prerequisite, some thoughts regarding the concept of analytical moral education will follow in this third section. Contrary to the forms of an "overly pedagogical position," which replaces primarily knowledge-oriented learning for social-therapeutic-compensatory functions, analytical moral pedagogy sees its task primarily in fostering analytical awareness. Since moral pedagogy only acknowledges the "power of the better argument" (Habermas, 1973a, 1973b) as a goal, it makes a stand against all irrational positions. Moral pedagogy also refutes the empty gesture of a "further critical exploration of reasons" (value clarification), which questions and doubts everything from the start, and thereby destroys every basis of rationality. This rationality, after all, takes for granted the unproblematic validity of certain rules of factual communication and life context. The latter constitute a stabilizing background-context consisting of processes of possible habitualization which render unnecessary the permanent tendency toward reflection and decision. A moral pedagogy which is primarily concerned with the analytic awareness of specific conditions of complex conflict- and life-situations and aspires to optimal development of the cognitive and affective prerequisites of moral decision-making, leaves it to the self to make a decision and to justify this decision. A decision which can be morally justified requires an awareness of the moral content of situations. This is by no means guaranteed by affective concern, but necessarily includes the process of analytical awareness. This condition can be satisfied more easily within the framework of the relatively artificial and highly organized process of learning in school, than can the creation of affective concern.

For every subject, even the potentially moral one, the claim for autonomy is constitutive in the dual sense of the term. Each child has the right to form his or her own opinion. At the same time, he or she must also learn to understand that when justifying proposed solutions to a dilemma, only those viewpoints that include the perspectives of the others can be accepted. The child must acquire the ability to express his or her own needs, interests, feelings, and convictions, and at the same time to consider the claims of others. How adequately the child is able to do this depends on two factors: first, on the latitude for unconstrained discussion in factual communication and life practice as well as in the context of institutionalized learning processes; second, on the child's level of development. Thus, what is meant by a moral point of view is defined with respect to the principle of morality of discourse as well as with respect to the developmental level of the child. Both the communication practice which the child has grown used to as well as the child's level of development are prerequisites for the potential application of a well-reasoned discourse principle. The subject must take responsibility for his or her moral decisions, but, at the same time, he or she is tied to the conditions of communicative action.

Cooperative forms of decision-making more than anything else do justice to this dual claim which confronts moral pedagogy. To be at liberty to form an opinion, to justify it, and to come to terms with possible objections, is something the child learns only when given a fair chance, as a member of a relaxed discourse community. Also, a group produces greater capacity to solve problems than do isolated individuals who try to argue out a dilemma in a monologue. The process of moral decision-making must therefore be organized cooperatively as a group activity, without, however, making younger children or those less able to adjudicate moral conflicts victims of the "tyranny" of group pressure. Activities should be organized in such a way that a child can experience directly what it means to be involved in the tension of an ongoing communication process based on real life experiences, while governed only by the universal conditions of rational communication, i.e., the principles of mutual justification and universalization. Understanding and applying these principles, of course, depends on the individual's level of development, that is, on the ability to differentiate and coordinate perspectives. These principles determine every act of defining a situation and solving a moral conflict.

When working together to define a situation, different viewpoints based on the contributions of each group member are constructed and weighed. The cooperative exploration of conflict situations is not separated from the process of working together in order to find a solution. Both tasks are intertwined, and take place more or less simultaneously. The process of problem solving proceeds from the level of *interpretation,* where empirical needs, interests, expectations, feelings, etc., are related to each other, to the level of *legitimation,* where different perspectives and viewpoints are coordinated in view of what is just or fair in the case. In the process of cooperative problem solving, children complement and correct individual viewpoints, questioning solutions that derive from one perspective only. If different perspectives are not taken into account and coordinated by the students, the teacher as an integral part of the learning group has to turn into an advocate for the neglected perspective, trying to open their eyes to interests, expectations, obligations related to it. The viewpoints on the problem, as well as the proposed solutions will be elaborated differently depending on the children's level of development. When looking for an optimal solution, the teacher can try to control the discussion by specific suggestions, but in the end he or she will have to rely on what the children produce spontaneously during group activity. A heterogeneously structured group will provide different forms of reasoning which will more or less do justice to the demand for complete coordination of relevant perspectives and viewpoints. Whether or not a child is able and willing to adopt certain forms of reasoning, to come to terms with them and use them for his or her own decision-making, depends as much on the communication practice, which he or she grows into, as on his or her level of development, level of development itself being a function of communication practice.

Whatever solutions the community of discourse produce is merely a relatively broad range of potential definitions of situations and solutions to problems. The process of cooperative problem solving therefore has a twofold limitation: (a) the limited nature of the definitions and solutions the group arrives at, due to the different levels of reasoning which are represented in the group, and (b) the extent to which each child will make use of these choices depending on level of development. As long as the teacher is clear about this twofold barrier he or she will avoid the risk of overburdening the child, since suggestions from the teacher's side which serve to construct more differentiated viewpoints and to elicit more flexible structures of reasoning will run into the same limitations.

ACKNOWLEDGMENT

The empirical data used in this paper come from the Project "Child Development and Social Structure," Max Planck Institute for Human Development and Education. Special thanks are given to Wolfgang Edelstein for helpful comments. The first author wants to thank the German Research Foundation (DFG) whose grant supported this research.

REFERENCES

Baier, K. (1958). *The moral point of view*. Ithaca: Cornell University.

Denzin, N. K. (1980). A phenomenology of emotion and deviance. *Zeitschrift für Soziologie, 9*, 251–261.

Habermas, J. (1973a). *Legitimationsprobleme im Spätkapitalismus*. Frankfurt: Suhrkamp.

Habermas, J. (1973b). Wahrheitstheorien. In H. Fahrenbach (Ed.), *Wirklichkeit und Reflexion* (pp. 211–265). Pfullingen: Neske.

Habermas, J. (1981). *Theorie des kommunikativen Handelns*, Vol. 1. Frankfurt: Suhrkamp.

Habermas, J. (1983). *Moralbewusstsein und kommunikatives Handeln*. Frankfurt: Suhrkamp.

Hare, R. M. (1963). *Freedom and reason*. Oxford: Clarendon Press.

Keller, (1984). Resolving conflicts in friendship: The development of moral understanding in everyday life. In J. Gewirtz & W. Kurtines. (Eds.), *Morality, moral behavior, and moral development* (pp. 140–158). New York: Wiley.

Keller, M. & Maute, M. (1983). Die Entwicklung interpersonaler und moralischer Sensibilität. In G. Lüer (Ed.), *Bericht über den 33. Kongress der Deutschen Gesellschaft für Psychologie in Mainz 1982.* (pp. 599–603). Göttingen: Hogrefe.

Keller, M. & Reuss, S. (1984). An action theoretical reconstruction of the development of social cognitive competence. *Human Development, 27*, 211–220.

Kohlberg, L. (1976). Moral stages and moralization: The cognitive developmental approach. In T. Lickona (Ed.), *Moral development and behavior* (pp. 31–53). New York: Holt, Rinehart & Winston.

Kohlberg, L. (1981). *Essays on moral development. Vol. 1: The philosophy of moral development*. San Francisco: Harper and Row.

Mead, G. H. (1934). *Mind, self and society*. Chicago: University of Chicago Press.

Oser, F. (1981). *Moralisches Urteil in Gruppen. Soziales Handeln, Verteilungsgerechtigkeit, Stufen der interaktiven Entwicklung und ihre erzieherische Stimulation*. Frankfurt: Suhrkamp.

Selman, R. L. (1980). *The growth of interpersonal understanding*. New York: Academic Press.

Singer, M. G. (1961). *Generalization in ethics*. New York: Knopf.

II APPLICATIONS AND INTERVENTIONS
A. THE FAMILY

5 Parents as Moral Educators

Thomas Lickona
State University of New York
College at Cortland

In the graduate courses I teach, I have shared with teachers what I naively thought they would receive as good news: namely, the Gallup Poll's finding that four out of five United States citizens favor "instruction in the schools that would deal with morals and moral behavior." Teachers, I quickly discovered, are not overjoyed at this finding. "Parents are copping out," they say. "They want schools to do a job which they ought to be doing themselves."

Good teachers have always done some form of moral education, implicit or explicit, and will continue to do so. But they are absolutely correct, of course, to remind us of what we have always known: Morality begins at home. Raising good and decent children has always been the central challenge of parenthood. Oddly enough, of the three major theories of moral growth—social learning theory, cognitive-developmental psychology, and psychoanalysis—only psychoanalytic theory grants a special role for parents (who are seen as objects of identification) in the moral formation of the child. No current theory, taken alone, begins to do justice to the complexity and importance of the parent's role as a moral educator.

The evidence is all around us, however, that the job of moral education, today more than ever, demands an active collaboration between the family and the school. Wynne (1982) has carefully documented two unmistakable trends over the last 20–30 years: (1) a steady rise in self-destructive behavior by young people—drug abuse, drinking, teenage pregnancy, and suicide (the suicide rate among teens, for example, has nearly tripled during the last 25 years); and (2) a similar rise in other destructive behavior—violence, vandalism, abusive treatment of authority figures, cruelty toward peers, and juvenile crime (half the serious crimes in the United States are now committed by youths between 10 and

127

17). To these two trends one could add a third: the rise of a new morality, an ethic of selfishness—looking out for number one, or what social historian Christopher Lasch (1978) calls "the culture of narcissism." In a recent study of American college graduates of the 1970s, Levine (1981) concludes that young people have a "Titanic mentality"; they think the ship of society is headed for disaster, but they want to go first class. Their goal is not to better the world as they find it, but to make money, have status, and live well.

I am not certain whether these trends are limited to the United States or—as I suspect—characteristic of much of the Western world. But in my own country, at least, the pattern seems disturbingly clear: Young people are increasingly engaged in hurting and abusing themselves and others, and decreasingly concerned about becoming responsible, contributing members of the human community.

How to remedy this state of affairs? Clearly, moral education in the schools is needed; so are efforts to create the societal conditions—political, economic, institutional, spiritual—that help people develop morally and lead good lives. But however much we stress action on these fronts, we must also turn a spotlight on the role of parents in bringing young people to moral maturity. That role begins, of course, in early childhood, as I have argued elsewhere (Lickona, 1983), but it remains vitally important throughout the adolescent years. The conventional wisdom, unfortunately, holds that peers rush in and parents fade out as the moral socializers of adolescents. "Parents Relegated to Scrap Heap During Teens," said a recent newspaper headline. If parents believe this gloomy forecast, and too many do, it becomes a self-fulfilling prophecy. In order to believe otherwise, they need help in developing a clear conception of how they can act as deliberate and effective moral educators as long as their children are with them.

Over the last 10 years, I have conducted workshops for parents on fostering moral development in the family, interviewed parents about their efforts to raise moral children, listened to their questions and concerns as a family counselor, and learned about the complex and humbling business of parenting from my

TABLE 5.1
Raising Moral Children: Nine Big Ideas

1. Morality is respect
2. A morality of respect develops slowly, through stages
3. Foster mutual respect
4. Set a good example
5. Teach by telling
6. Help children learn to think for themselves
7. Help children take on real responsibilities
8. Balance independence and control
9. Love children

experiences as a father of two sons, one now in midadolescence. From these experiences, and from my reading of the research literature, I have developed a set of interrelated points that I offer to parents as nine major concepts or "big ideas" about raising moral children (see Table 5.1). I will present these nine ideas here as I present them to parents, ground them in supporting theory and research, and indicate where I think further research would be helpful. Finally, I will indicate along the way some of the parallel processes of moral education that can be carried out in both home and school.

1.   MORALITY IS RESPECT

Before parents or teachers can develop morality in children, they need to be clear about what it is. The first big idea says that the core of morality is respect for self and others—for the rights, dignity, and worth of all persons.

There is more to morality than respect, of course. A traditional religious family, for example, might also want to foster moral values such as humility, chastity, and love of God and neighbor. But in a pluralistic society, respect for persons is common moral ground. It is something that all people, regardless of what else they believe, can agree on. Indeed, the best-known expression of the principle of respect—the Golden Rule—can be found in religions and cultures all over the world.

2.   A MORALITY OF RESPECT DEVELOPS SLOWLY, THROUGH STAGES

The second big idea is that a morality of respect doesn't burst forth, full-formed, at a particular age. Rather it develops, slowly, through a series of stages. When the dust settles at the end of the century, that idea will, I think, be reckoned as one of developmental psychology's enduring contributions. Current differences among moral psychologists about how to describe the stages should not obscure what research increasingly confirms: that growing up morally, like growing up intellectually, is a process of developing an increasingly complex and comprehensive theory of how the world works; and that the broad sweep of moral development, regardless of which developmentalist paints the picture, is from selfishness to conformity to principled morality.

The idea of moral stages (Kohlberg, 1976) has profound implications for parenting. It calls parents, first of all, to think of the child as a developing person, as a thinker with a point of view, not as a blank slate but as an active architect busy constructing a moral world view. For most parents, who may be only barely conscious of their own thinking processes, thinking of their child as a thinker is quite new. In practical terms, a developmental view calls for a parent to *meet children where they are,* to "plug into" their level of understanding. That, in turn, means two things. First, it means speaking the language of a child's present stage, establishing rapport and communication by "going with the flow" of the child's present construction of morality. It means appealing, for example, to a Stage 1 child's belief that he should obey ("David, this is a chance to obey"); to a Stage 2 child's sense of tit-for-tat fairness ("I did a favor for you yesterday, now I'm asking a favor of you"); to a Stage 3 child's concern for meeting others' expectations and living up to his self-image ("I'm disappointed by your behavior—you can do better than that"), and so on.

Second, meeting children where they are means challenging their present moral logic with reasoning which is one stage higher. This may be easier for parents to do in the home where they can deal with their child one-on-one, than it is for teachers to do in the thick of moral discussion in the classroom, but there are opportunities for challenging reasoning in both domains. One challenges a Stage 1 child, for example, to see that two-way fairness is a better reason for cooperating than fear of punishment; a Stage 2 child to see that a family doesn't work very well if everybody just looks out for himself; a Stage 3 youngster to see that doing what others expect of you doesn't solve problems when some people want you to do one thing and other people want you to do something else.

One might wonder, "Can parents really diagnose a child's moral stage, given the fact that trained researchers sometimes find that a formidable task?" I would submit that when you live with children in their natural social ecology, you do not need to be a trained scorer to identify their dominant moral orientation to the world. There is nothing subtle, for example, about the what's-in-it-for-me fairness of Stage 2; children at this stage drive parents to distraction with their rigid notion of equality, constant negotiation, and cries of "It's not fair!" Likewise, the young teenager's Stage 3 obsession with "What will people think of me?"—death seemingly being preferable to peer disapproval—hardly takes a professional psychologist to spot. A moral stage approach simply helps parents understand the moral reasoning that lies behind classic behavior patterns that parents readily recognize.

There are times, of course, when it takes some questioning—"Why do you think it was wrong to steal that?" "What's the most important reason why you should tell me the truth?"—to make contact with a child's operative moral reasoning in a particular situation. And even if questioning doesn't produce easy-to-stage answers (it often won't), parents can still get a rough feel for the developmental maturity of their child's thinking. That in turn will help them know at what level to pitch their reasoning.

There is at least some research (Berkowitz, 1981; Berkowitz, Gibbs, & Broughton, 1980) to indicate that people advance in their moral reasoning when they are exposed to or required to interact with reasoning slightly (no more than one stage) above their own. The hypothesis offered here is that a judicious combination of going with the flow (by appealing to the logic of the child's present dominant stage) and challenge (making a higher-stage appeal) will lead to more harmonious parent-child relations and better moral reasoning than either accommodation or challenge alone. Elsewhere (Lickona, 1983) I have detailed various ways that parents can try to go with the flow and challenge moral reasoning at each developmental stage.

3. FOSTER MUTUAL RESPECT

One of the most important lessons a parent can teach children is that morality is a two-way street. Respect is reciprocal. Do unto others as you would have them do unto you.

Parents teach the lesson of mutual respect by respecting their child and requiring their child to respect them in return. A liberal-romantic view of the child, prevalent in the 60s, assumed that if we treated children respectfully, they would automatically respect us and others. A developmental view is not so optimistic; it knows that children, who are at immature levels of moral development, must frequently be reminded and even required to reciprocate the respect that is given them.

Mutual respect is never as important as it is in adolescence, when the stresses of accelerating development and rising peer pressure put new strains on parent-child relations. Although some conflict between parents and teenagers is virtually inevitable, respect appears to have widespread efficacy in calming the troubled waters. Pikas (1961), in his survey of 656 Swedish adolescents, found that adolescents tended to accept parental authority when it was based on rational concern for their welfare. (Parents who take pains to make clear the rational basis of their concern are showing one form of respect for their teenager.) However, Swedish adolescents rejected parental authority when it appeared to stem from their parents' desire to dominate or exploit them.

One way to foster mutual respect between parents and children is to take what I call a "fairness approach" to discipline and conflict in the home. The basic rationale for this approach is the idea that all children, even young ones, come equipped with at least a beginning sense of fairness and that the continuing development of that sense of fairness is a crucial part of moral development. The fairness approach requires parent and child to pool their ideas in a cooperative effort to solve the problem at hand.

To establish a fairness approach in the home, parents I have worked with sometimes find it helpful to hold a sit-down, 10-step fairness discussion. The steps of the fairness discussion are listed in Table 5.2. Steps 1 through 6 are aimed at achieving mutual understanding between parent and child as the foundation for the subsequent problem-solving steps. These first 6 steps require the participants to engage in the kind of systematic role-taking that Piaget (1965) and Kohlberg (1976) regard as the *sine qua non* of moral development. Steps 7

TABLE 5.2
Steps in a Fairness Discussion

A. *Achieving Mutual Understanding*
1. State the purpose of the discussion (to find a fair solution).
2. State intent to understand each other's feelings about the problem.
3. State your feeling about the problem.
4. Ask your child for his feelings about the problem.
5. Paraphrase your child's feelings to show understanding.
6. Ask your child to paraphrase your feelings.

B. *Solving the Problem*
7. Together brainstorm fair solutions to the problem.
8. Agree upon a solution that everyone thinks fair; sign a "fairness agreement."
9. Plan implementation of solution and follow-up; evaluate discussion.

C. *Evaluating the Solution*
10. Hold a follow-up discussion to evaluate how the solution is working.

through 9 are aimed at solving the problem. Step 10 is aimed at evaluating the solution after it has been implemented to see how well it is working and what can be done, if necessary, to make it work better.

As an example of how a fairness discussion can work even with young children, consider the following account by a mother. She describes her first fairness discussion with her two children, James, age 7, and Elizabeth, age 5. "The problem we discussed," she says, "is one that had been disturbing to our family for quite a while."

Step 1: Parent states purpose of discussion.
> Mother: James and Elizabeth, we're having a problem with you two getting along. I'd like to talk with you about it and see if we can come up with a fair solution.

Step 2: Parent states intent to achieve understanding.
> Mother: First, I want you to know and understand how I feel about this situation, and then I want to find out how each of you feel.

Step 3: Parent states feelings about problem.
> Mother: Kids, I get so irritated when I see the two of you fighting with each other or hitting one another. When I get irritated I start to yell at you, and everything becomes upset. I would like to see the two of you try a little harder to get along.

Step 4: Parent elicits children's feelings.
> Mother: Now, I've told you how I feel. I'd like to hear each of your feelings about this.

> James: Elizabeth always wants to do everything I do. She wants to sit in the same seat that I do, and she wants to play with the same toys. Sometimes she hits me, too.

Elizabeth: James punches me. He makes me cry. He won't play with me. I don't
like it when you yell, Mommy.

Step 5: Parent paraphrases children's feelings.

Mother: Okay, I want to make sure that I understand what you said. James,
you feel Elizabeth is always in your way—wanting to sit with you
and play with you. Also, you don't like it when she hits you. Elizabeth, you say that James makes you cry when he hits you and won't
play with you. And you don't want me to yell because it upsets you.

Step 6: Children paraphrase parent's feelings.

Mother: Can you remember what I said about the situation?

James: You want us to try not to fight because it upsets you and everybody
else. Right?

Mother: That's right, James. Elizabeth, do you understand that?

Elizabeth: Yes.

Step 7: All brainstorm fair solutions.

Mother: You know what I'd like us to do together? I'd like us to make this
situation better. All the things we put on the list have to be fair to
everyone. Okay? (Children nod.) Elizabeth, do you understand what
"fair" means?

Elizabeth: Yes, Mommy. It means everybody has to like it.

Mother's commentary: Together we came up with these possible solutions:

1. Don't hit.
2. James should try to teach Elizabeth some of his games.
3. Mommy shouldn't yell.
4. Elizabeth should try to find things to do by herself sometimes.
5. Everyone should try to say and do nice things.

Step 8: All reach and sign a fairness agreement.

We agreed on the following solutions as being fair:

1. No hitting or yelling by anyone—Mommy, James, or Elizabeth.
2. James should try to play with Elizabeth at least once a day.
3. Elizabeth should try to play by herself sometimes.
4. Everyone should try to say and do nice things.

We all signed our contract and promised to try our best.

Step 9: All plan implementation and follow-up; evaluate meeting.

We decided to post our solutions on the refrigerator where all could see them. Next
to our solutions we put a paper to be used to keep a list of nice things said and done
during the next two days. James agreed to write down whatever Elizabeth wished to
have recorded on the list.

We agreed to start immediately with our plan and to inform Dad about it when he
got home. We decided we would meet again in two days to see how our plan was
progressing.

I asked the children how they liked our fairness meeting. They said they were
glad to know that I cared about them. They were also pleased to know that I
realized I had to change, too. They weren't the only ones who had been acting
badly.

Step 10: Follow-up meeting to evaluate solution.

In our follow-up meeting we began by reading the list of nice things that people had said and done during the last two days. We decided that everyone had indeed tried to be kinder. Then we went over each of our solutions, and we all contributed a comment about how well the plan was working.

> Mother: James, I'm so pleased that you've been trying to include Elizabeth in your playing. Do you realize that I've had to speak to you only twice in two days? I think that's quite an improvement. And Elizabeth, you are certainly trying to be nicer to everyone.

> James: I'm glad you're not yelling, Mommy. And I don't think Elizabeth has hit me at all.

> Elizabeth: James played with me, and he let me sit in the bean bag with him yesterday.

To the questions, 'Is our plan working?' and 'Are we all trying to be fair?' we all answered with a resounding yes. To the question, 'Can we make our plan work even better?' we answered that we would remind ourselves of our agreement at the beginning of each day and would have another meeting in a week's time to see if we were each still following our plan.

This mother concluded: Our household is now a much happier one. We continue to add to the list of nice things said to and done for others, and Dad has also gotten involved. I can foresee using this method in dealing with other problems that come up with my children and even with my husband. The fairness meeting seems to be a good way to get things out into the open. Often we do not think about how the other person views a situation, and it does us good to hear the other side of the story.

Sometimes a fairness discussion can be shortened to a single step: a quick, on-the-spot settlement. For example, a 5-year-old wanted to play for 30 minutes with his 10-year-old brother, while the older brother wanted to have private time. With brief parental mediation, they agreed to 15 minutes of play and 15 minutes of private time as a fair compromise.

Does a fairness approach to rules and discipline mean that children never suffer any negative consequences for their lapses? Not at all. Consequences, even stiff ones, can be built into the fairness agreement: Pick up your toys after you have been playing with them or lose them for two days; have the car home by midnight or lose driving privileges for a month. The critical condition is that the consequences be seen as fair by both parent and child.

How does a fairness approach foster moral development? First of all, it requires children to think morally—to "decenter" and consider the needs of others as well as their own. It sets a good example for children by treating them with respect for their rights and feelings as people and by showing that reason rather than power can be used to resolve conflicts. It teaches a child responsibility by making him an active partner in the solution of conflicts. Finally, a fairness approach gives children valuable practice in the skills of communication and problem-solving. It thereby equips them to deal effectively and justly with the myriad problems they will encounter as they make their way in their widening social and moral world.

4. SET A GOOD EXAMPLE

The fourth big idea about parenting for moral development is one of the oldest: Set a good example. There is an impressive modeling literature which confirms everyday observation: Children are influenced by what they see others do. A spate of television studies (National Institute of Mental Health, 1982), for example, demonstrates that children who watch violence on the screen are more likely to use violence in life. Besides trying to provide a positive moral example themselves, parents obviously need to be vigilant regarding the other models that children are exposed to in their social-moral environment.

In the interviews I conduct with parents and teachers, I ask them, "How did your parents influence your moral development?" Far and away, the most common answer I get speaks of the example a parent sets. One young woman, a dedicated teacher who also opens her home to people needing a meal or shelter, remembered her mother's moral courage:

> My mother had a tremendous sense of justice. She was always involved in causes. One of my earliest childhood memories is that of my mother being arrested for leading a PTA crusade. She said they wouldn't leave the Capitol steps until they saw the governor.
>
> It was my mother who taught me from my earliest years always to stand up for what I thought was right. I don't remember much talking about it. The beauty was in what she did. My mother is the corner I've woven my web in.

Other people remember quieter ways in which their parents stood up for moral principle. A young woman recalls the time when she was 7 and they had recently moved to Philadelphia. An Asian family wished to purchase a house in their middle-class, all-white neighborhood, and the neighbors were circulating a petition against it. "My mother was the only person who refused to sign," said this young woman, "and when the family moved in despite the petition, she made them a cake to welcome them."

Rosenhan (1969) provides similar documentation of the power of parental example. He was able to classify young American civil rights workers in the 1960s into two groups: "fully committed students," who had worked in the deep South, often at personal risk, for a year or more; and "partially committed students," who had taken only one or two low-risk "freedom rides" and whose commitment seemed more talk than action.

Partially committed students, Rosenhan's interviews disclosed, usually disliked their parents. They often remembered them as preaching one thing and practicing another, especially toward members of out-groups. One student, for example, went on a tirade about how easily his father condoned dishonesty when the victims were people he did not like.

Fully committed civil rights workers, on the other hand, typically looked up to their parents as persons who lived by their moral ideals. One young man remembered vividly how his father had carried him on his shoulders in a parade to protest the execution of Sacco and Vanzetti, two political radicals believed by many to have been framed for murder. Another student recalled how his father, outraged by Nazi atrocities, had signed up for service in World War II despite bad health and old age.

Many parents of adolescents unfortunately assume that their influence as moral models ends with childhood. It doesn't have to. Whether it continues into the teens depends on a number of variables, such as how adolescents feel about their parents, and that is obviously affected by how parents treat them. Hoffman and Saltzstein (1967), in their study of seventh-graders, found that parents who were high in power assertion (unilateral control) had children who were low in admiration of their parents and desire to be like them. Elder (1963) found that junior high school and high school students were more likely to model themselves after their parents and to associate with parent-approved peers if their parents used reason to explain their decisions and demands.

It becomes obvious that the important processes of raising moral children do not operate independently. Respecting children and teaching by example clearly interact. If parents do not respect adolescents as persons with minds and feelings, they greatly reduce their chances of being effective moral models.

5. TEACH BY TELLING

The fifth big idea I propose to parents is also drawn from the wisdom of the ages: We teach by telling. This is the notion that it's not only important to practice what you preach, but it's also important to preach what you practice.

Direct moral teaching has, unfortunately, been viewed with disdain by two leading movements in moral education. Values clarification has called it "moralizing" and "no longer a valid teaching tool." Similarly, Kohlbergian-Piagetian moral education has until recently scorned old-fashioned values teaching as manipulative indoctrination which didn't respect the child as a thinker and didn't work anyway. Kohlberg (1980, this volume), however, says that dealing with the moral—or immoral—behavior of some 50 adolescents in his Just Community high school cured him of his belief that nondirective Piagetian facilitation was adequate moral leadership. Students take years to construct a new moral stage; stealing has to be stopped right away. The school staff, therefore, must vigorously advocate the honesty necessary for trust and community. I came to similar conclusions regarding the role of moral authority via my work with elementary school teachers and life as a parent; one simply has to manage behavior.

Behavior management, however, turns out to be the occasion for a deeper, more important kind of moral education: that of transmitting values, or what I call "teaching by telling." Direct values transmission has, of course, been around for a long time—as long as values themselves. Before contemporary individualism led us to believe that we should be completely self-determining, autonomous moral agents, people used to take it for granted that each generation had a moral heritage to pass on to the next. Kilpatrick (in press) suggests that we should regard the best of this generational legacy as a moral treasure that young people might not come to on their own; indeed, in any society worth its salt, adults would show a lack of virtue if they did not pass on a moral heritage to their children. Lasch (1978) argues that we have become so narcissistic, so encapsulated and diminished by our self-centered pursuits, at least partly because we are prisoners of the present, ignorant of the past, cut off from the enduring values that have traditionally helped people to form an identity and ground their moral being in something larger than themselves.

Adolescents will surely add to and alter the values that we try to pass on to them. But if we pass on something, they start with a foundation. One can easily extend this point to the school. If young people today are, as Robert Coles has said, "awash on a sea of relativism," it may be partly because teachers as well as parents do not seem to stand for anything, do not express positions on the great moral issues of the day, do not react even to the moral events in their immediate environment, do not talk or act as if morality really matters.

Is there research evidence that direct moral teaching has positive moral effects? Baumrind (1975), in a review of the literature, concludes that, at least within American society, families who maintain and communicate a strong belief system seem able to keep their youth from destructive drug use and radical alienation. Döbert and Nunner-Winkler (1982, this volume) report that parents who frequently "moralize"—point out the moral issue in a situation—have children who are more advanced in their moral reasoning than children of parents who do not do this kind of teaching. London (1970) investigated the backgrounds of "rescuers," people who had risked their lives and/or their fortunes to save Jews from the Nazis. Rescuers consistently remembered their parents as strong, good people who both preached and practiced morality. London quotes one man, involved in the rescue of more than 200 Jews over a 4-year period, as exemplifying this pattern:

> You inherit something from the parents, from the grandparents. My mother said to me when we were small, and even when we were bigger, 'Regardless of what you do with your life, be honest. When it comes to the day you have to make a decision, make the right one. It could be a hard one. But even the hard ones should be the right ones.' (p. 243)

Thus research again confirms common belief: Parents' direct moral teaching can have a profound influence on the conscience of their children.

6.   HELP CHILDREN LEARN TO THINK
FOR THEMSELVES

Telling children or adolescents what we believe gives them important value content, grist for their moral mill. Obviously they need to *think* about that content, to exercise and expand the structures of their own moral reasoning. The sixth big idea is that we raise moral children by empowering them to think for themselves.

How does a parent do that? Not with a big stick or a cold shoulder, according to Hoffman and Saltzstein's (1967) study of seventh-graders. They found that parental power assertion related negatively not only to parent-child identification, but also to a child's moral judgment. Parents who used a lot of power assertion ("Shut your mouth!" "Do what I say if you know what's good for you") tended to have children with an "external conscience," more concerned with getting caught than with the rightness or wrongness of following a rule. Parents who used a lot of shaming and love withdrawal ("You're acting like a baby," "I don't want to speak to you") tended to have children with a rigid, "conventional conscience," who, for example, said that it would be wrong for a person to tell a lie to protect a classmate from cruelty or to steal to save your dying wife. By contrast, parents who used a lot of "induction"—other-oriented reasoning ("How did so-and-so feel when you did that?")—tended to have children with a "humanist-flexible conscience," able to weigh extenuating circumstances and make moral judgments according to the spirit rather than the letter of the law.

Other research has used Kohlberg's framework to illuminate styles and effects of parental reasoning. Holstein (1972) studied 53 families with eighth-grade youngsters in a professional community in San Francisco. She found that parents who scored at Stage 5 of moral reasoning on a Kohlberg pretest were likely to take their adolescent's opinions seriously in family discussions about how to resolve hypothetical moral dilemmas. Teenagers in these families responded to their parents' encouragement by using up to 40% of the discussion time. Parents who scored at Kohlberg's conventional stages, however, behaved quite differently; they were likely to explain to their child how they were right and to expect their child to conform to their judgment. Only one adolescent in these families used more than 20% of family discussion time. In the pretest Kohlberg interviews, children of parents who encouraged their participation were likely to score at Stage 3, whereas children of low-encouraging parents were typically still at Stage 1 or Stage 2 of moral reasoning.

Grimes (1974) worked with the families of fifth-and sixth-graders rather than with the families of adolescents. At the end of a 10-week course in moral discussion for both mothers and children, all but one of the 11 participating children made significant movement on Kohlberg's scale from Stage 2 to Stage 3. In contrast, a group of children who went through the same moral discussion course in their classroom showed much less progress; only half of them made gains.

Two recent research reviews (Leming, 1981; Lockwood, 1978) conclude that Socratic moral discussion in the classroom produces stable stage gains in moral reasoning for about half the students. Some students are interested in moral discussions and take them seriously; others do not. When students see their own parents wrestling with moral dilemmas, however, and openly sharing their thoughts and feelings, moral discussion may take on new importance. Grimes, in fact, comments on the intense interest children showed as they listened to their parents talking in the group about how they thought a dilemma should be resolved. Schools may not ordinarily be able to bring parents into the classroom; but with a little imagination they could find a way to involve the family in moral discussion—perhaps by having students interview their parents about a moral dilemma or bring the dilemma up for discussion at the dinner table.

Edwards (1981) observes that the rational, democratic mode—the discussion style that proved effective in the Holstein and Grimes studies—is not the cultural ideal in many non-Western societies that it is in the middle and upper classes of the United States. Does democratic, induction-style reasoning predict advanced moral judgment in other and different cultures? At least one study suggests that it does. Parikh (1975) carried out a procedure parallel to Holstein's, using professional families of adolescents in an urban area of India. The extent of parents' encouragement of adolescents' participation in moral dilemma discussion and the extent of parents' use of induction reasoning in general showed a strong positive relation to adolescents' moral judgment (much stronger than their relation to either adolescents' IQ or logical cognition stage).

7. HELP CHILDREN TAKE ON REAL RESPONSIBILITIES

Morality is not a spectator sport. In at least one important sense, however, adolescents are on the sidelines of the moral life: They typically lack real responsibilities of the kind that foster moral maturity. Kohler (1981) charges American society with creating an empty adolescence, devoid of opportunities for work, service to others, and beginning citizenship. She wrote: "We ask young people to prepare for a nebulous future without allowing them to participate in the here and now. By denying young people an immediate role in our society, we prolong their dependence, undermine their self-esteem, and cripple their capacity to care" (p. 34).

The problem of the empty adolescence is, of course, a relatively recent phenomenon, since a long, psychosocial adolescence is itself a modern creation. In the days of agricultural and early industrial societies, for example, families were large, and simple survival demanded contributions from everyone, even young children. As children grew, Kohler observes, "they gradually assumed more and more responsibility until, almost without noticing it, they became adults with jobs and families of their own" (p. 34).

Erikson (1968) points out that delaying adult responsibility has an advantage: Affluent societies grant their young a "psychosocial moratorium" so they may have the time and security to find the unique niche in society through which they can best contribute. We know from Whiting and Whiting's cross-cultural research (1975), however, that children become responsible when they have responsibility, and they become self-centered when they do not. A prolonged adolescence may be, as Erikson suggests, conducive to identity development in a complex society. But it is increasingly clear that we do a disservice to young people and retard their development as moral agents if we shield them from all responsible involvement in the lives of others.

Acting on that awareness, some schools have provided opportunities for adolescents to participate in society in meaningful and responsible ways: through historical restoration projects, service programs for senior citizens, tutoring for young or handicapped children, or peer counseling. And there is at least some evidence (see, e.g., Mosher, 1980) that such programs have positive effects on the ego and moral development of the youth who participate. Increasingly, I think, parents are seeing the need for similar moves in the home toward requiring children and adolescents to share the responsibilities as well as the benefits of family life.

I would predict—and one could design a family intervention study to test this—that children will sooner make the transition from self-centered Stage 2 moral reasoning to other-oriented Stage 3 reasoning when they are expected to function as contributing members of their family. If that transition can be accomplished in childhood, instead of delayed until adolescence, secondary schools would be able to focus on helping adolescents take the next step, from Stage 3 participation in their immediate group to Stage 4 participation in the wider world, rather than expending valuable energy on controlling selfish and disruptive behavior.

8.   BALANCE INDEPENDENCE AND CONTROL

The eighth big idea is that wise parenting seeks to balance two things that are always somewhat in tension: the child's desire to be independent and the parent's need to exercise control.

Baumrind (1975) offers a good operational description of this balance. Labeling it "authoritative" parenting (as contrasted to "authoritarian" or "permissive" parenting), she wrote:

> Authoritative control includes the following attitudes and practices: the child is
> directed firmly, consistently, and rationally; issues rather than personalities are

focused on; the parent both explains reasons behind demands and encourages verbal give-and-take; the parent uses power when necessary; the parent values both obedience to adult requirements and independence in the child; the parent sets standards and enforces them firmly but does not regard self as infallible; the parent listens to the child but does not base decisions solely on the child's desires. (p. 130)

Becker (1964) reviews evidence indicating that *authoritarian* discipline (irrationally restrictive compared to Baumrind's authoritative style) leads to "fearful, dependent, and submissive behaviors, a dulling of intellectual strivings, and inhibited hostility." Maccoby (1980), in a more recent review, cites a variety of studies showing that children reared under a heavy-handed authoritarian regime are lacking in empathy, low in self-esteem, poor in internalization of moral standards, and low in effective peer interaction. All of this calls to mind the ample evidence, already cited, that parents who use power in a way that does not respect children seem to retard moral growth. What's the evidence that the other extreme of parenting—permissiveness—is bad for moral development? Peck and Havighurst (1960) found that highly self-centered adolescents came from highly permissive families. And Middleton and Putney (1963) report that parental discipline that is seen by teenagers as *either* very strict or very permissive is associated with lack of parent-child closeness and with the child's rebellion against the parent's viewpoints.

Baumrind (see Maccoby, 1980) has produced direct evidence for the efficacy of the authoritative balance between independence and control in her studies of children that began when they were nursery schoolers and followed them until they were nine. She also reports briefly (1975) on an unpublished study of 103 tenth-graders. Among these adolescents she identified a small group—15 students—that she labeled "Principled Humanists." These were highly achieving, highly responsible teenagers who said they felt good about authority arrangements in their families and—what is germane to the present issue—described their parents as "firm but democratic."

Azrak (1980) did a family intervention study that bears on this issue in an interesting way—and suggests why parents need to address their adolescent's demands for independence if they wish to maintain moral clout. Azrak ran a 10-week course in a suburb of Boston for 19 parents (seven couples and five mothers) of seventh-ninth graders. Parents were taught to consistently apply inductive reasoning in everyday discipline encounters, and were helped to understand how children differ in their reasoning about right and wrong at different stages of moral development.

In an earlier pilot study, Azrak says, he observed that parents tended to feel personally rejected when their early adolescent began to pull away from close family ties. He had also observed that adolescents who participated in the pilot program were more willing to talk about different moral viewpoints on a discipline situation when their parents were willing to talk about issues of separation and independence.

The subsequent course intervention (in which only the parents took part) bore this out. When adolescents perceived their parents as addressing separation issues, parents reported less resistance to discipline and more interest in higher-stage moral reasons for behaving. And adolescents whose parents participated in the course, compared to a control group whose parents did not, showed significant progress toward Stage 3 moral reasoning. Azrak wrote:

> The parents' attention to the disengagement process facilitated their children's transition from Stage 2 to Stage 3 morality. The parents learned that they could actively promote both the disengagement process and moral reasoning by providing an atmosphere of trust and predictability whenever they observed separation strivings in their children. . . . A discussion about going out with the gang on Saturday night instead of accompanying the family to the movies could be used to facilitate the separation process and also to negotiate a Stage 3 contract about what time the child should be home. (p. 364)

In short, it appears that a spoonful of independence helps the moral medicine go down. When teenagers feel recognized as independent persons, they're more willing to accept parents' controls and listen to their moral reasoning.

9. LOVE CHILDREN

We know intuitively, I think, that there is something more basic than whether parents respect children, set a good example, pass on values, teach them to think, give them responsibility, or balance independence and control. Important as all of these things are, there is something still more fundamental on which everything else builds. What is prior to all other moral influences, I submit, is love.

Parental warmth and nurturance, while certainly not the only antecedents of mature conscience, have been consistently and positively linked in the research literature to children's moral development (Hoffman, 1970; Staub, 1978, 1979). The lack of parental love is a salient factor in the background of delinquents; the presence of love has been a prominent member of the constellation of factors that appear to bring children to moral maturity.

Holstein (1972) turned up clear evidence of the interaction between parents' affection and a child's moral reasoning development. Holstein found that a mother's level of moral reasoning was a strong predictor of her adolescent's; when she was principled in her judgment, her child was very likely to have developed to the conventional moral stages (3 and 4). For fathers, however, there appeared to be no relationship at all. Principled fathers were just as likely to have preconventional (Stages 1 and 2) children as they were to have conventional-reasoning children.

Puzzled by this, Holstein probed further. She compared what she called "unsuccessful fathers" (principled themselves but with children still reasoning at a preconventional level) with "successful fathers" (principled themselves and with children who had developed to the conventional moral stages). When the 13-year-old children of both groups of fathers were asked to rate how often their fathers showed affection to them or played with them, the successful fathers emerged as much warmer than unsuccessful fathers and much more involved with their youngsters. Moral reasoning thus appears to grow best when it's nurtured by love.

Why this is so is a matter of theoretical speculation. Research has not yet mapped all the variables that connect the heart and the mind. One of them may well be self-esteem. Coppersmith's research (1967) with pre-adolescents finds that high self-esteem children, who can stand by their own judgment amidst peers and have an easier time making friends, come from families which show their child lots of love and appreciation through everyday expressions of affection and concern. (Parents of *low* self-esteem children tend to be highly critical of their youngsters and to treat them as a burden.) A child who feels good about himself appears to be more likely to exercise his own powers of moral reasoning and to seek out social relationships that afford the opportunity for role-taking and hence the opportunity for developing more advanced moral judgment.

I suspect, however, that the relationship between love and moral development goes deeper than the provision of role-taking opportunities. Consider the following passage from the autobiography of Christiaan Barnard (1974), originator of the heart transplant:

> Whenever we were ill, my father got up at night to doctor us. I suffered from festering toenails that pained so much I would cry in bed. My father used to draw out the fester with a poultice made of milk and bread crumbs, or Sunlight soap and sugar. And when I had a cold, he would rub my chest with Vicks and cover it with a red flannel cloth. Sunday afternoons we walked together to the top of the hill by the dam. Once there, we would sit on a rock and look down at the town below us. Then I would tell my problems to my father, and he would speak of his to me. (p. 21)

The British philosopher Richards Peters (1970) has said that the chief business of moral education is getting people to care. In the passage I have just quoted, the son is clearly learning to care by being cared for. He is learning that other people—their needs, their feelings—are important. He is learning that human relationships, and all that they require of us, are to be taken seriously. And that is the first step toward taking morality seriously.

To understand why some people take morality seriously and others do not, why some care deeply about leading a moral life, and others hardly at all, would require us to look at many factors. One of them, I think, is the quality of the affective bond between parent and child.

In adolescence, a positive relationship between parent and child has a special importance. Adolescents have a special need for a parent's moral counsel to counterbalance the growing influence of peers, to protect them from their own developmental immaturities, and to help them learn to use their powers of moral reasoning to deal with the increasingly complex and stressful world that confronts them. They are more likely to accept a parent's guidance when it is offered in a context of love.

These, then, are nine ideas that can guide parents in the raising of moral children: Think of morality as respect for persons, support and challenge a child's present developmental stage, promote mutual respect, set a good example, teach values directly, stimulate children's moral reasoning, give them meaningful responsibilities, balance independence and control, and give them love. I submit that all of these processes can be—indeed, have been—carried out in one or another form in both home and the school. While their applications may differ, the same basic principles can guide the work of parents and teachers in their roles as moral educators.

Although I think we know a good deal about how to help young people grow morally, much remains to be learned. The Kohlbergian moral stage studies have typically focused on the Stage 2-Stage 3 shift; we need studies of those influences that stimulate transition to the society-wide perspective of Stage 4 and the principled moral perspective of Stage 5. Stage gains, moreover, have to date been measured in terms of vertical development—progress up the ladder of Kohlberg's moral stages.

Horizontal development—the process of actually *using* one's highest available stage with increasing frequency to deal with real-life problems—has not been assessed, even though horizontal development is the bottom-line outcome that parents and educators are justifiably interested in. We also need studies of families as interacting systems (what happens when parents take different approaches, for example?), and longitudinal studies that ask, "What are the long-term effects of this or that parenting style?" and "Does effective parenting style vary as a function of a child's developmental stage?" Finally, we need studies that look at home-school interaction and ask, "What kinds of home-school collaboration increase children's moral development beyond the effects of school or family alone?"

Though the evidence isn't all in, it seems obvious, to return to my opening point, that moral education is too big a job for schools to tackle alone. Parents are indispensable partners in that enterprise and remain so throughout adolescence. How to make that partnership a working reality in the moral education of our children is a task that lies before us.

REFERENCES

Azrak, R. (1980). Parents as moral educators. In R. Mosher (Ed.), *Moral education* (pp. 356–365). New York: Praeger.

Barnard, C. (1974). Selections from *One life*. In J. L. Milgram & D. J. Sciarra (Eds.), *Childhood revisited* (pp. 11–30). New York: Macmillan.

Baumrind, D. (1975). Early socialization and adolescent competence. In S. E. Dragastin & G. H. Elder (Eds.), *Adolescence in the life cycle* (pp. 117–143). New York: Wiley.

Becker, W. C. (1964). Consequences of different kinds of parental discipline. In M. L. Hoffman & L. W. Hoffman (Eds.), *Review of child development research*, Vol. 1 (pp. 169–208). New York: Russell Sage Foundation.

Berkowitz, M. W. (1981). A critical appraisal of the educational and psychological perspectives on moral discussion. *The Journal of Educational Thought, 15*, 20–33.

Berkowitz, M. W., Gibbs, J. C., & Broughton, J. M. (1980). The relation of moral judgment stage disparity to developmental effects of peer dialogues. *Merrill-Palmer Quarterly, 26*, 341–357.

Coopersmith, S. (1967). *The antecedents of self-esteem*. San Francisco: W. H. Freeman.

Döbert, R. & Nunner-Winkler, G. (1982). *Moral climate in the family: Impact on adolescents' stage of moral development*. Paper presented to International Symposium on Moral Education, University of Fribourg, Switzerland.

Edwards, C. P. (1981). The comparative study of the development of moral judgment and reasoning. In R. H. Munroe, R. L. Munroe, & B. Whiting (Eds.), *Handbook of cross-cultural human development* (pp. 501–528). New York: Garland.

Elder, G. H. (1963). Parental power legitimation and its effect on the adolescent. *Sociometry, 26*, 50–65.

Erikson, E. H. (1968). *Identity: Youth and crisis*. New York: Norton.

Grimes, P. (1974). *Teaching moral reasoning to 11-year-olds and their mothers*. Unpublished doctoral dissertation, Boston University, School of Education.

Hoffman, M. L. (1970). Moral development. In P. H. Mussen (Ed.), *Carmichael's manual of child psychology* Vol. 2 (pp. 261–359). New York: Wiley.

Hoffman, M. L. & Saltzstein, H. D. (1967). Parent discipline and the child's moral development. *Journal of Personality and Social Psychology, 5*, 45–57.

Holstein, C. (1972). The relation of children's moral judgment level to that of their parents and to communication patterns in the family. In R. C. Smart & M. S. Smart (Eds.), *Readings in child development and relationships*. New York: Macmillan.

Kilpatrick, K. (in press). Storytelling and virtue. In *Psychological foundations of moral education*. Lanham, MD: University Press of America.

Kohlberg, L. (1976). Moral stages and moralization. In T. Lickona (Ed.), *Moral development and behavior* (pp. 31–53). New York: Holt, Rinehart, and Winston.

Kohlberg, L. (1980). Educating for a just society: An updated and revised statement. In B. Munsey (Ed.), *Moral development, moral education, and Kohlberg* (pp. 455–470). Birmingham, AL: Religious Education.

Kohler, M. C. (1981). Youth participation: The key to responsibility. *Phi Delta Kappan, 5*, 34–38.

Lasch, C. (1978). *The culture of narcissism*. New York: Norton.

Leming, J. S. (1981). Curriculum effectiveness in moral values education: A review of research. *Journal of Moral Education, 10*, 147–164.

Levine, A. (1981). *When dreams and heroes died: A portrait of today's college students*. San Francisco: Jossey-Bass.

Lickona, T. (1983). *Raising good children: Helping your child through the stages of moral development*. New York: Bantam Books.

Lockwood, A. (1978). The effects of value clarification and moral development curricula on school-age subjects: A critical review of recent research. *Review of Educational Research, 48*, 325–364.

London, P. (1970). The rescuers: Motivational hypotheses about Christians who saved Jews from the Nazis. In J. Macauley & L. Berkowitz (Eds.), *Altruism and helping behavior* (pp. 251–268). New York: Academic.

Maccoby, E. (1980). *Social development: Psychological growth and the parent-child relationship*. New York: Harcourt Brace Jovanovich.

Middleton, R. & Putney, S. (1963). Political expression of adolescent rebellion. *American Journal of Sociology, 68,* 527–535.

Mosher, R. (1980). *Moral education: A first generation of research and development.* New York: Praeger.

National Institute of Mental Health (1982). *Television and behavior: Ten years of scientific progress and implications for the 80's* (DHHS Publication No. ADM 82–1195). Washington DC: U.S. Government Printing Office.

Parikh, B. (1975). *Moral judgment development and its relation to family environmental factors in Indian and American urban upper-middle-class families.* Unpublished doctoral dissertation, Boston University.

Peck, R. F. & Havighurst, R. J. (1960). *The psychology of character development.* New York: Wiley.

Peters, R. S. (1970). Concrete principles and the rational passion. In *Moral education: Five lectures* (pp. 29–56). Cambridge, MA: Harvard University Press.

Piaget, J. (1965). *The moral judgment of the child.* New York: Free Press.

Pikas, A. (1961). Children's attitudes toward rational versus inhibiting parental authority. *Journal of Abnormal and Social Psychology, 62,* 315–321.

Rosenhan, D. L. (1969). Some origins of concern for others. In P. Mussen, J. Langer & M. Covington (Eds.), *Trends and issues in developmental psychology* (pp. 132–153). New York: Holt, Rinehart, and Winston.

Staub, E. (1978). *Positive social behavior and morality. Vol. 1: Social and personal influences.* New York: Academic.

Staub, E. (1979). *Positive social behavior and morality. Vol. 2: Socialization and development.* New York: Academic.

Whiting, B. & Whiting, J. W. M. (1975). *Children of six cultures.* Cambridge, MA: Harvard University.

Wynne, E. G. (Ed.). (1982). *Character policy: An emerging issue.* Washington, DC: University Press of America.

6

Moral Development and Personal Reliability: The Impact of the Family on Two Aspects of Moral Consciousness in Adolescence

Rainer Döbert
Freie Universität
Berlin, West Germany

Gertrud Nunner-Winkler
Max-Planck-Institut für Psychologische Forschung
Munich, West Germany

Within theories of cognitive development the role of the family has been rather neglected. In contrast to this we will address some of Piaget's ideas about the importance of certain aspects of family interaction that influence morality. This influence, we maintain, pertains not only to moral development but also to moral commitment or reliability, an aspect of moral consciousness which has received much less attention in cognitive research. After an introductory theoretical discussion we will use our own data to show that different aspects of the intrafamilial interaction are responsible for moral development and moral reliability.

THE ROLE OF PEERS AND THE FAMILY IN COGNITIVE THEORIES OF SOCIALIZATION

The role the family is said to play in the socialization of the child depends not the least on the learning mechanisms which different theories assume to be at work. For it is the learning mechanisms which describe in detail the form of the interaction between the child and the socialization milieu. Where a theory views the child mainly as a passive recipient or regards a mere reproduction or adoption of a given pattern of orientation as the product of socialization, the family must be held the dominant factor, for the family is the first, the affectively most important, and a very enduring factor of influence. Thus it is not surprising that learning and psychoanalytic theories of socialization, far apart as they may be in their other basic assumptions, do agree on this point: identification, internalization, or modeling guarantee a direct reproduction of parental patterns of orientation. Classical and instrumental conditioning allow the shaping of the child's personality in accordance with conscious or unconscious educational goals of the parent. In both cases the child's personality development can almost completely be deduced from a knowledge of the familial milieu.

In cognitive theories of development the situation is somewhat more complicated, since they impute to the child an active structuring of his or her environment and assume complex interactions between environmental stimulations and the child's coping strategies. This is not to deny that the learning mechanisms postulated by competing theories actually do take effect. They are, however, responsible only for the content aspect of patterns of orientation and thus do not concern that which cognitive theories are primarily aiming at, namely those, in principle, universal strategies of information processing (operations) which build on one another according to an ontogenetic developmental logic. Those developmental sequences of cognitive structures apparently can only be speeded up or slowed down, but not essentially changed through specific environmental conditions. Besides, a wide variety of rather different environmental experiences seems to lead to the same result: The concrete-operational stage normally reached by all, looks no different in children from authoritarian families than in those from anti-authoritarian families. This, of course, implies that the relationship between organism and learning milieu can only be defined in relatively formal terms. By and large the bare minimum is postulated: namely that there must be a differential in the complexity of the environment on the one hand, and subjective coping strategies on the other. On this very general level the interaction between organism and environment is seen as a process of equilibration in which the organism either changes its cognitive operations and adapts them to new experiences (accommodation) or else subsumes new experiences under categories already mastered (assimilation). Cognitive conflicts are the motor of development; they arise when the subject's expectations are disappointed and there is the danger of failing to adequately handle either the physical or the social reality. Failures impend when reality is not adequately conceptualized, that is, when in the field of socio-cognitive development, for example, the orientations of the significant others are not correctly identified and role-taking has been ineffective.

Role-taking and interactive experiences play the same role in socio-cognitive development as the propounding of hypotheses and the manipulation of physical objects in cognitive development. On this level of abstraction, adequate role-taking opportunities seem an obvious requirement of social learning milieus (Kohlberg, 1969). This general qualification of learning milieus, however, does not allow one to mark specific spheres of interaction as particularly relevant for socio-cognitive development: family, peer groups, and school all satisfy this

criterion equally. At the most it might be postulated that children should participate in many spheres of interaction so that their role-taking abilities are broadly
trained. These purely formal considerations are rather unsatisfactory theoretically, however. Thus, specifying more detailed causal connections between specific aspects of the development of a competence and certain traits of learning
milieus has been attempted. In the following we shall concentrate on those
considerations that are relevant for moral development.

In this field of research several adherents of Piagetian theory have pointed to
the preeminent importance of peer interaction, thereby, however, somewhat
simplifying Piaget's position. In connecting learning milieus and moral development, Piaget starts from one main developmental trend, namely the transition
from heteronomous to autonomous morality. In order to trace morally stimulating social conditions Piaget first attempts to clarify what types of relationships
have to hold between individuals for whom the rules of autonomous morality are
to be valid. The imperatives of autonomous morality are not perceived as external prescriptions. In case several individuals are concerned, this can only mean
that none of them can enforce one-sided regulations to which the others could not
agree. In short, reciprocal respect among all participants is presupposed. In
authoritarian relationships characterized by unilateral respect, autonomous morality cannot emerge. Since the child's relationship to his or her parents is one of
unilateral respect, Piaget does not see the family as a central cause of development. The child experiences reciprocal and cooperative relationships primarily in
the peer group which thus should be the prime cause of moral development. To
quote Piaget (1977): "Any relation with other persons, in which unilateral respect takes place, leads to heteronomy. Autonomy therefore appears only with
reciprocity, when mutual respect is strong enough to make the individual feel
from within the desire to treat others as he himself would wish to be treated" (p.
189).

Piaget sees peer interaction as a necessary condition for the acquisition of
moral autonomy, yet he certainly has not underestimated the role of the family
for the constitution and development of moral consciousness. First of all morality
is only constituted for children through their being integrated into the authority
structure of the familial system. The feeling of moral obligation necessary even
for autonomous morality (sticking to self-imposed duties) is based on unilateral
respect. As Piaget (1977) said: "Moral constraint is characterized by unilateral
respect. Now, as M. Bovet has clearly shown, this respect is the source of moral
obligation and of the sense of duty: Every command coming from a respected
person is the startingpoint of an obligatory rule" (p. 188). Were the relevance of
the family for moral consciousness reducible to this constitutive function, "family" still would be a variable of low explanatory power for individual differences
in levels of moral judgment. "Family" could help to explain only those cases in
which actors interpret reality almost exclusively in instrumental, amoral terms
(e.g., socio-psychopathy or extreme Machiavellianism).

Piaget, however, mentions quite a few traits of the family system that are egalitarian and thus apt to promote the development of autonomous morality. First of all, he points out that the parent-child relation is not merely one of unilateral respect and constraint but also one of affective reciprocity which forms the basis for the spontaneous taking over of moral norms characteristic of autonomous morality. In Piaget's (1977) own words:

> The relation between parents and children are certainly not only those of constraint. There is a spontaneous mutual affection, which from the first prompts the child to acts of generosity and even of self-sacrifice, to very touching demonstrations which are in no way prescribed. And here no doubt is the starting point for that morality of good which we shall see developing alongside the morality of right or duty, and which in some persons completely replaces it. The good is a product of cooperations (p. 188).

Furthermore it is to be noted that the parent-child interaction is structured not just by power but also by the parental orientation to binding standards. To the extent that parents keep these standards and make this plain to the child, the child experiences a further moment of equality and reciprocity in the family: The parents are subject to binding standards in the same way as the child (cf. Piaget, 1977). Thus, the created "atmosphere of reciprocal support and understanding" strengthens autonomous morality.

Also, it must not be forgotten that the parent-child interaction changes qualitatively with the increasing age of the child. The whole socialization process culminates, after all, in the child's detachment from the family of origin. Independence is granted to the adolescent as a quasi-ascribed status. Thus, as the child grows older, the parent-child interaction gradually takes on more egalitarian traits. As Piaget (1977) notes: "A sense of justice . . . can develop only through the progress made by cooperation and mutual respect—cooperation between children to begin with, and then between child and adult as the child approaches adolescence and comes, secretly at least, to consider himself as the adult's equal" (p. 308).

Another aspect of reciprocity that has especially been pointed out by Damon (1982) may be added to those egalitarian traits of the family system mentioned by Piaget. Piaget's criteria of equality and reciprocity are formulated in terms of manifest behavior, so that the use of parental authority per se must seem an expression of inequality. Damon calls this assumption into question by conceptualizing parental authority from the beginning as an example of legitimate domination. "The core of the concept of authority is the process of exchanging obedience against the exercise of accepted leadership qualities" (p. 119). Thus a principle of reciprocity can be recognized to underlie the manifestly very different actions of parents (command) and children (submission). To the extent that this conceptualization of the family as a case of 'legitimate domination' is valid, the peer group loses much of its significance for the explanation of moral development in cognitivistic theories. To generalize this consideration: It may well be doubtful whether the common identification of concrete institutions with specific organizational principles (equality/inequality) is at all theoretically meaningful. This of course would also apply to the institution of the peer group, which by definition seems to embody equality of rights. Here as well, as H. Bertram (1978) rightly pointed out, the manifest organizational principle need not take effect: Conformist compliance to group pressure may very well prevail instead of autonomous cooperation.

The egalitarian traits of the family system thus far mentioned refer exclusively to parent-child interaction. Our data, however, suggest one further aspect that is usually neglected in research projects in socialization theory. The common understanding is that only those parental actions, norms and educational goals that are imediately directed at the child are of importance for the child's socialization. In action systems, however, it is not only the participant actors who learn but also the observer (latent learning processes), and the child is a constant observer of the conjugal subsystem of the family. To the extent that the conjugal subsystem has egalitarian traits, the child is witness to a type of interaction that is supposed to promote autonomous morality. Piaget (1977) clearly did see this chance to learn through the mere observation of interactions: "It is obvious that since in our modern societies the common morality which regulates the relations of adults to each other is that of cooperation, the development of child morality will be accelerated by the examples that surround it" (p. 313). Piaget here draws on the Durkheimian diagnosis of developmental trends of modern societies (from "gerontocratic theocracy to egalitarian democracy"). Within the family this trend is manifested (among other things) by a weakening of the patriarchy in favor of modern partnership. Since the child's life is mainly oriented to the family it experiences this societal trend primarily as it manifests itself in his or her parents' interactions. This experience should be more influential the closer the affective tie between parent and child.

In summary, Piaget's theory does contain clues to an adequate consideration of the family's role in the moral development of the child. That is, Piaget's own emphasis on the preeminent importance of peer group interaction for the development of autonomous morality is by no means conclusive. Thus, Youniss' (1982) critique of mainstream socialization research and his inclusion of peer group interaction may very well have been legitimate and necessary. Still, it is overstating the case to imply that within the Piagetian tradition the family had no import as a cause of development.

HYPOTHESES ABOUT TWO ASPECTS OF MORALITY AND THEIR FAMILIAL ANTECEDENTS

Moral Reliability

Within congnitivist research the discussion of the impact of the family on morality centers nearly exclusively on the development of structures of moral judgment. What usually is omitted is the behavioral relevance of moral judgment. We assume that this is mediated by the commitment to moral rules which is manifested in *moral reliability,* a trait which is also a central criterion for the naive evaluation of people. Everyday language reveals the recognition that the mere knowledge of valid norms does not guarantee conformity in action. By reliability we mean the willingness and capacity to realize in principle accessible moral insights in action even if competing motives and ego goals have to be postponed. The qualification "in principle accessible" is necessary, since a deviation from a given level of competence is possible on two levels of consciousness. Under the pressure of amoral interest the actor may not only consciously betray his or her moral convictions and deviate, he or she may also, and this in fact will more often be the case, subconsciously try to come up with a definition of the situation that conforms to his or her interest, so as to cover up the violation of norms (rationalization, cf. Blasi, this volume; Döbert & Nunner-Winkler, 1978, 1980). Drawing upon Rest's recent systematization (1983), one could localize the concept of reliability as belonging to his third of four components of moral action. The actor has to define the situation cognitively (Component I), determine the ideal course of moral action (Component II), weigh this ideal course of action against alternatives guided by other interests and decide for the moral course of action (Component III), and finally actually behaviorally follow through on this decision (Component IV). Whenever an actor successfully completes all these stages we call him or her "reliable." An actor can be "unreliable" in two ways: (1) He or she can openly decide to give preference to nonmoral goals (Component III) or (2) the actor can subconsciously change the definition of the situation (Component I) in such a way that another course of action can be substituted for the ideal one (Component II). Both types of deviation from what the actor in a concrete situation could recognize to be the right action decision must be counted as indicators of a lack of reliability.

This dimension is analytically independent of the structural aspect of patterns of orientation that are dealt with in given typological or developmental models. These consider different conceptualizations of moral conflicts. Irrespective, however, of whether an individual follows an autonomous morality and comprehends valid moral rules as a self-imposed order or as an unquestionable tradition (cf. Kohlberg, 1969; Piaget, 1977) and irrespective of whether an individual, in solving moral conflicts, rigidly observes the rules or rather takes the needs of others involved into consideration (cf. B. Bertram, 1976; H. Bertram, 1978; Hoffman & Saltzstein, 1967; Saltzstein, 1976), the question is whether the actor will stick to the at least recognizable ideal course of moral action even under stress and will thus qualify as reliable. Since unreliable actors (subsequently referred to as "strategists") simply act instrumentally in the service of their self-interests, they may be confused with preconventional moral reasoners. This confusion arises from a misconceptualization of preconventional morality. If one reduces preconventionality to merely avoiding negative consequences or merely pursuing own interests, our strategists would indeed become identical with preconventionals. But conceptualizing preconventionality in this way would amount to excluding preconventional thinking from the scheme of *moral* development altogether. This statement, of course, presupposes that children can differentiate between situations in which moral rules are relevant and those which are morally neutral and in which self-interests can legitimately be realized. There can be no doubt that at least among adolescents a clear-cut distinction between moral and extra-moral (instrumental) realms has been achieved. Thus, preconventional moral thinking in this age group is *not* identical with bluntly instrumental action.[1] If it is instrumental action it is instrumental action which has been checked against another criterion, namely, that "you have to recognize that other people have their interests too" (Kohlberg, 1976, p. 34), interests which have to be respected. A preconventional can thus be either reliable or a strategist depending on his willingness to check the pursuit of interests against this second criterion. Despite the analytical independence of moral judgment level and moral reliability, we do expect a relationship between moral orientation and reliability. Thus, for example, a B-type moral orientation in which the needs of others are focused on (Colby, Gibbs, Kohlberg, Speicher-Dubin & Power, 1979) will favor reliability and not have its own interests stand out quite as prominently. In contrast, low reliability is to be expected in the case of Kohlberg's preconventional morality, since at that stage attention is focused primarily on costs of action for ego, thus the temptation to infringe on the rules is enhanced. On the other hand postconventionals should be more reliable, since insight into the moral necessity of certain regulations per se motivates one to act accordingly (competence motive). As will soon be shown, our data do support this hypothesis.

We shall now inquire into those *familial constellations* that favor reliability. For a variety of reasons we have assumed that the affective quality of the parent-child relationship (warmth) is of central importance for the development of reliability. First, a Piagetian line of argumentation (one that he, however, connected too closely with processes of structural development) can be modified and generalized. In the statement about the correlation of affective warmth and moral commitment quoted above, Piaget maintains that warm parent-child relationships primarily further the willingness to do good (i.e., supererogatory acts as contrasted with a mere fulfillment of duties). This implied link between an ethic of the supererogatory and autonomous morality is not compelling, however, and in fact it is not supported by the results of recent research in altruism. It has been shown that even very small children differ in the empathy and helpfulness displayed. These may be held to indicate stage-neutral motivational aspects of moral consciousness. Therefore, detaching Piaget's idea from the stage concept

---

[1]In our first study of the moral reasoning of adolescents we found it necessary to distinguish between five types of instrumental argumentation: genuine preconventional thinking, pure instrumentalism, segmental instrumentalism, protest instrumentalism, and subcultural instrumentalism. For a discussion cf. Döbert and Nunner-Winkler (1975, pp. 126–130).

and generalizing it beyond the sphere of the supererogatory, the following hypothesis may be advanced: Positive affective parent-child relations will lead to high reliability since the child will fulfill his duties for love of his parents and do even more than what is required. Of course this chain of reasoning almost reverses the function of reciprocal affective relationships in Piaget's theory of moral consciousness. Due to the affective bonds to his parents, the child allows himself to be implanted with non-egalitarian, dogmatic-heteronomous aspects of orientations. Additionally, taking into account that in warm parent-child relationships the child experiences unconditional and full acceptance will increase the plausibility of the above hypothesis. The child thus comes to know a stable environment in which he can rely upon having his needs considered. So the basis for an orientation to consensus that is constitutive of moral consciousness is laid. Since "basic trust" (Erikson, 1966) has been established, a thoroughgoing instrumentalizing of the social world is unlikely to occur.

We do not, however, assume, as do psychoanalytic thinkers, that 'basic trust' can definitely be established in early childhood. A supportive familial environment is necessary not just for the genesis, but also for the maintenance, of interpersonal trust and thus for the basis of reliability (especially in early adolescence). Even in adolescence a positive affective climate and the kind of parental control that, from the child's point of view, can be seen as an expression of interest and a sense of responsibility, can thus be expected to correlate with reliability. This correlation, however, will be weakened by opposing trends (detachment from the parents, gains in the level of reflectivity) typical for that age group.

The Level of Moral Judgment

The theoretical construct of *moral development* has been adopted from the Kohlberg tradition. In the following discussion of the relevance of *familial milieus* for the development of moral judgment structures, direct and indirect causal variables have to be distinguished. To illustrate this distinction let us again take up Piaget's hypothesis concerning the development of moral judgment. According to Piaget, parents, who in interacting with their child follow moral rules and not arbitrary impulses, further their child's development. Thse rule-guided socialization practices favor autonomous morality because the parent-child relationship displays egalitarian traits. Those parents make it quite clear that they themselves are bound to obey moral rules the same way the child is. We do not look upon this line of reasoning as very convincing. For what is actually more important is the fact that parents with such a style of interaction do work out the potential moral content of conflicts much more clearly. They tell the child: This situation comprises a moral problem. And by pointing out the moral relevance of conflicts, irrespective of the developmental level on which solutions are sought, they further the reliability of their child. The child comes to know when situations have moral relevance and that they have to be dealt with on moral terms. Still, insofar as the attainment of higher levels of moral judgment requires practice, i.e., a moralization of action conflicts, an indirect influence of those aspects of parental behavior can be assumed.

We expect a direct influence on development to result from the way parents treat each other. Especially important are parental styles of conflict resolution, since morality, by definition, deals with potential conflicts. In their conflict behavior parents can display to their child an egalitarian practice that, unlike the parent-child interaction, is not impaired by an almost insurmountable competence and power differential.[2] Now the implications of the egalitarian style of conflict resolution for developmental advancement do not result from the norm of equality per se; equality is found at all stages, though in different versions. The main impact results from the interactive consequences of following this norm: simple and one-sided solutions cannot be enforced. Instead, solutions that coordinate all interests have to be searched for by as inclusive a consideration of relevant situational parameters as possible. That is to say, equality is effective as a procedural principle that compels parents to strive for higher stage forms of conflict resolution. These considerations tie in well with basic assumptions of cognitivist theories; i.e., in these internal discrepancies, imbalances and contradictions (on the basis of an imputed need for consistency) count as the motor of development. In the realm of interactive experiences, discrepancies and contradictions arise when actors have to realize that prevailing regulations of social interaction are no longer functional so that social frictions arise that may even escalate into open conflicts. So social conflicts are for the development of interactive competence what mere logical contradictions are for cognitive development. Whenever these conflicts are approached with a consensual orientation, a strong pressure towards moral learning is produced. This consensual orientation is most easily rendered visible when differences in interests are openly acknowledged and fairly bargained; that is, negotiated in an egalitarian, situationally adequate manner without recourse to one-sided power strategies. In sum, egalitarian styles of conflict resolution are expected to lead to postconventional structures of judgment; power and status-oriented styles of conflict resolution and conflict suppression due to an exaggerated need for harmony block the transition to post-conventional structures.

METHOD

The following data are based on the (partial) coding of a study of 112 male and female adolescents between 14 and 22 years of age from different SES strata. We questioned the adolescents in 4–6 hour open-ended interviews about the follow-

---

[2]Kohlberg (1974) has clearly pointed out in his analysis of sex role stereotyping that from the child's perspective even biologically given differences in size may suffice to indicate differences in power.

ing topics: the course of adolescent crisis, experiences in school and on the job market, moral judgment, ego development, value orientations and political socialization, intrafamilial milieu and peer group involvement, coping and defense mechanisms, and aspects of ego-strength. Only a small part of the data collected will be reported here. (For other results cf. Döbert & Nunner-Winkler 1978, 1980, 1982).

Aspects of Moral Consciousness

Reliability and level of moral consciousness were coded using open-ended responses to the following three moral dillemmas:

1. There was a woman who had very bad cancer, and there was no treatment known to medicine that would have saved her. Her doctor knew that she had only about six months to live. She was in terrible pain, but she was so weak that a good dose of a pain-killer like ether or morphine would make her die sooner. She was delirious and almost crazy with pain, and in her calm periods she would ask the doctor to give her enough ether to kill her. She said she couldn't stand the pain and she was going to die in a few months anyway. (Colby, Gibbs, Kohlberg, Speicher-Dubin, & Power, 1979).

2. Johann and Karl are friends. Johann does not have a driver's license. One evening he "borrows" his parents' car and goes on a ride with Karl. In the darkness he overlooks a badly lit motor cycle and hits it. The motor cyclist falls off yet does not seem dangerously hurt.

3. You advertised your car to be sold. The first customer succeeded in bargaining an $80 reduction. You come to an agreement and you promise to keep the car for him while he returns home to get the money. In the meantime another customer shows interest in your car. He is willing to pay the full price.

Two types of questions were posed. First, we asked "should" questions, referring to the "ideal" course of moral action (Rest's Component II). Answers to the should questions (What should the doctor do? What should Johann do? What should Karl do? What should you do?) were used for coding Kohlberg's *levels of moral judgment*. Then we also asked "would" questions, referring to the hypothetically chosen course of action (Rest's Component III) (What would the doctor/the driver/you most like to do? What would he/you actually do?). Reactions to the would questions were used for coding *reliability*. In the last two dilemmas it is quite obvious that problems of reliability come into play. In this age group all subjects, irrespective of their level of moral judgment, know that hit-and-run offenses are inexcusable and that promises are to be kept. Hypothetically choosing a course of action that openly violates these norms strongly bespeaks of strategic orientations for even without incurring actual costs the actor gives preference to amoral interests. Indirect evidence for reliability does, however, also follow from the first dilemma. Subjects may simplify the dilemma by ignoring the woman's suffering in their definition of the situation, taking only the doctor's interests into account in their action decision. Such a one-sided selective definition of the situation indicates a lack of reliability, because ego goals are unconsciously realized.

Using this information about conscious or unconscious hypothetical violation of moral commands, two extreme groups were respectively defined. The strategist label was attached to subjects who gave clearly strategic reasons for action in at least two of the three dilemmas (actually most strategists gave instrumental reasons in all three). For example, in the car-selling dilemma: "I'd give it to the second. First, one looks after oneself"; "The second, that's more advantageous and there's been no contract. It's the first's own fault that he did not carry the money with him"; In the mercy-killing dilemma, deciding against the woman's plea: "I'd have to go to prison for that"; In the driver's escape dilemma: "Yes, I'd run off—it's his own fault, after all he had no lights." The reliable label was attached to those subjects who, in none of the three dilemmas, mentioned any instrumental reasons and in their choice of action flawlessly followed their moral judgments. Subjects were also classified as reliable if their deviation followed from a basically consensual orientation (car-selling: "If it were a question of $200, I'd wait for the first to return and again start bargaining"). Thus 16% (18) of the subjects were classified as strategists, 38% (43) as reliable and 46% (51) were neither full-fledged strategists nor consistent reliables.

Family Variables

For a description of the intrafamilial milieu we can refer to standardized instruments as well as to qualitative data. Unluckily, this part of the interview has been less extensive than might have been desirable. Thus these data are limited, since we did not want to stretch the interviews even longer and since only the adolescents, and not their parents, were questioned. We recorded aspects of the parent-child relationship, of the conjugal subsystem, as well as parental value orientations. For the measurement of the *parent-child relationship, open-ended questions* were used, such as: "On the whole—how do you get along with your parents? How do you parents punish you? If there is a fight—what is it about (clothes, appearance, going out) and how does it come off?" We also presented the subjects a shortened version of the *Shafer-Parent-Behavior Inventory* (cf. Stephenson, 1966). This instrument measures affective climate and control. It contains items such as: "My father/mother understands and supports me when I'm having problems." "My father/mother grants my own domains to me."

We also confronted subjects with several *conflict stories* typical for *parents and adolescents*; some of those were adopted from Steinkamp and Stief (1978); the others we devised ourselves. A sample conflict follows: "On weekends you sometimes wash your father's car. Afterwards you may always drive the car into the garage. All of a sudden you inadervently dent the fender at the gateway. What do your parents do in that situation?'' (all of the conflict stories are listed in Appendix A). The *relationship between the parents* was ascertained by *open-ended* questions, such as: ''Do your parents often/rarely quarrel? How do fights come off? Would you consider your parents' marriage a good one?'' We also gave the subjects a *list of typical parental strategies in conflict situations.* Each subject had to check all reactions typical of his father and mother. The list contained items such as: ''My father/mother eagerly tries to calm down my mother/father. My father/mother won't let my mother/father get a word in and flies at her/him right away. My father/mother gives in and comes round'' (the conflict strategies are listed in Appendix B).

Finally subjects had to indicate the importance they assumed their parents would place on a set of *value orientations,* such as ''I have led a decent life.'' ''I thoroughly enjoyed life.'' ''I made a lot of friends.'' etc. (cf. Schoole, 1973).

Evaluation

The qualitative material was coded in inductively extracted categories. Besides an analysis of differences in means between groups of subjects (postconventional vs. non-postconventional; strategists vs. reliables) a cluster analysis was computed, since this allows for the detection of different or even contrasting developmental paths. In the cluster analysis individuals are grouped according to their similarity in the independent variable (family constellations). For testing causal constellations for moral development we mainly used the percentage of postconventionals produced in different familial constellations. We also checked the distribution of individuals with advanced or retarded moral development (i.e., moral stage considerably above or below the average stage reached by their age-mates) over different family types.

RESULTS AND DISCUSSION

Relationship between Moral Stage and Moral Reliability

The results confirm the postulated *analytical* independence of reliability and moral development. The fact that reliables are distributed almost evenly over the three moral levels (even the preconventionals contribute one-third to the group of reliables) and that almost 40% of the strategists come from the conventional and postconventional levels, clearly demonstrate that reliability is not identical with higher moral development or strategic thinking with preconventionality (see Table 6.1). An independent confirmation of this analytical independence results from another piece of evidence we have concerning our subjects. In discussing

TABLE 6.1
Relationship between Level of Moral Judgment and Reliability
(Percentage)

	Preconventionals	Conventionals	Postconventionals	
Strategists	61	28	11	100
Reliables	33	37	30	100

whether to resist the military draft, 67% of the strategists, as compared to only 46% of the preconventionals use instrumental reasons only. Thus, more than half of the preconventionals in this context use moral arguments.

At the same time the hypothesized *empirical* relations between the two dimensions are borne out: the preconventionals contribute disproportionately to the group of strategists. On the other hand postconventionality and reliability are linked as had been expected. Of all the postconventionals, only 7% are strategists while 48% are reliables. Splitting up the postconventional subjects into two groups, one of which exclusively presents postconventional arguments and one that does so only occasionally, reveals that only half of the latter, but two-thirds of the former, are reliables. A finer grading of postconventional judgment will thus yield a closer correspondence to reliability, quite in line with Kohlberg's hypothesis of competence motivation. Structure apparently does contribute to reliability.

Parent-child Interaction and Reliability

Whatever the antecedents of reliability, it must be noted that there are decidedly more reliables than strategists. Even unfavorable family conditions, that is, still produce a minimum percentage of reliables. This suggests that human sociality is part of a relatively well protected basic make-up.

Affective Warmth.   Our core hypothesis that moral reliability is mainly dependent on affective warmth in the parent-child relationship could not fully be confirmed. In different family milieus (produced by a cluster analysis of responses to the *Shafer Parent-Behavior-Inventory*) reliables could be found in approximately equal proportions. The probability of strategists in the different family types, however, varied in the expected direction.

As Table 6.2 demonstrates, strategists are underrepresented in families that are characterized by a very good parent-child relationship (5%); they are overrepresented, however, in families, in which the affective relations between parent and child are disturbed and characterized by indifference, rejection and neglect of the child (47%).

TABLE 6.2
Relation between Parent–Child Relationships and Reliability

Parent–Child Relationship	n	Strategists	Reliables
1. Both parents positive affective/no or low control	56	5% (3)	38% (21)
2. At least 1 parent positive affective/and/or control	41	20% (8)	39% (16)
3. No parent positive affective and no control	15	47% (7)	40% (6)

The difference between row 1 and 3 for the strategists is significant, p = 0.001, Fisher exact text[3]

Parent-Child Conflicts.   What about the explanatory power of the other variables? Further determinants of moral reliability will most profitably be looked for where the regulation of at least potentially moralizable conflicts is at stake. In case of child misdemeanor, parents have to decide whether and how to punish the child and what rules and prohibitions to insist upon. Now the first striking result is that the general *open-ended question* about punishments typically imposed by parents shows no difference between reliables and strategists. Fifty-nine percent of the strategists and 56% of the reliables mention concrete sanctions (beating; ban on TV; ban on going out; cut down on allowances); 35% of strategists and 26% of reliables report verbal sanctions (talking, scolding, admonitions, indignation).

A more detailed analysis of parental reactions in the *parent-child-conflict stories* presented, however, does reveal differences that, taken together, point to a more intense moralization of the situation by parents of reliables. The largest differences are found in those two situations where a third party is hurt (cigarette machine and fight stories). In the cigarette machine story, 75% of the parents of reliables but only 33% of the parents of strategists evince moral-psychological reactions (difference significant at level .01), i.e., they were disappointed, inquire into the reasons for the offense and demand repair. In the fight story, 55% of the parents of the reliables as compared to only 31% ot the strategists are indignant, demand an apology and point out the unfairness of the act. In other situations differences are not quite as strong, but in the same direction.

It is also noteworthy that certain types of reactions are specific to parents of reliables and strategists, respectively. In the exam situation, e.g., the decision itself (child may go/ought to take books along/may not go) does not differentiate between the two groups of subjects. Yet only parents of reliables appeal to the child's own sense of responsibility, and clearly the taking of responsibility for the consequences of one's action is a central moral category. Also only parents of reliables demand apologies and reparation, which again means that they insist on

---

[3]For calculating the value of *p* in all tests for significance, the Fisher Exact Test has been used. In the following, p-values are reported intermittently just to give a hint at what size difference becomes significant.

the moral responsibility of the child. On the other hand, purely amoral parental reactions (e.g., cigarette machine: giving advice in case of detection) are only found among strategists. Furthermore it seems that parents of reliables also enforce their moral demands more strictly: In the conflict story about the volume of the radio, 43% of strategists' parents, but only 18% of the reliables' parents just continue scolding, even though scolding thus far had obviously been ineffective ("warned several times"). The parents of reliables, in contrast, do not tolerate their child's inconsiderateness: 44% (as compared to 21% of the parents of strategists) interfere physically, whereas 26% (as compared to 0%) pull out the plug or turn off the radio. But in contrast to the strategists' parents they do not take the radio away, indicating that, after all, they do consider the child able to control himself and not turn on the radio again.

This interpretation deviates somewhat from the interpretation Steinkamp and Stief (1978) give to their similar data, whereby they represent a whole trend of educational philosophy. This deviation concerns the understanding of the rationality of parental behavior. Whenever parental behavior is interpreted, some standard of appropriateness is made use of. These standards remain implicit or are even (shamefully?) covered up in most socialization studies. We want to at least expose the problematic. What we take to be an indicator of a legitimate insistence of parents upon their own interests (turning off the radio), Steinkamp and Stief (1978) see as a power-oriented reaction. Such power-oriented reactions let the child "primarily feel the negative consequences of his lapse" while "reasons are not given and an understanding of parental actions and their underlying expectations is not awakened," This "irrational exercise of authority," according to their theory, produces weak egos. Their interpretation is based on a very problematic conceptualization of rationality, one that in any case does not consider the situational adequacy of concrete actions. To give an example: Much to their surprise they find in their study that parental sanctioning techniques vary strongly across different situations. This they take for "inconsistent problem solving behavior," and as an indicator of a lack of a "strategy of problem solving" (p. 158). We, however, find it more plausible to take just this flexibility as an expression of the rationality of parental socialization practices. The situations used by Steinkamp and Stief are so different that using the same socialization techniques over and over again cannot be held to indicate situational adequacy, which is certainly one aspect of rationality. One may wonder whether sociological theory may claim to present criteria of rationality that obviously fail to grasp the complex functioning of everyday intuitions about rationality. In our study, the vast majority of those adolescents who successfully had mastered the crisis of detachment said that, on the whole, parental prohibitions and punishments were quite reasonable and just, although at the time they themselves had violently resisted them. We think that sociological theorizing cannot just ignore these kinds of appraisals.

All in all, parents of reliables recur to moral standards in conflicts with their children and by that demonstrate that the situations are analyzable from the moral point of view. Thus the child becomes sensitive to morality and his or her reliability increases. Theoretically this means that one of the determinants of moral consciousness works differently than had been assumed by Piaget: The equal orientations of parents to standards does not directly further moral development, but rather moral commitment, i.e., reliability. Thus, although affective variables do contribute to the explanation of reliability, what does seem more important is the moralization of the situation, i.e., the moral climate, and that means that even here cognitive factors operate. These factors would be classified with Piaget's empirical, rather than structural, aspect of cognition, however: The parents tell the child only that moral standards (of whatever stage) *do* apply to a given situation.

Parental Value-Orientations, the Parents' Relationship and the Child's Reliability

Now, are there any other aspects of the family's interactive milieu besides the quality of the parent-child interaction that might explain the probabilities of strategists vs. reliables? One might think of variables that characterize the parents' personality and the quality of their relationship. For example, parents who respect each other as moral persons present to the child a model of moral thinking and action. On the other hand, it is not very plausible that this more latent indirect influence on behavior should be any stronger or even as strong as parents' direct socialization behavior. In fact, however, the pertinent results are as powerful as those reported before.

Parental Value Orientations.   The responses to the list of value orientations show that fathers of strategists esteem hedonistic-egocentric values highly. They deem it definitely important "to take delight in the beautiful things in life" (47% of the strategists' parents vs. 10% of parents of reliables think it highly important; conversely: 7% of the strategists' parents vs. 27% of parents of reliables think it unimportant); "to enjoy life fully" (important: 47% vs. 15%; unimportant: 13% vs. 44%); and strategists' fathers deem it quite important "to gain all sorts of experiences." Strategists' fathers also have a more conventional occupational role orientation; e.g., they want to "advance on their job and enjoy general prestige." Conversely, parents of reliables attach more importance to "making many friends" (important: parents of reliables 32% vs. 7% of strategists' parents, p = .02; unimportant: 24% vs. 60%); and "to being there for others whenever they need help" (important: 51% vs. 10%, p = .14; unimportant: 10% vs. 24%). If one adds to this finding the fact that fathers of reliables combine their social orientation with a strong need for autonomy (they "do not want to put up with anything from anybody" and take care "never to need other people") one may conclude that they have reached a higher level of ego development than the strategists' fathers.

Fewer items differentiate between mothers and the differences are smaller. As compared to mothers of reliables, the strategists' mothers—though not employed at a higher rate—attach more importance to the occupational sphere ("advance on the job," "work as fulfillment") and less to traditional female role attributes ("doing everything for the family," "beautiful things," "religious convictions"). The individual differences noted between parents of strategists and reliables may not seem particularly impressive—taken together, however, they do give a consistent picture. Strategists are growing up in a familial milieu in which interpersonal relations are undervalued and the pursuit of self-centered goals is emphasized. Thus, irrespective of the level of structural learning, it is made more plain to reliables on the content side that living together, and with it the realm of morality, play an important role in human life.

Conflict between Parents.   Differences also showed up in the quality of the parental relationship as indicated in the answers to the *open-ended questions* about the marriage relationship. Reliables rate their parents' marriage higher (50% poor or broken marriages of the strategists' parents in contrast with 26% poor or broken marriages of the parents of the reliables). Similarly, conflict behavior as measured by the standardized *list of conflict strategies* (Appendix B) differs among parents of reliables and strategists. Arranging the conflict strategies in the order of their relative frequency and constructing a hypothetical dialogue between fathers and mothers reveals quite a clear picture: Taking just the most frequently used strategies the following pattern for the parents of strategists will result: "Father will not give in and keeps starting all over again" (50%); "Mother attempts to appease father" (63%); "Father furiously leaves the apartment" (43%); "Mother cries" (63%); "Father won't let mother get a word in edgewise" (43%); "Mother gives in and comes round" (50%). For the reliables the hypothetical scene would read as follows: "Mother won't give in" (43%); "Father does not listen any more" (38%); "Mother starts talking of something else" (33%); "Father tries hard to appease mother" (33%); "Mother gives in and comes round" (30%); "Father starts talking of something else" (30%).

The differences in those two patterns are striking: Parents of strategists only use complementary strategies, whereby the father enforces his will by all means and mother exclusively employs submissive strategies. Parents of reliables, in contrast, pretty much use corresponding strategies with the intention of either reaching consensus or—if this is not possible—of cooling. A cluster analysis of parental conflict strategies gives a more differentiated picture that does, however, confirm first impressions. The cluster analysis produced five types of family constellations:

1. *Incomplete families:* comprising families without father or without mother.

2. *Families with an authoritarian father*: Father "keeps starting all over again," "won't let mother get a word in edgewise," while mother "gives in," "comes round," "cries," i.e. employs sex role specific appeasement strategies.

3. *Mother-dominant families*: Mother "won't speak to my father till he comes round," "won't give in," "won't listen any more." Father "tries very hard to appease mother," "starts talking of something else after a while."

4. *Families with few conflicts in which rational conflict-solving strategies are used symmetrically with the intention of reaching consensus*: Father/mother "wait till they both have calmed down," "try hard to appease the other."

5. *Families with intense symmetrically staged conflicts*: Father/mother "yell at each other," "won't give in," "keep starting all over again."

The distribution of strategists and reliables over the different types of family constellations is presented in Table 6.3. This distribution suggests that—irrespective of the level of moral judgment—the likelihood of instrumental vs. moral orientations depends upon whether and to what extent parents in conflicts still do consider a common good. A high percentage of strategists is produced in *families with an authoritarian father* (39% vs. 8% in all other complete families, p = .02) and in *incomplete families*. By his behavior the father in group 2 signifies that what matters is enforcing one's own will and that the legitimacy of reciprocal wants need not even be reflected upon. He acts egocentrically and thus offers a model for acting strategically rather than morally. The high percentage of strategists in the *incomplete families* may indicate that children interpret their parents' divorce as a breach of trust towards the child and as totally revoking any willingness to come to an understanding. Also, several subjects reported that their single parent, in looking for a new partner, found having a child to be quite troublesome. On the other hand this constellation does produce at least an average quota of reliables. This may be due to the fact that children perceive their parents as especially committed and creditable if parents take their educational duties seriously in that difficult situation. Reliables, in contrast, are more fre-

TABLE 6.3
Relation between Parental Styles of Conflict Resolution and
Reliability

Groups	n	Strategists		Reliables	
1. Father/mother missing	9	44%	(4)	33%	(3)
2. Authoritarian father	18	39%	(7)	22%	(4)
3. Dominant mother	29	3%	(1)	41%	(12)
4. Few/symmetrical conflicts	45	11%	(5)	36%	(16)
5. Open staging of conflicts	11	9%	(1)	73%	(8)
	112	16%	(18)	38%	(43)

quent in mother-dominant families and especially in families with open conflicts. *Mother dominance* in group 3 obviously means something different than the authoritarian dominance of the father in group 1: Total submission is not required. No doubt, the mother dominates, yet it is specific for this constellation that conjugal harmony keeps being reestablished by masking rather than by settling factual disputes. Mother's dominance may also be held to remain embedded in the sex-specific family orientation that per se represents an altruistic element. The parents with *open conflicts* demonstrate to their children that conflicts can be settled in an open and violent manner without jeopardizing the basic loyalty of the relationship. Each has the same right to introduce his or her own needs; thus the stage-independent minimal condition of morality, namely reciprocal respect towards each other, is guaranteed. Despite violent conflicts, parents thus present to the child a model of a relationship that is subject to moral rules and incorporates fairness.

The qualitative data indicate that a model of parental fairness impresses adolescents even when they themselves have vehement conflicts with parents in the course of an intense crisis of adolescence. For example, one subject painted a rather derogatory picture of his parents and reported escalating rows that ended in his being thrown out. Even so, he picked up moral principles from the example his parents gave:

I: Could you briefly describe how you're getting along with your parents?

S: Right now? Well, I've already said that they find me ridiculous and think I have no character, since right now I'm on a crazy trip and they hope that one day I may return to normal social life and lead the same Philistine life they do, maybe even more so. And secretly they dream that one day I will become terrifically rich, so as to allow them a decent old age—which of course I'd never do.

I: Have you had specific conflicts with your parents, recently?

S: Of course. For 25 years my father has been an arse-crawler in the company; he's always pussyfooted, and that's caused dissonance; because I've always done what I thought and said what I thought and I've always been plain-spoken.

I: Would you raise your kids the way your parents did—or would you bring them up differently?

S: Ha, ha—180 degrees around.

I: Did your parents quarrel often, sometimes, never?

S: Well, sometimes—but never a real fight; in their direct relationship, in their marriage I've never noticed that they've had conflicts, so that one of them would have beat it or something like that, or that they hit each other, never. In that respect I've really gotten quite a few ethical principles from home, as far as that goes.

I: Who do you take after more—your mother or your father?

S: If one can at all talk about taking after—then I got a couple of negative things from the old man; positive things—well, that's difficult to say,—positive things at most from the good sides, from the companionship of the old folks, there I've gotten something from both.

The relatively strong influence of the parental conflict behavior on the child's reliability came as a surprise. We had primarily expected an influence of this variable on the level of the moral judgment of the child. This—as will be seen—really is the case. Now, of course, an influence on structural development presupposes that situations are at all interpreted from a moral point of view and this pertains to reliability. Thus parental conflict-solving behavior has an impact on moral reliability and moral development at the same time. Now taking all the results on reliability together a rather consistent picture emerges: The explicit moralization of educational conflicts, the strong interpersonal-ethical value orientations, the fair way in which the marital partners treat each other and, even in conflicts, respect each other as persons constitute a moral learning climate that has its main impact on the cognitive realm; yet what is learned is nothing structural. The child is only made to see—via content learning—that action problems are to be approached with moral categories (irrespective of stage level). This conceptualization of a moral learning climate clearly differs from Kohlberg's conception of the moral community. For the latter, responsible participation in decision processes is constitutive. Besides the moral community is supposed to be a main motor of development.

The Bearing of the Intrafamilial Milieu on the Level of Moral Consciousness

A moral climate may be a necessary condition for moral development but it certainly is not a sufficient one. Our data indicate that additional and more specific conditions are required for higher levels of moral reasoning to appear. Table 6.4 confirms this. A comparison of the percentage of postconventionals and reliables in mother-dominant families reveals that this family constellation does produce a relatively high quota of reliables, yet it has the lowest quota of postconventionals. Here we thus find the structure-independent path to reliability that is implied in the analytical independence of development and reliability. This group also has the highest quota of mothers to whom their children attribute clearly family-centered value orientations ("I've done my utmost for my family"; 85% mothers in this group vs. 76% of all reliables vs. 59% of all strategists). In these families the mother offers a model of altruistic self-sacrifice and can also push corresponding patterns of behavior through, because she has the dominant role in the family. This form of mother dominance renders a bargaining of interests practically superfluous. The binding norm for the mother as well as for other members of the family is that individual interests are to be subordinated to the common good without ado. On the postconventional level, however, system interests and individual interests are well balanced and individual interests precisely are not reduced to the common good.

In this respect, interactions of parents in groups 4 and 5 differ from those in group 3: Equality in the parental relationship presupposes that the common good

TABLE 6.4
Level of Moral Judgment and Parental Strategies of Conflict
Resolution

Group	n	Postconventionals	Reliables
1. Father/mother missing	9	11% (1)	33% (3)
2. Authoritarian father	18	17% (3)	22% (4)
3. Dominant mother	29	10% (3)	41% (12)
4. Few/symmetrical conflicts	45	36% (16)	36% (16)
5. Open staging of conflicts	11	64% (7)	73% (8)
	112	27% (30)	38% (43)

has to be agreed upon every time anew. This explains why egalitarian styles of conflict resolution on the part of the parents do stimulate postconventional thinking: an above average quota of postconventionals can only be found in groups 4 and 5 (41% vs. only 13% in the remaining complete families). Thus Piaget's hypothesis that an egalitarian environment is highly important for moral development is borne out to some degree. Yet at the same time the difference in the percentages of postconventionals in groups 4 and 5 (36% vs. 64% in Table 6.4) indicates that even more important than egalitarian relationships per se are their interactive consequences. If equality were the main factor, why should a rather conflict-free symmetrical relationship produce less postconventionals than highly conflictual symmetrical relationships? The difference between group 4 and group 5 could be explained by taking into account that parents in group 5 quite often have to ''invent'' solutions for their conflicts that balance diverging interests. Thereby the functions of interactive rules become transparent. This consequence of an egalitarian relationship is less frequently called for in group 4: On the whole parents already are in an agreement so that complex interactive coordinations need not be accomplished forever anew. There is still another, perhaps even more plausible interpretation of these data: The chaotic milieu produced by the parents' continual quarreling initiates thinking processes in their children that lead to the invention of better (hypothetical) patterns of interaction. In this case we are dealing with children with an ego development that surpasses that of their parents. The assessment of parental socialization techniques given in the discussion of parent-child conflict stories suggests that at least for some subjects this is the case. In either case, however, it holds true that the main effects produced are due to the *procedural and not the content aspect of an egalitarian style of conflict regulation,* namely due to the consequences this style produces for all involved and not due to its mere existence.

This style of interaction evidently proves to be a motor of development not just at the threshold between conventional and postconventional thinking: A classification of subjects at all stages according to whether their moral development is more retarded or more advanced than that of their age-mates shows that

56% of the advanced and 26% of the retarded subjects come from symmetrical families, while only 39% of the advanced as contrasted with 68% of the retarded subjects come from asymmetrical families. The assumption that it is the form of the interaction process that is decisive for development finds another—indirect—confirmation in the fact that content variables, e.g., parental value orientations and positive affective parent-child relations, are of practically no import for the development of postconventional structures.

In sum, as Piaget had hypothesized, egalitarian marriage relationships further moral development, but the concept of equality has to be differentiated. There is a content and a procedural aspect of equality. The content aspect seems to contribute somewhat to moral development but equality fully unfolds its dynamics only through its procedural implications. It is further to be noted that there is a path to reliability which seems even to hamper moral development. Speculatively one may suggest that the altruistic self sacrifice of dominant mothers prevents children from delimiting their ego clearly against the familial system, a process necessary for postconventional thinking.

FINAL COMMENT

By and large our hypotheses stood the test and a rather consistent picture can be said to have emerged. It is especially worthy of note that according to our results, even reliability seems to be strongly dependent on cognitive factors. But it depends not primarily on competence as maintained by Kohlberg, but above all on the stage-independent ability to conceive of situations as moralizable. Reliability thus is shaped by both of those main forms of non-heritable knowledge distinguished by Piaget (1967)[4]: mainly by empirical and secondarily also by structural aspects of knowledge. Surely it is also striking that variables not dealing directly with parent-child interaction (value orientations, parental styles of conflict resolution) were by no means less effective than those parental actions that were directly aimed at the child (affective parent-child relations, socialization techniques).

We believe that an explanation of the latter result must refer to the particularity of the adolescence phase. For one thing, it is obvious that the struggle for autonomy characteristic of that developmental phase might lead to a kind of reactance on the part of the adolescent. The parental socialization techniques may seem to threaten the child's independence and the child may attempt to evade all control. Besides, the ability to reflectively grasp everyday life is growing in that developmental phase. The intrafamilial milieu forfeits its causal

---

[4]In a different context we have encountered this concurrence of both types of knowledge in the form of an interplay of formal and material role-taking (cf. Döbert & Nunner-Winkler, 1982).

efficacy to the extent that the adolescent enters an extended living space, escapes the naive embeddedness in given family constellations and gains reflective distance towards his own home. The likelihood of such reflective breaking of interaction patterns is increased by the spread of sociological knowledge about favorable, as opposed to unfavorable, socialization milieus. Given parental behaviors are no longer taken as a matter of course, but are questioned for their adequacy. Shortcomings can be blamed on the parents themselves. Both factors, i.e., the heightened reflectivity due to psychic growth processes and the cultural legitimizing of critique directed towards parental socialization styles, taken together result in a weakening of the causal effectiveness of processes that up until then had determined behavior. They can be objectified, countered and thus made ineffective. Indirect influences, in contrast, are much harder to see through. Parental conflict solving styles, for example, are neither focused upon in public discussion nor held by the socializee to be of direct concern to himself.

Appendix A

Parent-child conflict stories

1. *Car washing:* On weekends you sometimes wash your father's car. Afterwards you may always drive the car into the garage. All of a sudden you inadvertently dent the fender at the gateway. What do your parents do in that situation?
2. *Radio:* You turn your radio (record-player) on full volume at night. The noise bothers your parents who want to watch TV. They have already urged you several times to turn the volume down. (Steinkamp & Stief 1978).
3. *Exam:* After the Easter vacation an important exam is awaiting you, and you are poorly prepared for it. You had planned on a little trip with friends for the holiday. Your parents want you to use the time to study for the exam. You, however, do not want to forgo the trip.
4. *Being late:* You promised to be home at ten o'clock, but you don't come in until midnight.
5. *Cigarette machine:* Your parents find out that you and a couple of your friends broke open a cigarette machine.
6. *Fighting:* Your parents are told that a couple of times you've beaten up a feeble boy from the neighborhood (Steinkamp & Stief, 1978)

Appendix B

Conflict solution strategies

1. My father/mother will not speak to my mother/father any more until she/he is willing to give in.
2. My father/mother furiously leaves the apartment and when he/she returns everything is O.K. again.
3. My father/mother tries hard to appease my mother/father.
4. My father/mother will not come round and keeps starting all over again.
5. My father/mother stops listening and gets busy with other things.
6. My father/mother waits till both have calmed down and then attempts to get things straight in a cool talk.
7. My father/mother won't let my mother/father get a word in edgewise and flies at her/him right away.
8. My father/mother after a while starts talking of something else as if nothing had happened.
9. My father/mother gives in and comes round.
10. My father/mother says that that's enough and he/she'd soon beat it.
11. My father/mother yell at each other.
12. My father/mother tries to win the children over to his/her side.
13. My father/mother tries to relieve tension by a joke.
14. My father/mother makes sarcastic and scornful remarks.
15. My father/mother hits the bottle.
16. My father/mother bursts into tears.
17. My father/mother produces physical complaints (headache, stomachache, heart-attacks).

18. My father/mother takes it out on the children.
19. My father/mother acts as if nothing had happened, but you can tell that he/she is annoyed.

ACKNOWLEDGMENTS

This is a revised version of an article originally published under the title: Moralisches Urteilsniveau und Verlässlichkeit. Die Familie als Lernumwelt für kognitive und motivationale Aspekte des moralischen Bewusstseins in der Adoleszenz, in G. Lind, H. A. Hartmann, R. Wakenhut (Eds.), *Moralisches Urteilen und soziale Umwelt*. Weinheim, Basel: Beltz Verlag (1983). We would like to thank the editors and the publisher for the permission to publish the translation of this article in this volume.

We deeply appreciate the help given by the heads of the Munich Labor Office and specially by Mrs. Griesang and Dr. Popp in recruiting subjects. Also, we would like to thank O. Nunner for doing statistical calculations. For critical remarks and helpful suggestions we owe thanks to M. Berkowitz.

REFERENCES

Bertram, B. (1976). *Typen moralischen Urteilens*. Unpublished doctoral dissertation, University of Düsseldorf, West Germany.

Bertram, H. (1978). *Gesellschaft, Familie und moralisches Urteil. Analysen kognitiver, familialer and sozialstruktureller Bedingungszusammenhänge moralischer Entwicklung*. Weinheim, Basel: Beltz.

Colby, A. Gibbs, J. C., Kohlberg, L., Speicher-Dubin, B., & Power, C. (1979). *Assessing moral stages: A Manual*. Cambridge, MA: Center for Moral Education, Harvard University.

Damon, W. (1982). Zur Entwicklung der sozialen Kognition des Kindes. Zwei Zugänge zum Verständis von sozialer Kognition. In W. Edelstein & M. Keller (Eds.), *Perspektivität und interpretation Zur Entwicklung des sozialen Verstehens* (pp. 110–145). Frankfurt: Suhrkamp.

Döbert, R. & Nunner-Winkler, G. (1975). *Adoleszenzkrise und Identitätsbildung*. Frankfurt: Suhrkamp.

Döbert, R. & Nunner-Winkler, G. (1978). Performanzbestimmende Aspekte des moralischen Bewusstsein. In Portele (Ed.), *Sozialisation und Moral* (pp. 101–121). Weinheim, Basel: Beltz.

Döbert, R. & Nunner-Winkler, G. (1980). Jugendliche 'schlagen über die Stränge.' Abwehr- und Bewältigungsstrategien in moralisierbaren Handlungssituationen. In L. Eckensberger & R. Silbereisen (Eds.), *Entwicklung sozialer Kognitionen: Modelle, Theorien, Methoden, Anwendung* (pp. 267–298). Stuttgart: Klettcotta.

Döbert, R. & Nunner-Winkler, G. (1982). Formale und materiale Rollenübernahme: Das Verstehen von Selbstmordmotiven im Jugendalter. In W. Edelstein & M. Keller (Eds.), *Perspektivität und Interpretation* (pp. 320–374). Frankfurt: Suhrkamp.

Erikson, E. H. (1966). Wachstum und Krisen der gesunden Persönlichkeit. In E. H. Erikson (Ed.), *Identität und Lebenszyklus* (pp. 51–107). Frankfurt: Suhrkamp.

Hoffman, M. L. & Saltzstein, H. D. (1967). Parent discipline and the child's moral development. *Journal of Personality and Social Psychology, 5*, 45–47.

Kohlberg, L. (1969). Stage and sequence: The cognitive-developmental approach to socialization. In D. Goslin (Ed.), *Handbook of socialization theory and research* (pp. 347–480). Chicago: Rand-McNally.

Kohlberg, L. (1974). Analyse der Geschlechtsrollen-konzepte und-attitüden bei Kindern unter dem Aspekt der kognitiven Entwicklung. In L. Kohlberg, (Ed.), *Zur kognitiven Entwicklung des Kindes* (p. 334–471). Frankfurt: Suhrkamp.

Kohlberg, L. (1976). Moral stages and moralization: The cognitive-developmental approach. In T. Lickona (Ed.), *Moral development and behavior: Theory, research, and social issues* (pp. 31–53). New York: Holt, Rinehart & Winston.

Piaget, J. (1967). *Biologie et connaissance.* Paris: Edition Gallimard.

Piaget, J. (1977). *The moral judgment of the child.* Baltimore: Penguin Education Books.

Rest, J. R. (1983). Morality. In P. Mussen (Ed.), *Handbook of child psychology,* Volume III 4th edition. (pp. 556–629). New York: Wiley.

York: Wiley.

Saltzstein, H. D. (1976). Social influence and moral development. A perspective on the role of parents and peers. In T. Lickona (Ed.), *Moral development and behavior: Theory, research and social issues* (pp. 253–265). New York: Holt, Rinehart and Winston.

Schoole, C. (1973). Social antecedents of adult psychological functioning. *American Journal of Sociology, 78,* 299–322.

Steinkamp, G. & Stief, W. H. (1978). *Lebensbedingungen und Sozialisation. Die Abhängigkeit von Sozialisationsprozessen in der Familie von ihrer Stellung im Verteilungssystem ökonomischer, sozialer und kultureller Ressourcen und Partizipationschancen.* Opladen: Westdeutscher Verlag.

Stephenson, G. M. (1966). *The Development of conscience.* London: Routledge & Kegan Paul.

Youniss, J. (1982). Die Entwicklung und Funktion von Freundschaftsbeziehungen. In W. Edelstein & M. Keller (Eds.), *Perspektivität und Interpretation Zur Entwicklung des sozialen Verstehens* (pp. 78–109). Frankfurt: Suhrkamp.

7 The Role of Affective Processes in Moral Judgment Performance

Susanne Villenave-Cremer
Lutz H. Eckensberger
University of the Saarland, Fed. Rep. Germany

This article addresses the interrelation between cognitive structuring and dealing with affects in conflict situations as well as with the influence affects may have on the performance of moral judgments. It is assumed that moral discussions of conflict situations implying high ego-concern are more likely to induce defense mechanisms than those situations which are rather ego-distant, and that defense mechanisms, according to Haan (1977), inhibit the unfolding of moral competence. Since life conflicts are more ego-involving than hypothetical moral dilemmas, we expect that deficiences of moral stage scores in real-life conflicts may be due to defense processes, while more equilibrated scores in both types of conflict may be due to coping.

Several hypotheses are examined in the following study by comparing moral stage patterns (in real life conflicts vs. hypothetical dilemmas) with directly, independently measured coping/defense indicators in real-life conflicts. At least indirectly, earlier studies have revealed some empirical evidence that differences between moral judgments in real-life conflicts and moral judgments in hypothetical conflicts correlate with emotional disturbance in those cases where the real-life moral score falls below the hypothetical moral score (Gilligan & Belenky, 1980; Haan, 1975; Selman & Jaquette, 1978). These studies are, however, based either on "extreme" situations, even on critical life events (political activities: Haan, 1975; abortion: Gilligan & Belenky, 1980) or on deviant subjects (Selman & Jaquette, 1978). Furthermore, they follow a rather nonspecific relation between moral stages and affective processes. The research presented here focuses on usual daily-life conflicts which are compared to hypothetical moral judgments, and in addition, tries to benefit from a recent attempt to explicate the "deep structure" in the stages of moral development (Eckensberger

& Reinshagen, 1980) in terms of action structures. Although this reformulation of Kohlberg's theory closely follows his empirical basis, it differs in important aspects from his stage interpretations, aspects which are especially fruitful if the relationship between cognitive structures and affective processes is considered.

The clarification of the role of affective processes in moral judgment has implications, not only for the theory of moral development in general, but especially for the domain of moral intervention research. Intervention studies up to now have either attempted to improve moral reasoning through discussions of moral dilemmas or through improvements of the justice structure and level of democracy in prisons and school-settings (cf. Berkowitz, this volume; Kohlberg, this volume; Oser, 1981a; Power, this volume; Power & Higgins, 1981). They do not aim at the improvement of *theoretical* moral judgment but rather at the improvement of moral judgment *in real life contexts*. Given the empirical evidence concerning the influence of affective processes on moral judgment cited earlier, however, these strategies are deficient as long as they are primarily concerned only with cognitive processes.

Whether a subject is able to apply his or her moral competence to a real-life context seems not only to be a structural problem but rather a problem of affectively dealing with personal needs and self-interests in a situation. Therefore, it is no wonder that the usual cognitive interventions succeed much more in theoretical moral judgment than in moral discussions of real-life conflicts (Oser, 1981b). If these arguments can furthermore be affirmed empirically, it would suggest that interventions should focus more on the discrepancies between affective needs, self-interests, and moral considerations if they are to make possible an optimal unfolding of moral competence. This, surely, is a proposition that contradicts Kohlberg's tendency to theoretically and methodologically exclude affective processes from analysis, and consequently from intervention studies, as well.

THE RELATIONSHIP BETWEEN COGNITION AND AFFECT IN MORAL JUDGMENT

Affects may have considerable influence on moral judgment with regard to (a) *the constitution of moral judgment in ontogenesis* and (b) *the realization of moral competence in a concrete situation.*

In Kohlberg's theory of moral development both aspects have been recognized, but not discussed or considered in adequate detail. In fact, in order to work out the "purely" cognitive structural component of moral judgment, Kohlberg tends to radically exclude affective aspects from theoretical and empirical analysis. With regard to ontogeny Kohlberg (1969, p. 349) emphasizes the constitutional aspect of affect on moral development in one of his fundamental postulates. "Affective development and functioning and cognitive development and functioning are not distinct realms. 'Affective' and 'cognitive' development are parallel, they represent different perspectives and contexts in defining structural change.'' This postulate, at first sight, corresponds exactly to Piaget's (1981a) proposition about the relationship of affect and cognition. If you look carefully, however, you recognize that Kohlberg does not expand this concept any further in the elaboration of his theory. He merely mentions, for instance, that empathy is the emotional presupposition of moral judgment (Kohlberg, 1969) without any further explication of its function for moral development. By contrast, Piaget (1932/1981b) conceptualizes moral judgment in accord with the above-cited parallelism postulate as a result of the interaction between affect and cognition. He denies that cognitions are separable from affects in moral judgments. Affect and cognition in interaction both constitute moral development.

With regard to the microprocess of a simple moral judgment, the impact of affect on the subject's ability to realize his moral structure in moral conflict is recognized by Kohlberg, at least on the methodological level, in that he minimizes the influence of emotion and self-interest by giving subjects hypothetical moral dilemmas that should exclude considerable personal involvement in the conflict. This procedure is probably based upon the assumption that affective needs and self-interests may deteriorate the performance of moral judgment (Döbert & Nunner-Winkler, 1978). Kohlberg, in this way, hopes to come to an optimal approximation of the cognitive structural component of morality (competence), again by tentative exclusion of affect. Although Kohlberg's method may reduce the probability of interfering affects, it cannot guarantee the subject's impartiality because ego involvement may occur even in a hypothetical dilemma if there is any reactivation of conflict experience in the subject. Without a doubt, however, the subject should be *relatively* less concerned by a hypothetical dilemma than by a real-life conflict. For example, you may assume that a medical doctor is personally concerned by the Kohlberg's hypothetical mercy-killing dilemma (Colby, Kohlberg, Gibbs, & Lieberman, 1983, p. 79) because of his professional experience. Nevertheless, he will be even more concerned if he is thinking about a similar conflict which he has experienced or is currently experiencing himself.

Nevertheless, the amount of ego-concern and the impact of affective processes can hardly be assessed in any individual case without including these variables in the analysis. This is especially true for real-life conflicts, but, in a limited sense, for hypothetical conflicts, too. Thus, to come to an adequate comprehension of practical moral judgment we have to ask in which way and to what degree affective processes influence moral judgment performance.

Haan (1977) and Döbert and Nunner-Winkler (1978, 1980) investigate this problem. They use ego-psychology based concepts of coping and defense, two distinct forms of dealing with affects, in order to clarify the impact of affect on moral judgment. The underlying dynamic of these ego-processes can be distinguished from the dynamic underlying moral competence: The latter is based on the *subject's attempt to maintain a consistent self*. There are various situations that can threaten the consistency of the self. But what, precisely, are threatening aspects in the case of moral conflict? According to Döbert and Nunner-Winkler (1978) these are *discrepancies between moral consciousness* (what one thinks one *should* do) and *action impulse* (how one really acts or how one thinks one *would* act). In other words, it concerns the subject's dealing with unacceptable impulses of action. In the case of defense the subject will obscure these discrepancies by manipulating certain situational aspects in his argumentation.

The defense mechanisms include "some element of negating intersubjective truth and reality" (Haan, 1977, p. 37). *Defense will thus result, on the moral judgment performance level, in a somewhat irrational, nonlogical, incomplete reconstruction and solution of the conflict situation* because the subject is forced to ignore or distort certain aspects of conflict if he wants to create congruence between ego-oriented action impulses and moral consciousness in order to avoid, for example, feelings of guilt. By contrast, in the case of *coping* the subject will tolerate such discrepancies and will deal with them so as to come to a final solution of a conflict situation. In other words, *the subject, in his judgment performance, will consider all aspects of the situation that are available to him according to his level of moral competence.*

The above characterizations of coping and defense reflect the main criterion used both by Haan (1977) and by Döbert and Nunner-Winkler (1980) to distinguish them: *situational accuracy* (or *adequacy*). Defense, with its tendency to distort or to ignore certain aspects of conflict, does not resolve a conflict accurately or adequately whereas coping does. Unfortunately, this criterion is very hard to conceptualize and to operationalize; one attempt will be presented later in the section on the empirical investigation.

Returning to the relationship between cognition and affect in moral judgment, Haan's (1977) and Döbert and Nunner-Winkler's (1978, 1980) findings indicate that defense hinders, while coping makes possible, the unfolding of moral competence. According to this perspective *coping,* not merely logical and social-cognitive abilities, is a necessary condition for the unfolding of moral judgment.

AN ACTION-THEORETICAL APPROACH TO MORAL COMPETENCE AND AFFECTIVE PROCESSES IN CONFLICT-SOLVING

Intercorrelations of data derived from different theory-families remain meaningless unless some "transformatory concept" or common theoretical language is developed (Klausner, 1973). Since coping/defense processes and moral judgment have their origins in different theory traditions, it is apparent that a common theoretical language is a necessary prerequisite for clarifying the interrelations of the two concepts. In the present context, action-theoretical terms are chosen.

Eckensberger and Reinshagen (1980) proposed a reformulation of Kohlberg's stage theory of moral judgment in action theoretical terms. This reformulation was based upon the analysis of the Kohlberg scoring manuals available in the 1970s. Although a detailed explication of this analysis is clearly beyond the scope of this chapter, a short introduction is necessary here, because the results of this reformulation, generally not familiar to the American reader, differ from Kohlberg's stage interpretation in some important aspects relevant in the present context. The basic motive for this kind of an analysis was the desire to improve the determination of the deep structure of the stages. Eckensberger and Reinshagen (1980) argued that the explication of the stage-structures by Kohlberg is theoretically as well as empirically deficient, even after the criterion of *social perspective* was chosen (cf. Kohlberg, 1976). Although many arguments which cannot be summarized here have been elaborated, one argument may be helpful in this context. Since the social perspective taken at each stage of moral development is theoretically as well as empirically only a necessary but not a sufficient condition for a moral stage, then obviously the definition of a moral stage in terms of social perspective-taking cannot be a sufficient one.[1]

The approach chosen by Eckensberger and Reinshagen (1980) is a rather simple one as summarized in the following steps[2]:

1. An action can be evaluated under (at least) two aspects: (a) Under the aspect of *prudence*, one only analyzes whether a chosen means is practically

---

[1]One could argue that the above points are no longer valid because (a) the most recent publication of Kohlberg's longitudinal data (Colby et al., 1983) demonstrates the tremendous validity of various aspects of the theory, especially its claim that there are no developmental regressions of stages; and (b) the new manuals distinguish much better between content and structure than did their predecessors. Both arguments, however, are not convincing. If one looks at the longitudinal data as well as at the manuals, then it becomes evident, that, in test theoretical terms, the stages have historically increased in difficulty. Most subjects are now scored somewhere between stages 3 and 4, and subjects who were scored at stage 6 before (e.g., those who refused to conform in the Milgram obedience experiments; see Kohlberg and Candee, 1984) are now scored at stage 4B. Consequently, the probability of regressions decreases drastically. Furthermore, with reference to the second argument, a recent attempt to empirically analyze whether in fact content and structure are independently defined in the most recent manuals leads to the result (Eckensberger, 1983; Eckensberger & Burgard, 1983) that the *existence* of criterion judgments (i.e., those scoring units which form an intersection of three content aspects of judgments: the chosen issue, the applied norm, and the chosen ethical orientation, called element) are highly related to stages (Kendall's Tau ranges from .70 to .80, p. < .01). This demonstrates that neither is the content of the stages held constant in those criterion judgments, as it is claimed by Kohlberg and his associates (Colby, Gibbs, Kohlberg, Speicher-Dubin & Candee, 1982), nor is the structure of the stages sufficiently defined in the manual, because it is still greatly determined by (or at least interrelated with) content.

[2]The reformulation has now also been empirically tested by a cross-sectional design. Although the *stage sequence* cannot be demonstrated sufficiently by this design, the data generally do not falsify the interpretation of Eckensberger and Reinshagen (1980). Although they lead to further complications, they also lead to further clarifications.

adequate in order to reach an intended consequence (goal); and (b) under an *ethical-moral* aspect, one analyzes whether an action helps or harms the interests of others (person, groups, principles), i.e., to what extent it is *conflicting* with other actions (or actors).

2. The consideration of or respect for interests of others is, however, already contained in laws, rules, duties, obligations, etc., given in a specific society. They only exist because conflicts exist. They, therefore, are *reifications* of *means* for conflict solution, i.e., to a large extent reifications of moral judgments.

3. Moral judgments are, therefore, normative (evaluative) cognitions about *conflicts,* including their genesis as well as their solutions. They can refer to *concrete conflicts* of actions with *other actions* (actors), or to conflicts with *reifications* of actions (laws, rules, etc. in systems).

4. To define the structure of ideals of conflict solutions (moral judgments), therefore, at first the structural components of an action have to be defined. In general, structure can be defined by elements and their interrelations. In particular the elements of an action are: the *goals, means, results, and consequences.* And the *relations* between these elements are given by different thought-processes: *Means* are related to *goals* by *final* thought (means are chosen *in order to* attain a goal); *consequences* and *results* are related to *means* either *causally* (*because* a certain means is chosen, *therefore,* a certain result follows, and *because* a certain result occurs, *therefore,* certain consequences follow) or *functionally* (the consequence may be interpreted as a function of a result, etc.). Also *intended consequences* are related to *goals* by *intentional* thought (intended consequences are identical with goals). It is this thought process which first makes possible a distinction between *intended* and *unintended consequences.*

5. A *moral dilemma* then is a situation, in which (a) at least two actions form a conflict, and (b) the negative (unintended) consequences of *one* action are *logically* implied in positive (intended) consequences of the *other* action, and *vice versa.*

6. In their attempt to define the structure of Kohlberg's stages in action-theory terms, Eckensberger and Reinshagen (1980) kept as close as possible to the theory's empirical basis. First they analyzed existing dilemmas, then they reconstructed the actual moral judgments from the Kohlberg stage scoring manuals in action-theory terms.

7. The first step (analysis of dilemmas) leads to the conclusion that the Kohlberg dilemmas represent structurally quite different types of conflicts. Eckensberger and Reinshagen (1980) at first worked on a type of moral dilemma which Holstein (1976) describes as follows: "The actor (moral agent) finds himself in conflict with established authority invested either in a person or in a set of rules relevant to the situation in question" (p. 52). This type of conflict is best represented in Kohlberg's "Joe" dilemma, which concerns a father's unfairly broken promise and subsequent demand to his son (Colby et al., 1983, p.

79)[3]. To come to an *equilibrated* solution of any conflict of this type, the subject has to consider three parameters (within the Joe dilemma): (a) There are two agents with different goals (Joe wants to go to camp, the father wants to go on a fishing trip); (b) the possibilities for reaching these goals are mutually exclusive because the means are restricted (there is only enough money for one of them). In other words, there is a *logical implication* of intersection of positive intended consequences for the one and negative unintended consequences for the other (if Joe goes to camp, his father cannot go fishing although this *is not intended* by Joe, and *vice versa*); and (c) the means are in a dominance relationship (the father is more powerful than Joe).

8. The result of the second step (the analysis of the stages themselves) can be summarized as follows: (a) The stages of moral judgment in the Eckensberger and Reinshagen model differ in the complexity of the perceived conflict-solving and action structures. The various stages are created by the fact that, in the argumentation of the conflict's solution, different numbers and kinds of action elements and different numbers and kinds of implications in the conflict are taken into account by the subject; (b) since stage 4½ was included in the analysis (because of reasons that cannot be elaboraed here), the analysis referred to stages 1, 2, 3, 4, 4½ and 5 (stage 6 has been excluded for being a metaethical position, and only one possible position among many others); and (c) although many aspects of the analysis are in accordance with Kohlberg's stage interpretation, there are three basic differences the reader should keep in mind, especially for the formulation of the hypotheses. First, the stages are clustered differently: In contrast to Kohlberg, *stages 1, 2 and 3* are assumed to belong to one "level," namely the level of the "concrete individual," and *stages 4, 4½ and 5* are affiliated with the second level of moral judgment that represents judgments concerning the relation of the subject to whole systems. Second and most important, however, is the interpretation that the second "level" represents only a "horizontal decalage" of judgments, i.e., only the *elements* (goals, means, results, consequences) are interpreted in a more *abstract* and qualitatively different manner (as *reifications* of actions) than the first level. The *structure of the stages themselves*, however, is repeated on the second level: *Stage 1* and *4* are structurally identical; so are *2* and *4½* and *3* and *5*. Third, it is true, however, that the reformulated *stage 3* (the reformulation also took into account the data of Holstein, 1976) is more "*equilibrated*" than is *stage 3* in Kohlberg's terms.

---

[3]Joe dilemma: Joe is a 14-year-old boy who wanted to go to camp very much. His father promised him he could go if he saved up the money for it himself. So Joe worked hard at his paper route and saved up the $40 it cost to go to camp and a little more besides. But just before camp was going to start, his father changed his mind. Some of his friends decided to go on a special fishing trip, and Joe's father was short of money. So he told Joe to give him the money he had saved from the paper route. Joe didn't want to give up going to camp, so he thinks of refusing to give his father the money.

A rough description of the reformulated stages may read as follows: At *stages 1 and 4* the conflict is *localized* in conflicting means of persons (stage 1), or in a conflict between the means of a person and rules (laws) attached to role positions (stage 4). These means and rules are both interpreted as inevitably dominant. At the same time the employment of actions means (stage 1) or the application of laws (stage 4) are viewed rather rigidly, i.e., as if obeying natural laws. From this it follows that the consequences of the conflict situation are rather inevitable, too: At *stage 1* one necessarily has trouble (punishment), and at *stage 4* the role positons are defined rather rigidly as implying certain rights. Hence, the dilemma situation is *accepted,* and the *solution* of the conflict abandons personal goals at both stages.

At *stages 2 and 4½* the conflict is *not localized* in the means but in the goals (ends) of the conflicting people or system aspects in a situation. Either conflicting goals of concrete persons (stage 2) or ends of whole systems (stage 4½) are considered justified. Therefore the dilemma situation is *not accepted.* At the same time, means/ends relations are reconstructed as being rather *flexible* and *final* (not quasi-casual). From this it follows that the *solution* of the conflict at *stage 2* is seen in the necessity to invent new means (often situation-bound), and at *stage 4½* they are made relative, are arbitrarily redefined, or also changed.

At *stages 3 and 5* the dilemma is *perceived* (analyzed) completely and it is *fully accepted as a dilemma.* At both stages the conflict is *localized in* complete action plans, and it is realized (a) that the action means are in a dominance relationship, (b) that the conflicting parties both have justified goals, and (c) that the realization of both actions is logically impossible. This is true for the goals of concrete individuals (stage 3) as well as for the ends of whole systems and role-positions, seen at *stage 5.* Hence, at both stages the dilemma is *solved* by transcending it. This, however, can be done only by constructing a higher goal, common to both (conflicting) parties. Therefore at both stages the dilemma solution is *equilibrated*; they only differ with reference to the interpretation of a dilemma as being localized between concrete subjects or between subjects and roles (systems).

It is important, however, to realize that under the perspective elaborated here, dilemmas exist which *stage 3* can already be seen to adequately solve. These are dilemmas which take place between single subjects who are defined by their concrete relationship like father-son, husband-wife, etc. In other words, the subjects do not have to discuss these dilemmas with reference to concepts like roles, society, etc.

If we now turn to the concepts of coping and defense, it is easy to see that they can be fruitfully linked to the stage structures, defined in action terms. This is so because they refer to the ''adequacy'' or ''completeness'' of the analysis of a given situation. While defense is defined as a psychological mechanism that results in ignoring or distorting aspects of situations, in our case conflicts, coping is defined as a process that allows for full consideration of all relevant aspects in a situation. If these conceptualizations are applied to the given stage structures, then it can be defined more precisely under what conditions coping is a necessary prerequisite and under what conditions defense processes may be involved in a judgment. Because *stages 3 and 5* (in the action theoretical reformulation) by necessity imply a completely undistorted analysis of the situation, these stages presuppose coping. On the other hand, *stages 1, 2, 4 and 4½* are deficient structures (under the aspect of complete reconstruction of the dilemma). They are either the result of cognitive (competence) deficiencies or of defense processes that distort the judgment competence at the performance level. This, however, implies that it is not possible to decide for these latter stages what the moral judgment performance represents: cognitive structure, affective processes, or both. Consequently, it does not suffice to only measure the cognitive structure but it is also necessary to analyze affective processes in moral judgment.

THE EMPIRICAL STUDY

Sample, Design and Method of Data Gathering

The following empirical study is a first attempt to look for some evidence concerning affective processes in moral judgment performance. It is based upon data which were originally collected for another purpose (Villenave-Cremer & Hartmüller, 1978), namely, to clarify the child-rearing context of the moral judgment of mothers and daughters. The authors decided to use these data because the study's design had some features that were relevant for a first test of the present concern.

Sixteen mothers and their 12-to 14-year-old daughters were interviewed, simultaneously but in separate rooms, with regard to *their conflict-solving strategies in the family*. The subjects were asked to give examples of real-life conflicts (RLC) in the family, and to describe in detail those situations in which the daughter's actions or intentions conflicted with the goals and/or interests of her mother. They were also asked to describe the course of conflict solutions in detail, as well as their interpretation and evaluation of the course and type of conflict solutions. These interviews required an average of three quarters of an hour, ranging from half an hour to a full hour. In addition, all subjects were presented with Kohlberg's *hypothetical Joe dilemma* (see footnote 3, p. 181; German version: Eckensberger, Reinshagen & Eckensberger, 1975). On average one quarter of an hour was required for this part of the interview. For present purposes we shall focus on the analysis of the mothers' discussions of the hypothetical dilemma. The type of conflicts represented in the Joe dilemma and in the mother-daughter situations are rather similar in that both are conflicts within families and deal with individuals (not social systems). On the other hand, there are important differences, crucial in the present context: Mothers and daughters in the RLCs are real agents, both are personally involved, the mother's authority is real, both have personal values about the educational situation, and the responsibility of the mother is real. Hence all goals, desires, and preferences are evaluated not only structurally but also with reference to the involved egos. The analysis and solution of these conflicts therefore is not only cognitively-based but additionally serves the function of maintaining the agent's ego-consistency. Consequently within these RLCs the probability of defense mechanisms that lead to a distortion or selective analysis of the situation is very high. The hypothetical Joe dilemma, on the other hand, is constructed in such a way that it can be solved by rather ego-distant role-taking processes and ego-detached evaluative processes in principle. There are also no *real* consequences for the arguing subjects (mothers or daughters). Hence the probability of the occurrence of defense mechanisms is at least smaller than in the RLCs.

Some weaknesses and dangers arise when data are analyzed under a different point of view from that under which they were originally collected and, in fact, we must admit that there exist some restrictions in the present data concerning the quality of the interviews. Their original purpose was primarily to investigate details of child-rearing processes; this is irrelevant for our present question. In addition, the ''ought'' component of conflict-solving strategies was unfortunately neglected in the original data collection.

The analysis was done in three steps: mothers' real-life conflicts (RLC) and hypothetical moral dilemmas (HMD) of the Kohlberg-type were analyzed in the frame of reference of moral stage structure, defined in action-theoretical terms (Eckensberger & Reinshagen, 1980). Second, stage structures in RLCs and HMDs were not interpreted solely as approximations of cognitive competence; instead specific *differences* between RLCs and HMDs within subjects were interpreted as indicators of the existence of defense mechanisms, which are due to a higher ego-concern (threat) of the RLCs. Also, identical stages in RLCs and HMDs within the same subject were interpreted as indicators of coping mechanisms (see following section). Third, these interpretations were tested by independently-derived indices of defense and/or coping mechanisms derived from the mothers' and the daughters' real-life conflict reports.

Hypotheses

A given solution to a moral conflict can be interpreted as the result of two different psychological processes: (a) the subject's moral (cognitive) competence which is applied to the complexity of the conflict situation; and (b) the subject's dealing with affects in conflict situations that are more or less threatening for the subject's ego. In order to maintain a consistent self the subject will defend if he or she cannot bear reality and the subject will cope if he or she is able to bear the conflict.

The hypotheses are based on the distinction between complete moral stage structure (stages 3 and 5) and incomplete moral stage structure (stages 1, 2, 4, and 4½) and their relations to coping and defense strategies.

Hypothesis 1: We expect the usage of complete stages 3 and/or 5 in reasoning about hypothetical moral dilemmas to be a necessary condition for usage of a complete stage in reasoning about real life conflicts.

HMD is a better estimation of moral competence, because ego-involvement and consequently the probability of defense mechanisms that deteriorate moral judgment is lower than in the RLC.

There is one theoretical problem to be mentioned: According to the Piagetian hypothesis that structures are first manifested in concrete action contexts and only later in theoretical reflection, higher stage arguments in real life conflicts have been structurally interpreted as indicating stage transition. Gilligan and Belenky (1980) and Haan (1975) contribute empirical evidence to this assumption. But in contrast to our study, the real life conflicts in these studies are critical life events experienced by young adults (abortion, student protest) that appropriately encourage moral growth. We don't expect the daily-life conflicts between mothers and daughters to substantially encourage moral growth. Rather, we expect them to be integrated in the mothers' cognitive moral structure and usual defense/coping patterns.

Hypothesis 2: (a) If the RLC level is stage 1, 2, 4, or 4½, and the HMD level is stage 3 or 5, then the subject is defending in the RLC. (b) If the moral stage in both types of conflict is either stage 3 or 5 the subject is coping.

The existence of coping/defense processes can be logically deduced from these two patterns of RLC stage and HMD stage. First, since stages 3 and 5, in terms of the action-theoretical reformulation of Kohlberg's stage theory of moral development (cf. Eckensberger & Reinshagen, 1980), represent equilibrated types of moral reasoning, they are based upon a complete situation-adequate analysis of the conflict and, therefore, presuppose affective coping. Second, since stages 1, 2, 4 and 4½ by contrast represent unequilibrated types of moral reasoning, they are non-complete and non-situationally adequate but may be due to either deficient moral structures, defense mechanisms, or both.

On the basis of these arguments *no conclusions* can be made with respect to coping and defense if the moral stages in both types of conflicts are below stages 3 and 5 because the subjects in these cases may show a deficient cognitive competence, defense processes, or both.

The described cases represent the four possible combinations of stage pattern in the two types of conflicts (RLC, HMD) and the two major forms of moral stages (complete conflict restructuring: stages 3 and 5; incomplete conflict restructuring: stages 1, 2, 4 and 4½) as well as the conclusions that can be drawn from them with respect to coping and defense mechanisms. They are schematically presented in Table 7.1.

TABLE 7.1
Summary Table of the Relation between Stages of Moral Judgments
(HMD: Hypothetical Moral Dilemma; RLC: Real-Life Conflict) and
Coping/Defense Mechanisms

Stages	*RLC*	*Assumed Affective Processes*	*HMD*	*Stages*
complete (equilibrated) solution	3,5	coping	3,5	complete (equilibrated) solution
		probably not / *will occur* / *defense*		
non-complete solution	1,2 4,4½	no expectation	1,2 4,4½	non-complete solution

Method of Analysis

Hypothesis 1 is simply to be examined by the comparison of the moral stages in the two types of conflicts of every subject. In hypotheses 2a and 2b the propositions that the defined stage patterns represent coping or defense in the RLC are examined by a comparison with an independent measurement of coping and defense in the real-life conflicts.

Before reporting the results and the testing of the hypotheses, we will explicate first our definitions of stage scores and, second, the criteria for assessing coping and defense processes.

Definition of Stage Scores in RLCs and HMDs

The interviews about RLCs and HMDs were both scored in terms of the action-theoretical structures characteristic for each moral stage. In the following, stage criteria are given that are derived from stage descriptions (see p. 182), and scoring examples are selected for purposes of illustration. Examples for HMD-scores are taken from those parts of the Kohlberg manual (Eckensberger, Reinshagen & Eckensberger, 1975) which have been analyzed in action theoretical terms (Eckensberger & Reinshagen, 1980). They refer to the Joe dilemma.

The reader is reminded that the internal relationship of stages and levels of development differ from Kohlberg's theory: The first level consists of stages 1, 2 and 3, the second of stages 4, 4½ and 5. The latter is structurally identical to the former (in terms of action elements) but differs in abstraction.

Stages 1 and 4
Common structural criteria of scoring:

1. The means of the agents are *seen and accepted* in their dominance relationship.
2. The employment of action means by the more powerful agent is viewed rigidly as if it were a natural law.
3. The less powerful agent abandons his goal. Frequent contents: Stage 1: obedience, avoidance of punishment Stage 4: law, normative order, well-being of the group, sanctions.

Examples
Joe dilemma: "Joe should give up the money because his father is more powerful; if he does not, he will be punished." (Stage 1)
"The father has the right to demand the money." (Stage 4)
Real-life conflict in mother-daughter dyad: Here dealing with the question why the daughter shouldn't come home too late: M: "The daughter will get house arrest if she doesn't come home on time." I: "Do you tell her why you are punishing her?" M: "Why? She can tell time! She already knows she has to obey the rules!" I: "Why should she obey the rules?" M: "Because we have to learn that. There have to be some rules we obey, unless one is born a 'playboy' or a 'playgirl' " (Stage 4, M).

Stages 2 and 4½
Common structural criteria of scoring:

1. The relationship between means and goals as well as the goals of the actions are considered. The appropriateness of means is discussed.
2. The use of means is *final*: There is an attempt to help both agents to their goals. This view of conflict results in the following solution strategies:
3. *Equifinal action means* are constructed; inventions of alternative means lead to a positive result for both people. (In the hypothetical dilemma the solution tends to be unrealistic in ignoring the inevitably negative consequences for one of the two persons. In the real-life conflict there is often no solution proposal; the subjects are frequently quite helpless.)
   Frequent contents:
   Stage 2: self- and other-interests, welfare of the individual, negative reciprocity, exchange.
   Stage 4½: "greatest good for the greatest number," freedom, welfare, autonomy.

Examples
Joe dilemma: "The only way the father can rightfully demand the money is if he promises to pay it back immediately." (Stage 2)

Real-life conflicts in mother-daughter dyad: Here dealing with the question, why the daughters shouldn't receive their boyfriends in their rooms: "It bothers me personally. I like for them to stay here (in the living room) . . . but they go on up to their own world. And find nothing there. I tell them that I'd rather . . . but then they argue that all their things are upstairs and they won't do anything anyway . . . What should I do? I can only tell them I don't like it . . . should I use force? I don't think that's the right way. The older they get, the more freedom they'll want to have." (Stage 4½, 3M) Helping with household chores: "I often think they want to have some duties . . . sometimes it happens that my husband and I are working in the garden, doing all kinds of things, and they (the children) are nowhere to be found! On the other hand they also need something besides school and homework, and they shouldn't be tied to the house again with chores of some kind." (Stage 2, 11M).

Stages 3 and 5
  Common structural criteria of scoring:

1. The action means are recognized in their dominance-relationship.
2. The goals of both people are considered.
3. Reciprocal crossings of action consequences are discussed.
4. The subject goes beyond the conflict and looks for *higher* goals which represent common interests of both agents and which may permit a decision and a solution to the conflict.
  Frequent contents:
  Stage 3: Personal relationship, social recognition, interpersonal well-being, obligations and trust.
  Stage 5: Conscience and self-regulation, civic rights and social justice.

Examples
Joe dilemma: "Trust is not one-sided . . . it's very important in an interpersonal relationship. If one person doesn't trust another person, then that person won't trust him either." (Stage 3)
Real-life conflict: Here dealing with the question of why the mother should insist that the daughter make an effort at school: "I tell her that I believe that with her intellectual ability she should be able to handle school work, and I really do believe that. That it's only a question of determination and effort, and that as parents we can't be responsible for demanding nothing of her because otherwise we would cut off her chances of making it in our society." (Stage 5, 2M)

Definitions of Coping and Defense Criteria

In order to test whether the stage-specific variations in moral judgment scores from RLCs and HMDs can be justifiable interpreted as indicators of defense or coping processes, some criteria are necessary that go beyond the consideration developed so far. They have been derived from two sources: (a) from the mother interviews; (b) from the agreement/disagreement in the mothers' and daughters' interviews with respect to the analysis and/or interpretation of the same conflicts.

For our purpose, we did not differentiate all the defense/coping mechanisms distinguished by Haan (1977); we only determined whether or not defense is present. Nevertheless, the concept of coping/defense we used is rather close to that given by Haan (1977). The criterion of "accuracy" or "situation adequacy," crucial for the distinction between coping and defense, is operationalized in our study by the following differentiation:

Situational Accuracy. This refers to the subject's dealing with objective situation characteristics; in the case of defense, the subject manipulates the facts of a conflict in the argumentation. (Certain forms of "denial" [Haan, 1977] may belong to this category.) Situational accuracy was excluded from analysis for two main reasons: (a) We defined defense as a tendency to ignore and distort situational aspects. Applied to the objective characteristics of a conflict, confusion with the moral stage criteria, defined above, cannot be avoided because we cannot distinguish whether a person ignores some objective characteristics of conflict because of a threat to his self-consistency or whether he ignores some aspect for cognitive reasons; and (b) *distortion* of objective situation aspects, which could only be taken from a comparison of mother and daughter interviews, did not occur in the sample.

Affective Accuracy. In the case of defense, affective accuracy is characterized by ignoring and distorting one's own feelings as well as those of others; in the case of coping it is characterized by a tendency to recognize accurately one's own feelings as well as those of others and to tolerate one's own (and others') unacceptable impulses and to deal with them. The affective accuracy of the mothers was analyzed under two aspects: *accuracy in respect to the self* and *empathic accuracy.* These two kinds of accuracy, to be described and illustrated shortly, are not completely independent of each other. A mother who receives a defense-score in the first category cannot receive a coping-score in the second (for example, a mother cannot take into account the daughter's perception of the mother's feelings if the mother distorts or ignores her own affective and cognitive processes).

Affective Accuracy in Respect to the Self. This aspect of accuracy refers to the adequacy of self-description of affective processes in relation to cognitive processes. A defense-score was given in the following cases:

1. If there was a total lack of affective statements in the interview (cf. Haan: "intellectualization").

2. If there were obviously inadequate and exaggerated emotional reactions with respect to the facts of the situation (cf. Haan: "projection").

3. If descriptions of affects, motives, interests (etc.) of the mother, relevant for the mother's analysis of the conflict and its solution, appeared in the daughter's interview but not in the mother's interview (cf. Haan: "intellectualization").

4. If the mother demonstrated an excessive conformity and submission to the husband (cf. Haan: "reaction formation").

A *coping-score* was given in the following cases:

1. If the mother differentiated between her emotions and the facts of the situation (cf. Haan: "objectivism").

2. If the mother differentiated between her own and her daughter's affects (cf. Haan: "empathy").

3. If the mother gave differentiated descriptions of her emotions and the related cognitions in a conflict (cf. Haan: "objectivity").

Empathic Accuracy.   This aspect of accuracy refers to the accuracy of understanding the daughter's feelings and cognitions. A *defense score* was given in the following cases:

1. If there was a complete lack of empathic reflections in the mother's interview.

2. If discrepancies between the mother's description of the daughter and the daughter's self-description occurred and the daughter was coping according to the coping criteria with respect to the self (see above).

3. If the mother gave a very vague unlikely interpretation of the daughter's feelings or cognitions.

A *coping score* was given in the following cases:

1. If there was a large amount of agreement between the daughter's self-description and interpretation and the mother's understanding of the daughter.

2. If the interpretation of the daughter's motives, disposition, and cognitive orientation was differentiated and logical.

Before the results are presented, some rather general problems with the analysis of the interviews should be mentioned. First, it was very difficult to determine conflict units for the analysis of the real-life conflicts in respect to conflict-solving because the interviews were conducted with a minimum of a priori structure, and the manner in which the different mothers described their conflicts varied considerably. In some cases, one finds precise descriptions of the course of conflict-situations, for example, what happened when the daughter wanted to wear jeans to visit a play. In other cases, one finds the formulation of general problems and some short examples to illustrate them; for instance, the problem of a daughter's having little motivation to go to school. In other cases, one finds conflicts where other persons are involved. Finally, one finds reflections and evaluations in respect to childrearing methods (punishment, permissiveness, etc.). In short, the data are most heterogeneous. Nevertheless the *content* of the conflicts across the sample were quite homogeneous: school, dressing, coming home too late; dates and activities with peers; conflict with sisters and brothers. It was decided, therefore, to look for all statements and descriptions made about one content, similar to the issues in the Kohlberg dilemmas.

Secondly, in some cases a considerable part of the interview was purely descriptive (details of mother's interventions and situations but no evaluations or cognitions about it). In this event there were no indicators for scoring. Nevertheless, the range of scorable conflict-solving foundations is fairly high. It varies from two to seven units. The highest stage score determined a subject's final moral judgment score, accounting for the structural theorist's perspective that a subject cannot produce by chance a stage argument above his own competence (cf. Döbert & Nunner-Winkler, 1978; Eckensberger, Villenave-Cremer & Reinshagen, 1980).

RESULTS AND TEST OF THE HYPOTHESES

Table 7.2 summarizes the analysis of the data from the 16 mothers. As Table 7.2 demonstrates, all but two mothers argued at stage 3 in the hypothetical Joe dilemma, a result which is frequently reported with adult women (cf. Holstein, 1976). In some cases there were indications of more abstract arguments, in the direction of stage 5. In no case, however, could stage 5 be scored reliably, and these cases are therefore noted in parentheses. With reference to the expected coping/defense strategies, derived from the stage patterns in RLCs and HMDs for two mothers (both lower than stage 3), no expectation could be formulated. For the remaining 14 mothers, 5 were classified as copers and 9 as defenders. One mother in the defender group, however, could not be positively identified as either a coper or a defender when the additional criteria summarized above were applied.

The *first hypothesis* is supported. Not one of the mothers received a higher moral judgment score in the RLC than in the HMD. This was also true for those two mothers who had scores lower than stage 3 in the RLC. (Compare columns 1 and 2, Table 7.2.)

The *second hypothesis* was tested by means of Fisher's exact probability test (Lienert, 1973). The empirical distribution deviated only in one single case (subject 3) from the expected distribution; hence no distribution was more ex-

TABLE 7.2
Stage-Scores of 16 Mothers in Real-Life Conflicts (RLCs) and
Hypothetical Moral Dilemmas (HDM) Compared with Coping and
Defense Expectancies and Actual Coping and Defense Processes

Subject Number	Moral Stage Score in RLC	Moral Stage Score in HMD	Theoretically Expected Coping/Defense Mechanisms	Empirically Defined Coping/Defense Mechanisms
2	3 (5)	3 (5)	C	C
8	3	3	C	C
10	3	3	C	C
13	3	3 (5)	C	C
16	3	3 (5)	C	C
1	1;2	3	D	D
6	1;2	3	D	D
7	1;2	3	D	D
5	2	3	D	D
9	2	3	D	D
12	2	3	D	unscorable
14	2	3	D	D
15	2	3	D	D
3	2 (4½)	3 (5)	D	C
4	1	2	no exp.	D
11	2	2	no exp.	C

treme than the empirically determined one ($p < 0.0047$). The second hypothesis, therefore, is also supported. (Compare columns 3 and 4 in Table 7.2.)

DISCUSSION

Cognitive competence has been the core concept in analyzing reasons and justifications for action choices in moral dilemmas of the Kohlberg-type, and affective processes have only been dealt with as cognitive arguments. The influence of affective processes in analyzing and solving a moral dilemma has unfortunately been neglected so far by most researchers, and irregularities between stage scores from different dilemmas and/or issues involved in a dilemma were primarily interpreted in structural terms, e.g., as an indicator of domain specificity of thinking (cf. Eckensberger, Villenave-Cremer, & Reinshagen, 1980) or as an indicator of stage transition (Gilligan & Belenky, 1980; Haan, 1975). The argument put forward here, however, is that a specific performance of a subject in discussing a moral dilemma cannot be interpreted solely as an approximation of this cognitive competence, because it may be the result of two analytically independent but dynamically interacting processes: cognitions and affects. Moral performance can only be regarded as an indicator of cognitive competence as long as the subject copes with all affective processes involved. This, however, can only be assumed if it is methodologically controlled.

Coping/defense mechanisms must be measured even more independently than was possible in the present study; nevertheless the authors assert that the inclusion of affective processes in the measurement and interpretation of moral judgment is necessary. It is highly probable that in the analysis of real-life conflicts as well as in the case of hypothetical dilemmas the diagnosis of the existence of affective processes may contribute to a better understanding of many results which are as yet unclear. For instance, several aspects of Gilligan's (1977; Gilligan & Belenky, 1980) analysis of abortion-conflicts, whether they lead to a different morality with regard to justice or whether they are regressions or in fact progressions, would be clarified if one knew the amount of coping and/or defense in these arguments. Also, the predominance of stage 4 arguments in adults may be due more to the emotionally "economic" function of stage 4 arguments (taking the system perspective is sometimes much easier emotionally than to confront it with individual rights).

Finally, the implications of the results for intervention strategies, mentioned in the introduction section, should be reiterated here. Since the data in fact demonstrate that, at least under certain conditions, differences between performances in moral judgments can be fruitfully interpreted as results of defense mechanisms, it is no longer plausible in these situations to stimulate only the cognitive aspects (role taking abilities, etc.) of moral judgment. It would be more promising, instead, to at first give people a chance to realize their moral competence in performance by helping them to cope with feelings that otherwise may distort their perception and analysis of these situations, and consequently may distort or deform their moral judgments as well. It is assumed that only then are subjects given even a chance that cognitive interventions can work. To maximize the likelihood of success, both "sides of the coin," the cognitive and affective aspects of moral judgment, should be considered in intervention strategies in the future.

REFERENCES

Colby, A., Gibbs, J., Kohlberg, L., Speicher-Dubin, G., & Candee, D. (1982). *Standard form scoring manual*. Center for Moral Education: Harvard University.

Colby, A., Kohlberg, L., Gibbs, J., & Lieberman, M. (1983). A longitudinal study of moral judgment. *Monographs of the Society for Research in Child Development, 48*, 1–2.

Döbert, R. & Nunner-Winkler, G. (1978). Performanzbestimmende Aspekte des moralischen Bewusstseins. In G. Portele (Ed.), *Sozialisation und Moral* (pp. 101–121). Weinheim: Beltz.

Döbert, R. & Nunner-Winkler, G. (1980). Jugendliche "schlagen über die stränge." Abwehr- und Bewältigungsstrategien in moralisierbaren Handlungssituationen. In L. H. Eckensberger & R. K. Silbereisen (Eds.), *Entwicklung Sozialer Kognitionen* (pp. 267–298). Stuttgart: Klett-Cotta.

Eckensberger, L. H. (1983). Zur ontogenese des Normenbewußtseins. *Arbeiten der Fachrichtung Psychologie*. Saarbrücken: Universität des Saarlandes.

Eckensberger, L. H. & Burgard, P. (1983). *Zur Entwicklung von Konfliktlösungsvorstellungen*. Unpublished report. University of the Saarland, Department of Psychology, West Germany.

Eckensberger, L. H. & Reinshagen, H. (1980). Kohlberg's Stufentheorie der Entwicklung des moralischen Urteils. Ein Versuch ihrer Reinterpretation im Bezugsrahmen handlungstheoretischer Konzepte. In L. H. Eckensberger & R. K. Silbereisen (Eds.), *Entwicklung sozialer Kognitionen* (pp. 65—132). Stuttgart: Klett-Cotta.

Eckensberger, L. H., Villenave-Cremer, S., & Reinshagen, H. (1980). Kritische Darstellung von Methoden zur Erfassung des moralischen Urteils. In L. H. Eckensberger & R. K. Silbereisen (Eds.), *Entwicklung sozialer Kognitionen* (pp. 335–377). Stuttgart: Klett-Cotta.

Eckensberger, U., Reinshagen, H., & Eckensberger, L. H. (1975). *Kohlberg's Interview zum moralischen Urteil III. Auswertungsmanual—Form A*. Fachrichtungsarbeit an der Universität des Saarlandes, Fachrichtung Psychologie, Saarbrücken (available from L. H. Eckensberger, Universität des Saarlandes, Fachrichtung Psychologie, D-6600 Saarbrücken, West Germany).

Gilligan, C. (1977). In a different voice: Women's conception of the self and of morality. *Harvard Educational Review, 47*, 481–517.

Gilligan, C. & Belenky, M. E. (1980). A naturalistic study of abortion decisions. *New Directions for Child Development, 7*, 69–90.

Haan, N. (1975). Hypothetical and actual moral reasoning in a situation of civil disobedience. *Journal of Personality and Social Psychology, 32*, 255–270.

Haan, N. (1977). *Coping and defending: Processes of self-environment organization*. New York: Academic.

Holstein, C. B. (1976). Irreversible stepwise sequence in the development of moral judgments: A longitudinal study of males and females. *Child Development, 47*, 61–67.

Klausner, S. Z. (1973). Life-span environmental psychology: Methodological issues. In P. B. Baltes & K. W. Schaie (Eds.), *Life-span developmental psychology: Personality and socialization* (pp. 72–94). New York: Academic.

Kohlberg, L. (1969). Stage and sequence: The cognitive developmental approach to socialization. In D. A. Goslin (Ed.), *Handbook of socialization theory and research* (pp. 347–480). Chicago: Rand McNally.

Kohlberg, L. (1976). Moral stages and moralization: The cognitive developmental approach. In T. Lickona (Ed.), *Moral development and behavior* (pp. 31–53). New York: Holt, Rinehart & Winston.

Kohlberg, L. & Candee, D. (1984). The relationship of moral judgment to moral action. In L. Kohlberg, *The psychology of moral development* (pp. 498–581). San Francisco: Harper and Row.

Lienert, G. A. (1973). *Verteilungsfreie Methoden in der Biostatistik*. Band I. Meisenheim: Anton Hain.

Oser, F. (1981a). Moralische Erziehung als Intervention. *Unterrichtswissenschaft, 3*, 207–224.

Oser, F. (1981b). *Moralisches Urteil in Gruppen, soziales Handeln, Verteilungsgerechtigkeit*. Frankfurt: Surkhamp.

Piaget, J. (1981a). *Intelligence and affectivity: Their relationship during child development*. (T. A. Brown & C. E. Kaegi, trans.). Annual Reviews, Inc.,: Palo Alto.

Piaget, J. (1981b). *Das moralische Urteil beim Kinde*. Frankfurt: Suhrkamp. (Orig. 1932).

Power, C. & Higgins, A. (1981). Moralische Atmosphäre und Lernen. *Unterrichtswissenschaft, 3*, 225–240.

Selman, R. & Jaquette, D. (1978). Stability and oscillation in interpersonal awareness: A clinical developmental analysis. In C. B. Keasy (Ed.), *Twenty-fifth Nebraska symposium on motivation*, (261–304). Lincoln: University of Nebraska.

Villenave-Cremer, S. & Hartmüller, G. (1978). *Zusammenhänge zwischen dem moralischen Urteil der Mutter, Variablen der Eltern-Kind-Interaktion und der moralischen Entwicklung des Kindes*. Unpublished Diplom-Thesis. University of the Saarland, Saarbrücken, West Germany.

APPLICATIONS AND INTERVENTIONS
B. THE SCHOOL

8 The Role of Discussion in Moral Education

Marvin W. Berkowitz
Marquette University
Milwaukee, WI

Developmental moral education, based upon Kohlberg's (1984) study of moral reasoning, has been manifested in a variety of settings and forms of application. One component which is prominent in most forms of developmental moral education is peer moral discussion. Indeed, the first attempts at moral education based on Kohlberg's theory (e.g., Blatt, 1969) were comprised entirely of peer discussions of moral dilemmas. Even more recent and different procedures such as democratic governance (Power, this volume) and counselor training (Sprinthall, 1980) include peer moral discussion as a core ingredient. This paper will explore adolescent moral discussion as a form of moral education from the standpoints of both psychological research and educational practice. First, what we know and what we think we know about moral discussion will be considered. Included in this section will be reflections about what research has taught us. Then moral discussion as a process of structural development will be addressed and a program of research aimed at uncovering the developmental features of adolescent moral discussion will be presented. Finally, an attempt will be made to integrate these two analyses and to consider where this perspective can take moral education and research in the future.

PEER DISCUSSION IN MORAL EDUCATION

Moral education is one of those intriguing domains where psychological researchers and educational practitioners share a literature. Not surprisingly, as is typical when two disciplines are joined, there have been some confusions, miscommunications, and misinterpretations. Many of the problems center around moral discussion.

Research, theory and practice have produced an educational Zeitgeist that, like some theoretical juggernaut, has taken on a momentum and life of its own. Hence, it has become quite difficult to separate myth from fact. I shall try to address how moral discussion, the most pervasive element in moral education today, influences the development of moral thinking in adolescents.

Kohlbergian moral discussion originated in the doctoral work of Moshe Blatt (1969) under Kohlberg's direction. Blatt used the discussion of hypothetical moral dilemmas as a method for educating for moral development. His original study and subsequent applications by himself and others (Blatt & Kohlberg, 1975; Colby, Kohlberg, Fenton, Speicher-Dubin & Lieberman, 1977; Mosher, 1980) relied heavily upon research by two of Kohlberg's colleagues (Rest, 1973; Turiel, 1966) for their theoretical justifications. Reviews of this literature are plentiful (Berkowitz, 1981; Higgins, 1980; Lockwood, 1978; Sprinthall, 1980), so we will merely summarize some of the conclusions prevalent in this literature.

The moral discussion literature seems generally to include contradictory conclusions about whether exposure to reasoning one stage above one's own leads optimally to moral development. A further conclusion frequently based on the research literature is that interactions by students at a variety of stages is important for moral education to be effective. Teacher facilitation of moral discussion is also typically considered essential to the success of a moral discussion education curriculum. Finally, cognitive conflict is assumed to be a necessary condition for development to result from moral discussion.

Now let us explore in a bit more detail what it is that we actually do know from the research on moral discussion in education. The so-called ''+1 convention'' may be the most problematic variable in the literature (c.f. Berkowitz, 1981; Lockwood, 1978; Rest, 1980). While the moral education literature does reveal a diversity of interpretations of the psychological research underlying the convention that discussion facilitators need to present reasoning one stage above that of their students, it is nonetheless a widely accepted convention (e.g., Arbuthnot & Faust, 1981). Unfortunately, it is not a convention that has strong empirical support. From my own analyses of examples of moral discussions led by the experts in the field, it appears to be largely a mythical beast (Berkowitz, 1981). Educators simply do not seem to produce ''+1'' reasoning in moral discussion. Furthermore, despite the recent teacher training book by Arbuthnot and Faust (1981) which argues that "the capacity for +1 reasoning relative to one's students is required to carry out certain of the moral educator's tasks, and therefore, seems essential for optimally effective moral education" (p. 110), one has to agree with Fraenkel (1978) that such "moral educator's tasks" are highly impractical and unrealistic. This seems especially true in light of my failure to find +1 behavior in expert-led discussions. We can perhaps derive a clearer understanding of this controversy and of moral discussion processes by examining the next two variables concerning the form of moral discussion, i.e., classroom stage mixture and teacher facilitation.

A number of studies have indicated that student stage mixture may be an appropriate substitute for the +1 convention. Colby, Kohlberg, Fenton, Speicher-Dubin and Lieberman (1977) have concluded, based upon their massive study of moral discussion classroom programs in civic education, that classroom student heterogeneity of moral reasoning is central to the success of such programs. In our own research we have demonstrated that heterogeneous dyads develop significantly more than homogeneous dyads in a moral dialogue program (Berkowitz, Gibbs & Broughton, 1980). In studying non-moral stage development, Mugny, Perret-Clermont and Doise (1981) conclude that heterogeneous groupings typically produce more development than do homogeneous groups, except for pairings of transitional subjects, who are probably producing a mixture of stages of reasoning. This is all certainly quite consistent with Piagetian theory (1932/1965) that argues for the power of peer interaction in promoting moral development, and is furthermore consistent with Kohlberg's (1980) recent synthesis of the theories of Piaget and Durkheim that argues for the authority and influence of the peer group in moral education and development. Despite this theory and research, the definitive study on the effects of peer stage mixtures in moral discussion programs awaits realization. Nevertheless, we may conjecture that student stage heterogeneity may serve to provide the so-called +1 reasoning that teachers are urged to but typically do not seem to provide. In other words, the exposure to higher stage reasoning that is theorized to be necessary for development resulting from moral discussion may be produced by peers, not by experts such as group leaders or teachers. This again would be quite consistent with the Durkheimian model and with Piaget's original formulation.

A sidelight on the stage mixture issue is the question of absolute stage. There is evidence that suggests that moral discussion programs are more effective for low stage students than for high stage students. Lockwood (1978), in his critical review of the moral education intervention literature, concludes that there is little evidence for the effectiveness of moral interventions in producing development beyond stage 3. Likewise, in a non-moral domain, Mugny, Perret-Clermont and Doise (1981) report that the most consistent gains are found for low and intermediate subjects, although their definitions are relative to a single stage of development rather than across the entire spectrum of logical stages.

The third variable we mentioned, teacher facilitation, is also related to the +1 controversy outlined above. There are actually two issues here: (1) Is teacher facilitation necessary for successful moral education?; and (2) if so, what form should it take? Again, we do not have adequate bases for answering these questions definitively, but, fortunately, we do have enough information to begin to examine them. Except for some control groups in the Blatt and Kohlberg (1975) study that showed mixed results, educators have not adequately explored the potential of peer-led moral discussion programs. In the psychological literature, a number of investigations have shown that peer interaction without adult facilitation can be quite successful (e.g., Berkowitz, Gibbs & Broughton, 1980; Maitland & Goldman, 1974). This is certainly not an argument *against* teacher facilitation, but it does serve to suggest that such teacher roles *may* be expendable. Once again we do need more research in this area. As for the second question, the educational curriculum literature is replete with suggestions for "teacher roles," "teacher techniques," "facilitator behaviors," etc. They range from the +1 directions already discussed (Arbuthnot & Faust, 1981) to facilitation of peer interaction (Galbraith & Jones, 1976). They include small group construction, dilemma writing, "Socratic" probing and a wide variety of other behaviors. While most of these have not been directly studied, it seems fair to conclude from our previous discussions that behaviors that enhance the likelihood of students at different stages interacting in discussions of moral justifications will be successful moral education techniques.

A fourth assumption about the form that moral discussion programs of education should take concerns cognitive conflict. This is perhaps the most fundamental of the ingredients and one that differs in an important respect from the +1 convention, student interaction, class composition, and teacher facilitation. Cognitive conflict is a "first order" variable in moral education whereas +1, peer interaction, class composition and teacher facilitation are "second order" variables. By this, I mean that the second order components are all designed to cause the first order component. For example, peer interaction is assumed to be effective because it produces disequilibrium or cognitive conflict (Mugny, Perret-Clermont & Doise, 1981). Disequilibrium, or, more colloquially, cognitive conflict, is a fundamental element in Piagetian structural theory. It is the dynamic counterpart to static structure. Indeed, in his later writings Piaget (e.g., 1971) seemed to focus more on process than he had previously. Actually, for some time Piaget (1967) had contended that: "What is important for psychological explication is not equilibrium as a state but, rather, the actual process of equilibration. Equilibrium is only a result, whereas the process as such has greater expository value" (p. 101). While it is abundantly clear that structural development theory contends that the equilibration process demands that cognitive conflict occur for structural shifts to ensue, the moral education literature has largely ignored this process dimension of moral development, except perhaps for theoretical treatments. Research on cognitive conflict in moral education has been largely nonexistent, and, for this reason, educational practice has either ignored it or has simply had to engage in untested attempts at manipulations that are assumed to be likely to result in cognitive conflict.

We therefore will discuss cognitive conflict as a variable in our second section of this paper on the processes of moral development and education. First, let us examine another area that can shed some light on the issue of the role of moral discussion in moral development and education, i.e., the family. While the family is traditionally assumed to be the major force in the moral growth of children and adolescents, it has not been studied as extensively by moral stage researchers as might be expected. This is due at least in part to the perspective of stage theory on the role of the family in moral development. Both Piaget (1932/1965) and Kohlberg (1969) have historically deemphasized the importance of the family in moral development. A recent review of the literature on the role of childrearing on moral development (Speicher-Dubin, 1982) suggests that parents may have much more impact than has previously been suggested.

Two variables have been studied repeatedly in this small but informative literature: (1) parent stage of moral reasoning, and (2) parental childrearing techniques. We may think of the former as somewhat parallel to the $+1$ variable and the latter as parallel to the group interaction variable, although the similarities are far from exact. For example, only one study (Parikh, 1980) separated out the effects of the two variables completely. Parikh found them to both be highly significant in predicting child stage, but also to be highly redundant. It is clear that parent stage is related to childrearing technique, with higher stage parents using induction, the technique most positively related to higher child stage. Nevertheless, the literature in general does permit some conclusions about the role of the family in child moral development (see Lickona, this volume, for a broader review of this literature).

One of the most pronounced findings is that, across different cultures and diverse measures of both parenting and moral stage, induction is a parenting technique that is related to higher stages of reasoning in offspring (Hoffman & Saltzstein, 1967; Holstein, 1969; Parikh, 1980; Peck & Havighurst, 1960; Speicher-Dubin, 1982). Induction is a technique that is best typified by discussion and reasoning. Hoffman and Saltzstein defined induction as an appeal, in discipline, to the consequences of the child's actions. Holstein used the term "encouragement" to represent taking the child's opinion into account in making decisions. Other researchers used similar definitions. We may thus conclude that opportunities for democratic decision-making (Peck & Havighurst, 1960), reasoning about discipline (Hoffman & Saltzstein, 1967; Parikh, 1980), and expressing one's opinion (Holstein, 1969) in the family will lead to greater child moral development. Furthermore, in training studies, Grimes (reviewed in Higgins, 1980) Azrak (1980) and Stanley (1980) report significant child moral development when parents are included in moral discussions. Grimes found significantly greater development when mothers were included in moral discussions with their children than in the also significant traditional classroom discussions. Stanley uncovered part of the process by noting that only the successful parent group, i.e., parents trained *with* their adolescents, showed a decrease in authoritarian decision-making in family discussions. This seems quite similar to the parallel effects of moral discussion in the classroom.

The role of parents' stages is somewhat less clear. As Speicher-Dubin (1982) points out, there is a clear and consistent relationship between the parents' stages and the stages of their children. However, as we have already noted, parent stage is related to parenting technique. We therefore need to know if it is the technique of reasoning with one's child or the stage of the parents' reasoning that leads to the child's development, or both. Unfortunately, only parent technique has been studied directly in parenting situations. That is, no direct assessment of spontaneous parent moral reasoning has been done. Olejnik (1980) has found, however, in simulations with college students that post-conventional students use conventional reasoning and both conventionals and pre-conventional students use pre-conventional reasoning in messages intended for children. This, however, while suggestive still leaves the question largely open.

It is important to note that since these studies are often quasi-naturalistic, they do not typically study pretest and posttest change in moral reasoning. Rather, they correlate current stage of reasoning with family conditions (cf. Speicher-Dubin, 1982). We therefore cannot infer any causal mechanisms. We don't know, for instance, if parent stage causes parenting style which causes child development or if parenting style causes parent and child stage, or if some other entirely different process is at work. The training studies do, however, allow us to infer process.

Let us now briefly review what we have concluded thus far about moral education. First, there are many confusions about what the psychological research literature prescribes for moral education through peer discussion. Second, the need for exposure to teacher-produced higher stages of reasoning is not supported. Third, peer interaction, especially in stage heterogeneous moral discussions, is an important part of moral education programs. Fourth, the literature on the role of parenting in moral development supports the moral education literature in suggesting that the largely egalitarian moral discussion process may be more central to moral stage growth than the transmission of content.

The central role of the moral educator then becomes the facilitation of open peer discussion of moral issues. Let us now turn to a discussion of the process dimension of moral education and development.

MORAL DISCUSSION AS DEVELOPMENTAL PROCESS

We have already defined what we have termed "first order" and "second order" variables in moral education. This is largely parallel to what empirical researchers term dependent and independent variables, respectively. We cannot directly control the dependent variable, indeed it is dependent upon that which we can directly control, i.e., the independent variable. In this case, we cannot directly manipulate cognitive conflict, an intra-individual variable (Mugny, Perret-Clermont & Doise, 1981). Rather, we influence cognitive conflict by manipulating second order variables such as class composition. This leads us to a new distinction. The second order variables give us only limited understanding of the developmental process. We may term this "predictive" or "conditional" understanding. That is, by understanding *which* second order variables have which effects, we are able to predict the success or failure of a moral education intervention, i.e., we know the conditions under which such education will produce development. However, we do not know precisely *how* the effects are produced. In other words, we do not know the first order process. If we study cognitive conflict directly, however, we will have a different form of understanding, which I will call "causal" or "process" understanding. In other words, we can come to understand how those second order conditions cause development.

Unfortunately, successful attempts to directly measure the first order process of disequilibration do not exist. Our initial attempt at this enterprise (Berkowitz, Broughton & Gibbs, 1977) was somewhat less than revolutionary. We have since taken a middle ground stance by exploring the disequilibrating features of the adolescent discussion process. Research by Maria Taranto (1984) with our data set is intended to more directly explore the disequilibration process in adolescent moral dialogue by focusing on centrations and decentrations, much as has been suggested by Bearison (1982) with child moral discussion. Thus, our discussion of developmental process does not directly assess disequilibrium; rather, it explores the interactional bases for moral discussion. We may think of peer discussion as a variable that intervenes between what we have called second order variables and the first order variable of cognitive conflict.

As has been suggested by Piaget (1967) and others (e.g., Miller, 1981), the study of process should take precedence over the study of structure. Yet, what we find in the literature is an almost total disregard for the study of developmental process, especially peer discussion. Over the past 7 years, the beginnings of a literature on developmental process have emerged. At first, process was inferred if an intervention was successful. Then two quite different research groups began remarkably similar attempts at studying process in the development of Piagetian concrete operations. Miller and Brownell (1975) published a study that analyzed the interactions of conserver-nonconserver dyads and related their behaviors to developmental outcomes of the interactions; in the same year Doise and his colleagues began publishing similar data (Doise, Mugny & Perret-Clermont, 1975). Even more surprising is the fact that the former are American developmental psychologists interested in cognitive development and were adopting social interaction as a method, while Doise and his colleagues are Swiss psychologists interested in social interactions and were using cognitive variables as content. While the American branch of this research has not flourished, the Swiss movement is becoming a significant force in developmental and social psychology. At about the same time these studies were beginning, John Broughton and I were developing a similar interest independent of either Miller or Doise. We noted that disequilibrium was often implicated in moral educational process by inference, but that no one had yet directly assessed it. Unfortunately, as I have already noted, our attempt to directly assess disequilibration was somewhat less than successful (Berkowitz, Broughton & Gibbs, 1977).

While the American conservationists gave up that line of research, and Doise and his colleagues were focused more directly on the second order dimensions of peer interaction such as stage mixture, our plan of attack shifted and John Gibbs and I began to look for the "developmental features" of moral discussion. We wanted to uncover the discourse process of moral development. Elsewhere I have termed this process "the social construction of knowledge" (Berkowitz, 1980). The aspect of this process that we specifically explored is the dialogic interaction of reasoning structures, or, in our terms, "transactive" discussion. We have defined transactive discussion as "reasoning that operates on the reasoning of another" (Berkowitz & Gibbs, 1983). We view such discussion as dialectical in its ideal form, with Ego's (the speaker's) reasoning confronting Alter's (the listener's) in a dynamic and constructive interplay.

It is interesting to note that Bill Damon (Damon & Killen, 1982) and David Bearison (1982) are attempting to construct similar schemes with young children. Mugny, Perret-Clermont and Doise (1981) have inferred such processes in their research. All of these investigations, however, have been directed toward young children. Because we are studying adolescent moral discourse, we see a qualitative difference in the form of moral discussion between the subjects in these studies and the subjects in our own.

This points to a marked neglect of one particular developmental perspective in this literature. Typically, authors do not consider the structural capacities of their subjects as relevant to their interactional performance. They merely see interaction as affecting structural development. Max Miller (1980) has most directly confronted this issue in his investigation of the development of moral discourse. He has acknowledged that it is a developmental phenomenon and has, quite bravely, attempted to determine the parallelism between the development of moral discourse and the development of logical and social thinking. Nevertheless, his subjects are all young children as well and his work is, self-admittedly, quite preliminary.

When we originally began this research, we noted the work of Scott Miller (Miller & Brownell, 1975) with young children and the conservation task. One reason for our choice of adolescence as the age group to study was the relative immaturity of the communication skills that Miller and Brownell were limited to assessing. Furthermore, we noted Piaget's (1972) description of the nature of formal operational discussion:

> From the social point of view, there is also an important conquest. Firstly, hypothetical reasoning changes the nature of discussions: a fruitful and constructive discussion means that by using hypotheses we can adopt the point of view of the adversary (although not necessarily believing it) and draw the logical consequences it implies. In this way, we can judge its value after having verified the consequences. (p. 4)

Let us now take a closer look at (1) how we discovered transactive discussion, (2) its features, and (3) our empirical evidence for its existence and validity. We began our research with two different but complimentary perspectives. On one hand we had our a priori theoretical assumptions about what the adolescent manifestation of disequilibrating discourse should look like. On the other hand, we realized that we needed to refine our theoretical ideas with concrete data. We borrowed this "mutual bootstrapping" approach to theory construction from Kohlberg's (1981) work in the development of a moral stage scoring manual. Our basic theoretical assumption was that adolescent disequilibrating discourse should include an active reflection and operation upon the reasoning of a discussion partner.

In order to shape these notions with data, we began a moral discussion intervention with adolescents. Since these data are published elsewhere (Berkowitz, Gibbs & Broughton, 1980), I will merely summarize them here. We asked 30 same-sex undergraduate dyads to engage in a series of weekly to biweekly moral dialogues to be preceded and followed by a Kohlberg standard moral judgment interview. Dyads were paired on the bases of content differences (action choices in moral dilemmas), and stage differences (based on the pretest interview). Dyads were either at the same stage of moral reasoning, less than a full stage apart or approximately one full stage apart. We discovered that the group with less than a full stage disparity developed approximately one third of a stage on the average (about the norm for most successful moral reasoning interventions), which was significantly greater than any of the other groups, including a control group that engaged in no discussions. Despite these significant differences we were interested in the dialogues themselves. We found that some dyads in the "success" group did not develop and some from the unsuccessful groups did. We hypothesized that the nature of their dialogues should explain this so-called error variance.

The next step was to explore some of those dialogues in order to develop our understanding of disequilibrating dialogue. We compared success dialogues with non-success dialogues and discovered what you have been introduced to as transactive discussion. In doing so, we have identified 18 types of dialogue behavior which we classify as either higher order or lower order (Berkowitz & Gibbs, 1979). In Table 8.1, where all 18 transacts are presented, the higher order forms are followed in parentheses by the letter O representing Operational Transaction, and the lower order forms by the letters R for Representational or E for Elicitational. There are also a few hybrid transacts. The Operational Transacts fit our definition of transaction fully; i.e., they are characterized by a transformation of Alter's reasoning via integration, logical analysis or some other operation. An example of higher order Operational Transacts, and a model of the ideal transact as well, is Integration/Common Ground. In this case, Ego (the speaker) attempts to dialectically integrate his or her own reasoning with Alter's reasoning. Another example is Contradiction, where Ego points out how Alter is contradicting him or herself.

Representational Transacts are best likened to lower order reflective counseling behaviors (e.g., Carkhuff, 1969; cf. Berkowitz & Prestby, 1980) in that they

TABLE 8.1
Table of Transacts

1. *Feedback Request (E)*
   Do you understand or agree with my position?
2. *Clarification (O)*
   (a) No. What I am trying to say is the following.
   (b) Here's a clarification of my position to aid in your understanding.
3. *Competitive Clarification (O)*
   My position is not necessarily what you take it to be.
4. *Refinement (O)*
   (a) I must refine my position or point as a concession to your position or point (Subordinative mode).
   (b) I can elaborate or qualify my position to defend against your critique (Superordinative mode).
5. *Paraphrase (R/E)*
   (a) I can understand and paraphrase your position or reasoning.
   (b) Is my paraphrase of your reasoning accurate?
6. *Justification Request (E)*
   Why do you say that?
7. *Completion (R/O)*
   I can complete or continue your unfinished reasoning.
8. *Extension (O)*
   (a) Here's a further thought or an elaboration offered in the spirit of your position.
   (b) Are you implying the following by your reasoning?
9. *Competitive Paraphrase (R/O)*
   Here's a paraphrase of your reasoning that highlights its weakness.
10. *Contradiction (O)*
    There is a logical inconsistency in your reasoning.
11. *Reasoning Critique (O)*
    (a) Your reasoning misses an important distinction, or involves a superfluous distinction.
    (b) Your position implicitly involves an assumption that is questionable ("premise attack")
    (c) Your reasoning does not necessarily lead to your conclusion/opinion, or your opinion has not been sufficiently justified.
    (d) Your reasoning applies equally well to the opposite opinion.
12. *Competitive Extension (O)*
    (a) Would you go to this implausible extreme with your reasoning?
    (b) Your reasoning can be extended to the following extreme, with which neither of us would agree.
13. *Counter Consideration (O)*
    Here is a thought or element that cannot be incorporated into your position.
14. *Juxtaposition (R)*
    Your position is X and my position is Y.
15. *Common Ground/Integration (O)*
    (a) We can combine our positions into a common view.
    (b) Here's a general premise common to both of our positions.
16. *Dyad Paraphrase (R)*
    Here is a paraphrase of a shared position.
17. *Competitive Juxtaposition (R)*
    I will make a concession to your position, but also reaffirm part of my position.
18. *Comparative Critique (O)*
    (a) Your reasoning is less adequate than mine because it is incompatible with the important consideration here.
    (b) Your position makes a distinction which is seen as superfluous in light of my position, or misses an important distinction which my position makes.
    (c) I can analyze your example to show that it does not pose a challenge to my position.

are simply representations of Alter's reasoning, without any transformation. The classic lower order Representational Transact is exemplified by our category of Paraphrase. Here Ego simply repeats Alter's reasoning, unchanged except for vocabulary. Elicitational Transacts are actually exceptions to the rule. They are really facilitating behaviors that we have found to be correlated to transaction. An example is our category of Feedback Request in which Ego requests feedback from Alter concerning Alter's processing of Ego's reasoning. The three Hybrid Transacts are ambiguous or complex transacts.

Once we had identified and described the 18 transacts, we wrote a manual for coding them (Berkowitz & Gibbs, 1979). Then it was necessary to validate the scheme. To do so, we selected the middle (third) of the 5 discussions that the original intervention subjects had engaged in as our data set. We had 30 dyads to study. The typed transcripts of their discussions were blinded for subject identities and coded by myself, with interrater reliability cases coded by John Gibbs, a trained graduate student coder, and a self-trained undergraduate coder. Again, since these data have been reported elsewhere (Berkowitz & Gibbs, 1983), they will only be summarized here.

Our predominant index for validity was whether the degree of transactive behavior in the dialogues could differentiate between the dialogues of dyads that evidenced pre-to-posttest moral stage change from those that did not. Using a density measure of transactivity (percentage of statements that were transactive), we found significantly more overall transaction in the "change dyads" than the "non-changers." When we distinguished between Operational and Representational types of Transaction (Elicitational Transacts were pooled with Representational Transacts), only Operational types significantly discriminated between the two groups (see Table 8.2). Subsequent analyses of all the dialogues of the 30 dyads suggest that neither type alone significantly accounts for the moral stage growth, but that both together do (Berkowitz, 1983). The summary density measure used here was the mean number of Transacts per page of the transcribed dialogue (see Table 8.3).

We next wanted to determine the relative contribution of transactive behavior to discriminating between the two groups. In two multiple regression analyses, we found the degree of Operational Transaction to be the single most significant source of variance, with almost no overlap with the second and more traditional

TABLE 8.2
Percentages of Total Statements in Each Transact Category for
Pretest to Posttest Moral Stage Changers and Non-Changers

	All Transacts	Representational Transacts	Operational Transacts
Non-Changers	20	7.2	12.9
Changers	27	8.8	17.8

TABLE 8.3
Mean Operational, Representational and Total Transaction for
Pretest to Posttest Moral Stage Changers and Non-Changers
(All Four Discussions)

| Group | Transact Measure | | | |
	MOPP	MRPP	MTPP	N
Non-Changers	0.92	0.44	1.36	14
Changers	1.12	0.59	1.71	16

variable, stage disparity between dyadic partners. Furthermore, our measures of interrater agreement (Pearson correlations) average over .87 for myself and John Gibbs, over .76 for myself and the trained graduate student, and .70 for myself and the self-trained undergraduate (Berkowitz & Gibbs, 1983).

At this point, we felt that we had demonstrated both the validity and reliability of transactive discussion.

ROLE OF TRANSACTIVE DISCUSSION
IN MORAL EDUCATION

One cynical but important question this raises is, So what? In other words, what can we do with this scheme? Let us reflect back now on our preceding analysis of the moral education discussion literature. We had concluded that we seemed to have some reasonable understanding of what I have termed second order, or predictive, variables of moral discussion, such as group stage heterogeneity, although we did uncover significant disagreement and confusion over some variables, such as teacher +1 modeling. We also noted, however, that we had a very limited understanding of first order or process variables in moral discussion. Indeed, this was a principal reason for the research that led to the discovery of transactive moral discussion. I would claim that we have clearly approximated a first order process variable in moral discussion. Furthermore, it seems to account for more variance in the developmental effects of moral discussion than does the more traditional second order variable of stage disparity. What we may have then is a variable that can significantly increase the power of moral discussion education programs. How then can we utilize this laboratory discovery to improve moral education?

One critique I have often leveled at moral educators and theorists is that there seems to be an acceptance of an implicit assumption that optimal facilitator behavior is non-spontaneous and needs to be trained, but that optimal student discussion behavior is spontaneous and therefore requires no training. This does not seem to me to be a very reasonable assumption. It is assumed that if the right classroom or school atmosphere is established *by trained teacher behavior* then optimal student behavior will necessarily follow. Note the unidirectionality of this model. Teachers are instructed to "get the kids to X" or "make sure that students don't Y," as if the ability to X or Y must be innate, and teachers need only trigger or suppress their appearance. I contend that students are not spontaneously proficient in moral discussion skills. Certainly, we did find about 15% of spontaneous adolescent moral discussion to be Operational Transaction and a further 8% to be Representational Transaction. There was a significant difference between the moral stage changers and non-changers on these variables. I would guess that these are not upper limits we observed, and that training could increase the degree of transactive behavior in a moral discussion. Unfortunately, we have not yet run the training study that would test this hypothesis. We have, however, done some preliminary research that may shed some light on the issue. In an undergraduate peer counselor training program, John Prestby and I assessed the differences in moral discussion behavior between the counselors and three control groups. As we had predicted, the training of lower order reflective counseling skills produced the highest degree of Representational Transactive behavior and lowest degree of Operational Transactive behavior in the peer counselors. This Training by Transact Type interaction was statistically significant (Berkowitz & Prestby, 1980). We have shown these data to the personnel running the peer counselor program and have convinced them to include some more confrontive and directive counseling skills in their training. They have done so and we have collected a new round of data. Unfortunately, these data have not yet been analyzed. We do not have high hopes for this study, however, since we discovered after the fact that the additional training was limited to only one 1-hour session. It is very clear from the literature, however, that adolescents can be trained successfully in general communication skills. Furthermore, peer counselor training has led to moral development (e.g., Mosher, 1980; Sprinthall, 1980). We have further noted in our research that pairing students to maximize moral opinion differences, such as whether the fabled Heinz (see p. 29, this volume) should steal the drug, increases the length of discussions. It also appears that a desensitization period for nonfamiliar discussants may increase the length of discussions as well as the density of transaction in the discussions. We, therefore, will assume that students can also be trained in transactive behavior. We actually are assuming two points here: (1) that transactive behavior in a discussion *causes* the ensuing moral stage development; and (2) that individual differences in spontaneous moral discussion behavior are alterable to a significant degree through training. We have in actuality demonstrated neither of these as of yet. The training study we are planning will test both, however.

TRANSACTIVE DISCUSSION IN THE FAMILY

Previously, in discussing moral discourse, we examined the literature on moral development in the family. As we have noted, this literature has a high degree of similarity and relevance to the moral education literature. We now will turn again to family phenomena to learn more about transactive moral discussion. Sally Powers (1982) has been working in Stuart Hauser's laboratory on the role of family interactions in moral development. As part of a much larger project (Hauser, Jacobson, Noam & Powers, 1983; Hauser, Powers, Jacobson & Noam, in press), she has created a highly comprehensive coding scheme for analyzing mother-father-adolescent "trialogues" of moral dilemmas. Part of the coding scheme is an adaptation of the Berkowitz and Gibbs (1979) transactive coding scheme. In a study of over 50 families, Powers has questioned whether families with higher stage adolescents use more transaction than families with lower stage adolescents. She bases this hypothesis on the Berkowitz and Gibbs (1983) finding that higher degrees of transaction are related to greater gains in moral development. Hence, families whose children have achieved higher stages of moral reasoning may be using more transaction in their family discussion of moral issues. To test this, videotapes of each family discussing their individual positions about the Heinz dilemma were analyzed for degree of transaction in the discussion.

While the results are not perfectly consistent, there was a significant positive correlation between the adolescents' stages of moral reasoning and their own transaction in the discussions. However, only one of six correlations between mothers' or fathers' transaction and the adolescents' stages was significant and in this case mothers' transaction was *negatively* correlated to adolescent stage. This appears to be due, at least in part, to group differences in the sample. Families of both psychiatrically institutionalized adolescents and non-psychiatric adolescents were studied. The mother transaction/adolescent stage correlation was not significant for either of the groups individually. Adolescents' transaction was positively and significantly related to their own stages in the total sample and in the psychiatric group, but not in the control group. Thus, we see some evidence for the child's stage to be related to his/her own discourse, but not related to father's discourse and possibly negatively related to mother's discourse.

Powers (1982) also looked at parents' transaction and their own stages. Mothers show a confusing pattern, with no total sample relationship, and with a significant positive correlation for the control group and a significant negative correlation for the psychiatric group. Fathers had a non-significant positive trend for the total sample, which seemed due to the strongly significant positive correlation for the control group. Overall then, parents' transaction was not significantly related to their own stages for the total sample, was positively related for both parents in the control group, and was negative for the mothers and non-significant for the fathers in the psychiatric group.

What can we conclude from these results? We certainly now have further evidence that transaction is related to moral growth. Nevertheless, the results are somewhat inconsistent, and at this point, still somewhat incomplete. When we consider the relation of transaction to one's own stage of moral reasoning for mother, father and adolescent, four out of nine correlations for the two subgroups and the total sample are positive and significant, one is negative and significant and four are nonsignificant (three positive, one negative with one of the former approaching significance). On the other hand, when we look at the relation of parents' transaction to their child's stage of moral reasoning, we find five nonsignificant correlations and one significant negative correlation. It appears that one's own stage may be related positively to one's transaction, but not to one's parents' transaction. Some of the inconsistency has been explained by Powers (personal communication) as potentially due to her revision of the transact coding scheme, which she feels may have dulled its precision. She has noted that one of her coding category groups includes Representational Transacts, which we have already shown to be at best weakly related to moral growth. Indeed, she reports this coding group to be negatively related to adolescent stage in her study and predicts that an analysis of Operational versus Representational Transaction may bolster her results. Despite such problems, however, we can conclude that transaction in family moral discussions is a meaningful variable. Whether laboratory family discussion is really indicative of family interactions in the home is certainly open to question, as Broughton (1982) has noted for the entire literature on moral discussion. Since Powers did not assess development that could be directly related to the discussions she assessed, we must be cautious in relating the interaction analyses to the adolescents' stages. There are many other variables operating in the home that might cause differential rates of moral development. Finally, we cannot determine causality from these data. That is, we do not know whether the transaction caused the development, vice versa or if some third variable caused both.

Powers' (1982) results do raise another interesting question, one that we have been interested in for some time. *Whose* transaction in a discussion is most related to Ego's development: Ego's or Alter's? Powers' data suggest it may be Ego's. Traditionally, in the literature it is assumed that it is Alter's discourse that causes development, such as in the +1 phenomenon. Another position, which Broughton (1982) has labeled "egalitarian romanticism," suggests that all discussants should benefit from a discussion, although American researchers tend to find only the lower stage member developing while the Swiss researchers sometimes find both members of a dyad developing. This question certainly deserves further study.

FORMAL OPERATIONS AND TRANSACTIVE DISCUSSION

Another question that remains unanswered concerns the source of transactive discussion. As noted in the Preface to this volume, research and practice in moral education has long overemphasized adolescence and de-emphasized other life stages. The research in transactive discourse is not an exception. Ironically, this research has stemmed from the discipline of developmental psychology. Nevertheless, the development of such discourse has been sorely neglected to date, except for the pioneering work of Max Miller (1980).

One way that we have attempted to tackle this developmental issue has been to look for developmental precursors to the use of transaction in adolescence. We have long been interested in Piaget's contention that formal operations implies a particular form of discussion. We have also long been aware of the logical basis for many of the Operational Transacts. We have, therefore, hypothesized for some time that formal operations may be necessary for some of the Operational Transacts.

Before we proceed further, however, let us examine a conversation between two ninth grade boys (approximately 13 or 14 years old) that I overheard on a public bus and have reconstructed. You may recognize this exchange as a good example of developmental play (what I term "practice/play") in the service of exercising nascent formal operational structures. These two boys were in essence playing "put down" on a public bus. They were using a concept which they called "hornybird." It seemed to have a clearly derogatory connotation which appeared to be derived from its homosexual and hypersexual features. What you will be reading is a reconstruction and excerpt, since I was remiss in my duty as a social scientist and did not have recording equipment with me at the time. I will simply refer to the boys as "A" and "B."

A1. You are a hornybird.
B1. No. *You* are a hornybird.
A2. You are the biggest hornybird I've ever seen.
B2. You are the hornybird of hornybirds.
A3. No, I'm not, you hornybird. You're such a hornybird I can't believe it.
B3. You must be a hornybird because you don't have a girlfriend.
A4. Your mother is my girlfriend.
B4. Oh, big man! You'd be afraid to go near my mother.
A5. Oh, no I wouldn't.
B5. Why don't you ask her out then? Because you're a hornybird—that's why!
A6. I will so ask her out. Besides, you're the hornybird—not me. Hornybirds are always confused.
B6. Right and you're confused if you think I am the hornybird, so that proves you are a hornybird, you hornybird.
A7. Hornybirds always deny they are hornybirds. That's a sure test of being a hornybird, and you said you're not a hornybird, so that makes you a hornybird.
B7. Are you a hornybird?
A8. I used to be a hornybird. I admit it, but I'm not anymore, you hornybird.
B8. Ah, so you deny you are a hornybird. That makes you a hornybird.
A9. I didn't deny it. I admitted I *used to be*. Only non-hornybirds can admit they used to be hornybirds.

B9. Are you a hornybird now?

A10. I used to be.

B10. Are you a hornybird now?

A11. No.

B11. Aha! That proves it! You are a hornybird. You said hornybirds always deny they are hornybirds and you just denied it, you hornybird.

A12. But non-hornybirds can also deny it, and I am not a hornybird. But hornybirds are also always accusing non-hornybirds of being hornybirds. Are you calling me a hornybird?

B12. Yeah, but . . .

A13. No "buts." You are accusing me of being a hornybird, so that not only makes you a hornybird, hornybird, hornybird, but proves that I am not a hornybird. Besides, I've seen that Elaine that you went out with. What a pig! (At this point the two exited from the bus, to my disappointment and the relief of all the other passengers, two of whom were seniors in the same high school as the two discussants. One of the older students remarked at their passing, "What infants! They must have just taken freshman logic!")

We can note a number of interesting aspects of this exchange. First, note the conflictual mode of the discussion. It need not be malicious to be conflictual. Indeed, a good dialectical theorist should tell us that conflict can be cooperative and constructive. Second, note the sequence of strategies employed. At first, assertion and denial are the tactics used to apply the derogatory label "hornybird" to each other (statements A1-A3). Then, in statement B3, B begins to try to "prove" his accusation. A counters in A4 with a standard "put-down" which leads the discussion to regress into daring and name calling (statements B4-B5). In A6, A again attempts a logical "proof." These proofs are based on spontaneously generated characteristics of the derogatory concept "hornybird." B simply elaborates and applies A's criterion to A in B6. Then, A generates a new logical proof in statement A7 which produces a lengthy and interesting logical battle (B7-B12). In A12 and A13, A produces a resolution and a new proof which, along with A's return to name calling, concludes the argument.

We can note from this exchange that the new acquisition of formal logical thinking in adolescence may influence the nature of discourse, particularly discourse which is directed at resolving differences and conflicts, as Max Miller (1980) has suggested. These two adolescent boys seemed to be employing their nascent logical structures to reconcile their difference of opinion concerning which of them is to carry the burden of the label "hornybird." Let us now look at a somewhat less colorful but more rigorous investigation of this relationship between moral discourse and logical thinking.

We (Gibbs, Schnell, Berkowitz & Goldstein, 1984) have administered a measure of formal operational reasoning (Tobin & Capie, 1981) to college undergraduates and created 40 same-sex pairings of both formal, both transitional or both non-formal scores on this Test of Logical Thinking (TOLT). On a scale of 0–

10, formal reasoning has been operationalized as 6 and above, transitional as 2 or 3, and non-formal as 0 or 1. We then asked the dyads to engage in a tape-recorded moral dialogue of a pre-determined dilemma. As in our prior research, we transcribed the recordings and scored the discussions for transaction.

Since we only hypothesized that Operational Transaction would be related to formal operations and since only Operational Transaction has been found to be significantly related to stage development, we coded only Operational Transaction. Furthermore, it is important to note that the coding scheme used for these analyses is a working revision of the set of categories in Table 8.1.

Using a chi-squared analysis, we found a significant trend for formal reasoners to be more likely than transitionals who were more likely than nonformals to evidence high levels of transactive behavior; $X^2 (2) = 25.6, p < .0001$, as can be seen in Table 8.4. The frequencies of nontransaction are 9, 20 and 11 for the formal, transitional and nonformal individuals respectively, while there were 31 formal, but only 8 transitional and 1 nonformal subjects exhibiting any transaction. The overall mean percentages of statements that were Operational Transacts were 7% for the formal reasoners, 1.9% for the transitionals and 0.4% for the nonformal reasoners. The generally low percentages of transaction are due to two factors. First, they are limited only to Operational Transaction. Second, these discussions were the first interactions for each dyad. This is a variable which seems to reduce both the length and form of the discussion.

The "acid" test of our hypothesis is whether *non*formal, as opposed to *low* or *high* formal, thinkers produce *any* transaction in their dialogues. While TOLT scores of zero or even one are extremely rare in an undergraduate population, the data just presented include 12 individuals with TOLT scores of zero or one. Eleven of those 12 evidence *no* transaction at all. Thus, the results support our hypothesis of the relationship between formal operations and Operational Transaction.

We find a similar and compatible conclusion in Mugny, Perret-Clermont and Doise's (1981) review of their own research in the social-cognitive process of logical development. They note that "in order for the predicted cognitive acquisition to take place, the child should already possess certain 'prerequisites'

TABLE 8.4
Transactivity by Level of Formal Operations

| Operational Level | Transactivity | | |
	Present	Absent	Mean %
Formal	31	9	7.0
Transitional	8	20	1.9
Nonformal	1	11	0.4

which render him or her capable in some way of playing a significant part in an active confrontation and discussion with his partner'' (p. 322). Similarly, Miller (1980), as we have noted, has attempted to explore the parallels between logical thinking, social thinking and moral discussion skill development in children. For adolescents, this readiness that Mugny et al. refer to should be based in the acquisition of formal reasoning, as we have tried to demonstrate.

FUTURE DIRECTIONS

Where do we go from here? That is always the easiest and most enjoyable point of conjecture, largely because it does not require commitment or action. As I have suggested elsewhere for professional ethics education (Berkowitz, 1982), we need to build into moral education procedures for both assessing and training discussion skills and prerequisite skills in students. For adolescents, we need to determine readiness for transaction by assessing the degree of development of formal reasoning structures. If the structures are present, we need to train the transactive behaviors, and if they are not, we need to facilitate logical develop- ment first. I have begun experimenting with some one-trial training procedures, but have not yet systematically developed a training model. I would hope for the development of such a model to be influenced largely by moral educators them- selves rather than by researchers and psychologists.

As I have already mentioned, we are also currently planning a laboratory training study, but I would expect that to be followed eventually by actual applications of our model of transactive discussion in classrooms. Furthermore, I would hope to assess the effects of such curricula.

Fritz Oser and I have also begun to explore the nature of child and pre- adolescent moral discourse. Max Miller (1980), and William Damon (Damon & Killen, 1982) have already begun such work with children. David Bearison (1982) has begun some parallel work in social cognition with children. We can further learn much from the work of Mugny, Perret-Clermont and Doise (1981) in the area of logico-mathematical thinking with children. Hopefully, all of this work will lead to a life-span understanding of socio-moral interaction and its relationship to development. Such knowledge, may lead to better education for morality and social maturity.

REFERENCES

Arbuthnot, J. & Faust, D. (1981). *Teaching moral reasoning: Theory and practice.* San Francisco: Harper & Row.

Azrak, R. (1980). Parents as moral educators. In R. L. Mosher (Ed.), *Moral education: A first generation of research and development* (pp. 356–365). New York: Praeger.

Bearison, D. J. (1982). New directions in studies of social interaction and cognitive growth. In F. Serafica (Ed.), *Social-cognitive development in context* (pp. 199–221). New York: Guilford.

Berkowitz, M. W. (1980). *The social construction of knowledge.* Paper presented at the Tenth Annual Symposium of the Jean Piaget Society, Philadelphia.

Berkowitz, M. W. (1981). A critical appraisal of the educational and psychological perspectives on moral discussion. *Journal of Educational Thought, 15,* 20–33.

Berkowitz, M. W. (1982). The role of discussion in ethics training. *Topics in Clinical Nursing, 4,* 33–48.

Berkowitz, M. W. (1983). *The process of moral development through discourse.* Paper presented at the biennial meeting of the International Society for the Study of Behavioral Development, Munich, West Germany.

Berkowitz, M. W., Broughton, J. M., & Gibbs, J. C. (1977). *Equilibration in moral reasoning development: A new methodology.* Paper presented at the Seventh Annual Symposium of the Jean Piaget Society, Philadelphia.

Berkowitz, M. W. & Gibbs, J. C. (1979). *A preliminary manual for coding Transactive features of dyadic discussion.* Unpublished manuscript, Marquette University, Milwaukee.

Berkowitz, M. W. & Gibbs, J. C. (1983). Measuring the developmental features of moral discussion. *Merrill-Palmer Quarterly, 29,* 399–410.

Berkowitz, M. W., Gibbs, J. C., & Broughton, J. M. (1980). The relation of moral judgment stage disparity to developmental effects of peer dialogues. *Merrill-Palmer Quarterly, 26,* 341–357.

Berkowitz, M. W. & Prestby, J. (1980). *Transactive communication in peer counseling.* Paper presented at the Eighty-eighth Annual Convention of the American Psychological Association, Montreal.

Blatt, M. (1969). *Studies on the effects of classroom discussion upon children's moral development.* Unpublished doctoral dissertation, Harvard University.

Blatt, M. & Kohlberg, L. (1975). The effects of classroom moral discussion upon children's level of moral judgment. *Journal of Moral Education, 4,* 129–161.

Broughton, J. M. (1982). Cognitive interaction and the development of sociality: A commentary on Damon and Killen. *Merrill-Palmer Quarterly, 28,* 369–378.

Carkhuff, R. R. (1969). *Helping and human relations. Vols. 1 and 2.* New York: Holt, Rinehart and Winston.

Colby, A., Kohlberg, L., Fenton, Speicher-Dubin, B., & Lieberman. (1977). Secondary school moral discussion programs led by social studies teachers. *Journal of Moral Education, 6,* 90–111.

Damon, W. & Killen, M. (1982). Peer interaction and the process of change in children's moral reasoning. *Merrill-Palmer Quarterly, 28,* 347–368.

Doise, W., Mugny, G., & Perret-Clermont, A. N. (1975). Social interaction and the development of cognitive operations. *European Journal of Social Psychology, 5,* 367–383.

Fraenkel, J. R. (1978). The Kohlberg bandwagon: Some reservations. In P. Scharf (Ed.), *Readings in moral education* (pp. 250–263). Minneapolis: Winston.

Galbraith, R. E. & Jones, T. M. (1976). *Moral reasoning: A teaching handbook for adapting Kohlberg to the classroom.* St. Paul, MN: Greenhaven.

Gibbs, J. C., Schnell, S. V., Berkowitz, M. W., & Goldstein, D. S. (1984). *Relations between formal operational reasoning and logical modes of social conflict resolution.* Unpublished manuscript, Ohio State University, Columbus, OH.

Hauser, S., Jacobson, A., Noam, G., & Powers, S. (1983). Ego development and self-image complexity in early adolescence: Longitudinal studies of psychiatric and diabetic patients. *Archives of General Psychiatry, 40,* 325–332.

Hauser, S., Powers, S., Jacobson, A., & Noam, G. (In press). *Working with adolescents: Ego development and family processes.* New York: Free Press.

Higgins, A. (1980). Research and measurement issues in moral education interventions. In R. L.

Mosher (Ed.), *Moral education: A first generation of research and development* (pp. 92–107). New York: Praeger.

Hoffman, M. L. & Saltzstein, H. D. (1967). Parent discipline and child's moral development. *Journal of Personality and Social Psychology, 5,* 45–57.

Holstein, C. B. (1969). *Parental consensus and interaction in relation to the child's moral judgment.* Unpublished doctoral dissertation, University of California, Berkeley.

Kohlberg, L. (1969). Stage and sequence: The cognitive developmental approach to socialization. In D. A. Goslin (Ed.), *Handbook of socialization theory and research* (pp. 347–480). Chicago: Rand-McNally.

Kohlberg, L. (1980). High school democracy and educating for a just society. In R. L. Mosher (Ed.), *Moral education: A first generation of research and development* (pp. 20–57). New York: Praeger.

Kohlberg, L. (1981). *The meaning and measurement of moral development (Volume XIII: 1979 Heinz Werner Memorial Lectures).* Worcester, MA: Clark University.

Kohlberg, L. (1984). *The psychology of moral development.* San Francisco: Harper and Row.

Lockwood, A. L. (1978). The effects of values clarification and moral development curricula on school-age subjects: A critical review of recent research. *Review of Educational Research, 48,* 325–364.

Maitland, K. A. & Goldman, J. R. (1974). Moral judgment as a function of peer group interaction. *Journal of Personality and Social Psychology, 30,* 699–704.

Miller, M. (1980). *Learning how to contradict and still pursue a common end: The ontogenesis of moral argumentation.* Unpublished manuscript, Max-Planck Institute, Starnberg, Germany.

Miller, S. A. (1981). Conceptions of number. *The Genetic Epistemologist, 10,* 1–3.

Miller, S. A. & Brownell, C. A. (1975). Peers, persuasion, and Piaget: Dyadic interaction between conservers and non-conservers. *Child Development, 46,* 992–997.

Mosher, R. L. (Ed.) (1980). *Moral education: A first generation of research and development.* New York: Praeger.

Mugny, G., Perret-Clermont, A., & Doise, W. (1981). Interpersonal coordination and sociological differences in the construction of intellect. In G. M. Stephenson & J. M. Davis (Eds.), *Progress in applied social psychology,* Vol. 1 (pp. 315–344). New York: Wiley.

Olejnik, A. B. (1980). Adults' moral reasoning with children. *Child Development, 51,* 1285–1288.

Parikh, B. (1980). Development of moral judgment and its relation to family environmental factors in Indian and American families. *Child Development, 51,* 1030–1039.

Peck, R. F. & Havighurst, R. J. (1960). *The psychology of character development.* New York: Wiley.

Piaget, J. (1965). *The moral judgment of the child.* (C. M. Gabain, Trans.), New York: Free Press. (First published in English, London: Kegan Paul, 1932).

Piaget, J. (1967). *Six psychological studies.* New York: Vintage Books.

Piaget, J. (1971). *Biology and knowledge: An essay on the relations between organic regulations and cognitive processes.* Chicago: University of Chicago.

Piaget, J. (1972). Intellectual evolution from adolescence to adulthood. *Human Development, 15,* 1–12.

Powers, S. I. (1982). *Family interaction and parental moral development as a context for adolescent moral development.* Unpublished doctoral dissertation, Harvard University.

Rest, J. (1973). Patterns of preference and comprehension in moral judgment. *Journal of Personality, 41,* 86–109.

Rest, J. (1980). Developmental psychology and value education. In B. Munsey (Ed.), *Moral development, moral education, and Kohlberg: Basic issues in philosophy, psychology, religion and education* (pp. 101–129). Birmingham, AL: Religious Education.

Speicher-Dubin, B. (1982). *Parental moral judgment, child moral judgment and family interaction: A correlational study.* Unpublished doctoral dissertation, Harvard University.

Sprinthall, N. A. (1980). Psychology for secondary schools: The saber-tooth curriculum revisited? *American Psychologist, 35,* 336–347.

Stanley, S. (1980). The family and moral education. In R. L. Mosher (Ed.), *Moral education: A first generation of research and development* (pp. 341–355). New York: Praeger.

Taranto, M. A. (1984). *Microprocesses in moral conflict dialogues.* Paper presented at the Fourteenth Annual Symposium of the Jean Piaget Society, Philadelphia.

Tobin, K. C. & Capie, W. (1981). The development and validation of a group test of logical thinking. *Educational and Psychological Measurement, 41,* 413–423.

Turiel, E. (1966). An experimental test of the sequentiality of developmental stages in the child's moral judgments. *Journal of Personality and Social Psychology, 3,* 611–618.

9 Democratic Moral Education In The Large Public High School

Clark Power
University of Notre Dame
Notre Dame, Indiana

In the fall of 1981 Brookline High School, a semi-urban public school with approximately 2000 students and 200 faculty held its first Town Meeting, a democratic assembly of representatives from the student body, faculty, administration, and support staff. That meeting inaugurated one of the first large scale attempts to apply the cognitive developmental approach to democratic schooling. This approach grew out of Kohlberg (this volume) and Mosher's (1978, 1980) work consulting for three alternative high schools—S.W.S. (School Within-A-School) in Brookline (MA), Cluster in Cambridge (MA), and S.A.S. (Scarsdale Alternative School) in Scarsdale (NY). Experience in these experimental schools suggested organizational structures and intervention strategies for the Brookline High School (B.H.S.) Democracy Project.

In the first section of this chapter I will outline how these alternative schools were organized and how they functioned in order to give some substance to what I mean by the developmental approach to democratic education. Since Kohlberg (1980) and Mosher (1980) present somewhat differing accounts of how they undertook their tasks in the alternative schools, I will address the question of whether they, nevertheless, share a general approach applicable to the average large, public high school. In the second section I will argue that large, bureaucratized high schools tend to produce a moral atmosphere conducive to disciplinary breakdown. The democratic approach, as developed by Kohlberg and Mosher, offers a way of responding to disciplinary breakdown by providing an alternative organizational structure for the public high school. Finally I will discuss how the democratic approach is becoming institutionalized in a large high school, specifically B.H.S., and how those of us involved in the Democracy Project at B.H.S. have undertaken the task of staff preparation.

THE DEVELOPMENTAL APPROACH TO DEMOCRATIC
SCHOOLING: THE ALTERNATIVE HIGH SCHOOLS

The major architects of the particular approach we have taken in the B.H.S. Project are Kohlberg (this volume) and Mosher (1980). Although their formulations of democratic theory and practice differ on their conceptionalization of community, I believe their views are similar enough to regard them as generally sharing a common approach. Both emphasize the importance of direct participatory democracy as a way of promoting the development of all students in the school. Both focus on moral issues as comprising a major part of the agenda for democratic meetings. The alternative schools for which both consulted were quite similar in organization and functioning. Each school had a student enrollment of less than 125 and a staff of less than 10. Once a week all staff and students in these schools gathered for what was called a "Community Meeting" in Cluster and S.A.S. and a "Town Meeting" in S.W.S. In the Community and Town Meetings, staff and students engaged in discussions about problems in the school and made decisions through majority vote.

Although Community and Town Meetings were the focal points of democratic participation in these schools, democracy was, in Mosher's (1978) words, "a way of life." Classes were small and discussions were frequent. All schools established small faculty-student committees, for example, Cluster's Discipline Committee and S.W.S.'s Agenda Committee. Outside of meetings and classes, in hallways, offices, lounges and empty classrooms, students and staff from each of these schools could be seen discussing anything from current events to the agenda for their next meeting. There was no question that the staff and students were involved in a common project and felt a strong sense of responsibility for the quality of their shared academic, social, and moral life.

What makes Kohlberg and Mosher's approach to high school democracy unique is the way in which they integrated democratic principles with cognitive developmental theory. This was done in two ways in the alternative schools. First, they used the techniques of moral discussion described by Berkowitz (this volume) to enhance the quality of discussion in the democratic meetings. Second, they relied upon their assessment of the students' moral stages to guide them in selecting the kinds of issues that might best promote the students' development. For example, in Cluster school, which had a high proportion of students between stages 2 and 3, Kohlberg endeavored to foster development to stages 3 and 4. In S.W.S. and S.A.S., which had a high proportion of students between stages 3 and 4, Kohlberg and Mosher tried to encourage development to stages 4 and 5. While Kohlberg and Mosher were concerned with the individual development of students in the alternative schools, their primary focus was on group development. Kohlberg (this volume) conceptualizes group development as the development of a school's moral atmosphere and emphasizes the extent to which norms and values supportive of the moral community are institutionalized. Mosher (1980) articulates his notion of group development as the progressive establishment of democracy.

For Kohlberg and Mosher, knowledge about a school's level of development serves a purpose analogous to knowledge about the stage of an individual. According to the cognitive developmental theory of "optimal cognitive mismatch" the educator should stimulate individual development by directing the teaching process at or slightly above the individual's stage. Providing stimulation below or significantly above the individual's stage will be unproductive. In terms of promoting group development, Kohlberg and Mosher charge consultants and staff with a responsibility to become democratic leaders, guiding the group to a higher level of development. Acting as a democratic leader requires that one has both a realistic sense of the present limited level of the group and an ideal for future group development. To encourage groups to face issues which their members do not recognize as vital to the present life of the group is self-defeating. To refrain from prodding the group is to squander an opportunity to promote both individual and collective development.

Kohlberg and Mosher differ over how active a leadership role the consultant and teachers should assume in a high school democracy. Kohlberg (1980, this volume) recommends a strong, advocacy role for the consultant and educator. In contrast, Mosher has great faith in the spontaneous development of the group and is reluctant to endorse a leadership role which would interfere with that process. The tension between their positions reflects in part the tension of the democratic, developmental educator, who must give direction but still be sensitive to the will of the group. Neither Kohlberg nor Mosher thinks this tension should be collapsed. Kohlberg clearly stipulates that when teachers act as advocates, they have both a moral responsibility to respect the principles of democracy and a pedagogical responsibility to engage the school's level of moral atmosphere development. In his role as consultant, Mosher's (1978, 1980) theoretical reluctance to vigorously advocate was tempered somewhat by his firm support of proposals for affirmative action, greater student responsibility for disciplinary decisions, and mandatory group meetings. These proposals met considerable staff and student resistance and raised serious questions for S.W.S. members about the kind of school they wished to create.

While advocacy appears to be an issue for any democratic program based on developmental theory, it becomes a crucial issue for democratic programs with a strong community ideology, such as Cluster and S.A.S. In these programs, staff speak for communal ideals in advocating norms and values that reflect a sense of collective responsibility. In Cluster the most dramatic illustrations of a sense of collective responsibility were decisions in favor of collective restitution for victims of theft and property loss. In S.A.S. the best examples come from decisions to deal with members of the community who break the rules of the group by collectively agreeing to help them uphold the rules in the future. In S.W.S. there were no comparable decisions; in fact, during one meeting in which there was a specific proposal for collective restitution, a staff member summarized the thrust of the majority of arguments by stating "This is not a collective responsibility school. This is an individual responsibility school." This difference between the "collective responsibility schools," Cluster and S.A.S., and the "individual responsibility school," S.W.S., reflects a difference in the theories of community entertained by Kohlberg and Mosher and in the particular kinds of advocacy that followed from those theories. Mosher's sense of community is more restricted than is Kohlberg's. For Mosher, community is based on a willingness to cooperate in a democratic way to resolve conflicts. Advocacy is a matter of individuals making proposals to the group without the obligation of having to represent the will of the group or the shared ideals of community. In terms of applicability, Mosher's model better accommodates to the pluralism of the large public school and makes less of a demand on staff to deal with an unfamiliar ideology of community than does Kohlberg's model. For these reasons the B.H.S. Democracy Project relied primarily on Mosher's model for the initial phase of the project with the expectation that Kohlberg's communitarian model would become more applicable in a later phase of the project.

Studies on the effectiveness of the democratic approach indicate that it has been reasonably successful in promoting individual and group development. Modest gains have been found in Cluster and S.A.S. students' moral development (Kohlberg, this volume). The moral atmospheres of all the alternative high schools have been assessed as significantly more positive than their regular school counterparts (Kohlberg, this volume). The moral atmospheres of the alternative schools were characterized by a high degree of commitment to community and to such shared normative values as caring and trust. Positive changes in the moral atmospheres of the schools have been accompanied by positive changes in student behavior. Successes have been noted in dealing with the problems of stealing (Power & Reimer, 1978), racial integration (Kohlberg, 1980; Reimer & Power, 1980), low levels of academic participation and aspiration (Power & Higgins, 1982), and alcohol and drug use (Kohlberg, Lieberman, Power & Higgins, 1981). Mosher (1980) found that in S.W.S. there was significantly greater student participation in community activities outside of school than in comparison schools.

Although a good case appears to have been made for the small, democratic alternative high school, many educators have asked if this approach is applicable to the large public school. This question raises a prior question: Is there a need for this kind of approach in large public schools? Before beginning to describe how a large high school might think about adapting a democratic approach for moral education, I will indicate some problems common to large public high schools that I believe call for a democratic approach.

THE MORAL ATMOSPHERE OF THE LARGE
HIGH SCHOOL

School Culture and Crime

The need for democratic moral education is perhaps most evident when one considers the high rates of violence, crime and vandalism in contemporary high schools. As I hope to show, these problems are not simply due to permissive teachers or to psychologically disordered students. The problems of crime and disruption in our schools have their origins in a declining school culture or, more specifically, in a low level of moral atmosphere. There is a growing body of research that indicates that large, highly bureaucratized schools tend to produce an environment that has a negative effect on students' sense of moral responsibility and behavior.

In a review of research on school crime, Garbarino (1978) notes in dismay that schools currently provide an excellent "growth medium for crime" and that some of the tactics schools currently employ to combat crime, such as security guards, may actually backfire, further eroding relationships among staff and students and leading to increased crime. He argues that attempts to deal with school crime, if they are to succeed, must be based on an ecological sensitivity that does not focus narrowly on student achievement or individual development but on the school environment. What makes a school an excellent medium for crime? Garbarino points to the following: large school size, curricular specialization, neglect of character development as a responsibility of the school, and a lack of adult feedback to students.

Since 1930 the total number of schools in the United States has decreased three-fold, whereas the number of students has doubled (Guthrie, 1979). An impressive body of studies demonstrates that large group size is dysfunctional to a school organization. The classic study of Barker and Gump (1964) demonstrated that a greater percentage of students in small schools participated in school activities, held positions of responsibility, and felt more challenged academically and socially than did students in large schools. Large schools, although offering more facilities and a greater variety of courses and activities than small schools, fall short in providing an atmosphere conducive to social cohesiveness and cooperation. Furthermore, the studies indicate that large schools have the most detrimental effect on academically marginal students.

The increased size of schools has brought with it a more diversified and specialized curriculum, more elaborate educational facilities such as computer centers, labs, and large libraries, and distinct support services within the school, such as administrators in charge of school discipline and security, guidance and adjustment counselors, and social workers. Indeeed, a major impetus towards large schools has been increased economy and efficiency in providing these resources (Fox, 1980). The tradeoff for greater specialization is a greater segmentation of the students' experience in school. Teachers, administrators, and counselors are bureaucratically organized into distinct departments, offices, and centers throughout the school; and coordination is infrequent and difficult. Thus, student contact with staff is limited by the particular expertise of the staff member and there is little or no coordination among staff in order to monitor the overall well-being of the student.

When disciplinary problems arise in such a school, there are specialized personnel (administrators and counselors) available whose role it is to see that these problems are dealt with as efficiently as possible. This division of labor supposedly frees teachers and students to concentrate more fully on the curriculum. However, it also limits their sense of responsibility for the school as a whole and wastes an invaluable opportunity for moral education. When school discipline is treated within a highly bureaucratized context, the moral dimension of disciplinary problems is often lost. Instead of regarding disciplinary problems as symbolic of a moral breakdown in the school community, administrators and counselors tend to treat them as failures to properly manage and control behavior.

Moral Atmosphere Analysis

According to our analysis of moral atmosphere, treating disciplinary problems solely as matters of social control creates a climate of mistrust and fear which only exacerbates the problems in the school. I will now turn to our moral atmosphere analysis and indicate what we mean by a ''low'' or a ''deficient'' moral atmosphere and how it can lead to problems with school discipline. In doing so I will shift my focus from schools in general to B.H.S. and discuss baseline data we collected from moral atmosphere interviews with B.H.S. students.

Our method of assessing moral atmosphere consists of presenting students with several dilemmas which typically occur in high schools. For example, should a student volunteer to help an unpopular classmate, if helping requires considerable self-sacrifice? Should a student succumb to peer pressure to smoke marijuana on a class trip? Should a student intervene in some way on observing a theft taking place in class? Should a student agree to integrate a racially-imbalanced class? These dilemmas are designed to elicit not only individual students' socio-moral reasoning but also their perception of the norms and values that are shared by fellow-students. In focusing on student perceptions of shared norms and values, we probe specifically in the following areas:

1. How do students value their school as an institution (Degree of Community Value)?
2. To what extent do students, as members of the same school, share norms and values of care, respect for rules, trust, and integration (Degree of collectivity)?

3. How committed are students to uphold norms and rules of the school (Phase of the norm)?
4. What shared understandings do students have of the norms and values which regulate their interactions in school (Collective stage)?

Degree of Community Value

Our first dimension of moral atmosphere, Degree of Community Value, concerns how students value their school as an institution. Our interest in pursuing this question is to determine, first, whether students value their school at all. If they do, then the question becomes in what way they value the school. Do they value it instrumentally as a place to get a good education, prepare for a job, have a good time, etc., or do they value it intrinsically as a community of care and shared responsibility? Here is a response from a B.H.S. student, Jay, when he was asked whether his school was a community.

Nobody really takes pride in the school except a few who are good students or very good athletes. Where people don't take pride in something, go out of their way to help each other, the community doesn't really benefit. It doesn't promote the welfare of the school. Kids go vandalize a lot. There is no sense of caring, helping each-other.

Later in the interview, when asked about marijuana use, Jay went on to say that the goal of B.H.S. was "to learn" and that students should realize that coming to class "stoned" would have a negative effect on the school. Jay tells us in these and other comments that he values B.H.S. as a place where learning goes on and where friends can enjoy each other's company. Jay does feel obliged to maintain the learning atmosphere of the school by not getting high on drugs and by maintaining a positive attitude. However, he adds that there are many students who do not share his sense of commitment to the school. While Jay has overstated the problem of community at B.H.S. by saying "nobody takes pride in the school," he correctly points out that the students who do not take pride are those "marginal students" who do not participate in extracurricular activities or who are having academic difficulties.

The way in which students value their school is crucial, not only with respect to reducing negative behavior in school, such as crime and vandalism, but also in promoting positive behavior, such as a sense of caring that cuts across divisions between ethnic groups and social cliques. We can begin to expect students to feel a sense of responsibility for the school and its members only when they feel a genuine attachment to the school as a community. As Durkheim (1973) has so forceably argued, discipline and attachment to the group are two essential elements of morality and moral education. If students are to accept the constraints of group norms and rules, they must be attracted to a group that they perceive as desirable and good. From our perspective, the fundamental problem that must be addressed in large high schools such as B.H.S., is the detachment of many students from the school. Often, instead of seeing themselves as actively constituting the core identity of the school as a community, they see themselves passively as the recipients or non-recipients of benefits from an impersonal institution. Thus, even a school with an outstanding reputation for its curriculum, faculty and plethora of extra curricular activities, such as B.H.S., can fail to meet student needs for participation in a genuine community of care.

Degree of Collectivity

Our second dimension, Degree of Collectivity, concerns the extent to which norms and values are shared by students and staff in the school. When asked about helping out in school, Jay tells us that students are more "worried about themselves" than others and that, in the case of being called upon to help an unpopular student, would likely say 'Let him worry about it himself, (and) do it himself somehow.' When asked about B.H.S.'s response to marijuana use, he says, "they are much too divided to handle the problem as a community." He reveals that most students would smoke marijuana on a class trip, and, even if they had promised not to, would say " 'who cares, I am going to do it' . . . They think it is the cool thing to do." These statements indicate that the B.H.S. students have not developed shared norms and values, at least with respect to matters of caring and drug use. Their sense of obligation for helping and rule-following is based almost entirely on individual concerns with little or no peer support in evidence. In fact, Jay tells us that the student peer group sometimes applies social pressure to break the rules ("they think smoking is cool . . . you are expected to smoke . . .") and to not be caring ("there is pressure if somebody is an outcast, it is hard to come out and do something for them").

Clearly a major difficulty in many schools such as B.H.S. is the gap between the expectations of adult authorities and the student culture. Sometimes, as in the case of marijuana use, adult and student norms may be in opposition. Attempts to enforce such a norm through a coercive use of authority only widens the gap between adult and student, often leading to a "catch us if you can" response to adult threats. In problem areas such as stealing, adult authorities and most students happen to have a similar moral evaluation that stealing is wrong, but they typically do not have a shared norm of trust or respect for property based upon an agreed upon expectation as members of the same community. Although students and staff say, "*I* think stealing is wrong," they have not established, through discussion and agreement, enough of a collective sense to say "*We* think stealing is wrong and a violation of our community." Becoming a community entails sharing norms and values out of a sense of group membership. Our research indicates there is little reason to expect that norms and values will instantaneously come to be shared once school authorities articulate them. What seems to be required is that all members of the school explicitly discuss common problems and agree upon solutions.

Phase of the Norm

The third area addressed by our moral atmosphere research, the Phase of the Norm, is the extent to which members of the school are committed to uphold the norms and rules of the school. We may expect that if a school has not developed a shared sense of obligation to follow norms, there will be little or no sense of a shared obligation to enforce them. In fact, Jay and other students state that it would be "dangerous" to report another student for smoking marijuana because students have a strongly held peer group norm against reporting a fellow student for any kind of offense. While Jay feels obligated to obey B.H.S.'s drug rule, he does not feel it prudent or even obligatory for him to enforce this rule. Responsibility for enforcing rules belongs to those who make up the rules. He states that:

> A faculty member should enforce the rules, because they are the ones setting up the laws . . . whereas a student wouldn't have that responsibility . . . If they (students) were student leaders or in the student government they might . . . I think the average student is under no obligation to report them (those violating the drug rule) . . . WHY? The student is more of a follower and the teacher is generally a leader. They have set up the laws, so they have to hold them up.

As we can see from these remarks, Jay sharply distinguishes the responsibility of those in leadership roles and most students. This division of labor makes it difficult, if not impossible, for faculty to effectively enforce a rule against marijuana smoking, for example, and it only widens the gap between the adult and peer cultures in the school.

Collective Stage

The fourth area which we examine in our moral atmosphere interview, Collective Stage, refers to the moral adequacy of the norms and values shared by members of the school. This is a very difficult area to assess in schools that have few if any norms with a high degree of collectivity, that is, few genuinely shared norms. Those which are shared to a degree, such as a norm against "ratting" on a fellow student or against helping a student who is not a member of one's clique, are not shared out of a sense of a moral obligation but out of a desire for behavioral conformity with the peer group. Although it is difficult to use Kohlberg's scoring system for prescriptive moral reasoning to assess the stage of descriptions of behavioral norms made normative by the presence of peer pressure, we have tried to do so when possible. We generally find that students appeal to concerns scorable from a stage 1 fear of being beaten up if they fail to conform to a stage 2/3 concern for being accepted as a member of their clique if they do conform. The stages used in describing these peer group norms are in most cases a stage or more below the moral judgment competence of students, as assessed by Kohlberg's Standard Moral Judgment Interview.

When students in B.H.S. reported a shared rationale for upholding school rules against drug use and stealing, the most frequent justification given was the fear of being caught and punished, a stage 2 justification according to Kohlberg's scoring system. This reasoning was far below the competence of most of the students in the school, whose stages of moral judgment were generally between stages 3 and 4. One explanation for the prevalence of this stage 2 reasoning about school rules has to do with the failure of adult authorities and students to develop shared norms and a shared sense of responsibility for upholding those norms. If the staff fails to influence students to make an internal commitment to school norms and rules, their only means of social control consists of external measures of threat and coercion. These measures do not appeal to the higher moral sentiments of students. For example, when administrators respond to stealing and vandalism with guards, locks, and threats of criminal prosecution, students are not challenged to understand and commit themselves to upholding the values of private and public property. Nor are they inclined to think of their school as a community.

The Written Moral Atmosphere Test

Having illustrated the conceptual scheme utilized in our moral atmosphere analysis with examples taken from clinical moral atmosphere interviews administered in B.H.S., I will now present baseline data on B.H.S. obtained with written moral atmosphere interviews. We designed the written atmosphere interviews to follow the format of Rest's (1979) Defining Issues Test. We took the same dilemmas we used in the clinical interview and asked students to agree or disagree with typical responses to them and to rank certain ones in order of importance.

This test has the obvious practical advantages of greater ease in administration and scoring over the more cumbersome clinical interview format. More importantly the pencil and paper format may conceptually be a more suitable method of data gathering than the clinical interview. The clinical interview is a production task which requires students to present their own descriptions of the environment. The difficulty with such a method is that students with reasoning competencies at moral stages below the stage of the moral atmosphere may lack the competence to generate stage descriptions. The pencil and paper interview is a recognition task, which simply requires that students choose from among a variety of descriptions of the moral atmosphere. This method makes it possible for students at lower stages to identify prototype responses at higher stages that may be most descriptive of their school's moral atmosphere.

TABLE 9.1
Summary Comparison of Means on Degree of Collectivity, Phase
and Stage

	Degree of Collectivity		Phase		Stage	
	Self	Other	Self	Other	Self	Other
SWS n = 22	4.6	3.8	3.4	3.0	326	294
BHS n = 33	3.7	2.8	2.6	1.8	293	271
F	12.5***	7.3**	5.0*	10.7**	10.6**	5.6*

***$p < .001$, **$p < .01$, *$p < .05$

Looking at Table 9.1, which compares B.H.S. with S.W.S., the alternative high school housed in B.H.S., we see that S.W.S. scores significantly higher on the following dimensions of the moral atmosphere: Degree of Collectivity, Phase of the Norm, and Collective Stage. These results are summary scores, taken across four dilemmas. Note that this table provides two scores for each dimension: a "self" score and an "other" score. Students are asked to make two sets of responses, first from their own perspective and then from the perspective of most others in the group. Degree of Collectivity and Phase statements were arranged to form Gutman Scales. Degree of Collectivity and Phase Scores were simply calculated by adding positive responses. Stage scores were calculated to yield a score similar to Kohlberg's Moral Maturity Score.

These results are similar to those obtained with the clinical interview (Kohlberg, this volume). Thus we have some reason for confidence in our assessment instrument and in our finding that there is a significant difference between the moral atmospheres of S.W.S. and B.H.S. Since S.W.S. had long followed the democratic approach we wished to pursue in B.H.S., it is fitting to regard its moral atmosphere development as a goal and a possibility for B.H.S.

THE BROOKLINE DEMOCRACY PROJECT

The Origins of the Project

The origins of the current project, which applies a developmental approach to democratic moral education, go back to 1979 when the Department of Justice warned the town of Brookline about escalating racial and ethnic violence. In response to numerous incidents in the town and in the high school, B.H.S. participated in a thorough school climate study by a local consulting firm. This study indicated there were very serious problems of school climate in the high school, problems that contributed not only to racial incidents but also to widespread disciplinary problems and student alienation. The study also showed that S.W.S. had developed a very different, positive school climate and recommended S.W.S. serve as a model for reform in the larger high school. The three most significant recommendations of the study were as follows: (1) to establish socially significant, small sub-units within the high school, which would be racially and ethnically diverse; (2) to increase student and staff contact outside of courses; and (3) to increase student participation in decision-making.

The first action taken on these recommendations was to hire Robert McCarthy as headmaster in 1980. Before taking the Brookline job, McCarthy had successfully initiated a Town Meeting form of representative democracy in a high school of approximately 600 students. With the help of Robert Kenney, a doctoral student working with Ralph Mosher, and members of the high school staff, McCarthy led discussions during the school year 1980/1981 among faculty and students about the particular form democracy should take in the high school. At the end of the school year the choice was narrowed to a Town Meeting model, advocated by McCarthy, versus an *ad hoc* committee model, advocated by several faculty. A school-wide referendum involving students and staff chose the Town Meeting model. The Town Meeting structure called for a representative body composed of 45 students and 30 staff (faculty, administrators, secretaries, custodians and cafeteria workers). All seats on the Town Meeting board are elected, with the exception of three student seats which are reserved for appointed representatives of minority groups with insufficient elected representation.

The second action taken on the school climate recommendations was to initiate a Fairness Committee. The Fairness Committee's structure and procedures developed out of Elsa Wasserman's (1980) effort to introduce some of the democratic practices evolved in the Cluster School into the large Cambridge High School as well as from McCarthy's (Kenney, 1983) experience establishing a Judiciary Committee in his previous school. The Fairness Committee is composed of a volunteer group of approximately 15 students and 4 faculty. It meets in order to resolve disagreements among individuals and subgroups and to hear appeals of disciplinary decisions. The Fairness Committee's most outstanding contribution, when it was first established, was to quiet tensions between rival groups of students who, during free periods, congregated in various doorways and on landings referred to as their "turf." Many students complained about being harassed when they passed through these "turf" areas, which led school administrators to threaten to outlaw them. The Fairness Committee provided a public forum for the different parties to work out an agreement that allowed for informal congregating but forbade blocking passage or harassment.

The third action taken on the school climate recommendations was to establish a Democracy Project (with funding from a federal E.S.A.A. grant) that would support existing programs, such as Town Meeting and Fairness Committee, and would establish new programs as needed. In 1981 I was hired as projector director. With the help of Mosher, who continues to consult for this project, and Kenney, I attempted to work out with the Brookline High School staff a broad theoretical and practical orientation to democratic decision-making and moral atmosphere. I also proposed an overarching plan for the project, which I saw as unfolding in three phases. In the first phase priority would be given to representative structures, such as Town Meeting and Fairness Committee, which would introduce democratic decision making on a school-wide basis. In the second phase, the focus of attention would be on establishing direct, participatory democratic decision-making structures within the school's existing administrative subunits. B.H.S. is divided into four large administrative subunits, called houses, each with 500 students from all grade levels. The houses are further subdivided into 20 homerooms. I envisioned each house having three or four Disciplinary Committees made up of approximately 8 to 10 students and 2 staff, which would deal with students who violated school rules. Membership on the Disciplinary Committees would be through random selection and members would rotate quarterly. The homerooms would be used for discussions of major problems in the school such as stealing, vandalism, and racial tensions in order to prepare students and staff for school-wide referenda on major rules and policies. In the third phase of the project, the houses themselves would be broken into smaller units, modeled on the alternative high schools.

Staff Development

The first and most important issue we faced in our project was staff development. As we saw the issue, we had a dilemma. We could either delay the implementation of each phase of our project in order to spend time preparing staff for future involvement or we could forge ahead and provide on-the-job training. We chose the latter course, partly because funding was limited to a short period of time and partly because we thought it pedagogically most sound. We felt that the best way to address staff concerns, such as whether democracy would lead to a tyranny of the student majority or to a loss of respect for adult authority, would be to encourage them to answer their own questions through their actual participation on a Town Meeting or Fairness Committee. From our perspective, experience would be far more convincing than theoretical arguments for why democracy should work or assurances by project staff that democracy had worked elsewhere. What the staff members on Town Meeting and Fairness Committee discovered was that there was very little bloc-voting by staff or students on any decision and that staff were as likely to disagree among themselves as they were with students. Also, they found that Town Meeting and Fairness Committee led to a deeper respect for authority in the school. As both staff and students took a legislative perspective in making decisions on rules and policies of the school, they became concerned with strengthening the authority of their decisions and policies by making them fairer and better understood and accepted. The head-master and housemasters found that the Town Meeting and Fairness Committee assisted them in their roles by making the problems of school discipline and inter-ethnic relations more public and by building a broader base of support for school rules.

The most difficult question of authority which surfaced in both Town Meeting and Fairness Committee was where to draw the line between democratic authori-ty and the professional authority of the teacher. McCarthy and I agreed that Town Meeting and Fairness Committee should confine themselves to issues that dealt with disciplinary rules in the school and with inter-group relations among students or staff and students. Rather than establish more detailed guidelines, we left room for borderline cases, such as grading, to be resolved as they arose. The first borderline case concerned a new plus-minus grading policy that had been adopted by the administration with faculty consultation at the end of the previous school year. A small group of students argued that this policy was unfair because it might arbitrarily lower grades and because students should have had some input into the original decision. They enlisted support from several faculty mem-bers who thought the plus-minus decision had been adopted without sufficient study and discussion. Instead of trying to resolve whether Town Meeting had the prerogative to overturn the previously decided grading policy, the dissident students and staff were authorized by Town Meeting to form a committee, which was required to include proponents and critics of the new policy, and to report their committee's recommendations to Town Meeting. After a semester of re-search into the issue and polls of student and faculty reactions following the first issuance of grades, the committee unanimously recommended that the new plus-minus policy be continued.

The second case arose out of a complaint by several students that their teacher had given them a major homework assignment over the Christmas holiday that interfered with previous travel arrangements. These students initially proposed a rule that would prohibit any major assignments over a holiday period. However, they readily agreed to a compromise providing that teachers who wished to give major assignments over a holiday period must allow sufficient time for students to complete the assignment either before or after the holiday period. Most of the faculty had balked at the initial proposal because they felt it undermined their authority as teachers to determine what was a fitting homework assignment. However, they voted for the compromise proposal, which they recognized was addressed specifically to a fairness issue.

The third case concerned a grievance, filed with the Fairness Committee by several students, that their teacher had given a disproportionately high percent-age of low grades on a test. The Fairness Committee offered to serve as a mediator between the faculty member and the students. The teacher refused the mediation and the students urged that the Fairness Committee hold hearings to adjudicate this case. After considerable discussion the Fairness Committee de-cided the issue was within the professional jurisdiction of the teacher and declined to hear the case. Committee members expressed their ambivalence about this decision and recommended that the faculty form a professional review board for such cases. These three cases served to clarify the distinction between judgments based on professional competence and judgments based on considerations of fairness although a "gray area" still remained. They also demonstrated that democracy could overcome faculty and student mistrust and antagonism, making possible increased cooperation.

Although we found that the staff could resolve certain issues through their experience in democratic decision-making bodies, we also believed we should supplement this experience with more formalized training for two reasons. First, we observed a need for the staff to become more reflective about their interactions in Town Meeting so that the meetings could have a greater educational impact on the students. Second, we wished to transfer the executive responsibility for the planning of the meetings from the project staff to the school staff as soon as possible. This would entail sharing with the school staff our theory of developmental democratic education with a specific focus on how Town Meetings could be directed to improve the moral atmosphere of the school. Thus we viewed staff training as a guided reflection on experience, relating theory to practice. By focusing staff training on a common base of experience, the resulting educational process could be one of genuine dialogue and exchange, rather than a simple transfer of information from trainer to staff. In this exchange, we recognized that trainers and staff could learn from each other and, indeed, had to learn from each other, if the project were to succeed.

Dewey (1964) noted that there are two distinct perspectives on the kind of staff training we wished to provide: a laboratory and an apprenticeship point of view. Both the laboratory and apprenticeship ideas stress the need for learning through practical experience but they differ greatly in how they relate theory to practice. According to the apprenticeship point of view, the purpose of practice is to attain mastery and skills in a defined area. Thus we may endeavor to train teachers to effectively employ a variety of moral and democratic discussion skills by having them practice techniques in their classes and in meetings. Developmental theory is secondary and subordinate to the acquisition of these skills. According to the laboratory point of view, the purpose of practice is to grasp the theoretical principles and methods which can then inform the independent acquisition of specific skills and proficiencies. Taking the laboratory approach to training teachers to be moral educators entails guiding teachers in the construction of their own theories of democratic moral education by helping them to reflect on meetings as case studies, illustrating general principles of ethics, moral psychology and sociology. Only after teachers are able to analyze the significance of interactions in democratic meetings according to developmental theory can they thoughtfully and critically construct their own pedagogical practices. As Dewey (1964) noted, it is not enough for teachers to master the mechanics of teaching because they may be lacking the insight to discern whether their teaching is having a meaningful influence on their students. Teachers must have developed the ability to penetrate into the "soul-action" of their students. They must always be "students of mind activity," always growing as "inspirers and directors of soul-life" (Dewey, 1964, p. 321).

The Shift from Representative to Direct, Participatory Democracy

In addition to addressing staff uneasiness about sharing decision-making with students, we also faced vehement objection from some staff that the B.H.S. Democracy Project was not serving the students it was specifically designated to serve—the alienated and isolated. Staff members correctly pointed out that the few minority students who belonged to Town Meeting and Fairness Committee were already well integrated into the school and thus hardly represented the disaffected student cliques in B.H.S. Some of the staff urged that the project suspend efforts at democratization and focus on consciousness-raising activities in the school. They believed that a truly representative democracy would only be possible after a great amount of student and staff preparation. In their view, democracy was an end or a goal of socio-moral education but not a means. In our view, democracy was both a means and an end. We thought that through democracy the building of B.H.S. as an integrated academic community could become a common project, uniting all students and staff. Our approach to the problem of reaching alienated and isolated students was to create, in the second phase of our project, democratic structures among smaller groupings of students in which all students would be required to participate. This entailed a massive mobilization of the staff who would have to help organize and direct these groupings.

We initiated staff preparation for the second phase by holding small group discussions with them about how members of B.H.S. might be able to respond to disciplinary problems such as stealing through a democratic process. By selecting a disciplinary problem as an issue we helped allay some fears that democracy would lead to laissez-faire neglect of school discipline or to a preoccupation with the trivial matters that typically make up student council agendas. Following these staff meetings, we began discussing the problem of stealing in Fairness Committee and Town Meeting—amassing statistics about the extent and seriousness of the problem and soliciting suggestions about how to deal with it. A student survey indicated that one in five students was a victim of theft during a semester. Proposals for resolving the problem included toughening up the penalties for stealing, upgrading security, and building a greater sense of shared responsibility for individual property and school property.

The Homeroom Discussions

Next, we designed a format for homeroom meetings to replicate the Town Meeting discussion of the issue. We stipulated that procedures similar to those used in Town Meeting were to be used in conducting these meetings. Town Meeting members were asked to assist the staff in chairing these meetings. The decision to hold these discussions in homerooms as opposed to classes was a controversial one. Most faculty felt they had better rapport with the students they taught for 50 minutes a day than they had with the students they saw for attendance-taking and announcements 10 minutes a day. The major drawback to using classes for the discussion was that in most cases students were tracked, that is, they were grouped by ability or achievement level. This meant that many classrooms would not represent the diversity of the student body. Homerooms on the other hand were heterogeneous, as students were randomly assigned to them. The fact that homerooms were less cohesive than classrooms was in our estimation a reason in favor of selecting them as a good starting place for building an integrated community through democratic decision-making.

Final preparations for the homeroom discussions entailed assigning all staff to a homeroom and providing them with detailed instructions for conducting the meeting. Two 50-minute discussions were held on the stealing problem. During these discussions, we directed students' attention to the seriousness of the problem and to their responsibility for building a climate of trust in the school. During the course of these discussions the influence of a student peer culture which permitted theft and protected those who stole became apparent. As one student described the situation, "You shouldn't steal, but the way society is everybody steals . . . If somebody is going to steal then more power to them. If you can get away with it you might as well." Students were so accustomed to theft at school that some blamed careless victims rather than the thieves. As one student put it, "If somebody is going to be dumb enough to bring something valuable to school they deserve to get it stolen."

In the second homeroom discussion of stealing, a specific proposal was advanced for a change in the penalties for stealing. With minor modifications, that proposal then was voted upon and accepted in a school-wide referendum. These discussions of stealing and the ones to follow concerning the problem of lateness were intended to introduce the idea of direct participatory decision-making to members of B.H.S. We did not expect that they would have an immediate, dramatic impact on the moral atmosphere or on student behavior. Experience in the alternative schools indicated that moral atmosphere development was a slow process that required repeated efforts to address problems.

The Disciplinary Committee

In addition to inaugurating homeroom discussions, the second phase of our project called for the establishment of House Disciplinary Committees. We pilot tested two D.C.s (Disciplinary Committees) in one of the houses. The first cases house administrators sent to the D.C. concerned students who were habitually late for class and students who flagrantly skipped classes. In resolving these the administrators looked upon the D.C. as a peer counseling group. The students proved to be quite adept at probing why a student was late or missing class and often showed a sympathetic understanding for the excuses given. Typically our first D.C.s concluded with students offering arguments why rules should be upheld and then establishing a probation period with the threat of a severe penalty if the rule-breaker did not act more responsibly. Often students on the D.C. would become aware that students who presented disciplinary problems did not really feel a part of the school, and they would offer to help them by finding an extracurricular activity to match their interests. The administrators working with the D.C. described it as "energizing" and one of the more rewarding experiences they had. They also felt that the D.C. had much more success in dealing with difficult cases than they had alone. In our consultations with administrators and students on the D.C., we stressed the importance of thinking of the D.C. as more than a peer counseling group but as a group representing the school community. This meant that D.C. members had to assume a responsibility not only to help the students called to the D.C. to get through school, but also to help develop a sense of respect and concern for the school community.

THE FUTURE OF THE PROJECT

Because the B.H.S. Democracy Project is not yet 3 years old it is difficult to predict whether it will succeed and become a model for other large, public schools. A staff evaluation undertaken by DeVos and Higgins (1982) at the end of the first year of the project found that a solid majority of the faculty supported its goals and the institutions of Town Meeting, Fairness Committee and homeroom discussions. Three-fourths of the faculty felt the project contributed to student understanding of democracy and two-thirds felt the project increased the students' sense of belonging to the school and cooperation. There was, however, a considerable amount of faculty ambivalence about democratizing decisions. As one faculty member put it, "A part of me feels the responsible adults should run the affairs of the school. Another part realizes that if we do not make the students share in the decision-making, we have not done our part in helping them to become responsible individuals."

Clearly much work needs to be done in order to assist the faculty in working out a sense of their role as developmental moral educators in a democratic school. Nevertheless, data from this evaluation and data collected at the end of each homeroom discussion indicate that most faculty members are willing to cooperate with the project as long as they are confident that it can have tangible effects on students and on the atmosphere of the school.

In terms of the phases of the implementation of the project, little development has occurred beyond the first phase. Town Meeting has slowly become institutionalized as an important part of B.H.S.'s governance structure. In a recent assessment of the history and progress of the project, Kenney (1983) concluded optimistically that Town Meeting is evolving and providing an increasing impetus for a more widespread democratization of the school. Whether the growth of Town Meeting will eventually lead in the direction of the second and third phases of the project is still an open question. The number of homeroom discussions and D.C. meetings declined in the second year of the project with a cut in the number of project staff. However, grassroots staff and student commitment to these institutions may actually have increased according to Kenney (1983) based upon evidence from Town Meeting discussions and supportive comments from administrators. Whatever the future of the Democracy Project at B.H.S. may be, we have learned a great deal about high school democracy and moral education by working with talented and committed staff and students. I believe members of B.H.S. have taken some very important steps that have brought about a greater sense of fairness and cooperation in the school and will provide a model for the future of democratic moral education.

REFERENCES

Barker, R. G. & Gump, P. (1964). *Big school, small school.* Stanford, CA: Stanford University.

DeVos, E. & Higgins, A. (1982). *Evaluation report for Brookline High School's E.S.A.A. Project.* Unpublished manuscript.

Dewey, J. (1964). The relationship of theory to practice in education. In R. D. Archambauld (Ed.), *John Dewey on education: Selected writings* (pp. 313–338). New York: Modern Library.

Durkheim, E. (1973). *Moral education: A study in the theory and application of the sociology of education.* New York: Free Press.

Fox, W. F. (1980). *Relationships between size of schools and school districts and the cost of education.* Technical Bulletin No. 1621. Washington, DC: Economics, Statistics, and Cooperative Services, Department of Agriculture.

Garbarino, T. (1978). The human ecology of school crime. In National Council on Crime and Delinquency, *Theoretical Perspectives on School Crime, Vol. 1* (pp. 353–389). Hackensack, NJ: New Gate Resource Center.

Guthrie, T. W. (1979). Organization scale and school success. *Educational Evaluation and Policy Analysis, 1,* 17–27.

Kenney, R. (1983). *The creation of a democratic high school: A psychosocial approach.* Unpublished doctoral dissertation, Boston University.

Kohlberg, L. (1980). High school democracy and educating for a just society. In R. Mosher (Ed.), *Moral education: A first generation of research and development* (pp. 20–57). New York: Praeger.

Kohlberg, L., Lieberman, M., Power, C., & Higgins, A. (1981). Evaluating Scarsdale's "just community school" and its curriculum. *Moral Education Forum, 6,* 31–42.

Mosher, R. (1978). A democratic high school: Damn it, your feet are always in the water. In N. A. Sprinthall and R. Mosher (Eds.), *Value development . . . as the aim of education* (pp. 69–116). Schenectady, NY: Character Research.

Mosher, R. (1980). A democratic school: Coming of age. In R. Mosher (Ed.), *Moral education: A first generation of research and development* (pp. 279–301). New York: Praeger.

Power, C. & Higgins, A. (1982). *The just community approach to moral education: Developing the moral atmosphere of the school.* Paper presented at the American Educational Research Association, New York.

Power, C. & Reimer, J. (1978). Moral atmosphere: An educational bridge between moral judgment and moral action. In W. Damon (Ed.), *New directions for child development: Moral development* (pp. 105–116). San Francisco: Jossey-Bass.

Reimer, J. & Power, C. (1980). Educating for democratic community: Some unresolved dilemmas. In R. Mosher (Ed.), *Moral education: A first generation of research and development* (pp. 303–320). New York: Praeger.

Rest, J. R. (1979). *Development in judging moral issues.* Minneapolis: University of Minnesota.

Wasserman, E. (1980). An alternative high school based on Kohlberg's just community approach to education. In R. Mosher (Ed.), *Moral education: A first generation of research and development* (pp. 265–278). New York: Praeger.

APPLICATIONS AND INTERVENTIONS
C.   THE WORKPLACE AND PROFESSIONAL TRAINING

10 Work Climate and Socio-Moral Development in Two Worker-Owned Companies

Ann Higgins
Frederick Gordon
Harvard University

For the past 3 years a group based at the Harvard Graduate School of Education has sought to theoretically and empirically investigate democratic organizations. This group has oriented toward practical projects in work democratization, both in worker-owned businesses and in "Quality of Work Life" projects of union-management cooperation. We intend our research to aid consultants to these two types of democratic organizations by providing systematic organizational assessments. We are developing a data base on a number of firms that will allow us to make comparative assessments. In addition, we are investigating theoretical questions concerning the relationship between work environments and the socio-moral development of adults.

The firms we discuss in this chapter have converted their structure of legal ownership. By converting to a cooperative structure, control which had previously been held by the owners is transferred to all individuals working in the organization on a one person/one vote basis; thus, each person owns one "voting share."

This change in the formal legal structure puts enormous stress on the organizational structures through which the enterprise is governed and on the people's attitudes and their norms of socially appropriate action. Often, organizations become democratic legally, but the relations between management and managed remain conventional. Alternatively, an organization may rid itself of its old style leadership in the name of democracy, but have no institutions for self-management to take its place. The result is typically frustration and chaos.

Under normal circumstances, various aspects of an organization are in equilibrium. Traditional organizations remain in equilibrium because the legal form (private ownership), mode of governance (authoritarian), worker attitudes (limited identification with the aims of the organization and development of a workers' culture to defend against managerial directives), and even technology (the breakdown of work into simplified and repetitious standard units so that it can be carefully monitored by management) all complement and reinforce one another. Changing one aspect of a work organization in the direction of democratization may not improve the organization immediately and, in fact, may destabilize it, creating tension on the level of individual psychological and social functioning and dysfunction at the level of the organization.

If the tensions are not identified and addressed, we believe, workers will come to feel that the "democratization" process has created problems that they do not understand well and that seem unresolvable. If the problems created by the change in ownership structure are not understood and resolved, the sort of cynicism that Johanneson and Whyte (1978) see as widespread in worker take-overs will establish itself and be difficult to reverse.

A THEORETICAL PERSPECTIVE

Following upon the work of the moral atmosphere of schools (see Kohlberg, this volume) we are developing a theory of the "work climate" of organizations. Our theoretical interest lay in developing concepts and measures that would bridge moral psychology and sociology. According to Durkheim (1933/1968), a group creates collective norms, which are group phenomena, sui generis. Group norms are collectively shared expectations about what should and should not be done by a member of the group under specified circumstances. Group norms also usually define appropriate attitudes that should be associated with particular behaviors (Mills, 1967). Groups create sets of norms that form systems in order to insure and regulate complex patterns of action. These systems of related norms form a social structure of the group that we call the *normative structure*. The normative structure of an organization is a primary component of its work climate.

More basically, we believe that moral action usually takes place in a social or group context and that the context has a profound influence on the moral decision-making of individuals. Individual moral decisions in real life almost always are made in the context of group norms. Furthermore, individual moral action is often a function of these norms.

Durkheim also wrote about the sense of attachment to the group, which in the school moral atmosphere research is discussed as the sense of community and the way in which students in a school value their school as a community. In our research on the work climate, we do not look directly at workers' and managers' sense of community, but we evaluate their sense of attachment to the organization and the reasons for their feelings of attachment or loyalty by assessing individual values. To understand more completely the work climate of an organization, we must understand the underlying values people hold and bring to bear as justifications for upholding or violating the organization's norms.

Although norms are group phenomena, values are individual. All individuals within a group may act in ways consistent with the group's norms, but their motivations for doing so most likely vary. Furthermore, the motivations or underlying values for upholding norms may be related to an individual's feelings of attachment to the organization or to his or her basic assumptions about what it means to be a moral person.

Individual values influence and, to some extent, determine the particular norms generated by a group or organization. They also define for each individual the actions he or she believes (1) are consistent with the group's normative structure and (2) constitute violations of the group's norms. Individual values also may reveal a person's assumptions about, and understanding of, the ways in which he or she is the same or different from other members of the group or organization. Insofar as this is true, individual values constitute a basis for people in an organization with shared or common norms to form allegiances to particular other individuals or subgroups within the organization.

Although values are expressions of an individual's moral identity and are recognized as springing from the individual's beliefs and assumptions about who he or she is, people recognize that they may and do share certain values with others. This is especially true in homogeneous organizations that have explicit and well defined purposes, goals or beliefs.

The modern workplace is most often not of the homogeneous type, but rather demands only behavioral conformity to work-related norms in addition to recognition and acceptance of the power and authority structures within the organization. However, some companies consciously attempt to create an image and encourage their employees to manifest that image by persuading them to adopt certain company-wide goals or values. This is usually done most successfully by appealing to more basic underlying individual values of the employees. Companies that are successful in creating common goals and an accompanying set of shared values as well as having common or collective norms are said to have a "corporate culture."

Our developing theory of work climate maintains that all organizations or workplaces have a "culture"; however, in many cases the depth and richness of the culture remain unrecognized and latent. By conceptualizing the work climate as the complex interrelationships of the various layers of the organization, from the visible actions and behaviors of the members to the normative structures that guide action to the underlying values of individuals that give meaning to both norms and behavior, we are attempting to construct a theory of organizations that truly does bridge moral psychology and sociology. Moreover, we think that such a theory will be better able to predict not only the development of organizations over time but also the potential problems or rifts that break apart or destroy the normative structure of a seemingly well functioning organization.

We stated earlier that when the workers of a company become its owners and, in a broad sense, its managers, tensions arise and cynicism and frustration can easily replace the initial feelings of pride and euphoria. We said the process of democratizing the functional management and production structures often raises problems for the worker-owners that they see as unresolvable or insuperable. To understand why this commonly happens, it is necessary to understand in more depth the role of the moral psychology of individuals.

In a democratic worker-owned firm, people must communicate with, confront, and successfully negotiate with all other members, many of whom are unlike themselves in culture, race, class, sex, and/or education. Although it is characteristic of much democratic theory to maintain that such diversity in a community or organization is beneficial to the development of democratic structures within it and to the development of more tolerance or democratic traits within the individual members, that diversity does not guarantee tolerance. Instead of people becoming more appreciative of their differences and willing to imagine a situation or problem from each other's perspectives, the work of democratization may, under certain conditions, create divisions which dialogue cannot easily bridge. The contact of diverse social groups may not lessen but may actually inflame differences and engender racism, sexism, or various hierarchical divisions on the basis of innate or acquired abilities.

The freezing of various subgroups into stereotypical conceptions has moral psychological ramifications. The understanding of the other as the basis of role-taking is narrowed and moral role-taking, as such, collapses. The perspective of the stereotyped group is not considered, save in its capacity to cause irritation or disruption. The stereotyped person is not seen as a morally autonomous individual with a point of view worthy of consideration. His or her values, norms and actions are not conceived as being the possible object of deliberate, rational choice, but rather as "facts of nature," and heaped together with physical and material conditions. Thus, the collapse of moral role-taking is the manifestation of the denial of moral dignity to the other. Stereotyping, therefore, constitutes an arresting or regression of individual socio-moral development, either globally or in its expression in particular situations or with particular segments of the social world.

Necessarily related to the moral psychological ramifications of a stereotypical conception of various subgroups within an organization are the sociological ramifications. Identification of stereotyped subgroups tends to split the organization so that it is no longer a community, but forms two or more separate groups which no longer share a common understanding of the normative structure of the organization. Communication and coordination suffer, negotiation becomes impossible, and the original organization may split apart.

It is important, therefore, to discover when diversity in a democratic organization or community leads to tolerance and an appreciation of differences, and when it splits a group and dehumanizes relations. In our research, we seek to analyze the relationship of the normative structure of an organization to the salient values expressed by individuals or groups for upholding or violating the norms of the organization. We have identified several cases in which the relationship between norms and values creates conditions under which individual moral role-taking may fail, stereotypic conceptions of subgroups may emerge, and an organization may divide or fall into disarray.

Cases of Norm-Value Relationships

The first case is one in which an organization has a common normative structure but has within it subgroups which hold different salient values that do not overlap at all, i.e., which are mutually exclusive. If one or more subgroups assert their values as being the necessary basis for upholding the normative structure of the organization or as being the necessary basis for organizational membership, then the normative structure of the organization is put under great strain. The inherent weakness of an organization in this situation is that moral role-taking among subgroups with mutually exclusive values is difficult and stereotypic conceptions are likely to exist, therefore making communication and negotiation about problems a limited process that ultimately fails. However, if the subgroups have some combination of overlapping salient values then the subgroup members will be able to engage in moral role-taking, stereotypic conceptions of subgroups will be less likely to emerge, and the possibility exists for the organization to ground its common normative structure on the set of overlapping values of the various subgroups.

The second case is one in which the organization does not have a common or shared normative structure but rather has a shared value, such as a common goal or sense of mission, which knits the organization together. If the shared organizational value or common purpose is weakened and strong mutually exclusive normative subgroups exist then different actions by the various subgroup members guided by their norms will be interpreted by other subgroups as underming the common purpose or mission. Moral role-taking and the avoidance of stereotyping the other will be difficult to maintain and the organization will be threatened. However, if the subgroups have some combination of overlapping salient norms, then the subgroup members will be more likely to engage in moral role-taking, misinterpretation of actions will be less likely to occur, and the organization will be able to function with adequate stability.

The alternatives in the third case represent both the most inherently unstable and stable structures. The unstable case is an organization comprised of subgroups that have both mutually exclusive norms and values, creating a confederation, at best. The extreme example, although not rare, is one in which organizational subgroups have in common not only norms and values, but also race, ethnicity, sex, class or education. The tendency for others to freeze that configuration into something that could be called ''group character'' is great. Thus, when such a group is viewed as containing not only a contingent combination of attributes but as having a necessary essence, moral role-taking is impossible, therefore limiting problem-solving to superficial, short-lived and uneasy compromises. The stable case is an organization comprised of subgroups, all of whom share at least one salient norm or value with one other subgroup. This knits together the organization into a complex set of relationships and minimizes the emergence of stereotypic conceptions of subgroups by each other because there exist demands within each subgroup for members to take the perspective of other subgroup members who are to some degree different from themselves. Moral role-taking within each subgroup then enhances the chance of moral role-taking among subgroups.

To summarize the central dynamic conceptualization of the relations among values, norms and actions in the different cases, we would argue that in an idealized conception of moral role-taking, conflicts about particular actions are referred back to specific norms under which they are subsumed and these norms are, in turn, referred back to the values which justify them. Therefore, moral argumentation is discussion that recognizes each of the three aspects and their relationships—one's own and others' values, their relation to norms and the ways in which norms should guide concrete actions. In contrast, when one is in conflict with a stereotyped other, the differentiation between the other's actions, norms and values collapses into a single essence that simultaneously may threaten the one's interpretation of one's own action, one's norms, and one's values—in sum, one's identity as a moral being.

In this chapter we analyze data collected at one point in time about the work climate of two worker-owned firms as examples of the first two cases. We can only anecdotally report how the relations among norms and the relations among values in each company has affected change over time in organizational stability. Longitudinal analysis of the work climate of one of these companies is being done currently by Mackin (1984) in his dissertation research. Before presenting the two case studies, we need to introduce our methodology and the way we have operationalized the concepts of norm and value that comprise the core of work climate as we have defined it.

THE METHODOLOGY AND MEASUREMENT
OF WORK CLIMATE

In traditionally managed and owned firms, the contradictions and weaknesses of the work climate often remain hidden or implicit. In democratically governed worker-owned companies, the work climate becomes explicit and results in the "moralization" of work, e.g., people can judge and criticize each others' commitment to the work and the way of working, using the newly legitimate basis of cooperative ownership. As a consequence, the democratic process reveals the contradictions and weaknesses that may be inherent in the work climate. Instead of understanding that flaws in the work climate create barriers to the successful democratic resolution of problems, the democratic process and governance structure itself is sometimes falsely identified as the only or major barrier. Therefore, we believe that it is especially critical for a new worker-owned company to receive useful information about its work climate in order to enhance the capacity of its workers to more fully engage in democratic problem solving and governance.

Our method of data collection is qualitative; we conduct in-depth, open-ended interviews with a sample of people representative of a cross-section of a firm. Our method of data analysis, however, is both qualitative and quantitative. The richness of interview material enables us to paint a portrait of a firm using the language of the workers themselves, thus offering them a description of the company's problems, strengths and alternative solutions that are immediately comprehensible and usable. In addition, because of the conceptual structure of work climate, we are able to characterize its aspects and their relationships using a quantitative methodology which allows us to compare one company with another and to chart the change of one company over time. This section, then, gives the operational definition and quantifiable aspects of the theoretical terms introduced in the previous section.

Norms

Since one major focus of our approach is on the normative culture of an organization, we identify the most important work-related norms and then analyze each norm in terms of three aspects. As stated earlier, a norm is a collectively shared expectation about what should and should not be done by members of a group in specified circumstances.

The first aspect of a norm we consider is its origin or source of legitimation. Although norms are group phenomena, they may have quite different bases of legitimation—through explicit discussion and agreement; through the tendency of members to conform to a set of behaviors without explicit discussion, through the imposition of directives from an authority, or through any individual's proposal of a set of expectations for the group that he or she has learned in another group.

The categorization scheme is ordinal. Norms at the higher levels originate within the group and are prescribed for the group by the speaker as a member qua member of the group speaking in the name of the group. Norms at the lower levels more often do not originate within the group, are more often seen as conformist tendencies or following orders or rules rather than as binding expectations, and are described by the speaker who speaks in his or her own name as an informant only, rather than as a group member qua member. Thus, this scheme distinguishes true group norms from behavioral conformity, rule-following, and individuals' values about how the group should function.

The categorization scheme for the source of legitimation of norms is similar to the scheme for identifying the degree of collectiveness of norms that is used in analyzing the moral atmosphere of schools (see Kohlberg, this volume). Table 10.1 gives the descriptions of the sources of legitimation for norms.

The second indicator of the strength of the normative culture of an organization is the extent to which norms have regulative power over the behavior of the group members. We term this aspect the phase of the norm. It is a measure of commitment to and institutionalization of a norm or set of norms. It also measures the developing institutionalization or decay of a norm over time. The phase scheme forms a Guttman Scale in which each higher phase implies all lower phases. The phase scheme moves from proposal to the group that it adopt a norm, to acceptance of the idea, to an expectation that the norm exists and will be upheld (the first phase that registers the existance of a true norm), and finally to disapproving or sanctioning of norm violations (see Table 10.2).

The third aspect is the "moral stage" of representation of a norm. This is a structural analysis of the articulation of the norm and the reasons given in support

TABLE 10.1
Source of Legitimation of Norms

Levels:	
0	*Denial:* Of any norm related to the action or policy in question. Source is the individual. Descriptive mode.
1	*Rejection:* Of the idea that a norm or agreement about a particular action or policy would be followed by members of the group. Source is the individual. Descriptive mode.
2	*Conscience:* An action in accordance with a norm should not be expected by the group because it should be left to each individual's free choice. Source is the individual. Prescriptive mode.
3	*Individual:* An action is performed that is consistent with maintaining the group norm but group membership is not yet the source. Source is in the individual person's history. Descriptive or prescritive mode.
4	*Delegated Authority:* An action is performed that is consistent with the norm articulated by authority, designated by management.
	(a) Source is authority having effective, real power of enforcement. Prescriptive mode.
	(b) Source is authority as figurehead, without power of enforcement. Descriptive mode.
5	*Personal Authority:* An action is performed that is consistent with the norm articulated by someone whose basis of authority rests upon personal attributes, such as charisma, trust or loyalty. Source is the personal authority. Prescriptive or descriptive mode.
6	*Technical Competence Authority:* An action is performed that is consistent with the norm articulated by someone whose authority rests upon respect for his/her expertise or experience. Source is the authority as expert. Prescriptive or descriptive mode.
7	*Representative Authority:* An action is performed that is consistent with the norm articulated by an authority who has been formally elected to be the group spokesperson. Source is the elected authority. Prescriptive or descriptive mode.

TABLE 10.1 (*Continued*)

Levels:	
8	*Aggregate-alienated:* The group or subgroup has a tendency to act in accordance with the norm but the speaker disagrees and does not conform behaviorally. Source is the observation of consistent behavior of others noted by the speaker. Descriptive mode, but can be prescriptive.
9	*Aggregate-accepted:* The group or subgroup has a tendency to act in accordance with the norm and the speaker agrees. Source is the observation of both the speaker's own self-consistent behavior and the consistent behavior of others. Prescriptive or descriptive mode.
10	*Democratic-proposal:* The speaker thinks that the group or subgroup members should ratify a new norm or agree to uphold an existent norm more strongly. Source is the individual speaker *as* a member of a democratic (formal or informal) group. Prescriptive mode.
11	*Democratic [limited]-alienated:* The group or subgroup has articulated a norm that is shared by a substantial portion of the members but not by the speaker. The speaker may differentiate his/her own perspective. Source is the knowledge of an explicit and shared norm reported by the alienated speaker. Prescriptive mode.
12	*Democratic [limited]:* The group or subgroup has articulated a norm that is shared by a substantial portion of the members including the speaker *as* members of the group. Source is the speaker *as* a group member. Prescriptive mode.
13	*Democratic-collective:* The group or subgroup has articulated a norm that is shared by all members *as* members of the group. Source is the speaker *as* a group member speaking *for or in the name of the group.* Prescriptive mode.

TABLE 10.2
Phases of a Norm

Nonexistence	0	No norm exists, nor has been proposed, nor has been instituted.
Proposal	1	Proposal *or* Institution by Authority or Policy. An individual or organizational entity proposes a norm for group acceptance or institutes a norm for group acceptance.
Acceptance	2	Having an Ideal. A norm is accepted as an ideal or policy of the group but neither formally nor informally agreed to.
	3	Having an Agreement. A norm is accepted and either formally or informally agreed to, but it is not yet an expectation, that is, considered binding on members.
Expectation	4	Having an Expectation. A norm is assumed to be accepted and is expected to be upheld, that is, considered binding on members.
	5	Being Disappointed. A norm is expected and considered binding on members and when it is *not* upheld members are disappointed.
Enforcement	6	Expressing Disapproval and/or Attempting Persuasion. A norm is expected and is considered binding on members and informal attempts are made, including public disclosure, to persuade nonconformers or violators to live up to the established norm.
	7	Calling for Punishment or Reporting. A norm is expected and individuals bound by it use agreed upon or formal procedures for reporting or calling for the punishment of nonconformers or violators.

TABLE 10.3
Complexity of Social Conception

0	Anomic	The individual speaker expresses no awareness of any subgroup or group norms as governing the organization.
1	Alienated negative	The individual speaker rejects the salient norms of the group or organization and offers no counter-norms.
2	Alienated positive	The individual speaker rejects the salient norms of the group but offers counter norms which may or may not coincide with those of a subgroup of which he or she is a member.
3	Integrated	The individual speaker accepts the norms of the subgroup or group of which he or she is a member.
4	Integrative	The individual speaker recognizes that the differences in norms of subgroups are complementary for the organization as a whole.

of it. When a norm originates through discussion and explicit agreement and is at a high phase, then most members offer a commonly understood and shared reason which has structural properties scorable within the Kohlberg (1981) moral stage theory. The stage of representation of a truly collective norm, therefore, is the shared meaning a norm has for the functioning of the group and not the average stage of the individuals within it. Norms originating in other ways and/or at low phases are not scorable for moral stage, but rather the reasons given in support of such norms usually indicate the individual's own stage of reasoning and set of values.

There are two additional steps we take in analyzing the normative culture of an organization. After characterizing each norm in terms of the above three aspects, we identify the members in the organization that hold particular constellations of norms and thus, characterize the normative culture in terms of normative subgroups. Normative subgroups may share an organization-wide norm but also have particular norms of their own.

Lastly, we analyze each individual member's understanding of the number, complexity and interrelationships of normative subgroups to each other. This we term the complexity of social conception. When analyzing the data from an entire organization, scoring individuals for their level of complexity of social conception allows us to describe the organization based on the most widely agreed upon social conception and to consider individuals with variant conceptions as incompetent informants. It is also usually the case that the interviews of such individuals are marked by feelings of and statements about alienation from fellow workers or the organization as a whole. This ordinal categorization scheme appears in Table 10.3.

Values

We define values as expressions of an individual's identity springing from the individual's belief and assumptions about who he or she is or should be. Thus our definition includes ideas of one's moral identity as well as conscious motivations of either a moral or pragmatic nature. Motivations of which a person is unaware as well as psychological defenses and coping strategies are excluded from this definition and, in fact, are presently excluded from our overall analysis since our goal is to define the social structure of the work climate of an organization.

We identify and analyze values in order to understand the motivational basis for people's adherence to organization and/or subgroup norms and their commitment to the organization or work group. Since one's work-related values express identification with the firm, our categorization scheme of values is termed Individual Identity and Identification. Table 10.4 outlines this 7-point ordinal scale and gives examples. A dimension of abstractness underlies this measure. Examples at the concrete end are valuing money or convenience; examples in the midrange are valuing relations with specific other workers or the atmosphere of the company; examples at the abstract end are valuing professional goals or an ideal societal organization. The first, second and third most important values of each person are registered on this scale. This method gives us a measure of the level of abstractness or generality in creating a value profile of the organization.

The second way of generating a profile of the values of an organization involves a weighting of the three most important values for each person. The

TABLE 10.4

Individual Identity and Identification [Values about the Meaning of Work and the Meaning of the Workplace]

		Examples
1	No Values	"The kinds of things that people do here mean nothing to me."
		"I could care less about what this company is trying to achieve."
2	Values Outside Company	"I like working here because I'm learning skills I can use elsewhere."
		"I work to support my family."
3	Valuing Concrete Work	"I like working with my hands."
		"I like to see something that I have made at the end of the day."
4	Valuing Particular Others	"I like working with these people, Helen and Jim."
		"I like working here because I can make friends whom I can rely on."
5	Valuing The Company	"I like the way this company runs."
		"I want this company to succeed."
6	Valuing Professional Norms	"I like doing work where my work is in accordance with objective standards."
7	Valuing Abstract Ideals	"I like working here because the company embodies values which I believe in."
		"I like working here because this company is working towards an ideal society."

most important value counts as 1, the second as ½, and the third as ¼. These weighted values are then summed to obtain the most salient values of the organization as a whole. This method captures and orders the particular values that exist in the firm.

We identify value subgroups similarly to the way in which we identify normative subgroups. After identifying the four or five most salient values within the organization, we separate the members into value subgroups by assessing who holds which of the most salient values.

Individual Moral Judgment Stage

The moral stage of individuals in a firm is assessed because we think that complex organizations require modes of resolving conflict that are increasingly morally adequate, in which people are capable of coordinating numerous points of view and interests in a way that allows them to justly settle problems. In a conventional organization, management makes these judgments. A democratic firm, we believe, requires of all its members complex role-taking and judgments of what is fair. Reciprocally, a democratic organization ought to stimulate its members to take the perspective of others and of the organization as a whole and thereby ought to develop the capacity to coordinate contending interests and enhance moral development.

We assess moral stage using a hypothetical work moral dilemma, created from pilot data and our experience of workplaces. The dilemma focuses on the norm of working hard. Probe questions explore both a hypothetical situation and a real-life situation given by the interviewee about the workplace.

In the remainder of the chapter we introduce two worker-owned firms and discuss and contrast their normative cultures and value profiles looking at the implications for each company's stability and evaluating the extent to which the governance of each has been democratized. In the course of the discussion we address issues highlighted in the two general cases.

TWO CASE STUDIES: NORTH COUNTRY RESTORATION AND SOUTHLAND SEWING[1]

The first company we studied, North Country Restoration, was founded by college graduates who were part of the 1960's counter-culture and who wanted to do fine carpentry and construction work, especially the reconstruction of architecturally worthy old buildings. The company did well and, as it grew, it brought

---

[1]The names of these companies are fictitious in keeping with our commitment to protect their privacy.

in more traditional carpenters who had extensive training and experience and expressed the craft's values and norms.

From its inception, the ideology of North Country was democratic but the actual governance and decision-making processes were informal with familiarity constituting the basis for inclusion or exclusion in making decisions. This type of governance depended on strong personal bonds and a close community. However, when North Country became a larger, more complex organization, familial, informal democratic governance merged with cronyism and inefficiency. In addition, the company took on difficult projects that challenged the skills of its workers and that they attacked with a tremendous ''we can do anything'' attitude. But bidding on some of the contracts was sloppy and not enough attention was paid to the costs in production.

The personal basis for making decisions became inadequate for three reasons. First, there was a problem of communication. Sharing information about work was a natural part of the interaction among the original group but those not part of the inner core were often not informed about when supplies would be delivered, when plans had to be ready, or when jobs were scheduled to be begun and completed.

Second, there was the problem of equity. In spite of a stock distribution plan, the founders retained control of the company and the newer employees had neither the same right to ownership nor governance. Entitlement, in other words, was not based on equitable principles but rather on the accidents of who knew whom and who was there first.

Third, standards for how the work ought to be done were not made explicit to all and, thus, were not commonly shared. The original group developed standards based on what they felt defined high quality work and communicated those to one another only by what work they let pass and what work they did over. But as North Country grew the founders could not check everything. Standards were never codified nor did they become explicitly shared norms. The quality of the work began to vary widely from carelessness to a meticulousness not justifiable on a cost basis.

Serious financial troubles ensued and threatened the success and life of North Country. The legitimacy of the founders' management strategies was severely questioned by the more recently hired professional carpenters who demanded to be more involved in running North Country and to be a part of its internal informal democracy. At that point the founders called in the Industrial Cooperative Association (ICA)[2] to advise them about setting up the legal basis for formal democratic ownership by converting to a cooperative structure.

---

[2]The Industrial Cooperative Association of Somerville, Massachusetts is a consulting firm that specializes in working with cooperatives and advising and educating traditionally owned businesses, cities and towns about the advantages and feasibility of creating worker-owned enterprises.

After becoming a legal cooperative, the members seized their newly won democratic control and demoted the president, who subsequently left the company. The newly elected governing board also fired two workers, saying the company didn't need them and had to cut costs. The new management, which was a combination of new and founding members, could not coordinate its decisions and activities; North Country drifted but with consultation from the ICA began to codify and institute procedures for the transfer of information within the company, for personnel decisions, and for work evaluation. It was during this period of transition that we did our interviews in cooperation with the educational and consultative aims of the ICA.

We must add a sad postscript to this description of a budding legally democratic cooperative. North Country continued to make progress as a cooperative in the year and a half following our interviews; however the collapse of the economic underpinnings of the construction industry in the United States, especially in the Northeast, led to the closing down of North Country Restoration. A second round of interviews done shortly before its demise indicate that despite the crushing economic conditions, North Country's work climate was positive and quite strong. As indicated earlier, the longitudinal analysis of this company is currently being done by Mackin (1984).

The second study we will report here was of Southland Sewing, a garment producing firm located in an area of the southern United States which is economically poor, has a high degree of social class uniformity and strong racial unity. This company employed primarily black women workers with some white women employees as well. It was and still is run by a black man who had run successful private businesses previously and had led an earlier attempt to found a garment firm financed by and run for the benefit of the same local community.

The founding of Southland Sewing was based in the Civil Rights Movement and its president has had a strong reputation as a leader in the movement for civil rights and black economic independence. Thus, Southland Sewing was somewhat unique from its beginning in being a primarily black factory managed by a black person. Moreover, the president personally desired to see Southland Sewing become a worker-owned cooperative and to that end sought consultation from the ICA in the third year of the company's life.

Southland Sewing did adopt the legal structure to become a cooperative, which required each member to buy one voting stock share and to participate in the election of a board of directors. During this transition, ICA identified two major barriers to the company's growth and successful democratization. First, work was done in shifts on assembly-lines. Second, the manager, supervisors and workers were having difficulty redefining the patterns of authority within the new legal structure. The complementary nature of these problems exacerbated poor communication and confusion about the role and authority of the democratically elected board of directors which was comprised of on-line workers as well as supervisors and the manager. Subsequently, unevenness in productivity increased and became a critical issue. Because garment factories must secure individual contracts for work and because, at that time, the garment industry was depressed due to the American economy, it looked as if becoming a democratically governed cooperative may have only added to Southland Sewing's fragility.

The Normative Cultures of North Country Restoration and Southland Sewing

As stated earlier, the three main problems North Country Restoration faced when it converted to a legal worker-owned cooperative were a lack of effective channels for the flow of information, lack of formal and real equity and a lack of professional standards for evaluation of both workers and the work.

The interviews showed that the source of these problems, the informality and personal nature of the company, held within it the beginnings of the solution. As one worker stated,

> Even if there was a more clearly delineated power structure before, still the spirit of the company was that everybody had some sort of say, whether it was on a management level or a more spiritual level. So in spite of the power structure from before, I think that people who were in the company, who did not have the power then, were also responsible for forming the whole thing. As a result of what the whole was, that was our history. You can't say that, well, that's just the history of the board of direcors that made the decisions while the old president was here. It's everybody's history.

The normative culture of North Country reflected this sense of group cohesion and shared history. It was a company rich in several shared norms about work and holding a collective norm about sociality and helping each other. The four norms related to work were (1) working hard, (2) upholding professional standards or doing high quality work, (3) productivity, and (4) responsibility to complete the work. All of these norms had as their source of legitimation a basic, if nascent, agreement to conform to certain patterns of behavior and are scored as aggregate level norms.

The aggregate level of the source of legitimation for the norm of working hard is illustrated in the following quotation. "I think in general people do work hard and most people work very conscientiously. I think the motivation is mostly peer pressure, that essentially there are very few policies." The norm of working hard was seen by almost all those we interviewed as an aggregate level norm that was collective but known through informal means and behavioral conformity. It was not discussed and explicitly agreed upon, a level we would call "democratic collective," nor did its legitimacy come from management directives, a level we would term "authority-based."

The strength or phase of the working hard norm was phase 7, indicating that compliance to the norm was assumed and that enforcement of violations was expected by the majority of the members. When asked what happened when the norm of working hard was violated, a worker gave us an example of phase 7. He said,'' If it were an isolated incident, they might just say 'Get yourself in gear, you know you're not working.' If the isolated incidents turn into the way it is practiced, then they express it officially.'' Finally, our analysis of the reasoning supporting this norm showed that it was construed as a Stage 4 norm.

The professionalism and quality, responsibility and productivity norms were not as systematically probed as was the working hard norm, but rather were spontaneously raised by most of the people we interviewed. These three norms were also at the aggregate level, but at a slightly lower stage (Stage 3/4), and at lower phases (between phases 4 and 6); workers assumed others accepted the norms (phase 4), were disappointed when violations occurred (phase 5), and sometimes spoke out against violations (phase 6).

The following statements are representative of these three work-related norms. One man told us he came to North Country because it had a reputation for upholding professional standards:

> At the same time that I started, another man started, and we both had expectations that we would be working with a class act of carpenters and that we would be expected to live up to a certain standard. So we felt that by being accepted in the company we would possess that standard ourselves and that we would be working with people who also possessed this standard, which made me feel good. And I find that to be true pretty much.

The norm of productivity was explained by a supervisor:

> Keeping a good site going, that's important. You know what I'm talking about. Do the job. if you don't want to do the job, then, well, that's the construction business. You're going into productivity here. I mean, if the guy wants to sit and debate for half an hour, then I lose out on an hour's time. Anyone that would work under me would just have to have that confidence in me that I do know. And I expect that from anybody above me.

The norm of responsibility for completing a job was typically talked about in terms of the necessity of crews or teams to work together. One person described it this way:

> For everyone to be on the job, for the good of the job so that it comes in on budget and so that it's easier for the supervisor to really depend on the crew being there. It just makes things work, I think, for the company as a whole. If everyone deals that way, you get a little more into depending on people. If you can assume that support, which is, if everyone is responsible, you can assume that they arc going to

be there. I think people do expect each other to be responsible. I think that's an expectation of us as a unit, as a group.

The particular work-related norm of responsibility stated above rested on the feeling of group solidarity. This idea of community or solidarity is the value of affiliation shared by many at North Country but it also has a normative manifestation. The one strong norm that is not directly related to work is that of helping each other both on the job and outside by talking over personal problems and/or socializing together. An example of this broadly defined norm of social cooperation was given by one of the board members. He said:

We are not here on this earth just to work. We are working together but we all realize that there's a lot more to life than that. Everybody's got time for everyone else. We get together outside work and that becomes part of my conception of them as people and of what I expect as a result of that.

When asked how this idea was expressed, he continued:

Just by your actions. It's a friend relationship and we try to watch out for everyone else. If you can help them, help them. It's somewhat egalitarian as far as you can go. Most people feel that way.

Nearly half of the group interviewed (11 of 26) articulated this norm of cooperation and sociality. It was an aggregate level norm understood as being Stage 3/4. The average phase at the time of the interviews was phase 4, i.e., people assumed it was accepted by others.

Although there was widespread agreement about the salient norms that guided work and social interactions among the members, individual members were unsure about how strongly their peers felt about upholding the norms and could not predict what actions others would take if the norms were violated. Since the expressions of hesitancy were pervasive, they were not the basis for the formation of normative subgroups. However, we will see when describing North Country's value profile that there were value subgroups, which we interpret as one reason for the hesitancy and/or inability of members to predict the extent to which others were willing to uphold the commonly perceived norms.

To summarize the normative culture of North Country Restoration, we saw a company with several broadly defined and wide ranging work-related norms that served as assumed standards regulating the quality of work and the productivity of the workers. The work-related norms were buttressed by a norm of cooperation and sociality and the valuing of affiliation. From this analysis we conclude that North Country was then a positive illustration of our second case, that members of a company with broadly shared norms feel they understand each other's actions and can take each other's perspectives.

In contrast, the normative culture of Southland Sewing was less rich, being comprised of only two work-related norms and one norm of cooperation. Furthermore, clear normative subgroups existed at Southland Sewing. The interviews showed a deep division in people's conceptions of the roles of worker and manager, which our analysis of the norms confirmed. The two work-related norms were seen as originating with management and some felt they were imposed in an authoritarian manner. Thus, we identified two normative subgroups in relation to the work norms. On the other hand, a norm of helping and cooperation among the workers seemed to spring spontaneously from the worker culture and was widely shared.

As will be discussed, confusion arose when a representative board was elected; new worker-board members did not know if they were still workers or had "joined management" and other workers resented these women "taking privileges" and "acting like a boss." We speculated that prior to electing a board and implementing other democratic procedures there were two fairly stable subgroups, the managers and the workers. By setting up democratic decision-making in the form of an elected representative board, the old subgroups began to break up and some workers, especially board members, began to align themselves with the managers, thus creating new subgroups, one composed only of workers and one composed of some workers and managers. Less than half of the people we interviewed belonged to the latter subgroup (8 of 20), and four of them held managerial positions. In order to better understand this shift we will analyze each of the three salient norms at Southland Sewing.

The two work-related norms were (1) working hard and (2) maintaining productivity. The norm of working hard was seen as arising from the management; authority's demands were its source of legitimation. This norm was construed as a Stage 2 norm by the women who felt it was imposed on them. Others construed it as a Stage 2/3 norm and felt the authority of the management had been to some extent delegated by the board through a democratic process.

A stark but not uncommon version of this norm was stated by one machine operater, a member of the worker-only subgroup, who said, "The supervisors tell you what to do and they are the boss, and we are here to do what they tell us to do." One of the supervisors, representative of the other subgroup, felt her authority was considered legitimate in the eyes of some of the workers as well as in her own eyes since her authority had been delegated to her by them. She said, "I just go right out and tell them what I expect of them in every aspect. And they don't pay me no mind sometimes, but I feel a little bit proud of myself because sometimes they will listen to me."

The phase of the working hard norm or its strength in the company came primarily from the manager-worker subgroup. The average phase was 7 in our scheme, which is a call for the norm to be enforced by authorities after violations have occurred. One member of the worker-only subgroup said, "I believe the supervisors should report because the others have reason to believe that the person next to them is doing it (reporting) to show them up. I feel it should be someone that she (who is not working hard) knows is watching and that she has to do better. Its her equals that are sitting next door to her.'' Another worker defended the idea that management's job was to uphold the norm because she felt ''people and groups would resent a fellow worker telling them what to do.'' Yet another worker cited confidentiality as the reason for authority handling violations.

The norm of maintaining productivity had a similar structure. Its basis of legitimation lay in its proposal by management. This norm was held by only the manager-worker subgroup who felt that supervisors were exercising legitimately delegated authority. This norm was articulated as a Stage 3 idea and its acceptance was assumed (phase 4).

The one norm that originated from the workers' culture and was widely shared by most workers and some supervisors was the norm of caring and cooperation. This norm was spontaneously given by almost two-thirds of the people interviewed. It was scored as an aggregate level norm at phase 4, assumed acceptance. The norm was understood and articulated as a Stage 3 or 3/4 idea.

The content of the norm of caring and cooperation came out of the ideal of Christian love and the religious culture of the southeast part of the United States. The following quotation is a version of the Golden Rule:

> I expect people to treat me in a decent manner. If I do bad work and it comes back, I'll do it again. I'm a Christian and I use my Christianity here. I want people to treat me like I treat them. We have to have a certain amount of respect and love for each other or this place could become hell to work in.

A second version of the norm reflected the altruistic side of Christian love. A machine operator said:

> When you're working with people sometimes they're nasty and there's a good reason for being that way. You should approach the person with a friendly attitude. Let them know you care. Everyone wants a friend and if you let them know you are a friend and you're concerned, most of the time that solves the problem.

Thus, at the time of our interviews Southland Sewing had only one norm shared by most of its members. People's understanding of the work-related norms revealed both the old split between workers and managers and a newly emerging split between a group of managers and worker board-members and the other workers. Although the new democratic structure of the board brought to light people's differing conceptions of the appropriate roles and behaviors of workers and managers by shifting people into new structures and roles, our analysis clearly shows that democratization did not give rise to the role conceptions nor to the difficulties in communication and motivation that accompanied them.

When discussion began about creating a board of directors, many women did not want to serve. Some thought it would be a sham without real power or authority. Some thought it would be disloyal to other workers for them to seek a place on the board. The workers' feelings about the board and their ability to use the board and to participate in general meetings was described by several people as problematic. One of the supervisors commented:

> When we have a board meeting, they won't raise their hand. They won't ask a single question. And as soon as the meeting is over, they say, 'Come here Joan, let me ask you this.' I say, 'Why didn't you bring this up in the meeting? I can't answer all these questions.' See, this worker-owned thing is something new to them and I think it's going to take time for them to get adjusted. They have been working under managers and they just never had a chance to express themselves, but if somebody would start to talk, I think it would grow and then everybody would know everybody's feelings.

Many workers were concerned with whether the board members were making the right decisions. One operator said:

> Sometimes it's good to be in a cooperative, but sometimes it's bad. Too many hands in one pie making the decisions. People might vote for a decision which might not be a good one. It's not what you think, but what is best.

A few people were hesitant to have "uneducated" workers on the board and expressed some mistrust of others' capabilities. This mistrust was exacerbated by the budding self-definition of some board members who decided that they had become managers, and were not just workers. One woman commented, "Some operators that are on the board feel like they should have a little more privileges than the others. They feel like they should be able to have a few minutes a day or come to work late sometimes."

A second aspect of privilege was knowledge received as a board member that was not yet known generally. At that time the company did not have guidelines or policies about the flow of information. One person complained, "As soon as some of them were out of the board meeting they were telling their buddies things that were happening they really had no right to spread. I informed the manager since I knew it would start problems."

The shipping clerk who saw herself as part of management described why she thought some worker board members may have felt entitled to privileges in terms of the old well-established conception of the manager role. "I think they view management as a glorious position, not realizing the time and effort that management has put into the company. They feel being in charge means signing checks rather than being ready to sweep the floor or do whatever is required."

These views illustrate that the workers' role conceptions had come from the larger culture and their own past experiences in subordinate roles. When the ownership structure changed and demands were made on workers to develop more flexible role definitions, the potential for misunderstanding increased among workers. In our report to the consultants at the ICA we emphasized these problems and offered a strategy that, we hoped, would help the ICA in its program of educating the members of Southland Sewing about the role of the board, teaching board members the skills and giving them the information they needed to make sound policies and decisions, and creating a work climate conducive to the increased participation of all members.

Our suggestion came from the complaints of a few stronger and more dedicated members. One woman, when asked about cooperation, stated the issue succinctly. She said, "It's the attitude that 'I'm not going to overdo, since these others aren't doing the amount I'm doing.' They expect each other to work hard, but they don't expect it of themselves."

It seemed to us that if Southland Sewing and its consultants could use the strong norm of caring and helping as a basis for building a norm of positive cooperation in the workplace through working together and working hard there would be two benefits. A new norm generated by the group of cooperation about work-related issues would in time replace the existent authority based work-related norms, and the kind of discussion necessary for this transformation would become a critical component of the ongoing education process.

This analysis illustrates the negative side of our second case, that when members of a company belong to different normative subgroups they are less capable of understanding each other's actions and of taking each other's perspectives, and they criticize each other for not fulfilling their functional roles.

The Value Profiles of the Two Worker-Owned Companies

Our analyses of the value profiles identified four categories that encompass the most important values in both companies. The value categories were then given relative weightings as discussed in the methodology section above. We report the weighted importance of each value category in terms of a percentage which represents the number of workers X the weight each worker assigned to values included in each value category.

In North Country Restoration the two strongest value categories were, first, an intrinsic interest in doing professional quality work (with a score of 30%), and second, affiliative motivations (28%). Motivations which are best described as ideological, valuing democratic processes and a participative workplace, were ranked third (27%). Instrumental motivations of money and the convenience of the workplace comprised the fourth and much weaker value category (10%).

The same four value categories accurately represented the most important values at Southland Sewing; however, the order of their importance was strikingly different. The fact that this firm is located in a poor rural section of the

South with high unemployment was reflected in the strongest cluster of values given by its members, that of making money, having steady employment and the convenience of the workplace (38%). The second strongest motivator was ideological, which included valuing being a member of a black enterprise, valuing the leadership of a native son, and valuing democratic processes and worker ownership. (23%). Intrinsic interest in the work as represented by valuing professional standards and managerial expertise was rated third (19%). Although cooperation and helping was a strong norm in Southland Sewing, affiliation was the weakest value category (10%). A comparison of the value profiles of these two companies is given in Fig. 10.1.

With these profiles of the differential importance of the four clusters of values, we predicted that the commonly experienced economic adversity would affect the work climate of the two companies differently. We thought the construction workers would not tolerate having to do low skilled, unchallenging jobs, which seemed necessary to keep the company afloat, since the intrinsic interest of the work was North Country's most salient value. In contrast, we thought the sewers would be willing to do monotonous, large jobs sewing thousands of a single garment in order to have steady employment. Although North Country succumbed to the bad economic times and Southland Sewing survived, the impact of the economic situation on the construction industry in the Northeast was so grave that we cannot say whether the construction workers would have

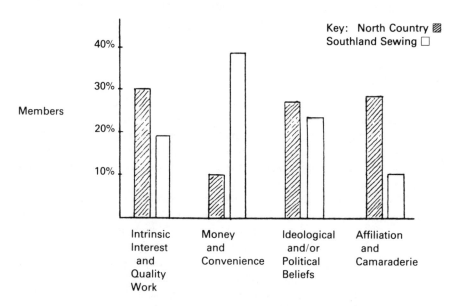

FIG. 10.1   First four weighted values held by members of North Country Restoration and Southland Sewing (in percent).

Intrinsic Interest
and Quality Work

	Present	Absent
Present	61% (16)	8% (2)
Affiliation		
Absent	19% (5)	12% (3)

FIG. 10.2   Members of North Country Restoration who held two most important weighted values (in percent).

rejected low skilled jobs because of their values since so little work of any kind was available.

Furthermore, since ideological or political motives were not of primary importance for either company even though both were worker-owned and democratically run, we speculated that democracy might be sacrificed at some future time to more salient interests unless the democratic processes themselves were generating stronger democratic values that would then direct policy decisions.

Turning now to look at the distribution of these values among individuals, we identified value subgroups and thus, gained more insight into the value profiles of each organization. As North Country Restoration grew and brought in more traditional carpenters, it seemed likely that two value subgroups would have developed, one subgroup of the ''hip'' founders characterized by affiliative values and a second subgroup of experienced carpenters characterized by professional craft values and an intrinsic interest in work. Contrary to that likely expectation, we found that a full 61% of the workers held both of these most salient values (see Fig. 10.2). North Country Restoration had succeeded in merging the affiliative motivations of the founders with the professionalism of the experienced but not college-educated craftsmen.

As we described earlier, North Country Restoration had gone through a major split and demoted its original president at the time it became a legal worker-owned cooperative. Shortly thereafter, that president and several founders quit. These actions seem to indicate that value subgroups did exist and that their respective members had great difficulty in taking the other group's perspectives. As a result the company became polarized. We speculate that those who left were less able to adopt and integrate the values of the separate subgroups than were those who stayed. Thus, our analysis of the value profile of North Country after some founders had left combined with knowledge of its history illustrates the negative side of our first case, that a break in a company is likely to occur when it is under stress and its work climate is grounded in distinct value subgroups. In summary, however, at the time of our research the analyses of both the normative culture and the value profile of North Country show that it had a strong, complex and unified work climate.

In contrast, at Southland Sewing only 15% (3) of the people held both of the most salient values, instrumentally valuing the company as a convenient place to earn money and identifying with it ideologically (see Fig. 10.3). Those who believed in the organization's political and ideological purpose were not the same individuals as those who were there only to earn a modest living. In fact, a year after our work there, the president and board of Southland Sewing made the difficult decision to lay off a substantial number of workers and later to rehire only the "best." The company was able to do this without destroying the fabric of the work climate. We suggest this was possible because the work-related norms had not yet developed a democratic basis and the emphasis upon being a black enterprise with black leadership remained the primary ideology rather than democratic ownership. This interpretation of decisions made a year after our research in a positive illustration of our first case. It shows that a decision to drastically cut a workforce is tolerated by workers in a company that has distinct value subgroups grounded in traditional role definitions of workers and managers. Furthermore, it seems democracy was still embedded in a broader ideological context and within a network of values insuring the company's survival, the need for money and the convenience of the workplace.

On the other hand, the apparent strength of Southland Sewing seems to come from its broad-based norm of cooperation and care, in combination with an expressed trust in its leadership and managerial expertise; these two values seemed to underlie the work norms, not only for the normative subgroup that

Money and Convenience
Extrinsic Reward

	Present	Absent
Present (Ideology)	15% (3)	35% (7)
Absent	30% (6)	20% (4)

FIG. 10.3   Members of Southland Sewing who held two most important weighted values (in percent).

gave legitimacy to the authority's power but for many in the worker-only sub-group as well.

The Influence of Individual Moral Stage

In understanding why North Country was able to maintain itself and develop for some time despite the depressed economy, the changes brought about by the legal restructuring of ownership and the increased democracy, we should look at the average stage of individual moral reasoning. The new president and one board member used Stage 4/5 reasoning and all other board members reasoned at Stage 4. The old leadership who stayed on was comprised of one who reasoned at Stage 3, two who reasoned at Stage 4, and two who reasoned at Stage 4/5. Although the mean stage of moral judgment used by the workers in our sample was Stage 4, half used Stages 3 or 3/4.

Recall that the stage of the norms at North Country tended to be Stage 3/4. This half stage discrepancy between the stage of the norms and the average stage of the individual members indicates that the work climate of North Country was not developmentally challenging for most of its members.

The relation between average moral judgment stage and the stage of the norm of cooperation at Southland Sewing showed congruency; both were Stage 3. The work-related norms were understood as being either Stage 2 or 2/3, a half or whole stage lower than the average individual moral stage, a situation similar to that at North Country. At Southland Sewing the management personnel reasoned at Stages 3 or 3/4. The workers' reasoning ranged from Stage 2/3 to Stage 3/4. This indicates that the work climate of Southland Sewing, like North Country, would not provide the context for development for most of its members.

Theoretically, a company and workforce that are able to create norms understood at a stage higher than the mean individual stage should create a work climate that is seen as challenging and exciting and, thus, would lead to the moral development of individuals within it. Similarly, a work climate with norms congruent with or below the average stage of the individuals would not lead to further individual development for most of the workers within it. Longitudinal research studies are needed to test these relationships.

CONCLUSION

Our original hypotheses held that diversity among groups in an organization is conducive to socio-moral development of the individuals as long as that diversity can be managed. The failure to manage allows the collapse of adequate role-taking and the emergence of stereotyping and labeling. When differences among individuals in an organization are not the bases for separation and grouping then the opportunities for role-taking are high and the dangers of stereotyping remain fairly low. This made us optimistic about the kind of diversity in norms and values manifested at North Country at the time of our research. While the organization experienced some stress between "craft" and "affiliation" values, many workers held both. Moreover, most of its members shared several work-related norms as well as normative manifestations of the affiliation value. We therefore expected that the tensions would not have led to polarization and may have led to enhanced role-taking between the more traditional craft workers and the college-educated refugees from the "hip" counterculture. In contrast, our analysis of the work climate of Southland Sewing showed that all of its members shared only one norm, the norm of cooperation. The work-related norms were defined differently by two normative subgroups that existed within the organization. Furthermore, the organization was split between those who held ideological values and those who valued working there for the material benefits. The danger of polarization and stereotyping, with the collapse of moral role-taking, seemed greater for this company.

The ability to recognize the fragility of organizations and whether they represent environments conducive to socio-moral development is a critical aspect of our work climate research. Typically, we work with a consultant whose role it is to actively intervene in the democratization process. In the case of North Country, we were able, working with the consultant, to present the organization itself with our analysis of the diversity existing within it, which members had not recognized before. Many members had tended to view those with different norms and values with considerable irritation and as having simply failed according to their own code. The interpretation of the commonly held norms and of the different value subgroups enabled the members to understand the diversity in more positive terms. It also strengthened the influence of those members who bridged both worlds. This understanding, we think, is a necessary, big step toward enhancing socio-moral development of individuals in the workplace.

The use of the research to identify organizational stress and environments of manageable diversity is only one way that research can aid the democratization process. It can also explain the ways that workers understand democracy and the democratization process, as we illustrated when discussing the newly elected board at Southland Sewing. Knowing this is critical for determining how to intervene. In Southland Sewing the consultant began an educational intervention to teach the board members accounting and marketing so they could make better informed and more responsible decisions. Work climate research can also direct change by identifying problems of norm phase and source of legitimation. In each case, work climate analysis can inform the practitioner and aid the self-reflection of the organization's members.

Work Climate as the "Hidden Curriculum"

Workers and managers learn and are educated informally and often times formally in the workplace. Formal education in traditionally owned and operated firms is done by personnel and development offices that seek out or create seminars for employees. These programs may introduce employees to new knowledge and skills or may only enhance and focus the knowledge and hone the skills of the already educated or experienced. In most cases the ultimate goal of the education that a company gives its employees is to increase productivity and profits. However, more immediate and individually beneficial goals often coexist with the "bottom line" goals. The explicit focus of this kind of education is on new content: new ideas, new knowledge, new skills or new techniques.

Another kind of formal education that is becoming widespread takes the form of modifying the lines of communication and increasing the sharing of knowledge and, sometimes, power. This education comes through labor-management participation programs, the institution of quality circles and other interventions to enhance the quality of worklife within a company. Although more firms and unions are developing the capacity to conduct such programs themselves, it is still most common for an outside consultant to come in and train core personnel. In these cases, a second and more implicit goal of education is added: to teach people new functions, new roles, or how to redefine or combine old functions by utilizing a new process.

Although formal education may or may not exist in a company, a process of informal education always goes on. It is the "unstudied or hidden curriculum" of the workplace. Members of an organization are socialized into its culture, they learn what should be done and what they can and cannot do. In our work we seek to make the "hidden curriculum" explicit and recognize it as the work climate of an organization. In a similar vein, Kohlberg and his colleagues (see Kohlberg, this volume) have developed a theory of the "moral atmosphere" which explicates the "unstudied curriculum" of the schools.

Because the work climate of a firm plays an influential role in determining what kind of policies and changes will be proposed and how they will be implemented, we think that it is important to make it manifest; thus it becomes a third kind of formal or explicit education. This is especially important when a company becomes worker-owned and democratically governed.

For instance, when a company decides to institute an employee stock ownership plan (ESOP) or to become a cooperative, we think extensive education that would include an explanation of the work climate ought to be done in order for workers and managers to evaluate the basis and merits of the new ownership structure. After the decision, further education concerning the implications of the new ownership structure for the governance of the company and for defining and understanding the new rights and obligations of the workers and managers is critical. This educational process would be most valid and useful if it were based on knowledge of the history and development of the existing work climate. The consulting relationship and collaboration between the ICA and the two cooperatives we have described are examples in which education about the "hidden curriculum" or work climate has been combined with education focused on learning new ideas, skills and roles.

Beyond suggesting that organizational education should recognize and utilize the work climate of an organization, we also think that educational experiences in the workplace, as in academe, should have intrinsic value to the individual and should promote personal, social and moral development.

The theory and methodology of work climate that we have illustrated in this chapter provide two bases for justifying and defining educational programs in the workplace. Because our theory of work climate is based, in part, on Kohlberg's (1981) theory of individual moral development, we make the same claims as he concerning the structural, invariant and sequential development of individuals' reasoning about social and moral issues. More importantly, we also accept another theoretical tenet of cognitive developmental theory: that development occurs through the interaction of the individual with the physical and social environment.

Therefore, experiences in the workplace that are truly educational for adults are those that promote cognitive, social and moral development. Assessing individual moral judgment stage in relation to the stage of the norms of a workplace over time would allow us to ascertain its educational potential for the development of the individuals within it. This method of assessment is grounded in a theory and body of research that is non-relativistic, universal and, thus, applicable to any work environment.

Finally, as we discussed earlier, the method of analysis we employ to understand work climate can specify both the direction and the content of an educational program for particular firms at particular points in time.

Democratization in the workplace is becoming increasingly widespread in the United States. Our experience with this movement seems to indicate that it fails as often as it succeeds, and that democratization programs as ready-made formulas imported with no regard to organizational culture seldom succeed. Our research aims to provide those who intervene in the democratization of an organization with an understanding of its culture, of the fragility of the democratization process, and of the dangers to socio-moral development when differences among groups become unmanageable. Therefore, it supports and clarifies processes to democratize and make educational an environment that generally influences the worker more by the unspoken rules of culture than by any overt program of learning.

REFERENCES

Durkheim, E. (1968). *The division of labor in society.* New York: Free Press. (Originally published 1933).

Johanneson, J. & Whyte, W. F. (1978). *Organizational strategies for preserving jobs and strengthening local economies.* Department of Labor Grant #91–36–76–39.

Kohlberg, L. (1981). *Essays on moral development, Vol. 1: The philosophy of moral development.* San Francisco: Harper and Row.

Mackin, C. (1984). *The social psychology of ownership: Moral atmosphere in a cooperatively owned workplace.* Unpublished dissertation, Harvard Graduate School of Education.

Mills, T. M. (1967). *The sociology of small groups.* Englewood Cliffs, NJ: Prentice-Hall.

11 But It Does Move: The Difficulty of Gradual Change in Moral Development

Fritz Oser
Andre Schläfli
University of Fribourg
Switzerland

The title of this chapter was written after the 1633 trial at which Galileo was forced by the Roman inquisition to repudiate his theory of the heliocentric system. In spite of pressure from the church, he was convinced that the earth revolved around the sun, even though this was not apparent to the eye.

We are likewise convinced that the development of socio-moral judgment, which has been stimulated by education, does advance. We conclude this in spite of the fact that direct progress can not yet be sufficiently measured, because the measuring instruments are too coarse, the treatments are too imprecise and the change appears too general. But development does move, even though no direct progress is apparent. Our educational behavior can, therefore, prepare, support, stimulate and diversify this development. We would like to show definitely that (a) the moral learning process requires *a clearer description* of the educational treatment than has been the case in many intervention studies up until now; (b) the path to a higher level of moral judgment is possible only by using a transformational model that explains *the preconditions of disequilibrated systems*; and (c) that a developmental psychological theory, such as that of Kohlberg (1958, 1979), can also be used as a basis of intervention if the learning process is not masked by measurement problems. Thus, that which lies hidden behind education must be made apparent. That hidden movement must come to light. The empirical background of our attempt to do this is based in an intervention study that was carried out with apprentices employed at the "Schweizerische Kreditanstalt Bank" in Basel, Switzerland.

APPRENTICES AND SOCIO-MORAL LEARNING

Before we outline the specific theories and problems that underlie our intervention study, we would like to justify our theoretical intention. Our goal was, in conjunction with the stimulation of the development of socio-moral judgment, to train the "practical" rationality of the apprentices, with emphasis not just on professional skills and morals but on the extent of responsibility one should feel towards the whole firm, the improvement of social relations and a greater socio-moral awareness as well. Admittedly, apprentices are encouraged to learn fixed values of professional morals, such as punctuality, adherence to safety regulations and precision in their work. Similarly, they are encouraged to optimize those skills specific to their profession. The place of work, as part of a more or less complex complete structure of a firm does, however, demand more from the person who fills this role than the mere knowledge and habits required to perform the work. The place of work is not just a place of production; it is also a place where one spends a significant portion of one's life. Provided that the apprentice learns to see a more complex and better equilibrated system of justice, which comes near to the universally accepted pattern of human intercourse within the firm and with respect to the firm's activity within society, then socio-moral development will take place. And here the firms, like vocational schools, have an enormous deficit to record, because this goal cannot be achieved through instruction given by the state and society. Moreover, the introduction of a few fine general goods into the main ideas on educating apprentices does not help anyone either. The apprentices are after all employees and citizens, who in the end have the same responsibility as high school and college students. They are people who have to develop their social and moral identity.

Various interventions within the Kohlberg paradigm, which we assume are familiar to the reader, have shown that it is possible to bring people to a *higher level of socio-moral judgment* by using cognitive stimulation (cf. chapters in this volume by Berkowitz, Higgins & Gordon, Kohlberg, Power). Until now, these attempts have been carried out with high schools and college students, and prisoners. The apprentice has, however, been neglected. That is to say, the large group among the population who are trained for nonacademic professions, or those who are employed in a profession or other occupation who require retraining in a field specific to their profession have not been involved in moral education until now.

What does it mean when we talk about bringing apprentices to a higher level of socio-moral judgment? First of all, what does greater judgment mean, according to Kohlberg? Let us suppose that an apprentice is suddenly placed in a situation of conflict where, because of the loss of a colleague, working overtime, and filling in for the colleague is necessary, which means losing some free time. Let us suppose it develops into a subliminal conflict between the master and the apprentice. How do a Stage 1 apprentice and a Stage 4 apprentice (according to Kohlberg's model of moral reasoning development) view this conflict? A Stage 1 apprentice, by definition, does not take the interests of other people into consideration. This individual cannot establish any relationship between two different points of view. If this Stage 1 person nevertheless feels that the conflict must be overcome, is is only to avoid a sanction (e.g., dismissal). On the other hand, a

Stage 4 person can consider the personal interests of everyone within the system; he or she adopts—albeit with reservations—the role of a cooperative member. He or she sees that in fulfilling actual duties, a contribution is made to the success of a community.

The path to higher levels of socio-moral judgment—as strategic behavior—has been traditionally achieved with the help of *special treatment* (see the following section). However, in spite of these studies, we still have little systematic knowledge of the effects of belonging to a higher level in professional and private life. The general approach is aimed at (a) variables which can be described as absolutely necessary for such interventions and (b) variables which *make the intervention easier*. The variables which are necessary for change are those without which a higher level cannot be reached. Direct stimulation with dilemma situations belongs to this category. The variables making intervention easier are facets of the transformation to a different level, such as a greater moral sensitivity, a better moral climate, a changed hierarchy of values, greater metacognitive knowledge, etc.

Many studies have established that it is possible, *but not easy,* to undergo a change in level according to Kohlberg. If it were easy, then the construct of "moral judgment" would have no stability. But we should not abandon this difficult approach because a higher level guarantees better moral conduct, a more adequate way of viewing justice, greater social responsibility and a higher balance of normative realities. Because it is now so difficult to stimulate development to a higher level, we have placed the stress in our examination on the variables that make an intervention easier. At this point it will be useful to consider a few technical explanations about these facilitating variables.

EARLIER STUDIES

Since the first intervention study carried out by Blatt and Kohlberg (1975), two important developmental stimuli have been repeatedly discussed. The first is the so-called "+1-Convention" in which argument patterns are transformed to the next higher stage by the discussion of moral dilemmas and by the introduction of argumentation material one stage above the reasoning of the student. This is the active form. Secondly, it is accepted that the process of moral growth takes place in such a way that a just moral climate of a given naturalistic setting would have to be created and then, almost "automatically," a higher moral judgment would develop. This is the passive form. Both forms rely on the idea that certain stimulating conditions further the natural process of moral development. In both cases, the idea inaugurated by Kohlberg is present; i.e., that development should be taken as the goal of education; thus the so-called Development-Education Paradigm.

Both themes have since been further developed. The +1-Convention has been improved by Berkowitz and his colleagues (Berkowitz, 1981, 1983, this volume;

Berkowitz & Gibbs, 1983; Berkowitz, Gibbs & Broughton, 1980). In a series of examinations they showed that (a) the $+1/3$-Condition with peer dyads leads to better results than the $+1$-Condition and (b) that the form of dialogue is important. The more "operational transactive" dialogue form used, the better the result. By "operational transactive" they mean that the partners transform their respective mutual statements actively, for example by the critical analysis of the logic of an argument (other so-called operational transacts are: competitive clarification, refinement, expanding, contradiction, criticism, etc.). They also describe "representational" transacts, by which they mean "passive representing" of the statement of a partner (paraphrasing, questioning about agreement, and requests for justification, etc.).

The moral climate as a stimulation of a higher moral level was applied in prisons (Hickey & Scharf, 1980) and in schools (Lieberman, 1980, 1981; Mosher, 1980; Power, 1979; Reimer & Power, 1980). Lieberman (1981) thinks that, by the stimulation of a moral community, the production and recognition of moral arguments increases, the level of moral argumentation is raised (gradual progress), and there is an even higher identification with group norms. In general, with this approach, it can be said that by participation in the meetings of the whole community, and by discussion of "real" problems, the moral level, in the sense of stages, increases considerably (see also Kohlberg, this volume).

In spite of these two fairly hopeful approaches, which have been applied in many studies, a whole series of problems remains: how transformation in fact takes place; which transitions occur with the greatest ease or with the greatest difficulty; what developmental psychological oriented "catching up" of growth means; what the implications are for the treatment if people have reached the highest possible level for the time being (ceiling effect); what should be meant by equilibration and disequilibration; at what moments treaments are in fact effective (functional treatment validity); why short-term interventions are so frequently ineffective; why the measuring instrument (development stage) is too coarse. We would in particular like to examine the question of the description of the transformation process as such, and in doing so to also examine the question of functional treatment validity.

THE DEVELOPMENT-EDUCATION PARADIGM AND ITS GENERALIZATION TO THE DIVERSITY OF SOCIO-MORAL PARTIAL LEARNING PROCESSES: A CRITICISM OF PREVIOUS RESEARCH

In order to examine these questions, we must look at the original approaches and ask ourselves whether, other than the Berkowitz approach, there are more far-reaching methods for stimulating socio-moral judgment. Previous research has been distinguished very often by the "concealment" of that very information which interests us, namely what actually happens in a treatment. First of all, the mixture of different influences would have to be mentioned. For example, in the study of Sullivan (1980) four treatments are reported: Phase 1, focused moral discussions with the +1-Convention; Phase 2, advice on morals, empathy training and role-playing; Phase 3, presentation of the theory of moral development and moral philosophy; Phase 4, subjects' teaching morality to and founding a "Just Community." The dependent variables are a growth in the moral stage and growth on the Loevinger (1976) ego scale. If we examine this study more closely, it is not absolutely clear what in fact influences the two dependent variables. Is it the development supported by education? Is it one of the phases? Do the individual phases interact? There are almost no parallel studies in existence, so that we cannot speak of a treatment validity (Cook & Campbell, 1979).

Secondly it must be stressed that most studies say little about the treatment. Schläfli, Rest and Thoma (1984) were able to show in 56 treatment studies on moral education, which used the Defining Issue Test (DIT) developed by Rest in the early 70s, that most authors describe the treatment only symbolically: some say "Film Input," others refer to the "Galbraith-Jones" method, and others use "empathy training" or employ discussions of the Kohlberg theory or literary or political problems, etc. Out of 56 studies, 36 produced significant results and 20 were not significant.

Schläfli, et al reach the following conclusions:

—When successful methods were analyzed, it was found that both the interventions with the classic approach (dilemma discussion) and studies with additional affectively-oriented exercises (DPE-Studies) produced changes in moral judgment;

—In studies of merely socially-oriented content, no changes could be achieved.

—Short-term interventions (under 10 hours) produced no effects.

—There was no difference in effects between medium- and long-term interventions.

Unfortunately in almost all the studies compiled, it is actually only stage development that is assessed (cf. Lockwood, 1978; Mosher, 1980; Rest 1979). The treatment validity is not reflected, i.e., what takes place in additional learning processes is interpreted as though it would further development in any case. Most researchers do not attempt to evaluate other dimensions, such as the type of atmosphere in the course, the change in moral sensitivity in the face of ethical questions, etc. These extensions of existing work have nevertheless facilitated this interpretation and may have given new impetus for further resarch.

We wanted to profit from these conclusions in our own study. Thus, one of our main aims was to examine whether intervention could be arranged in such a way that a large proportion of the influences could be mentioned. We maintain that moral education should be carried out under a developmental-psychological or rather genetic-structural approach, even if reaching the next stage is not a reasonable immediate goal. This should take place on the one hand by considering all the prerequisites necessary for moral-educational success (logical prerequisites, perspective-taking prerequisite, moral empathy training, interpersonal awareness training, etc.) and on the other hand by the partition of the actual stimulation and learning process into partial learning-processes, which have been presented as stimuli by different conditions.

For this extended approach, there are, however, many references already, for example, the Lieberman study (1981). This is a curriculum developed with Strom and Parsons (Strom, Parsons & Lieberman, 1980) in which no growth in the field of the development of moral judgment and no growth on Loevinger's (1976) Ego-development scale was recorded. On the other hand, development of interpersonal awareness according to Selman's measure (1976a) was discernible. This shows clearly that *in the process of moral discourse seen from an educational standpoint more takes place than a mere stimulation to higher moral development*. The problem remains, however, that in spite of all, it is mostly only development that is measured; the rest goes by the board. In her informative review article, Higgins (1980) describes three sorts of interventions: (a) direct moral discussion of real-life dilemmas with natural groups; (b) direct moral discussion and deliberate psychological education; and (c) direct moral discussion in social studies curricula. Using this as a base, it can be stated that there are more and more studies that measure something other than so-called moral maturity, which represents a widening of the range of dependent variables, and thus risks a break from the system of measuring stages. In a similar vein, Bebeau, Rest and Yamoor (1982) have examined the moral sensitivity of dental students. In doing this, they developed an instrument "to assess an individual's ability to recognize the ethical issues often hidden in professional problems" (p. 1). Jennings, Higgins and Power (1980) also measure not only the level of moral judgment, but "Behavioral Change," "Parental Perceptions of Effects on their Children" and "Social Atmosphere and Change" as well. Lempert (1982) too, speaks in a similar way of the extent and quality of (a) moral experiences in connection with social interests, norms and the conflict of values; (b) general understanding and the support of co-workers or colleagues; (c) statements about social and self-responsibility; and (d) statements about democracy and institutions. These approaches and similar ones hope, by a diversification of the dependent variables, to carry out a large change and expansion of the Kohlberg concept. But ultimately, they do still refer to the dependent variable of moral stage change. The independent variable is furthermore—in spite of the representation of Higgins—an unexplained phenomenon. Shaver (1983) thus justifiably puts forward the claim that the treatment or the teaching method should be better controlled. He says: "The formulation of adequate a priori decision rules so that verification involves checks on whether behaviors conform to specified teaching methods rather than post hoc judgements based on differences in behavior is crucial but not difficult'' (p. 8). Not only the stability of the treatment reliability (cf. Patry, 1981, p. 4) is meant by this, but also the logic of the connection of means and aims. The derivation of such a connection is not an appropriate question for us here. *That would be formulating a question prematurely, but one should first of all postulate this connection for oneself.*

In spite of the problems mentioned, it of course appears that educational interventions in the moral field cannot go back beyond Kohlberg especially with regard to te stimulation to a higher stage and to the stimulation of a just socio-moral atmosphere. It is thus necessary to differentiate each treatment so that the *functional validity* (i.e., that technique A influences B in a clearly described manner) of individual partial learning aims is controlled (a) in the direction of those practical processes which are relevant within a structural conception of morality, and (b) in the direction of additionally necessary moral aims. The differentiation of such treatment-facilitating influences is, therefore, important because often development (a) cannot be increased at will within a given age group, (b) can only be sensibly stimulated if demonstrable catching up processes are under discussion, and (c) must be striven for as a process even if no higher stage, or rather no additional increase on a moral scale, is possible for prerequisite reasons (cognitive maturity, age, social competence, etc.). However, all these connections underly our acting which is geared towards understanding. In this field, with the exception of certain information-transmitting procedures, whatever the aim is, we are dealing with the realization or normative demands for validity in practical discourse.

TWO MODELS OF TRANSFORMATION AND THEIR INTEGRATION

We have established that it is difficult to achieve developmental progress on the moral scale in Kohlberg's terms by the influence of education. We have also established that (a) in much research the given treatment is insufficiently described or is merely attributed to coincidence, and (b) the developmental psychological measure is a milestone measure which explains too superficially what happens. For this reason, we would now like to introduce both a *transformation model* and an *aim-means model* and combine the two, so that the above-mentioned problems are at least partly removed. We believe that development moves forward, even if this is not immediately apparent or even if what development is actually taking place has to be broken down into different parts to be more accurately assessed or identified.

There are four basic elements to the transformation model:

1. The starting point is the assumption that an equilibrated cognitive structure of a subject faced with problems is confronted in such a way that the problems cannot be sufficiently overcome. The person is, therefore, in a state of disequilibrium. This is externally expressed by the fact that the person makes cognitive contradictions, feels that excessive demands are being made of him, and is unsure in his thinking pattern. This can lead to processes such as defense, denial and insufficient surmounting of problems, etc.

2. The existing cognitive structure becomes "shaken" and, at the same time, new important elements are discovered. These elements can now be worked on and integrated. In this phase, the person is inconsistent in problem solving. He relativizes his position and alternates between different opinions and solutions.

3. There follows a phase of the integration of the new elements during which other valences and conditions of the previous elements emerge. The new elements thus seem of greater importance, which leads to a transformation or to the reduction of the importance of the old elements. The person emphasizes new features, stresses the importance of his current knowledge, disassociates himself and practices the new way of thinking.

4. Finally, the newly acquired structure is transferred to different content areas and, thereby, practiced and strengthened.

By the representation of these processes, the "inside" of moral growth is captured. The general pedagogical formula as developed by Selman (1976b) in order to stimulate these internal processes is: 1. The presentation of problems or dilemmas; 2. The guarantee of optimal learning controversies; 3. The stimulation of argumentation material of a higher stage; and 4. The making aware that the change occurring, with regard to the original judgment is only a small part of the whole.

For this reason, we present the second, more additive model. This aims-means model entails the following elements:

1. A part of the qualitative change consists of *moral sensitization*. This can be achieved in two ways: (a) by the "seeing" of the moral standpoint, as such (cf. Baier, 1958) and (b) by the exhausting of moral realities in a decision situation. After an intervention, it should be established that the moral standpoint is perceived more quickly and, at the same time, that when they are re-discussing the same dilemma, people assume role-playing more or systematically introduce more points of view.

2. A further part of the qualitative changes in transformations of structural level must become obvious from one's hierarchy of values. Value hierarchies are changed in such a way that, when taking an upward step, spiritual, cultural, and communicative values are preferred, whereas when taking a downward step, material and external values are preferred. An intervention must change the

hierarchy because higher levels also implicitly contain spiritual, cultural, and communicative values.

3. There is an ability that is the basic prerequisite for moral decision-making and that Kohlberg neglects: moral *conflict-solving ability*. This ability has two sides. The first deals with getting into the conflict, and not just by artificial dilemmas but especially by social opinion differences. And the second side involves the interpreting of the conflict as the learning process, as "warming to the transformation," which can be used for developmental purposes.

4. There is a presumed influence on the change in stages in connection with *the knowledge about psychological stage theory* itself (Boyd, 1976). The higher the stage and the greater the knowledge, the more likely it is that an increase in moral values will occur. We describe this as the extent of metacognition with regard to the genetic-structural moral approach, or as theory-learning.

5. We accept that empathy and frankness towards others is a characteristic of the higher stages. If this ability is trained, we then have the guarantee that prerequisites for a change in level are fulfilled.

6. The moral climate is a prerequisite for change in stage. That is, the higher the stage, the greater the extent of mutual trust, of acceptance of mutual seeking of truth, and of the assumption of equal participation and proportional rights.

These six elements are, therefore, "signs," which represent transformation. If we can categorize changes in these six fields, we then say that a progression in stage has been achieved, even when the developmental psychological measurement of stage in Kohlberg's terms is not yet in force. For these six measurements are movements without which there can be no transformation in stage. It could, therefore, be said that achieving positive changes in these six fields does actually signify development, provided that the basis is a stimulation of moral conflict. For this reason, we can make the assumption that development also takes place if prerequisites are first stimulated by pushing them along. Hence also the title: "But it Does Move."

In our intervention, we have placed the six fields under the heading "aim-means." We have admittedly striven for the stimulation of higher levels in general by discussion of more general dilemmas specific to the profession; furthermore we have also formulated the six dimensions as aims which could probably be achieved by certain methods. Fig. 11.1 gives an overall view of this "correlation."

Figure 11.1 shows that all the individual measurements contribute to a change in the socio-moral stage, but also that the results of the individual aim-means connections clearly represent an indication of a change in stage. These fields are examined empirically below and in such a way that the treatment and the corresponding results become apparent for every field of stimulation. To complete the transformation model, we suggest on the one hand the aim-means variation and a simultaneous stimulation in the traditional sense on the other hand.

expected result

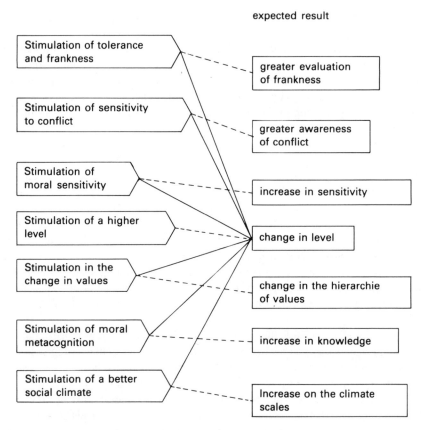

FIG. 11.1 Influencing factors, which were changed into aim-means connections, and which are decisive in the stimulation of higher moral levels.

THE INTERVENTION WITH BANK APPRENTICES

Overview and Method

The participants were young people between the ages of 16 and 20 who were completing their banking apprenticeships. With regard to this, we would like to say something about the Swiss system of apprenticeships, which differs considerably from that in the United States. At the age of 16, about 75% of the young people in Switzerland decide to follow 2–4 year apprenticeships. The apprenticeship takes place in a large or small firm and involves "on the job" training. The apprentice works for three days in the office, supervised by trained teachers. On the remaining two days, the apprentice goes to a state school. The apprentices participating in our intervention have the benefit of going to a firm school. The one-week course on socio-moral learning took place within this framework.

The intervention course was carried out in autumn 1981 with 50 apprentices. Two weeks before the preliminary test, the apprentices were given detailed information about the intention of the project; out of 53 apprentices, 50 decided to take part. The pretests and posttests took place before and after the course. The participants in the first of two courses were second year apprentices and office apprentices; those in the second course were first and third year apprentices. For each course we had a complete working week at our disposal and we worked approximately 8 hours a day, very often in groups. In order to guarantee that the teaching aims were followed optimally, during group work as well, three teaching assistants helped us.

Another group of twenty first year apprentices served as a control group. The delayed posttests took place six months later. Forty-seven of the 50 test subjects taking part in the course participated in both the preliminary and final tests. Thirty-one participated in the delayed posttest. (Third year apprentices were unable to be present because of exams.)

Goals

We intended to achieve the furtherance of socio-moral judgment by means of education, in accordance with our theoretical model. In so doing, the time aspect was important. In previous intervention studies the program was spread over a period of 4 to 8 months. What interested us was whether an intensive multitreatment program carried out in a 40-hour week of instruction could change the apprentices' socio-moral judgment. In the course of a whole week, intensive interaction between the course participants was possible.

More specifically, the influencing elements were the goals we strove for as teaching aims, corresponding to Fig. 11.1 (our intervention model). The contents for the program were also formulated according to these teaching aims. Our overall goal was stimulation of higher moral stage levels in Kohlberg's terms. Although we did, of course, attempt to stimulate subjects to a higher level directly, with the help of often re-introduced dilemmas, in the Kohlberg sense, we also had six intermediate goals:

1. *Moral sensitization.* This element involved an expansion of the cognitive structure to different, new moral contents. In this way, we hoped that the apprentices would learn to consider new, more varied moral objectives in the solution of dilemmas.

2. *Stimulation in the change in values.* We were also interested to know whether the apprentices become aware of more ideal values to a great extent, or whether they prefer more material values. Will they tend to prefer and support ideas and statements from the course which require an involvement in society?

Will apprentices, as a result of the course, support and prefer democratic values and behavior oriented to moral principals even if they possibly cause negative personal consequences?

3. *Stimulation of sensitivity to conflict.* We make the assumption that apprentices become aware, during the week of the course, that a dilemma consists of conflicting elementary issues. Will the sensitivity to conflict increase because of this? We do at least assume they may perceive the dilemma in a more conflicting way.

4. *Moral metacognition—Knowledge of the stage theory.* In our work, what we refer to as moral metacognition is the knowledge of the Kohlberg theory and its conversion into socio-moral discussions. This teaching aim was more of the exploratory kind. Until our work, there had hardly been any examinations of the effect of the understanding of the theory on young people. In this context, we were interested in the following questions, among others: How will the apprentices react to the understanding of the stage theory? Can the apprentices actively apply the knowledge acquired in their argumentation? Are they able to bring this theory into practice?

5. *Stimulation of tolerance and frankness.* This teaching aim almost became a motto throughout the whole work. An attempt was made, with the help of operative conversational rules (active listening, the understanding and respect of other opinions etc.), to acquire other modes of behavior in communication with others. A particular matter of concern here was the furtherance of tolerance towards other people and different opinions. We were interested to see whether the apprentices learned to use the conversational rules and put them into practice. From reports, interviews and course evaluations, we hoped to see that the apprentices "believed" that after the course they were more open, more tolerant and showed more empathy towards others.

6. *Stimulation of a better social climate.* There is an intervening variable involved here. We considered that a positive course atmosphere was a basic prerequisite for all teaching aims in order that certain changes could be achieved. Will the atmosphere improve during the week? If so, are there differences between the two course groups?

Operationalizing the Influencing Elements in Practice

For the purpose of translating the teaching aims into concrete teaching material, different methods were applied. Group discussions of dilemmas, role-playing, and games and strategies to make the subjects aware of the value of consciousness were employed. By means of oral and written tests certain dispositions and skills were said to be acquired. By showing the concrete applicability of the themes dealt with, we attempted to further the willingness of the apprentices to apply what they had learned in their everyday lives. The connection between each of the aims and the means applied cannot be dealt with in greater detail here.

Evaluation. In our case we were dealing with a field experimental design with a nonequivalent control group. The different teaching aims were evaluated with interviews, questionnaires and reports.

RESULTS

The Furthering of Socio-Moral Judgment.   In the interviews no increase in stage could be established with the somewhat crude Kohlberg instrument. About 70% remained at the same level, 13% showed a slight increase and 17% a slight regression. This study also supported the theoretical assumption that in a short time no stage increase should be expected (see Table 11.1). (On the other hand, when other instruments were used, changes were visible). Table 11.1 presents the pretest and posttest Moral Maturity Scores (MMS), which are essentially weighted mean stage scores multiplied by 100. In contrast to Kohlberg, we concentrated on one dilemma, Kohlberg's Heinz dilemma. Because of a lack of time, it was not possible to deal with two dilemmas in detail. The Heinz dilemma was not considered as a moral problem by the apprentices because there are good health insurance programs in Switzerland, depending on the apprentices' own choice, and possibilities to borrow money from the banks. This fact made the conducting and evaluation of interviews difficult.

TABLE 11.1
Results of the Experimental and Control Groups with Regard to the
MMS (Moral Maturity Scores)*

Group		Time	
		Pretest	*Posttest*
Experimental Group	x̄	278.4	273.3
N = 44	s	23.0	28.2
Control Group	x̄	286.5	292.5
N = 20	s	23.0	19.8

Group: F(1, 62) = 5.19ˣ
Time: F(1, 62) = 1.47
Group × Time: F(1, 62) = 1.16

x = significant to α = 0.05
xx = significant to α = 0.01
*All calculations of statistical significance in Tables 11.1–11.9 were made with the two-way analysis of variance for repeated measurements with the SPSS-program.

From Table 11.1, we can see that the stage construct shows an impressive consistency over a period of time. As many other intervention studies have shown, it does in fact seem very difficult to bring about a change in stage in a short space of time.

It must be pointed out that 90% of the apprentices were reasoning at Stages 2, 2/3 or 3. Kohlberg (1979) found in longitudinal studies that 16–18 year-olds were seldom above Stage 3/4. Stage 4 was frequently reached by 25–30 year olds. Furthermore, because bank apprentices were already generally at a higher stage, it was particularly difficult to achieve an increase in stage with this group anyway.

Rest (1979) showed that individuals who enter into active employment stagnate in their moral development. We are, however, of the opinion that the course sensitized the apprentices in the long run to socio-moral matters.

Stage change was also assessed with questionnaires on moral judgment (MUT by Lind, 1983, and UKT by Hinder, 1982a) and significant changes did emerge in comparing the experimental groups with the control group. This does point to a certain furthering of socio-moral judgment (see Table 11.2).

Furthering of Moral Sensitivity.   During the course, many different sorts of dilemmas were discussed. In these discussions the apprentices were supposed to learn how to become aware of their own argumentation and the subject matter to which the argument refers. Both of these are interdependent, that is to say the subject matter influences the moral argument, which in turn contains the subject matter (e.g., Heinz steals because he loves his wife, or Heinz steals because he

TABLE 11.2
Comparison of the Pretest and Posttest Means of the Measured
Level Values from the UKT (JCT, Judgment Consistency Test) for the
Experimental Group versus the Control Group

		Time	
Group		*Pretest*	*Posttest*
Experimental	x̄	70.4	82.2
N = 41	s	27.9	17.6
Control	x̄	82.1	82.1
N = 21	s	21.0	21.1

Group:	$F(1, 60) = 1.24$
Time:	$F(1, 60) = 6.83^{xx}$
Group × Time:	$F(1, 60) × 4.10^{x}$

x = significant to $\alpha = 0.05$
xx = significant to $\alpha = 0.01$

TABLE 11.3
Frequency of Moral Issues: Mean Scores in the Interview and of the
JCT for the Experimental and Control Group

Group		Time	
		Pretest	*Posttest*
Experimental Group	X̄	9.4	12.1
N = 38	S	2.2	3.2
Control Group	X̄	9.8	10.4
N = 18	S	2.7	2.7

Group: $F(1, 54) = 1.24$
Time: $F(1, 54) = 17.98^{xx}$
Group × Time: $F(1, 54) = 4.14^{x}$

x = significant to $\alpha = 0.05$
xx = significant to $\alpha = 0.01$

wants to save his wife's life). If different sorts of moral subject matter are considered in the argument, then it is to be assumed that the type of socio-moral argumentation is more diverse and contains more perspectives.

The first question of the Heinz-dilemma was evaluated. The apprentices were asked to say everything that came into their minds with regard to the first question. Only the subject matter that Kohlberg considered as moral subject matter in his manual was coded. The following came into that category: Authority (Obedience, punishment), Property, Relationships (Love), Law, Life, Conscience, Truthfulness, Social Contract, Fundamental Rights.

From Table 11.3, we can see that the experimental group uses significantly more moral subject matter in its socio-moral argumentation than the control group. This result clearly shows that the apprentices have increasingly referred to moral subject matter in their argumentation. This could signify a preparatory step for the next stage up because of Stage 4, the next step up, the social system must be considered as a whole. In order to understand this system better, more varied subject matter must be included in the socio-moral argumentation as well. This result cannot be attributed to increased length of explanation in the posttest because the control group did not differ from the experimental group in the length of its statements.

Stimulation in Change in Values.   During the intervention, personal values were spoken about and discussed. Complex socio-moral argumentation is required so that one is aware of one's own values. In the course, no attempt was made to lecture to the apprentices about the values that appeared to be the right ones to us. The participants were supposed to become aware of their own values and be sensitized to values that would be desirable for them. In the first part of the questionnaire on values, the apprentices listed those values that were important to them personally. They could name a maximum of 17. On the average, the experimental group noted 12 values and the controls 11. In a further exercise, the apprentices were supposed to put their five most important values in order. In Table 11.4 we have shown the five values named most frequently.

It shows that in the control group, apart from insignificant changes in order, no changes occurred in the individual hierarchy of values. On the other hand, in the experimental group, values such as "tolerance," "health" and "self-confidence" appeared. It seems likely that the social intercourse in the course, which was molded by the conversational rules and by the behavior of the course leader, had an influence on the apprentices' opinions on values.

It is typical that nothing explicit was ever said about the value "tolerance." However the behavior of the course leader, the acceptance of the most diverse opinions and the request to the apprentices that they express their opinions openly all led to this success. It is gratifying that, 6 months after the course, this hierarchy still remained. The value "frankness" did, however, disappear again; this was apparently a direct effect of the course, and did not last. The value "health" is an ideal value, which increased its value in the final test, and was considered by the apprentices in the delayed posttest as very important. This in fact emerged from every discussion as being something of great importance. In the delayed posttest the value "peace" gained in importance but probably as a result of actual peace demonstrations.

The percentages of all values listed is given in Table 11.5. The values were analyzed independently by two evaluators using a category system devised by Hinder (1982b). There was a 95% agreement rate. The ideal categories like love—self-discovery, social and interpersonal values recorded an increase of 19% in the experimental group; whereas in the control group there was an increase of only 3%. The material categories like body, knowledge, pleasure, property and money decreased in the experimental group by 18% and in the control group by only 1%. Categories like friendship and family remained unchanged as expected. These results were also confirmed in a questionnaire.

Furthering of Sensitivity to Conflict.   We were of the opinion in the course that it is not worth avoiding conflicts, but rather that it is important to face existing moral conflicts and to tackle them. The conflict was not shown as being something bad, but rather as something that furthers personal development. Both before and after the intervention, the apprentices assessed how they perceived the Heinz dilemma and the Euthanasia dilemma on a seven-item scale. There were items such as "the dilemma makes me depressed," "there is a conflict involved," etc. (The assessment was carried out in the framework of the testing of a new measuring process for the raising of moral judgment: Judgment-Consistency-Test, JCT).

In Table 11.6, the results of the sub-test "sensitization to conflict" are summarized. The experimental group found the dilemmas (Heinz dilemma and Euthanasia dilemma) in the posttest more reliable to conflict. The controls on the other hand showed a significant decrease in the sensitivity to conflict when confronted by a dilemma. It would appear that the frequent dilemma discussions lead to that confrontation of values contained in the dilemma being perceived and experienced as more liable to conflict. The apprentices were not afraid to show that they were personally affected by the dilemmas and that they were in a situation of conflict.

The decrease in the control group's conflict sensitivity scores could be attributed to the fact that they were already acquainted with the dilemmas the second time and no longer regarded them as being problematical or liable to cause conflict. In personal conversations the apprentices confirmed that they valued this way of solving conflicts and that in the future they would not simply try to avoid the conflicts.

Moral Metacognition.   The following results refer only to the experimental group because they concern the contents of the course. Shown in Fig. 11.2 is how well the apprentices understood the information about the stages.

The apprentices were administered a test to identify five stage arguments from the Heinz dilemma of the JCT. They also had to produce arguments for each stage in response to the question "Why should one not steal?". Figure 2 shows that for the most part stages 1 and 5 were correctly identified. On the other hand, apprentices had difficulties in discriminating among stages 2, 3, and 4. The upper curve indicates that the apprentices supposedly believed they had understood all the stages. The third curve shows that the apprentices could produce stages 1 and 2 particularly well and stage 3 moderately well. This result corresponds to the theory that the previous levels can be reproduced but levels above their own cannot be reproduced, or only partly. It is interesting that only 40% identified the correct stages, whereas 54% were able to reconstruct them. According to the memory theories, recognition is normally easier than production. It can be stated in the end that it was not wholly possible to make the stages completely clear to the apprentices. On the one hand it seems that the theory can only be passed on with difficulty. On the other hand, the theory makes many interesting ethical discussions possible. At the same time various elements of the course were held together by the theory. The apprentices expressed in reports as well that they found difficulties in putting the knowledge of the theory into practice. From the metacognition questionnaire we gained further information as to how the apprentices assessed the usage of the socio-moral theory in different spheres of life. Table 11.7 presents the posttest and delayed posttest results.

TABLE 11.4
Individual Hierarchy of Values: Illustration of Those Values Most Important to the Apprentices

I Total Values of the Experimental Group

	Pretest N = 44			Posttest N = 44			Delayed Posttest (6 months after the posttest) N = 31**	
Order	Value	% Frequency*	Order	Value	% Frequency	Order	Value	% Frequency
1	Love	60.0%	1	Love	65.9%	1	Love	73.3%
2	Friendship	60.0%	2	Friendship	54.4%	2	Friendship	70.0%
3	Profession, Prof. Success, Working Climate	35.0%	3	+Health	40.4%	3	+Health	43.3%
4	Sport	27.0%	4	Tolerance and understanding towards others, giving time and attention to others and respecting	31.9%	4	+Peace	38.7%
5	Comradeship, Friends	25.4%	5	Profession, Professional Success	27.6%	5	+Tolerance, understanding towards others, respecting others' opinions	30.0%
6	Money	23.5%	6	+Family	25.5%	6	+Family (especially good family relations)	30.0%
7	Freedom	17.6%	7	Freedom	25.5%	7	Travel	23.3%
8	Free Time	15.6%	8	+Self-Confidence ability to express one's own opinions	21.2%	8	Money	23.3%

II Total Values of the Control Group

| | N = 21 | | | N = 21 | |
Order	Value	% Frequency	Order	Value	% Frequency
1	Friendship	66.6%	1	Love	66.6%
2	Love	61.9%	2	Profession, Apprenticeship	66.6%
3	Prof., Apprenticeship	47.6%	3	Friendship	52.0%
4	Family, Brothers and Sisters	38.0%	4	Sport	42.8%
5	Money	28.5%	5	Music	38.5%
6	Sport	28.5%	6	Family	33.3%
7	Music	23.8%	7	Money	23.8%
8	Personal Freedom Heit	19.0%	8	Free time	19.0%

+ Newly chosen values.

*The percentage frequency refers to the number of apprentices who place any one value in the first five of their most important values. 60% signifies that for example 60% of the apprentices placed the value "love" in the first five places.

**Thirteen students were unable to participate in the delayed posttest.

TABLE 11.5
Proportion of the Percentage Differences for Ideals, Affiliative, and
Material Value Categories for the Experimental and Control Groups

Categories	Group	Pretest %	Posttest %	Delayed Posttest %
Ideals	Experimental Group			
	N = 44	21.4	40.1	
	Control Group			42.2
	N = 21	23.4	26.5	
Material	Experimental Group			
	N = 44	54.9	36.8	
	Control Group			39.6
	N = 21	55.0	54.0	
Friendship	Experimental Group			
	N = 44	24.0	23.1	
Family	Control Group			18.2
	N = 21	21.6	19.5	

TABLE 11.6
Comparisons of Mean Sensitivity to Conflict from the Pretest and
Posttest Heinz and Euthanasia Dilemmas of the Experimental and
Control Groups

Group		Time	
		Pretest	Posttest
Experimental Group	X	32.7	35.1
N = 40	S	7.6	6.4
Control Group	X	34.2	31.8
N = 20	S	5.2	5.6

Group:	$F_{(58, 1)} = 0.32$
Time:	$F_{(58, 1)} = 0.76$
Group × Time:	$F_{(58, 1)} = 6.35$xx

x = significant to $\alpha = 0.05$
xx = significant to $\alpha = 0.01$

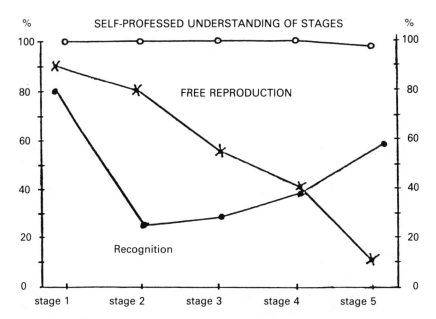

FIG. 11.2   Experimental subjects' estimated supposed understanding of stages, percentage proportions of correct recognition of stage items, and percentage proportions of correct free stage reproductions.

About 50% believed in the posttest that they would be able to apply the knowledge of the theory. In the delayed posttest, however, only 20% were of this opinion, and only in question 2 did 40% agree that they would apply the knowledge about socio-moral levels when arguing in discussions. Thus the participants in the course clearly rejected the idea that they would use this knowledge in solving conflicts. This was the expected result. (In addition to this knowledge therefore, elements of Gordon's conflict-solving method were also taught). The stage theory appears to be too abstract and too theoretical for the apprentices. Perhaps the practical application with the various sorts of argumentation was also used too little. All this does of course confirm the thesis of research in the field of structural genetic theories; that is, that knowledge of developmental levels is of use to instructors, but does not help the pupil in any way. For it is only at the higher levels that the learning of theories is fruitful (cf. Regenbogen, in press).

We are nevertheless of the opinion that it would be worthwhile to teach the theory again in another course. However, the manner of presentation and the time taken to introduce the theory would have to be considered anew.

Stimulation of Tolerance and Frankness.   As far as this teaching aim was concerned, we have mainly qualitative data (apprentices' reports) and subjective course assessments to present. All in all, we can conclude that the apprentices

TABLE 11.7
Metacognition Questionnaire Results Based on Knowledge of the
Theory of Socio-Moral Judgment

	Experimental Groups	Posttest	Delayed Posttest
Question 1	N = 31	%	%
Will you be able to make a decision about socio-moral levels more easily in the future when in a situation of conflict on account of knowledge acquired on the course?	Yes	42	23
	No	10	32
	Don't Know	48	45
Question 2			
As a result of any knowledge acquired on the course, would you be able to argue more easily about socio-moral stages in the future?	Yes	58	39
	No	10	33
	Don't Know	32	28
Question 3			
Does the knowledge about stages help in solving conflicts/problems in your everyday life?	Yes	19	19
	No	35	65
	Don't Know	46	16
Question 4			
In your private conversations in the future will you bear the distinction in qualities of stage arguments in mind?	Yes	64	23
	No	16	58
	Don't Know	20	19
Question 5			
Will you bear the distinction in stages in mind in your professional conversation?	Yes	55	23
	No	23	58
	Don't Know	22	19
Question 6			
Will you bear the distinction in stages in mind when you see news or commentaries in the newspaper, on the television or at the cinema?	Yes	48	23
	No	34	54
	Don't Know	18	23

themselves found they could be more open towards their colleagues. The conversational rules learned in the course were conducive to this (such as, for example, active listening).

In Table 11.8, we see that the results of questions 7 and 8 are about conversational rules in contrast to the questions in Table 11.7 which deal with the usefulness of socio-moral judgment. Respectively, 66% and 87% of the apprentices stressed in the delayed posttest that the conversational rules for discussions would be of particular personal use when solving conflicts and in discussions. Only one person rejected this latter idea.

In written reports, the apprentices noted that they had profited most in the following ways:

(a) Learning about conversational rules.
(b) Getting to know themselves and others better.
(c) Learning how to get along better with others.
(d) Being able to discuss things more easily.
(e) Thinking about one's own actions.

These learning effects outlined by the apprentices were mainly intended with teaching aim 5. In personal conversations, the apprentices later confirmed that they had come to appreciate the method of solving conflicts by frankness and tolerance. They did, however, notice that with certain apprentice supervisors, problems could arise because these people had not followed the course. Those individuals would prefer to suppress conflicts or solve them by punishment. At the end of the course, the apprentices filled out an overall course assessment. The items (see Table 11.9) about frankness, empathy and tolerance towards others were considered very positively the apprentices.

The stability of judgment also remained constant over a period of time. A large proportion of the apprentices believed they had effectively learned something in this area. The course leaders and teachers in the bank also confirmed that they had noticed progress among the apprentices in this respect.

Stimulation of a Better Social Climate. In order to make possible a change in tolerance, self-confidence, and socio-moral judgment, a positive moral atmosphere and trust between the course leaders and apprentices was necessary.

TABLE 11.8
Metacognition Questionnaire Percentage Results with Regard to
Knowledge of the Conversational Rules

	Experimental Groups	*Posttest*	*Post-Posttest*
Question 7			
Will you apply the conversational rules	Yes	84	87
learned in your future discussions?	No	0	0
	Don't Know	16	13
Question 8			
Will the conversational rules be of use to	Yes	58	66
you in your personal conflicts with	No	6	3
other people?	Don't Know	36	31

The introduction of conversational rules was a significant step in the creation of a positive atmosphere. It was also important that the course leaders showed themselves to be models of tolerance and empathy, etc. There are certain data which show that the creation of a positive atmosphere was a success. The discussion leaders observed an improvement in the atmosphere among the first course group on the second day, and among the second group on the third day. This was clearly expressed in group evaluation discussion.

This subjective impression was empirically tested. Every day, the apprentices filled in a form evaluating the day's work, which contained the same questions each time. The subtest "atmosphere" contains items such as "I feel at ease," "I enjoyed the day," "the discussions were open," etc.

We see in Table 11.10 that the atmosphere improved constantly throoughout the week. The data agree with the conclusions of the discussion leaders, i.e., the atmosphere improved in the first course on the second day and in the second course on the third day. On the fourth day we again noticed a strong increase in positive climate values in the second course. A conflict existing at that time between some of the apprentices and the training and apprentice leaders was tackled. It appears that the solution of real conflicts by the means given in the model was very highly regarded and had a positive effect on the atmosphere. The video recordings also confirm that the atmosphere between the apprentices and the course leaders was positive. This observation was also made by an independent advisor. The good atmosphere was, however, not achieved merely through

TABLE 11.9
Percentage of Affirmative and Negative Responses to the Subjective
Course Evaluation Items in the Total Evaluation for the Course

In Comparison to the Time Before the Course:	Yes % T 1 (T 2) Posttest (Delayed Posttest) N = 50 (N = 31)	No % T 1 (T 2) Posttest (Delayed Posttest) N = 50 (N = 31)
1 I believe I can argue and discuss better	96 (82)	4 (18)
2 I believe I can listen to others more easily in discussions	96 (82)	4 (18)
7 I believe I can think over my decisions and actions more carefully	94 (82)	6 (18)
9 I believe that I can better consider different interests and viewpoints which affect me and other people	98 (82)	2 (18)
10 I believe that I can empathize with others more easily	94 (69)	6 (31)
12 I have gotten to know my colleagues better than before	100 (91)	0 (9)

TABLE 11.10
Comparison of the Means of the Daily Atmosphere Assessments for
Both Experimental Groups

Group		Time			
		Monday	Tuesday	Wednesday	Thursday
Experimental Group 1	x̄	17.0	19.2	20.0	20.5
N = 14	s	1.7	3.0	3.1	2.1
Experimentsl Group 2	x̄	16.7	16.7	20.7	21.7
N = 18	s	2.8	2.1	1.8	1.6

Group comparison over the whole week
Group: $F(1, 30) = 0.15$
Time: $F(1, 30) = 24.9**$

Comparison of the increase from Monday to Tuesday Effects
Time (Mon–Tue): $F(1, 30) = 4.82*$
Group × Time: $F(1, 30) = 3.55*$

Comparison of the increase from Tuesday to Wednesday Effects
Time (Tue–Wed): $F(1, 30) = 4.53*$
Group × Time: $F(1, 30) = 9.12**$

Comparison in the increase from the Wednesday to the Thursday Effects
Time (Wed–Thu): $F(1, 30) = 13.61**$
Group × Time: $F(1, 30) = 1.84$

* = significant to $\alpha = 0.05$
** = significant to $\alpha = 0.01$

automatic acceptance by the course leaders of the demands of the apprentices. It was worked on intensively throughout the week of the course and any conflicts arising between course leaders and apprentices were solved openly.

We believe that a positive atmosphere is an indispensable condition if tolerance, frankness and reflection about oneself are to become at all possible. This is also confirmed by other researchers who have looked into socio-moral education (Hersh, Paolitto & Reimer, 1979; Hickey & Scharf, 1980, Kohlberg, 1978, in press).

CONCLUDING COMMENTARY

In their very fine book about educating for justice, Aufenanger, Garz and Zutavern write (1981, p. 9) that it is easy to understand human rights and similarly great objectives, but that nonindoctrinative educating for justice within concrete educational activity is both very important and very difficult to achieve. And it is especially apprentices, whose training is above all geared to production, who should have a right to acquire a higher socio-moral competence and thereby a greater social identity. The application of "practical" reason, which becomes useful in a socio-moral intervention (and because of this application also becomes instructive), does however have many facets. We have considered which of these facets are the most important and which is the structural-genetic basic stream that carries them. On the basis of the stimulation to a higher level of development (variables requiring intervention) the following goals were striven for: (a) an increase in moral sensitization, (b) a stimulation in the change in values, (c) a stimulation of the sensitivity towards conflict, (d) an increase in moral metacognition, (e) an increase in tolerance and frankness and (f) an improvement in the social climate. Even if the developmental stage has not been changed directly, all the results of the six facets point to the fact that the way has been conclusively smoothed for such a change. The results achieved are, in each case, evidence that the training of socio-moral competence is possible in the training of apprentices as a supplement to training them for success in their profession. Apprentices express themselves more freely, they become more tolerant with regard to possible plausibility structures and more sensitive about morals. They acquire a greater understanding of the normative networks which determine their system and their thinking. They are able to cope with more conflicts and assume responsibility for all the things that concern people working within a firm, that is to say the social working climate. What we have striven for, and achieved, must however be judged by the general human goal of education toward social autonomy and competence. This means that higher socio-moral development enables an individual who has the requisite thinking ability to attain the highest universal principles of justice and of society with which he can understand and tackle what he encounters in his dealings with others in his work.

We would now like to round off these conclusions with an excerpt from a nonrepresentative report written by an apprentice about the course. The apprentices are of course the most important participants in this study. Further reports have been published in the HASMU-Bulletin (1981, no. 2).

The course surprised me in a quite positive way. At the beginning, I was apprehensive about the discussion, but that soon changed. You really could feel that the participants in the course and especially the course leaders took you seriously. The week was marked by honesty, friendliness and general pleasantness which lead to the 'teaching' being very relaxed. We did not follow one set timetable, but whenever possible the course leaders gave their attention to details and problems. This was especially noticable in the small group. The aim of the week was to create a better understanding with those around us, and to be able to control and respectively understand ourselves. On the last day of the week, each participant was able to put what he had learned into practice. Among people in the course it was find but I found that there were difficulties with "outsiders," that is to say people who weren't in the course. This one week seems to be far too short to me. Everything was all right in theory, but how and when do you apply what you have learned in real life? So, all that I'm left with is a tear in my eye and the wish that the course could be continued. Instruction like this in every state school would, as far as I can see, be ' too good to be true.

ACKNOWLEDGMENT

The project was carried out within the Swiss National Program "Education and active life" (Education et vie active: EVA)

REFERENCES

Aufenanger, S., Garz, D., & Zutavern, M. (1981). *Erziehung zur Gerechtigkeit.* Munich: Koesel.

Baier, K. (1958). *The moral point of view.* Ithaca, NY: Cornell University.

Bebeau, J. M., Rest, J. R., & Yamoor, C. M. (1982). *Development of profession-specific tests of ethical sensitivity: An example in dentistry.* Unpublished manuscript, Unversity of Minnesota.

Berkowitz, M. W. (1981). A critical appraisal of the educational and psychological perspectives on moral discussion. *The Journal of Educational Thought, 15,* 20–33.

Berkowitz, M. W. (1983). *The process of moral development through discourse.* Paper presented at the meeting of the International Society for the Study of Behavioral Development, Munich.

Berkowitz, M. W. & Gibbs, J. C. (1983). Measuring the developmental features of moral discussion. *Merrill-Palmer Quarterly, 29,* 399–410.

Berkowitz, M. W., Gibbs, J. C., & Broughton, J. M. (1980). The relation of moral judgment stage disparity to developmental effects of peer dialogues. *Merrill-Palmer Quarterly, 26,* 341–357.

Blatt, M. & Kohlberg, L. (1975). The effects of classroom moral discussion upon children's level of moral judgment. *Journal of Moral Education, 4,* 129–161.

Boyd, D. (1976). The problem of sophomoritis: An educational proposal. *Journal of Moral Education, 6,* 36–42.

Cook, T. D. & Campbell, D. T. (1979). *Quasi experimentation.* Chicago: Rand McNally.

HASMU-Bulletin (1981). Number 2. Pädagogisches Institut der Universität Freiburg, Switzerland.

Hersh, R., Paolitto, D., & Reimer, J. (1979). *Promoting moral growth: From Piaget to Kohlberg.* New York: Longman.

Hickey, J. E. & Scharf, P. L. (1980). *Toward a just correctional system.* San Francisco: Jossey-Bass.

Higgins, A. (1980). Research and measurement issues in moral education interventions. In R. L. Mosher (Ed.), *Moral education: A first generation of research and development* (pp. 92–107). New York: Praeger.

Hinder, E. (1982a). *Der Urteils-Konsistenz-Test.* Unpublished manuscript, University of Freiburg, Switzerland.

Hinder, E. (1982b). *Auswertungsmanual für Freiantworten des Wertfragebogens. 1. Teil.* Unpublished manuscript, University of Freiburg, Switzerland.

Jennings, W., Higgins, A., & Power, C. (1980). *Preliminary program evaluation.* Unpublished manuscript, Harvard University Center for Moral Education, Cambridge, MA.

Kohlberg, L. (1958). *The development of mode of moral thinking and choice in the years 10 to 16.* Unpublished doctoral dissertation, University of Chicago.

Kohlberg, L. (1978). Revisions in the theory and practice of moral development. In W. Damon (Ed.), *New directions for child development: Moral development* (pp. 83–88). San Francisco: Jossey-Bass.

Kohlberg, L. (1979). *The meaning and measurement of moral development.* Worcester, MA: Clark University.

Kohlberg, L. (in press). *Der Just Community Ansatz der Moralerziehung in Theorie und Praxis.* Frankfurt: Suhrkamp.

Lempert, W. (1982). Moralische Urteilsfähigkeit: Ebenen und Stufen, Anwendungsbereiche und Anwendungsbedingungen, Entwicklungspfade und Entwicklungskontexte. Zur Explikation und Extrapolation logischer und soziologischer Implikationen der Theorie Kohlbergs. *Zeitschrift für Sozializationsforschung und Erziehungs-soziologie, 2,* 113–126.

Lieberman, M. (1980). New directions in evaluating moral educational programs. In L. Kuhmerker, M. Mentkowksi, & V. L. Erickson (Eds.), *Evaluating moral development* (pp. 13–26). Schenectady, NY: Character Research.

Lieberman, M. (1981). Facing history and ourselves: A project evaluation. *Moral education forum, 2,* 36–41.

Lind, G. (1983). *Moralische Urteilskompentenz und berufliche Ausbildung.* Berichte zur Erziehungswissenschaft aus dem Pädagogischen Institut, Number 36. University of Freiburg, Switzerland.

Lockwood, A. L. (1978). The effects of values clarification and moral development curricula on school-age subjects: A critical review of recent research. *Review of Educational Research, 48,* 325–364.

Loevinger, J. (1976). *Ego development.* San Francisco: Jossey-Bass.

Mosher, R. L. (Ed.) (1980). *Moral education: A first generation of research and development.* New York: Praeger.

Patry, J.-L. (1981). *Zur Validität der unabhängigen Variable in N=1-Designs mit natürlichen Treatments.* Unpublished manuscript, Pädagogisches Institut, Freiburg, Switzerland.

Power, C. (1979). *The moral atmosphere of a just community high school: A four year longitudinal study.* Unpublished doctoral dissertation, Harvard University.

Regenbogen, A. (in press). Gerechtigkeit als Lernprozess. In *Denken und Handeln. Günter Freudenberg zum 60. Geburgstag.* University of Osnabrück: Osnabrück Philosophische Schriften.

Reimer, J. & Power, C. (1980). Educating for democratic community: Some unresolved dilemmas. In R. L. Mosher (Ed.), *Moral education: A first generation of research and development* (pp. 303–320). New York: Praeger.

Rest, J. R. (1979). *Development in judging moral issues.* Minneapolis: University of Minnesota.

Schläfli, A., Rest, J. R., & Thoma, S. (1984). *Does moral education improve morol judgment? A meta-analysis of intervention studies using the DIT.* Unpublished manuscript, University of Minnesota.

Selman, R. (1976a). Toward a structural analysis of developing interpersonal relationship concepts: Research with normal and disturbed preadolescent boys. In A. Pick (Ed.), *Tenth Annual Minnesota Symposium on Child Psychology* (pp. 156–200). Minneapolis: University of Minnesota.

Selman, R. L. (1976b). *Friendship—caught in the middle.* White Plains, NY: Guidance Associates.

Shaver, J. (1983). The verification of indepedent variables in teaching methods research. *Educational Researcher, 12,* 3–9.

Strom, M., Parsons, W., & Lieberman, M. (1980). *Facing history and ourselves: Holocaust and human behavior.* Brookline Public School application to Joint Dissemination Review Panel, Washington, D.C. Brookline Public Schools, Brookline, MA.

Sullivan, P. (1980). Moral education for adolescents. In R. L. Mosher (Ed.), *Moral education: A first generation of research and development* (pp. 165–187). New York: Praeger.

12 Classical Ethics and Live Patient Simulations in the Moral Education of Health Care Professionals

Daniel Candee
Center for Moral Education
Harvard University

In this chapter I discuss several new ideas in moral education that have emerged out of my work with practicing health care professionals. The work began with physicians and later expanded to include nurses as well. The impetus for these ideas came from the fact that the activities of health care workers, and no doubt other professionals as well, reveal a set of considerations not usually encountered in school settings. These considerations stem from the fact that a professional is often accountable to a client whose goals must be considered and to whom one's decisions must often be defended. For these reasons moral education in this area must devote particular attention to the actual decisions reached and the manner in which the client's views are consulted.

MORAL THOUGHT AND MORAL ACTION

A fruitful way to organize both research and educational ideas in this area is to use a model of the relationship of moral thought to moral action. One such model is proposed by Rest (1982, 1983, and this volume). Rest outlines a sequence of steps that must be carried out as one goes from encountering a situation to making a moral judgment to taking a moral action. Rest is careful not to claim that these steps follow a necessary order. Rather, he considers the steps to be components which encompass several psychological skills within them. They include the following: (1) interpreting the situation—being aware of social cues and defining them as potential moral problems; (2) formulating the morally ideal course of action, "integrating the various considerations—person A's needs, person B's needs, personal needs, expectations founded on previous promises or roles or instituted practices'' (Rest, 1982, p. 32) usually by the use of a moral principle or decision rule; (3) deciding what one actually intends to do—comparing the ideal moral behavior to behaviors that appear to maximize other values; (4) executing and implementing what one intends to do—having the perseverence, ''will power'' and skills to carry out one's intended action.

The scope of Rest's model is particularly relevant for describing moral reasoning and behavior in a clinical setting. There, potentially moral situations exist in contexts where physiological or nonmoral behavioral problems are in the forefront. The health care professional must be able to perceive, reason about, and develop a plan to resolve moral problems that appear in a multi-problem context.

An alternative but compatible model of the judgment-action relationship is proposed by Kohlberg and Candee (1984). They, along with Blasi (1980), have reviewed a large number of studies and found that the vast majority display a monotonic relationship between stage of moral reasoning and action. That is, they find that in carefully defined situations a given action is performed more often by persons at each higher stage of moral reasoning as measured by Kohlberg's Standard Moral Judgment Interview. These studies point out that the principles used to resolve moral problems are directly linked with the decisions one makes. The structure of one's moral thought is clearly related to the moral conclusions one draws. Thus, if we in the field of moral education are concerned with students making optimal moral decisions, there is good reason to focus on the process by which these decisions are reached.

MORAL REASONING AND CLINICAL PERFORMANCE

Moral reasoning would be of little interest to an educator working with practicing clinicians if it could not be shown that such reasoning was related to clinical performance. For the last 8 years I have been working with T. Joseph Sheehan and others at The University of Connecticut Health Center studying this problem. We began by investigating the proposition that moral reasoning was, in fact, a significant and identifiable factor in physician performance. To test this we obtained ratings in 18 areas of clinical performance from faculty members at seven different hospitals. Data were provided for 372 residents in both pediatrics and internal medicine. Residency, in the United States, is the period of on-the-job training following graduation from medical school. Our results showed an average correlation of $r = .20$ between moral reasoning as measured by the Defining Issues Test (DIT) and an overall rating of clinical performance, within a single residency program. This correlation improved to $r = .33$ when we combined all seven programs into one sample and increased again to $r = .59$ when adjusted for program quality. A correlation of $r = .47$ was found when, for two subsamples, Kohlberg's standard Moral Judgment Interview was used in place of the DIT (reported in Sheehan, Husted, Candee, Cook and Bargen, 1980). A second study (Candee, Sheehan, Cook, Husted and Bargen, 1982) demonstrated that residents whose moral reasoning was more developed expressed attitudes towards the treatment of critical illness that took greater account of patient or family requests and of the subsequent quality of life.

These studies established a link between a physician's moral thinking and his or her clinical performance. However, our measures of performance remained at the level of verbal report—faculty impressions in the case of the Sheehan study, physicians' attitudes in the case of the Candee study. Over the past 2 years we have attempted to overcome our previous limitations by observing clinical performance as it actually occurs between doctor and patient. In order to do this we created two simulated cases dramatized by actor-patients who were seen by doctors in a clinical setting. I discuss these simulations more thoroughly later in this chapter.

Results of our current research again showed a significant relationship between moral reasoning and clinical performance. This time performance was observed on the simulated patient encounters ($r = .26$), as well as through faculty rating ($r = .38$). In addition, we constructed a special interview, called the Role Concept Interview (RCI) to assess the physician's reasoning about his or her job. This measure also correlated with clinical performance ($r = .38$ with simulated patient encounters and $r = .51$ with faculty ratings). A recent report of our work (Sheehan, Candee, Wilms, Donnelly and Husted, 1984) outlines a path-analytic model relating the various measures. In that paper we present evidence for a model in which moral reasoning and role concepts affect clinical behavior through the formulation of specific plans of action. This statistical model is consistent with the theoretical approaches of both Rest and of Kohlberg and Candee. It is also consistent with a general model of the relationship between attitudes and behavior proposed by Fishbein and Ajzen (1975) and recently tested using path-analytic equations by Bentler and Speckart (1979).

MORAL EDUCATION MEASURES AND TECHNIQUES

Having demonstrated that, at least in the settings where we have studied it, moral reasoning is a significant component of clinical performance, I began to think about how to teach moral reasoning with the goal of ultimately improving performance.

Table 12.1 presents a sequence of steps that I have used to guide my efforts in moral education and measurement for several years. Next to each step is the component of Rest's model that seems to subsume it. For each step in the model, I propose a skill to be taught and an instrument by which to measure that skill. The reason for including measures along with methods for each step is that I

TABLE 12.1
The Relationship of Moral Reasoning Process to Rest Components

Steps in Reasoning Process	Rest Component
1. Identify as a moral dilemma	Interpreting the situation
2. Gather and elicit claims	Interpreting the situation
3. Establish bases for claims	Formulating the morally ideal action
4. Determine validity of each claim	Formulating the morally ideal action
5. Determine priority of claims	Formulating the morally ideal action
6. Communicate decision to other	Deciding the actual action
7. Negotiate decision with other	Deciding the actual action
8. Implement action plan	Implementing action

believe they are inseperable. Any skill that is worth measuring is worth teaching and any skill worth teaching is worth measuring.

There are two sources from which I derive my ideas about both teaching methods and instruments. The first consists of several courses on moral education that I have been teaching. One involved working with groups of five or six pediatric residents over the course of 2 years at Kings County Hospital, a high-volume urban hospital in Brooklyn, New York. Another is a course that teaches clinical reasoning (ethics and diagnosis) to 100 practicing nurses. A third course is an annual summer institute in moral education given at the Center for Moral Education, aimed primarily at secondary school teachers and administrators. The second source of my ideas is our recent study at the University of Connecticut, described in part earlier, in which we have videotaped doctor-patient interactions.

Each source has yielded different kinds of methods and measures. I shall go through each step of the moral reasoning process, drawing first from my work with practicing doctors and nurses. This source has yielded relatively formal instruments by which practitioners are aided in making individual moral decisions. They are most appropriate to steps 1–5 of the following model, which focus on individual decision-making. Later in the chapter I discuss the use of videotapes to measure and teach some of these same components, from an interactive point of view.

Step 1: Identify as a Moral Dilemma

Measures.   The first step in the reasoning process is to identify a dilemma as being potentially moral. This skill has been greatly overlooked in recent moral education. In classroom settings a dilemma is usually prepackaged to be moral. It has already been framed so that a moral problem is central. Even in Just Community situations (cf. Kohlberg, this volume), problems that are brought before the community are almost always done so because they are known to contain moral aspects.

We measure the ability to identify a moral problem by presenting a series of clinical cases followed by four or five questions about the case. Only one of the questions clearly raises moral issues or turns the case into a moral dilemma. The student is asked to mark the item that "best transforms the situation so as to pose an ethical dilemma." An example is as follows:

Joan Fitzpatrick is an 84-year-old woman who lives alone and has no relatives or close friends. Over the past year she has developed problems with her balance, has fallen often, and has had difficulty managing her medications and household activities. The Visiting Nurse's Association (VNA) recommends that she enter a nursing home. However, Mrs. Fitzpatrick steadfastly refuses to even consider giving up her house and entering a nursing home.

—a) Should the VNA staff nurse arrange for a home health aide to help Mrs Fitzpatrick manage her household activities?

—b) Should the VNA staff nurse seek a court order to have Mrs Fitzpatrick placed into a nursing home despite her wish to live by herself?

—c) Should the VNA staff nurse try labeling medications with color codes and leave specific instructions as to which color code should be taken at specific times?

—d) Should the VNA staff nurse request that Mrs Fitzpatrick obtain a lifeline beeper which she can use to signal for help if she falls and is injured?

The correct answer in the example is letter "b." The other responses involve various strategies to make Mrs Fitzpatrick's life at home more manageable. However, only question "b" presents a clear moral conflict, in this case between the nurse's belief that Mrs Fitzpatrick would be better off in a nursing home and Mrs Fitzpatrick's desire to remain at home. Our test, called the Domain Discrimination Test, presently consists of five cases such as the one presented above. As with all of the other tests there are two distinct but parallel forms.

We have done little specific teaching in the area beyond pointing out the characteristics that comprise a moral dilemma. My guess is that this skill is best learned by exposing students to a large number of situations, some moral and some not, and pointing out the differences. It is a skill that may best be learned by example, not logic.

Steps 2–3: Gather Claims and Establish Their Bases

Measures. We move now to the next two steps in the moral reasoning process, gathering moral claims and establishing their bases. This skill consists of determining which persons are involved in a moral situation and what each individual wants. We define a moral claim as what a person wants or feels he or she is entitled to. We define a basis as the best moral argument that supports the claim as judged from the viewpoint of the individual making the claim. The purpose of being able to delineate persons, claims and bases is that having "set up the problem" a student is in a better position to resolve it. We test this skill by presenting subjects with a case and asking them to list the relevant parties, their claims and the bases of those claims. The test, called the Hypothesis Generation Test, consists of two cases on each form. Here is a sample item and one subject's response:

> Margaret Hestor, 30, is admitted to the hospital for a diagnostic D&C. Over the years her surgeon, Dr. Benton, has proven himself to be a good surgeon who has been willing to work long hours or help out by taking a case on short notice. However, during Ms Hestor's operation Dr. Benton accidently severs the uterine artery, requiring the removal of the uterus. Later, Dr. Benton tells Ms. Hestor that the pathological findings discovered during surgery warranted an immediate hysterectomy. Ms. Hestor becomes upset and asks the peri-operative nurse who was present during the operation whether the hysterectomy was necessary. The nurse knows that reporting the accident and exposing Dr. Benton's story would probably lead to the dismissal of an otherwise very good surgeon.

	Person	Claim	Basis
☑	Ms. Hestor	To be told the truth	She has a fundamental right to know
X	Dr. Benton	It was an accident	He has the human right to error
X	Nurse	The patient has a right to know	While the doctor made a surgical error he compounded it by lying

As can be seen in the sample item, the subject identified three persons as being involved in this moral situation, Ms. Hestor, Dr. Benton, and the peri-operative nurse. Clearly, these are the three central characters. Occasionally, other respondents included the hospital or the effects on society as other "persons." At present we have not analyzed the correlates of such extended responses. While leaving out one of the three central characters certainly seems to be a crucial omission we do not know whether adding peripheral characters is a significant comission.

Both claims and bases are classified into three groups, acceptable, semi-acceptable, and not acceptable. The criterion for acceptability of a *claim* is that the content of the claim be the basic issue that we have imposed on the case, that the claim be stated in terms of what a person wants or is entitled to, and that the claim make sense in terms of the clinical situation. Responses that could be rephrased to be acceptable, either by keeping the content and altering the form or by keeping the form and altering the content are considered to be "semi-acceptable." Responses that are inappropriate both in form and content are classified as "not acceptable."

The criteria for acceptability of a *basis* is that it present a moral argument or lend moral support for the individual's claim. Two necessary but not sufficient conditions are that the basis must be sensible in terms of the clinical situation (e.g., not refer to outcomes that are very unlikely to occur) and that it be logically related to the claim it is supporting. However, the key criterion is that the basis be phrased in moral language. To help us with an operational definition of moral language we employ the system of moral elements used in scoring Kohlberg's Moral Judgment Interview (Colby, Kohlberg, Gibbs, Candee, Speicher-Dubin, and Hewer, in press). This list includes elements derived from three major ethical approaches or "theories": justice, utility, and perfectionism. The most recognizable elements are rights, duties, welfare, and approbation (good and bad persons). A basis that clearly includes any one of these elements and that satisfies the more basic criteria of situational relevance and logical relationship to its claim is considered acceptable.

The case mentioned earlier has been set up to oppose the patient's right to know the truth with either the utility that may be lost by jeopardizing the career of an otherwise good surgeon or, alternatively, with the fairness of the surgeon's losing his job after years of meritorious service. The response for Ms. Hestor given by our sample subject is acceptable both in terms of claim and basis. The content of the claim is one of the issues that was built into the situation, that is, the patient's right to know the truth about her operation. In addition, the claim is phrased in terms of what the patient wants or is entitled to. In both a philosophic and psychological sense it is indeed "a claim." Similarly, the basis of the claim is acceptable. It is logically related to the claim, it is sensible in terms of the story and most important it is phrased in moral language, "the *right* to know." The acceptability of Ms. Hestor's claim and basis is indicated by the check in the left hand margin.

The remaining responses given by our sample subject illustrate responses that are not considered acceptable. For example, the claim for Dr. Benton is not acceptable because it states a fact ("it was an accident"). It does not state what Dr. Benton wants or is entitled to. The basis for this claim ("he has the human right to error") is classified as "semi-acceptable." It is clearly stated in moral language and contains the moral element "having a right" (see list of moral elements in Colby et al., in press). These two criteria are necessary but not sufficient conditions for acceptability. The difficulty with this response lies in its content. There is no generally recognized "human right to error." The response may be rephrased to read "in light of his previous efforts it would be unfair not to allow him one error" or "it would be unfair to fire him because of one error." These rephrased responses refer to the issue of deservingness or "just desserts," both clearly recognized moral categories. It may well be that this is what the respondent intended to communicate. However, one of the goals of our program is to teach health professionals to be more precise about the moral nature of their justifications, to think more carefully about whether something that is considered a right is, in fact a right, or at least whether the subject can give a reasonable argument for why it should be considered a right. Notice also that in classifying responses we do not attempt to judge whether the position attributed to each character in the dilemma is morally "right." We are concerned only with whether the position is stated in moral language and is sound enough to be morally arguable.

The claim given for the third person, the nurse, is acceptable. However, the basis, "while the doctor made a surgical error he compounded it by lying," is not acceptable. Again, this response merely states a fact about the case. It does not give a clear moral basis or lend moral support to the claim. As is often the case, we can reinterpret the subject's response to suggest that because of the doctor's apparent lying the patient has a greater than ordinary interest in having the truth be known. But, this rephrasing is a considerable leap from the subject's actual words. Where a response cannot stand clearly on its own it cannot be classified in the "acceptable" category. The fact that neither of the claim-basis combinations are acceptable for either the doctor or the nurse is indicated by an 'x' next to those persons in the example above.

A total score for this measure is compiled by awarding 3 points for acceptable responses, 2 for semi-acceptable responses and 1 for unacceptable responses. The omission of a crucial character (nurse, patient or doctor) is scored as if it were an unacceptable response.

Educational Methods.   We have found that filling out a form similar to the one above is a valuable way for students to organize data about cases. In our course with practicing nurses we present a case, often based on a film or video, and have students indicate persons, claims and bases. Discussion with groups as large as 100 can be held by writing the persons, claims and bases on the board as they are suggested. Group discussion, lead by a teacher or moderator can begin at the point of asking, "Does this qualify as a moral basis for a particular claim?" More often, establishing claims and bases serves to set the stage for the next two steps, determining the validity and priority of claims.

Steps 4 and 5: Establishing Validity and Determining Priority of Claims

Steps 4 and 5 in the moral reasoning process focus on the resolution of moral problems. This is done by determining which of the proposed claims are valid and which take priority. In order to make these decisions I suggest that we draw upon concepts of classical moral philosophy. The two most widely used criteria on which philosophers have sought to justify their moral beliefs are teleology (from the Greek word telos—end), which defines "right" action in terms of the consequences it produces, and deontology (from the Greek work deont—binding upon) which defines right actions as those in accordance with inherently valid principles and duties. Teleology (hereafter called by its most common form, utilitarianism) leads one to calculate the probable consequences of commiting a given act and to consider the ratio of benefit to harm thus produced. Deontology, one version of which is formalism, is best exemplified by Kant's categorical imperative (i.e., act so that the maxim of your action can be a universal law) and by his dictum to treat individuals as ends not simply as means (Kant, 1959). Deontology leads one to look at the duties (imperatives) binding upon one in a situation and to respect the rights and autonomy of others (treat as ends not means), regardless of the utilitarian consequences.

Candee and Puka (1984) demonstrate in detail how a controversial case in medical ethics can be resolved using both of these approaches. In the following paragraphs I will evoke the highlights of that discussion in order to illustrate the educational application of these approaches. Let us consider the following case:

> In 1971, at Johns Hopkins Hospital a baby was born who, shortly after birth, was clinically diagnosed to have Down's Syndrome, a condition associated with mental retardation. The baby also had a duodenal atresia, a constriction of a portion of the intestine that prevents the passage of food. It leads to death if not surgically corrected. Surgery for this condition carries a relatively small risk.
>
> The mother of the baby, a nurse, was so distressed on learning the diagnosis that she refused to give consent for the operation to remove the intestinal blockage. Her husband accepted the decision, believing that as a nurse, his wife was more knowledgeable about this matter than he. The physician in the case indicated to the parents that children with Down's Syndrome often have IQ's of between 50 and 80, can perform simple jobs, are usually happy, and can live a long time. This failed to change their minds. The doctors at the hospital did not attempt to thwart the parents' decision through a court order. In the hospital, after about 2 weeks, the child died of starvation [Reiser, Dyck & Curran, 1977, p. 536].

Were the doctors at Hopkins right or wrong to have allowed the baby to starve?

The first step in resolving any moral problem is to gather claims, to determine who wants what. Among those persons who will be directly affected by the present decision are the parents, who would like to avoid the difficulty of rearing a retarded baby, the doctors, who are willing to accede to the wishes of the parents, and the baby who, we can assume, would like to live as normal a life as possible.

Next, we should establish feasible alternatives. The purpose of moral decision-making is to determine which of the feasible alternatives is morally best. In the present case, the alternatives would seem to include performing surgery, allowing the baby to die (passive euthanasia), or actually ending the baby's life (active euthanasia).

At this point, utilitarian and deontological approaches diverge. Students are encouraged to apply both approaches to solving the problem. If both point to the same solution one feels on firm moral ground making that choice. If the two approaches point to opposite solutions, at least it should become clear which moral features are being supported and which are being sacrificed by making a particular choice. Further, if each approach is applied conscientiously then the resulting choice will be morally justifiable, at least from the viewpoint of one of the theories.

Utilitarian Approach.   I will now briefly describe the suggested procedure for decision-making following each approach. The goal of utilitarianism is to determine which action will lead to the greatest ratio of benefit to harm for all persons involved in the dilemma. (This can be done for each act or by formulating a rule which, if followed regularly in similar situations, will likely maximize good). In order to calculate the utilitarian ratio it is necessary to predict the possible outcomes (consequences) of each action, the probability of each outcome occurring, and the desirability of those outcomes for the child, for the parents and for society. This method of determining utilities relies heavily on Brody (1976, chap. 2).

A list of utilities for each feasible alternative appears in Table 12.2. This table is presented from the baby's point of view. Looking in column 2 ("Outcome") we see that there are three possible outcomes for each alternative action. The

TABLE 12.2
Utility of Alternative Medical Treatments (Child's Perspective)

Alternative Treatment	Outcome	Probability	Value	Utility	Alt Value	Alt Utility
Surgery	Normal IQ	.02	1.00	.02	(1.00)	(.02)
	60 IQ	.49	1.00	.49	(.50)	(.25)
	40 IQ	.49	1.00	.49	(.20)	(.10)
	Total utility			1.00		(.37)
Passive euthanasia	Die quickly	.10	.30	.03		
	Die slowly	.80	.10	.08		
	Die very slowly and painfully	.10	.00	.00		
	Total utility			.11		
Active euthanasia	Die quickly	1.00	.30	.30		
	Die slowly	.00	.10	.00		
	Die very slowly and painfully	.00	.00	.00		
	Total utility			.30		

outcomes range from better to worse. The task of determining utilities is to try to give some numerical weight to both the probability of each outcome occurring (column 3) and the value of each outcome (column 4). For example, the first line of Table 12.2 shows that the outcome of having a normal IQ might be highly valued by the child (value = 1.00 on a scale of 0 to 1, see column 4). However, it is very unlikely to occur (probability = .02). Thus, the total utility for this outcome is $1.00 \times .02 = .02$ (column 5).

At this point, let us distinguish between the method used to assign weights to probabilities and the method used to assign weights to value. The probability of an outcome occurring is a theoretically finite number. We may not always know what this number is, but in many cases we can gain a reasonably accurate estimate by consulting previous research or by polling experienced clinicians. The probability of a Downs Syndrome baby growing up to have an IQ of 60 or 40, as presented in Table 12.2, was obtained by consulting a large survey of studies in this area conducted by Rynders, Spiker, and Horrobin (1978). We allow a 2% chance that the child will have a normal IQ since the clinical diagnosis of Downs Syndrome may be in error. Other probabilities contained in Table 12.2 under the alternatives of passive or active euthanasia were established more clinically. The point here is that much critical information in resolving moral problems is not a matter of guess-work or personal opinion. By using the method described here, or any related one, the student learns what aspects of moral decision-making are matters of establishing fact and what aspects rely solely on one's nonempirical choice of values.

Because it is recognized that not all persons will give the same "value" to an outcome we allow, for illustrative purposes, a list of "alternative values." In the current example we may find that certain moral reasoners do not give as much value to the prospect of living with an IQ of 60 or 40 as they do to living with a normal IQ. These are reflected in the column labeled "alternative values" (column 6, Table 12.2). Since utilities are a product of probability times value, lowering the value of the outcomes in Table 12.2 lowers their utility (see last column).

The purpose of the "alternative values" column in Table 12.2 is simply to illustrate the point that two moral reasoners may differ in the values they assign to different outcomes. An individual actually using this format would have only one values column.

The total utility for an alternative is determined by adding the individual utilities for each possible outcome within that alternative. A comparison of total utilities in Table 12.2 shows that, using the original values, the alternative of performing surgery is clearly the best choice. Using the "alternative utilities," surgery is still the best choice, but this time it is only marginally so.

A complete calculation of maximum utilities requires that we construct two other tables, one from the viewpoint of the parents and one from the viewpoint of "society." The parents' perspective is shown in Table 12.3. One of the major

TABLE 12.3
Utility of Alternative Medical Treatments (Parents' Perspective)

Alternative Treatment	Outcome	Probability	Value	Utility	Alt Value	Alt Utility
Surgery	Normal IQ	.02	1.00	.02	(1.00)	(.02)
	60 IQ	.49	.30	.15	(.00)	(.00)
	40 IQ	.49	.10	.05	(.00)	(.00)
	Total utility			.22		(.02)
Passive euthanasia	Die quickly	.10	.50	.05		
	Die slowly	.80	.50	.40		
	Die very slowly and painfully	.10	.00	.00		
	Total utility			.45		
Active euthanasia	Die quickly	1.00	.50	.50		
	Die slowly	.00	.50	.00		
	Die very slowly and painfully	.00	.00	.00		
	Total utility			.50		

differences between this table and Table 12.2 (child's perspective) is that, in general, the prospect of rearing a child with an IQ of 60 or 40 will be a more lowly valued outcome when viewed from the parents' perspective. In fact, for the particular parents in the example, the value of rearing a retarded child may be zero (see alternative values).

Just as the value for the surgery alternative decreases as we move from the child's perspective to that of the parents, so the value of the euthanasia outcomes increases. Notice that while the value weightings changes considerably from the child's perspective (Table 12.2) to that of the parent (Table 12.3) the probabilities of each outcome occurring remain the same. Value judgments may be different for each moral reasoner. Probabilities, within limits set by consulting different sources of information, are not.

The final step in the utilitarian approach is to combine utilities for each alternative from both the child's and the parents' perspectives. Doing so (Table 12.4) reveals that, given the probabilities and original set of values, surgery is the most useful option. This is primarily due to the clear advantage that surgery has for the child, even though it is recognized that the child will almost certainly be mentally disabled. In comparison, the disadvantages of surgery to the parent are not as great.

However, if we accept the alternative utilities shown in Table 12.4, we arrive at a different conclusion. A comparison of these utilities indicates that euthanasia, particularly active euthanasia, is the preferred choice. The change between the two sets of utilities in Table 12.4 rests primarily on the value that the child would give to living with an IQ significantly below normal. If that value is high, then the surgery alternative has great utility. If it is not, then the surgery alternative becomes least attractive. A smaller but still significant change between the original and alternative utilities is the contribution made to the surgery alternative by the parents. If the parents find some value in rearing a mentally disabled child (as in the original utilities) then the surgery alternative is more likely to be useful. If they do not (as in the alternative utilities) then the surgery alternative becomes less useful.

Educational Technique (Utilitarian Approach).   We ask students to practice the utilitarian approach by resolving a case using only that theory. If time permits we ask students to fill out forms similar to those shown in Tables 12.2–12.4. This can be done individually or in groups. If the procedure is done in groups then one person fills out the table reflecting the group's agreed upon decisons.

A second technique for presenting the utilitarian approach is to list a number of consequences for each alternative and to ask the student to indicate how many units of happiness or unhappiness he or she believes the alternative will create. This technique essentially duplicates the value columns of the tables. It does not easily allow for a consideration of probabilities. However, it does have the advantage of posing the consequences in an immediate and structured manner.

I suggest using the longer method where time allows and where the goal is to teach students both to set up and resolve a moral problem from the utilitarian point of view. However, if the purpose is simply to give students the experience of using utilitarian considerations then the shorter method might be appropriate. The longer method lets a student establish a utilitarian solution "from scratch." The shorter method gives a student "the flavor" of utilitarianism. This method takes about 30 minutes, can be done in groups of up to 30 students, and rather

TABLE 12.4
Utility of Alternative Medical Treatments (Combined Perspectives)

Alternative Treatment	Utility For		
	Child	Parents	Combined
Using original utilities[a]			
Surgery	1.00	.22	1.22
Passive euthanasia	.11	.45	.56
Active euthanasia	.30	.50	.80
Using alternative utilities[b]			
Surgery	.37	.02	.39
Passive euthanasia	.11	.45	.56
Active euthanasia	.30	.50	.80

[a]See total utilities for each alternative Tables 1–2.

[b]See total utility in parentheses for surgery alternative, Tables 1 and 2. Other utilities are same as original.

quickly allows students to discover the strengths and shortcomings of utilitarianism.

After resolving the problem, all groups meet in a common lecture hall and share their discoveries. Although we have no specific test based on the utilitarian approach it is not hard to imagine using responses to the forms in Tables 12.2–12.4 as the basis for constructing a test.

Deontological Approach.   Having considered a teleological approach to solving our sample dilemma, I now demonstrate the perspective of deontology. Deontology denies what teleology asserts. That is, in the deontological perspective, the moral rightness of an act is determined not by the consequences it produces, but by qualities intrinsic to the act itself. The key to deontological thinking centers around two questions: "What rights are claimed, and by what principles are they valid?," and, "What duties are owed by whom and to whom?"

These rights and duties may be listed in terms of claims, using the format described earlier (p. 302). For the previous example, three rights-claims seem relevant: the child's claim to life, the parents' claim to liberty in their own lives, and the parents' claim to the freedom of being able to make decisions affecting their child.

In order to determine which claims are valid in this situation and to establish a set of priorities among valid claims, several important questions must be answered. For the baby in the current example key questions may include the following: Does the neonate qualify for the status of personhood? (it is often argued that rights are associated with the status of personhood). Does the retarded neonate have or will it have a sense of self that may be considered to constitute a "point of view"? (if it does not we need not be concerned with respecting that point of view), and thirdly, If the infant does have a right here is it a right to require the surgery or only a right not to be harmed?

Although our procedure can help get students to the point where they know they must pose certain questions in order to determine the validity of claims, it cannot tell them which questions to ask. We have found that having students observe the way others have reasoned about ethical dilemmas, most often through written articles. is valuable here.

The second right-claim to consider in our current example concerns the parents' liberty. Clearly, rearing a retarded child places especially serious limits on the activities of its parents. The key question to be asked here is whether the parents have a duty to rear the child. If they do, then the surgical interference is justified. On the other hand, forcing the parents to keep and rear the baby when they have no special duty to do so would violate their rights. Arguments both for and against a parental duty are presented in Candee and Puka (1984). If it has been determined that the baby has rights then the position taken here is critical to deciding whose claims take precedence, the parents' or the baby's.

Educational Technique (Deontological Approach).   We have found that one very good format for resolving moral problems using the deontological approach is the Hypothesis Generation Test (claims and bases) described earlier. Claims such as the baby's claim to live, the parent's claim to liberty and the parent's claim to custody over the child would all be listed in the claims column. The moral concerns that support each of these claims would be listed in the basis column. The discussion of which claims are valid and which take precedence, as demonstrated earlier, is the essence of the deontological approach. Particular rights and duties enter the discussion as they support or oppose a given claim.

This format is also appropriate for claims of utility. Arguments, such as, the parents do not want the child to live because the harm they will suffer outweighs the happiness the child will receive, can be treated as a claim and supporting basis. The validity of such a claim, may be determined by the utilitarian method presented above. If valid, the claim may then be evaluated either against other utilitarian claims or against deontological claims using the Hypothesis Generation format. This process can be carried out individually, in small groups or in large classes.

To this point we have discussed steps 1–5 of the moral reasoning process. In doing so I have suggested several measures and methods that can be used to help students organize their thinking about ethical problems. These include the Domain Discrimination Test, The Hypothesis Generation Test (persons, claims and bases), and the utilitarian and deontological approaches to resolving conflicts among claims.

Steps 1–8 as Measured through Videotaped Clinical Encounters

We turn now to the other major source of ideas for moral education among health care professionals, the use of videotaped clinical encounters. This procedure differs from those discussed earlier in that it is interactive. Previously, we examined steps 1–5 of the moral reasoning process as they appear to an individual moral reasoner. We will now examine those same steps, but this time from the viewpoint of an observer watching a two-person interaction. In addition to measuring steps 1–5, the use of videotapes allows us to gain information about the remaining steps in the moral reasoning process, step 6 (communicating), step 7 (negotiating) and step 8 (implementing) a moral decision.

The first scenario involves a daughter who has been called into the doctor's office to receive a report about her 74-year old mother who is in a nursing home. The mother has been becoming more senile and sometimes does not even recognize her daughter during visits. Within the last few days the mother developed a life-threatening infection. The doctor who had been treating the mother was called out of town and the case was left for the resident. Although the resident has never seen the mother, he or she must decide, along with the daughter,

whether to take immediate, aggressive action which would require hospitalization in order to save the mother's life or whether to let the mother die in the
nursing home.

The residents in these situations had been informed that the patient is simulated. However, we have found through pretesting and through the reports of other
researchers that the behavior elicited in simulations is indistinguishable from
normal doctor-patient interactions. If a doctor is accustomed to treating patients
in a certain manner he or she does not suddenly change in front of our cameras.

On the contrary, residents consider the situation to be so life-like that one
resident later scolded the primary physician, who also happened to be the department chairman, for going out of town when the mother was so seriously ill. In
another scenario a resident spent 5 minutes trying to find time in which to hold a
follow-up session between himself and the "simulated patient" to be sure that
the patient's "disease" was improving.

I will use an excerpt from one videotaped session to illustrate an interaction in
which the resident's behavior was less than ideal. The resident took a position in
favor of admitting the mother to the hospital and did not try to elicit the
daughter's views. The daughter is trained to be neutral at first to see how the
doctor will structure the interaction. However, after the doctor makes his or her
position known the daughter is instructed to introduce several concerns that go
against the doctor's recommendation. What we are looking for is the manner in
which the doctor responds to these counter-suggestions. Noteworthy in the following interaction is the degree to which the resident avoids talking about the
moral problem, in this case the quality of life. Instead she defends against the
subject by devoting an inordinate amount of time to lecturing about the medical
aspects of the case. In this scenario I refer to the daughter as the patient (P) since
she is the person with whom the doctor (D) interacts. The resident, the primary
physician and the patient were all women.

D: I have a note from Dr. Smith and she told me about the problem with your
mother. What has happened because of her urinary incontinence is that they put a
catheter into her bladder. This will help her skin because if your skin is wet it will
eventually break down. [The doctor gives a long lecture about the effect of
catheters and their vulnerability to infection]. What we'll do is give her antibiotics
in her vein. They usually don't have a reaction to antibiotics. The nursing home
can't handle IV's so she'll have to go to the hospital.
P: IS IT REALLY NECESSARY TO TAKE HER TO THE HOSPITAL? SHE
WAS UPSET ENOUGH WHEN WE BROUGHT HER TO THE NURSING
HOME. NOW, TO MOVE HER AGAIN. . .
D: No, she definitely has to go because this is the way we have to treat her problem.
P: SHE'S BEEN SO SICK I HATE TO SEE HER GO THROUGH ALL THIS
NOW.
D: No, it's really necessary that she go to the hospital.
P: WHAT WILL THE REST OF HER CONDITION BE? SHE'S SO SENILE.

D: It will be the same as before this happened. She will respond well to the antibiotics.

As pointed out above, this interaction is marked by the resident's avoidance of the moral issue and by her inability to elicit the patient's own agenda. These characteristics are captured as part of a 66-item rating form which we developed especially to code the interactions. The form is known as the Moral Behavior Analysis (MBA). A sample item appears below:

Does the doctor make an effort to discover the patient's agenda (e.g., asks, "what are your major concerns?")?
a) Asks patient directly
b) Asks patient vaguely
c) Does not ask, but responds when patient initiates
d) Does not ask, and ignores when patient initiates

Resident 1 was scored in category 'd' on the above item. The patient attempted to introduce the possibility that her mother not be sent to the hospital. The doctor essentially ignored this concern by insisting that the mother be hospitalized and by asserting the medically tenuous claim that she would respond well to antibiotics. On other items, Resident 1 was rated as rarely listening to the patient's concerns, blocking the patient's initiative, and rarely acknowledging the patient's concerns. Among the 66 items on the MBA is an overall rating made on a 7-point scale. Three raters independently scored each resident. Resident 1 was given a score of 6.0 which fell between the categories of "definite problems" and "unsatisfactory." Her moral judgment score was stage 3/4 which falls in the lowest 10% of American-born residents we have studied.

A contrasting performance was exhibited by Resident 2. The scenario in this situation is different. It involves a husband who has contracted gonorrhea during an affair and whose wife must be examined for possible infection. Here the patient is trained to suggest that his wife would be resistant to an exam and/or that the revelation of his affair would destroy their marriage. The doctor's decision is one of whether or not to take the responsibility of working with the patient to find an acceptable solution to telling his wife. Unlike Resident 1, Resident 2 tackles the moral issue directly. The doctor, who is again a woman, ties the issue of the husband telling his wife to the wife's own welfare and to the quality of the marriage. She identifies the patient's concerns and poses the permissible moral choices as clear alternatives.

D: You are not the first person this has happened to but I know when it's you it feels like 100% . . . You have to decide which alternative you want. I don't think there is a choice about treating her but there is a choice about how your wife is to be told.
P: I KNOW SHE IS GOING TO ASK. SHE'S AN INTELLIGENT WOMAN.

D: Do you think if you explained it to her it would be better than her having to ask her gynecologist and his saying, "I'm looking for gonorrhea."? Is your marriage something you value?
P: I DO CARE ABOUT MY MARRIAGE BUT I DON'T SEE HOW EXPLAIN-ING MY INFIDELITY IS GOING TO HELP MATTERS.
D: Maybe the culture won't grow. Or, you can talk to the gynecologist yourself. Do you have a physician or minister you have gone to with your wife? Maybe you would be more comfortable with these options?

The scores of Resident 2 on the MBA were, for most items, the opposite of those of Resident 1. Resident 2 was scored as encouraging patient initiative, asking directly about the patient's agenda, and both attending to and acknowledging the patient's concerns. The overall performance score of Resident 2 was 1.5 (1.0 = excellent). Her moral judgment score was Stage 5.

The items on the MBA were originally developed after surveying a dozen rating forms used at various universities to rate medical students or residents. The items were designed to be behaviorally specific in order to reduce the degree of inference required. In addition, they were designed to apply cross-situationally, to cases where either moral or medical issues were prominent. The MBA was subsequently factor-analyzed. Final factors were derived on the basis of both empirical loadings and the theoretical expanded version of Rest's (1983, this volume) model, which we developed. Review of the empirical loadings necessitated relatively few changes. Several of the theoretical factors were combined into single factors. Only a few items had to be deleted from the theoretical factors for empirical reasons. The resulting factors are as follows:

Factor 1: Mutual-Moral-Sensitive: (Measures Steps 1–5).   This factor is a composite of three theoretically distinct groups of items. Mutual items are scored when the physician demonstrates a model of the doctor-patient relationship in which both the doctor's and patient's input are required. A representative item asks the scorer to, "Rate the quality of balance in the physician-patient exchange in terms of treating one another respectfully, allowing equal opportunity for listening, speaking, idea generation, and idea initiation: (a) high reciprocity, (b) moderate mutuality (imbalanced in either direction), (c) non-mutual (nearly unidirectional)."

Items that reflect sensitivity were discussed in the analysis of Residents 1 and 2. They include, among many others, discovering the patient's agenda, encouraging patient initiative, and acknowledging tbe patient's concerns. Moral items were scored in the positive direction if the physician recognized the basic moral conflict in the scenario, as evidenced by statements such as, "What is quality of life all about?," or "I think honesty is called for in a situation like this."

Together, factor 1 seems to measure steps 1–5 of the moral reasoning process (identifying the situation as a moral problem, determining claims, and taking an initial position in terms of resolution). Whereas our earlier measures of steps 1–5 were based on the viewpoint of the individual moral reasoner, the MBA measures are based on observed interaction. However, it is only at the level of the roughest analogy that the MBA and the tests described earlier can be said to be measuring the same constructs. The steps in the moral reasoning process, as well as Rest's components, are simply heuristic devices that map broad roadmarks on the reasoning-to-action path.

Factor 2: Efficiency.   Included in this factor are items such as "has a master plan," "avoids jargon," "avoids unnecessary detail," and "is efficient, gets directly to the moral problem." This factor does not correspond to any single step in the moral reasoning process. Rather, it can be thought of as describing a "master step" which enables the organized, efficient execution of all other steps.

Factor 3: Patient Education: (Measures Steps 6–8).   Items in this factor include, "checks for patient's understanding of the procedure," "asks about patient's ability to carry out management plan for the medical or moral problem," and "takes account of the patient's environment and habits when interpreting the medical complaint and when considering therapy." These items focus on the act of communicating moral decisions to a client (step 6), in particular as it involves matching patient characteristics with possible treatments. This is an especially important skill for health care professionals since no treatment plan, no matter how morally conceived, will achieve its intended results if the patient is unable or unwilling to carry it out. The give-and-take involved in formulating such a plan involves the skills identified in step 7, negotiation. Although we do not follow a physician's behavior through to a true phase of implementation, the discussion of a workable plan, as measured by this factor and the next, at least provides a partial measure of the implementation step (step 8).

Factor 4: Treatment Plan.   Included here are the items, "discusses urgency and treatability," and "explains diagnosis and management clearly." While factor 3 focused on tailoring a treatment plan to the patient's characteristics, factor 4 focuses on communicating the details of the plan to the patient. While it may appear that factors 3 and 4 are concerned only with the technical and therapeutic aspects of treatment they are not without moral meaning. We believe that the construction of a clear treatment plan, responsive to the characteristics of the patient, may ultimately stem from a respect for the personality of the patient.

Other significant factors include one composed of body language items (affect, variation in tone), and another composed of morally relevant social skills (introduces self, explains relationship to institution, uses names of equal status).

Educational Techniques

Using the simulations and instruments described above we have devised a procedure for providing residents with systematic feedback based on watching videotapes of their own performances. The procedure relies on two other measures not yet discussed.

One measure, mentioned only briefly earlier, is the Role Concept Interview. It consists of eight semi-structured questions designed to elicit the physician's philosophy of his or her job and of the ideal doctor-patient relationship. The questions include, What are your satisfactions (and dissatisfactions) with medicine?, Do you have a philosophy or ideas that you keep in the back of your mind as you go about your job?, What do you think makes a good doctor-patient relationship? and What do you consider are your strengths (and weaknesses) as a physician? The interview is conducted personally, is probed, and analyzed using a formal scoring system.

The second measure, the Flanders Interaction Analysis (FIA), is a system of coding continuous interaction between two or more persons. It was originally developed to record classroom interactions (Flanders, 1966) and was adapted for use here. The system contains 10 categories of either doctor or patient behavior. Every 3 seconds the observer places the behavior presently occurring into one of the categories. By pairing each sequence of behavior, a 100-cell matrix is achieved. Analysis of this matrix yields several summary categories. Three of the most useful categories are the degree of doctor talk (i.e., the proportion of interactions in which the doctor is talking), the degree of patient-initiated response, and the degree to which the doctor recognizes patient feelings. These along with other summary categories yield a description of the balance and nature of the doctor-patient relationship.

The specific procedure for providing educational feedback is as follows:

1. Show the resident a transcript of his or her Role Concept Interview. Ask what ideas stand out as most representative of his or her thinking. Point out those that we believe to be most salient.

2. Ask the resident how he or she might expect the most salient philosophies to be manifest in actual clinical behavior. Point out ways in which we expect the philosophy to be manifest. These ideas provide a self-anchoring standard against which actual behavior can be judged.

3. Show the videotape of the resident's encounter with the simulated patient.

4. Stop the tape at a point where we or the resident think a behavior confirming or contradicting his or her ideal philosophy has been exhibited. Ask the resident what was going on in his or her mind at that time, i.e., what he or she was trying to accomplish. If a problem is identified ask the resident how it might be overcome. Suggest possible solutions.

5. At the completion of the videotape present the resident with the results of the FIA and MBA analyses. The analyses serve two purposes. One is to give the

resident a normative sense of his or her own behavior, a comparison of his or her behavior with others. The second is to confirm or disconfirm the presence of strengths and weaknesses which the resident attributed to him or herself while watching the tape.

6. Review suggestions for change.

Additional steps may include showing the resident videotapes of others to exemplify alternative behaviors or repeating the above procedure with additional scenarios. The principle behind the suggested feedback procedure is to have residents observe discrepancies between their own actual behavior and their notions of ideal physician behavior. The resident's initial impressions can be confirmed or qualified by the MBA and the FIA. For example, most residents feel that they explain disease mechanisms well to patients. However, many residents have never actually seen themselves doing so and few have factual data as to whether their explanations are overly-detailed or overly-brief compared to other residents. By providing empirical data concerning certain physician behaviors we can present the resident with a more accurate picture of his or her own performance.

In the area of remediation, our goal is to suggest a list of general skills, statements, and questions that can be employed by the resident when difficulties are encountered. We do not try to change the resident's personality or attitude toward treatment but rather we try to give him or her the tools to effectively handle problematic situations. In the case of a resident who gives overly-detailed explanations, such as Resident 1, we may suggest that she routinely ask the patient after two or three minutes, "Is this too much detail for you or would you like more information?" In this way residents can improve their ability to handle morally problematic cases. The most immediate goal that we expect to achieve is for residents' actual behavior to become more consistent with their goals.

Future Directions

We have used the feedback procedure suggested here with a number of residents at The University of Connecticut Health Center. We now have a grant to continue the program, adding role-taking exercises and pencil and paper versions of the simulations. At the Boston College School of Nursing we are entering the second year of a 3-year grant in which we will combine the teaching of classical ethics with videotaped simulations. The course is designed so that nurses will first discuss ethical issues in the classroom and then have the opportunity to experience these same issues as they occur in clinical encounters. The program will allow us to integrate the tests and techniques used to make individual moral decisions discussed in the beginning of this chapter (steps 1–5) with the measures and methods of moral reasoning as they occur in a clinical interaction, as described in the latter part of the chapter (steps 1–8).

ACKNOWLEDGMENTS

The following organizations have supported work reported in this chapter: The Commonwealth Fund, The National Fund for Medical Education, The National Institute of Health, The State University of New York Downstate Medical Center, The University of Connecticut Health Center and the Boston College School of Nursing.

REFERENCES

Bentler, P. M. & Speckart, G. (1979). Models of attitude-behavior relations. *Psychological Review, 86*, 452–464.

Blasi, A. (1980). Bridging moral cognition and moral action: A critical review of the literature. *Psychological Bulletin, 88*, 1–45.

Brody, H. (1976). *Ethical decisions in medicine.* Boston: Little Brown & Co.

Candee, D. & Puka, B. (1984). An analytic approach to resolving problems in medical ethics. *Journal of Medical Ethics, 2*, 61–70.

Candee, D., Sheehan, T. J., Cook, C. D., Husted, S., & Bargen, M. (1982). Moral reasoning and decisions in dilemmas of neonatal care. *Pediatric research, 16*, 846–850.

Colby, A., Kohlberg, L., Gibbs, J., Candee, D., Speicher-Dubin B., & Hewer, A., (in press). *The measurement of moral judgment: a manual and its results.* New York: Cambridge University.

Flanders, N. (1966). *Interaction analysis in the classroom: A manual for observers.* Ann Arbor, MI: University of Michigan.

Fishbein, M. & Ajzen, I. (1975). *Beliefs, attitude, intention and behavior: An introduction to theory and research.* Reading, Ma.: Addison-Wesley.

Kant, I. (1959). *Foundations of the metaphysic of morals.* (L. W. Beck, trans.). New York: The Liberal Arts Press.

Kohlberg, L. & Candee, D. (1984). The relationship of moral judgment to moral action. In L. Kohlberg, *Essays on moral development. Vol. 2: The psychology of moral development.* (pp. 498–581) San Francisco: Harper & Row.

Reiser, S., Dyck, A., & Curran, W. (1977). *Ethics in medicine.* Cambridge,MA: MIT Press.

Rest, J. (1982). A psychologist looks at the teaching of ethics. *The Hastings Center Report*, February, 29–36.

Rest, J. (1983). Morality. In J. H..Flavell & E. M. Markman (Eds.), *Cognitive development*, volume in P. H. Mussen (Ed.), *Manual of child psychology* (4th ed.) (pp. 556–629). New York: Wiley.

Rynders, J., Spiker, D., & Horrobin, M. (1978). Underestimating the educability of Down's syndrome children: examination of methodological problems in recent literature. *American Journal of Mental Deficiencies, 5*, 440–448.

Sheehan, T. J., Candee, D., Wilms, J., Donnelly, J., & Husted, S. (1984). *Structural equation models of moral reasoning and physician performance.* Paper presented at annual meeting of the American Educational Research Association, New Orleans.

Sheehan, T. J., Husted., S., Candee, D., Cook., C., & Bargen, M. (1980). Moral judgment as a predictor of clinical performance. *Evaluation and the Health Professions, 3*, 393–404.

APPLICATIONS AND INTERVENTIONS
D. CLINICAL SETTINGS

13

Stage, Phase, and Style: The Developmental Dynamics of the Self

Gil G. Noam
Harvard Medical School
McLean Hospital, and
The Clinical-Developmental Institute

Psychoanalytic theorists focus primarily on psychosexual and object-relational interpretations in the study of adolescent development. Cognitive psychologists in the Piagetian tradition focus on the structural transformations of the abstract adolescent thinker. And, lifespan-developmental researchers are chiefly interested in the adolescent tasks and their resolutions. Although these traditions have yielded considerable insights into the adolescent experience, important questions remain unanswered. What is the organizing principle of the adolescent self? Is there a structural-developmental basis to the developing self? And if so, how do the underlying developmental structures relate to adolescent psychosocial tasks?

This chapter addresses some of these broad issues by distinguishing between two central theoretical traditions: "structural-development" and "functional-development." Although these approaches have been described elsewhere in detail (Noam, in press; Noam, Kohlberg, & Snarey, 1983), I argue in this chapter that a structural-functional model of the self offers an important view of the developmental dynamic in adolescence—that is, those principles promoting or impeding the growth and shape of the self. This work grows out of an attempt to bridge Kohlberg's cognitive-developmental model with personality psychology and clinical theory. Structural psychology in the Kohlberg tradition must integrate the systematic changes of life transitions if it will contribute more fully to a lifespan personality theory. For example, what is lost in our analyses of an individual who remains in Kohlberg's interpersonal Stage (3) from early adolescence through middle and late adulthood if we do not include in our examination of the underlying moral structure the important epochs in the person's life? Similarly, a description of the eras in the life cycle without a view of cognitive and personality transformations rarely reaches the deeper levels of meaning these life events hold for the experiencing person. Out of this dual critique emerges the model outlined in this chapter: a dynamic of stage (organizations of meaning in the structural tradition) and phase (task organizations at different points of the life span).

Defining personality styles as evolving at each new stage of ego development, personality theorists in the Piagetian tradition (e.g., Kegan, 1982; Loevinger, 1976) have provided an alternative path to trait psychological formulations. This approach, however, has supported a view of the person without history. Styles have their natural history and can be traced longitudinally and even reconstructively as biographical continuities of the human's experience of self and relationships. The recent focus in the literature on gender differences (e.g., Chodorow, 1978; Gilligan, 1982) has also facilitated renewed interest in differences of orientations throughout life. The study of these differences, however, usually leads back to a dichotomous perspective with little emphasis on the underlying structural reorganizations of styles at different stages. In the framework presented here another goal is to show the importance of stylistic differences and their transformations and contribution to structural personality development. The three components of development (stage, phase and style), often mistakenly interpreted as a single aspect of the self, are interconnected and allow us to observe different aspects of the self across the lifespan.

Given the scope of this work, the purpose of this chapter is to introduce terms and create a context for discussion through examples interpreted from a stage, phase, and style perspective. In future work longitudinal, empirical research (presently under way) and in-depth clinical observations will explore the research potential of the model.

FUNCTIONAL AND STRUCTURAL MODELS: PHASE AND STAGE

Recent progress bridging developmental and personality psychology has led to the emergence of a developmental personality psychology. Most prominent in this effort are Jane Loevinger's model of ego development and theories building on Kohlberg's theory of moral development. For Loevinger (1976), the ego is the master personality trait around which the whole personality is constructed. Her concept of ego development draws on the theoretical traditions of interpersonal, cognitive, and character psychology. Loevinger's perspective emphasizes the individual's integrative processes and overall frame of reference. It assumes that each person has a customary orientation to self and world and that there are stages and transitions along which these frames of reference can be organized (Hauser, 1976). Her stages are differentiated along dimensions of impulse control, conscious concerns, and interpersonal and cognitive styles.

In a tradition more directly linked with Piaget's paradigm is research in structural self or self-other psychology. This school of thought also builds upon the work of Kohlberg and expands it in areas relevant to a theory of self— interpersonal mutuality (Gilligan, 1982), perspective-taking (Selman, 1980), faith (Fowler, 1981; Oser, Power, Gmuender, Fritzsche, & Widmer, 1980), and epistemology (Broughton, 1978). A number of theorists are working on more explicit developmental theories of the self (Blasi, 1983; Damon & Hart, 1982; Kegan, 1982; Lyons, 1983; Noam, in press). Underlying most of these conceptualizations, and basic to my model, are the following principles (see also Kohlberg, 1969; Noam, Kohlberg, & Snarey, 1983):

1. The self is both intrapsychic and interpersonal, organized through an underlying social-developmental structure. The development of the self involves underlying transformations of cognitive structures that are understood as organizational wholes or as systems of internal relations, rather than by elements of association. Structure refers to the general characteristics of shape, pattern and organization of response rather than to the rate or intensity of response or its pairing with particular stimuli.

2. The development of the self is defined by underlying logics of the self, in other words, as levels of self-other perspectives. These have been described similarly in a variety of theories building on Baldwin, Mead, Piaget and Kohlberg. Because of the combination of its strong social-developmental orientation (as compared to more biological interpretations), its link to the cognitive logic in the Piaget tradition, and its empirical strength, I build on Selman's (1980) perspective-taking levels in the development of this model. Many insights come from the parallel stage descriptions of Kegan (1982), Loevinger (1976) and Fowler (1981) who all, much like Kohlberg (1969), tap the underlying social perspective between self and other.

3. The self develops throughout life in a progression of qualitative stages of equilibration (and disequilibration) that give the variety of social experiences cohesion, or an overall "meaning organization." The development of the self always means moving toward greater equilibrium in the organism-environment interaction. This balance—between external objects and internal assimilating and accommodating structures—represents knowledge, truth, logic and adaptation, as well as self-other perspective.

4. The balance of equilibration of self and other is more than a momentary act and represents periods of underlying stability; thus the concept of stage or structure of the self. Structures are whole entities or systems rather than aggregates of elements independent of the whole. Elements of structured wholes are defined by the laws governing the roles they play. The elements derive their power as phenomena only as parts of a whole. The structure that orders the elements raises them to a form that they do not possess in isolation.

5. There is a fundamental unity of personality organization and development termed the ego or the self. Although various strands of social development exist (psychosexual development, moral development, etc.) these strands are united by their common reference to a single concept of self in a single social world. Social development is, in essence, the restructuring of the concept of self in its relationship to other persons in a common social world with social standards. In addition to the unity of social development stages due to general cognitive development, there is a further unity of development due to a common holistic factor, termed here self-other perspective.

6. The self (and social cognition in general) always involves role-taking, that is, awareness that the other is in some way both like and unlike the self, and that the other knows or is responsive to the self in a system of complementary expectations. Accordingly, developmental changes in the social self reflect parallel changes in conceptions of the social world.

7. Recently developmental descriptions of the lifecycle have made use of a spiral model (e.g., Kegan, 1982; Vaillant and Milofsky, 1981). Kegan has described the self as progressing in spiral form in which a number of stages are placed on a more affiliative side of a helix, and others on a more differentiating side. This idea has also been put forward by Vaillant and Milofsky for Erikson's stages. I am not utilizing the analogy of the helix in this chapter, because I want to highlight the continuous and biographical aspects of the life course, but the distinction between more inclusive and more differentiating stages in the lifecycle provides a useful bridge for the relationship between stages and styles in my model.

Two Terms: Self-Logic and Life Experience

Structural-developmental theories of the self, with their emphasis on transformation, in stepwise progression of an underlying self-other perspective, enhance our ability to distinguish between the *self-logic* (Edelstein & Noam, 1982) and *life experience*. The term self-logic refers to the underlying perspective that coordinates the view the person holds of him or herself, of important others, and of the relationship between self and other. Subsumed under the highest principle of the developing self, the self-logic gives structure to a multitude of experiences, including self-observation and understanding of social situations. There is accumulating evidence that structural stages also relate to processes of distortion (defenses) and psychiatric symptoms (see Noam, 1984 and Noam, Hauser, Santostefano, Garrison, Jacobson, Powers, & Mead, 1984 for results and an overview of the literature).

Life experience refers to the important and shaping life events that mark the biographical path of a person. Early family relations, first separations, entrance into school, adolescent friendships and love relationships, occupational training, marriage, and children are only a few key events in a person's (and cohort's) life. Each one of these new experiences occurs in the context of important relationships in which closeness, distance, change, and achievement of goals must be negotiated. The history of these relationships as they are internalized and become part of a person's memory and repertoire, gives life experience continued power throughout the lifespan. I do not mean to imply a superficial life task notion, but rather a complex set of shaping, disappointing and enhancing experiences of the self in relation to important others throughout the life cycle. These life experiences relate to the self-logic because they occur within the context of a given self-organization at a certain point in a person's life. The actual meaning these experiences carry for the future of a person's life and even for the future shape of a person's transforming self will depend greatly on the life experiences, i.e., family support, school achievement, etc.

The strength of all accounts of the self building on Piaget and Kohlberg is the focus on an organization of meaning attributed to self and other. Each new stage brings out a new equilibration (and disequilibration) of what is understood as who the self is in relation to self and other. New and more complex forms of understanding of the relationship between the self and the other also bring out new wishes and desires, needs and gratifications traditionally studied as motivational systems. Conflict, always inherent in interpersonal relationships, emerges as something new at each developmental position. That the web of desires, thoughts, and feelings are at least in part organized by an understanding of self and other leads to my use of the German term *Sinnstrukturen,* loosely translated as *meaning organizations* that address the self-logic as it relates to the relationship of self to self, and self to other. Each new stage is defined by an underlying logic and a meaning organization. Table 13.1 summarizes the stages of self-other perspective as used in this model. In general, the stages parallel in part Selman's descriptions of self-other perspective, while adding an important early stage and expanding his model into adulthood. Because the model presented here is also the basis for the development of a self coding system, Selman's extensive empirical work provides important support, although it needed more detailed descriptions of the transformations of the self. Figure 13.1 places the stages on two sides of a developmental progression and compares them to Kohlberg's stages of moral development.

Kohlberg and Kramer (1969) have argued that a structural model of moral development (and the self) implies (a) that the nature of each new stage has a definite structure, defined by a logical system, and (b) that each higher stage is logically, cognitively, or philosophically more adequate than the preceding stage and logically includes it. Kohlberg and Kramer state that "the price it [a structural model] pays, however, is abstraction from life history". As long as our focus has been Piaget's epistemic subject or Kohlberg's moral self, the "price was well worth paying," because it opened our view far beyond the specifics of the contextualized content. But as we turn to the self and personality develop-

TABLE 13.1
Self–Other Perspectives Important for the Adolescent Phase

1B *Subjective Self–Other*

The egocentric perspective already present in Stage 1A persists in this stage, even though an important developmental shift has occurred: object permanence has been achieved, thus the person can hold images over time, leading to the inner representation of others. But there is no consideration of the other's interest as different from the self's. There is an emerging awareness of the distinction of physical and psychological characteristics in people, but mostly, actions are evaluated in terms of physical consequences. For that reason the self protects itself by hiding from or submitting to powerful authority figures that can inflict physical harm. Others are seen as suppliers and there is considerable dependence on them. The concrete perspective on the self leads to a dichotomous view of being good or bad. Impulsive responses are typical and feelings are expressed in action language.

---

2 *The Reciprocal–Instrumental Self–Other*

The second-level perspective creates the possibility of understanding self interests and goals as separate from the intent of others. Conflicting interests between self and other are resolved through instrumental exchange. The person can step out of the concrete bounds of the self and thus create "two-way" reciprocity. This perspective also changes the self's relationship to itself. There now is the conceptual distinction of outer appearance of the "public self" and "inner hidden self." This creates the possibility of planned deception, through which the self can affirm its boundaries. Conflict usually does not lead to submission or impulsive action, but to self protective assertion of control. The negative outcome is opportunism, exploitation, and manipulation. The positive outcome is the mastery of the tool world, the ability to control feelings and to concentrate on tasks. The limitation of the reciprocal–instrumental stage is the isolation of two exchange-partners whose relationship is not guided primarily by trust and altruism but by interest.

---

3 *The Mutual Self–Other*

At the mutual self–other perspective the person understands others *in relationship* coordinated through a generalized perspective. The person experiences different points of view through the "Golden Rule" of seeing reality also through the eyes of another person. This perspective creates the context for altruistic actions and surpassing the bounds of self interest. Attitudes and values are seen as persisting over time often leading to stereotypes like "I am that kind of personality. . . " These "self-traits" in addition to the new perspective the self can take on itself leads to more complex self-observational capacities. The limitations of the mutual stage are, however, an over-identification with the views of the other and conformist social behavior. It is very crucial for the self to be liked and appreciated in order to feel a sense of esteem. Typical feelings of low self-esteem are linked to a sense of abandonment and feeling "lost in the world."

---

4 *The Systemic Self–Other*

At the systemic-perspective stage the societal point of view is distinguished from the interpersonal one. Multiple mutual perspectives can be integrated into a systemic one. When the self takes a systemic perspective on relationships, the communication between people is seen as existing on a number of levels simultaneously. Individual relations are interpreted in terms of their place within a larger system of roles and rules. System-maintenance of the self becomes the hallmark of Stage 4.

TABLE 13.1 (*Continued*)

The person views the self as having control over his or her destiny. It is also the point, however, at which the person realizes the existence of parts of the self not easily managed by the system's control, i.e., the discovery of unconscious motivations. The societal perspective also brings out strong motivations of achievement, duty, and competition. The limitations of the systemic self–other perspective is the attempt to overcontrol self and other, to reflect on social relations too much in terms of power, role, and status and to take so many perspectives on self and other that obsessive–compulsive indecision can result. These contradictions are reintegrated into a new whole at the Integrated (5) and Universal (6) self–other perspectives. These are, however, positions not relevant to the adolescent phase.

SELF-OTHER PERSPECTIVES

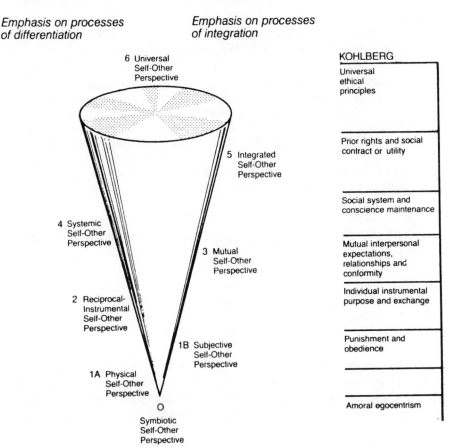

FIG. 13.1.

ment throughout life, this abstraction creates a problematic view of central concerns of psychosocial adaptation at each important point of life.

In analyzing the adolescent revolution, Kohlberg and Gilligan (1971) state that "for many people it never occurs at all" and that almost 50% of American adults never reach adolescence in the cognitive sense. Of those who do, most develop it (formal operations) in early adolescence (age 11–15), whereas others do not reach full formal reasoning until the 20s (p. 1065) The description of the adolescent crisis progresses, however, with the adolescent shifting from the grip of a conventional construction of reality to post-conformist doubt and freedom. What is adolescence for the 50% of Americans who never reach adolescence in the cognitive sense? Would it not be useful to investigate the other adolescences, organized by the principles of earlier cognitive structures such as concrete operations?

When we turn to functional approaches, on the other hand, we are usually confronted with very detailed descriptions of life tasks and their resolutions in different phases of life. Adolescent research is guided by concepts of social and biological time tables. Neugarten (1964) defines this orientation:

> Every society is age-graded, and every society has a system of social expectations regarding age-appropriate behavior. The individual passes through a socially regulated cycle from birth to death as inexorably as he passes through the biological cycle: a succession of socially delineated age statuses, each with its recognized rights, duties, and obligations. There exists a socially prescribed timetable for the ordering of major life events: a time in the life span when men and women are expected to marry, a time to raise children, a time to retire. This normative pattern is adhered to, more or less consistently, by most persons within a given social group. . . (p. 16).

Although this approach points to important age-specific developmental markers of adolescence, the underlying meaning organizations, the strong points of structural-developmental psychology remain hidden.

When other more psychoanalytic-minded psychologists from the functional school point to the subject of who experiences and thinks about the life tasks, it is done by positing an ideal version of crisis and adaptation. The normative move of the adolescent's identity crisis (Erikson, 1968), the establishment of a life dream of the young adult (Levinson, 1978), or the generative keeping of meaning in the transition from adulthood to old age (Vaillant and Milofsky, 1981) are all ways in which *one* crisis of meaning is seen as occurring within *one* life phase. Phase and stage are organized as one conceptual whole, thus providing no context for the differential analysis of underlying self-logic and phasic tasks.[1]

---

[1]Erikson (1968) began to trace earlier forms of the adolescent identity crisis but left it to others to explore the meaning of this enterprise for a theory of ego development.

It is of great importance, however, to study the detailed descriptions, empirical findings, and theoretical elaborations of the functional schools in order to truly grasp the social and biological time tables in different cultures and subgroups that mark the transition points of the life maps between the two great poles, birth and death. It is not the observing self that can be the sole subject of our investigations, but the experiencing, thinking, and acting person who shapes and adapts to the cycle of growth, in the context of social opportunities and limitations. The meaning attributed to an individual, intergenerational and collective life cycle is that of the life tasks and their resolutions as well as the underlying perspective that shapes and is shaped by the dynamic between what I call *stage and phase*.

Stage and Phase: Adolescent Worlds

Self-logic, as mentioned earlier, refers to the process and structure of meaning attributed to self, other, life history, and life task. That there is coherence to this experience, and that it is organized by core principles derived from cognitive-developmental psychology is a premise of this line of work. Thus, an adolescent can be organizing adolescence at a variety of different stages of meaning organization. Adolescents can function at the subjective stage, the instrumental stage, mutual stage and even the systemic one (ranging from Stage 1 to Stage 4 in Kohlberg's theory, as shown in Fig. 13.2).

I view these different meaning organizations within this life phase as an exciting possibility for subdividing adolescence from a constructive-developmental perspective and for talking of the concept of different adolescent worlds. At each stage of the self (and within each transition), the adolescent phasic tasks (such as inclusion in the peer group, romantic relationships, etc.) can be experienced, understood, and solved in very different ways. Figure 13.2 shows how typical adolescent tasks can be addressed within a variety of adolescent worlds.

To the left of the cone some typical adolescent tasks are shown. Most adolescents in our culture, independent of their self-other perspective, will have to adapt to the new phasic demands that are significantly different for girls and boys, members of different ethnic groups and socioeconomic classes. There are, however, overarching and changing demands established by the culture, social structure and maturational factors. To the right of the cone paralleling the stages of self-other perspectives the labels for the adolescent world are shown. Building on Erikson's crisis model, I introduce four adolescent conflicts. This approach might clarify the importance of conceptually separating age and stage before integrating it into a larger dynamic of the developing self. Although the chapter format does not allow for great detail to the adolescent worlds, two case vignettes will help bring it to life.

Erikson's *identity versus identity defusion* provides an excellent description of the transition from the mutual self-other perspective to the systemic one. During this transition, the adolescent emerges out of a definition of self that is strongly

STAGE AND PHASE

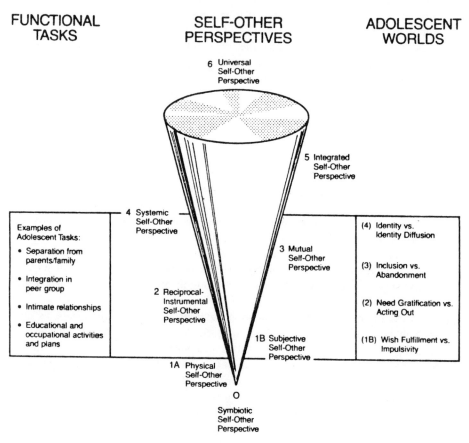

FIG. 13.2.

tied to the family and the peer group in an effort to create a context for self-chosen choices and commitments. In fact, group and family repudiation can be important aspects in this transition. At the mutual self-other stage, the adolescent conflict manifests itself quite differently. The conflict between *inclusion versus abandonment* is tied to the meaning organization where the adolescent is capable of experiencing the world predominantly through the eyes of others. In this process it becomes crucial how others view the self. The inclusion into a peer group and an intimate friendship becomes central in defining "who I am." The adolescent experiences great pain at any disruption of the intimate bond and feels abandoned. Although these experiences are painful at any stage in adolescence (or any other phase of the life cycle), at the mutual stage the loss of other is experienced as loss of self. In contrast to the systemic and the mutual self-other perspective, the conflict at the reciprocal-instrumental self-other perspective is quite different again. I call the two poles of the conflict *need gratification versus acting out* in order to point to the strengths and weaknesses at this developmental position: The adolescent understands that others have their own goals and motives and engages in mutually beneficial exchanges. The adolescent also tries to find ways to get his or her needs met, something again relevant to all stages and ages. But, because a true ability to understand and experience the world in accordance with the golden rule is not yet achieved, the instrumental aspects in relationships are not fully balanced by empathy and selfless love. The *acting out,* an imperfect term because it is used by clinicians to describe many behaviors, is meant to point to a willful and planned aspect of behavior rather than momentary reactions called impulsivity. The adolescent at this stage easily feels victimized and, as part of the reciprocal-instrumental point of view, tries "to get even and to break out." At the earlier position the stage I term subjective (1B), the conflict for the adolescent is *wish fulfillment versus impulsivity*. The adolescent who still has not fully made the transition from preoperations to concrete operations is guided by fantasy and a belief that the world is run the way the wishes emerge and are fulfilled in the self. Seemingly contradictory to the moment-to-moment expectations is a system of rigid and punitive rules that stands external to the self's wishes. Again this conflict has a strong general adolescent "ring" but at this stage there is no system able to translate the fantasy and wishes into a world where tools and concrete knowledge can guide the behavior over time. The vulnerability is the impulsive, submissive as well as grandiose response to the exteral environment. Even though it is possible to go back one step earlier and to posit an adolescent conflict at the physical self-other perspective it is rare to find a young person fully arrested at the stage of a 15- to 20-month old toddler (Margaret Mahler's separation individuation phase; Mahler, Pine & Bergman, 1975). We enter the realm of most severe psychopathology, not a topic of this chapter, when we find adolescents at the physical or symbiotic self-other perspective. I have previously shown (Noam, in press) that patients who are seen by clinicians as being arrested at these early stages usually show important signs of continued self-development even though conflicts stemming from the early experiences reemerge in later developmental positions.

The following excerpts from two clinical research interviews are from a longitudinal study of adolescent and family development (Hauser, Powers, Noam, Jacobson, Weiss & Follonsbee, 1984; Noam, et al., 1984; Powers, Hauser, Schwartz, Noam, & Jacobson, 1983).[2] They illustrate the difference between the adolescent tasks of (a) separating from parents and (b) recreating a

---

[2]The Adolescent and Family Development Project was funded by a variety of foundations, including the NIMH (5K02-MH-70178 Dr. Hauser), Biomedical Research Grant, NIH (RR05484 Drs. Hauser and Noam), the Spencer Foundation and the McArthur Foundation.

new image of who they are and what the relationship to the parents means in two developmental positions: the reciprocal-instrumental and the mutual self-other perspective.

Reciprocal-instrumental Self-Other Perspective.   Jim is a hospitalized 15-year-old adolescent who was referred for evaluation by the court. He had broken into a number of stores, was unwilling to cooperate with his parents' rules or to negotiate agreeable terms. When asked about his father, he responded:

A: Oh, he's a nice guy. We do a lot of stuff together.
I: Like what?
A: Go fishin' (brief pause) stuff like that. Go out.
I: Any memory really stand out in your mind between you and him?
A: Not really.
I: How would you describe him to someone like me who's never met him before?
A: How would I describe him?
I: Yeah.
A: What do you mean "How would I describe him? How he is? What he looks like?
I: Yeah, any of those things. Yeah, I never met him before; how would you put a picture together?
A: I don't know.
I: What's the first thing that comes to your mind?
A: Nice guy.
I: Nice guy?
A: Yeah, uh, he has black hair. He's tall. About 6 foot. /Hm/Just a nice guy; I don't know.
I: How about your mother; what's she like?
A: She she's a nice lady. She's short/Huh/.
I: Must be quite a combination 'cause 6 feet is a good size.
A: Yes, my mother's short. My mother's only about 5'7", 5'6".
I: That's not so short. Seems short to you compared to him?
A: I'm taller (yawning) than my mother.
I: Try to say more about her 'cause that would be helpful to know about the ins and outs of that. Sounds more complicated than with your father.
A: Yeah, oh my mother, she used to be what they call a *bitch*. (laughs) All the time, you know, naggin' all the time. She bitches.
I: What is she bitching about?
A: Like when I do something she doesn't want me to do, or shit.

Using this short excerpt from a longer clinical research interview it is important to see whether this somewhat problematic dialogue between interviewer and subject gives us a window into a typical adolescent struggle of defining the self in relationship to the parents as providers, models, and limit setters. What is the meaning of these struggles? The reader should trust that no other parts of the interview reveal a more complex social perspective. The fact that Jim was hospitalized for acting-out delinquent behavior can be interpreted as overpowering his family experience, suggesting, perhaps, that the data should really be analyzed from a psychopathological rather than a developmental perspective. It is the goal of this line of exploration, however, to bridge clinical and developmental theories into a broader framework of clinical-developmental psychology. Thus, I interpret Jim's description of his father and mother to be typical for the second level of the self-other perspective in which the self understands others' needs and direction as separate and guided by their own interest. Similarly the self views itself as a separate agent involved in pursuing goals that lead to getting what "I want." Similarities and differences between parents are seen in terms of size (a leftover from earlier stages) that can be translated into who can dominate whom. The fact that Jim is taller and stronger than his mother makes it hard to accept her as a full authority figure. Nor does there appear to be tolerance for ambiguity or ambivalence, that the mother could care *and* not give him what he wants. The relationship to the parents is marked by (mainly) physical separation (storming out, for example) in order to secure and to enhance boundaries and to ensure willful and undeterred mobility.

Mutual Self-Other Perspective.   Jean, also a 15-year-old, was hospitalized for an in-depth evaluation after a suicidal gesture. She had stopped going to school, stayed in the basement of the house and drank liquor "to drown the hopeless feelings." She talks about her parents quite differently.

I: Well, tell me a little bit about your father.
A: No.
I: No? How come?
A: 'Cause.
I: Are you mad at him?
A: No. I love him I do, but I don't wanna. He gets me mad 'cause he always tries to make me feel guilty about everything (unclear). He should be here.
I: Your father?
A: He should be here and I should be home.
I: Hmm. Oh, do you think he has a lot of psychological problems?
A: Yes, I can psychoanalyze him.
I: I am sure. What do you think is wrong with him?
A: I think (unclear)—he won't forget things that happened in the past and he keeps reliving them.
I: What kinds of things?
A: He doesn't want me to get hurt the same way he did.
I: Who hurt him?
A: My mother.
I: Hmm. How did she hurt him?
A: By leaving him.

Jean has reached the mutual self-other perspective. I call her adolescent conflict inclusion versus abandonment. At this stage, the adolescent derives a central definition of selfhood through the identification with others and especially significant, close relationships. Separation and conflict is understood in psychological rather than physical or power terms and often elicits a heightened psychological vulnerability. She can understand the problems of the father from the father's point of view—to protect her from his hurt. Jean is thrown into a terrible dilemma as she realizes that she cannot identify with both her father and her mother, because the mother has hurt the father by leaving him. She cannot integrate their separation, because it means a "separation from herself." She views her relationship with her father psychologically and with a perspective on the past, whereas Jim did not. Seeing the family problems from the mother's *and* the father's perspective does not mean that she has the capacity of integrating their divergent views into a larger system that maintains identity across conflict areas. Her loneliness, depression, and her suicidal gesture could be connected to an underlying sense of abandonment.

I have called this model a process dynamic, because I have observed in both clinical and educational contexts that the dynamic between life phase and life stage is important in understanding developmental progress and arrest. One example of the relationship of phase and stage is *age-stage-dysynchrony*.

Age-Stage Dysynchrony

Given the differentiated social and interpersonal norms in complex post-industrial societies, the relatively undifferentiated self-systems of the earlier subjective and reciprocal-instrumental self-other stages make it difficult to solve the social demands of adolescence. Comparing 76 psychiatrically hospitalized adolescents with 70 nonhospitalized adolescents (Noam, 1984; Noam, Powers, Hauser, & Jacobson, 1981), we found that the great majority of the hospitalized adolescents functioned at preconformist (Loevinger) and preconventional (Kohlberg) levels, whereas the control group functioned at the higher conventional stages. The fact that adolescents at all levels of development (from Stage 1 to Stage 4) could be found in both samples speaks to the usefulness of the concept of different adolescent worlds.

Stage developmental analyses might prove a framework for addressing psychopathology (at least in part) as Age-stage dysynchrony. Tasks of a given life phase can be approached in very different ways depending on the frame of reference or meaning applied at a self-other stage. Important tasks of adolescence, such as reworking the relationships with parents and other authority figures and the inevitable anxieties and frustrations in the move into the peer group, might be especially difficult at earlier stages of the self. The self-protectiveness at the reciprocal-instrumental self-other stage or the lack of impulse control at the subjective self-other perspective (developmentally adequate at earlier phases in the life cycle) becomes inadequate for coping with many adolescent issues. The mutual self-other stage brings with it important developmental gains: the establishment of mutuality through the golden rule, and the ability to delay gratification of needs. These gains bring out new and more complex abilities to deal with adolescent tasks and conflict situations. The example of Jean shows that more advanced development of the self does not necessarily provide a shield against psychopathology. But Jean's ability to view interpersonal conflict psychologically ultimately provided her with a set of more complex and adaptive tools to resolve the adolescent task of separating from the parents as well as finding new forms of relating to them.

In summary, all adolescents, while participating in important social interaction and pushed forward through biological growth, also face major occupational, educational, and interpersonal shifts. These transitions are best described as socially mediated tasks around love, work, and learning. The self-system will determine (in part) the meaning given these shifts and the ways the person will respond to these demands. The distinction between stage and phase in adolescence can enhance our understanding of different adolescent worlds.

STAGE AND STYLE

I have noted earlier that the constructivist synthesis presented here has three components. I have discussed the stage-phase relationship and now turn to the stage-style distinction (the terms *style* and *orientation* are used interchangeably in this discussion).

Styles of personality have always been a source of interest to psychologists and philosophers. Various traditions within psychology have described stylistic distinctions including trait psychology, psychoanalytic ego psychology (e.g., Shapiro, 1965), object relations theory (e.g., Balint, 1959), and Jungian psychology (e.g., Jung, 1923/1971; Neumann, 1948; Von Franz & Hillman, 1971). Numerous longitudinal studies support the hypothesis that certain dimensions of psychological functioning remain stable over time, e.g., reflectivity versus impulsivity (Kagan & Kogen, 1970), and temperament (Thomas & Chess 1978). These studies vary greatly in the characteristics discussed as well as in their focus and scope, yet the research and the theoretical work speaks to the fundamental nature of elements of consistency.

Although these various traditions all recognize and attempt to describe orientations of personality, they fail to take full account of their developmental implications. Jung, most notably, describes the changes of orientation as a function of maturity. He posits that as the individual reaches the later adult stages of development, the orientation that has not been dominant becomes incorporated into the personality. This causes somewhat of a reversal or transcendence of orientation in later life, as introverts begin to become more extroverted and vice versa. But Jung lacks a systematic, empirically valid theory of life-span development in which to ground an understanding of the changes of style.

Chess and Thomas (1978), in their observation of temperament differences in infants, imply a biological component in temperamental differences, which could also have some basis for styles in general. My own view is closer to the psychoanalytic object relations school (e.g., Fairbairn, 1982; Winnicott, 1958). Fairbairn asserts that the ego is object-relational from the beginning and its energies are directed toward interpersonal experiences. Experiences in the interpersonal field (*infant-caregiver matrix*) are internalized and lay the ground for future experiences of self and others (see Noam, Higgins, & Goethals, 1982). These basic experiences of closeness and distance, support and frustration, conflict and conflict resolution within the early family configuration lead to what I call a *self-world grammar*. In these early interactions, the child develops typical ways of relating to self and others. Beyond the family, school and peer environments provide social experiences that help shape patterns of interaction. It is important to note, however, that this grammar is generative in nature, providing some rules for its dynamic for the future developmental transformations.

In the structural-developmental tradition, as mentioned before, most systems have ignored continuities of development and focused on the qualitative reorganizations at each new level. Loevinger's ego stages and Kegan's levels of the self are examples of models that do not address subtypes within a given ego or self-position. Both interpret stylistic issues as emerging out of each stage position.

Kohlberg's (1958) dissertation was based on an ideal-typological method in which structure and content were not clearly separated. In the later revisions, structural stages and Piaget-based substages distinguished more clearly between structure and content. In his attempt to address this issue he has distinguished more clearly the status of *substages* (i.e., A and B, and more recently the Piagetian types of morality, autonomy and heteronomy).

We found those subtypes necessary to account for autonomous action in those who had not reached post-conventional or principled reasoning. In addition to the potential usefulness of a Piagetian typology to relate judgment to action, we thought it would be useful in the way in which Piaget originally intended, as an index of the type of social relationships in which the individual was embedded, those of hierarchical authority or those of egalitarian cooperation and solidarity. We expected these to vary by culture, class and peer group participation independent of stage. (Kohlberg 1984, p. 664)

But although Kohlberg's substages are the most elaborate empirical system of distinguishing between orientations and hard stages, (Kohlberg, Levine and Hewer, 1983) he has not described the process or the developmental dynamic between developmental stage and orientations.

Recent criticisms of the Kohlberg system, at least in part, revolve around differences of orientation. Gilligan (1982) and Lyons (1983) posit two modes of morality that are identified with two modes of the self. These different perspectives are reflected in two different moral ideologies, because separation is justified by an ethic of rights, whereas attachment is supported by an ethic of care (Gilligan, 1982). Although some skepticism remains warranted on philosophical, psychological, and empirical grounds regarding a normative theory of moral care distinguishable from a moral theory of justice, a clear focus on the self-in relation with others, shows promise. The model presented here, however, attempts also to address a lack of theoretical clarity in Gilligan's work. There is no evidence that the connected self described by Gilligan and her co-workers is structured by different cognitive or role-taking principles than the differentiating self (a position held by Lyons, [1983]). Nowhere have the authors clarified the underlying logic of the self nor the status of its developmental lines. The lack of distinction between stage and style contributes greatly to the difficulties of placing the work conceptually. There is a need to distinguish structure and content where differences in styles can be analyzed conceptually apart from underlying structural perspectives. This distinction can then lead to the investigation of the dynamic of stage and style, without having to posit a different cognitive psychology for men and women before data can support such a claim.

Relational and Boundary Styles

I am suggesting two overarching orientations with two connected suborientations. I am distinguishing between a boundary and a relational style, which in their extreme forms are expressed as self-style and other style. These styles describe a consistent orientation of self and relationship in the face of important developmental transformations. The brevity of the following descriptions of styles can easily lead to misunderstanding. There is no value judgment intended regarding the two families of style. Neither boundary nor relational styles are per se better or more developed. The extreme forms in both cases are considered less desireable and closer to psychopathology. Also, all individuals engage in both relational and boundary activities depending on situation and type of relationship. The notion of style suggests a preference for one of these attitudes.

The relational style describes a focus on the self in the interpersonal context. People with relational styles focus much energy on the establishment, enhancement, and maintenance of relationships. The self is defined as a living part of these relationships and the individual is concerned with acceptance by others. The relational person wants to care for others and to be cared for by them. This person will go to great lengths to avoid separations from others or disharmony with them. To this end they will sacrifice and avoid negative emotions such as anger, which differentiates the self from others. In its extreme form, the relational orientation becomes an other style, defined by the self's losing itself in the other. The person merges with the wishes, needs, interests and directions of the other and ceases to experience the possibility of existing separately. The dependency leads to submission of the will to the other and a loss of boundaries of where self begins and other ends.

The boundary types focus on their independence and self control. They maintain a boundary to protect the sense of self and use individual power, mastery, and achievement to maintain a differentiating posture. The boundary-oriented individual is preoccupied with self-reliance and can be contemptuous of those who need help. These persons are oriented toward task rather than process and are usually more ideational. In relationships they ask the question "How am I different from you?" In its extreme form, the boundary style becomes a self-style in which the self is consumed with its own interests and wishes and ceases to orient to others except as they relate to the self's needs. The person either pursues his life goals totally separately from others ("extreme loner") or uses others as an audience for mirroring the self ("narcissist").

Earlier, I described the position of the self moving from an affiliative side to a more individuated side of the cone back to a more inclusive one. The developmental dynamic presented here is an attempt to capture relationships between styles and stages. Figure 13.3 shows interaction patterns between stage and style. Family, school and peer environments shape early self-world grammars and thus influence the future history of self-other transformations. Boundary and self styles will be more syntonic with the side of the cone emphasizing processes of differentiation. Relational and other styles are syntonic with the side emphasizing processes of integration and inclusion. These harmonizing effects can lead to a fuller state of equilibration at a given stage (matching), but can also contribute to delays in development. An individual may have difficulty entering into the transition from a stage that is syntonic with the stylistic orientation to one that is more dystonic (interlocking). The result may be a defensive avoidance of the new experiences that could otherwise lead to a structural reorganization (defensive overassimilation). Matching and interlocking positions, as shown in Fig. 13.3, can interrupt the momentum of development because new accomodation is experienced fundamentally as ego-dystonic. Only powerful new social experiences and phasic demands will trigger developmental reorganization, often experienced as particularly painful.

A stage-style discrepancy can lead to acceleration of development in which the internal tension between new needs and typical style pushes toward a new synthesis at a more advanced developmental level. It can also lead to a creative attempt to integrate confusing and contradictory wishes, goals and aspirations within a given stage. This view helps in understanding why many people are far from balanced even when functioning within an equilibrated structure. When accelerated development occurs, it is often observed later that the important milestones were achieved in a superficial or "as-if" manner, in need of reworking. When a longer balancing between conflicting stage and style occurs, there is a greater possibility for more integration of the two styles.

STAGE AND STYLE

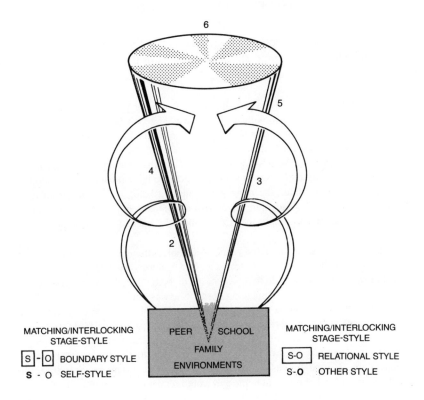

*Emphasis on processes
of differentiation*

*Emphasis on processes
of integration*

MATCHING/INTERLOCKING
STAGE-STYLE

S - O   BOUNDARY STYLE

S - O   SELF-STYLE

PEER   SCHOOL

FAMILY

ENVIRONMENTS

MATCHING/INTERLOCKING
STAGE-STYLE

S-O   RELATIONAL STYLE

S-**O**   OTHER STYLE

One misunderstanding could easily arise from this description: Two internal processes in their relationship to each other determine developmental patterns. But stage and style continuously emerge out of the self's interaction with the social world, with internalized earlier relationships and the idealized version of future interpersonal experiences. Thus the meaning organization will shape and be shaped by important relationships as will the boundaries be placed in real relationships bringing the history of relationships to life. Systematic longitudinal analysis will need to shed more light on this dynamic, which I have observed in detail through research cases and in clinical contexts in which patients were given developmental stage measures and were observed during transitional periods. A clinical example may clarify the theoretical distinctions presented in this chapter.

THE DYNAMIC OF STAGE, PHASE AND STYLE: THE EXAMPLE OF MELISSA

I have examined the concepts of stage, phase and style separately and in pairs. Now I will attempt to integrate all three elements of the model. To do so, I will rely upon a clinical case analysis.

Melissa was 15 when she was hospitalized at a major psychiatric institution. A thin, attractive, and frail-looking girl, she was angry at her parents, staff, and therapists. She had "gotten into trouble with her family" and continuously fought with her mother who favored her younger sister. All the bad occurrences in the family were blamed on Melissa, who began to feel that nothing she did made any difference, "so why try?" Her mother responded to her demands for attention by stating that Melissa should be more grown up and help. The mother wanted assistance from her older daughter, rather than additional requests. Melissa was seen as an independent and responsive little child who spent more time playing by herself.

Melissa did well in the early years of school, although she became a loner, withdrawn from her peers and her teachers. She became very independent and took great pride in being able to do things alone, to do better than the other students, and to speak only when she had something to say. She was rarely seen in the schoolyard playing with others, but usually stayed by herself, thinking, and observing. She became fascinated with observations of nature such as subtyping birds, trees, and flowers. Her knowledge in these areas impressed her teachers and she developed the idea that one day she would become a great scientist in her own laboratory. Melissa made some friends but they were somewhat distant relationships. She looked forward to her books at home and would retreat into her room. She does not remember feeling depressed, but she began to trust only herself. The valued father stayed longer and longer hours at work, the mother focused more and more on the little sister.

Although she found ways of coping with her family problems in latency, the situation became intolerable after she reached puberty. She was still not interested in a peer group and close friends. A family move left her and the whole family isolated; she began to fight with her mother over any issue. Her mother could not make her do anything and any request led to a hostile response. Her father retreated even further, and her mother smothered her sister even more. Melissa was not able to maintain a sphere of success in school; she began to be truant and to associate with the more delinquent children in her class. But she also felt herself to be an outsider there and usually went into stores by herself to steal. She had lost any interest in pursuing plans for college and a career and had also stopped reading books. When her mother began to confront her about her schoolwork, Melissa began to fight with her by throwing things at her (on two occasions even knives), and storming out of the house. She became a "Youth Services Case" when she was seen wandering the streets alone at night and her mother called the police to search for her. At about this time when she was caught stealing and possessing marijuana, the court recommended a psychiatric evaluation and possible residential treatment.

Before continuing with the description of Melissa's development, I interpret this material in light of the model presented earlier.

Melissa's early experiences, frustration, and continued aloneness led to a detached stance. The rejecting mother who favored the sister and the absent father contributed to a self-reliance and distrust in the availability of important others. The view that "I have to do it alone," "I have to look after myself because no one else will do it," generalized to school life. Melissa stayed away from playing with classmates and became interested in observing nature. When other children experienced the excitements of group play, Melissa began to talk to herself. She also stayed away from the teachers and wanted to find solutions by herself. All of these descriptions point to a boundary style. Melissa's early experiences suggest a relationship between the etiology of style and family context. Her place in the web of complex family interaction supported the loner, distant and removed side in herself. In latency, the boundary style still was directed in productive age appropriate activities: observing the natural world. The concrete reciprocal-instrumental stage supported the orderly division of self and world, of facts and feelings. It can be hypothesized that the strong separations at home led to a strengthening of the boundary style during the latency years, a time when boundaries are strengthened in most children. In Melissa's case, the process of boundary establishment took extreme forms and was not balanced by supportive relationships. When she had reached adolescence and continued to function at the reciprocal-instrumental stage she began to get into trouble. An interlock occurred in which Melissa's boundary style and the reciprocal-instrumental perspective, together with a strong distrust of relationships, led to a developmental arrest. Phasic demands of adolescence as described earlier in this chapter create a tension for adolescents at the second level, because the reworking of the relationship with parents and the creation of new intimacy with peers demand more complex self-understanding and conflict resolution, usually achieved at the mutual self stage. For Melissa, the switch from latency studiousness at Stage 2 to adolescent rebellion at Stage 2 was radical even though there was no change of underlying stage-organization. The example provides some evidence regarding the importance of making explicit the relationship between stage and phase, because the differences are not in self-logic but in task resolution. Melissa's retreat had become far more dangerous to herself and her family and the problems were made more severe by the adolescent demands on separation that could not be contained within the family.

Melissa began treatment at the hospital with a young therapist whose approach was formal and who wanted to discuss her thinking about herself and her family. He was conducting what one could call insight-oriented therapy geared toward a more advanced level of self-observation and self-reflection. It is not surprising that she rejected this notion and felt victimized and yet again, misunderstood. The transference interpretation of the therapist, that she was repeating with him what she had experienced with her family, was greeted with a mixture of laughter, contempt, and disbelief. The therapy relationship broke down.

When I began seeing her, I could build upon her earlier therapy experience and was aware of her concrete and externalizing stance. I did not interpret it mainly as defensive, but as reflecting a momentary developmental ceiling. I had to answer her continuous question? "What do I get out of this?" Her manipulations, distancing maneuvers, but also a wish to be close to people emerged. While she was fighting with me and other staff about many authority issues, she also began to build important peer relations, took in a cat, and, after another few months, began a very intensive friendship with a girl of similar background called Joanne. She described the excitement of having someone with whom to share secrets and whom she could trust, but did not want to detail the reports.

Melissa's therapist had pushed for too much intimacy and self-reflection; her history of disappointments, her boundary style in connection with her reciprocal-instrumental stage position did not allow for his therapy model to be successfully applied. The more supportive approval that respected both her limited self-observation and boundaries proved successful, because it avoided unnecessary power struggles. Her movement into the peer group and the establishment of an intense friendship in which she began sharing some of her disappointments in her family all reflect a move into the mutual self-position. This move took almost 10 months and was accompanied by many set-backs, such as her running away when angry, or when she felt victimized.

Many misunderstandings occurred in the friendship of the two girls, because Melissa wanted to spend much time alone and Joanne's idea of a best friend was someone with whom to spend almost all of one's time. The adolescent task of creating important relationships outside the home was magnified by the hospitalization. The establishment of an important therapy relationship, peer interaction in groups, and a best friend slowly led to the overcoming of the age-stage dysynchrony. Melissa's transformation into the mutual self-perspective led to more affiliative needs but even then she retained a boundary style (need to be alone, anger, and distancing, etc.) The boundary style had gotten more complex (not only action orientation, but more inward reflection). The affiliative needs that came to the foreground at this developmental position brought out the hidden style, the dialectic counterposition to the dominant style. Each new developmental transition creates a new possibility for a more integrated and ballanced use of both styles.

In the next phase of treatment, Melissa began to make use of me in a very different way. She thought more about her past, about future aspirations, and the pain of being part of a rejecting family, but also about her own participation in the painful struggles with her family. She became a very engaged student and put a great deal of thought into planning a career—marine biology—with fantasies of travel to remote areas for scientific explorations. Her friendship with Joanne had become less important, because Melissa felt that Joanne had become too "clingy" and not interested in living her own life. Melissa had, by now, moved to a residential school and was preparing for college entry.

Melissa's move out of the mutual self-stage occurred much faster than the move into Stage 3. Her boundary style in tension with the mutual self-system led to an accelerated movement into a transition to Stage 4. The themes of distance and observation, which had led to good scholastic achievement in latency and to contempt, rage, and externalization in adolescence reemerged, but this time in a more complex self-system: the systemic self. Much as important relationships can be fostering development, the turning to the self in difficult times can lead to a growth-producing internal dialogue. The experience of aloneness can create the context for a new internal system that gives structure to the feelings. It became quite important to work with Melissa against a new sense of isolation. She channeled her boundary needs into more adaptive directions: future aspirations, biographic considerations about "who I am" and "where I come from" and the goals of far travels in the Darwin tradition.

In summary, Melissa was confronted in adolescense with tasks she was unable to resolve at the reciprocal-instrumental level. Having to work out a new relationship to parents and teachers, develop plans for later love and work provided her with the experiences leading to structural accommodation. Her earlier disappointments coupled with her latency experiences of solitude and reflection had created a boundary style (clearly with relational yearnings). The transition into the mutual self-other perspective often felt like going against the "natural grain" of doing things. The intense relationship with Joanne was a period in which more relational experiences were integrated, modifying the rigid self-protection. Melissa became more ballanced, integrating her relational needs with her strong wishes for distance and solitude. The move into herself, fostered by intense family conflict that made it necessary for her to "sort things out", contributed to an accelerated transition toward the systemic self-other perspective. This transition was experienced as much more ego-syntonic than the earlier transition into the mutual self-other perspective. The earlier transition required trust in others, the transition into the systemic stage required the trust in the self. The hope of a future integration points to the phase of adulthood and new developmental transformations that will encompass in a new whole boundary and relational styles.

CONCLUSION

The heuristic presented here and illustrated through selected examples has emerged from extensive case observations. More are needed. Careful therapeutic observations and longitudinal research analyses will contribute increasing detail to knowledge of this developmental dynamic. Toward these ends my colleagues and I have emphasized two areas. First, I have developed a semi-structured research instrument, the *Stage-Phase-and-Style Interview*. The interview focuses on the requirements of the adolescent phase and reviews the subject's perspective, choice, and reasoning concerning these functional tasks and their resolutions (e.g., separation from home, choices of work, school and friends.) In addition, the boundary, self, relational, and other styles are established by a set of questions dealing with the way relationships are experienced and how interpersonal boundaries are set.

A second area of research concerns our efforts to describe developmental patterns as they relate to underlying meaning organizations, task resolution, and continuities of styles. At present a coding group at Harvard (Gil Noam, Sally Powers, Robert Kilkenny, Jeffrey Beedy) is developing a manual for the analysis of longitudinal interviews from a stage, phase and style perspective. To date, this work has demonstrated both the strength of the Kohlberg paradigm for the study of the self, personality change, and psychopathology as well as the need to account more fully for personality transformations in adolescence and adulthood. Such an observation contains at once the perspective and the conclusion of the model of the developing self presented here. That is, only with observations over time—longitudinal analyses, in-depth clinical studies—can we begin to reconstruct the developmental processes and their relationships to each other.

ACKNOWLEDGMENTS

I want to acknowledge Gayle Elkins' editorial help and Christopher Recklitis' contribution to the discussion of styles. Marvin Berkowitz, Wolfgang Edelstein, Stuart Hauser and Maryanne Wolf gave excellent comments and Barbara Panza, Mark Sarasohn, and Margaret Lufkin have patiently worked with me on draft after draft.

REFERENCES

Balint, M. (1959). *Thrills and regressions*. New York: International University Press.
Blasi, A. (1983). The self and cognition. In B. Lee & G. Noam (Eds.), *Developmental approaches to the self*. New York: Plenum.
Broughton, J. (1978). The development of concepts of self, mind, reality, and knowledge. *New Directions for Child Development, 1*, 75–100.

Chess, S. & Thomas, A. (1978). Temperamental individuality from childhood to adolescence. In S. Chess & A. Thomas (Eds.), *Annual progress in child psychiatry and child development* (pp. 223–232). New York: Brunner/Mazel.

Chodorow, N. (1978). *The reproduction of mothering: Psychoanalysis and the sociology of gender.* Berkeley: University of California.

Damon, W. & Hart, D. (1982). The development of self-understanding from infancy through adolescence. *Child Development, 53* (4) 841–864.

Edelstein, W. & Noam, G. (1982). Regulatory structures of the self and post-formal operations in adulthood. *Human Development, 15,* 407–422.

Erikson, E. H. (1968). *Identity, youth and crisis.* New York: Norton.

Fairbairn, W. R. D. (1982). *Psychoanalytic studies of the personality.* Boston, MA: Routledge, Kegan & Paul.

Fowler, J. W. (1981). *Stages of faith.* New York: Harper & Row.

Gilligan, C. (1982). *In a different voice.* Cambridge, MA: Harvard University.

Hauser, S. T. (1976). Loevinger's model and measure of ego development: A critical review. *Psychological Bulletin, 83*(5), 928–955.

Hauser, S. T., Powers, S. I., Noam, G., Jacobson, A. M., Weiss, B., & Follonsbee, D. J. (1984). Familial contexts of adolescent ego development. *Child Development, 55,* 195–213.

Jung, C. G. (1971). *Psychological types* (rev. ed.) Bollinger Series (Vol. 6). Princeton, NJ: Princeton University (original work published 1923).

Kagan, J. & Kogen, N. (1970). Individuality and cognitive performance. In P. H. Mussen (Ed.), *Carmichael's manual of child psychology,* 3rd ed., Vol. 2 (pp. 1273–1366). New York: Wiley.

Kegan, R. (1982). *The evolving self.* Cambridge, MA: Harvard University.

Kohlberg, L. (1958). *The development of modes of moral thinking and choice in years 10 to 16.* Unpublished doctoral dissertation, University of Chicago.

Kohlberg, L. (1969). Stage and sequence. The cognitive developmental approach to socialization. In D. Goslin (Ed.), *Handbook of socialization, theory and research* (pp. 347–480). New York: Rand Mcnally.

Kohlberg, L. (1984). *Essays on moral development. Vol. 2 The psychology of moral development.* San Francisco: Harper Row.

Kohlberg, L. & Gilligan, C. (1971). The adolescent as a philosopher: The discovery of the self in a postconventional world. *Daedalus, 100* (4), 1051–1086.

Kohlberg, L. & Kramer, R. (1969). Continuities and discontinuities in childhood and adult moral development. *Human Development, 12,* 93–120.

Kohlberg, L., Levine, C., & Hewer, A. (1983). Moral stages: A current formulation and a response to critics. *Contributions to human development* (Vol. 10). New York: S. Karger.

Levinson, D. J. (1978). *The seasons of a man's life.* New York: Knopf.

Loevinger, J. (1976). *Ego development.* San Francisco: Jossey-Bass.

Lyons, N. (1983). Two modes of self and morality. *Harvard Educational Review, 41,* 325–378.

Mahler, M., Pine, F., & Bergman, A. (1975) *The psychological birth of the human infant.* New York: Basic Books.

Neugarten, B. L. (1964) *Personality in middle and late life: Empirical studies.* New York: Atherton.

Neumann, E. (1948). *The great mother.* Princeton, NJ: Princeton University.

Noam, G. (1984). *Self, morality, and biography: Studies in clinical-development psychology.* Unpublished doctoral dissertation: Harvard University.

Noam, G. (in press). Marking time in the midst of the hardest movement: Adolescent borderline disorders in lifespan perspective. In K. Fields, B. Kohler, & E. Wolf, (Eds.) *Learning and Meaning.* New York: International University.

Noam, G., Hauser, S. T., Santostefano, S., Garrison, W., Jacobson, A., Powers, S., & Mead, M. (1984). Ego development and psychopathology: Study of hospitalized adolescents. *Child Development, 55,* 184–194.

Noam, G., Higgins, R., & Goethals, G. (1982). Psychoanalytic approaches to developmental psychology. In Wolman (Ed.), *Handbook of developmental psychology* (pp. 23–43). Englewood, NJ: Prentice-Hall.

Noam, G., Kohlberg, L., & Snarey, J. (1983). Steps toward a model of the self. In B. Lee & G. Noam (Eds.), *Developmental approaches to the self* (pp. 59–134). New York: Plenum.

Noam, G., Powers, S., Hauser, S., & Jacobson, A. (1981). *Moral development in a group of psychiatric adolescent patients and high school students.* Paper presented at the meeting of the Society for Research in Child Development, Boston.

Oser, F., Power, C., Gmuender, P., Fritzsche, U., & Widmer, K. (1980). Stages of religious judgment. In J. Fowler (Ed.), *Inward moral and religious maturity* (pp. 277–315). Morristown, NJ: Silver Burdett.

Powers, S., Hauser, S. T., Schwartz, J. M., Noam, G., & Jacobson, A. M. (1983). Adolescent ego development and family interaction: A structural-developmental perspective. In H. D. Grotevant & C. R. Cooner (Eds.). *Adolescent development in the family New Directions in Child Development* (No, 22, pp. 5–26). San Francisco: Jossey-Bass.

Selman, R. L. (1980). *The growth of interpersonal understanding: Developmental and clinical analyses.* New York: Academic.

Shapiro, D. (1965). *Neurotic styles.* New York: Basic Books.

Vailliant, G. & Milofsky, E. (1981). Natural history of male psychological health IX: Emprical evidence for Erikson's model of the life cycle. *American Journal of Psychiatry, 138,* (11), 1433–1440.

Von Franz, M. L. & Hillman, J. (1971). . *Lectures on Jung's typology,* Dallas, Texas: Spring Publications.

Winnicott, D. W. (1958). *Through pediatrics to psychoanalysis.* New York: Basic Books.

14 Moral Reasoning in the Assessment and Outcome of Suicidal Breakdown

Alexandra Hewer
Center for Moral and Personality Development
Harvard University
Clinical Developmental Institute
Belmont, Massachusetts

Habermas (in press), noting the recent turn toward hermeneuticism in the social sciences, remarks:

> Only to the extent that the interpreter grasps the reasons that allow the author's utterance to appear as rational does he understand what the author could have meant. Thus the interpreter understands the meaning of his text only to the extent that he sees why the author felt himself entitled to put forward as true certain assertions, to recognize as right certain values and norms, to express as sincere certain experiences.

The two longitudinal case studies presented in this chapter can be seen as attempts to make evident the reasons that allowed each young person to genuinely believe that his own suicide was justifiable. Developmental changes in reasoning, especially about the value of life, are then documented in each case, revealing the cognitive basis of each young person's coming to newly value his own life and to choose living over suicide. Thus, these analyses map a life-saving change in subjective perception. Stable recovery from suicidal breakdown is explained or made plausible not by reference to changes in material circumstances, but rather by reference to structural developmental changes in value assumptions; i.e., to changes in the *meanings* that material circumstances held for each subject.

Kohlberg acknowledges that "hermeneutic objectivism" is the scientific position he takes in designing his theory of moral development (Kohlberg, Levine, & Hewer, 1983. p. 15). Scorers of Kohlberg's Moral Judgment Interview (see Colby & Kohlberg, in press; Colby, Kohlberg, Gibbs, Candee, Speicher-Dubin, Hewer, & Power, 1982), and of other structural-developmental measures of social cognition, take the position of at first trying to see the world through the interviewee's eyes. This involves running with the same capabilities, and running up against the same limits of current thinking, as the subject experiences as he or she tries to resolve hypothetical or real-life conflict situations. Later in the scoring process, with the aid of a scoring manual, the formal structural properties of these capabilities and limits are recognized by the scorer as belonging to this or that particular structurally defined socio-moral perspective, classifiable on a developmental scale as a stage of reasoning.

The case analyses presented here use Kohlberg's measure and another structural-developmental interview. The analyses assume that the reasons why, for instance, someone feels him or herself entitled to put forward certain assertions as true can be grasped by reference to structural-developmental stages of cognition, such as Kohlberg's stages of moral reasoning. That is, derived from Piagetian genetic epistemological theory, these stages reveal the epistemic bases of the subjects' experiences. Insofar as others can be directly acquainted with these epistemic bases, the subjects' experiences are knowable or shareable.

The reader is directed to the Appendix, which presents an amalgam of structural-developmental stages investigated by Kohlberg (1976) in the moral domain and by Kegan (1982) in the broader domain of self-other differentiation. These stages assume a Piagetian cognitive-developmental theory of hierarchical equilibrative structuring of interactions between organism and environment. Each stage of development is bounded by its particular limit of psycho-social perspective-taking, and development is invariantly sequential. The case analyses refer to development in terms of these stages.

Subjects

The subjects of the case studies are middle-class, white males, called Woody and Paul (Names have been changed to protect confidentiality). They have been admitted as inpatients on a psychiatric unit of a city hospital after making serious suicide attempts, that is, attempts that, by their cirumstances and methods, were highly lethal and would have succeeded but for unforseeable accidents. Both received the psychiatric diagnosis of "Borderline Personality" organization. Woody stays on the unit for 2 months and is transferred to another inpatient psychiatric facility. Paul stays on the unit for 1 month and is discharged to continue regular psychotherapy while living at home. While on the unit Woody and Paul agree to participate in a research study. They are interviewed with Kohlberg's Moral Judgment Interview and a second semi-structured clinical interview. At this time Woody is age 18 and Paul is age 20. One year after discharge Woody and Paul are reinterviewed with these measures. Woody is still in the hospital, shows more sadness about his life, but is maintaining the first sexual love relationship of his life. Paul still lives at home, has been fairly regularly in psychotherapy and reports some improvement in his work relationships. Neither has reattempted suicide nor do they report feeling seriously suicidal.

Measures

The *Moral Judgment Interview* (MJI) (Colby et al., 1982; Colby & Kohlberg, in press) is a semi-structured test in which the subject reasons through a series of three moral dilemmas. The aim in each case is to arrive at what the subject considers the best resolutions of the moral conflicts the stories pose. A dilemma or "story" pits two moral issues against each other. The most well-known story involves a husband, Heinz, who must decide whether to steal a drug to save his dying wife after all reasonable and legal means to obtain the drug have failed. The two issues in opposition here are the value of life and the value of law. Regardless of the subject's preferred choice of action, a set of standard interviewer probes helps elicit the subject's best reasoning about each issue. Responses in favor of stealing the drug are classified under the Life Issue, responses opposed to stealing the drug are classified under the Law Issue. Thus the key psychological function being measured by the MJI is not the subject's decision whether to steal or not to steal the drug, but rather his or her assumptions and reasons underlying either decision. These assumptions and reasons are in turn analyzed for sociomoral structure in terms of particular justice operations, and (more pertinently for the present study) in terms of level of social perspective-taking (see Kohlberg, Levine, & Hewer, 1983). This structure or stage of reasoning is used by the subject to perceive the moral conflict and to frame his or her view of its fair resolution. A standard interview consists of three dilemmas, generating reasoning about six moral issues. A subject receives a stage score for each of the six issues, and a final "global" stage score is assigned on a 9-point scale comprising five pure stages (Stages 1 through 5) and four mixed or "transitional" stages (e.g., Stage 1, ½, 2, etc.). Interviews are analyzed using a complex scoring manual (see Colby et al., 1982; Colby & Kohlberg, in press). Readers unfamiliar with the nature of Kohlberg's stages of moral reasoning are referred to Kohlberg (1976), or to the Appendix.)

The *Clinical Interview* (CI) (see Rogers, 1983; Hewer, 1983a) is designed to gather information about problems and conflicts in the subjects' own lives and to elicit interpretations of their experience and management of breakdown. Questions probe three areas of subjective understanding: (1) what led up to hospitalization, and what (if any) changes there have been in these matters; (2) understanding and management of real-life relationships with significant others; and (3) how subjects see themselves and perceive maturing vs. staying the same. Material from the CI is analyzed for structural stage in level of perspective-taking (see Rogers, 1983, and the Appendix).

The weaving together of material from the MJI and CI for each subject, followed over time is the substance of the detailed case studies that follow. The first aim of the analyses is to suggest that these suicides are not simply the impulsively "crazy" acts of Borderline Personality organizations, but are coherent, albeit despairing, expressions of meaning organizations that can be clearly distinguished in cognitive-developmental terms. A second aim is to make evident the connection between each subject's recovery and a process of structural developmental reorganization. This process enables subjects to reject their former suicidal positions by taking a structurally new perspective on both the value of life and on their experience of self.

CASE 1 - WOODY

Woody is first interviewed 5 weeks after his suicide attempt. He says at that time that he no longer wishes to be dead. He is white, age 18 at hospital admission, and comes from a professional family background. Up until his suicide attempt he was not aware of depressed feelings. At both interview times his global score in the MJI shows mixed or transitional Stage 4/5 reasoning, but, as we shall see, the reasoning he uses to justify his own suicide is Stage 4 reasoning, which he already rejects.

Retrospective Suicide Analysis

In describing what led up to his suicide attempt, Woody tells of his hopes as a freshman at a prestigious university to become a "Renaissance man and participate in changing the world." He had been outstanding in high school at anything he set his mind to and had an image of leadership among his peers, which he explained in the statement "I was so arrogant. I was supposed to be an elder statesman." Woody seems to have taken ideological self-consistency particularly seriously: "In my family I made an extra effort to follow the Judeo-Christian ethic and made a deliberate effort to call other people when they didn't." But he also entertained a love of acting, music and platonic socializing. However, he abandoned these activities on entering the university for the sake of better concentrating on his goal of changing the world. Everything came to rest on academic training and performance.

The situation that consciously led him to try to take his own life was being unable to write a freshman paper to his satisfaction. There were no complaints from his professors but it seems clear he began to suffer from a sense of personal failure which he saw as incompetence. He says in the CI:

> I had a *crisis in competence,* as I called it then, which in itself is indicative of something. The final last straw was that I found myself incapable of doing academic work. My brain wouldn't work. I couldn't take mental leaps. I felt that there was a hurdle in front of me that I couldn't get over and *it was my fault.* What I had

written was garbage. I told myself "This is something you have to do, you seem unable to do it, go back and do it." People are often put in situations where they have to do something and *I felt this was my test of being a human being.* I'd gotten all these things. All my life I've been going to the best schools, I've lived a life of great luxury. I've worked very hard but I'd enjoyed it and had incredible help from my environment and *this was the time when I had to prove myself. It seemed perfectly reasonable to me and I couldn't do it.*

His crisis, then, is construed as failing to perform what he agrees is a "perfectly reasonable" obligation. The obligation, in turn, is construed with a sensitivity to socio-economic role. His brain, the trained instrument that must carry out the obligation to which he has freely committed himself, is letting him down. He is thus obstructed from carrying out a social duty he views as existing independently of professors', parents' or friends' personal expectations of him. It is the independent perspective and sense of social objectivity in these thoughts that indicates their Stage 4 organization.

Woody carried out his attempted suicide in conditions of privacy, experiencing frustration at its physical difficulty but apparently experiencing no mental or emotional difficulty at the task. In fact he emphasizes that it seemed an act like any other in the sense of requiring consistent work for its successful completion. His account shows a conscientious calmness that the doctors saw as lack of proper emotion. He relates the event in a way that shows it was not an explosion of chaotic or disorganized thought, conveying an unglamorous sense of conviction about his actions. He continues in the CI:

There was a sensation of pain but it didn't have the stopping effect that pain normally has. There was no instinct of self-preservation, no moment when something clicked. *I was waiting for something to click and it never did.*

I suggest we take seriously the idea that his self-execution was supported by convinced judgment, and that no competing judgment of a systematically argued excuse or reprieve intervened. Insofar as the worth of his own life was on trial, then it was as if no organized case for the defense "clicked" into place to mediate the case for the prosecution. There is no ultimate redeeming feature within Stage 4 reasoning to excuse social failure of this perceived sort.

Let us turn now to the MJI material to see what can be added to our understanding of why Woody had been convinced he was without worth, or that his death was justified. In the Heinz dilemma, the interviewer probes Woody's reasoning on the value of life in general. Woody suggests that a country's legal system will oppose systematic stealing but that Heinz is right to steal the life-saving drug for his wife because "no human institution can foster death." This reasoning apparently uses a post-conventional, i.e., post-Stage 4, social perspective. The interviewer tests out this scoring hunch by trying to disconfirm it. The

interviewer offers a conventional Stage 4 countersuggestion which posits maintenance of a social system as an ultimate value taking precedence over any individual right to life. Although Woody resists the countersuggestion in the present,
he also asserts that at the time of his suicide he would have accepted its conventional logic.

> BUT SHOULD ALL HUMAN INSTITUTIONS CONSIDER ALL LIVES
> EQUALLY? PRESUMABLY THEY COULD ALLOW THE DEATH OF SOME
> AND NOT OTHERS IN ORDER TO SURVIVE? OR SHOULD THEY TREAT
> ALL LIVES EQUALLY?[1]
>
> Well, you are contrasting two principles that have been the center of debate in
> ethical philosophy for a long time. That of treating lives equally versus the max-
> imization of the survival of society where individual lives become relative to that
> good. And which side will I take? *Five weeks ago* I would have taken the latter side
> but now I'll say all lives should be treated equally, and that if there is an absolute
> moral sense then there's no reason for thinking a philosopher is any better than a
> janitor in an absolute sense. If you wanted a society to survive, well then of course
> you would kill the philosopher. That was a joke.

If we trust Woody's self knowledge here, then the implication is that at the time
he attempted suicide his reasoning about the value of life, and presumably the
worth of his own life, was evaluated within a Stage 4 perspective. Five weeks
later, at the time of this interview, he is already reaching beyond that perspective
in his ideas about absolute moral worth in which janitor and philosopher are
equal. This is accomplished by differentiating people from their roles in the
prevailing social system and in turn integrating them into a new category, as
members of a species that exists prior to particular social organization. This view
expresses a qualitative change in the form of social perspective-taking and a
move to principled or post-conventional moral reasoning (transitional Stage 4/5).

What we find in the next section are the emotional catalysts and accompani-
ments to this developmental transition. The transition is from a societally construed self, its single-system referenced duties, and its "crisis in competence"
towards moral post-conventionality and a new form of ego integrity and self-
composure—described by Kegan (1982) as interdependent systems equilibrium
(see the Appendix, Stage 5).

Post-Suicidal Recovery Analysis

As we have already previewed, part of Woody's recovery from suicidal despair
and part of his coming to feel justified in living involves a structural reworking of
his assumptions about the value of life in general. The MJI and CI material
together reveal some of the emotional and personal aspects of this developmental

---

[1]In all quotations from interview data, words spoken by the interviewer are capitalized.

movement as he describes metamorphosing feelings about the worth of his own life and of those like him in their societal dysfunctionality or "incompetence." He confides:

> The suicidal act itself and what followed has been the swiftest humbling I've ever received—moving from one who is independent to one who is dependent. . . One week I was a student and the next, there I was in a lunatic asylum with all these crazy people, and discovering that they were no more crazy than myself, and not crazy at all. And it wasn't hard to make a mental leap from these people and myself to people who have done much worse things or much more inexplicable things. And I was amazed to find that every person in the entire ward was an interesting person with all sorts of qualities that made them attractive. And they've asked me why I haven't gotten angry at people. I am so delighted to find that everybody here has something I can like about them. And I'm delighted to find that highblown academic intellectual liberal philosophy actually has some emotional bearing. That's something really hard to get at.

As Woody loses some more conventionally snobbish preconceptions, we again see that human value is no longer relativized by an ultimate concern with promoting the optimal functioning and established standards of a social system. That is, a Stage 4 social perspective is not taken.

Significantly, I think, there are several places in the interview material where Woody connects this moral reconceptualization of the value of life with a newly formed appreciation of interdependent interaction. For instance, in another part of the MJI, Woody argues that it is important to keep promises and contracts "because false communication limits the uses of communication." The interviewer probes why he thinks it important to preserve communication and he replies:

> Because it permits interdependence. And why do you want to permit interdependence? Because I found 5 weeks ago (at suicide) that my great goal was independence and being able to handle a big problem myself, and thinking it was weakness to ask for help. Well, it would not have been a weakness to ask for help, and, if I had, then this wouldn't have happened and I would be considerably stronger. And I think that applies to almost everything. That strength comes from interdependence as opposed to independence. Therefore false communication is a weakness.

This new valuing of interdependent dialogue and communicative interaction is echoed in his reasoning about the value of law. In the MJI he says:

> I think humans need only one law, and that is that they won't kill themselves, they won't kill each other. After that anything is possible. You can yell and scream at each other until you're blue in the face, and build countries and nations and get rid of them and do whatever you like, but you can't kill because that makes argument impossible. . . And so I get a little astonished when on the ward people are still afraid of me hurting myself.

What Woody seems to be building in these thoughts is a new concept of strength that he applies to himself and to human survival in general. His previous sense of strength or integrity was tied to experiences of independent self-sufficiency that were tested by, for example, the ability to consistently adhere to a Judeo-Christian ethic; i.e., to single-system conviction and consistency. The new development in his thinking is an ability to conceptualize strength, integrity, truth, and what is right as differentiable from any one particular ideology, as freed from specific content. These values become newly identified with the form of dialogue itself, with communication and interplay. This distinction is used by Habermas (1979) and by Kohlberg et al. (1983) to define dialectical cognition in mature ego and post-conventional moral organization: Habermas refers to a highest level of "communicative competence" and Kohlberg refers to a highest stage of justice reasoning or of "ideal role-taking."

In the analysis so far, Woody's recovery from suicidal living is supported in his own view by changes in perception of the value of life and of the value of independence versus interdependence. The suggestion has been that these issues are bound up in changing his understanding of personal integrity and strength, and I have been arguing that all these changes are expressions of rejecting Stage 4 structuring of social reality, and are expressions of developmental progress. The changing natures of personal integrity and strength are also strikingly involved in a third area of recovery experience that Woody describes in the CI. This is his insight into the existence and power of the unconscious as a source of his reasoning and behavior. As we shall see, his perception of the role of the unconscious in his life involves further elaboration of the themes of integrity, dialogue between interdependent systems, and strength, into a new area of conflict perception. That is to say, this third aspect of crisis raises issues concerning the exercise of power, the nature of justified authority, and the nature of self-control. This debate resembles the changing conception of integrity and strength, which we have already traced.

In the CI, Woody says that before his recent suicide attempt he had not taken the notion of the unconscious very seriously. He adds:

> It took me an event of this magnitude to look far enough to see other examples in my life when my unconscious has behaved for me. And in that sense I'm profoundly grateful for it. Before this happened I very strongly felt that my rational intelligence was capable of keeping all irrational forces under control.

Here it is as if the unconscious was lost or subjugated under the authority of a single-system (Stage 4) view of what rationality must be. He goes on:

> I used to submerge anger, lust, jealousy, depression, disappointment, all those things that I felt were unnecessary to a good human life, mainly because they seemed irrational. But they are necessary. Well, they are there, and it's better to let

them come to the surface so they can be recognized rather than have them come out in strange ways. I would like to move towards being as reasonable but as healthy as possible.

We seem to be seeing here the beginning of a, so to speak, more democratic conversation between two systems of organization: the "rational" and the unconscious. The psychological possibility of this happening is evidence that structural transition and reorganization is taking place. This is so because, from the point of view of maintaining the power or authority of a Stage 4 single-system view of rationality, admitting the unconscious into one's ontology as a competing or alternative organizing system of motivation is necessarily a revolutionary threat. In the past it seems that a Stage 4 construction of authority was rigidly or unaccommodatively defended by Woody's denial or delegitimization of "irrationally" organized emotions. But in the act of suicide the Stage 4 view of rationality loses its authority because, as Woody admits, the competing unconscious system actually won for a while in organizing and carrying through his attempted execution: "Something clicked and everything I did from then on was simply deranged." By this important admission, by letting in this insight, Woody is able to grasp a developmental opportunity out of the defeat of Stage 4 authority and Stage 4 self-control that his suicide represents. The developmental opportunity lies in recognizing the need to more democratically dialogue with or integrate the "irrational" system of emotions into a concept of rationality that is itself structurally intersystemic. This means giving up an old and bankrupt form of self and self-control. It also means finding a new form of self and of its control in the ongoing process of structural development. This is the suggestion of the following passage from the CI at followup:

I inherited from my mother a problem: how to get power and how to use it when you've got it . . . that's why I took my life. But now the more I think about it, there's a pleasure in sitting back and *allowing things to happen as they happen rather than controlling*. That typified the first quarter of my life and it's no fun at all. It's very uncomfortable and as far as I know there's nothing creative I've done that's really good that came from that kind of discipline. *There's a certain authority that comes in the long run from sitting back*—but I'd hesitate to call it authority.

In this analysis I have drawn on material in which Woody describes changes in his interpretation of the value of life, and of the nature of strength, integrity, self-control and authority. Woody has cited these changes as new ways of resolving old conflicts and as new insurance against suicide. I have tried to suggest how these subjective experiences of change are expressions of a structural revolution in which Stage 4 views are found bankrupt and rejected while the construction of a Stage 5 social perspective is underway. Kegan (1982) has noted that, relatively speaking, all prior stages of structural-equilibrative development are logically and experientially limited in comparison with later developmental stages. He also has commented of the Stage 4/5 transition that it allows tolerance of paradox and carries an ''opened up'' quality in comparison with its ''sealed up'' more restricted Stage 4 predecessor. This more accommodating ''opened up'' quality rings through Woody's closing remarks of the CI as he contrasts child and adult parts of himself in a changing view of the nature of maturity. He says: ''The adult part of me has to do with compassion, reasonableness, tolerance. The ability to adapt to changing situations with compassion. . . This affable quality: resiliance, softness, flexibility. Almost a kind of wisdom.''

CASE 2 - PAUL

Paul is also first interviewed about 5 weeks after his suicide attempt. He is white, age 20 at first interview, and is also from a professional family background. Paul dropped out of college after one semester, then started and gave up a series of jobs. He has shared apartments with friends, periodically returning home to live with his parents. He was living at his parents' house at the time of his suicide attempt. He says he has been very depressed for the 5 years before his suicide attempt. While in the hospital he seems indefinite about wanting to live. At the time of first interview, while on the psychiatric unit, Paul uses predominantly Stage 3 reasoning on the MJI and justifies his own suicide in Stage 3 terms. In the year followup his reasoning on the MJI has become transitional with a Stage 3/4 global score. At followup Paul seems much more convinced about his decision to live and has not reattempted suicide.

Retrospective Suicide Analysis

Paul says that, prior to his suicide attempt, he had been feeling more upset at the end of a love relationship than he could really explain to himself. It had been the last in a long line of what he felt were failed relationships. They seemed to start out well in the sense that his lovers admired his precocity and uniqueness, but they ended with the lovers feeling he was immature and dependent. Paul had also been frustrated in a recent attempt to get a job. This had also been the most recent in a long line of failures. He cannot seem to turn the jobs into careers; he gets bored, feels uncomfortable with the other people at work, and leaves without explanation. Aware of these thoughts, Paul says he became ''overwhelmed by feelings of failure'' and decided to end his life ''feeling undepressed for the first time in a long while.''

In a suicide note to named family members Paul found it important to say that he loved them very much and that everyone should get over his death as soon as possible to ''continue (their) productive lives.'' He added ''I wouldn't know anything about that.'' When asked in the CI what it would take for him to value his own life, he answers vaguely "being successful," explaining that this means other people knowing him as the best at something or other. There is a suggestion in all this that being of worth is determined by popular opinion. At the same time he is agonizingly aware that he is not thought of by others as a success, that people do not call him productive. The conduct of his own life seems to fall short of shared norms and conventional practices and this is painful to him. His suicide note ends by saying that everyone will be all right, even "happier," without him. He later recalls: "Part of why I attempted suicide was to get out of people's hair and *stop letting people down.*"

If we take Paul seriously here, then the implication is that in Paul's logic at this time there is an absolute duty to live up to expectations, and also that one's own self-expectations and others' expectations of the self are not clearly differentiated. This belief also operates axiomatically in Stage 3 social perspective-taking. If one cannot live up to normed expectations then the ultimate purpose of actions and of life seems to be gone. Put another way, the hypothetical argument "Just because people don't like you and don't approve of what you do does not mean that you as a person have no value" counts as self-contradictory within the interpersonal logic of Stage 3 structure.

Both Woody and Paul seem to be aware of having suffered before their suicide attempts, not so much from experiences of loss as from experiences in which they feel they have failed. Each in his own way could be described as having felt he could not carry on his work. However, the experienced relation of self to world in carrying on work was distinct in each case. It was distinguished by level of socio-moral perspective-taking, evidenced on the MJI and CI. Woody's experience of failure was to not live up to impersonal societal role obligations. Paul's failure was that he made people he knew unhappy. Woody's failure is inexcusable within a Stage 4 organization because it undermines the Stage 4 social-system-maintenance frame of reference itself. Similarly Paul's failure—letting down personally known people—undermines the Stage 3 interpersonally organized frame of reference itself, and is in that sense ultimately inexcusable within Stage 3 logic.

In the MJI Paul himself reflects on the self-destructive aspect of letting people down, as he reasons about the importance of contract and promise-keeping. Asked why it is important to keep a promise, Paul replies:

> Well, this hits home as far as I'm concerned. And it becomes very upsetting when you've kept so few promises and lied so many times that your word doesn't hold very much weight. It's important to have trust because, well, *what a person says or does seems pretty insignificant if the people who are hearing that don't believe it or don't put much weight in it.* I'm trying to think of something else but I can't.

In the interpersonal Stage 3 world view, who one is and what one believes is not yet differentiated from others' opinions. Just this differentiation will mark the coming independence of a Stage 4 self-construction. In contrast, at Stage 3, a means of confirming self-integrity is being able to share in others' approval of oneself and in others' approval of one's personal reputation. Viability within Stage 3 organization rests on not undermining the experience of "we." This concern emerges clearly in Paul's reasoning about the value of life in the MJI, where he does not seem to have a justification for valuing human life that is independent of someone else giving it value through positive personal feeling for the person whose life it is. For example:

WHY SHOULD HEINZ TRY TO SAVE HIS WIFE'S LIFE?
Well, actually it didn't say anything about—I just assumed that it was his wife and he loved her. But it didn't say anything about that did it? It didn't say "his wife, whom he loved dearly, is dying" did it?

SO IF HE DOESN'T LOVE HER?
Well, he clearly has some feeling for her if he's that set on keeping her alive.

In this passage the interviewer notes that Paul seems to find the existence of close personal feelings the single most critical feature in deciding whether it is right to break a law in order to save a life. This would be a characteristic of Stage 3 reasoning. The interviewer then tries to disprove this scoring hunch by counter-suggesting the absence of loving feelings. The opportunity is thus offered to Paul to frame a more impartial Stage 4 argument for the value of life—an argument that could attach positive value to life independently of actual personal feeling. Significantly, the opportunity is passed over by Paul who persists in framing the situation within Stage 3 logic. Paul then continues:

And I don't approve of the druggist putting money over human life. WHY? Well, I guess that he would have no—I mean—*Well, I guess there's really no good reason for him to put that woman that he doesn't know over his $2,000.* But I'm looking at it from her husband's point of view.

WELL, WHY DO YOU THINK IN GENERAL THAT MONEY SHOULDN'T BE PUT OVER LIFE?
I feel like a real shit not being able to answer this one.

In this passage the interviewer is reminded of a transitional Stage 3/4 point in the MJI scoring manual when Paul begins to express a hierarchy of values in implying that life should be more important than money. Paul is asked to elaborate this suggestion, but again passes up the opportunity and remakes a Stage 3 appeal to absence of a close relationship as the determining factor the druggist should act upon. Nevertheless, Paul's closing remark suggests he himself begins to sense the inadequacy of the Stage 3 perspective. What comes through these responses is a systematic difficulty Paul has in even getting to grips with a concept of human value if it is not identified with a concept of immediate loving affiliation. In a Stage 3 interpersonal epistemology these concepts are not yet differentiated.

In the CI we again find the characteristic Stage 3 confusion of facts about the self with others' opinions about the self. In the CI this perspective is taken in regard to ego rather than moral issues. Paul says: "One weakness in my relationship with my mother is that she has a tendency to say "Oh come on, dear, that's not really you," or "You don't really feel that way." And that's sometimes all it takes for me to decide "Yeah, she's right" and just disregard how I was really feeling."

However, perhaps the fact that Paul is able to reflect on his relationship with his mother, in a way that seems dissatisfied with its Stage 3 limitations, suggests that a transitional perspective is already taking shape. The same tacit criticism is audible in his description of what he felt immediately before he tried to kill himself: "I would do or perform whatever people ask of me without imposing my own will." At this point in time, however, he seems unable to experience himself as distinct from this way of behaving. In rejecting the behavior he rejects himself.

The sense of personal failure, then, has two aspects in Paul's case. The first is described by Paul on followup as "I didn't see how I was going to stop letting people down. I couldn't see any other way out (than suicide)." We can describe this as a failure of integrity within a Stage 3 socio-moral perspective, a failure to live up to its terms. The second aspect of failure is a beginning perception of the limitation or lack of integrity of Stage 3 organization itself. This is the recognition of a confusion between what the self feels, believes, and wills with what interpersonally known others feel, believe and will.

Post-Suicide Recovery Analysis

Unlike Woody, who quite rapidly after his suicide attempt came to actively reject it, Paul's initial "recovery" while on the hospital unit seems without personal will:

> "It was mostly the staff and my parents that contributed to the change (from acting suicidally). It was necessary that I back down from my standpoint and decide, okay, you're better to judge."

We know from the MJI that during hospitalization Paul is using a Stage 3 perspective. It may be more accurate to say that Paul's remark expresses the activity of a Stage 3 will that is still fused with the wills of personally known others. In just that sense he does not impose an independent will. Significantly, at followup a year after discharge, and when Paul is using transitional Stage 3/4 reasoning on the MJI, he says of this initial "recovery" that "I was railroaded."

The lack of Stage 4 independent agency in Paul's first recovery statement contrasts with Woody's self assertive perspective: "It was *my* opinion 2 days after waking up in the hospital that something was terribly wrong." I am suggesting that Paul's initial recovery is not a thoroughgoing developmental passage, for in his initial recovery statement we do not find the self related differently to others in any qualitative sense. There is the same deferential identification with others' definitions of what is the case. The only change is that the social environment is colluding to bolster a more positive Stage 3 perception of the self's worth. Others are insisting that Paul is after all interpersonally valued, and that to think otherwise is mistaken. In this we can see that what is true is still identified with shared opinion, and that if others believe he is of value then that is both necessary and sufficient for Paul to value his life, or at least to devalue his death choice.

Between hospital discharge and followup Paul spends many months in individual psychotherapy and lives with his family. Other changes take place besides his coming to judge that he was railroaded back to life by well-wishers. He becomes more agentive, and freed from the tyranny of others' personal feeling about him. This shows in the fact that it becomes tolerable to him to define himself in a way that *risks* others' good opinion of him. This psychological position has not been tolerable or ultimately viable within the prior Stage 3 organization. An example of this change can be seen in his self-description in the followup CI: "I'm much more up front about myself. So people can take care of themselves and not have me let them down." Paradoxically, being prepared to take this risk seems to herald a new capacity to be close with people, to be with them as an independent person, rather than as an appearance in their perceptions or object of their opinions. Some appreciation of this emerging Stage 4 freedom may lie behind Paul's remark on followup: "I can tell how good I feel by how much I listen to others and participate and don't care if my hair is messed up."

As previously noted, at first interview Paul was already showing some transitional awareness of the bankruptcy of his Stage 3 perspective in the CI material when talking about his relationship with his mother. This transitionality is maintained and extended during the intervening year to a point where Paul experiences his beliefs and wishes as quite distinct from those of others, even in the case where their surface content is identical. This is clear in the CI when on followup he says that he wants to continue therapy, but not for the sake of harmony in the home nor to satisfy his parents, even though he knows they are delighted by his wish. *His* reason, not theirs, is that there are "issues *I* want to go into, like the job thing." Behind his words the ultimate purpose of life seems to be transitionally reshaping from fostering mutual approval (Stage 3) to a more autonomous commitment formation (Stage 4):

> You see, I want to make a commitment at some point. But I just don't feel ready to make it. I don't feel I know enough about what I want and what is right for me . . . I guess confused is really the way I'd describe myself right now.

It is significant, I think, that this confusion does not make Paul feel suicidal. This confusion can be seen as a property of transitionality, which itself demonstrates flexibility in structuring reality, in contrast to the rigidity or intransigence seen earlier in his defense of Stage 3 reasoning about the value of life, which underpinned his own sense of personal failure. In contrast, Paul's followup reasoning about the value of life on the MJI shows transitional development beyond a Stage 3 perspective. There is a more sustained assertion of a Stage 3/4 value hierarchy that places the value of life above the value of law than was evident at first interview.

> Two thousand dollars seems like such bullshit in comparison to trying to save Heinz's wife's life. *But there are really no laws around that. I don't see it as much of a conflict as I do that one has its place and so does the other, and one has more importance than the other.*

WHY IS THE HUMAN SPHERE MORE IMPORTANT THAN THE LEGAL?
It just flashed through my mind, may be the right to hold on to our possessions is almost a human right. It has laws attached to it. I don't know if I can answer why one is more important.

At transitional Stage 3/4 the hierarchy of values is based on emotional intuition as opposed to the logically analytical rationale of Stage 5 justifications of the hierarchy. A Stage 5 perspective can distinguish logical priority even among human rights. Thus the interviewer probed for a Stage 5 principled ordering of hierarchy but Paul responded with at best a beginning Stage 4 legalistic systems perspective on human rights. Nevertheless, his reasoning shows developmental advance over his previous Stage 3 reasoning about the value of life.

CONCLUSION TO THE CASE STUDIES

In the two preceding case studies we have been following passages from suicidal psychological breakdown to relative recovery when the subjects were no longer suicidal. Although their psychoanalytic diagnoses were identical (Boderline Personality organization) the case analyses have demonstrated that these selves and their worlds that have broken down are systematically different in structural-developmental organization. These differences had consequences for the meaning given to events, for the subjective experience of crisis, and for the subjective experience of improvement. An aim of the case studies was to show that although hospital physicians gave diagnoses of Borderline Personality to Woody and Paul, in part because their suicidal acts appeared impulsive and irrational, developmental analyses of their first-hand subjective experiences reveal the normal socio-logical and psycho-logical assumptions and considerations in which these suicidal acts seemed justified or made sense to the subjects. It was these socio-moral structural assumptions and considerations that the subjects themselves later judged invalid or limited and came to reject in their developmental passages to recovery. These two cases can both be called developmental passages because they involve constructive revision of the perspective and value assumptions of a previous structuring of social reality. Thus the case studies show how normal processes of cognitive restructuring were involved in dissipating or resolving the real life conflicts and issues to which Woody and Paul attributed their breakdowns. In particular, restructuring their perceptions of the value of life seems to function as an insurance against the experience of failure and lack of personal worth that Woody and Paul suffered from when they tried to kill themselves. Thus, besides revealing that different stages of meaning organization were involved in each breakdown experience, the case studies revealed a similarity between the cases in the process of recovery.

The tendency in structural developmental analyses is to become fixated on stages and to lose sight of process. I conclude the case studies by emphasizing their documentation of structural process because it seems to me that it is features of process rather than properties of stages *per se* that illuminate whatever abnormality or suicidal pathology we find in the cases.

In both cases we saw that Woody and Paul judged that real-life events showed their lives to be chronically failing. They were failing against what we can see as stage-related criteria of the value of life and of how life ought to be lived. At the time they attempted suicide neither Woody nor Paul could relinquish their criteria. Neither was able to restructure his view of the basic value of life until later. Thus, at suicide, life was simultaneously experienced as necessarily having to be a certain way, and also as personally unlivable that way: "It seemed perfectly reasonable to me and I couldn't do it" (Woody): "I didn't see how I was going to stop letting people down. I couldn't see any other way out" (Paul).

What seems to add the suicidally despairing aspect to what would otherwise be a puzzling existential dilemma is the rigidity or inflexibility of conviction. At first Woody and Paul are not able to respond to their perception of existential conflict by flexible inquiry, but rather feel stuck, paralyzed, and reason dogmatically in the face of conflict. At the time of their attempted suicides Woody and Paul are without doubt, without confusion and without disequilibrium in the matter of the value of life in general and of their own life in particular. At suicidal breakdown they follow through on their judgments about life worth by trying to remove themselves, convinced it is not within their control to just remove the failing behavior they are showing. In addition, at suicide, they are also unable to really doubt the structural bases upon which they judge the value of life, for they are still embedded in those structures and do not yet have a transitional disembedding perspective on the issue of the value of life. But, significantly, it is precisely this rigidity of conviction that changes and becomes more flexible in the stage-transitional process of recovery. At recovery, there begins to be what we may call transitional cognitive pheonomena: doubt and cognitive disequilibrium, confusion and rejection of previous stands, a tentative deepening of appreciation of facts and possibilities. As teachers we are familiar with these phenomena as characteristics of progressive classroom debate and inquiry. As clinicians we become interested in these phenomena because it is via these transitional processes that, for example, the bases upon which Woody and Paul value their lives begin to change. As a consequence it is no longer the value of the subject's own life that is felt to be contradicted by events, but rather it is the validity of the old way of valuing life that begins to be seen as contradicted by events.

Paul's case departs from this picture of a naturally restorative process in the middle of its history. This is during the period of his initial recovery, which he later describes as being "railroaded" back to life. In that first, nondevelopmental recovery he is able to avoid the prior contradictions to positively valuing his life because, rather than communicating to him that he has let them down, important others instead insist his life does have value. This social change of emphasis provides somewhat tenuous safety. That it proved inadequate life protection for the long haul is suggested by the fact that on followup, avoidance of conflict has been replaced by the restructuring engagement with conflict measurable in transitional Stage 3/4 reasoning on the MJI and described in the case study of his recovery.

DISCUSSION

These cases were taken from an ongoing research project investigating the structural-developmental dimensions of pathological breakdown in a group of adolescents and young adults (Hewer, 1983a; Rogers, 1983). The relevance of this research is hopefully directable to a wider audience than practicing clinical psychologists. There is a common ground shared by clinician and educator within the structural-developmental theoretical framework used in this chapter. Both types of professionals attend to natural processes of development and try to accompany the people living through developmental passages in a manner that assists the person in making sense of what seems to be happening in their lives. Both sorts of professionals try to create a setting and a relationship that promotes engagement with living and its conflicts, rather than withdrawal from them. Both types of professionals are concerned with the development of reality testing and the activity of intelligence in the sense of discrimination and choice making (intellect: from the Latin inter-, between + legere, choose). From a structural-developmental point of view, there is a shared understanding between educator and clinician that, structurally speaking, "growing up" depends on being able to experience conflict with tolerable anxiety, responding to it with disequilibrium and then re-equilibration within a more powerful structure of experience organization and knowledge. Piaget (1975/1978) remarked:

> It is worthwhile to note that however the nonbalance arises, it produces the driving force of development. Without this, knowledge remains static. The real source of

progress is to be sought in both the insufficiency responsible for the conflict and the improvement expressed in the equilibration. Without the non-balance there would be no increasing equilibration. Re-equilibration expresses the obtained improvement. (p. 13)

The preceding case studies have tried to map progress by revealing structuring insufficiencies responsible for conflict experience, and by indicating the substantive improvements in living and conflict management, including rejection of suicide, that accompanied structural progress. Döbert and Nunner-Winkler (1982) have made the point that stage structural developmental analyses of reasoning may be extremely cogent in showing why a person finds a certain state of affairs *problematic* or conflictual, but are not adequate in providing causal explanations of a person's *response* to the perceived problem. That is, formal structural analyses neither account for why someone would respond progressively by restructuring (as these two subjects eventually did), nor why they might respond suicidally (as these subjects did at first) or with some other form of stress expression such as stuttering. To the extent that I agree with Döbert and Nunner-Winkler's point, I would wish these studies to be seen as descriptive of a process of breakdown and recovery in conflict management, rather than as causally explanatory of suicidal response. They are primarily rational reconstructions of two people's judging first that suicide was justified, and later coming to reject this position. Recovering suicide cases are useful as markers of psychological breakdown and recovery in the face of conflict, and their study can be useful to those whose primary interest is conflict management rather than pathology. Structural developmental analyses such as those of the case studies discussed earlier ultimately show whether or not there is resistance to structural disequilibrium for subjects at different times. They fall short of explaining why there is resistance. It is interesting to note, however, that suicidologists from a variety of theoretical backgrounds and using a variety of tests and measures, have repeatedly found "inflexibility" a character feature correlating highly with suicide and its attempts (Lester & Lester, 1971). It may be that resistance to disequilibrium and restructuring is the structural-developmental analogue of this general inflexibility feature (see Hewer, 1983b for a further discussion of "equilibrative inflexibility" and "unaccommodative structural defense").

However, even if we accept Döbert and Nunner-Winkler's point that formal structural analyses can explain why there is conflict but cannot explain individual responses to conflict, nevertheless structural developmental approaches to educational practice can be of help to those who would create settings that nurture rather than impede the processes of structural equilibration and development (Gardner, 1983; Mosher, 1980). Here is the point where therapy and education become not parallel but identical enterprises—creating settings that are experienced as safe enough in which to relax rigid defenses, and that encourage free or flexible inquiry, so as to permit participation with others who are different, and engagement with conflict without intolerable anxiety.

Appendix

STRUCTURAL-DEVELOPMENTAL STAGES: AMALGAM OF KOHLBERG'S SOCIO-MORAL AND KEGAN'S SELF-OTHER STRUCTURAL ORGANIZATIONS

Stage 2 When Stage 2 organization operates, the moral domain and the level of perspective used in it are presocially and egocentrically referenced. Right acts are those which are instrumental in furthering the isolated self's hedonistic needs and wishes. Wrong acts are those with negative or thwarting consequences to the same. Experience is concretized. Not only is there an absence of abstract appreciation of "we-ness" that could include the self who sees through another's perspective, but also there is a view of the self as a concrete possession over which one has absolute ownership and use rights. The construction of self and its relation to other is shaped by an ability to author one's own impulse-filled wishes and to manage them over time through co-operative, postponed gratification. There is a kind of psychological tyranny of chance and opportunism, because who I am and what is true is not yet differentiated from chance and opportunism. For Stage 2 reasoners, events that risk the integrity of opportunistic autocracy and the power to manipulate, are the ultimate threats to stability: If I cannot get what I want, I am not viable.

Stage 3. When Stage 3 organization operates, the moral domain and the level of perspective used in it extends to face-to-face social relationships known by sociologists as the "primary group." It has the psychologic of interpersonalism, orienting to mutuality of feeling and shared norms of concordance and harmony in personally felt relations. The notion of "the good" is somewhat trapped in stereotypes of what is "nice" because the good is that which functions

365

to maintain approval from personally known others. The construction of self and its relationship to other is shaped by an ability to coordinate two egocentric perspectives into the construction of a "we" identity. There is a kind of psychological tyranny of the group in my self-definition and the definition of what is true, because who I am is not yet differentiated from (is confused with) personal relationship with the in-group, its mutuality of feeling and norm sharing. That is, there is confusion between what are *my* feelings and beliefs about this and that, and what are *others'*: what is good is that which meets with generalized personal approval. Crudely, if everyone agrees then it is right, and if I do not match up to the approved in-group stereotypes then I am not understandable to myself or to the world. For Stage 3 reasoners, events that risk the integrity of the shared context mobilize the self's defensive operations.

Stage 4.   The qualitative gain of Stage 4 over Stage 3 is in being able to coordinate and include disparate small group values in a secondary more complex social system perspective. At Stage 4, I bring a third party perspective to organizing experience, aware of itself looking at itself in relationship to others. I have become differentiated from the interpersonal "we," and "I" become an independent entity that comes to relationships with a separate identify. My self is not defined within personal relationships but rather within socio-cultural systems and ideologies. My level of perspective extends to broad impersonal society and perceives its cultural institutions. I construe myself and my actions in terms of societal powers and responsibilities. It is accepted at Stage 4 that an impersonal system with institutions, agencies and ethical codes of practice is needed to regulate and adjudicate the legitimate interests of quite disparate small groups. There is an ultimate focus not on mutuality of feeling (you do not have to feel as I do) but on systematic organization, consistency in performance of duty, and the determination of cases by systematic rule (you do have to rationalize as I do). There is a sort of tyranny of the system at Stage 4 because if something is consistent with the system then it is by definition not wrong. The system defends against or resists having its control relativized by a competing system, by systematic dissent. The self is identified with the system it is trying to run smoothly. Crudely, Stage 3's concern for niceness and approval gives way to an ultimate concern for consistency and respect. The ultimate question is no longer "Do you like me?" but rather "Will you show respect for the way I do things?" At Stage 4, concern for self is expressed in vigilance towards a hard-won sense of independence.

Stage 5.   When Stage 5 organization operates, a prior-to-society socio-moral perspective has been constructed and is used to coordinate claims of conflicting societies and ideological cultures within a moral domain extending to the globally human or species context. General principles rather than codified rules are the appropriate tools to resolve dispute and to determine the right and the true. This level of perspective is that which coordinates systems and is grounded in a concept of self as an individual human being differentiated from a particular culture but included in and subject to universal human conditions. In this sense the significance of oneself and one's actions have a global or species relevance. However, Kegan writes that whereas at Stage 4 one's feelings seem often to be regarded as a kind of recurring administrative problem which the successful ego-administrator resolves without damage to the smooth functioning of the organization, at Stage 5 the interior life gets freed-up or broken open, permitting a new dynamic flow of playfulness. This is the result of a new capacity of the self to move back and forth between psychic systems within itself and the other. Conflict and ambiguity both become recognizable and tolerable as interior conversation (not external threat as at Stage 4) in a more powerful psychologic which creates the space for systems to interpenetrate and be interdependent.

REFERENCES

Colby, A. & Kohlberg, L. (in press). Measuring moral judgment: *A theory and method of assessment*. Vols. 1 and 2. New York: Cambridge University.

Colby, A., Kohlberg, L., Gibbs, J., Candee, D., Speicher-Dubin, B., Hewer, A., & Power, C. (1982). *Standard Form Scoring Manual*. Cambridge: Moral Education Resource Foundation.

Döbert, R. & Nunner-Winkler, G. (1982). *Formal and material role-taking: The understanding of suicide among adolescents and young adults*. Unpublished manuscript, Max-Planck-Institute, Munich.

Gardner, E. (1983). *Moral education for the emotionally disturbed early adolscent*. Lexington, MA: D.C. Heath & Co.

Habermas, J. (1979). *Communication and the evolution of society*. (T. McCarthy, Trans.). Boston, MA: Beacon.

Habermas, J. (in press). Interpretive social science versus hermeneuticism. In N. Haan, R. Bellah & W. Sullivan (Eds.), *Social science as moral inquiry*. New York: Columbia University.

Hewer, A. (1983a). *A structural-developmental investigation of psychological breakdown and its management in a psychiatrically hospitalized group of adolescents and young adults*. Unpublished manuscript, Harvard University Graduate School of Education, Cambridge, MA.

Hewer, A. (1983b). *From conflict to suicide and revival: Disequilibrium and re-equilibration in experience of psychological breakdown and recovery*. Qualifying Paper, Harvard University Graduate School of Education, Cambridge, MA.

Kegan, R. (1982). *The Evolving self*. Cambridge, MA: Harvard University.

Kohlberg, L. (1976). Moral stages and moralization. In T. Lickona (Ed.), *Moral development and behavior: Theory research and social issues*. (pp. 31–53) New York: Holt, Rinehart and Winston.

Kohlberg, L., Levine, C., & Hewer, A. (1983). Moral stages: A current formulation and a response to critics. *Contributions to human development (Vol.10)*. New York: S. Karger.

Lester, G. & Lester, D. (1971). *Suicide*. Englewood Cliffs, New Jersey: Prentice Hall.

Mosher, R. (Ed.), (1980). *Moral education*. New York: Praeger.

Piaget, J. (1978). *The development of thought: Equilibration of cognitive structure*. Oxford, England: Basil Blackwell. (Original work published 1975).

Rogers, L. (1983). *Structural-developmental aspects of the experience of psychopathology in adolescents and young adults*. Unpublished manuscript, Harvard University Graduate School of Education, Cambridge, MA.

15 The Adolescent as Interpersonal Negotiator: Three Portraits of Social Development

Steven Brion-Meisels
The Judge Baker Guidance Center, Boston, MA.

Robert L. Selman
The Harvard Graduate School of Education

David is 15 years old. He wants to go to the movies with his friend Mark. When he comes into Mark's house, Mark is watching a football game on TV. David says, "Come on, let's go to the movies this afternoon." Mark doesn't want to go because he is more interested in watching the game. David says once more, "Come on, I wanna go." When Mark says no, David calls him a jerk and says, "OK. Forget it. You're stupid anyway. I'm leaving." He stomps out the door.

Amie is 15 years old. She wants to go to the movies with her friend Alice. When she comes into Alice's house, Alice is watching a basketball game on TV. Amie says, "Let's go to the movies." When Alice says she doesn't want to go, Amie tells her, "Come on, I really want to go. If you don't go, I'm not gonna come over to help you babysit anymore. You can just forget that."

Adam is 15 years old. He wants his friend Ray to go to the movies with him. When he comes into Ray's house, Ray is watching a soap on TV. Adam says, "Come on, let's go to the movies." Ray says he want to stay home. Adam tells him, "Come on, you'll really like it. You can always see the re-run of this. Besides I wanna go with someone. If you go with me now I'll help you babysit later."

Each of these adolescents has been involved in an important negotiation. Each has dealt with similar situations using a different strategy. They are representative of the kinds of situations in which adolescents often find themselves: caught between competing needs, often in new and confusing roles, and struggling to find new ways to resolve difficult conflicts.

Adults who work with adolescents, or who remember their own adolescence, can testify to the intense, confusing, and entangled changes that mark the years

369

between childhood and young adulthood. Biological, hormonal, affective, cognitive, and sociological changes—all combine in a compressed and critical series of transitions that affect the young adolescent's sense of self, as well as the relationship between this "new" self and the rest of the social world.

In terms of social development, these transitions represent an increase in the number and complexity of relationship-oriented tasks—for example, dealing with friends in a group context, changing classes in a high school environment, establishing working relationships with employers, and maintaining family ties despite increasing autonomy from parents. Furthermore, the transitions of early adolescence represent a move from one-way or dyadic relationships that involve only self-interested or reciprocal exchanges, to more stable relationships, for example, friendships that allow for mutual sharing and intimacy. Changes in tasks and relationships, combined with biological changes, create a new sense of the *self-in-relation-to-others*. This new sense of self is an essential element in a successful transition from childhood to adulthood.

The transitions of early adolescence take place in a number of different contexts, or situations: at home, at work, in school; with friends, with parents, with teachers and employers; in areas where the adolescent feels competent, as well as in areas where she or he feels fearfully incompetent. These changing situations require more sophisticated kinds of conceptual skills; they evoke (and are evoked by) a variety of new feelings. However, nested within all these complex and interactive variables, is one common process: negotiation. Each of these transitions requires that the adolescent *negotiate with others, to resolve some kind of social disequilibrium,* social disequilibria felt within the self as well as between self and other. A focus on the negotiation process and on the interpersonal strategies used by adolescents allows us to begin exploring some crucial developmental questions about the construction of a self-in-relation-to-others, a *social self.* For example, we can explore how adolescents resolve interpersonal conflicts with their friends, so that a stable and mutual friendship can be achieved. We can explore how adolescents negotiate conflicts in the workplace, with co-workers or employers, so that they can keep a job, create a positive employment record, and at the same time protect their personal interests and needs. We can explore how adolescents negotiate changes in their family roles, so that they can integrate their own needs for autonomy in a mutual relationship that maintains parental ties.

This chapter proposes a model for the study of certain aspects of interpersonal development, as well as a model of collaboration between theoretical and action research. As co-authors, we have brought to bear both independent and mutual interests in thinking about adolescent social development. Brion-Meisels's work is largely focused on psychological education, curriculum development, and the application of developmental theory and research in educational and clinical settings. Selman's work is largely focused on developmental research, methods of assessment, diagnosis and evaluation, and empirical work; this research draws on experiences in applied educational and clinical settings for purposes of constructing and validating basic social developmental theory. As collaborators on a project designed to improve the decision-making and negotiation strategies used by troubled adolescents, we have worked together to attempt to bridge the domains of theory and practice in the area of social competence.

Thus, our objective is to demonstrate how the events of a troubled adolescent's life, seen through the eyes of a practitioner, can be understood through the organizing lens of a developmental model of interpersonal behavior. We also show how real-world, fast-paced, intuitive observations in clinical contexts pose problems that challenge the normative model's validity—and force it to accommodate to the complex, rich reality of all adolescent life. Thus, we speak to two audiences, practitioners and researchers, to interest each in the other's work, and to demonstrate the importance of the joint study of "normality" and "pathology" in social development.

INTERPERSONAL NEGOTIATION STRATEGIES: A DEVELOPMENTAL APPROACH

Interpersonal negotiation strategies involve a sequence of interactions between two or more people in a meaningful social context; the negotiation attempts to resolve some kind of significant disequilibrium within and between the participants—that is, conflicting needs, interests or intentions. There are many ways to study this kind of interactive chain; however, our primary interests have been to study (a) the developmental aspects of interpersonal negotiation strategies (across ages, between normal and pathological groups, over time, and in different social contexts), and (b) the ways in which these strategies function in *naturalistic* educational contexts. These interests have determined both our research context and methods.

Thus far, we have examined negotiation strategies formally in three different settings, with three distinct groups of children and adolescents. One study observed and interviewed children age 8-11 in a 12-week, small-group after-school program in a public school. One focus for this study was to examine how normal pre-adolescent children begin to understand and use the negotiation strategies that allow for peer-group collaboration (Selman, Schorin, Stone, & Phelps, 1983). In a second study, we have observed and interviewed pairs of socially immature children age 8-11, in an on-going therapeutic intervention that is designed to help the children improve their ability to make and keep friends. One focus for this project is to understand how troubled pre-adolescents begin to rethink and modify dysfunctional negotiation strategies when placed in a structured, supportive context (Selman & Demorest, 1984). In the third study, which is the focus for this paper, we have observed and interviewed troubled adolescents who are involved in a therapeutic school curriculum called the Adolescent

Issues Program, whose goal is to help troubled youth improve their decision-making and self-control skills (Brion-Meisels, Lowenheim, & Rendeiro, 1982). One focus for this study has been to examine the interaction among cognitive, affective, and situational variables in determining an adolescent's choice of negotiation strategy. In all three studies, the context for studying the development of negotiation strategies has been one in which the self must work out new relationships with others—that is, a context in which we can observe a "new" social self in the process of being formed.

Our research thus far has combined the use of reflection-eliciting interviews and direct observational methods. Interviews with adolescents have adapted the open-ended techniques pioneered by Piaget (1932/1965), and Kohlberg (1969), by focusing on the presentation of common dilemmas that involve dealing with peers or adults around issues of sexuality, drugs, work and the law. The focus has been on ascertaining the strategies that adolescents believe are best used to deal with another individual in order to restore a state of interpersonal equilibrium. For example, one case asks the adolescent to resolve the following dilemma:

> John works in a grocery store after school. He is supposed to work for only 10 hours a week but his boss keeps asking him at the last minute to work really late on Friday night. Even though the boss pays him for his time, he doesn't like to be asked to work at the last minute. How do you think John should deal with his boss?

Responses are coded and analyzed in the context of a developmental model of interpersonal negotiation strategies. In our analysis, we are as interested in the strategies adolescents use to "deal with" others as in the actual decision (choice) they make in a given situation (e.g., to work late or go home).

Observations have focused on dyadic and small-group interactions in which there is a common task (e.g., a project, discussion, role-play, or problem-solving session). Two goals of our observations have been to collect and analyze episodes of interpersonal negotiation strategies, among peers and with adults, and to relate these observed strategies-in-use to the more reflective data collected through the interviews. In this way, we have begun to examine the interaction among thoughts, feelings, and the situation in determining the adolescent's choice of a negotiation strategy. In addition, the observations allows us to examine the emergence, over time, of a new social self—that is, of an adolescent in the process of working out new ways to relate to others and, thereby, a new sense of self in the social context.

Components of the Interpersonal Negotiation Strategies Levels System

The principal process we have used to categorize levels of negotiation strategies is the ability to understand and coordinate the social perspective of self and other(s) in resolving a conflict. Each new level of negotiation strategy is related to a new level of social perspective-taking (Selman, 1981). The relationship is explored in the case studies that follow, and is summarized in Table 15.1.

There are many ways to examine how an individual deals with the feelings that are brought to a negotiation situation. One strategy is to explore the degree to which he or she attempts to change the self to meet others' perceived needs versus the degree he or she attempts to change other to meet the self's needs. In our work, we have conceptualized this distinction by examining interpersonal episodes in which the adolescent's interpersonal orientation to affective diseq-uilibrium is to "transform" the *self*, or to "transform" the *other*. Although we have analyzed episodes in dichotomous terms (self- vs. other-transforming), most interactions contain elements of both orientations; and at the higher levels of our developmental sequence, orientations are integrated in collaborative strategies.

Variations in role and situation are often crucial in determining an adolescent's choice of strategy. For example, negotiating with an employer is a very different situation than negotiating with a peer. It has a different balance of power, it creates a different affective response, and it may necessitate different cognitive skills. Understanding the development and use of negotiation strategies as a vehicle for creating a new social self necessitates mapping out the situations in which an adolescent tries out new strategies, and analyzing emergent patterns.

Four Levels of Interpersonal Negotiation Strategies

Table 15.1 summarizes the four levels we have thus far begun to describe and analyze, and their relationship to cognitive and interpersonal orientation components. A brief description of each level will help concretize the information summarized in Table 15.1, and provide a framework for the case studies that follow.

Level 0: Impulsive (Unreflective) Physical Actions. Conceptually, level 0 strategies suggest a functional inability or unwillingness to take the perspective of others (and therefore a tendency to think of others as objects rather than subjects). In other words, we do *not* argue necessarily that an adolescent who uses a level 0 strategy to resolve a specific problem is not cognitively capable of taking the perspective of others. Rather, we argue that he or she does not take that perspective, and therefore, that the structure of the negotiation process will remain at a physicalistic level, because the adolescent relates to the other only as an object that must be changed or avoided. In affective terms, impulsive feelings may be directly expressed in the form of withdrawal, transforming the self, or physical force acting on the other. In either case, the self has been unable to find a common ground with others on which to negotiate or compromise.

The designation "0" has been chosen because it marks the initial entry point

TABLE 15.1
Four Levels of Perspective-Taking and Negotiation Strategies

Level of Interpersonal Negotiation Strategy	Level of Coordination of Social Perspectives	Interpersonal Orientation Used to Deal with Disequilibrium	
		Self-transforming Types	*Other-transforming Types*
Mutual, collaborative negotiations	3 — Needs of Self and Other are integrated in mutual, "3rd person" perspective	works out conflicts in terms of mutual needs and relationships collaborate	
Reciprocal (Orientation to Exchange) negotiations	2 — Needs of Self and Other are taken into account sequentially and reciprocally	accommodate barter go second ask for a reason	influence bribe barter, go first give a reason
Command or one-way negotiations: Obey	1 — Self is recognized as a subject with interests *separate* from Other.	obey give in be helpless wait for help	command bully assert
Impulsive, egocentric negotiations: Fight or flight	0 — "Other" is viewed as an "object"; Self in conflict with external forces	whine flee hide ignore	fight grab hit

of this developmental system. It does not connote the absence of a negotiation strategy, or the absence of other positive social qualities. Level 0 strategies are age-appropriate for young children and may function well in certain situations for older ones—an issue explored more fully in the case studies. In our developmental analysis, level 0 strategies represent the functional inability to use an understanding of self's or other's thoughts, feelings, or intentions in social interactions. Level 0 strategies include hitting or grabbing, or impulsive withdrawal or running away.

Level 1: One-Way Commands, Threats, or Obedience.   Level 1 strategies indicate an ability to recognize the existence of others (as subjects) and even to differentiate the perspective of self and others. However, level 1 strategies do not incorporate the needs of self and others in a reciprocal relationship. Rather than use exchanges or trades, these strategies rely on one-way commands or obedience to the commands of others. Affectively, they signify a self who asserts his or her own needs or gives in to the assertions of others, but who does not feel able to combine both sets of needs in a reciprocally-acceptable compromise. Level 1 strategies include giving repetitive commands, or going along obediently with the wishes of others.

Level 2: Reciprocal Exchanges.   These strategies represent an ability to consider the perspective of the self and other person, and to create exchanges that accommodate to both sets of needs in a simple, reciprocal kind of way. These strategies suggest a self who feels able to get what he or she needs without having to deny the needs of others or be swallowed up by them. Level 2 strategies do *not* represent an integration of self-and-other in a mutual relationship. However, they do allow for more complex and stable chains of interactions than do levels 0 or 1. Examples of level 2 strategies include: trading, bartering, making deals, convincing others to go along, exchanging favors, and making contracts.

Level 3: Mutual Collaborations.   These strategies represent, for us, a developmental milestone of normal adolescence—that is, the self's ability to participate in stable, on-going, mutually satisfying interactions. Conceptually, they represent the ability to integrate the needs of self and other into a strategy that considers both needs—and, in the process, may transform those individual needs into a new, mutual relationship. One example of this is the adolescent who is able to work out dating patterns that allow for autonomy (for the self) while recognizing his or her parents' need to feel responsible, involved, and in touch with their child's changing peer relationships. Level 3 strategies are also involved when an adolescent works out ways to "be himself" in front of friends, or assert his or her rights as a worker without denying the needs of an employer. These are major developmental accomplishments, and herald the emergence of a new social self, ready for the new roles of adulthood.

The Theoretical Foundation of the Model

The levels of interpersonal negotiation strategies just described can be understood to be developmental in two distinct but critically related senses. First, the levels are ontogenetic. By this, we mean that the developmental model in Table 15.1 is a classification system of ordering the expanding repertoire of interpersonal negotiation strategies as they naturally develop over the course of childhood and adolescence. In other words, it is theoretically asserted that with increasing chronological age, interpersonal negotiation strategies emerge in the sequence characterized by the levels. This can be seen in the specification of types of strategies listed in Table 15.1 at each level in the column Interpersonal Orientation Used to Deal with Disequilibrium.

Our preliminary research suggests the following age-related sequence: Level 0 strategies dominate the period of toddlerhood and early childhood. During the preschool and early elementary school years, children add to their repertoires the strategies classified at level 1 and, during the middle elementary and preadolescent years, level 2 strategies are added to the repertoire. Not until early adolescence, at the earliest, are level 3 strategies constructed to meet the social tasks and challenges of that epoch. We hypothesize that most adolescents have the capacity for using level 3 strategies. Troubled adolescents do not regularly *use* their capacity in a representative range of social situations. One clinical use of the developmental model is to map the contexts in which troubled adolescents are not able to *use* their optimal strategies—in order to understand and then intervene.

The model is developmental in a second and related sense. Once an individual has developed a strategy (or set of strategies) at a particular level, we must still ask *whether,* or in what ways, lower-level strategies are still available for use in particular situations. In other words, can the developmental model be used to characterize in some functional way (e.g., for purposes of assessment) the strategies of individuals who, ontogenetically speaking, have already constructed their way through the sequence? For instance, a 14-year-old with the capacity for level 3 strategies may behave in a way that "looks like" level 1. Whether the strategies of older individuals that look like those of younger individuals (i.e., those first constructing the lower levels) are actually "the same" or not is a critical question for any developmental theory. Our work with troubled children and adolescents has allowed us to map out patterns of strategies, and to think about whether the observable behavioral similarities are simply morphological, or whether they are functional and/or structural. In other words, we ask a series of assessment questions. Does an adolescent who regularly uses strategies of impulsivity and egocentrism (level 0) really feel like a toddler in those situations? Are his or her other thought or behavior patterns similarly regressed? Will he or she have other behavioral/social/cognitive characteristics of a toddler? Or, are these observable similarities only appearances? That is, does an impulsive egocentric strategy have very different meanings and functions in adolescence as compared with childhood? How do these meanings and functions differ? Is the use of a level 0 strategy more situationally determined for the adolescent? If so, what intervention strategies available in the adolescent's repertoire might be used to encourage the use of higher level strategies? In this paper we speak of a hierarchical repertoire of strategies *as if* lower level stategies are still available once higher level ones are constructed. However, the reader should interpret these as testable hypotheses, not as empirical facts or conclusions.

Another characteristic of the model worth re-emphasis is the attempt to integrate alternative ways of dealing with inner disequilibrium (self-transforming and other-transforming types of strategies) with developmental characteristics (levels). Once again, Table 15.1 provides specific examples of strategies classified according to each orientation at each level. The issue of a two-factor developmental definition of strategy level, and the issue of the developmental similarities underlying individual differences in orientation at each level are both discussed in more theoretical detail elsewhere (Selman, Demorest, & Krupa, 1984). Here, it is crucial to re-emphasize that strategies are neither traits nor people; rather, they are ways of dealing with self and other under conditions of disequilibrium. Empirical research and clinical observation together may begin to speak to the consistency of the strategies individuals use, as well as the factors that stimulate growth, regression, or oscillation in their utilization.

THREE PORTRAITS

The three portraits that follow demonstrate the utility of this model in a clinical-educational context. They are drawn from our work with adolescents who have long histories of interpersonal and academic failure. In this sense, the portraits are not representative of the changes most adolescents experience in their sense of self and their interpersonal relationships. However, each case concretizes a number of issues concerning the relationships of understanding, affect and situation. Together, they hint at the range and rich diversity of negotiation strategies used by most adolescents in coping with new relationships. Each case has implications for intervention.

David

David is 15 years old. He is being raised by his grandparents, because both his parents died when he was a toddler (one from illness, the other from a gunshot wound). David reads at a third grade level, and is extremely uncomfortable in most classroom situations; however, he is a superb athlete, comfortable in all group games, and in general, very social with peers. We have observed David in four different social contexts, using four different strategies.

In class, when David is asked to read, often he will first ignore the teacher's request, then ask to leave, then refuse to read, then either put his head down or storm out of the room swearing at anyone who happens to be around. This pattern of response holds for most academic requests, even when they are well within his capability and his interests. On his first school-sponsored job placement, David went to work for a few days, then decided he wanted to participate on a community basketball team that practiced during his work hours one day each week. David's response to this situation was to call in sick one day, and then quit, rather than work out a new work schedule.

With peers, David can be aggressive or collaborative, depending in part on the role he plays in the situation. For example, in a pick-up basketball game, we observed him order others around, take most of the shots, and generally dominate. In this situation, when an adult placed limits on his behavior, he ignored and resisted the adult's authority. However, when he plays the role of a team captain, Daivd includes others, mediates disputes, accepts the authority of the referee, and handles his own disappointment at losing with calm and good sportsmanship.

David's negotiation strategies are clearly affected by the situation in which he finds himself, and by the feelings these situations generate in him. The situations reported above include strategies we score at level 0 (grab, run away, quit); level 1 (bully, command), and Level 2 (share, exchange, mediate conflict). David uses a very different level of strategy in each of these situations.

However, in terms of frequency, David's negotiation strategies are usually level 0 or 1, and are largely inadequate for the range of new relationships he must develop. They are inflexible and do not generalize. For example, David seems able to use "high-level" strategies *only* in a situation where he feels totally comfortable, more competent than others, where the role of the other (e.g., a basketball referee) is readily predictable, and the situation presents alternative solutions that are easy for David to use. However, most situations in David's life do *not* fit these criteria. In situations where the perspective of the other is less clear to him (e.g., when a teacher tries to explain the importance of completing a classroom task), or where he feels less competent, he is unable to use a high-level strategy; his fear and his sense of helplessness lead him to hit out or run away, or put his jacket over his head to block out a painful world. Furthermore, whether his response is to run away, or hit out at others, his (Level 0) negotiation strategies suggest a self that is terribly isolated from others—trapped in his own psychological world and, therefore, unable to modulate his responses in a way that is comprehensible to others, unable to meet others on common ground. Beneath the apparently different responses (hit out vs. run away) lies a common core; for this reason, both responses are coded as Level 0 (see Table 15.1).

When David can take the perspective of others, feel comfortable and competent, and is in a situation where he can adequately generate solutions to problems, he is capable of high-level negotiation strategies. When any of these elements is missing, his strategies are less adequate, i.e., simpler, unmodulated, less adaptive and less successful in terms of accomplishing the social tasks of adolescence (forming stable and mutual relationships).

Amie

Amie is 15 years old; she lives with her mother and father (both of whom are chronically unemployed) and an older brother and sister. Her father has struggled for years with alcohol abuse, and has been institutionalized repeatedly. Amie's family has suffered greatly from this problem; although each member shows the physical, economic, social and psychological scars of their struggle, Amie feels like she carries most of the family's burden. Amie reads functionally, and is beginning to enjoy school work. She is extremely uncomfortable in peer groups, has difficulty making friends and asserting herself, and depends on adults for the support she needs to continue the struggle to find her "self" in social contexts.

In the classroom, Amie works by herself. When she has a problem with her work, she often sits and waits for the teacher to notice her. If the teacher does not respond, she will ask to take her work out to a work-study room; there she will sit again and wait for a counselor to help her. At her school-sponsored job (a day care center), Amie finishes all her tasks but has been unable to request help or ask for any new jobs.

Amie uses the counselors at her school to help her talk about problems, and try out new strategies for dealing with peers. She interacts often with one class-mate, but she either dominates (by making repetitive commands) or rejects (by calling her "stupid") or gives in to the needs of her new friend. In group situations, she withdraws into corners, or leaves the room; when asked for her ideas or suggestions, she shrugs and remains silent, or says simply, "I don't know."

Amie's strategies are much more consistent than those used by David. They are coded as level 0 (run away), and level 1 (command, give in, wait for help); only rarely can she use level 2 strategies (for example, in dealing with a third adult counselor). In most situations, Amie seems to demonstrate a consistent affective response (helplessness and withdrawal), and a consistent set of strat-egies (involving one-way perspective taking). Amie's strategies seem less deter-mined by variations in the situation than they are by her feelings about herself and her inability to take and use the perspectives of others in social interactions. For example, when she simply waits for the teacher to notice her, Amie suggests she is unable to figure out more than one way to capture an adult's attention. When she bullies or rejects her classmate, she suggests an inability to take the other's needs and interests into account when resolving a conflict. In either case, Amie seems to have a concept of her "self" which is still relatively isolated from others, i.e., unable to find common ground, and therefore, left to assert her own needs or give in to the needs of others.

Adam

Adam is 15 years old and lives with his mother in a public housing apartment. Although he is several years behind age norms in all academic areas, Adam is a hard worker who often requests work that is more difficult than he can handle. In addition, he is very social—both with adults and peers. He enjoys groups, and enjoys being the center of attention. However, Adam has a history of poor peer relations because of his desire to grab the spotlight and his lack of self-control; peers are intimidated or upset by his constant, high-energy chatter, and his hyperactive behavior. Adam has an easy time making friends and starting relationships with adults; however, he has more difficulty maintaining stable, long-term relationships with either peers or adults.

In the classroom, Adam is able to negotiate with his teachers around academic expectations and choices. For example, when asked to complete a math worksheet on decimals, Adam asks for help and then, after repeated attempts to complete the work, asks if he can try a different sheet first and then return to the assignment. This strategy suggests he can integrate his teacher's needs (that Adam work on his own math skills) with his own need (that he be given work he can successfully complete). During group discussions, Adam is able to communicate his ideas to the group, mediate interpersonal problems, and even become a spokesperson *for* the group. For example, when two students disagreed over who started an argument, Adam helped the class set up a mock trial, suggested defense and prosecutor roles, and worked hard to give each party an opportunity to voice his case. Adam's strategy helped his two classmates find a way to resolve their conflict. During group meetings, Adam can accurately predict adult responses to student suggestions, and can help the group formulate strategies for getting what they want (e.g., extra time for break after lunch, a school dance, etc.). In situations where he feels comfortable and competent, Adam is quite able to help other classmates express and act upon their own interests.

In less structured peer settings, Adam has a more difficult time controlling and channeling his interest in holding the group spotlight. For example, during group basketball games, he will try to dominate the game, and become angry or sullen when others challenge him. In these situations, Adam's strategies are verbal: He gives orders, assigns roles, becomes coach and referee, is upset when he is not the ''star'', and often has difficulty letting other students share in discussions. However, one important difference between Adam and David (or Amie) is that Adam can more easily shift strategies, with structure supplied by an adult and/or in response to changes in the situation. Because Adam more readily uses level 2 strategies, he has an ''extra'' repertoire of negotiation strategies that are unavailable to either David or Amie. In Adam's case, his use of level 2 strategies is both more stable and flexible than either David's or Amie's use of level 2 strategies.

In sum, Adam consistently demonstrates the ability to use what we have called level 2 strategies—that is, strategies which, although primarily focused on getting his own way, include and *communicate* a concern for the needs of self and other. For example, he recognizes the teacher's right to plan academic tasks for him, but also voices his own need for a change of pace; he helps classmates listen to each other and still actualizes his desire to be an important player in the brief classroom court scene. However, his strategies are also vulnerable to affective and situational factors—for example, on the basketball court, where he may feel less competent and more pressed to prove himself in front of his peers. In addition, it is unclear how Adam's coping style (for example, his constant high energy) will affect his ability to use his "best" level of negotiation strategies in more long-term relations—for example, in maintaining stable friendships or keeping a job at the restaurant.

CLOSING COMMENTS

The three cases selectively described here suggest some important ways in which it is possible to begin to map the relationship among cognitive, affective and situational variables in determining the development of negotiation strategies and the development of a social self. Each adolescent seems to be affected by the interaction of thoughts, feelings, and situations. However, David seems most vulnerable to situational stress; Amie carries with her a consistent, low-level set of strategies which keep her isolated from peers; Adam seems most able to use a consistently high set of strategies in different situations. For each adolescent, there are developmental processes (related to the level of coordination of social perspectives) which provide a framework for their repertoire of negotiation strategies.

The three case studies help also to clarify the relationship between interpersonal orientation and developmental level. On the one hand, we need to distinguish the *orientation* of an individual's strategy from the *developmental level* of the strategy he or she uses. For example, using the system described in Table 15.1, the three adolescents use strategies that fall in two orientations. David and Adam's strategies are both coded in the "Other-Transforming" orientation: They are active, they seek to get others to do what they want. David's strategies are more physical and impulsive than are Adam's (which are more verbal), but they both orient primarily toward changing others. Amie's strategies contrast strongly in orientation; she primarily transforms herself in order to fit the social situation. These differences in orientation (and in affective response to social conflict) may be due to an interaction of personality and socialization (for example, boys often being taught to change things, and girls to let others have their way). Similar socialization differences across differences in cultural values or social class may affect the orientation (or style) of strategy used by an individual. However, these differences in style or orientation may mask similarities in the (developmental) level of one's ability to take into account the needs and perspectives of others.

The differences in developmental level are not identical to differences in orientation. For example, Amie and David both use strategies coded as level 1 (Command or Obey), despite the difference in their orientation. In other words, beneath the surface differences in orientation lies a common structural (or organizational) similarity: an inability to take the perspective of the other person involved in a negotiation. Similarly, although both David and Adam use strategies that are primarily "other-transforming," in orientation, the strategies they use differ markedly in developmental levels: Adam more frequently includes the needs and perspectives of others in the strategies he uses to resolve interpersonal dilemmas.

The relationship among orientation, developmental level, and other personality variables (like "style"), suggests the richness and complexity of the social interactions of adolescence, and the difficulty of making simple assessments of social competence. Similarly, the relationship between having and using a specific level of strategy presents a complex interactive picture. For example, David demonstrates the capacity for at least three levels of strategy (0, 1, 2,) in different situations. In one sense, David *has* a level 2 strategy available in his repertoire. However, functionally, David does not *use* level 2 strategies with any consistency, in a broad range of crucial situations; therefore, in a very real sense, having the strategy does not help David, because he cannot use it to solve crucial interpersonal problems. In this sense, David's use of a level 0 strategy is fundamentally different from a young child's use of a Level 0 strategy: David's level 0 strategy is dysfunctional and problematic, and it prevents him from engaging in the stable interpersonal relationships that are the hallmark of emergent adulthood. David's social competence is, therefore, much more complex and difficult to assess than would first appear. We suggest his social competence can only be understood by taking into account the kind of relationships we have explored thus far—that is, the relationship among understanding, affect, and situation; among orientation and level, and the ways each of these interact with the specifics of different social situations. Understanding the development of complex social behaviors (like negotiation strategies) is a slow process of mapping out these relationships, over time and across contexts, in order to understand their richness as well as the mechanisms of change.

From both educational and clinical perspectives, we have operated on the belief that helping adolescents become more aware of their own negotiation strategies, and presenting new strategies to them, will in turn allow them to try out the new negotiation strategies they need for a successful transition into young adulthood. The claim that higher level strategies are better strategies is tentative and functional; it is intended to suggest some areas for further research, but also to contribute to the important here-and-now task of developing sound educational practice.

From the perspective of basic research, the study of interpersonal negotiation strategies contributes to the process of piecing together a more holistic picture of the development of social competence. Negotiation strategies stand at a middle ground between the underlying structure of cognitive and affective processes traditionally examined by cognitive-developmental and psychoanalytic researchers, and the situation-specific individual behaviors traditionally observed by social psychologists and behavioristic researchers. Negotiation strategies are an observable meeting ground for social thought and social behavior. To the extent that it is possible to analyze, categorize, and even "order" negotiation strategies along a developmental continuum, we can begin to generate hypotheses about the relationship between social thought and action—as this relationship develops over time, across situations, and in real-life social contexts.

REFERENCES

Brion-Meisels, S., Lowenheim, G., & Rendeiro, B. (1982). *The Adolescent issues project: program overview*. Unpublished manuscript. Judge Baker Guidance Center, 295 Longwood Avenue, Boston, MA 02115.

Kohlberg, L. (1969). Stage and sequence: The cognitive-developmental approach to socialization. In D. Goslin (Ed.), *Handbook of Socialization theory and research* (pp. 347–480). Chicago: Rand McNally.

Piaget, J. (1965). *The moral judgment of the child*. (M. Gabain, Trans.). New York: Free Press. (Original work published 1932).

Selman, R. (1981). The development of interpersonal competence: The role of understanding in conduct. *Developmental Review 1*, 401–422.

Selman, R. & Demorest, A. (1984). Observing troubled children's interpersonal negotiation strategies: Implications of and for a developmental model. *Child Development. 55*, 288–304.

Selman, R., Demorest, A., & Krupa, M. (1984). Interpersonal negotiations: Toward a developmental analysis. In W. Edelstein & J. Habermas, (Eds.) *Social interaction and social understanding*. Frankfurt: Suhrkamp Verlag.

Selman, R., Schorin, M., Stone, C., & Phelps, E. (1983). A naturalistic study of children's social understanding. *Developmental Psychology, 19*, 82–102.

CRITIQUES AND REVISIONS

16

Moral Intervention: A Skeptical Note

Wolfgang Edelstein
Max-Planck-Institute for Human Development and Education
Berlin, West Germany

This chapter outlines a dilemma. The writer is convinced, in principle, of the theoretical and empirical soundness, i.e., rational justification of Kohlberg's theory of moral development. Nonetheless he is skeptical about (a) the feasibility of moral intervention, (b) the nature of the effects and, correspondingly, (c) the wisdom of present applications of Kohlberg's theory to education. These objections, to be sure, appear somewhat contradictory. The doubts about the *wisdom* of application presuppose, in a way at least, its *feasibility,* and only if feasibility is given, may *effects* be problematic. Thus, my very objections may appear to defeat their intent.

Let me, however, start with a few remarks about what I shall *not* question in my comments. I do not propose alternatives to, nor doubts about, Kohlberg's theory. *First,* in spite of a number of anomalies in need of treatment I do *not* agree with those critics who propose a different *stage model* (e.g., Eckensberger & Reinshagen, 1980; Gibbs, 1977; Gilligan, 1982; Haan, 1978; Lempert 1982; and others). I believe that most, if not all of these alternatives, miss an important aspect of Kohlberg's theory, whatever their more or less plausible reasons for alternative stage constructions. Except Eckensberger, who proposes a formally modified stage system, these critics tend to substitute the *content* of specific metaethical convictions—care and responsibility, elements of a theory of the good life—for the strictly formal justice structures of Kohlberg's system.

Second, I do not purport to criticize Kohlberg's alleged *cultural bias.* Such criticism amounts to the adoption of a sociological-relativist position and this position implies the cultural relativity of moral value systems, including normative orientations (Bertram, 1980; Shweder, 1982; Simpson, 1974; and others). These critics miss the point of a neo-Kantian, formalist, universalist, pro-

387

cedurally-based ethic by resorting to *petitio principii,* i.e. by begging the question. Clearly, Kohlberg's *empirical* contentions may foster misapprehensions, which the *theoretical* core of his program does not warrant. Social evolutionary universalism does not imply empirical ubiquity. Universalizability is a formal norm, not just an empirical fact. Yet, obviously, validations based on cultural comparisons are important corroborations of Kohlberg's program, since they match theoretical universality with trans-contextual empirical data.

Third and finally, I do not intend to reject or criticize the *logic, methodology* or *empirical implementation* of either the construction of Kohlberg's system, the research design, the sampling or the scorring procedures (Gilligan & Murphy, 1979; Haan, Weiss, & Johnson, 1982; Habermas, 1983; Kurtines & Greif, 1974; Phillipps & Nicolayev, 1978). Much of the criticism levied at Kohlberg's research methodology has been refuted (Broughton, 1978; Colby, Kohlberg, Gibbs, & Lieberman, 1983; Oser, 1981) or even retracted (Kurtines, 1981). Other criticisms are debatable, and none appear decisive. What remains is important, but it fits with a melioristic attitude to research, and thus may be attended to in time to broaden the scope of the theory. However, it is not our objective to participate in this necessary exercise of criticism.

With regard to possible improvements of the theory, we stand on the shoulders of a giant. That privileged standpoint provides us with an awareness of unresolved questions that call for new research efforts. Kohlberg's theory is a cognitive-developmental theory of moral judgment competence. In the very light of this theory, we can see that a theory of *intervention into moral development* is part of a more encompassing theory of moral performance. That theory, at present, is, at best, a nascent theory. I see five classes of research questions in need of treatment in this context: (1) the relation between content and structure; (2) the relation between judgment and action; (3) the relation between competence and performance; (4) the relation between universals and cultural particulars; (5) and the relation between moral thinking and ego development. There is overlap between these problem classes, but they are not identical. Kohlberg himself and his colleagues as well as his scientific friends and allies have started research into these highly complex topics. Most of the alternative constructions proposed so far have failed to improve on Kohlberg's cognitive, universalistic, formalistic and developmental theory of moral competence. Further growth of the theory and the question of its application will presumably be decided in a somewhat different context. What is needed is a theoretical account of the conditions of moral performance. Moral judgment competence certainly is a privileged member of the set of these conditions. However, a theory that attempts to explain the social constitution of morality has to account for the effects of socio-cultural factors, social interaction and the dynamics of internalization on the emergence of morality in thinking and action.

To me, a skeptical note as to intervention appears warranted mainly for three reasons. *First,* as I see it, *intervention* into moral development, in contradistinction to the *construction* of Kohlberg's basic theory of moral cognition, is predicated on solutions to the performance problems the theory raises, and not on its constructive logic. Therefore, it is to these performance related problems that we turn in the following pages.

Second, constructivist educational intervention is based on the function of cognitive conflict in development. The strategy of choice in order to induce cognitive conflict is *discussion,* involving comparison and contrast. It is not clear at the moment whether the same discussion strategy will suffice for moral growth, as works for cognitive growth. The answer to that question will hinge on our convictions about the nature of moral communication. Ultimately our question is whether moral discourses can be equated with epistemic discussions. And that, again, has to do with the nature and progress of a theory of moral performances.

The *third* question deals with the *nature of school experience and school knowledge.* In the last resort it raises the question whether school as we know it and as it almost inevitably is organized today is capable of inducing growth as well as learning. It raises the question whether developmentally effective education is possible in a school that, for a number of complex historical, social, organizational and institutional reasons, is resistant to developmentally oriented action (Edelstein, 1979, 1983).

OPEN QUESTIONS OF A PERFORMANCE THEORY OF MORAL JUDGMENT AND MORAL ACTION

Let us now turn to the three possible objections just mentioned. I shall start with the problem raised by a performance theory of morality and then proceed to the other two problems—discourse structure and the institutional/organizational structure of the school. Since the latter two questions overlap, we shall not clearly distinguish between them. While the nature of school-based intervention raises serious questions about the feasibility and effects of moral intervention, this is not really the case with performance related problems of moral education. Rather they displace these questions: From influencing moral stage, intervention moves towards influencing the performance conditions that act as gatekeeping structures that dominate, as it were, the access to the functioning of moral performance itself. These performance conditions relate to the issues mentioned earlier as open questions about Kohlberg's theory.

The *first* of these issues concerns the relation between *structure and content.* This relation has to do with the reconciliation of the concrete morality of norms and values, of the choice based on specific perspectives as given in particular lifeworlds, with the formal deontological procedures called upon in order to resolve conflicting claims by appeal to mutually satisfying and universalizable "good reasons."

The *second* issue concerns the relation of *judgment and action*. This relation has to do with fundamental questions of validity—*not* because judgments are less valid moral acts than actions or because actions enjoy a higher status of relevance. Rather the problem arises because of the multiplicity of intermediate cognitions which determine the ultimately binding force of moral judgments in the face of a variety of performance conditions (Rest, this volume). I mention the existential pledge or personal vindication of moral judgment referred to by Blasi (1981) by his notion of *responsibility*. I mention the *ambiguities of action contexts* which prevent action from standing in a one to one correspondence to judgment. They call for specific sensitivities in order to define a situation as moral (Keller & Reuss, this volume). I mention, finally, the individual differences in standards of acceptability of moral action, to which Nisan (this volume) has called attention. For all these contingencies we rely on social-hermeneutic procedures in order to disentangle the concrete ambiguities of the relationship. Thus, the moral question: "What should I do?" by definition is asked in a context of potential action. "Is this what I have to do?" is the call for an explication of the moral action under the criterion of reason in light of the situation. "Is this what I meant to do?" or "Is this what I should have done?" is the request for a hermeneutic reconstruction of the act ex post facto in the light of judgment, action plan and motive as well as consequence of action. The evaluative component of the judgment/action relationship is an inescapable dimension to any contextuated act of moral judgment. Perhaps a more precise formulation would be: After the decontextualizing formalism of judgment has done its job, judgment itself calls for recontextualization—for an act of justice or fairness directed towards mutual understanding in a community in quest of agreement (Edelstein & Noam, 1982).

Let us pursue the *third* underattended issue. This issue concerns the relationship between *moral competence and moral performance*. Let me add immediately that *action* is not equated with performance, and judgment is not equated with competence. There are performance variations between judgments, about whose causes we know very little. We know too little about contextual, social or interpersonal reasons, about inner psychological-dynamic and situational causes for variation and décalage. Thus, performance conditions relate both to judgment and action, and differentially so. *Segmentation* in the social system may be a powerful inhibitor of generalization of moral judgment across domains—and this may be one of the strongest impediments to effective moral education. We address this issue later. Performance conditions affect the stage structure, the consistency of the whole of which a judgment, or an action, is a part; they touch on the topic of décalage, i.e., the problem of generalization across domains to which moral judgments are applied; they affect conditions of stage transition and regression. In a word, performance conditions may be at work in the *segmentation* of moral domains, either within the subjects or in social reality, or both, interactively.

Let us proceed to a *fourth* open question in Kohlberg's theory: the relation between *universals* and *cultural* particulars. To some extent this is another face of the structure-and-content problem. The formal universals of a cognitivist ethic match an evolutionary perspective in which developing principles of conflict resolution correspond to abstract principles of social organization and to transitions between these principles. But it is more difficult to locate their functioning on the level of concrete *culturally interpreted* interactions and claims, where conflicts constitute immediate action systems and trigger the operation of concrete moral rules endowed with a dignity of their own. Considerable affect has been aroused by Kohlberg's alleged cultural bias towards western type liberal constitutionalism. It is fair to point out that sociological relativism generates epistemological contradictions of its own (how to produce universally valid descriptions of particulars). Still, among Kohlberg's formal universals the role and place of particular and practical instances of moral conflict and conflict resolution is not well defined. Furthermore, while translation rules may be found that permit one to establish semantic equivalence between, say, the meaning of concrete reciprocity in Taiwan, Turkey, and Tucson, Arizona (but even that is difficult), it is less clear what specific transformation dynamics or conflict experience will move concrete reciprocity towards a system perspective within each of these cultures. For a theory of moralization, as well as for a theory of social evolution (for all universalist, formalist and cognitivist theories) this question is very important since it addresses the following problem: *How is higher order unity produced from cultural particulars?* That is, what are the mechanisms which generate the transitions? Is it the formal properties of conflict, independent of their content, or is it latent experiential commonalities among culturally distinctive contents that elicit converging transitions to higher order formal structures; structures that when attained redefine both conflict itself and the various type of conflict resolutions on the higher level.

This leads us to a *fifth* and final consideration of underattended issues in Kohlberg's theory. Culture, now seen in its function as an internalized structure of dispositions and valuations, represents a special set of performance conditions within a larger set of developmental conditions—the *developmental dynamics of the ego.* Culture operates selections among objects for cathexis and thereby creates distinctive saliencies among actions, and action-arousing emotional valences of interaction. Culture, besides defining the institutionally-sanctioned rules of conduct, defines (partly at least) the inner world of subjects, the semantic potential of motives, which confers a collective psychological structure on individuals in a culturally defined group.

Obviously, however, the performance conditions rooted in the inner nature of subjects are not confined to those collectively conferred on them by culture. More salient still are those developmental dynamics due to specifically cathected relationships and their vicissitudes. How moral judgment and moral action relate to super ego formation and defense is only beginning to be understood (Edelstein

& Noam, 1982; Kegan, 1979; Noam, this volume; Noam, Kohlberg, & Snarey, 1983; Snarey, Kohlberg, & Noam, 1983). Differential moral sensitivities, differential moral valences of situations depending on moral perception and moral reactivity of subjects to interpersonal experience demonstrate that moral judgment and moral action vary according to modes of processing experience that are characteristic of, or even idiosyncratic to, the psychic organization of the subject of experience. Within the structural paradigm, Blasi's (1976, 1981), Döbert and Nunner-Winkler's (1978), Keller's (1981), Keller and Reuss' (this volume) and Nisan's (this volume) studies have begun to throw light on the paramount importance of those performance conditions of moralization that are constituted by the developmental vicissitudes of the ego.

The Paradox of Moral Intervention in the School

Individual differences in moral performance conditions confront moral intervention with a difficult task. We can consider the relationships just analyzed as so many handicaps on the way. Moral education, while addressing the universal structure, is predicated on particular content as the basic matter on which educational action is grounded. The average school intervention in the form of moral discussion typically is limited to judgment alone, while moral action is merely the object of educational discourse—and yet the goal of educational intervention. Instructional activity has little control over whether the content under discussion is part of a segmented reality defying a universalizing argument, or whether segmentation severs judgment from action. We may legitimately ask whether school itself produces moral segmentation. That is, whether school, by attempting to influence moral development, creates moral school knowledge that may be quite separate from living moral experience in a similar way as proficiency in speaking one's native language generally appears quite separate from the knowledge of formal grammar imparted by school.

Thus moral intervention in a structuralist perspective faces a paradox: It addresses the moral competence of the mature subject adjudicating conflicts in a universalist attitude which involves the moral point of view and the original position as predicated on a universal substitution of perspectives. But the moral competence of the subject is incarnate in variable performance conditions. As pointed out before, among these performance conditions are social and situational factors as well as factors located in the ego dynamics of the person. To reach the subject, universalist moral instruction will have to be particularistic: It must enter the subject's skin and reconstruct, in a quasi-therapeutic attitude, the individual and collective history of those conditions. And that may appear to be a task more appropriate to the clinician than to the teacher. The very orientation of the school towards cognitive universalism may defeat or counteract the school's directed influence on the moral development of its students and leave what its intentional curriculum cannot achieve to the unexpected consequences of the hidden curriculum.

Lest a misunderstanding arise, a clarification is needed. Our doubts about intervention are not concerned with the feasibility of influencing cognitive behavior *per se*. We know that schooling produces cognitive effects. However, critics differ widely as to the nature of these effects. One does not have to join the ranks of the radical school critics and deschoolers to be critical of the cognitive functioning of school in post-traditional, and especially in "postmodern" society. Perhaps, school reformers have at times entertained an even more illusionary understanding of this institution than have the conservatives. Specifically, it appears naive to take school reforms, as we know them, for granted as structural devices for the improvement of learning, both cognitive and moral. We return to this topic later. Let us first specify a number of problems that haunt school-based intervention.

A first set of questions concerns the directionality of effects, i.e., the prediction of post-treatment change in a given context. As everybody knows, what Kohlberg did first was to establish adequate treatments, true to the theory and true to the structure of effects as anticipated. Obviously, the structure of treatments has to be intimately linked to the structure of constructivist theory. Intuitions of adequate treatment processes go back to Dewey's (1963) theory of experimental education and have been more recently expounded by Kohlberg and Mayer (1972). Conflict induction, discussion, discovery, and enrichment of sensory experience are among the repertoire of inductive instruction techniques. As to the organizational aspect of treatment, Kohlberg's construction of the Just Community Schools (as demonstrated in the studies by Power, 1979, this volume) is an attempt to establish structures of organic solidarity in order to produce didactically what in fact is presupposed by it. The organic solidarity supposedly implied in the school's social organization is expected to produce the conventional morality needed for it to function autonomously. But even if Durkheim's (1947) analytic reduction of forms of morality to forms of social organization is correct, it is not at all clear whether an artificial and willed organization of school, pedagogical authority and didactic division of labor among adolescents will produce the effect predicted from Durkheim. Durkheim's social forms are highly general and abstract ideal types. Schools are very concrete institutions. Can we expect these structures to function independently of the subjects' stages? Are they independent of local context? Of situation? Of need states? Can they function in independence of the particular history of particular institutions? And more generally, can we define the goal of moral progress as an objective, as a dependent variable in a treatment model with so many unknowns in the treatment definition?

However, let us assume, for the moment at least, that all of these questions could be answered in the affirmative, that feasibility of intervention could be established, that a technology of intervention could be made available. What about the predicted effects? Since morality is not made up of isolated elements of thought and action but constitutes a system which is a vital part of the system of personal identity, genuine moral growth will necessarily differ from, say, the potentially isolated acquisition of the rules of arithmetic or the incremental appropriation of foreign language skills. Successful moral rebalancing means the reorganization of personality in essential dimensions of thought, action and interaction. Are moral intervention strategies sufficiently responsive to unanticipated effects of intervention due to factors of time, place and organization, due to group structures and to the structure of performance conditions? What about the dynamics of intervention into personality which are taken into account as a matter of course in analogous interventions in the context of therapy, counseling and consulting? But perhaps all of these are less pressing than the converse, i.e., no-effect consequences and their possible causes, the induced immunity to growth that appears to some critics as the most fitting description of effects as produced by the change taking place in modern institutions of schooling.

There is a basic difference between practical discourse and strategic use of knowledge. A further possible objection to the feasibility of moral intervention may be more fundamental. This objection relates to the basic difference between the discourse model of moral growth and the strategic model of knowledge application. The discourse model describes the interaction, in practical discourse, of dissenting individuals in quest of agreement. They are oriented towards mutual understanding and have agreed to reciprocally binding procedures to reach consensus in communication (Habermas, 1981). The strategic model defines the functional or instrumental relationship to a goal, the utility function an action has for an actor intent to reach a goal. Formal schooling, whether we like it or not, has not been designed to function according to the discourse model of human communication oriented towards consensus. Rather, it is an enterprise of instrumental rationality. The goals built into its design are individual acquisition of knowledge, the increase of skills and the ability to abide by social regulations. I shall not here analyze the school's socio-historical difficulties in reaching these goals (cf. Edelstein, 1979, 1983). Instead, let us assume that school is indeed able to achieve these objectives. It could not but concern itself, first and foremost, with the establishment of an *observer's attitude* in the minds of the students. Instruction provides for the selection and demonstration of adequate descriptive propositions. Its job is to achieve respect for logically valid standards of truth for these descriptive propositions. The dialectical leap by which the "third person perspective," the neutral attitude required for objective learning, is transformed into a "first person perspective," the personal involvement required for normative learning, calls for a set of improbable conditions. Yet, this leap may be at the heart of any truly educative process. We can analyze, however, why this is bound to be a particularly improbable process if we consider the conditions of schooling decried by the deschoolers.

The school's well-founded instrumental goals require the construction of a set of descriptive statements and of standards for judging the truth value of these statements. Cognitive developmental theory has a kit of tools for the job, as modeled by theories of experiential education, discovery learning, cognitive conflict induction, etc. *Discussion* is the main device for constructive classification of knowledge in this sense. In contrast, moral discourse, like therapeutic discourse, requires reflexive communication consented by partners, independent, at the outset, of objective standards. All needs, all interest, all positions are permitted. No constraint is allowed, not even the constraint of discourse itself. Teaching, however, implies strategic intervention, an instrumental interaction geared towards effects, without granting the students permission to withdraw from dialogue in a mutual agreement co-established with the dialogue itself. Whereas the discovery of new knowledge as consistent with a constructivist epistemology places no burden on the teacher but to commit himself to some variety of the méthode clinique to stimulate the student to advance beyond the information given, this role is much more complex in the case of moral discourses. The construction of descriptive propositions differs from the establishment of agreement about the validity of normative statements. The exploration of truth merely presupposes a kind of methodological equality of teacher and taught, a Socratic perspective on the questionable truth of a given proposition. The validation of a normative statement calls for mutually unrestricted discourse among equals. That is why Piaget (1932/1965) maintains that morality is constructed in the *peer group* with its allegedly characteristic relationships of equality. A constructivist strategy of instruction relies on Socratic disequilibration of given states of knowledge in view of a reconstruction of reality. The equality of involvement among dissenting partners in moral discussions is something more, something more complex, and something different.

What I am driving at is that moral discourses are simultaneously located in an as yet unexplicated web of I-Thou relations and cognitive third person relationships. These simultaneously operating relationships generate transitions from first person to third and back in an ongoing validational process. This is, I think, the essential structure of therapeutic communication. Change is brought about by enlightenment under the condition of trust and affectively sustained mutuality. This is why significant others in the socialization process can entertain constructive, change-oriented discourses with children. Teachers in their institutional roles have serious difficulties here. Piaget's (1932/1965; see also Youniss, 1980) theorizing about relationships of constraint applies much more convincingly to *their* role than to parents'.

But in spite of certain recent leanings towards indoctrination, I anticipate Kohlberg's reply: It is not the teachers' job to enter moral discourses, he will say. It is their job to enable students to enter moral discourses. Just as it isn't the teachers' job to transfer cognitive knowledge by rote procedures, but to organize classrooms for the constructionist discovery of knowledge, likewise it isn't the teachers' job to provide moral instruction. What they are to do is to organize the prerequisites for moral discussions in the classroom.

CONTRADICTIONS BETWEEN MORAL DEVELOPMENT AND THE STRUCTURE AND FUNCTION OF SCHOOLING

Even so we need to confront two of the problems mentioned earlier. One relates to the nature of morality. The other concerns the nature of the school and school learning. Let me wind up this presentation by addressing these two problems in turn.

As the nature of the moral adjudication process is mutually involving communication among members of a discourse community in a situation of dissent about conflicting claims in view of reconciliation in terms of a principle of consensus (a norm), nobody will seriously enter this type of communication unless he is *involved* in dissent. Hypothetical involvement differs from real involvement in the nature or scope of the intervening cognitive conflict and the type of motivation coming into play. Thus, what school can affect, through the vicarious experience typical of its operations is not moral judgment and/or action—which can only emerge where subjects are directly involved in "moral" experience— but the performance conditions of (ulterior) judgment and action. What can be affected is the subjects' disposition to enter direct moral experience with some desirable prerequisites. School may influence the subject's moral sensitivity; it may influence either the average or the specific definitions of morally relevant situations; it may affect the saliency of certain moral issues, and so on. Moral discussions in the classroom thus can serve as (rational) gatekeepers for moral involvement, rather than affecting moral involvement itself.

What more, then, do we need, I hear Kohlberg say. That is all that school can do anyway in the cognitive domain—that is, *if* school is transformed, so that it can cope with this function, a task which, for structural reasons, school has considerable difficulties accomplishing today.

Therefore the critical question is whether, all other things being equal, the school is really in a position to function as a sensitizing device affecting the performance condition of moral judgment and moral action. When I talk about "school," what I have in mind is a structural idealization. I refer to an institutional order, bureaucratic regularities and rule-bound phenomena that characterize schooling in modern times. I do not deny that exceptions and alternatives are possible. I cannot analyze the socio-historical and evolutionary causes that have led to the present state of education. Elsewhere I have argued that with the emergence of posttraditional social organization, formal and abstract processes of education emerged as necessary substitutes for modes of cultural reproduction that had been typical of family-based subsistence economies. These economies were characterized by a low rate of change, intergenerational stability, a "cyclical" metaphor of life and predominantly concrete, yet transparent cognitive and moral operations (Edelstein, 1983).

I further argue that these processes, for structural reasons basic to the capitalistic mode of production, the division of labor, the division of generational roles and the division of knowledge were organized according to a factory model of functioning and knowledge acquisition (Edelstein, 1979, 1983; Schwartz, Schuldenfrei, & Lacey, 1978).

Let me draw the barest sketch of three types of consequences that I feel derive from the division of labor and factory models of schooling:

(*a*) Growth and change in humans proceed *developmentally,* i.e., by hierarchical reorganization of stages through which personality travels propelled by the operation of functional invariants on the objects of experience which they simultaneously organize. School is organized to operate by linear accumulation, i.e., according to the rationality of bureaucratic administration (birth cohorts, grades, timetables, chunks of curricular contents, etc.). Except for the fact that the developing subjects are the schools' administrative objects, the two trajectories have little in common. While "in the state of nature" learning corresponds to development and aliments it (developmental learning), industrial school learning is more or less divorced from development. School is an increasingly artificial context designed for the production of school learning which has few experiential correlates. Stage specific modes of inquiry tuned to the equilibrating action of assimilation and accommodation processes do not determine organized classroom learning. In return, school experience is increasingly characterized by boredom, lack of curiosity, and loss of motivation and thus progressively forfeits its function to help construct adequate models of reality for action in the world.

(*b*) Challenges to learning in such settings are highly ambiguous and contradictory. Precapitalist modes of cognitive socialization rested on immediately comprehensible experience, producing a natural community of developmentally guided learners. Where the industrial and administrative process has eliminated such natural (and naturally obtuse) communities, stage-bound susceptibilities for objects and collective sensibilities for conflicting claims would tend to emerge either at random or not at all. When, in response to failures, the industrial order of schools with its birth cohort organization, discipline and reward contingencies is changed into "a workplace" for children and adolescents, a setting that is planned to foster intrinsic motivation, to the distress of the reformers the very organization of reform has tended to reinforce what it was designed to counteract. Unexpectedly, when the factory discipline was abrogated in experiments of reform, to be superseded by more humane and more motivating forms of learning, students widely remained disinterested, unmotivated or rebellious. The organic solidarity of deeply involved students and characteristic patterns of intrinsically motivated cognitive growth often failed to emerge. The Just Community is conceptualized as a group bound together in organic solidarity and engaged in Deweyan practice.

This is Kohlberg's implicit or explicit presupposition for its functioning as a moralization device. What if that presupposition fails, and only its appearance remains—a kind of organic mimicry within mechanical conditions? Students, under such conditions, will tend to either operate on a preconventional level or segment their moral functioning.

(c) *Segmentation* is a functional cognitive analog to the dominant form of the division of labor: the division of institutions, the division of generations and the division of knowledge. Simultaneously, segmentation serves as a counter-universalization device, as a mechanism serving to balance the ever-growing burden of abstraction, formalization, and generalization. Thus, psycho-dynamically, segmentation functions as defense: regression, compartmentalization, or isolation. *Cognitively*, it functions as a device for the limitation of validity claims and the inhibition of generalization and transfer across domains. *Socially*, it serves to exclude individuals, groups, or problems from the extension of a norm or rule. In other words, segmentation serves the maintenance of limited validity. It contains validity within economically acceptable limits—of an institution, of a group, of a problem.

One of the most salient examples of segmentation is the school itself. Paradoxically, as a universalistic institution, its operations tend to substitute reality-based cognitions by a reality of its own, which we have called school knowledge. We cannot here analyze the social causes and mechanisms of the reduction of knowledge to school knowledge, nor spell out all its consequences and correlates. Phenomenologically, most people are aware of the self-serving and circular character of school knowledge—its abstracted nature and the social service system that profits from its maintenance. Frequently, school knowledge produces closed worlds with no traffic or transfer to experientially constituted knowledge domains outside the school curricula. And here is a particular peril for moral intervention worthy of attention.

There are two forms of segmentation or boundary setting that may affect the schools' explicit moral intervention: segmentation within school knowledge and confinement to school. The first type of segmentation may occur when moral intervention is confined to specific activities within the school schedule, as are other curricular activities, e.g. history, or mathematics. It is enormously difficult to dissolve cognitive boundaries and assure transfer of cognition between domains of application. The effect of social studies on voting behavior or political involvement among citizens is a case in point. This problem has been debated under the label of the *relevance* of school knowledge. Segmentation in this context means the assured irrelevance of knowledge through curricular confinement to the place a domain of knowledge has received in the syllabus and the time schedule of the school. Thus, we might institute a moral discussion hour with even potentially deep involvement of the participants, but without generalization beyond the limits of that institution.

The second form of segmentation is the confinement of cognitive structures developed through school intervention to the construction place, the school. As with school knowledge, we would then be confronted with school morality. This problem has been discussed under the label of *double morality*. Perhaps it would be more generous to discuss it in terms of restricted morality, a morality of rules limited to a particular setting. We sometimes criticize people for maintaining a moral facade. We then imply falsehood or deception. More often than not, however, we are just disappointed at the discovery that a person's moral stance is limited to a given institutional setting: It is only in the school, or in the office, or in private life, that his moral position prevails, and not across domains throughout his life (Sabini & Silver, 1982).

Segmentation is not a sickness vitiating Kohlberg's system of moral intervention in school. It is an ailment affecting the school as a party to the process of division of labor in modern society.

However, the illness may have a pernicious effect on the structure of moral discourse itself. Confined to school procedures and school knowledge, moral discourse may be transformed into a mere technique of discussion learned in order to comply with the rules of school knowledge. In reified form it might return to the bag of isolated virtues from which Kohlberg freed a universalistic, cognitive and constructivist morality. Only if educators succeed in overcoming the segmentation of school knowledge will analytic moral discussions influence the moral sensitivities and situational proclivities of the students across domains, and promise moral progress by transforming the performance conditions of moral judgment and moral action.

REFERENCES

Bertram, H. (1980). Moralische Sozialisation. In K. Hurrelmann & D. Ulrich (Eds.), *Handbuch der Sozialisationsforschung* (pp. 717–744). Weinheim: Beltz.

Blasi, A. (1976). Personal responsibility and ego development. In R. deCharms (Ed.), *They need not be pawns: Toward self-direction in the urban classroom* (pp. 177–199). New York: Irvington Publishers.

Blasi, A. (1981). *Autonomy in obedience. The development of distancing in socialized action.* Paper presented at the conference on "Structural approaches to the development of intersubjectivity," Ringberg, FRG. (German version in W. Edelstein & J. Habermas (Eds.), Soziale Interaktion und soziales Verstehen, Frankfurt: Suhrkamp 1984).

Broughton, J. (1978). The cognitive-developmental approach to morality: A reply to Kurtines and Greif. *Journal of Moral Education, 7,* 81–96.

Colby, A., Kohlberg, L., Gibbs, J., & Lieberman, M. (1983). A longitudinal study of moral judgment. *Monographs of the Society for Research in Child Development.* Serial No. 200, *48,* Nos. 1–2.

Dewey, J. (1963). *Experience and education.* New York: Collier.

Döbert, R. & Nunner-Winkler, G. (1978). Performanzbestimmende Aspekte des moralischen Bewußtseins. In G. Portele (Ed.), *Sozialisation und Moral* (pp. 101–121). Weinheim: Beltz.

Durkheim, E. (1947). *The division of labor in society*. Glencoe: Free Press.

Eckensberger, L. H. & Reinshagen, H. (1980). Kohlberg's Stufentheorie der Entwicklung des moralischen Urteils: Ein Versuch ihrer Reinterpretation im Bezugsrahmen handlungstheoretischer Konzepte. In L. H. Eckensberger, & R. K. Silbereisen (Eds.), *Entwicklung sozialer Kognitionen* (pp. 65–131). Stuttgart: Klett-Cotta.

Edelstein, W. (1979). *Universalistic theories of development—particularistic conditions of performance. Metatheoretical considerations and practical issues.* In *Psychology and early education. Cultural continuities and discontinuities.* Symposium conducted at the meeting of the International Society for the Study of Behavioral Development. Lund, Sweden.

Edelstein, W. (1983). Cultural constraints on development and the vicissitudes of progress. In F. S. Kessel & A. W. Siegel (Eds.), *The child and other cultural inventions. Psychology and society* (pp. 48–81). New York: Praeger.

Edelstein, W. & Noam, G. (1982). Regulatory structures of the self and 'postformal' stages in adulthood. *Human Development, 25,* 407–422.

Gibbs, J. C. (1977). Kohlberg's stages of moral judgment: A constructive critique. *Harvard Educational Review, 47,* 43–61.

Gilligan, C. (1982). *In a different voice.* Cambridge, MA.: Harvard University.

Gilligan, C. & Murphy, M. (1979). Development from adolescence to adulthood: The philosopher and the dilemma of the fact. In D. Kuhn (Ed.), *Intellectual development beyond childhood. New directions for child development,* No. 5 (pp. 85–99). San Francisco: Jossey Bass.

Haan, N. (1978). Two moralities in action contexts. *Journal of Personality and Social Psychology, 36,* 286–305.

Haan, N., Weiss, R., & Johnson, V. (1982). The role of logic in moral reasoning and development. *Developmental Psychology, 18,* 245–256.

Habermas, J. (1981). *Theorie des kommunikativen Handelns* (Vols. 1 and 2). Frankfurt: Suhrkamp.

Habermas, J. (1983). *Moralbewusstsein und kommunikatives Handeln.* Frankfurt: Suhrkamp.

Kegan, R. (1979). The evolving self. Process conception for ego psychology. *Counseling Psychology, 8,* 5–34.

Keller, M. (1981). *Children's explanations of moral transgressions: Competence and performance aspects.* Paper presented at the conference on "Structural approaches to the development of intersubjectivity," Ringberg, FRG. (German version in W. Edelstein & J. Habermas (Eds.), Soziale Interaktion und soziales Verstehen, Frankfurt: Suhrkamp 1984).

Kohlberg, L. & Mayer, R. (1972). Development as the aim of education. *Harvard Educational Review, 42,* 449–496.

Kurtines, W. (1981). *Discussion statement* at the "International Conference on Morality and Moral Development," Miami, FL.

Kurtines, W. & Greif, E. G. (1974). The development of moral thought: Review and evaluation of Kohlberg's approach. *Psychological Bulletin, 81,* 453–470.

Lempert, W. (1982). Moralische Urteilsfähigkeit. Zur Explikation und Extrapolation logischer und soziologischer Implikationen der Theorie Kohlbergs. *Zeitschrift für Sozialisationsforschung und Erziehungssoziologie, 2,* 113–126.

Noam, G., Kohlberg, L., & Snarey, J. (1983). Steps towards a model of the self. In B. Lee & G. Noam (Eds.), *Developmental approaches of the self* (pp. 59–141). New York: Plenum.

Oser, F. (1981). Die Theorie von Lawrence Kohlberg im Kreuzfeuer der Kritik—eine Verteidigung. *Bildungsforschung und Bildungspraxis, 3,* 51–64.

Phillips, D. C. & Nicolayev, J. (1978). Kohlbergian moral development: A progressing or degenerating research program? *Educational Theory, 28,* 286–301.

Piaget, J. (1965). *The moral judgment of the child.* (M. Gabain, Trans.). New York: Free Press. (Original work published 1932).

Power, C. (1979). *The moral atmosphere of a just community high school: A four year longitudinal study.* Unpublished doctoral dissertation, Harvard University.

Sabini, J. & Silver, M. (1982). *Moralities of everyday life*. Oxford: University Press.

Schwartz, B., Schuldenfrei, R., & Lacey, H. (1978). Operant psychology as factory psychology. *Behaviorism, 6*, 229–254.

Shweder, R. A. (1982). Beyond self-constructed knowledge: The study of culture and morality. *Merill-Palmer Quarterly, 28*, 41–69.

Simpson, E. L. (1974). Moral development research. A case of scientific cultural bias. *Human Development, 81*, 81–106.

Snarey, J., Kohlberg, L., & Noam, G. (1983). Ego development in perspective: Structural stage, functional phase, and cultural age-period models. *Developmental Review, 3*, 303–338.

Youniss, J. (1980). *Parents and peers in social development*. Chicago: University Press.

17 Limited Morality: A Concept and its Educational Implications

Mordecai Nisan
The Hebrew University
Jerusalem, Israel

Conceptions of moral education are guided by psychological theories of moral development and behavior. Two principal approaches can be distinguished in these theories, those of structuralization and those of internalization. The approaches differ on a number of dimensions (Nisan, 1983), with important educational implications. One realm of major educational importance that has not been explored sufficiently by either approach is that of the violation of moral norms, or immoral behavior. This realm is the focus of this chapter.

The structural approach tends to interpret immoral behavior as resulting from the absence of correct knowledge. This interpretation has a long philosophical history that can be traced back to Socrates. In its simplest form, it states that deviating individuals do so because they do not know the moral rules and principles. A more complex version of this theory holds that deviating individuals have a distorted view of reality, which cause them to "neutralize" their transgression (Sykes & Matza, 1957) and regard it as proper behavior. A more detailed version of this interpretation is proposed by Kohlberg (1971). It suggests that immoral behavior stems from individuals' failure to construct a proper moral principle. Because of this failure they do not identify the moral obligation of the situation, or respond to a quasi-obligation, that is, one which is in fact annulled by a superseding obligation. Making allowances for the specific ways in which a moral structure is applied to a situation, this view would also suggest that people may act immorally if they are incapable of properly applying their moral principle to a specific situation. It implies that moral education must find ways to help people construct a "high" moral principle and "train" them to apply this principle to complex situations.

403

The internalization approach tends to explain immoral behavior as the result of insufficient internalization of moral standards. Thus, according to Eysenck (1976), behavior is the mechanical result of an interplay of various response tendencies individuals have acquired through their specific learning. A much more complex form of this approach is inspired by psychoanalytic theory, which suggests that moral behavior is associated with the conflict between structural tendencies in personality. On the one hand, the tendency to pursue pleasure and self-interest is present, while on the other, there is a tendency to behave in accordance with those norms and inhibitions internalized by the child during its socialization. According to this view, immoral behavior indicates that the latter tendency was weaker than the former, that temptation has overcome the moral inhibitions. More recent versions of the internalization approach in the framework of social learning theory emphasize situational factors and introduce cognitive elements to the explanation of both moral judgement and self-control (Mischel, 1976). Here, too, the central element in interpreting moral deviation is the weakness of the moral tendency vis-a-vis the immoral one. This weakness partially results from the lack of suitable strategies of self-regulation. Mischel's (1974) studies of delay of gratification are an example of this view. This approach intimates that, to influence moral behavior, the moral tendency and its regulative strategy must be developed and reinforced. In its simple form it would recommend using learning techniques, such as reinforcement and models; in its more complex form it suggests, in addition, using various cognitive exercises.

It seems to me that neither of these approaches provides an exhaustive explanation of immoral behavior. Observation of daily life will suffice to show that immoral acts can be committed by individuals who are well aware that they are transgressing and that their specific act is morally wrong and should be avoided. Such actions cannot be explained by the cognitive approach unless we proceed from assumptions that will render the explanation unsupportable and unreasonable. Our observation of reality will also show that immoral acts can be committed not only with full recognition of the moral obligation, but even with deliberate planning and without apparent strong inner conflicts. These acts cannot be explained in terms of irresistible temptation or weakness of will. Of course, it is always possible to invent some mechanical explanation for immoral behavior, which ignores a person's cognition, but this we would not accept—for philosophical reasons concerning our view of people's nature and the definition of morality, and for psychological reasons regarding the appropriate paradigm for the study of morality.

This chapter outlines a different concept of immoral behavior and suggests its educational implications. Its premise is that moral judgment has a motivational power, in the sense that it guides individuals' behavior. This premise is based on psychological theories as well as on daily (naive) observations, which indicate that a powerful moral system exists. But, at the same time, we contend that human beings, even though they are aware of moral ways of behaving, tend to appropriate for themselves and others the right to deviate to a certain extent from the moral ideal. Thus we accept the thesis of the cognitive approach that moral behavior is dictated by moral judgment, but suggest that this influence is only partial. Individuals adopt the moral ideal, but what we call their "level of accepted morality" is not identical with this ideal; individuals may conclude that a given action is merely a "minor" violation that does not disturb their "moral balance." Hence individuals will permit themselves to commit this act, despite the knowledge that their behavior is morally wrong in terms of the moral ideal. Obviously, "temptations" and self-interest play an important part in people's considerations; they are the motivating force behind their actual behavior. But the interplay of forces is not mechanical. Nor is this a situation in which an urgent, immediate temptation is too strong for their will power. Here we have a judgment and a decision resulting from reflection and volition.

This conception suggests that immoral acts committed in daily life are, to a large extent, not the result of ignorance, primitive judgment or the incapacity to resist immediate temptation. Indeed, true moral transgressions in the strict sense are those committed deliberately, knowingly and voluntarily. From the research of Hartshorne and May (1928–1930) through the work of Turiel (1979), it has been found that moral knowledge barely increases with age. Turiel (1979; Nucci & Turiel, 1978) found that even 5-year-olds are already capable of distinguishing between moral rules and social conventions, perceiving the former, but not the latter, as intrinsically valid. Even though, according to Piaget (1932/1965) and Kohlberg, (1971) the moral structure of children changes with age, children of every age acknowledge the moral wrongness associated with various acts. Hence much moral deviation does not seem to derive from ignorance of the moral content or from a lack of insight into its moral validity. Our conception regards much of moral deviation as stemming from the attribution of a low moral weight and gravity to various transgressions, and from the existence of a "level of accepted morality" which is lower than the ideal. In the following, we examine this conception in more detail, and discuss its educational implications; finally we analyze a specific (but typical) program of moral education in the light of our approach.

Moral Judgment and Moral Choice

The type of immoral behavior we have described has two distinctive features: First of all, individuals allow themselves to deviate from what is right by their own judgment. Second, this deviation is limited, as otherwise it would mean a total abandonment of morality, which does not occur. In other words, the extent of the deviation is determined by some sort of a principle.

This description suggests that moral decision-making includes two consecutive processes: (a) *moral judgment* as to whether the behavior at issue is morally right or wrong; and (b) *moral choice* as to whether to perform the behavior or not. In claiming that a deviation may be made while individuals are fully aware that it is immoral to do so we imply that a *moral judgment* has been made in regard to the ''rightness'' of this behavior. This judgment is in terms of an ideal moral standard, designating the behavior at issue as either right or wrong. Responses to hypothetical dilemmas reflect this type of judgment. They refer to a decontextualized act, and are based on meager knowledge about the persons involved, their characteristics and their histories.

At the same time, in claiming that the performance of the act may be deliberate, not impulsive or arbitrary but according to some sort of a principle, we imply that a second decision takes place. We may call it a *moral choice*. It concerns the question: ''May I commit this specific act which I consider not right?'' Assuming that this question is asked when no fear of external sanctions is experienced, the mere question seems to imply an adoption of the moral order, and its meaning must be something like: ''Would it be acceptable for me to commit this sin?''

Now, it seems certain that there are some norms so absolute that they proscribe the raising of such a question. Thus the norm that forbids the taking of a life may sometimes be suspended or considered inapplicable (as during a war), but so long as it is seen as applicable, no deviation is acceptable. The identification and understanding of such absolutes (which may be culturally dependent) seems a worthy task for students of moral behavior.

However, everyday observations of such phenomena as ''white lies,'' private use of public property, evasion of income tax and a variety of other ''small'' sins suggest that certain behaviors under some conditions may indeed be considered ''acceptable'' deviations. We would like to suggest that ''acceptable'' should be understood in quantitive terms. This means that the moral decision is based on a quantitative principle. After they have judged an intended act as morally wrong, individuals may further ask themselves ''how bad'' is this specific act in this specific context and if it is an acceptable deviation for them at this point in their moral career. We will distinguish between two sorts of variables which seem to determine the answer to this question: (a) intrinsic features of the act under the given circumstances. These will determine what we call the ''seriousness'' of the transgression; and (b) individuals' factors—the moral state of people (what we call their ''moral balance'') and their ''level of accepted morality.'' All of these are variable across conditions and time, and have a quantitative dimension. The variables of the seriousness of transgression and ''level of accepted morality'' will be treated later. We now comment very briefly on the variable of the state of the person.

Unlike the moral judgment, the moral choice relates not to a decontextualized act, but to a person in a context. For the people who make a moral decision, this choice is perceived as an element in a continuous stream of behavior; it is considered against the background of, and as a part of, a series of moral (and nonmoral) behaviors. It seems reasonable therefore, to suggest that the persons making a moral choice take into account not only their evaluation of the intended act, but also their moral "state"—an overall evaluation of moral standing at that time. This evaluation seems to involve a sort of summary score, or a "moral balance," based on their overall behavior and in relation to individuals' ideal moral standard. Our basic premise that people adopt the moral order is thus extended to mean that people feel morally obliged not only to abide by moral norms, but also to adhere, in terms of their general behavior, to a personal moral standard.

The notion of an overall moral evaluation of a person in relation to a standard introduces the quantitative dimension of closeness to the standard. Indeed, people are willing to give themselves and others marks for moral "standing" if asked to do so on a questionnaire. These marks indicate that people are not seen as divided into villains and saints, but can only be classified by various gradations of virtue.

The distinction between moral judgment and moral choice, together with the quantitative dimension of moral evaluation, underlie our central thesis of *limited morality*.

LIMITED MORALITY

According to the concept of limited morality individuals do not aspire to perfect behavior in accordance with the moral ideal, but accept a certain distance from the ideal. Even though individuals aspire to be virtuous and honest, in accordance with their normative judgment, they do not aspire to be entirely righteous or saintly. Individuals allow themselves what they consider a "small" deviation from the ideal. Faced with the temptation to commit a transgression they may reason: "I know that this deed is wrong, but all things considered, the transgression is relatively small and I can allow myself to compromise somewhat in this case." Our thesis may be regarded as an expansion of the concept of supererogation into the sphere of transgression. Supererogation refers to acts that are perceived as recommendable but not obligatory. People who perform them are considered a saint, but if they do not, individuals are not necessarily sinners. They may tell themselves: "I know that it is morally desirable to perform these acts, but I am not and do not aspire to be righteous." In the context of supererogation this is an acceptable statement, for no clear border exists, for example, between helping one's fellow man and sacrificing oneself, and people are not actually expected to do the latter. Our thesis is that similar considerations are used in regard to clearly defined prohibitions as well. Here, too, people allow themselves to deviate from the absolute ideal in accordance with their own notions, even though in this sphere formal definitions do exist. Behavior according to the moral ideal may sometimes be considered parallel to self-sacrifice.

The concept of limited morality corresponds in certain respects to that of bounded rationality suggested by Simon (1957). Simon theorized that the limitations of human being's information processing capacity bring them to adopt a principle of "satisficing" rather than the "rational" principle of maximization of utility; people will suffice themselves with an "acceptable" alternative, rather than search and try for the best one. Later studies have pointed out further motivational limits to rationality (March, 1978). A study by Nisan and Koriat (1977) suggests that this type of "bound rationality" is already found in 6-year-olds. In this study children were asked to choose between one piece of chocolate today, and two pieces tomorrow, and also to tell what they thought a bright and a less intelligent child, respectively, would choose. The choices were placed before them in different orders. Most children thought that a bright child would choose two pieces of chocolate tomorrow. Nevertheless, a high percentage of the children chose for themselves one piece of chocolate today, even though they believed this to be the choice of less bright children. It thus seems that these young children already experience a discrepancy between their actual choice and their own conception of "rational" choice. They seem to be aware that their actual choice is a sort of "limited rationality."

While the concept of duty is unique to morality, it seems justified to draw a parallel between moral and rational behavior, not only because in some philosophical discussions the rational basis of moral behavior is emphasized (e.g., Rawls, 1971), but also because of the similarity of the typical conflict situations in both spheres. In both we find a type of higher-order tendency, which is considered superior to the opposed, highly temptational tendency. And while it is true that from the philosophical point of view, moral deviations are less expected, because moral obligation is regarded as overriding all other considerations and inclinations (Hare, 1963), psychologically they are less surprising than "rational" deviations. If people compromise rationality in matters of their own self-interest, they can certainly be expected to compromise morality, where the interests of others are at stake.

The right individuals arrogate themselves to deviate from the ideal is associated with a view of human nature, widely accepted, at least in western society, and most prominently represented (in psychology) by the Freudian approach. This view regards humans as the arena of a struggle between flesh and spirit, instinct and reason, egoistic and moral inclinations. Both sides are perceived as part of human nature and hence their struggle is inevitable and perpetual. This view intimates that it is impossible for individuals to be morally perfect and that every person surrenders from time to time to their weaknesses and must make compromises. A good person is therefore not necessarily a perfect person (such a one may even be "suspect"), but one who preserves a reasonable "moral balance." This conception is implicitly accepted by society as normative: certain transgressions, though morally rejected, are forgiven. This is not experienced as a contradiction, nor is there any indication that the norms are judged invalid. Even if we are willing to forgive certain transgressions and sins, we are not prepared to forgive their consistent commission. This indicates that the norm is considered valid and the forgiveness is associated with "limited morality." Religious ideologies, literary works and popular proverbs acknowledge the inevitability of occasional concessions, and distinguish between major and minor transgressions. Courts of justice also consider the degree of seriousness of violations. Some violations may be forgiven or only lightly punished, even if they are deliberate. The institutionalization of limited morality suggests that the boundaries of morality are transferred through direct socialization. Parents may instill in their children the conviction that they must behave morally, but don't have to be absolutely virtuous; that it is commendable to be saintly, but it is quite acceptable to be "human."

Seriousness of Transgression and Level of Accepted Morality

The limited morality thesis suggests that people's sense of moral duty demands that they preserve an appropriate level of morality, without necessarily being morally perfect. But individuals can arrogate the right to deviate from the ideal only if they are able to distinguish between various transgressions and to evaluate their seriousness. There is no doubt that trangressions are indeed judged by their degree of seriousness. Children and adults alike find it quite natural to do this, and a considerable degree of agreement exists as to the criteria for such an evaluation.

Several factors determining the seriousness of a transgression can be distinguished, some of them "rational," such as the damage caused to others, and others "non-rational," such as the gravity of socialization in regard to a certain norm. We will discuss two factors, which seem to be especially relevant in our context: (a) the degree of temptation in a given situation and, correspondingly, the effort required to resist it and abide by the norm; and (b) the prevalence of transgressions of this type. Our research shows that both 6-year-olds and adolescents believe a transgression committed because of a strong temptation is less serious than one committed although temptation was not very strong. These conclusions are based on judgment of the behavior of others, but may also be assumed to apply to judgments of one's own behavior. Thus, when a person is strongly tempted he regards his surrender as less serious than when he is less strongly tempted (all other things being equal).

We also found that children and adolescents alike believe that a person is less likely to commit a serious transgression than a minor one. We conclude that people faced with strong temptation or expecting to have to make a considerable effort in order to abide by the norm are more readily inclined to allow themselves to deviate. It should be made clear that we are not referring to cases where irresistible temptations lead directly to surrender, but rather to those in which temptation affects people's *judgment* of the seriousness of a transgression and this, in turn, inclines them to decide to commit it. The same applies to people's judgment of the required effort. Anticipating too great an effort may induce individuals not to abide by the norm, not because they cannot control themselves, but because they regard the demand as too great and hence the deviation from the norm as less serious and thus permissible. Although the temptation and the effort required to resist it are not necessarily the same, they are nevertheless closely related; hence the alternating use of the terms "moral effort" and "temptation." (It should be kept in mind that the variables "temptation" and "moral effort" are not the only ones to determine the seriousness of a transgression. An extremely strong temptation does not always detract from the seriousness of the transgression, for example when the damage caused to others is very great).

The second factor we mentioned is the frequency of a transgression. The more prevalent a transgression, the less serious it is believed to be (all other factors being equal). On the one hand, the prevalence of a transgression is an indication of its temptational nature, while, on the other, it raises the question of the justice of the demand to refrain from the transgression: If others allow themselves this transgression, I, too, am justified if I commit it *occasionally*. We have indeed found that children and adolescents tend to view prevalent transgressions as less serious. They also believe, not unexpectedly, that people are more likely to commit such transgressions than less common ones. In an extreme case of a very common transgression, people will regard the norm that forbids it as invalid, as one that normal people cannot be expected to abide by. Children evidently distinguish between "preached" norms and norms that are actually observed. They even learn to adopt such preached norms without applying them to their actual behavior (Bryan & Walbek, 1970).

The two mentioned factors, in combination with others not discussed here, allow people a certain latitude in their moral choice. Individuals may consider an act as temptational, as too demanding or as commonly "accepted," and therefore decide to deviate from their moral ideal. Such considerations are subjective to a great extent and therefore easily affected by defensive tendencies. This suggests a resemblance between our thesis concerning the evaluation of the seriousness of a transgression and those of Sykes and Matza (1957), but whereas they suggest the notion of neutralization, which negates the wrongness of the deed and regards it as justifiable behavior, we suggest that while acknowledging its wrongness, people may belittle the seriousness of a transgression and therefore *allow* themselves to commit it under certain circumstances (but not in an unlimited manner as in the case of neutralization).

The variable of the seriousness of a deed calls for an additional factor, if it is to explain level of limited morality. We have suggested that when making a moral choice, individuals take into account not only their evaluation of the intended act but also their "moral balance," a weighted summary of their moral state which they calculate on the basis of their overall behavior. Individuals thus need a standard by which they may judge whether the intended transgression would not take them too far from the ideal. This standard we may call the "level of accepted morality'' (LAM). It is the level of moral balance individuals set for themselves as that from which they may not descend.

It may be assumed that the LAM is affected by people's views of themselves and of the behavior of others. If individuals believe themselves to be weak and incapable of making a strong moral effort, their LAM will be low. If, on the other hand, individuals see themselves as strong and capable of coping with any temptation and demand, their LAM will be high. Individuals' LAMs are also affected by the behavior of other people, which sets a norm in regard to the level of socially accepted morality.

Reaching a moral decision in the manner suggested here is a process that compels people to refer to the moral ideal. To judge the seriousness of behavior and to evaluate their moral balance, individuals must represent in their mind their version of the moral ideal as well as their LAM. These representations aid in both the evaluation and the motivational control of behavior. Even though people make compromises, they still hold on to an absolute moral ideal, being fully aware that the less they yield the better person they will be. This conviction, which is reinforced by society's normative system, helps individuals keep their strong egoistic inclinations under control, preventing the total erosion of their moral faculties.

The seriousness of the transgression and the LAM are variables that significantly affect people's moral behavior. The normal daily temptations to transgressions do not require complicated judgments since people generally know the norm and accept its validity (in terms of the ideal morality). Nor do such situations present strong, irresistible temptation. In these cases individuals' choices depend on their evaluation of whether a specific transgression will lower their moral balance to below their LAM, and, hence, on the importance and seriousness they attribute to this transgression as well as on their momentary moral balance. The easier it is for individuals to belittle the transgression, and the more justifications they are offered to lower their LAM, the more they will be inclined to commit the transgression.

Sense of Moral Control

The concept of limited morality offers moral education an aim—not exclusive, of course—different from those derived from the main approaches towards moral development (namely the cognitive-developmental approach, which stresses the advancement of moral reasoning, and the internalization approaches, which stress inculcation of specific contents). The idea that people accept the moral order, but, knowing the weaknesses of human nature, allow themselves and others to compromise, points at an educational aim that seems justifiable: to help individuals behave in a manner they accept as proper and to narrow the gap between individuals' ideals and their actual behavior. Such an aim may be conceived as education towards self-actualization, and towards the realization of

one's higher-order motivations (Allstone, 1977). Several educational conceptions pursue a similar aim—to bring the pupil closer to an intrinsic ideal
(Kohlberg & Mayer, 1972).

The aim derived from the concept of limited morality seems reasonable and
contains nothing to deter the educator; it does not involve the formidable objectives of acquiring or developing structures and values individuals were unable to
acquire in their natural environment, of changing their personality structure, or
of breaking down their defenses. Limited morality implies that immoral acts may
be deliberate behavior, the choice of which takes into consideration the severity
of the transgression, the moral balance and the LAM. It thus seems to fit Rest's
(this volume) Component III of moral judgment. Presumably, all the considerations mentioned can be influenced and are therefore continuous objects of moral
education. Moral education would aim at narrowing the gap between behavior
and the moral ideal, by exposing the importance and seriousness of different
types of behavior on the one hand, and by raising people's LAMs on the other.
These are doubtless worthy objectives which seem to be all the more reasonable
as they agree with the basic inclination, presumably present even in children, to
adhere to a chosen ideal.

These two objectives—exposing the importance and seriousness of moral
behaviors, and raising the LAM—seem to have different emphases; the former
stresses an objective standard of evaluation; the latter, a subjective standard.
Psychologically, this distinction seems justified, but it must be noted that conceptually the two objectives are interrelated and partly overlapping. Thus, people
with high LAMs will attribute relatively great importance and seriousness to
every moral act. And although the severity of an act is determined, inter alia, by
such objective factors as the damage caused to others, subjective factors such as
the degree of temptation and emotional arousal also play a role. On the other
hand, the LAM, though in the first place a personal standard, is also partly
influenced by "objective" factors, such as, for example, the "LAM" of one's
group. Obviously, the two objectives are inter-dependent and affect each other.
Nevertheless, their different emphases indicate that they proceed from different
directions: the former from the importance and seriousness of the intended behavior and the relevant norm, the latter from the people's perception of their
ability to approach the ideal, and their evaluation of the prevailing LAM in
society. Both directions seem relevant to the two objectives, but depending on
the social and educational conditions, one or the other may be emphasized.

We may gain a better understanding of, and insight into, the objectives
mentioned above through an analogy with a framework and a concept recently
deemed central in the explanation of behavior—the sense of control (Bandura,
1977; Rotter, 1966; Seligman, 1975). The belief of individuals in their ability to
control outcomes in their environment has been found to be related to their
willingness to make an effort and hence indeed to succeed itself (Jones, 1977).
Dweck (1975), for example, found a difference between children who tried to

justify their failures by referring to their poor abilities and those who ascribed their failures to insufficient effort. The former tended to give up, while the latter were induced to try harder. The sense of control is thus associated with the conviction that success depends on effort (in addition to ability, which remains an essential precondition). While discussions of the sense of control have dealt almost exclusively with people's subjective probability of success, we would tend to emphasize, in the context of *moral* sense of control, individuals' evaluations of the effort required in carrying out a specific task. We would predict that people who evaluate the required effort as "reasonable" will be more willing to make this effort. Thus, the seemingly paradoxical lack of effort to accomplish something individuals are evidently interested in may readily be explained in terms of their *beliefs* that the desired outcome cannot be achieved, or, as we have added, requires a tremendous effort.

In light of all the foregoing we may now speak of a "sense of *moral* control." A high sense of moral control implies that individuals judge it possible to behave in close agreement with the moral ideal; that they are convinced that they themselves can behave in this manner; and that they believe that the required effort is not too great. These convictions seem to lead to, or correlate with, a number of attitudes and perceptions: the people in question will be more readily prepared to make a moral effort; they will have a higher LAM; they will ascribe immoral behavior to insufficient effort and not to inability to resist temptation; and consequently, they will attribute greater moral significance to various acts. These attitudes are, of course, closely related to the educational objectives ensuing from the model of limited morality. "Gaining a sense of moral control" may thus be used as a convenient summarizing concept, covering, though not exhaustively, the essence of the objectives we have derived from our model.

A THEORETICAL ANALYSIS OF A PROGRAM OF VALUE EDUCATION

In this section we apply the theoretical framework to an ongoing program of value education. Our analysis may provide a somewhat new look at the program, which may be described as "traditional" moral training through moral practice.

The program is conducted in a secondary school for girls, as part of its compulsory curriculum. It requires that every student invest 3 hours per week in helping a person in the community. A person in need of help (an aged or disabled person, a child in a children's home, etc.) is assigned to every student and visit him at least once a week at a fixed time. The program gives the student a responsibility she cannot treat lightly; someone is waiting for her and trusts that she will come. In addition to this practical service, the program also includes theoretical study of the subject of helping others, which is incorporated in the graduation examinations. The declared rationale of the program includes several of the usual goals of educational frameworks, such as development of sensitivity for people's needs, acquisition of values and formation of norms. However, we examine this program in light of objectives suggested by our theoretical analysis, i.e., formation of beliefs and perceptions regarding a person's moral abilities, regarding the moral weight of behaviors and norms, and regarding the moral behavior of people belonging to the reference group of the individual (affecting the individual's LAM). In this light we examine the following three components of the program: (a) a behavioral component—the activity of the individual student; (b) a social component—the behavior of the group; and (c) a cognitive component—the theoretical study of the subject of helping.

The central component of the program is the moral activity required from the individual. Her activity is moral in the sense that both society and individuals associate it with the moral idea of "being good." It may be said that an implicit assumption of the program is that although different modes of moral behavior can be distinguished (there is, for example, a difference between refraining from committing a transgression and performing a good deed), all belong to the same moral sphere. The effort involved in extending help to one's fellow man is similar, in an important sense, to the effort needed to refrain from committing a transgression. In both cases this effort is required to overcome the temptation of self-interest. This assumption is in accordance with the view of morality as an approach towards the ideal, which underlies our concept of limited morality. It is not an obvious assumption, but we will not elaborate it here.

The student's moral activity is expected to affect three perceptions which are deemed central by our analysis; her view of the value and importance of morally relevant acts (i.e., affecting the welfare of other people), her view of her own moral "capacity" and of the effort she may be expected to invest in moral acts, and her view of the social norm as to the moral level actually required (and acted by) members of society. A major determinant of the moral weight of an action, in the eyes of the actor, is its consequences to other people. A program that requires a continuous personal involvement with people in need is likely to affect the actor's view of the importance of moral actions by enhancing the awareness of the value and extent of their consequences. This is a common aim of programs of this type. In addition, our analysis brings to light the effects of the perceptions mentioned above. The student's own behavior is doubtless her most reliable source of knowledge of her moral capacity; if she persists in her moral efforts she may change her view of this capacity as well as her evaluation of the required effort. No less important is the effect of her persistence on her view of the social norm. Heider (1958) suggests that the source perceived as the most reliable for the knowledge of the social norm is the behavior of the individual himself. People are inclined to see their own behavior as a reflection of the norm, and different behavior as a deviation from the norm, resulting from the deviant's specific circumstances and characteristics. This may occur because the individual's own behavior is more salient in his consciousness. In any case, Heider's thesis has received empirical support (Hansen & Donoghue, 1977).

Yet there is no doubt that in a restricted social framework, such as a school, individual behavior unaccompanied by similar behavior in others will not easily come to be perceived by the behaving individual as an accepted norm. Here we encounter the second component of the program—the behavior of the other members of the reference group. Since here all members of the group participate in the same moral behavior, the conviction of a strong and generally accepted social norm is reinforced. At the same time, the behavior of her fellows also strengthens the individual's view of herself, which is largely influenced by social comparison (Suls & Miller, 1977).

The influences described may be expected to be exerted if the student behaves in the expected manner—not an easy, but a possible, accomplishment; and if that behavior is not perceived as coerced—a rather difficult condition. Coercion provokes counter-reactions or "reactance" (Brehm, 1981) and thus creates a need for additional moral efforts. It also causes individuals to feel that their moral capacity, and that of others as well, is weak; otherwise no coercion is needed.

The cognitive component of the program, the theoretical study, aims to resolve the problem of coercion. It includes regular lessons in which texts on the subject of helping one's neighbor and society are analyzed, and the problems faced by the students in their work are discussed. The cognitive component proceeds from the assumption that people's basic orientation is moral, or in cognitive-developmental terms that the educator can anchor the moral demand in the student's moral structure. By thus anchoring the demand the teacher gives it moral validity and at the same time weakens and hopefully even eliminates feelings of coercion. This specific program was introduced in a religious school where the moral content is anchored in religious duty. The students studied religious texts dealing with people's duty to help others, and in this context they scrutinized their own work. Helping behavior was thus perceived as part of their religious duty and a consequence of their belief. The external demand was thus presented—and hopefully also perceived—as a reminder and an encouragement to perform a moral act, rather than as a coercive command. We believe that a similar process is no less possible in a nonreligious framework. The demand to help one's fellow man can be anchored in moral structures like those described by Kohlberg's Stages 3 or 4, so that the individual sees the demand as derived from moral duty.

An important feature of the program, which is probably a necessary condition for success in anchoring the demand in the moral structure, is its continuity and length. The student is assigned a regular and continuous responsibility for a person. Only if the demand is consistent and continuous can it be regarded as of intrinsic value and not as an arbitrary demand of an external agent. Moreover, the continuity of the program and the assignment of a person almost guarantee that the student will try to cope with the program and to incorporate it in the context of her own moral orientation. The longer she is involved in helping an old man, for example, and the more she forms a relationship with him and learns about his situation, the more likely she is to ask herself such questions as: "Why am I doing this?", "Is it really my duty?", "What should the social institutions do in this matter?". These and similar questions reflect attempts to reach constructive understandings that lay the foundations in which the moral demand can be anchored.

The anchoring of the demand in the moral structure, and the continuity of the program also create the dynamics propounded by the dissonance theory (Festinger, 1957). Behavior extending over a long period of time confronts people with the conflict of self-interest and moral duty. There are two possible ways to solve this conflict. Individuals may tell themselves that this behavior was imposed on them or, on the other hand, that it agrees with their own moral ideal. The principal assumption of the present program, and for that matter, of every educational program based on behavior, is that the former solution will not work over the long run because it weakens people's self-image and sense of control; and probably more importantly, it does not agree with their "true" moral nature. People will therefore turn to the second solution, the acceptance of moral duty, even if there is only the slightest inducement to do so.

It is possible to formulate this analysis in terms of our summarizing concept—the sense of moral control. Positive moral behavior will arouse people's sense of moral control, because they have succeeded in making a moral effort and acting against their inclination to follow their egoistic needs. This has two consequences: on the one hand, people learn to respect their ability, and, on the other, they realize that the moral task requires a degree of effort which is not beyond their powers. These perceptions, in turn, will help to prevent attempts to justify or belittle transgressions with the claim that there was a strong temptation. However, studies on sense of control remind us that moral behavior is itself not sufficient, just as having successfully completed a task is not sufficient to change people's feelings of helplessness (Dweck, 1975). Experience must be accompanied by appropriate understanding and change in attribution of behavior to the sense of duty instead of to coercion. The theoretical teachings, anchoring the act of helping in the individuals' moral structures, may be considered as attempts at achieving such attributions.

Some Effects of the Program

A satisfactory evaluation of this program and its impact is not yet possible. While interviews and questionnaires completed by students have provided seemingly reliable data, the indispensable information as to long-term influence is not yet available, since the respondents were still in school and still engaged in the program. Nevertheless, some of the observations are valuable.

The most striking observation concerns the condition we have claimed is crucial for the program's success—the anchoring of its moral demand in moral structure. For many of the students the program has indeed provoked thinking about the situation and attempts at understanding it, combined with a feeling of being freed from coercion. These attempts started with criticisms of the activities and questioning of their justification, usefulness and so on. They presented difficult problems for the teachers and students, forcing them to cope with problems of both moral structure (principles) and moral content (e.g., morally relevant beliefs). Questions arose as to the definition of rights and duties, the effects of the extended help on the receiver's social functioning, and many other issues. The questions and doubts of the students about their activities, which we regard as indications of attempts at construction, sometimes found expression in their transferring to different activities, not only for egoistic reasons, but sometimes also for reasons of justice ("I didn't think they deserved to be helped.")

However, we received the impression that over the course of time, and beyond these hesitations, the two basic preconditions for the program's success were fulfilled. In general, the students behaved consistently and responsibly, and the feeling of coercion was reduced and in some cases even disappeared. The weakening of the feeling of coercion resulted from the conviction that the required behavior was part of the individual's moral framework, of the duties that people may and should be expected to fulfill.

Keeping in mind the limitations of our data, we point out very briefly the summary of respondents' answers to several questions that relate to the program's aims. We mention first two secondary findings regarding necessary conditions for success of the program. A substantial number of participants in the program came to acknowledge first that the need for help was much greater than they had thought initially, and second that they might have made a significant contribution by their help. These findings suggest the existence of the necessary basis for perceiving the helping behavior and the related norm as important. We turn now to results related to the main aims suggested by our theoretical analysis. The questionnaires revealed that participants in the program tended to agree that they were capable of making greater moral efforts than they had expected; the effort demanded of them by the program was reasonable and within the powers of every student and person in general; behavior for the purpose of helping others was much more prevalent than they had thought initially; some of their friends had shown admirable consistency and dedication; there is a real, and not only a theoretical, moral duty to help others in accordance with every person's capacity and inclination. Participants also came to distinguish between help based on empathy and sympathy, and that based on a moral duty, which requires an effort beyond one's personal inclinations. Although we do not know the depth, extent and stability of these influences, they seem to indicate the potential of this educational method.

CONCLUDING REMARKS

We conclude by pointing out a basic assumption of the suggested educational approach that should be investigated. The approach of moral education through moral practice is based on the assumption of a general concept of people's moral abilities, a sort of sense of moral control, based on the accumulation of their moral experiences, and affecting moral behavior. It is assumed that beyond the differences in contents and contexts of various moral situations, individuals find a common denominator based on which they reach a generalization as to their moral capacity. This generalization does not deny a certain differentiation in perception of moral capacity, but assumes that beyond this it is still possible to speak of a generalized conception. A critical point from the educational point of view is the claim that this generalization has a significant influence on behavior in specific situations. It should be mentioned, however, that we still have no evidence in this regard, and even if we theoretically accept the generalization (as it is accepted in the sphere of sense of control), the effect may be small from the educational viewpoint. If this is true, the educator should be advised to resort to a different strategy—namely, to deal specifically with those norms and behaviors that are problematic.

Related to the above is the assumption, already mentioned, of a continuity extending from positive behavior, such as help to one's fellow man, and through to the avoidance of negative behavior, such as harming one's fellow man. This assumption is based on a phenomenological examination of the concepts of morality and of good and evil among human beings, which indicates (at least in Western culture) that good and bad are perceived as constituting two poles of one continuum, both related to a unitary factor, namely morality (although the weight of bad behavior is probably greater than that of good behavior in determining the moral balance, a phenomenon that is not confined to the sphere of morality; Kanouse & Hanson, 1971). While the assumption seems plausible, it should be pointed out that the nature and extent of the relationship between morally good and bad behavior has not yet been studied. Educational programs of the type described earlier are focused on positive behavior, for practical reasons. It is easy to design such a program, and probably impossible to design one which focuses on avoiding transgressions. But the very fact that it is simple to build one program and not the other may indicate that the two should be differentiated. If morally positive and negative behaviors are separated to a great extent, we probably need to speak about separate and different LAM's for good and bad behaviors, and indeed, about two separate faces of moral education—the avoidance of the bad and the approach to the good.

ACKNOWLEDGMENTS

Research described in this paper was supported by a grant from the United States-Israel Binational Science Foundation (BSF), Jerusalem, Israel. The paper was written while the author was a visiting researcher at the Max Planck Institute for Human Development and Education, Berlin. The support of the Institute is gratefully acknowledged.

REFERENCES

Allstone, W. (1977). Self-intervention and the structure of motivation, in T. Mischel (Ed.), *The self: Psychological and philosophical issues* (pp. 65–102). Oxford: Blackwell.

Bandura, A. (1977). Self-efficacy: Toward a unifying theory of behavioral change. *Psychological Review, 84*, 191–215.

Brehm, J. W. (1981). *Psychological reactance.* New York: Academic.

Bryan, J. H. & Walbek, N. H. (1970). Preaching and practicing generosity: Children's actions and reactions. *Child Development, 41*, 329–353.

Dweck, C. S. (1975). The Role of expectations and attributions in the alleviation of learned helplessness. *Journal of Personality and Social Psychology, 31*, 674–685.

Eysenck, H. J. (1976). The biology of morality. In T. Lickona (Ed.), *Moral development and behavior*, (pp. 108–123). New York: Holt, Rinehart and Winston.

Festinger, L. (1957). *A theory of cognitive dissonance.* Stanford, CA: Stanford University.

Hansen, R. D. & Donoghue, J. M. (1977). The power of consensus: Information derived from one's own and other's behavior. *Journal of Personality and Social Psychology, 35*, 294–302.

Hare, R. M. (1963). *Freedom and reason.* Oxford: Oxford University Press.

Hartshorne, H. & May, M. A. (1928–1930). *Studies in the nature of character. Vols. 1–3.* New York: Macmillan.

Heider, F. (1958). *The psychology of interpersonal relations.* New York: Wiley.

Jones, R. A. (1977). *Self-fulfilling prophecies.* Hillsdale, NJ: Erlbaum.

Kanouse, D. E. & Hanson, L. R. Jr. (1971). *Negativity in evaluation.* Morristown, NJ: General Learning.

Kohlberg, L. (1971). From is to ought: How to commit the naturalistic fallacy and get away with it in the study of moral development. In T. Mischel (Ed.), *Cognitive development and epistemology*, (pp. 151–235). New York: Academic.

Kohlberg, L. & Mayer, R. (1972). Development as the aim of education. *Harvard Educational Review, 42*, 449–496.

March, J. G. (1978). Bounded rationality, ambiguity and the engineering of choice. *The Bell Journal of Economics, 9*, 587–608.

Mischel, W. (1974). Processes in delay of gratification. In L. Berkowitz (Ed.), *Advances in Social Psychology*, Vol. 7, (pp. 249–292). New York: Academic.

Mischel, W. (1976). A Cognitive social-learning approach to morality and self-regulation. In T. Lickona (Ed.), *Moral development and behavior*, (pp. 84–107). New York: Holt, Rinehart and Winston.

Nisan, M. (1983, Hebrew). Two approaches to development of Moral Judgment—an attempt at integration. In M. Nisan and U. Last (Eds.), *Between education and psychology*, (pp. 383–407). Jerusalem: Magnes.

Nisan, M. & Koriat, A. (1977). Children's actual choices and their conception of the wise choice in a delay of gratification situation. *Child Development, 48*, 488–494.

Nucci, L. & Turiel, E. (1978). Social interactions and the development of social concepts in preschool children. *Child Development, 49*, 400–407.

Piaget, J. (1965). *The moral judgment of the child.* (M. Gabain, Trans.) New York: Free Press. (First published in English, London: Kegan Paul, 1932).

Rawls, J. (1971). *A theory of justice.* Cambridge, MA: Harvard University Press.

Rotter, J. B. (1966). Generalized expectancies for internal vs. external control of reinforcements. *Psychological Monographs, 80* (No. 609).

Seligman, M. E. P. (1975). *Helplessness: On depression, development and death.* San Francisco: Freeman.

Simon, H. (1957). *Models of man.* New York: Wiley.

Suls, J. M. & Miller, R. L. (Eds.) (1977). *Social comparison processes: Theoretical and empirical processes.* New York: Wiley.

Sykes, G. M. & Matza, D. (1957). Techniques of neutralization: A theory of delinquency. *American Sociological Review, 22,* 664–670.

Turiel, E. (1979). Distinct conceptual and developmental domains: Social conventions and morality. In H. E. Howe & C. B. Keasey (Eds.), *Nebraska Symposium on Motivation, 1977: Social cognitive development* (Vol. 25) (pp. 77–116). Lincoln, NE: University of Nebraska.

18 The Postconventional Level of Moral Development: Psychology or Philosophy?

Guido Küng
University of Fribourg, Switzerland

THE POSTULATION OF POSTCONVENTIONAL STAGES

Kohlberg (1981), elaborating and concretizing ideas of Piaget and Dewey, has empirically documented that there are distinct stages in the development of moral judgment, and he has demonstrated that these lead from an egocentric level to a second (conventional) level where social norms are recognized, and further on to a third (postconventional) level where an attempt is made to justify these norms in terms of general principles.

But not content to have mapped out in some detail how human beings can develop to this third level of principled morality, Kohlberg has tried to differentiate *within* the level of postconventional morality that form of moral judgment which would lead to the highest perfection. Taking his clue from the history of European philosophy, he distinguishes within the postconventional level a first stage, which corresponds to the position of classical liberalism and utilitarianism and a second stage, which corresponds to the Kantian position in the form given to it by John Rawls (1971). Taking into account the parallel subdivision of the two first levels into a total of four stages, these two stages become Stage 5 and Stage 6 in the scheme of overall moral reasoning development.

The entire line of development, from Stage 1 to Stage 6, can be viewed as a line of recognition of increasing reciprocity among the members of society. This line has Stage 6, the Kantian or Rawlsian stage, as its culminating point; because, at that stage, the moral autonomy of each human individual is recognized as an absolute value, i.e., when reaching Stage 6 the individual realizes that in moral reflection one has the duty to put oneself into the place of each of the other individuals ("ideal role taking").

421

But whereas the existence of the earlier stages is empirically well-established, the same is not true for Stage 6. Kohlberg had to admit that none of the individuals whom he has tested clearly belongs to Stage 6. Thus it is only in theory that Stage 6 is distinct from Stage 5. Furthermore, as far as philosophical theory is concerned, many philosophers do not regard the Rawlsian position as the highest ethical position. Some argue that the utilitarian approach suffices to do justice to the moral autonomy of the human being. Others, such as highly patriotic people, or Marxists, or religious thinkers criticize the Rawlsian position, because for them the liberation of their nation, or the socialist emancipation of mankind, or religious salvation are higher values than the moral autonomy attributed to each individual; they believe that in critical situations the moral autonomy of certain individuals must be sacrificed for the sake of these higher values (Küng, 1984).

As a matter of fact, Kohlberg himself has come to postulate a religious stage beyond the Rawlsian stage. Not that he agrees with those who claim there is something wrong with the Rawlsian position, but he believes that the Rawlsian insights can be considered from the wider perspective of religious wisdom. He recognized, therefore, as a further step on the way to perfection, the step where an individual realizes that human dignity has its roots in an all embracing Absolute, an Absolute which has been called 'God' or 'Nature,' or by some other name which denotes the Infinite. At first Kohlberg counted this ultimate religious stage among the stages of *moral* development and called it Stage 7. However, the investigations of religious consciousness by Fowler (1976, 1978) have led him to understand that there is a path of full scale religious development of the individual that takes place *alongside* moral development. Therefore, what had been called Stage 7 is now recognized to be better conceived as Stage 6 of the path of religious development. But this religious Stage 6 is conceived by Kohlberg (1981) as a continuation following upon the Rawlsian stage of moral development.

Jürgen Habermas (1975), who has become interested in the work of Kohlberg, also tried to continue the earlier Kohlbergian scheme by adding a seventh stage beyond the Rawlsian stage. In accordance with his neomarxist outlook, the additional stage proposed by Habermas is not a religious stage, but a stage of ultimate social emancipation, which adds to the ideals of utilitarianism (civil liberties and public welfare) and Kantianism (moral autonomy) the ideal of genuine political freedom in the socialist sense, characterized by a universalized interpretation of need (cf. Apel, 1980a, pp. 59–60).

THE SPECIAL NATURE OF THE POSTCONVENTIONAL LEVEL

Before going on to theorize about Stage 6 and beyond, it may be time to sit back and ask ourselves whether it makes sense to postulate the existence of a necessary sequence of developmental stages at the postconventional level. Could it not be that the postconventional level differs in so fundamental a way from the previous ones that it becomes quite implausible to expect that here, too, there should exist an unambiguous line of development (cf. Gilligan & Murphy, 1979)?

An individual who has reached the postconventional level has in a certain sense become *morally grown-up:* The individual has come to see him or herself as a member of society and has even reached the point where in his or her moral argumentations realizes that he or she can criticize the actually existing norms in terms of more general principles. Is it really reasonable to believe that on this level the further development of moral judgment will still follow a line that is the same for all individuals? Must we not admit that in choosing the general principles by which to criticize existing norms, adults can follow different directions, becoming *either* utilitarians, *or* Rawlsians, *or* Marxists, *or* anarchists, etc.? Must we not say that the individuals on the postconventional level have entered the level of *philosophical* discussion where progress is seldom progress by consensus but mostly progress by agreeing to disagree, each discussant improving his or her own line of thought?

The development from Stage 1 to Stage 5 is characterized by a successive broadening of scope due to a successive discovery of the basic psychological and sociological facts of life. First the individual notices the other as someone with whom he or she is interacting, then the person becomes aware of the existence of a social order, and finally realizes the changeability of the social order and thus the necessity of justifying its norms by an appeal to general principles. In contrast with this, the passage from the utilitarian to the Rawlsian position does not seem to involve a coming to know of further empirical facts. It mainly consists in the recognition that the moral autonomy of each individual is an absolute value. Is it reasonable to believe that all individuals that reach the postconventional level will proceed to rank their values in the same way?

With respect to the religious domain, Kohlberg has already recognized that there are basic options that are *not* to be ordered into a progressive sequence, but have their own specific developmental stages. Thus he believes that in the religious domain the highest developmental stage of an individual is *either* a theistic, *or* an atheistic, *or* a pantheistic one. Why should the same not be true in the moral domain, leaving utilitarianism, and Kantianism, and ethical intuitionism, etc. side by side, as so many basic options?

THREE ARGUMENTS IN FAVOR OF POSTCONVENTIONAL STAGES

Let us first see more systematically what kinds of arguments are being brought forward by those who try to establish the existence of developmental stages at the postconventional level. It seems to me that there are three main types. The first argument proceeds by way of extrapolation from a regularity discovered with respect to the previous stages. The other two deny my previous suggestion according to which an individual arriving at the postconventional level has already come to know all the basic facts of life. But let me present these arguments in concreto.

Argument 1 centers around the following claim: "The first stage of the postconventional level does not yet realize the *ideal of a maximum of reciprocity.*" This is the argument that Kohlberg puts forward in favor of the Rawlsian stage. It contends that moral development, from Stage 1 onward, can be viewed as an ascending line of increasing reciprocity and equilibrium. On entering the postconventional level, the individual realizes the importance of intersubjective discussion and of a common rational strategy to maximize the well-being of the members of society. But the individual does not yet realize the importance of reaching an equilibrium of *maximal* reciprocity, where the rights of every single individual are fully respected; that is, where no individual is ever treated as a mere means. Only at the Rawlsian stage is this insight being achieved.

Argument 2 can be characterized as follows: "The individuals at the initial stages of the postconventional level are not yet fully grown up because *there are more sociological facts to be mastered.*" This is the argument typically put forward by Marxists. They argue that the present economic crises, ecological problems, the errors of consumerism, and the danger of nuclear war, etc. show that there are basic sociological facts, basic social mechanisms, which have not yet been mastered. There must, therefore, exist future developmental stages we have not yet reached. Habermas tries to combine this Marxist argument with the first argument for maximal reciprocity.

Argument 3 is characterized as follows: "The individuals in the initial stages of the postconventional level are not yet fully grown-up because *the tragic nature of human existence has not yet been experienced and has not yet been coped with.*" This is the argument in favor of an ultimate religious stage. It reminds us of existential limit-situations of human life: of suffering, injustice and death. An individual reaches the sixth stage of religious development when he or she comes to understand and accept that even where human dignity is trampled upon and suffers, it is preserved on the higher plane of an all embracing Absolute.

Do these arguments convincingly establish that a sequence of stages exists at the postconventional level of moral development? This is not at all clear. Extrapolating a scheme that has worked for the earlier stages does not per se guarantee the reality of what we extrapolate concerning a later stage. Furthermore, as Kohlberg has realized with respect to the religious stage, the developments stimulated by the experience of new basic facts may belong to a *different* line of development.

CRITERIA FOR PSYCHOLOGICAL BLUEPRINTS
OF DEVELOPMENT

On the whole it is not very clear what criteria a Kohlbergian development scheme must satisfy. This lack of clarity is especially regrettable when it comes to the highest stages of development where the empirically verifying instances are necessarily less numerous. In the remainder of this chapter I discuss such criteria.

From the start, it is important to keep in mind the basic nature of the Kohlbergian scheme of development. On the one hand it belongs to empirical psychology and claims to fit the actual psychological development of human individuals. Thus, what it says must be *empirically significant*. But, on the other hand, a Kohlbergian scheme is not concerned with the actual "ups and downs" of development. It is not a report about both the "ups" and "downs," but rather a scheme of the "ups" only, namely a blueprint of the "logical" path the "ups" have to follow. That is, it claims to be a map of the progress human individuals can make, and in this respect it must embody a specific *conceptual* ("logical") *cogency*. Let us take up in turn these two features of empirical significance and conceptual cogency.

Empirical Significance and the Criterion of Real Psychological Attractiveness

A Kohlbergian scheme cannot be a purely conceptual derivation; it must be empirically significant. This means, first of all, that it must be empirically testable. However, as we have remarked, the highest stages are not frequently realized and thus cannot be easily tested. Nevertheless it seems to me that here, too, the requirement of empirical significance must play a role. One way this can happen is through extrapolation from an empirically verified line of development. But as we have already remarked, extrapolation does not per se guarantee the reality of what has been extrapolated. I believe therefore that a further criterion of empirical significance should be observed, namely that a psychological line of development differs from a purely philosophical derivation by the fact that in it each stage has a real *psychological attractiveness*.

Consider for example the Rawlsian position. It may be true that Rawlsian individuals can solve moral dilemmas which others cannot; that a Rawlsian group is in the most stable equilibrium; that the method of extrapolation recommends we accept the Rawlsian position as Stage 6 in the moral development scheme because it can be viewed as the culmination of a line of increasing reciprocity. But is it plausible to think that because of these advantages in real life individuals will be moved to adopt a Rawlsian position? I am inclined to believe that, as far as the progress from the utilitarian to the Rawlsian stage is concerned, the only motive that has some real psychological force is the Kantian insight. This insight tells us that moral autonomy is an absolute value, a value which forbids that a human individual ever be treated as a mere means. But is the real psychological force of this insight so strong that in all minds which reflect on values it will prevail against different philosophical considerations? If the real psychological attractiveness of the Kantian insight is not considerably superior to the attractiveness of considerations which competing philosophies present as *their* respective insights, then one must, I think, admit that at this point the blueprint of development has to show a split into different directions.

A psychologist who has strong philosophical convictions must beware of confusing the *psychological blueprint* of development with a *philosophical blueprint*. The psychological blueprint must be chosen so that factual experience will verify that all (or at least most) humans actually travel on its path, or paths. A philosophical blueprint, on the other hand, represents a path recommended by some philosophers, but it does *not* exclude the possibility that in real life most or even all people will take a different route.

I do not mean to say that in a psychology book the psychologist's philosophical convictions should never be mentioned. On the contrary, I quite agree that in a book about development and education, for instance, the philosophical discussions concerning the goals of education must occupy an important place. But philosophical theories (ideologies) and theories of empirical science should be clearly distinguished. One can and should argue forcefully for what one accepts as a philosophical truth. But one must be careful not to claim the status of empirical science for something that is not empirical science.

Of course each empirical theory has some metaphysical (and thus philosophical) presuppositions. But that is another matter not in question here. The affirmation that the Rawlsian position is Stage 6 in psychological development is not a presupposition of Kohlberg's empirical theory of moral development, but it is a theorem of this theory; a theorem that is erroneously added to this theory, because, as I argue, it does not satisfy all the necessary criteria.

I myself would say that philosophical reasons speak for the superiority of the Rawlsian over the utilitarian position. For these philosophical reasons the education of moral judgment should have as one of its goals the inclination to help people to attain the Rawlsian position. One can add that this philosophically recommended goal constitutes a harmonious extension of the empirically verified line of development, but one cannot claim that this goal is recommended by empirical psychology.[1]

---

[1]Despite this warning, it should be remarked that the philosophy of John Rawls has a strong empirical bent: His theory of justice aims to be a theory that fits the verdicts of our sense of fairness, just as linguistic theory fits the verdicts of our sense of grammatical correctness. But while the linguists are empirical scientists that do fieldwork and collect data from populations of native speakers, Rawls is a philosopher who relies mainly on his own insight, who uses himself, his own sense of fairness, as his main informant.

Conceptual Cogency and the Law of Conceptual Presupposition

As I have stated, a blueprint of psychological development is a blueprint of a progressive development, and as such it must embody a certain conceptual cogency. But what kind of cogency, what kind of "logical" order is the proper expression of this progressivity? Unfortunately this is far from clear, and very little has been said on this subject. But it would seem that at least one essential requirement can be formulated. The progressivity of a Kohlbergian scheme of development has its basis in a cognitive progress, and this suggests that it has to satisfy the following "logical" law: "Every higher stage must conceptually presuppose the lower stages;" or, more explicitly: "It must be the case that a higher stage cannot be conceived if the stages which are lower with respect to it have not been conceived before." Let us call this the *law of conceptual presupposition*.

Consider again the step from the utilitarian to the Rawlsian position. As I have argued, it does not satisfy the criterion of real psychological attractivity. But it can easily be made to satisfy the law of conceptual presupposition: If the Rawlsian position has as its principle: "No individual should ever be treated as a mere means, not even for the sake of the greatest happiness of the greatest number," then it is clear that it presupposes that one has already acquired the utilitarian notion of the greatest happiness of the greatest number. Notice, however, that if the Rawlsian position is characterized in a more loose way, for instance by the principle: "The moral autonomy of each person is an absolute value that may not be sacrificed to any other value," then it is no longer so evident that the law of conceptual presupposition is satisfied.

Blueprints of development do not have to be simple one-line schemes. It can easily be noticed that the law of conceptual presupposition does not exclude the possibility that a given lower stage may have *several* positions that are immediately above it; i.e., the law of conceptual presupposition allows for the possibility that the ascending line of development branches out into different directions. This means that instead of a one-line scheme we can also have a tree-like map. There may be even more complex patterns. Take for instance the following scheme:

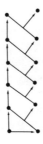

It is the scheme that Kohlberg attributes to moral and religious development taken together, when he claims that the religious development (here: the right side) runs alongside the moral development (here: the left side), with each religious stage presupposing the corresponding moral stage.

This is only one example, but a great many other complex schemes can readily be imagined. This suggests that a developmental theory that uses only a simple one-line scheme is probably a very poor and simplistic theory. But, of course, it is normal that one begins theory-building with simple theories, and that complexities are only brought in later on.

Whose Conception does the Law of Conceptual Presupposition Refer to? A further question can be raised in this context: "Does the law of conceptual presupposition refer to the conceptions of the psychologist or to those of the individuals which the psychologist is investigating?"

Strictly speaking, Kohlberg's investigation of moral development is centrally an investigation of the development of moral *judgment* (i.e., of the development of the ways in which human individuals argue about moral matters) and not an investigation of nonarticulated moral feelings or of moral conduct. It should therefore be clear that it is the conceptions occurring in the judgments of the individuals under investigation to which the law of conceptual presupposition is referring.

Of course, when theorizing about all human individuals, the psychologist is also talking about him or herself, and thus his or her own conceptions are also somewhat relevant, although they are not decisive. If the empirical character of Kohlberg's theory of moral development is to be preserved and if the theory is not to be changed into a philosophical theory, then the psychologist cannot be his or her own and only informant. And when for the sake of harmonization the psychologist formulates in his or her own language the principles to which all the individuals belonging to a certain stage of development appeal in their moral judgments, then it is essential that his or her formulations be faithful to the thoughts of those individuals.

Actually there is still a third possibility to be considered. Could the conceptions talked about in the law of conceptual presupposition not also be the collective conceptions of mankind, the ideas from the history of ideas? As a matter of fact the Kohlbergian scheme of development wants to be a blueprint of ontogenetic development, i.e., it claims to indicate the way by which an individual human being grows up. But could this *ontogenetic blueprint* not be related to what may be called the *socio-historical blueprint*? In biology it is said that the ontogenetic development of the individual recapitulates the phylogenetic development of its species. Could psychology not claim in a similar fashion, that the ontogenetic progress of the conceptions in the mind of an individual recapitulates in some respects the historical progress of the ideas in the development of mankind? Can it not be useful to study the historical development of philosophical movements in order to get clues to the ontogenetic development of conceptual schemes, and vice versa?

Habermas (1975) has tried to combine the Kohlbergian blueprint of the moral development of human individuals with a neo-Marxist blueprint of the history of mankind. And Apel explicitly recommends transferring the approach used with respect to the ontogenetic development of moral consciousness to the domain of social and cultural history. He admits, however, that the methodology of this transfer has not yet been adequately clarified (1980b, pp. 27–29; 1980c, pp. 85–89). Indeed one should not too rapidly conflate the ontogenetic and the socio-historical blueprint, and future investigations should analyze very carefully the essential differences that exist between the two kinds of development involved.

Of course one can try to rate great thinkers according to the stages of the Kohlbergian scheme. Kohlberg himself did this when he was looking for representatives of Stage 6 and Stage 7. But such an enterprise shows clearly that the analogy between the development of an individual and the history of mankind is limited. For instance, whereas a young child cannot yet belong to a high stage in the Kohlbergian scheme, there is no intrinsic reason why an early thinker should not already have reached the postconventional level.

LOGICAL ANALYSIS OF THE EXACT NATURE OF CONCEPTUAL PRESUPPOSITION

The crucial question concerning the law of conceptual presupposition is the following: "What kind of impossibility is meant, when it is said that a higher stage *cannot* be conceived unless the lower stages have been conceived before?" Is the impossibility in question a strict logical impossibility, or is it merely a high empirical unlikelihood (probability-that-not)? If it is an empirical unlikelihood, then what factors are relevant? If it is a strict logical impossibility, then how is it to be analyzed?

The earlier mentioned examples where the Rawlsian position was seen to conceptually presuppose the utilitarian position, suggests the following logical explanation: "Stage A conceptually presupposes stage B if and only if the principle of stage B deductively implies the principle of stage A (or at least a part of the principle of stage A)." But is this equivalence correct? Perhaps this deductive implication is not a sufficient condition for conceptual presupposition. Perhaps something has to be added to the right hand side of the equivalence. And it is also quite possible that such an explicit deductive implication is not a necessary condition; that the logical relation between the principles of stage B and the principles of stage A can also be of a different nature.

As far as logical analysis is concerned, the Kohlbergian scheme of moral development is in about as bad a shape as the Hegelian scheme of the dialectics of historical development! So far a sound formalization has not been found for either of them. But it makes a big difference that, unlike Hegelian dialectics, the Kohlbergian scheme of moral development can be empirically tested, at least up to the postconventional level. One should profit from this fact and try to establish exact formulations of the principles of those stages for which there is empirical evidence. Then the relations between the principles of each pair of successive stages should be examined from the logical point of view. Maybe one could then discover a logical connection that holds between the principles of each of these pairs. But, more likely than not, the logical connections may turn out to be different for the principles of different pairs. In this latter case we would have to say that in the law of conceptual presupposition the phrase 'conceptually presupposes' is ambiguous. This would mean that we would have no unambiguous criterion of conceptual cogency, and in this case the extension of the psychological blueprint into the empirically less accessible postconventional level would be a still more hazardous operation.

CONCLUSION

Reflecting on the problematic status of the postconventional stages in Kohlberg's scheme of moral development, we have come to appreciate in general the special nature of a Kohlbergian blueprint. We have seen that attention must be paid both to its *empirical* significance and to its *conceptual* (logical) cogency. Kohlbergian developmental schemes belong to empirical science, therefore even the stages in which they culminate have to be empirically grounded. On the other hand their stages are said to be steps in a progression, and as such they must follow each other with some kind of conceptual "necessity."

According to Kohlberg the progression of moral development follows a one-line scheme that culminates in one end point, but, as we have seen, the possibility of more complex structures that branch out in different directions must also be considered.

With regard to the postconventional level, we have noticed that the developments take on a new character at this level. It seems that on this level it is the philosophical (or religious) insights themselves, and not some other more subconscious source, that provides the moving force of development. We enter thus the domain of an empirical psychology of the development of philosophical conceptions. If such a discipline is at all possible then it would have to satisfy, among others, the following requirements:

(a) It would have to empirically investigate the degrees of real psychological attractiveness of competing philosophical insights. Presumably this attractiveness varies a great deal with the historical and social context into which the individuals are placed, but there may also be some universally verifiable features.

(b) It would have to clarify through logical analysis the nature of the relations of conceptual presupposition that hold between the empirically documented formulations of later and earlier conceptions.

(c) It would have to elaborate the differences and the connections between the ontogenetic development of the conceptions in the mind of an individual and the historical development of the ideas in the social consciousness of mankind.

REFERENCES

Apel, K.-O. (1980a). Geschichtliche Phasen der Herausforderung der praktischen Vernunft und Entwicklungsstufen des moralischen Bewusstseins. In *Funkkolleg Praktische Philosophie/Ethik, Studienbegleitbrief,* Vol 1 (pp. 38–60). Weinheim-Basel: Beltz.

Apel, K.-O. (1980b). Zur geschichtlichen entfaltung der vernunft. In *Funkkolleg Praktische Philosophie/Ethik, Studienbegleitbrief,* Vol. 2 (pp. 11–81). Weinheim-Basel: Beltz.

Apel, K.-O. (1980c). Die Notwendigkeit einer reflektierenden ethik. In *Funkkolleg Praktische Philosophie/Ethik, Studienbegleitbrief,* Vol. 2 (pp. 82–97). Weinheim-Basel: Beltz.

Fowler, J. W. (1976). Stages in faith: The structural developmental approach. In T. Hennessey (Ed.), *Values and moral development* (pp. 173–210). New York: Paulist.

Fowler, J. W. (1978). Mapping faith's structures: A developmental view. In J. Fowler & S. Keen (Eds.), *Life maps: Conversation on the journey of faith* (pp. 14–101). Waco, TX: Word Books.

Gilligan, C. & Murphy, J. E. (1979). From adolescence to adulthood: The moral dilemmas of reconciliation to reality. *Moral Education Forum, 4,* 3–13.

Habermas, J. (1975). Moral development and ego identity. *Telos, 24,* 41–55. (Text of the German original in J. Habermas, *Zur Rekonstruktion des historischen Materialismus* [pp. 63–91]. Frankfurt: Suhrkamp, 1976).

Kohlberg, L. (1981). *Essays on moral development. Vol. 1: The philosophy of moral development.* San Francisco: Harper & Row.

Küng, G. (1984). The marxist critique of Rawls. In J. J. O'Rourke, T. J. Blakeley & F. Rapp (Eds.), *Contemporary Marxism: Essays in honor of J. M. Bochenski* (pp. 237–243). Dordrecht: D. Reidel.

Rawls, J. (1971). *A theory of justice.* Cambridge, MA: Harvard University.

19 The Moral Personality: Reflections for Social Science and Education

Augusto Blasi
University of Massachusetts-Boston

In recent years, two approaches to moral education have shared a rather limited portion of the educational interest in North American schools. These two approaches are distinctly different, not only in their objectives and underlying philosophies, but also in their educational practices.

The first has been aptly called Values Clarification. Through a series of exercises, students are encouraged, first, to become aware of their own values (e.g., likes and dislikes, wishes, goals, ideals), of the way they order them, and of the degree of importance they attach to them. For instance, students are asked to list goals and desires, to choose among alternatives, to determine those values with which they identify most closely. They are also asked to state what they are willing to do to uphold their values: which ones they are ready to die for, or to fight for, or to argue for, etc. Having become aware of their values, students are asked to affirm them in public and to openly commit themselves to their pursuit: they write slogans on cardboards and demonstrate in the classroom, write letters to newspapers and telegrams to legislators. Finally, students analyze what they can do to produce changes, examine potential obstacles in detail both within themselves and in the environment, and draft contracts with themselves (Simon, Howe, & Kirschenbaum, 1972).

Some of these exercises may seem trivial. More seriously, in this approach, moral values are continuously mixed with nonmoral, even banal, values. Thus, the issues of violent political action and of race relations are discussed together with one's preferences about looks, the length of one's hair, or the season of the year. Everything is accepted. While the desirability of expressing one's values in action is stressed, the idea that values and their hierarchies can themselves be evaluated according to standards of rationality and universality is entirely ne-

433

glected (c.f. Colby, 1975; Kazepides, 1977; Lockwood, 1975). This approach, in sum, does not seem to understand the specific nature of moral values. But it understands quite well that any true value is rooted in one's personality, is owned and cherished by the individual, and generates commitment and effort.

The second approach, which I will simply call developmental moral education, was inspired by cognitive-developmental theory and particularly by Kohlberg's ideas (c.f., e.g., Galbraith and Jones, 1976; Hersch, Paolitto, & Reimer, 1979; Land & Slade, 1979; Scharf, McCoy, & Rory, 1979). Typically it revolves around the discussion of concrete moral dilemmas. The dilemmas may be those that the students themselves have experienced; but this is not necessary, because most dilemmas, whether real or fictional, whether they represent the students' own or other cultures, raise those questions and generate the type of intellectual conflicts that should stimulate development. Students are asked what one—anyone—should do in the dilemma situations and are continuously refocused on this question. Their choice is not simply accepted, but must be justified; the students' reasons, their implications and their adequacy are the real focus of the discussion. Behind the teacher's tolerance for the students' ways of reasoning, there is a clear understanding that moral criteria are not equally adequate. Students are asked to find the best reasons; teacher and peers alike, in their turn, challenge these reasons by pointing to contradictions or unacceptable consequences and by orienting the discussion toward a systematic comparison of different criteria.

This approach, therefore, in contrast with Values Clarification, clearly understands that moral values have special characteristics, that they must be rational, and that each person's ideas and values can and should be questioned. But it almost completely neglects those aspects that are precisely stressed by Values Clarification: that values belong to a person, that they elicit fidelity and pride, and that they shape and express one's identity.

Now we may ask: Is it possible to combine the positive aspects of these two approaches, namely, to educate people to view moral criteria as in principle rational, objective, and universal; to question their own ideas and evaluate them against standards of reason and truth; but, at the same time, to educate the whole person to the moral viewpoint, strengthening the love for justice and subordinating other interests to the moral interest? In sum, is it possible to influence the moral personality together with moral judgment? Logically prior questions are: Does the concept of moral personality make sense, philosophically and psychologically? What does psychology tell us about it? In what follows some considerations are offered, particularly about these two questions.

THE MEANINGS OF "MORAL PERSONALITY"

Assuming that moral action receives its essential meaning from moral understanding and moral judgment, one important question is: What are the relations between moral functioning, i.e., the tendency to behave morally with a certain degree of consistency and life-long purpose, and personality, or, to be more precise, those aspects of personality that are not directly involved in moral reasoning, moral understanding, and the construction of moral criteria?

It is possible to identify at least three different senses in which one can speak of personality characteristics as being relevant to moral functioning and, at least in this minimal sense, of moral personality.

According to a first meaning, personality is related to moral functioning (a) because a number of psychological processes are required to evaluate events and situations and to carry out in action the moral judgments that one has formulated, and (b) because these processes are themselves based on relatively stable psychological traits on which individuals differ. In other words, certain personality characteristics that are present in some individuals but absent in others, or that are available in different degrees to different people, are either necessary for or facilitate the formulation of moral judgments and the expression of these judgments in action.

One could list as examples the ability to process situations, the ability to focus one's attention on the successful realization of one's intentions, perseverance, courage, and the ability to delay gratification and to control one's impulses. In this category belong the coping and defensive mechanisms that have been the object, among others, of Haan's (1977) research. In this category should also be included the ability to take other people's perspective in all its developmental forms (cf., e.g., Kurdek, 1978; Selman, 1980; Shantz, 1975). Taking the part for the whole, I will refer to this first meaning by using the old fashioned term of "strong will."

That personality, in the sense just described, is related to moral functioning should be uncontroversial. However, these personality characteristics, including perspective-taking abilities, are, in themselves, neutral with respect to morality. They are general instrumental variables—one might call them "efficiency variables"—and can be used to sustain moral as well as immoral activity. In this context, therefore, the term "moral personality" is somewhat inappropriate.

However, because of their relation to moral functioning, one could argue that in certain cases there is a moral obligation to acquire or to strengthen one or more of these traits, to change one's will from "weak" to "strong." In these cases, the above personality characteristics and the effort to change oneself would acquire a moral meaning that would otherwise be absent. This moral meaning, again, does not derive from the traits themselves nor, at least directly, from judgments concerning the morality of actions, but from a general moral intention and orientation of the agent.

This leads us to the second meaning of moral personality. I am referring to the affective and motivational orientation that people have, in different degrees and types, towards virtue, justice, altruism, briefly, towards the moral as each person understands it. Under this heading one should include interest for the moral aspect of events, love and even passion for just solutions, commitment to live one's life according to one's moral understanding, and determination to effectively subordinate interests, wishes, and pleasures to the moral interest. One should also include what, in another context (Blasi, 1984) I called moral self or moral identity, i.e., the tendency to define oneself in moral terms or to view morality as a part of one's essential self.

I use the term *good will* to refer to the central affective and motivational orientation to morality that characterizes each person. This meaning of moral personality, in fact, seems to be closely related to the Kantian notion of good will (Kant, 1785/1964, 1788/1956). It also reflects a much older belief, rather common even now, that morality is a quality of persons more deeply than it is a characteristic of actions, that "being good" counts more than "doing the right action" in each instance.

To dissipate possible confusions, I should stress that those personality dispositions that constitute the good will assume that the agent has already understood what morality is and that he or she takes this understanding as a guide for his or her affects, for the ordering of his or her interests, and, ultimately, for the construction of his or her identity. I am not trying to replace moral cognition with moral personality, but to extend the influence of moral cognition, beyond individual actions, to the construction of one's personality. Those affective and motivational dispositions that make up the moral personality in this second sense will appear to be necessary the moment one understands that moral functioning, in contrast with other areas of human activity, involves the whole person and should become, ideally, a life-long project.

It has to be expected that the good will will make moral action more constant and dependable, either directly through its motivational power, or indirectly by motivating the development of a *strong will*. In this respect, moral personality in sense two shares with moral personality in sense one an instrumental value. Its value, however, is not purely instrumental as is the case for the strong will. Instead, the value and the necessity of the good will derive from the relations that exist between actions and agent. Because human agents have the capacity to transform time into history, they don't just act instance after instance, but unify their actions in projects with which they identify. Actions, then, either express a personality that already exists or modify the personality in order to express it. In sum, whereas "moral personality" in sense one is per se neutral with respect to morality, moral personality in sense two is intrinsically, though perhaps not primarily, moral. As a result, the effort to develop the good will has a moral meaning of its own, independently of its effects on specific actions.

Both senses of moral personality described so far involve the acquisition or the changing of personality characteristics, those that constitute the strong will and those that are included in the good will. Therefore, there may be activity directly aimed at shaping oneself that has moral meaning and establishes, at least in some cases, true moral obligation. However, the moral value of this activity and of the personality dispositions that result from it is either extrinsic and contingent on their effect on moral functioning (in the case of the strong will) or, though intrinsic and necessary, is indirect and derived from an understanding of morality in which personality may have no place. Both these meanings of moral personality, therefore, are perfectly compatible with the belief that morality, as such, is exclusively interpersonal.

But one could, and some do, speak of moral personality in a third sense. In this sense, certain aspects of one's personality and those activities that are aimed at them have an intrinsic moral value, irrespective of any external consequences that may follow and independent of interpersonal actions and relationships. For example, destroying one's intellectual capacities and one's dignity through alcohol or drugs, or selling one's freedom would be *prima facie* immoral, regardless of any interpersonal consequences. According to this third sense, moral personality is based on a personal morality.

Some seem to think that all morality is at bottom personal, insofar as it necessarily implies a basic choice of a mode of life for oneself (e.g., Taylor, 1976). But one could hold a more limited position and believe that, next to interpersonal morality, there is another dimension, genuinely moral, which concerns the agent and only the agent in his or her personhood.

Even this limited, the third sense of moral personality is controversial and is frequently regarded with suspicion or simply rejected. Such a rejection is clearly implied in the distinction between morality and the "good life." Whereas morality is universal, regulatory and prescriptive, interpersonal, and concerned with the minimal conditions for human welfare, good life issues would be mostly personal in content, relativistic, nonobligatory, and concerned with the pursuit of ideals. Examples of good life issues that are typically offered by the proponents of the distinction include finding congenial partners and friends, choosing a fulfilling occupation, becoming competent, developing special talents, and becoming increasingly rational. From this perspective, the moral question would be: "What should I do?"; the good life question, instead, is: "What kind of person do I want to be?" (cf. Hamm & Daniels, 1979).

Undoubtedly there are serious reasons for being cautious and even suspicious with regard to the idea of personal morality: One does not want to compromise the "objective," universalistic, and prescriptive character of morality, or confuse obligations with tastes, wishes, and preferences. That this is a real danger is demonstrated by the Values Clarification approach to moral education. On the other hand, it is possible to find examples of personal conduct that seem to be more clearly related to the typical form of moral thinking than the good life concerns listed earlier and about which it would not be absurd to speak of obligation. One could mention, besides tampering with one's freedom, not deceiving oneself in important matters and being authentically oneself. It is unquestionable that there are degrees of seriousness in these matters and that not every instance of inauthenticity would be the object of strict obligation, but this is also true of interpersonal morality.

That the acknowledgment of moral aspects in freedom and authenticity is relatively recent (see, e.g., Trilling, 1972), developmentally late, and perhaps rarely found in the general population, is no argument against its appropriateness and validity. The question may well revolve around whether one can apply to some personal issues the language of universal prescriptivity and whether it makes sense to ask, not only ''What kind of person do I want to be?,'' but also ''What kind of person should one, or must one, be?''

I do not wish to minimize the difficulties involved in making the distinction between morality and the good life. On the other hand, it is impossible to do justice, in this chapter, to the issue of personal morality and to the debate that it has generated. I can simply hint at the obvious educational implications of this issue. Assuming that the basis of morality lies in the intrinsic worth of persons, one may wonder whether it is possible to educate people concerning their duty of respecting others' personhood without sensitizing them to the obligation of respecting their own (I am not speaking of finding compatible partners or of fulfilling one's potentials). One may also ask whether it is possible to educate people concerning their right to have their personhood respected by others without opening their minds to the obligation of making themselves worthy of respect.

SOCIAL SCIENCE AND THE GOOD WILL

The first section described three meanings of ''moral personality'': The first consists of those traits of intelligence, determination, and control, which, though neutral in themselves, are needed to carry out one's moral intentions; the second, the good will, consists of a central affective and motivational orientation to morality; the third includes certain personality characteristics that have moral value in themselves, independently of their possible relation to interpersonal morality. These three meanings are not presented as alternative ways of thinking about the moral personality. One could think of them as complementary aspects or as forming an organic unity, in which the good will occupies the central role. The good will would be like the moral soul of the strong will, giving to it its moral meaning and its dynamic power; the good will would also strive toward the moral personality in the third sense, once the meaning of a personal morality is understood and accepted.

Starting from the aforementioned considerations, one can ask: What can social science and psychology in particular tell us about the good will, namely, about the ways people relate affectively to morality, about the importance that morality has in their lives and their self concept, about the degree of motivational power that moral interest can muster relative to other interests? When the concept of good will is properly understood, the answer is: nothing or next to nothing. Now, this situation may not seem surprising, but is interesting and demands an explanation. Psychology, in fact, has been concerned with moral functioning for a very long time, while, as already mentioned, the good will is rather commonly considered to play a central role in moral functioning. Moreover, whatever philosophers can say about the relations between moral knowledge and moral motivation, psychologists are precisely interested in the way various processes are functionally united and in the conditions that correlate with successful or unsuccessful integration. Many, for instance, particularly in recent years, have been stressing the importance of supplementing our knowledge of moral cognitive structures with the study of moral affect and moral motivation.

Why, then, this lack of interest for the good will? Of course, some ready answers come to mind: Science strives to divorce itself from values; moral feelings are private and therefore elusive and unreliable in their indicators; moral feelings are such an intimate part of the individual that the scientist must maintain some distance from them. These explanations, however, are at best incomplete and secondary. The total neglect on the part of psychology and education of the moral personality in the sense of good will seems to be one, perhaps central, aspect of a much broader picture; it seems indeed to be a necessary consequence of the mostly unarticulated guidelines that have directed the study of morality by social scientists.

It is possible in fact to identify three general trends that have characterized the scientific study of morality: secularization, fragmentation, and depersonalization of morality. Of the three, secularization is by far the most widespread and the most influential. It consists in transforming morality into morally neutral abilities and attitudes that are considered to be important for leading an efficient and well adjusted life in society. Briefly, the concept of morality has been replaced by the concept of character.

This explains the attraction that "instrumental virtues," what is called here the strong will, exercised for psychology, practically from the very beginning of its history. At the turn of the century, particularly in Germany and England, many were interested in the will, which was understood as determination and persistence of motives, and was even fused, at times, with the preseveration of ideas and actions (cf., for instance, Ach, 1910; Boyd 1911; Heymans & Wiersma, 1906–1909; Webb, 1915). The work of Hartshorne and May (1928; with Maller, 1929; with Shuttleworth, 1930), which signed a turning point and remains a milestone in the empirical study of "moral" traits, was directly influenced by the earlier work on the will. In Hartshorne and May's use, the term "character" indicates essentially the same personality processes that had previously been considered as elements of the will: resistance to temptation, persistence of motives, perseverance, and determination. From this pioneering effort derived the recent and contemporary study of a variety of "instrumental traits" and ego strength variables: attention, resistance to temptation, delay of gratification and control of fantasy, social responsibility, and tolerance of frustration.

The guiding spirit of all these studies, which occupy a very large portion of the psychological work on "moral" functioning, was aptly clarified by Webb in his 1915 study on character. Having pointed out that the experts do not concur on the definition of character, he continues:

> . . . another section of the community [i.e., not the experts] - the practical men of affairs - has had perforce to make some attack upon the problems involved in character. Some kind of estimation of a man's personal qualities must be made every day by business men, employers, committees, etc. and by all of us in appraising the desirability of persons to whom we are introduced. At this point it would be worth while to analyze, as far as possible, the basis upon which a business man makes such estimates when choosing a person for his employment (p. 3).

Character is seen, at the same time, as the basis for morality and as the set of those qualities that make an individual desirable for an employer. The secularization of morality, then, was achieved through a process of selection, by an overwhelming preference for morally neutral instrumental variables as object of study. The good will was replaced, first, by the strong will and, later, by ego strength.

The secularization of morality has also been achieved in another way, namely, by some sort of "naturalization" of those characteristics that are more specifically moral, such as kindness, empathy, and altruism. By naturalization I mean that these traits, when studied by psychologists, have been abstracted from what formally constitutes their morality, namely, from the agent's moral judgment and moral intention. Instead they have been approached like all other psychological characteristics, as deterministically originating either from the agent's biological make-up or from the agent's experiential history. Within this perspective, it makes little sense to speak of the agent's love and effort or of his or her obligation to pursue altruistic ideals, namely, characteristics that are central to the concept of good will. In sum, the secularization of morality in psychology consists in the fact that potentially moral virtues have been approached without paying attention to their "moral soul."

It is understandable now why even those psychologists who have been calling for an increased attention to affect in moral functioning (Aronfreed, 1976; Hoffman, 1976, 1978) had, and have, little chance of arriving at the good will. In most cases, affect seems to be necessarily tied to arousal of a quasi-physiological sort and to operate motivationally according to the tension-reduction model. As a result, the list of acceptable affects is rather limited and does not include, e.g., love for truth, passion for justice, or the good will as was previously described.

Fragmentation, the second characteristic of the psychological study of morality, takes the secularization tendency even further: It consists, not only in displacing the center of traits and attitudes from morality to functional adaptation, but in eliminating the center altogether. Early psychologists had assumed that a unitary character exists and thought to have found its center in the will. Webb (1915), whom I quoted earlier, reported data documenting the existence of a W (will) factor. Hartshorne and May started from the same assumption, and only to their regret had to acknowledge that their data did not support their expectation. It is irrelevant to my present purpose whether their conclusion was warranted by their data or whether a different methodology could have led these investigators to a different conclusion. The fact is that, from then on, psychologists easily abandoned the idea of a moral personality and were satisfied to study in isolation the various character traits (attention, resistance to temptation, etc.). None of these traits was assumed to be central; all were viewed as operating independently of each other.

The third tendency, toward depersonalization, is mostly relevent to moral education, particularly to that approach that is inspired by cognitive-developmental theory and, more generally, to any approach that stresses knowledge and reasoning. It consists in a tendency, on the part of both student and teacher, to deal with moral issues and moral knowledge as if they were irrelevant to, or could be divorced from, one's own personal life. In other words, some sort of professionalization may take place. What matters or, at least, what one focuses on are those conceptual and interpersonal skills that are useful in a classroom discussion: the ability to understand the implications of a dilemma, to generate reasons in support of one's choice, to pursuade and to defend one's opinion, to find the contradiction in others' reasoning. It may help to compare this approach to the type of professionalization that frequently occurs around the study of religion, in divinity schools, departments of religious studies, and seminaries. A theological doctrine is interesting in itself, as a coherent system of ideas or as reflecting certain cultural trends. One can become an expert in it, but confine one's expertise within the limits of the roles of writer, teacher, or student, entirely isolating it from one's own beliefs and life.

I do not wish to suggest that this kind of depersonalization is occurring frequently in developmental moral education, even less that it is a necessary consequence of the cognitive approach. But it seems to be a real danger, almost endemic in the nature of this approach.

It is intriguing to think that cognitive-developmentalism, the only psychological theory that, in approaching morality, carefully avoided both secularization and fragmentation, was accepted even to the present limited extent by the psychological and educational establishments, precisely because it lends itself to a depersonalized interpretation. If this is indeed the case, it may be possible to articulate the rules by which social sciences regulate their interest in moral functioning: Norms of practical living can be accepted as subject of research and teaching as long as they are not specifically moral; moral rules can be an acceptable subject for research and teaching as long as they are considered naturalistically and relativistically; the possibility of a universal and objective system of morality can be a proper subject for education and research as long as it is depersonalized.

CONCLUSION

If one should trust the present analysis, the state of affairs is rather sobering: Not only do psychology and social science have nothing to say about what I consider to be one central aspect in moral functioning, but their neglect, or avoidance, is a result of much broader and much stronger cultural currents. An education aimed at the good will, at least outside of the family environment, seems to go against the relativistic and bureaucratic grain of democracy, the way most of us live it. Many among us would feel embarrassed even at the thought of a good will curriculum for a public school system.

My suggestion, admittedly general and vague, would be to approach the problem in two steps: first, to educate our students to clearly think morally, separating moral issues and values from all other values. This is already being done in the cognitive-developmental approach to moral education.

The second step would be to encourage our students to relate to their knowledge, to truth as they know it, as *their very own*, namely, as knowledge and truth that they struggled for, constructed, for which they are responsible, and whose implications are their own to deal with. I am speaking now of all knowledge and truth, moral and nonmoral. Perhaps one mistake of the cognitive-developmental approach is to not fully realize that there are different ways and degrees of owning knowledge. One consists in understanding, i.e., in assimilating reality to one's intellectual structures. But a person is not just intellectual structures, and ownership can go far beyond assimilation.

Going back to the question from which this discussion started, it may be possible to combine the positive aspects of Values Clarification and of developmental moral education. But this requires that, at the very center of the educational process, a tension be maintained between the objective and universalistic aspect of knowledge and the subjective personal commitment to it (cf. Nagel, 1979, Ch. 14). Our students should learn to care about their beliefs, both because the beliefs are their own and because they are understood to be objectively true. When total involvement and personal commitment are not present, morality risks becoming abstract and ultimately sterile; when personal feelings and values are overemphasized, or more precisely, when they do not depend on and are not guided by knowledge and reason, the supraindividual nature of morality and the sense of genuine obligation are lost.

REFERENCES

Ach, N. (1910). *Über den Willensakt und das Temperament.* Leipzig: Quelle und Meyer.

Aronfreed, J. (1976). Moral development from the standpoint of a general psychological theory. In T. Lickona (Ed.), *Moral development and behavior* (pp. 54–69). New York: Holt, Rinehart, & Winston.

Blasi, A. (1984). Moral identity and its role in moral functioning. In J. L. Gewirtz & W. M. Kurtines (Eds.). *Morality, moral development, and moral behavior.* (pp. 128–139). New York: Wiley.

Boyd, E. B. (1911). *Motive force and motivation tracks.* London: Longmans.

Colby, A. (1975). Review of L. E. Raths, H. Merrill, & S. B. Simon, *Values and teaching,* and S. B. Simon, L. W. Howe, & H. Kirschenbaum, *Values Clarification: A handbook of practical strategies for teachers and students. Harvard Educational Review, 45,* 134–143.

Galbraith, R. B. & Jones, T. M. (1976). *Moral reasoning: A teaching handbook for adapting Kohlberg to the classroom.* Anoka, MN: Greenhaven.

Haan, N. (1977). *Coping and defending: Processes of self-environment organization.* New York: Academic.

Hamm, C. M. & Daniels, L. B. (1979). Moral education in relation to values education. In D. B. Cochrane, C. M. Hamm, & A. C. Kazepides (Eds.), *The domain of moral education* (pp. 17–34). New York: Paulist.

Hartshorne, H. & May, M. A. (1928). *Studies in the nature of character. Vol. I: Studies in deceit.* New York: Macmillan.

Hartshorne, H., May, M. A., & Maller, J. B. (1929). *Studies in the nature of character. Vol. 2: Studies in self-control.* New York: Macmillan.

Hartshorne, H., May, M. A., & Shuttleworth, F. K. (1930). *Studies in the nature of character. Vol. 3: Studies in the organization of character.* New York: Macmillan.

Hersch, R. H., Paolitto, D. P., & Reimer, J. (1979). *Promoting moral growth. From Piaget to Kohlberg.* New York: Longman.

Heymans, G. & Wiersma, E. (1906 to 1909). Beiträge zur speziellen Psychologie auf Grund einer Massenuntersuchung. *Zeitschrift für Psychologie, 42* to *51.*

Hoffman, M. L. (1976). Empathy, role-taking, guilt, and development of altruistic motives. In T. Lickona (Ed.), *Moral development and behavior* (pp. 124–143). New York: Holt, Rinehart, & Winston.

Hoffman, M. L. (1978). Empathy, its development and prosocial implications. In H. E. Howe, Jr., and C. B. Keasy (Eds.), *Nebraska symposium on motivation.* Vol. 25 (pp. 169–218). Lincoln, NE: Nebraska University.

Kant, I. (1956). *Critique of practical reason.* (L. W. Beck, Ed. and Trans.) New York: Liberal Arts. (Original work published 1788)

Kant, I. (1964). *Groundwork of the metaphysic of morals.* (H. J. Paton, Ed. and Trans.). New York: Harper & Row. (Original work published 1785)

Kazepides, A. C. (1977). The logic of values clarification. *Journal of Educational Thought, 11,* 99–111.

Kurdek, L. (1978). Perspective taking as the cognitive basis of children's moral development: A review of the literature. *Merrill Palmer Quarterly, 24,* 3–28.

Land, N. & Slade, A. (1979). *Stages: Understanding how you make moral decisions.* New York: Holt, Rinehart, & Winston.

Lockwood, A. L. (1975). A critical view of values clarification. *Teachers College Record, 77,* 35–50.

Nagel, T. (1979). *Mortal questions.* Cambridge: Cambridge University Press.

Scharf, P., McCoy, W., & Rory, D. (1979). *Growing up moral: Dilemmas for the intermediate grades.* Minneapolis: Winston.

Selman, R. L. (1980). *The growth of interpersonal understanding: Developmental and clinical analysis.* New York: Academic.

Shantz, C. U. (1975). The development of social cognition. In E. M. Hetherington (Ed.), *Review of child development research. Vol. 5* (pp. 257–324). Chicago: University of Chicago.

Simon, S. B., Howe, L. W., & Kirschenbaum, H. (1972). *Values clarification: A handbook of practical strategies for teachers and students.* New York: Hart Publications.

Taylor, C. (1976). Responsibility for self. In A. Rorty (Ed.), *The identities of persons* (pp. 281–299). Berkeley: University of California.

Trilling, L. (1972). *Sincerity and authenticity.* Cambridge, MA: Harvard University.

Webb, E. (1915). *Character and intelligence. An attempt at an exact study of character.* Cambridge, MA: Cambridge University.

Author Index

445

Subject Index